THE IDEAS
THAT
CONQUERED
THE WORLD

ALSO BY MICHAEL MANDELBAUM

The Nuclear Question:
The United States and Nuclear Weapons 1946–1976
(1979)

The Nuclear Revolution
(1981)

The Nuclear Future
(1983)

Reagan and Gorbachev
(CO-AUTHOR, 1987)

The Fate of Nations:
The Search For National Security
in the Nineteenth and Twentieth Centuries
(1988)

The Global Rivals
(CO-AUTHOR, 1988)

The Dawn of Peace in Europe
(1996)

Michael Mandelbaum

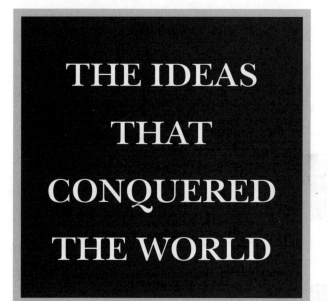

THE IDEAS THAT CONQUERED THE WORLD

PEACE, DEMOCRACY, AND FREE MARKETS
IN THE TWENTY-FIRST CENTURY

PublicAffairs Ltd

OXFORD

Originally published in the United States by PublicAffairs™,
a member of the Perseus Books Group, 2002.

Copyright © 2002 by Michael Mandelbuam.

Printed in the United States of America.

A CIP catalogue record for this book is available from the British Library.

The Ideas That Conquered the World

1-903985-44-7

FIRST EDITION

1 3 5 7 9 10 8 6 4 2

To Anne Mandelbaum, with love

CONTENTS

ACKNOWLEDGMENTS

I T IS A PLEASURE TO acknowledge the considerable help I have received in the writing of this book.

Four institutions and their leaders made it possible. First and foremost is the Council on Foreign Relations, where I have been a senior fellow since 1986. The Council's president, Leslie H. Gelb, suggested the book's topic and the approach to it that I have adopted and was instrumental in my becoming the Council's Whitney H. Shepardson Fellow for 1999–2000, when much of the work was done. Without him this book would not have been written. I am indebted as well for financial and other support to the Carnegie Corporation of New York City, with which I have had the privilege of being associated first during the presidency of David Hamburg and then during that of Vartan Gregorian, who have both been most supportive of my work. I am also happy to acknowledge the special help of David C. Speedie III, the chair of the Carnegie Program on International Peace and Security. At the Paul H. Nitze School of Advanced International Studies of The Johns Hopkins University, Paul Wolfowitz, the former dean, authorized an additional semester of leave to complete this work. This book began as a sequel to one I wrote for the Century Foundation, *The Dawn of Peace in Europe*, which was published by the Foundation (then the Twentieth Century Fund) in 1996. I thank the Foundation's president, Richard C. Leone, for his understanding when the project took a different path from the one I had initially planned.

The Council on Foreign Relations and the Chicago Council on Foreign Relations each organized seminars to discuss various chapters of the book. I am grateful to Lawrence J. Korb, vice president for studies of the Council on Foreign Relations, Professor James Kurth of Swarthmore College, and John Rielly, former president of the Chicago Council on Foreign Relations, for chairing these meetings. I thank all those who attended and would like to single out for particular appreciation for their comments the following participants: Robert Bowie, Ralph Buultjens, James Chace, Michael Elliott, Charles Elson, Adam Garfinkle, Neil Grabois, James F. Hoge Jr., Peter Kostant, Nicholas Lemann, Charles Lipson, Robert Manning, Eugene A. Matthews, Walter Russell Mead, John Mearsheimer, Rajan Menon, Philip Merrill, Karl Meyer, Don Oberdorfer, Daniel Rosen, John Munder Ross, Trudy Rubin, Ronald Tiersky, Fred Tipson, John Train, and Malcolm Wiener. David Stevens of the Council on Foreign Relations provided admirable research and logistical support.

Several of my colleagues at The Johns Hopkins School of Advanced International Studies also made helpful comments on the manuscript. They include Professors Fouad Ajami, Robert Chase, Charles Doran, Charles Pearson, James Riedel, and Riordan Roett. I am grateful to each of them.

I thank my agent, the peerless Morton L. Janklow, for placing the book and Peter Osnos, publisher, and Paul Golob, executive editor, of PublicAffairs for the skill and care with which they brought it to publication.

Some of the ideas in these pages began as newspaper columns for *Newsday*. I am grateful to James Klurfeld, editor of *Newsday*'s editorial pages, for his encouragement and to Noel Rubinton, editor of its op-ed page, for commissioning them. Other parts of this book originated in articles for *Foreign Affairs*, and I am grateful to that journal's editor, James F. Hoge Jr., and its former managing editor, Fareed Zakaria, for publishing them. I am particularly indebted to Thomas L. Friedman of *The New York Times* for many conversations that helped to shape my thinking on the subjects covered in Part Three of this book.

Last but certainly not least, I am deeply grateful to my wife, Anne Mandelbaum, to whom this book is dedicated. Her daily encouragement and support were indispensable, as was her brilliant editorial advice.

THE IDEAS

THAT

CONQUERED

THE WORLD

INTRODUCTION

O N THE MORNING of Tuesday, September 11, 2001, two hijacked commercial airliners flew directly into the twin towers of the World Trade Center, the tallest structures in New York City. The heat from the explosion of the two airplanes and the fires they set melted the steel supports of the 110-story buildings and they collapsed, killing more than 2,800 people. Almost simultaneously another hijacked airliner crashed into the headquarters of the American Department of Defense, the Pentagon, in Washington, D.C.

The events of September 11 qualify as the most spectacular, riveting, grim, costly, and searing acts of terrorism in history. The shock of the attacks reverberated around the United States and throughout the world. In their aftermath, September 11 was widely said to have been an historical watershed, a moment when the assumptions that had governed the way the world conducted its affairs were abruptly swept away.

In fact, the attacks did not usher in a new world. Instead, they illuminated the main features of the world that already existed, a world that had emerged in its full form a decade earlier but had been two centuries in the making. It is a world dominated by three major ideas: peace as the preferred basis for relations among countries; democracy as the optimal way to organize political life within them; and the free market as the indispensable vehicle for producing wealth. The world that peace, democracy, and free markets conquered and dominate, the world of the twenty-first century—its origins, its principal features, and its future—is the subject of this book.

Societies raise their grandest monuments to what their cultures value most highly. As the tallest buildings in a city noted for tall buildings, the twin towers of the World Trade Center were certainly monumental. They were the equivalent for the twenty-first century

United States of the great pyramid of Giza in ancient Egypt and the Cathedral of Chartres in medieval France. The institution that the World Trade Center symbolized, and to which it was dedicated, was the free market, the central activity of which is trade. The planet's dominant method for organizing economic activity, the market, did in fact occupy an exalted place in American society.

The market enjoyed a commanding position outside the United States as well and the September 11 attack also symbolized its global status. Once Manhattan's tallest structures had been the Empire State Building, named for New York itself, and the Chrysler Building, the headquarters of an American automobile manufacturer that by 2001 had become a subsidiary of a German corporation. The even taller buildings destroyed on September 11 were named not simply for trade but for *world* trade.

People from more than eighty different countries died in the fires and the collapse. Most of them, moreover, worked for firms concerned with one aspect or another of finance. Concentrated in lower Manhattan, the financial industry is the most cosmopolitan in the world because its product, money, is more portable and more widely utilized than any other. This product is the key to the international reach of markets: While purely local exchange can and does operate on the basis of barter, markets stretching beyond a particular time and place require money.

The money on which international commerce and industry depends is collected in lower Manhattan and from there distributed to every continent. The World Trade Center was thus symbolic of the network of commercial and financial exchanges that by the year 2001 had spread all over the planet. In choosing it as their target the terrorists perversely dramatized the supremacy of the free market and of the political system intimately associated with it in the United States and elsewhere, democracy, as defining features of the world of the twenty-first century.

The attacks on Washington and New York were acts of war, and the war they inaugurated, the American war against terrorism, became the first war of the new century. They recalled the surprise attack at Pearl Harbor sixty years earlier. Like that 1941 assault, the events of September 11 triggered a campaign against the attackers, with the American government mobilized for military action. The government dispatched forces to Afghanistan to root out the terrorists based there and to overthrow and replace the government that harbored them.

Yet the war against terrorism was unlike the conflict that began for the United States on December 7, 1941, or any of the other great wars of modern history—the European conflict touched off by the French Revolution at the end of the eighteenth century, the two World Wars of the twentieth century, and the four-decades-long political and military struggle known as the Cold War. The previous wars pitted mighty sovereign states against one another, all of them seeking the control of territory. They were waged by vast armies, which clashed in great battles—Waterloo, the Somme, Stalingrad—in which the fate of great nations and huge empires hung in the balance. In the Cuban missile crisis of 1962, when the United States and the Soviet Union confronted each other armed with nuclear weapons, the fate of the entire planet, of the human race itself, seemed to be at stake.

By these standards the war against terrorism scarcely qualified as a war at all. The United States conducted a campaign of aerial bombardment and modest mopping-up operations on the ground in Afghanistan. To wage this war, the aim of which was to protect their citizens against terrorist attacks, the United States and other countries relied less on their armed forces than on their intelligence services, local law enforcement agencies, border guards, and customs and immigration officials, as well as on their public health systems. The Pentagon, one of the targets of the September 11 attacks, was not the only nerve center of the American campaign against terrorism.

The attacks thus illustrated another defining feature of the world of the twenty-first century: the transformation, or at least the dramatic devaluation, of war—the age-old practice that, for the first two centuries of the modern age, did more to shape international relations than any other.

There was no possibility that the September 11 attacks would touch off a conflict anything like the great wars of the modern era, and the reason for this pointed to a third signal feature of the world of the twenty-first century. In the past, a blow to the international system's strongest power would have been welcomed by its rivals. In the wake of September 11, however, every significant government in the world declared its support for the United States.

For this there was an obvious reason: Every major government in the world supported the market-dominated world order that had come under attack and of which the United States served as the linchpin. While not every one subscribed to the political values symbolized by the other world-famous landmark at the tip of Manhattan island, the Statue of Liberty, all saw the free market as the path to what had become, in the twenty-first century, a supreme and undisputed national goal: the creation of wealth. Thus there was virtually no country that neither received nor hoped to receive capital from the New York financial community.

The market-centered international order of the twenty-first century commanded almost universal allegiance not only because every country saw potential benefit in it but also because there was no viable alternative. In the past, those who had challenged the existing order of things had equipped themselves with alternative programs for the organization of political and economic life. The slogan of the French Revolution expressed its aims: liberty, equality, fraternity. The revolutionaries of the nineteenth century who drew their inspiration from that great upheaval pursued concrete goals: the end of monarchical rule, the promulgation of constitutions, the establishment of nation-states instead of multinational empires. The revolutionaries of the twentieth century also had a slogan: "Workers of the world, unite!"—and a program: the abolition of private property and the installation in power of Communist parties. The perpetrators of the September 11 attacks had neither. They proposed nothing in place of what they sought to destroy. They acted in the name of a fanatical strain of Islam that was far removed from the precepts and customs of the great Islamic civilizations of history and that, insofar as it offered a political program of any kind, was intended to apply only to Muslims, who comprised approximately fifteen percent of the world's six billion inhabitants.

The events of September 11 therefore demonstrated that the dominant methods for organizing the universal tasks of political and economic organization had no serious rival in the world of the twenty-first century, and that is a third hallmark of it.

The commanding position of free markets and, to a lesser extent, democracy, the dramatic devaluation of war, and the absence of a plausible alternative to the global order of which these are the main elements characterize the conduct of human affairs at the outset of the third millennium. They also form the basis for the organization of this book, which is divided into three parts, each revolving around one of these three themes. In the pages that follow, the themes are taken up, however, in the reverse order: first comes the rise to a dominant position of markets and affiliated institutions and practices, then the dramatic changes in the role of war, and finally the reasons for and the implications of the supremacy of democracy and the free market. The themes appear in this sequence so as to tell the story of the world of the twenty-first century in chronological order. The book's first part concerns mainly the past, the second the present, and the third the future of the world that came under attack on September 11, 2001.

*

A book about the world of the twenty-first century begins by outlining its historical origins for three reasons. First, historical periods, like individual personalities, are the products of all the past experiences that shaped them. Both must be understood biographically, and the first part of *The Ideas That Conquered the World* offers a brief life history of the international order that the events of September 11 illuminated.

Second, because it is the product of two event-filled centuries of history, the world of the twenty-first century has deep roots. This helps to explain why the attacks on the United States did not fracture that world and provides the basis for believing that its main features will endure for some time. Third, the forces that created the market-dominated international order did not cease to operate with the collapse of Communism. They remain the most powerful influences on the world of the twenty-first century. For that reason, the past offers a preview of the future.

While the modern age, of which the world of the twenty-first century is the latest stage, is two hundred years old, Chapter 1 begins in the middle of the story, with the ideas presented as the basis of a new and better international order by the American president Woodrow Wilson in the wake of World War I. Eight decades later this set of ideas—peace, democracy, and free markets—had come to dominate international affairs, not in the sense that each was enthusiastically embraced and faithfully practiced everywhere but rather in the sense that they had no fully articulated and politically potent rivals. After Wilson first offered them to the world, victory in two subsequent conflicts was required for his "Wilsonian triad" to gain global ascendancy. One of them, World War II, was the bloodiest conflict in human history. The other, longer conflict ended with the triumph of the liberal, Wilsonian formulas for organizing political and economic life and remaining secure in a world of sovereign states. This second conflict, the Cold War, is the subject of Chapter 2, which addresses the paradox at its heart: It produced the same effects as the other great conflicts of the modern era—sweeping changes in the governments and the borders of much of the world—but without the familiar method of prolonged and intense fighting. The effects of the Cold War had a different cause, which is the oldest of all historical processes: the spread of new ideas, institutions, practices, and products from the world's "core," where they are created, to its "periphery," which adopts them.

The core and the periphery are made up of sovereign states, which are as important in the twenty-first century as in the past. They are the subjects of Chapter 3, which presents a political map of the contemporary world. As in the past, some countries are more important than others.

Germany and Japan have particular importance within the core because their conversion to free markets, democracy, and peace in the second half of the twentieth century, after having waged war against them in its first half, had a decisive influence on modern history. Their transformation from opponents to champions of liberalism immensely enhanced the standing of the Wilsonian triad in the world and provided a precedent for other would-be converts to these three liberal norms to follow.

The foremost member of the world's core at the outset of the twenty-first century, however, remains the United States. America stands at the core of the core. It was not accidental that an attack on the global order targeted Washington, its political capital, and New York, its economic center. The United States possesses the world's largest store of military and economic power and bears the heaviest responsibility for defending and sustaining the global institutions and practices that embody the Wilsonian triad. The fate of the global liberal order depends very substantially on the extent to which the United States is willing and able to fulfill these responsibilities, a matter that Chapter 3 considers.

Most countries of the periphery count for little in international affairs: What transpires within their borders affects only them. To this post-Cold War rule there are, however, three conspicuous exceptions. One is a region, the Middle East. The other two are major countries, Russia and China, which are part of the periphery in economic terms but for the purposes of security are countries of the core. Along with the policies of the United States, the national futures of Russia and China will have a greater impact on the world of the twenty-first century than any others. The reason is that the world is shaped by great power in concert with large ideas. The terrorists of September 11 had neither, but Russia and China each has the potential for both.

In the first decade of the new century neither of them had military might and economic power on a scale sufficient to challenge the existing international order, but both could achieve them in the future. Nor did either of them offer the world an alternative to the Wilsonian triad. But in the second half of the twentieth century each had done so. They had been the bearers of a political creed different from, and opposed to, Woodrow Wilson's liberal values and practices. Their illiberal ideology failed and Russia and China abandoned it. But in discarding orthodox Communism, neither fully embraced the Wilsonian triad. Each pursued a foreign policy that was not entirely peaceful, conducted its domestic politics in a way at best partly democratic, and operated an economic system that was only incompletely marketized. Because Russia and China could shake the reigning international order if they placed themselves in determined opposition to it, as the terrorists of September 11 could not, the future of each is a major theme of *The Ideas That Conquered the World*, and in particular of Part Two, which concerns war and peace.

In the Arthur Conan Doyle story "Silver Blaze," Sherlock Holmes calls attention to "the curious incident of the dog in the nighttime." Reminded that the dog in question did nothing in the nighttime, Holmes replies, "That was the curious incident." In the world of the twenty-first century, great war is the non-barking dog. And just as the dog's silence is the key to the mystery Holmes is investigating, so the transformed status of major war is crucial to the understanding of the world in the third century of the modern era.

Throughout this era, and for most of recorded history before it, the fact or threat of war on a large scale exercised a powerful and pervasive influence on the domestic and foreign affairs of sovereign states. The maxim of the ancient Greek historian Heraclitus held true: War is the father of all things. The minimal likelihood of such a conflict in the wake of the Cold War sets the twenty-first century dramatically apart from the two preceding eras.

The devaluation of war is as important a feature of the world of the twenty-first century as the rise of the market. The two are in fact closely connected: When the main business of governments ceased to be the defense of their sovereign borders, the way was cleared for the promotion and maintenance of smoothly functioning free markets to become their most important responsibility. And yet, while the third century of the modern age is more peaceful than the previous two, peace is far from universal. The terrorist network responsible for the attacks of September 11 was based in Afghanistan, a country consumed by armed conflict, and no account of the post-Cold War world would be complete—indeed no such account would be even adequate—without dealing with the places where conflict persists and with the reasons for its persistence. Moreover, even where the devaluation of armed conflict has gone furthest, this state of affairs is not irreversible. The future of the international order of the twenty-first century depends heavily on how durable peace turns out to be where it has been established.

The devaluation of major war is embodied in a great and underappreciated political innovation, one as important, in its own way, for international relations as the free market is for economics and democracy is for politics. In Europe, where organized violence achieved its greatest intensity in the five centuries preceding the twenty-first, a formula for peace emerged in the late twentieth century. This formula, common security, has two principles: the transparency of all national military forces and military operations, and the configuration of all such military forces so that they are suitable for defense but not for attack. Common security in Europe is the subject of Chapter 4.

Although the principles are universally applicable, only the countries of Europe and North America have mustered the political will to adopt them. The decision to establish a common security order stemmed from a number of related attitudes to armed conflict that are here grouped under the heading "warlessness." The Europeans and Americans implemented the principles of common security through a series of negotiated agreements limiting arms concluded at the end of the Cold War. The attitudes that contribute to warlessness grew and spread in the West over the second half of the twentieth century.

The commitment to common security at the outset of the new century was not uniform across Europe. It was shakiest in Russia, the security policies of which are also a subject of Chapter 4. Nor are the principles of common security firmly established in the other region besides Europe where a major war, a war that could not only destroy tall buildings but also shake the international order itself, could begin: East Asia. The prospects for war and peace in this region are the subject of Chapter 5.

In issues of war and peace in East Asia, China is cast in the same role that Russia plays in Europe. Neither retains the principled allegiance to a war-driven foreign policy that prevailed during its era of orthodox Communism. But both are less resolutely committed to peace than their neighbors and each is therefore the country within its region whose foreign and military policies are most important for the prospects of peace there.

Because the principles of common security are less well established in East Asia than in Europe, the chance of a major war there is greater, particularly in two parts of the region where American interests are directly engaged. One, the Korean peninsula, does not directly involve China. The other, the Taiwan Strait, qualifies as the most dangerous spot on the planet because China is involved.

While the world's core became, on the whole, more peaceful in the wake of the Cold War, much of the periphery followed the opposite course, growing more violent. In countries outside Europe and East Asia, the end of the Cold War caused an upsurge in violence. Chapter 6 explains how and why this occurred. One reason is that, with the end of the Soviet-American conflict of the second half of the twentieth century and the suspension, at least temporarily, of the kind of great-power rivalry that dominated international relations for centuries, the core countries had no interest in the periphery and so contributed nothing to stopping the violence there.

To this twenty-first century disconnection between the two principal parts of the international system, however, one region stands as a glaring exception: the Middle East. As Chapter 7 describes, the core countries, especially the most powerful of them, the United States, were obliged to take an interest in the Middle East because that region contained three sources of potential damage to the richest and most powerful members of the international system.

One, the most conspicuous in the wake of September 11, was terrorist networks, including the one responsible for attacking New York and Washington. Another was the world's largest reserves of oil, the mineral resource upon which the global economy was most dependent; a serious interruption in the flow of oil could do the kind of harm to the core countries usually associated with war. A third source of potential damage emanating from the Middle East was weapons of mass destruction, above all nuclear weapons, which might be acquired through the use of the revenues earned from the sale of oil and deployed or even used according to the fanatical convictions that animate terrorism. Chapter 7 assesses the threat posed by each of the three.

What are the prospects for Europe and East Asia to remain peaceful, and the world's periphery, especially the Middle East, to become peaceful in the course of the twenty-first century? They depend, according to a set of ideas widely held if not systematically articulated within the countries of the core, especially the United States, upon the progress of the other two parts of the Wilsonian triad—democratic government and free market economics. These are the subjects of the third part of this book. Having described and explained the origins of the world of the twenty-first century in Part One and investigated its defining condition—the devaluation of major war—in Part Two, the book moves, in Part Three, to a consideration of its central features, two of which—democracy and the market—came under symbolic attack on September 11, 2001.

The understanding of the world of the twenty-first century that prevails in the core countries—the "liberal theory of history"—consists of two propositions. One is that democracies tend to conduct peaceful foreign policies. The other is that where free markets are established, their working, over time, tends to promote democracy. Chapter 8 examines both propositions and finds them, with important qualifications, to have substantial validity. To the extent that they are valid, domestic politics and foreign policy depend, in the twenty-first century, on economics. The future of international relations, and of public life within the world's sovereign states, rests on the fate of the liberal method for organizing economic activity, the free market.

At the outset of the twenty-first century, two important things were true about the status of the free market. One was that, as a method of economic organization, it held a commanding position in the world. It was as close to a universally accepted institution as had ever existed in human history. Chapter 9 describes and explains the market's rise to global dominance. The other was that the construction and maintenance of a free market had proved to be far more difficult than had been imagined for most of the modern era. Virtually every sovereign state was engaged in the attempt, but the degree of success varied greatly among them. Drawing on the experiences of Russia and China, Chapter 10 explores the difficulties of establishing and operating a free market.

The construction of a working market economy depends chiefly on the efforts of the individual societies and governments involved—but not exclusively on them. It also depends on the vitality of the international economic order, especially the rules and institutions for assuring the unimpeded circulation, across sovereign borders, of goods and money. The economic history of the twentieth century teaches the lesson that national economies thrive to the extent that they have access to a global market. The collapse of international markets in the Great Depression of the 1930s had catastrophic economic and ultimately political effects the world over. A comparable twenty-first century collapse would be equally devastating.

The international economic order is the creation of the countries of the core. Its upkeep is their responsibility, and particularly that of the United States. Chapter 11 describes the evolution of the world's trade and monetary systems, while Chapter 12 assesses these systems' prospects in the twenty-first century.

While the attacks of September 11 aimed at the heart of the international order of the twenty-first century, their effect was more like that of a badly stubbed toe. They caused shock and pain. They led to a pause for checking and treating the injury. They produced heightened caution and vigilance and an effort to make sure that nothing similar happened again. But in their wake the world went on much as it had before. Terrorists could knock down the twin towers of the World Trade Center but they could not dislodge the system that these buildings embodied, which was pervasive, deeply rooted, and based on ideas and experiences that terrorism could not eradicate.

Terrorism poses a serious but not a mortal threat to the world of the twenty-first century. Nor, however, is it the only, or even necessarily the most serious, threat to the supremacy of the Wilsonian triad of peace, democracy, and free markets. The book's Conclusion surveys the other potential sources of disruption, most of which have their roots in the uneven capacity among the world's sovereign states to adopt the institutions and practices of the Wilsonian triad, even when they wish to do so. The threats include those considered in the preceding chapters—the national destinies of Russia, China and the United States, the spread and use of weapons of mass destruction, and global economic collapse. They include as well the growing inequality in wealth between the countries of the core and those of the periphery. The world also faces the possibility that a major change in the temperature of the Earth's atmosphere will disrupt existing patterns of life all over the planet, which, if it should occur, would be produced by the global expansion, rather than the failure, of market-driven industrial activity.

These final reflections conform to the dictum of the American philosopher and baseball player Yogi Berra, who once said: "Never make predictions—especially about the future." In this respect, both the Conclusion and preceding chapters resemble a preview of a baseball game, which can describe the rules, the field conditions, the important players, and the main strategies, and can say what is likely to happen in the contest, but can never foretell with certainty its result. Similarly, what the reader may expect to find in the pages that follow is everything important about the history of the twenty-first century except its outcome.

I

THE COLD WAR AND ITS LEGACY

"Germans conquered France in 20 days. It's already been two years, and [the] USA has still not subdued little Korea. What kind of strength is that? America's primary weapons ... are stockings, cigarettes, and other merchandise. They want to subjugate the world, yet they cannot subdue little Korea."

JOSEPH STALIN, 1952[1]

*

CHAPTER ONE

Wilson Victorious

F OR A BRIEF MOMENT in the winter of 1918–19, Woodrow
Wilson, the twenty-eighth American president, bestrode the
world like a colossus. When he arrived at the peace conference convened in Paris in the wake of World War I with a set of ideas for
remaking the international system so as to assure that another such
conflict could never take place, he commanded wider attention and
generated higher hopes than any American before or since. The
British writer H. G. Wells wrote that "humanity leapt to accept and
glorify Wilson. . . . It seized on him as its symbol. He was transfig-
ured in the eyes of men. He ceased to be a common statesman; he
became a Messiah."[2]

Wilson's ideas did not take hold, another terrible war erupted two
decades later, and his career came to be regarded as a failure, its
details forgotten by all but historians. At the outset of the twenty-
first century, however, these ideas had come to dominate the world.
His prescriptions for organizing political and economic life and for
conducting foreign policy are the keys to understanding the new
world that emerged when the great global conflict of the second half
of the twentieth century, the Cold War, came to an end.

THE NEW WORLD

T HE WORLD IN THE WAKE of the Cold War had the eerie aura of
a large city from which the major landmarks had suddenly

disappeared. The rivalry between East and West[3] that dominated international relations in the second half of the twentieth century was the geopolitical equivalent of a city skyline: massive, solid, familiar. By the end of 1991 it had vanished. Long-standing borders, long-serving governments, the familiar alignments and animosities by which the countries and peoples of the world had oriented themselves and to which they had geared both their foreign policies and domestic arrangements were gone. The new setting was initially defined by what was no longer there. The world after the fall of European Communism had entered the post-Cold War era.

Different though it was from what had gone before, however, the post-Cold War world was not totally unfamiliar. For the historically minded it evoked a feeling of déja vu. That impression was accurate: The world *had* passed this way before, in fact three times before. The aftermath of the Cold War was the last stage in a recurring historical pattern.

In the Cold War, for the fourth time in the course of two centuries a great power had made a bid for political and military dominance on the continent of Europe and beyond.[4] Each bid called into being an opposing coalition. On each occasion, after a bitter and prolonged conflict that included initial gains by the would-be master of Europe, the resisting coalition prevailed. On each occasion, the war destroyed the old political and economic order, creating the need to build a new one.

The French Revolution triggered the first of these cycles. The armies raised by the revolutionary regime and ultimately commanded by Napoleon swept over Europe and beyond, reaching east to Moscow and south to Egypt. The other European powers assembled in coalition three times to oppose the French but failed to defeat them. Finally, in 1815, a fourth coalition prevailed.

A century later imperial Germany sought the mastery of Europe. The resulting conflict was more destructive than any previous war. Of the 65 million men who fought, approximately 8.5 million were killed and another 21 million wounded.[5] On the eastern front Germany defeated imperial Russia and imposed a harsh peace. But in the West, the opposing coalition, with Britain and France at its core and with the late but crucial addition of the United States, which entered the war in 1917, finally broke German military power in the fall of 1918.

Two decades later, Germany, governed by the Nazi party and Adolf Hitler, again sought dominance in Europe. It was opposed and, after five and a half terrible years, defeated by the countries that had overcome imperial Germany in 1918. Nazi Germany's opponents were joined by the Soviet Union, the successor state to the Russian empire, the government of which had collapsed under the weight of its military failure in the previous war. In the Asia-Pacific region, Japan took the role of Germany, the power bent on conquest and domination, and was defeated largely by the efforts of the United States.

The fourth great conflict followed almost immediately. The Cold War conformed to the familiar pattern. The Soviet Union, its satellites, and its ideological allies aspired—at least rhetorically—to implant Communist regimes throughout Europe and ultimately the world over. The opposing coalition included the United States, the democracies of Western Europe, and Japan, and it prevailed. The collapse of Communism, and of the Soviet Union itself, brought the world, for the fourth time in modern history, to the final stage of the cycle.

This is the stage of reconstruction. On the three previous occasions the victors organized peace conferences to make plans for the postwar order. They drew new borders, installed new governments, founded new international institutions, and established new rules for international relations—or tried to do so. How well did they do? They have been judged, logically enough, by a single standard. In reconstructing a city gutted by fire, the first order of business is to make what is rebuilt fireproof. Since it is not possible to ensure that no fire is ever lit within the city limits, fireproofing involves minimizing the number of blazes that do break out, finding ways to keep them from spreading, and protecting the major structures against them—as well, of course, as organizing a fire department. Similarly, Europe's postwar reconstructions aimed, first and foremost, at avoiding wars such as those just concluded: preventing conflicts to the extent possible and, where prevention was not possible, containing them.

By this standard, the first postwar reconstruction, the foundations of which were laid at the Congress of Vienna in 1815, earns the highest marks. For the next century Europe was free of a major war. This was not simply a matter of good luck, coinciding with a period in which few political sparks were struck. To the contrary, the nineteenth century, with its industrial innovations and movements for social and political change, was more eventful, turbulent, and stressful than all the centuries of recorded history that preceded it.[6]

The period after World War II was the second most successful. To be sure, the Cold War era was not free from conflict and tension: In fact, war between the two rival blocs was a constant possibility. But for almost half a century no shot was fired in anger directly across the great East-West divide of the European continent. The two blocs waged wars by proxy outside Europe, but the two principal adversaries never fought each other directly.

Judged by what followed it, the least successful postwar reconstruction was the one after World War I, which brought Europe and the world a mere twenty-year respite from the horrors of major war. Yet it is this post-World War I settlement that bears the most instructive similarities to the international order after the collapse of Communism. It is in looking back at the aftermath of World War I that the sense of déja vu becomes most pronounced. To understand the problems and prospects facing the world after the collapse of Communism, a good place to begin is the failed effort at reconstruction in the wake of the First World War—and in particular the blueprint for the reconstruction of international affairs brought to the Paris peace conference of 1918–19 by the American president Woodrow Wilson.

PROPHET AND STATESMAN

WOODROW WILSON WAS the central figure at Paris,[7] arriving to extraordinary expectations. His country had remained neutral for most of the war, with Wilson trying unsuccessfully to play the role of mediator, before finally entering the conflict in 1917. Although American casualties were modest compared with the losses sustained by the powers that fought for the entire war (or in the case of Russia, most of it), the American entry had tipped the military balance against Germany. Alone among the leaders at Paris, Wilson insisted that his country would have no part of the claims of territory and economic compensation over which the European powers were fighting. His country, he emphasized, stood for new principles of international order that, once put into practice, would prevent a repetition of the ghastly conflict into which Europe had fallen in August 1914, which turned out to be the worst military catastrophe that the continent had ever experienced.[8] With his lofty ambitions and soaring rhetoric, Wilson seemed a political messiah who could spare the peoples of Europe another journey through the hell into which they had stumbled.

Wilson failed. At the heart of his program was the establishment of an international organization, the League of Nations, that was to play a central role in keeping the peace. Although the League was established, the United States Senate refused to ratify its charter, leaving Wilson's own country outside the organization, and in the end it turned out not to be effective in keeping the peace. It was not even a significant obstacle to the outbreak of World War II in 1939.

Eight decades after he stepped on to the international stage Woodrow Wilson remained a controversial figure. Retrospective judgments of the man, his policies, and his record were perhaps more sharply polarized than for any other figure in American political history. In this historical controversy both sides have a case. But the basis for Wilson's importance for the twenty-first century is something that historians seldom discuss.

Wilson's critics saw him as personally rigid, politically maladroit, and strategically naive—a man who concocted an unworkable scheme and then stubbornly resisted all efforts at improving it. They considered him a person whose responsibility for his own failure was mitigated only by the possibility that the cerebral hemorrhage he suffered in the midst of the political battle over American membership in the League of Nations impaired his faculties.

Wilson's defenders, by contrast, have regarded him as a visionary, a great reformer of world politics martyred by the pettiness and short-sightedness of his opponents. To them he was a prophet without honor in his own country who, if his program had been implemented, might well have been able to steer the world away from the disastrous course upon which it embarked in rejecting him.[9]

The case against Wilson is a strong one. He was indeed stubborn and self-righteous. His handling of the ratification of the League charter was a masterpiece of political incompetence. The questions that skeptics raised about how the League would function and what membership would mean for the United States were entirely reasonable. It would have been a dereliction of their duty for the members of the Senate not to have raised them. Just how, they asked, would the League prevent war? Article X of its charter committed all members not only "to respect" but also to "preserve as against external aggression the territorial integrity and existing political independence of all members of the League." If the League's Council found a country to have committed an act of aggression, and arbitration did not resolve the matter, would the Council's member countries, including the United States, be obligated to take up arms against the aggressor? If so, how did this square with the American Constitution, which reserved to the United States Congress the prerogative of declaring war? If, on the other hand, Article X of the Charter did *not* require an automatic military response to international law-breaking, was the League not fated to be a toothless, hollow creation, ineffective in preventing future wars?[10]

Wilson had no answer. At first he tried to dodge the question. Attempting to remain faithful to the Constitution while at the same time standing firmly behind his vision of the League as the key to world peace, he asserted that resolutions by the League Council would be morally although not legally binding—which neither answered the question nor squared the circle.[11] He implied that moral force could substitute for military force. But it was all too easy to imagine circumstances in which this would not be the case. History is full of examples of aggressors unswayed by moral condemnation. What would happen then? Wilson did not say.[12]

Still, Wilson's defenders do have a case.[13] In one important sense he was undoubtedly right: Europe needed a peace that conciliated Germany and it was this kind of peace—"peace without victory" was the phrase he used—that he sought to establish. But he was unable to produce such a peace because the war had been so costly that public opinion in the victorious powers, particularly Great Britain and France, demanded a settlement that could justify the sacrifices that had been made to win it. The publics insisted that the Germans pay reparations; but to the Germans this made the settlement harsh, unfair, and thoroughly unacceptable, sowing the seeds of the next conflict.

Moreover, some policies and decisions with which Wilson was associated, and that seemed in the immediate aftermath of the Paris peace conference to have been blunders, appear in a more favorable light decades later, if only because no one has since done better. If Wilson vested unrealistic hopes and expectations in the League of Nations, this was because it seemed to offer a solution to the problem he had gone to Paris to solve, the problem of war. With an effective global authority to keep them in check, he believed, sovereign states would not be free to commit the horrors they had perpetrated between 1914 and 1918. He was not the only person to conclude, in the wake of World War I, that a powerful international organization to keep the peace was rational, logical, and necessary.

All of these it might have been, but such an organization was not feasible. The experience with the League taught a lesson that held true thereafter: The world's sovereign states would not quickly, readily, or voluntarily surrender their sovereign prerogatives, whatever the price of retaining them. The international organization that was founded after World War II, the United Nations, embodied that lesson. The UN proved more durable than the League, but it was not a powerful institution and could not enforce peace. The question that Wilson had been unwilling and then unable to answer had long since been settled. The UN would not infringe on the sovereign prerogatives of its member states. The governments of these states were not prepared to submit to a supranational authority. The UN acted effectively on occasion, but only when its most powerful members agreed on the action and chose the UN as the vehicle for it. It did not have the power to compel the United States or any other country to go to war, or indeed to do anything at all.

Wilson and the other peacemakers at Paris were also retrospectively criticized for naivete in seeking to apply the principle of national self-determination to the multiethnic territories of central and southern Europe that the Austro-Hungarian Empire had ruled before World War I. But on this score they were not naive. Although they recognized that the eastern and southern parts of the continent could not be neatly parceled into ethnically homogeneous slices, they could not avoid dividing these territories in *some* fashion, as the Habsburg empire had already collapsed by the time the conference began.[14] It could certainly not have been reassembled,[15] although Wilson, wisely in retrospect, sought to preserve a measure of economic integration among the former Habsburg possessions. Recognizing that the successor states would inevitably contain substantial ethnic and national minorities within their borders, the peacemakers tried to devise a settlement that would protect them.[16] And while the borders drawn were often contested, most of them survived the twentieth century.

The case for Woodrow Wilson does not, however, rest solely on the proposition that he made the best of a bad situation. It is Wilson the prophet, not Wilson the statesman, who has a claim to the world's respect, or at least to its continuing interest. For his vision of a world transformed, of a new postwar order that would prevent any recurrence of the ordeal of 1914–18, went beyond the establishment of a League of Nations. The Wilsonian vision had three other components, each of which, the American president believed, would contribute to a more peaceful world: restraints on armaments, popular government, and the unimpeded flow of commerce across national borders. These other pillars of his program—this "Wilsonian triad"—are worth exploring in some detail, for together they form the setting of the world after the Cold War.

THE LIBERAL VISION

IN HIS STATEMENT setting forth what the United States hoped to accomplish by intervening in the European war—the "Fourteen Points" speech of January 8, 1918[17]—in his subsequent elaborations on those points, in his other major addresses on the war, and in his diplomacy at Paris, Woodrow Wilson presented his vision of the postwar international order. His was a program of international reform in which disarmament, democracy, and free trade were principal elements.

On January 8, Wilson called for the reduction of all national armaments to the lowest point consistent with national safety. He was convinced that the expansion of Europe's armed forces and the accumulation of weaponry by the continent's great powers before 1914 had contributed to the outbreak of the conflict. He believed that arms were themselves a cause of war.

Popular government was an equally important part of his vision. The United States had entered the war, according to the contemporaneous slogan, to make the world safe for democracy. Democracy was therefore a necessary condition of peace. The heart of democracy is self-government and the greatest obstacle to European self-government in the second decade of the twentieth century was imperial rule. Wilson's Fourteen Points speech thus called for the end of empires. This required the application, to territories under imperial rule, of the principle of national self-determination, a principle that Wilson considered necessary for the kind of democracy in which he believed.

In the same speech Wilson called for the removal of barriers to international trade and the establishment of equal trading conditions for all countries everywhere. Free trade was, with disarmament and democracy, a pillar of a peaceful world. At Paris, Wilson sought to dismantle the barriers to the free flow of commerce across international borders.[18]

Wilson's ideas are familiar. They reappeared in the statements of American aims in the next war by President Franklin D. Roosevelt, initially in the declaration of the Atlantic Charter that he issued with British Prime Minister Winston Churchill, in August 1941, four months before the United States entered the war. They entrenched themselves thereafter in the political rhetoric of the Western democracies.[19] They are staples of speeches by Western—especially American—political leaders on world politics and foreign policy. The Wilsonian ideas are so familiar that they have become the political equivalent of Muzak, scarcely registering on an audience whenever they are proclaimed. They are what all Western political leaders say they want and what the policies they are prescribing aim to achieve. Wilson's three precepts have become, over the course of the twentieth century, clichés. This is because they are considered the standard means to the universally desired and self-evidently worthy ends of peace, liberty, and prosperity. That these are the supreme ends of public life no one, at the outset of the twenty-first century, would venture to doubt.

But this was not always so. In the decades after Wilson unveiled his vision of international order, the means he had advocated were bitterly contested. And for most of recorded history the ends he proposed, far from being universally accepted, were all but unthinkable.

A century before Wilson's moment, and for all the centuries before that, the world in which every human being lived was what, after it had disappeared, came to be called traditional. Life was lived locally. Economic activity was almost entirely agricultural. Political authority was hereditary and arbitrary. Change in the daily routine of court, town, and village, when it occurred, was experienced as disruption rather than progress. The principal causes of change were dynastic succession, religious schism, and the weather. The three international goals that Wilson proclaimed and that came in the twentieth century to be regarded as unarguably desirable would have seemed distinctly odd to almost anyone living in the first half of the eighteenth century or earlier.

Peace would have seemed an odd goal because war was a natural feature of relations among sovereign states. War was not always desirable, of course, and a body of doctrine accumulated over the centuries to regulate its conduct, but the abolition of war was almost nowhere regarded as a serious human hope or purpose.[20]

If peace was a fantasy in the traditional world, liberty for all was widely considered a menace. Democracy was deemed tantamount to mob rule, as well as a departure from the divinely decreed, normal order of things. The educated few familiar with the history of the ancient world had learned from it that the rule of the *demos* (the people) had led to disaster.

As for prosperity, the third component of the Wilsonian triad, this too seemed beyond imagining. While it was true that exchange was a normal part of economic activity and that the discovery of new deposits of minerals, the opening of new trade routes, incremental improvements in the techniques of growing crops and making handcrafts, and the vagaries of the climate had caused the level of economic activity and the supplies of food and material possessions to rise and fall from time immemorial, the broadly based, self-sustaining economic growth that would characterize the nineteenth and twentieth centuries was something unknown to traditional societies.

The men who gathered at Vienna in 1815 to reconstruct Europe in the aftermath of almost two decades of war had sought to restore the political world that the Napoleonic wars had shaken to its foundations. Their successors at the end of World War I no longer thought that this was possible. The industrial revolution and the French Revolution, which the statesmen at Vienna had glimpsed, but the full power and the ultimate consequences of which they could not have realized, had swept away the traditional world.

The importance of the industrial and the French revolutions can scarcely be overstated. The first, which began in Great Britain in the middle of the eighteenth century, involved the substitution of inanimate for animate sources of power, the concomitant substitution of machines for human labor, and the use of new and more abundant (and ultimately man-made) materials. It led to the greatest change in human existence since the domestication of agriculture in the Neolithic age. The second, which substituted the popular will for dynastic inheritance as the basis for political legitimacy, was the most important event in Europe since the fall of the Roman Empire. The two revolutions formed the context for all that followed. They changed the way public affairs were conducted and individual life was lived, first in Europe and then in the rest of the world. Together they changed human life on Earth—decisively, irreversibly, and rapidly. So powerful was their impact that at Paris in 1919 assumptions about what the world was and what it could be that had been axiomatic as recently as 150 years before had been so decisively repudiated that no serious person could hold them.

The horrors of World War I, the result of the application of industrial techniques to warfare, had turned the abolition of the ancient practice of armed conflict into a practical necessity. The course of the nineteenth century, continuing the work of the French

Revolution, had progressively weakened the grip of dynastic rule in Europe, and World War I put an end to it.[21] And the extraordinary surge of economic activity, involving new sources of power that made possible new products and required new ways of producing them, had disrupted the settled agricultural life of more and more of the planet. In the nineteenth century, and to the present day, the industrial revolution, with its unimagined material wealth and its unprecedented squalor, has proven to be as close to an irresistible force as human history has known. Even before World War I, "the gods and kings of the past were powerless before the businessmen and steam-engines of the present."[22]

Wilson accepted the goals of the modern world but his vision of them was distinctive in two enduringly important ways. First, he offered a particular set of means to these ends. Wilsonianism provided a series of specific formulas for achieving peace, popular rule, and prosperity. Second, he asserted that the goals of liberty and prosperity also conduced to peace. The first of the three great aims of the modern world, the one World War I had made it imperative to achieve, was also, in the Wilsonian vision of the post-World War I order, a byproduct of the other two.

Although it was Woodrow Wilson who introduced these ideas to the world as the cure for the affliction of war, they did not originate with him. What came to be known as Wilsonianism was the product of a particular intellectual and political climate that had emerged from a particular historical experience. It arose in the late eighteenth and the nineteenth centuries in Great Britain and its political offspring, the United States.

The influential nineteenth century English political thinker Jeremy Bentham proposed the abolition of armaments as an avenue to peace, and the cause was taken up by the English peace societies that were founded in the first half of that century.[23] American revolutionaries at the end of the eighteenth century, especially the more radical of them, such as Thomas Paine, believed that the overthrow of the hereditary monarchies of Europe would relieve the world of the selfish, unnecessary wars that these monarchs were in the habit of waging.[24] As for commerce, the cause of free trade was a major issue in the nineteenth century politics of Great Britain, and some of its most enthusiastic proponents asserted that, beyond making countries richer, free trade would also make them more peaceful. The United States was not as firmly committed to free trade as was Great Britain, but the benefits of commerce and the desirability of promoting it were important themes in American political life from the founding of the republic.[25]

The putative relationship between democracy and free trade on the one hand, and peace on the other, was not central to the political life of either the United States or the United Kingdom before World War I. But that was because a great European and world war was not then a central concern in either country.[26] By the end of 1918 it had become the central issue, and one in urgent need of solution. Wilson bundled these Anglo-American ideas together and presented them as the solution the world was seeking, the application, to the world as a whole, of principles cultivated and practiced in Great Britain and the United States. The term ordinarily used to characterize the dominant forms of political thought and practice in the English-speaking world in the modern age is *liberalism*, standing for liberty, in contrast to the arbitrary restraints imposed by traditional politics and economics. Wilsonianism was and is the spirit of liberalism applied to international relations.

While in the nineteenth century the principal political divisions in Europe were within European countries, between the forces of liberalism and those of tradition, after World War I the great conflict pitted sovereign states, some of them liberal and others neither liberal nor traditional, against one another. The term often applied to liberalism's adversaries in World War II and the Cold War was "totalitarian." In the Cold War, the liberal bloc came to be known as the free world.

Liberalism's nineteenth century adversary could legitimately be called "conservatism" because it embodied the aspiration to conserve the old established ways and resist the changes that liberalism sought to bring about. (The word *reactionary* was also used; the forces of tradition reacted—negatively—to liberal changes.) Liberalism's twentieth century global adversaries, fascism and Communism, were not conservative at all but radical in pursuit of their ideological agendas.

The term conservative was widely used in the latter half of the twentieth century—but in connection with the central conflict *within* liberal states. This conflict was the ongoing and peaceful dispute, never to be finally resolved, over how far a government should go to provide social protection in the form of old-age pensions, unemployment assistance, and health care. Although sharply divided over this question, the parties to the dispute all accepted democratic politics and market economics and opposed the prescriptions and practices of the world's illiberal regimes. This was a quarrel within the liberal family. In the Anglo-American world those disposed to a greater role for government came to be known as liberals, while those favoring a lesser one were called conservatives—although the "conservative" position was closer to what the nineteenth century liberals had believed. (On the European continent, where the liberal tradition was less strong than in the Anglo-American world, the term for those arguing in favor of less government was historically more accurate: "neoliberals.")

The Wilsonian triad was liberal in the original and fundamental sense. Each of its component parts—democracy, free trade, and controls on armaments—involved restraints on the exercise of power by governments.[27] This principle has some claim to being the essence of political liberalism, which erects fences around certain spheres of social life into which the government is forbidden to intrude, thus creating space for individual liberty. Similarly, restrictions on arms limit one of the basic tools of statecraft and thereby circumscribe what sovereign states can do to one another. A market economy, which one of the earliest and certainly the most influential of its chroniclers, Adam Smith, called "a system of natural liberty,"[28] is liberal in that one of its central institutions is private property, which is controlled by individual owners rather than the government. Economic decisions, concerning what to produce and how, where and when to produce it, and to whom and at what price to sell it, are made by individuals according to the criterion of profitability rather than by government officials according to their own agendas. To be sure, government plays a role in a market economy. It produces some things; it sets some prices; it imposes taxes on privately owned property. But what it does is limited. As with democracy and restraints on armaments, market economics establishes zones that are off limits to the exercise of governmental power.

The three parts of Wilsonianism are liberal as well in that they establish explicit, impersonal, universal rules to govern politics, economics, and security. The essence of liberal government is fidelity to clear and visible procedures by which the public selects the government and by which it then governs. Of particular importance are the procedures for enacting and administering laws. In the liberal form of government, whatever outcome issues from adherence to the designated procedures counts as proper and just. The basic rules specifying these procedures are typically set out in a constitution.

Limits on armaments are also rules that sovereign states choose to follow. They are the partial equivalent, for relations among sovereign states, of the rules that govern public affairs within liberal political systems: partial, because they do not affect what states may do with the arms that they are permitted to possess.

Market economies work by rules as well. Producers strive for profits, which they earn when they satisfy the demands of consumers. In this way, as Adam Smith noted, the miracle of the market occurs: the pursuit of individual well-being by each leads to the greatest possible satisfaction for all. But this can only occur when all act according to common, well-understood rules.

The three parts of Wilson's triad are liberal, finally, in that all favor the interests of the individual. Political liberalism protects the individual against the state and gives him or her the power, via the ballot, to select and remove those in authority. The supreme goal of a market economy is to satisfy the desires of the individual consumer. Democracy is a system of popular sovereignty, the market economy one of consumer sovereignty. As for the third part of the triad, it is governments that conduct wars and war therefore enhances their power. Peace tilts the balance of power back toward the individual as well as preserving those individual lives that would be lost in war.

The liberal character of the Wilsonian triad stands in contrast to the principles that predominated before the modern era. Sovereign states sometimes observed the rules of war but virtually never agreed to limit their armaments. Peace, which Wilson believed required reducing if not abolishing armaments, arose from a military equilibrium among states that equipped themselves with the forces they believed they needed or could afford. The power politics that dominated international relations for virtually all of recorded history, and that Wilson hoped to transcend, produced peace not through constitutional arrangements governing military might but rather through a balance of power.[29]

Similarly, it was normal for the power of premodern governments over those they governed to be limited by custom, tradition, and the restrictions imposed by geography and technology rather than in the liberal manner by impersonal, universal rules. Constitutional liberalism was very much the exception, not the rule.

And while the twentieth century Communist governments' aspiration to control all economic activity was historically unusual, so, too, for almost all of recorded history, were the rule-bound market economies of that century and the previous one. In the largely agricultural economies in which all human beings lived before the modern age, governments rarely told farmers what to plant but did reserve the right to appropriate a share of their harvests when and as they chose.[30]

For Woodrow Wilson, the arbitrary, unfettered exercise of governmental power was all too typical of the autocratic, imperial governments that he held responsible for World War I and their abolition was therefore necessary to achieve lasting peace. The end of the continental empires was necessary because their characteristically illiberal practices—the uninhibited accumulation of arms, the arbitrary exercise of political power, and the self-interested interference with economic activity—led directly to war. Although Wilson did not put it in these terms, the political forces that had caused the war were the same ones that the Parisians who pulled down the Bastille in 1789 had been attacking: World War I had been caused by the persistence of the old regime.

If these three parts of Wilson's vision—limits on armaments, popular government, and the removal of barriers to commerce—had been established, the shortcomings of the fourth, his beloved League of Nations, might not have mattered, because by themselves the three would have made a conflict like World War I less likely to recur. But the Wilsonian triad was not established. In fact, it was not even securely established in the Anglo-American world from which it came: Britain did not favor self-government for its own imperial possessions, nor was it enthusiastic about limits on its navy, and the United States was not wholeheartedly devoted to free trade. But the most formidable difficulty in establishing the Wilsonian triad in practice was that out of the rubble of World War I emerged new rivals to liberalism. Fascism and Communism accepted two of the goals of modernity—popular sovereignty and economic growth—but prescribed radically illiberal means for achieving them. The contest for global primacy between the two of them and liberalism—two forms of modernity—would dominate the twentieth century.

The contest between international liberalism and fascist and Communist totalitarianism was over whether the popular will was properly expressed through the institutions and procedures of liberal democracy or through self-selected elite political parties presiding over extreme forms of state domination. It was also a contest over whether the wealth that the industrial revolution had made possible could be better achieved through the free market of the Anglo-American world or through much greater (in the case of fascism) or total (in the Communist case) control by the government of the basic economic tasks: investment, production, and distribution. As for international security, the illiberal version of modernity made war central, desirable, indeed necessary. In the face of such an attitude the liberal powers might well believe war to be unnatural and undesirable, but they could hardly afford to act as if it were impossible. Until late in the twentieth century genuine peace, let alone significant controls on armaments, was not a realistic prospect.

Woodrow Wilson believed that democracy, free markets, and arms restraints should be universally practiced. For most of the twentieth century after World War I they were far from universal. The idea that they could be, that these liberal norms could dominate the world, was, for the Western leaders who followed Wilson, little more than an attractive idea. It was something that would no doubt be beneficial if it ever came to pass but that showed no sign of ever doing so—until the end of the Cold War, when the hegemony of liberal ideas emerged as the defining feature of international life.

THE LIBERAL HEGEMONY

Déja vu, according to Freud, occurs when someone experiences in real life something that had previously appeared in a dream.[31] By this definition, the post-Cold War world is a textbook case. For as the twentieth century ended, what had been a dream for Woodrow Wilson had, to all appearances, come true. The new geopolitical landscape corresponded to the world Wilson had imagined, hoped for, and prophesied. A world dominated by the East-West conflict had given way to one in which liberal principles were unchallenged.

The control of armaments is a nineteenth century idea but a twentieth century invention. In Wilson's day no regulations governed the possession of weapons. In the wake of the Cold War many such regulations were in place. Most of them concerned a particular region and a particular type of armament. The region was Europe. By the time the Soviet Union collapsed, the European continent was as intensively regulated for military forces as the center of a major American city is for architecture. The European arms control regime, largely negotiated in the latter years of the Cold War and in the immediate post-Cold War period, was a set of military zoning ordinances: strict, elaborate, and designed to produce a stable balance of forces even as zoning laws are intended to produce an ensemble of height and space that is both esthetically appealing and commercially viable. The most heavily regulated arms were those known as "weapons of mass destruction." This category included nuclear weapons, but also, by convention, chemical and biological armaments.

As for democracy, it was rare in Wilson's era. World War I was won by a coalition of countries—the United States, Great Britain, France, and the British dominions of Canada, Australia, and New Zealand—that virtually exhausted the list of the world's functioning democracies, in which governments were freely elected and the laws that such governments enacted were scrupulously followed. But at the end of the Cold War, eighty years later, the goal for which the United States had fought World War I had evidently been achieved: Much of the world was democratic. In the 1999–2000 report of

Freedom House, an American organization that tracks and seeks to promote the progress of political liberty in the world, eighty-five of the world's 192 countries were classified as "free" and sixty more as "partly free." This was a far higher score, even adjusting for the vastly expanded number of independent countries, than the world would have earned in Wilson's day. It is a higher score than the Freedom House ratings of twenty or ten years earlier.[32]

The third Wilsonian precept, international commerce, was also a notable feature of the post-Cold War world. Between 1950 and 1996, the world's exports increased by volume sixteen times over. (Total economic output increased sixfold.) In most countries merchandise exports[33] as a percentage of the Gross Domestic Product were considerably higher in the wake of the Cold War than they had been on the eve of World War I.[34]

Many countries that had gained independence after World War II began their lives as sovereign states determined to restrict at least the inward flow of products made elsewhere. But by the 1990s they had lowered or abolished many of the barriers they had erected. The World Trade Organization, established in 1997 to further the principles of free trade, had 132 members, with thirty additional countries seeking to join. And the flow of capital across borders had increased even more dramatically than trade. [35]

At the same time, an increasing number of countries adopted liberal principles for organizing economic activity within their borders as well as across them. The role of government in economic management shrank, while that of market principles in decisions about production and distribution expanded. Liberal economic ideas penetrated even those parts of the world that had been, at the height of the Cold War, most hostile to them.[36] In 1997 Wang Zhongyu, the Minister of the State Economic and Trade Commission (his title itself a badge of official economic illiberalism) of the People's Republic of China, said, "We must have a system where the strong survive and the weak fail. That is the lesson of the market economy."[37] This statement came from a senior official of a country where, within living memory, someone suspected of following the "capitalist road" would have been imprisoned or shot. A term that became common in the wake of the Cold War bore witness to the strength of liberal economic ideas and practices: globalization. While it had a variety of implications, the word had a core meaning: the spread of free markets everywhere.

Another sign of the victory of economic liberalism was the status and power of the two principal international financial institutions, the World Bank and the International Monetary Fund (IMF). Both had their headquarters in Washington, D.C., the capital of the country that had been most vocal in its proclamations of support for free markets. Both were committed to propagating these principles and both—the Fund more so than the Bank—possessed a crucial instrument for doing so: money. The IMF was the Vatican of free-market economics, but more powerful than the Bishop of Rome. Stalin's sneering rhetorical question about the power of the Church—"How many divisions does the Pope have?"—was wholly inappropriate for the late-twentieth century citadel of liberal economic orthodoxy. For without so much as a palace guard the IMF had, in the wake of the Cold War, acquired the power to induce governments to adopt sweeping policies, with serious economic effects, that were often, in the short run, deeply disadvantageous to their own people. In exchange for loans to governments the IMF typically insisted on adherence to a strict free-market regimen. That regimen could be harsh, a Spartan diet leading to economic austerity that was sometimes intense and prolonged. The IMF may have been extremely unpopular in some countries but in the wake of the Cold War it was nearly omnipresent. Its organizational tentacles seemed to be irresistible to any country in economic distress or simply not as wealthy as the rich industrial democracies. In the year 2000 a total of eighty-three countries were involved in IMF lending programs of one kind or another, including virtually all of those that had emerged from Communist rule in Europe.[38] It became a mark of seriousness, almost a condition of sovereignty, to have such a program.[39]

While the liberal internationalism that Woodrow Wilson had brought to Paris was, in the wake of the Cold War, more popular and more widely practiced than ever before, its tenets were not universally established. Restrictions on weaponry could not in fact be said to be firmly established anywhere. The geographic reach of statutory limits on arms extended only to Europe, and even those limits were fragile. The treaties mandating them depended on voluntary compliance. The rules governing weapons of mass destruction were global in scope but they did not command universal compliance and were not matched by comparably broad protocols that applied to other kinds of weapons. Indeed, the very idea that restrictions on arms could make an important, let alone an indispensable, contribution to peace was not universally accepted.

Liberal politics and liberal economics were far better established than arms control, not only in practice but in theory. Behind popular, constitutional politics stood a rich tradition of scholarship and debate reaching back at least as far as the seventeenth century English philosophers Thomas Hobbes and John Locke. The comparable tradition for market economics was not quite as venerable, but its roots could be traced to the eighteenth century and to another formidable thinker, Adam Smith. No such admired tradition stood behind the idea that reducing weaponry was a key to international peace.

While more deeply and widely established, the form of government Wilson had thought integral to peace was not universal, either. In the initial post-Cold War decade, democracy became a cause to which a good deal of lip service was paid, especially by rulers who did not actually favor it but who found it convenient to claim that they did. Many countries had governments that looked like the British parliamentary model or the American federal system but did not function as they did. In the eighteenth century Grigori Potemkin, a minister of the Russian empress Catherine the Great, lined a route on which she was traveling with impressive-appearing but flimsy, hastily erected structures in order to persuade her that large settlements had been built there. They are known to history as "Potemkin villages." In the same spirit, many of the post-Cold War "Potemkin democracies" were intended, among other things, to deceive the powerful of the international system, who could be counted on to confer economic favors on regimes classified as "democratic." On the map of the world with degrees of democracy in shades of red, large stretches of the planet—in Africa, the Arab Middle East, and much of the former Soviet Union—could qualify only for the palest of pinks. The government of the most populous country in the world, the People's Republic of China, made the suppression of political liberty a matter of firm principle and daily practice.

Free trade, and the market economics that underlie it, were more widely accepted and practiced than either of the other two parts of the Wilsonian triad. While resolutely opposed to liberal politics, the Chinese government emphatically favored, at least rhetorically, liberal economics. Still, obstacles to commerce continued to exist throughout the international system, although they were fewer and more modest, and erecting and maintaining them were less respectable, than in Wilson's day.

Nor, finally, was the world fully liberal in the way that had mattered most to Wilson: It was anything but wholly peaceful. In the last decade of the twentieth century the threat of a major conflict like the three that had dominated the twentieth century had receded sharply, but lesser wars were numerous.

In the wake of the Cold War liberal internationalism was not, therefore, universal. It was, instead, hegemonic. The term "hegemony" comes originally from ancient Greece. There it referred to the fact of preponderance and the exercise of leadership or predominant influence by one Greek city-state, usually within the context of a confederacy of several of them. The hegemon towered over the others. Similarly, international liberalism was a towering presence in the post-Cold War world. It provided the most widely adopted set of political and economic principles and institutions. It was practiced and promoted by the most powerful members of the international system. It was the world's orthodoxy and had no serious, fully articulated rival as a set of principles for organizing the world's military relations, politics, and economics.[40] Not all sovereign states accepted each of the three features of international liberalism or were able to practice them. But there were no alternative principles. Asked where in Paris he would most like to live, a French architect is said to have picked the Eiffel Tower on the grounds that this was the only place in the city from which he would not have to look at it. Liberalism is the Eiffel Tower of the twenty-first century.*

As with the Eiffel Tower, the liberal world order of the twenty-

*This account of the past two centuries recalls a tradition of historical understanding popular in Great Britain and the United States known as the "Whig interpretation," which pre-first century did not please everybody. Its opponents were noisy, determined, and sometimes violent. Their ranks included the Middle Eastern terrorists who perpetrated the attacks of September 11, 2001. They included, as well, the thousands of Westerners who gathered to protest the international economic policies of the wealthy countries at the meeting of the World Trade Organization in Seattle in December 1999 and the meeting of the Group of Eight—the wealthy industrial democracies plus Russia—at Genoa in July 2001.

While both groups disliked—detested is perhaps a more accurate word—the liberal practices and institutions that dominated the world of the twenty-first century, and both sought to destroy them, neither had any real hope of success and neither offered anything to put in place of what they were assaulting. In the wake of the September 11 attacks a European marching to protest the military operations the United States undertook in response carried a placard that read "Civilization is genocide." The slogan captured the emptiness of the opposition to the Wilsonian triad: It was at once incoherent and idiotic.

The international system was therefore like a fixed price menu from which a diner could accept or reject different items. He or she could choose to skip the hors d'oeuvre, or the main course, or the dessert—or to go hungry altogether. In the first post-Cold War

---

sented the rise of liberty as the central theme of the national experience of the two countries. With the horrors of the twentieth century it fell out of favor in both countries. (On this point see William McNeill, *The Shape of European History*, New York: Oxford University Press, 1974, p. 3. The original study of this approach to historical understanding by the English historian Herbert Butterfield, *The Whig Interpretation of History*, London: G. Bell and Sons, 1931, had, in fact, a revisionist theme, arguing that one of the staples of the interpretation, the identification of Protestantism, the Reformation, and Martin Luther with the rise of liberty, was inaccurate.)

The version outlined here is Whig history with a vengeance, for it encompasses not only the nineteenth century, as the original English version did, but the twentieth as well; not only the United States and the United Kingdom but the entire world; and not only politics but also economics and international relations. This version of the outcome of the Cold War and its place in the history of the modern world also has an affinity with the theme of Francis Fukuyama's book *The End of History and the Last Man* (New York: Avon Books, 1993 paperback). The end of the Cold War does not mark the end of history except in one specialized but important meaning of the term—which happens to be the meaning that Fukuyama employed: the triumph and hegemony of liberal forms.

decade Burma, Cuba, Iraq and North Korea did reject international liberalism in its entirety and their people did in fact go hungry. But there was no other menu, no other series of equally appetizing political and economic choices from which to order. The political and economic weather varied from country to country in the wake of the Cold War but the global climate was unmistakably liberal. International liberalism had no shortage of critics, but no one was offering an alternative.

The Potemkin democracies and faux-market economies with their rigged stock markets and government monopolies, for all their failures to meet liberal standards, were eloquent testimony to the liberal hegemony. They were hypocritical enterprises; but, as La Rochefoucauld observed, hypocrisy is the tribute that vice pays to virtue. At the dawn of the twenty-first century liberalism was deemed the essence of virtue. And most countries went beyond simply paying symbolic tribute to international liberalism. Most tried to adopt at least some of its features. Their efforts to do so dominated the global agenda at the beginning of the twenty-first century.

THE POST-COLD WAR AGENDA

T HE END OF the first post-Cold War decade was the equivalent, for the history of the modern world, of one of the high Rocky Mountain passes on the trails that pioneers followed across North America in the nineteenth century. It was a vantage point from which the shape of the historical terrain already covered could be seen in sharp relief, and from which the outlines of what lay ahead could also be discerned.

The past, the history of the modern era through the Cold War, divided into two parts. The struggle between the world's centuries-old political and economic practices, institutions, and assumptions and the forces that created the modern world dominated the "long nineteenth century,"[41] from the French Revolution to World War I. This struggle pitted free markets, free elections, and a predilection for peaceful international conduct against more regulated and controlled economic activity, monarchical rule, and the acceptance of

war as a normal instrument of statecraft. At the end of World War I
the old regime lay in ruins. The mighty engine of the industrial revolution had destroyed the hopes of preserving a static, rural, agricultural way of economic life. The French Revolution had promulgated
the idea that the people, not the princes, should rule, and after a cen-
tury-long rearguard action the princes gave way, their last bastions
flattened by World War I. The great conflict that ended dynastic
rule in Europe also deprived the practice of war of legitimacy. The
slaughter in the trenches lent urgency to a view that, even in its
Anglo-American cradle, only a minority had held—namely that war
had to be abolished.

In the "short twentieth century," from World War I to the end of
the Cold War, two versions of modernity clashed. Instead of liberal
practices and institutions the illiberal version favored smothering
control of economic activity, the repression of independent politics,
and the active promotion of warfare. In World War II the liberal
world made common cause with one branch of illiberalism, Soviet
Communism, against two others—Nazi Germany and Imperial
Japan. The Cold War matched the two victors of World War II. Liberalism prevailed and emerged without the mortal challenge it had
faced in the nineteenth and twentieth centuries.

The perspective of the post-Cold War era also brings into focus
Woodrow Wilson's niche in modern history. His is a singular place
in company of the outsized Western leaders of the first half of
the twentieth century. Like David Lloyd George and Georges
Clemenceau, like Winston Churchill and Franklin D. Roosevelt, he
presided over one of the countries of the victorious coalition in one
of the two great wars of the century. But he was a different kind of
political figure than they. He lacked the personal and political char-
acteristics that made them successful war leaders, the guile of Lloyd
George and Roosevelt, the iron determination of Clemenceau and
Churchill. He was neither a lion nor a fox. Nor was he as important
to victory as they: The United States entered World War I relatively
late and made a modest, albeit crucial, contribution to its outcome.

In one important way he had more in common with Lenin and
Hitler. All three were the bearers, on the world stage, of a system.
Each system was grounded in a particular feature of social life—lib-

erty in Wilson's case, class and race for the other two. Each feature underlay the social and political arrangements of a particular great power, the government of which sought to spread its system abroad.

The differences between Wilson and the founders of twentieth century illiberalism, however, are more striking than the similarities. Lenin and Hitler were central to the establishment of Communism and fascism. It is difficult to imagine the victory of their ideas in their countries without them. This is not so for Wilson, who packaged and presented in dramatic fashion ideas that had been current for decades. Woodrow Wilson was the Henry Ford of international liberalism, taking what had already been invented and offering it to the world.

Most important, the content of the Wilsonian triad was the opposite of what Lenin and Hitler inflicted upon the world. The difference between the American president and the European dictators was the difference between liberty and oppression, between prosperity and stagnation, between peace and war. And, of course, Wilson's ideas triumphed. By the end of the twentieth century the ideologies of Lenin and Hitler were discredited, the institutions they had built had been abandoned, the sovereign states they had led, as defined by the borders within which they had exercised authority, no longer existed. By contrast, although when Wilson unveiled his ideas at Paris they were utopian, eight decades later they had become pedestrian.

From the high ground of the first post-Cold War decade the future, not surprisingly, was less clear than the past. But the geopolitical terrain after the Cold War clearly differed from that of the era that had preceded it. The post-Cold War world, like the world of the Cold War, did not lack problems, conflicts, or uncertainties. But while in the earlier period almost all of these stemmed from the great global conflict between liberalism and Communist illiberalism, in the later one most had their origins in the conditions created by the end of that conflict through its resolution in liberalism's favor.

More than that, the outline of the post-Cold War era was discernible. Its central theme, the plot of international history in the wake of the great East-West conflict, was the defense, the maintenance, and the extension of the three parts of the Wilsonian triad. Nor was this simply a detached, lofty perspective on the post-Cold

War world far removed from the hurly-burly at ground level. This was the theme of post-Cold War history, in the era's first decade, as those who were making that history understood and experienced it.

The more powerful states in the international system deliberately sought to propagate liberalism. They propagated it even when they were not consciously seeking to do so; they were magnets as well as missionaries. Lesser states, especially those not fully liberal, were attracted, repelled, exhilarated and offended—but at all events powerfully affected—by liberalism. It was the compass point by which they took their bearings. They understood their own politics, economics, and foreign policies as responses to the liberal hegemony even when they sought to evade it.

The liberal practices and institutions that Woodrow Wilson first brought to the center of the world's attention, and that stand at the heart of the international history of the post-Cold War period, come in two varieties. A system of arms restraints is, by definition, international, involving more than one country. Its relations with others determine the security of any particular member of the international system. Democracy, by contrast, is domestic in scope. Whether one country is democratic has nothing *necessarily* to do with whether there are other democracies, although the international popularity of democratic norms certainly affected their prospects within particular countries. Building and maintaining a democracy is like assembling and maintaining a computer. Organizing and maintaining an arms control regime is like assembling and maintaining a network that links different computers together. Establishing and maintaining a liberal economic order involves both: Sovereign states have distinct national economies but these are also part of an international network.

The procedures by which international and domestic liberalism are established differ. The first requires international negotiation. Deliberate acts of policy by governments interacting with one another create arms limitations. This is not so for democracy and the market economy. But they, too, have an international dimension; and here, too, sovereign states affect each other, although in a less direct way.

Like individuals, collectives can change by observing and learning. Arms control spreads by active cooperation, democracy and the market economy by imitation. The first involves what sovereign states do, the second what happens within societies. The first is the business of governments, the second the result of social forces that are anonymous, pervasive, and not readily controlled.

Still, the two are closely related. Sovereign states are willing to comply with liberal norms beyond their borders to the extent that liberal institutions, practices, and values are established within them.[42] Thus, for the prospects for the Wilsonian triad in the post-Cold War world, social forces are just as important as government policies—perhaps more so. This, as it happens, was true of the Cold War as well. Indeed, for the way that conflict came to an end, the social forces that contribute to imitation in the international system were decisive. An assessment of the world of the twenty-first century therefore requires a revised understanding of the global rivalry between liberalism and Communism that dominated the second half of the twentieth century, a conflict similar to, but also crucially different from, the three great global conflicts of the modern era that preceded it, an event that was, but also was not, a war.

CHAPTER TWO

The Cold War Reconsidered

IN A GROUP PORTRAIT of the major wars of the modern period the Cold War would certainly deserve a place. It bears an unmistakable family resemblance to the Napoleonic wars and World Wars I and II. Yet in important respects the Cold War was not like the others, and grouping it with them is like including the dog in a family portrait: The pet may be a valued and familiar member of the household, but it stands out as unmistakably different.

It is in fact the differences rather than the similarities between the Cold War and the other great conflicts that account for what is, for the post-Cold War era, most important about it: the global dominance of liberal, Wilsonian institutions and practices that it left in its wake. At the root of the differences between the great East-West rivalry of the second half of the twentieth century and the others is the fact that the term "Cold War" refers not only to a conflict but to an historical era. This era was one chapter in the ongoing history of the modern age, which began with the French and the industrial revolutions of the late eighteenth century. As such, the Cold War was the setting for a human practice even older, more pervasive, and ultimately more powerful than warfare; and it was this practice, the transmission of culture, that created the world of the twenty-first century.

THE FOURTH MAJOR WAR

L IKE THE OTHER major conflicts of the modern era, in the Cold War both sides deployed large armies and powerful arms in pursuit of incompatible goals. Like the others, two powerful coalitions faced each other. Like them, its geographic scope was a wide one, indeed the widest of all, waged as it was across the entire planet and even extending into outer space.

As in the major wars that preceded it, the opposing governments in the Cold War mobilized the societies they governed. They conscripted citizens into their armed forces and devoted appreciable parts of their national wealth, raised by taxation and borrowing, to the conflict. Like the two World Wars, the Cold War saw the systematic application of scientific research and industrial technology to the manufacture of weaponry, leading, in all three cases, to arms races between the opposing coalitions.

The Cold War also resembled the other three in its consequences. These great conflicts had the same impact on the international system that revolutions have on particular countries. They changed everything: the hierarchy of power in the world, the location of borders, the character of regimes—after all four wars the government of the losing power fell, to be succeeded by one more like that of the winners—and even the rules for relations between and among sovereign states.[1]

And yet the Cold War also differed from the others, with two specific differences having particular importance: its legacy, and the manner in which it ended.

The distinctive legacy was the sweeping victory of international liberalism. Liberal precepts had barely been introduced at the time of the Napoleonic wars and Napoleon represented them in a way that was, by the standards of the late twentieth century, at best imperfect. Napoleon and his principles, such as they were, in any case suffered defeat. World War I, won by liberal powers, marked the downfall of the forces of tradition, but that war gave rise to the two types of illiberalism—fascism and communism—that for the next seven decades contested the principles that Woodrow Wilson had introduced. World War II ended in defeat for the first of these varieties of illiberalism but in victory for the second. The Soviet Union was a mainstay of the victorious coalition and its armies and its ideas emerged from that conflict with greater power and prestige than they had enjoyed before the war. It was only after the Cold War that the principles to which Woodrow Wilson had given voice achieved unchallenged status.

THE LIBERAL VICTORY

O NE REASON FOR the sweeping character of the liberal triumph is that, although powers embodying different principles of political legitimacy and sometimes differing economic organization waged the three preceding great wars, the Cold War was more explicitly a contest of systems than any of its predecessors. Both sides said so. The American president, Harry Truman, asserted in 1947, at the outset of the struggle, that "at the present moment in world history nearly every nation must choose between alternative ways of life." The speech in which he uttered those words formed the basis for what came to be known as the Truman Doctrine, according to which "it must be the policy of the United States to support free peoples who are resisting attempted subjugation by armed minorities or by outside pressures." For the United States, the Truman Doctrine served as a declaration of war.

The leaders of the Soviet Union paid more attention than did the West to the systemic character of the contest, placing greater emphasis on its non-military aspects. They used the term "correlation of forces" to convey the idea that the balance of power between the two rival camps had to be measured in political, economic, and ideological terms as well as by the strength of their respective armed forces.[2] The Soviet state was created in opposition to, and for the purpose of displacing, the capitalist democracies of the West. The Bolsheviks who seized power in Russia in World War I assumed that socialist revolution would swiftly follow elsewhere in Europe, and the failure of events to follow this course surprised and dismayed them.[3]

It was all but inevitable that a conflict between the United States and the Union of Soviet Socialist Republics would be a contest of political ideas, for these countries had been founded upon political ideas. Neither was the political expression of an ethnic or linguistic community settled for centuries on the same territory. Each was founded to put into practice a specific set of principles. In both cases these principles were new and untried when the country was founded but, in the view of both sets of founders, were nonetheless universally applicable. Each country's identity, its justification for existing, and its purpose in the world were grounded in its political principles—which were mutually incompatible.

Another feature of the Cold War made it explicitly a contest of systems: In the years following World War II a number of formerly united countries were left divided between liberal and Communist regimes. Germany, Korea, and China thus became the political equivalents of a scientific experiment to test the consequences of practicing one or the other of the two systems.[4] The political, social, and economic histories of these divided countries were like the studies of identical twins who are separated at birth; because the twins' genes are identical, the differences between them must be caused by environmental influences.

The parallel Cold War histories of divided countries offered the purest possible tests of the difference it makes to live under one or the other system. They could hardly have been understood in any other way. These histories were more than simply an interesting experiment; they were the heart of a world historical contest. By the standards that both sides accepted, the liberal system triumphed.

The liberal economic order proved the more productive one. West Germany became more prosperous than East Germany, South Korea than North Korea, Taiwan than China.[5] And the liberal political order proved far more attractive. Evidence of the unpopularity of the Communist political system was the fact that those it governed were not permitted to modify, question, or even freely to discuss it—no doubt for fear of what they would say. Nor, for the most part, were they allowed to leave. When they could, many did. In all three countries the flow of emigration proceeded in only one direction: from communism to liberalism.

The outcome of the contest of systems was decisive not only in what might be called the margin of victory—that is, in how far the liberal order outperformed the Communist one—but also in its geographic breadth. Economically, Communism failed everywhere: in Europe, in Asia, in Latin America, and in Africa. Its failure was indisputable and freely acknowledged. In June 1991 Boris Yeltsin, who came to preside over the wreckage of Communist Russia, said that the Soviet Union's experience with Marxism-Leninism had "proved that there is no place for this idea."[6] Liberalism emerged from the Cold War in a commanding position because the Cold War had been explicitly a contest between liberal and illiberal principles, and in that contest liberalism scored a decisive victory.

Liberalism triumphed decisively for another reason. The winning coalition was united, and united in favor of liberal principles. This had not been so in the past. The winners in 1815 were not liberal at all. It was the old regime, the forces of tradition, that triumphed on the battlefield.[7] The winning coalition in World War I was not, as it had been a century earlier, an illiberal one, but neither was it united. In the wake of the war France wished to punish Germany and annex German territory; the United States shared neither goal. Neither Great Britain nor the United States fully subscribed to the vision of uninhibited global trade and the British sought a larger navy and merchant marine than the American president deemed prudent.[8] Nor were the victors entirely prepared to practice the liberal political principles they urged on others. Britain and France supported national self-determination in the European empires that they had defeated but did not offer it to the non-European subjects of their own overseas empires.

Some of the differences that surfaced after World War I reappeared during the next great war. The American president Franklin Roosevelt opposed imperial rule. Roosevelt's British counterpart and wartime partner, Winston Churchill, insisted on maintaining the British empire. He did not succeed in doing so, nor did the French manage to keep theirs. The deepest and most consequential cleavage within the winning coalition in 1945, however, divided the Soviet Union from the West. It proved unbridgeable.

In the wake of the Cold War, by contrast, none of the victors had any reservations about the Wilsonian triad. With the exception of West Germany, none sought what had been the normal prize of military victory for centuries: territorial gain.[9] Insofar as the power of their common principles to shape the postwar world depended on the breadth of their common commitment to them, that power was formidable indeed.

The Cold War differed from the previous great conflicts of the modern age in a second way, one even more striking than the first. It ended without military victory. Indeed it lacked in Europe what the other three conflicts had in abundance and what is the essence of war: combat. True, on the European continent between the 1940s and the 1990s two great opposing armed forces were raised, equipped, deployed, and maintained. But in all that time not a shot was fired in anger.[10] In the previous wars, military victory was the cause of political change. Defeated, disarmed, and demoralized, the vanquished submitted to the preferences of the victors. This was not so in the Cold War, a fact that raises a large question: Why did that conflict end at all?[11]

The losing side, the Communist bloc, was not defeated on the battlefield. The sweeping political changes that followed the three previous wars had come about because the losers were in no position to refuse them. But throughout the Cold War, until the very end, the Communist authorities *were* in a position to refuse. In strictly military terms the great East-West conflict of the second half of the twentieth century was a standoff.* There was no military reason for it to end as it did, which is why almost no one expected what happened.

Understanding the outcome of the Cold War—why it ended, how it ended, and how the way it ended has shaped the post-Cold War era—requires taking into account the ways in which, for all its similarities to the three great conflicts of the modern era, it was not a war. Here analogies are helpful. The Cold War can usefully be com-

---

*If anything, in military terms the Communist side had the upper hand. Its military forces ended World War II in control of Europe as far west as the middle of Germany. At the end of the 1940s Communists had won control of the Chinese mainland. In the 1960s they took control of the island of Cuba, a mere ninety miles from the coast of their great antagonist, the United States. In the 1970s Communist forces conquered all of formerly French Indochina. International liberalism made no comparable military gains.

pared to three quite different aspects of social life with which it nonetheless has important features in common: the process of evolution in nature; competition among rival firms in a market; and religious conversion.

ANALOGIES

L IKE THE Cold War, evolution—the process by which life in all its forms developed—was a protracted affair. The time scale of evolution is immensely longer—hundreds of millions of years—but the East-West conflict was long in comparison with other wars[12] and, as in the case of evolution, considerable time passed without major visible changes.[13]

Evolution does not ordinarily involve direct clashes between different life forms, just as the Cold War lacked battles between the two blocs.[14] But through the process of evolution some species survive and others die out. So it was with the Cold War, as the result of which a political species, European Communism, became effectively extinct.[15]

The mechanism by which evolution proceeds illustrates another feature of the Cold War. It involves three interrelated processes: replication, mutation, and adaptation. Changes in the design of species establish themselves as they are reproduced over generations of that species. Traits are reproduced if they are conducive to survival; that is, if creatures bearing those traits tend to reproduce themselves more successfully than those that lack them. Traits that survive, that are "selected," are, in this sense, adaptive. Similarly, the liberal system survived the Cold War not because it conquered the illiberal one but because its features proved to be better adapted to their common environment.

The analogy to evolution points to another significant aspect of the Cold War. What was adaptive in one set of circumstances came to be maladaptive in another. Dinosaurs died out because the conditions in which they lived altered. But for a period of time they thrived, just as for a substantial part of its life Communism seemed robust and formidable, with the potential to extend its reach all over the planet. Then the environment in which liberalism and Communism functioned changed, to the fatal disadvantage of Communism.[16]

The Cold War differed from the process of evolution through natural selection in two important ways, and the differences are as instructive as the similarities. First, different species not only do not fight, they do not compete directly against each other. They are programmed to try to reproduce themselves but not to inhibit the reproduction of others.[17] Evolution is thus a set of parallel processes. The Cold War, by contrast, was an interactive one. In the second half of the twentieth century liberal and illiberal systems competed with each other in every way except through direct combat in Europe. Moreover, and this is the second salient difference, both sides deliberately waged the Cold War competition. Evolution through natural selection is not deliberate. Species do not consciously adopt strategies to adapt and survive, as the two sides in the Cold War did.[18] Here the Cold War can more usefully be compared to the competition of private firms attempting to sell the same product.[19]

Like the two great political-military blocs during the Cold War, such firms do compete directly although not, ordinarily, violently. A gain in market share for one is usually a loss for its competitors. (This is not always so. The overall size of a market can expand, permitting gains for more than one firm.) Competent firms do adopt conscious strategies, as, of course, did the leaders of the liberal and illiberal camps during the Cold War. They devote time, effort, and resources to creating a superior product, making it at the lowest possible cost, and persuading consumers to buy it.

Mikhail Gorbachev, the last leader of the Soviet Union, who set in motion the changes that ultimately led to its disintegration, may be compared to an executive who takes charge of a failing firm and implements a radical strategy to close the gap with its rivals, only to have this strategy backfire, making things worse and leading ultimately to his firm's collapse into bankruptcy.[20] The element of purpose, of conscious design, is relevant at two levels for commercial competition, as it was for the Cold War: the firm decides on a strategy for selling its product, and the success or failure of that strategy depends on how many consumers decide to purchase and re-purchase it.

By this analogy the Communist variety of twentieth century illiberalism was rejected by consumers. The Soviet Union and its clients and allies lost the wherewithal to sustain themselves and experienced the political equivalent of bankruptcy. The analogy extends further: A collapsed firm is often taken over by a rival. This is, in a sense, what happened when the Cold War ended. The Communist world came under new management, which was committed, at least in theory, to the operating principles of its former rival.

Sovereign states cannot literally go bankrupt, with a court assigning their assets to their creditors, but Communist countries did experience considerable economic distress. They were deeply indebted, with economic output stalling and then falling.[21] The Communist regimes lost the political allegiance of those they governed. The term for what governments need to remain politically viable and what the Communist regimes lacked—credibility—is a cognate of the word for what is necessary for commercial viability—credit. The two come from the same root, *credere*, the Latin for "to believe." The end for Communism came when the political equivalent of its customers, the constituency for its product, the people it governed, ceased to believe in it.

Where the crucial issue of belief is concerned, however, the comparison between the Cold War and commercial competition misleads as well as illuminates. In both cases changes of belief have powerful effects. But the intensity and the scope of the beliefs at issue were far greater in the case of the Cold War. The terminology of economics does not, in fact, use the word *belief*. Consumers are said to express *preferences*. Many are lightly held, and consumers frequently change them. Changes of allegiance from one political and economic system to another are more consequential and less reversible. Such an allegiance is not a preference, it is a commitment, with the greater weight that that term conveys. The Cold War ended with a change of mind, but one involving an emotional upheaval less like a switch of brand loyalty than like religious conversion.

Conversion from one faith to another has historically tended to bring with it changes not only of belief but also of daily routine and even personal identity. This was true of the shift from Communism to liberalism in the wake of the Cold War. As a secular version of a change of religious affiliation, the Cold War and its outcome had two distinct although overlapping stages: the loss of faith in the precepts of the old system and the embrace of those of the new one. This two-step process, moreover, took place at two distinct, although again closely related, levels: among the governed and in the ranks of the governors.

For both groups, the loss of faith no doubt proceeded in gradual and cumulative fashion, involving the accretion of doubts and reservations about, growing into objections to, the orthodoxy. There were, perhaps, moments of epiphany as well, flashes of clarity and insight like the one experienced by Saul on the road to Damascus.[22]

Attitudes are powerful but slippery social facts. They are difficult to track and measure and the best twentieth-century instrument for doing so—survey research based on interviews—was, for political reasons, impossible to apply to the Communist world. Still, there can be no doubt that belief in the ruling system in the Communist world ebbed over time from what was probably its high point in the immediate aftermath of World War II. Nor can there be any doubt that this was crucial to the end of the Cold War.[23] The waning of belief surely had a number of causes. In some places the system had never commanded profound allegiance. In Central and Eastern Europe, especially in Poland, it had been alien and unwelcome from the outset, having been imposed by the conquering Red Army. However, the most prominent cause of the erosion of belief, the one most widely noted at the time and the one most closely tied to the post-Cold War policies of the governments that succeeded Communist ones, was economic failure. In the contest with liberalism to harness the forces of the industrial revolution to produce wealth, the Communist system came in a distant second. But another feature of this variety of illiberalism played a critical role in provoking a loss of faith in the system and deserves mention.

Communism was not only a method for wielding political authority and a set of principles for organizing economic activity: It was also a system for mass murder. Violence, brutality, persecution, and the killing of innocent people on a vast scale were its hallmarks. The Soviet and Chinese regimes practiced terror on a larger scale than had ever before been seen in the world. These regimes also provoked, and presided over, the two worst famines of the twentieth century. Measured by the numbers of people who died, they were probably the worst in human history.[24] Stalin's victims, by one estimate, numbered between thirty and forty million people; Mao's, thirty-five million.[25] If the proportion of the civilian population killed by the regime is the standard for judging the turpitude of the government, then the Communist Khmer Rouge, which ruled Cambodia between 1975 and 1979, probably deserves first prize, putting to death two million out of its seven million people.[26] Overthrowing Communism because it failed to deliver a sufficiently high standard of living was therefore like imprisoning the American mobster Al Capone, a man responsible for many murders, for his failure to pay income tax: The crime that was eventually punished was hardly the worst he committed. But the downfall of Communism in Europe did have something to do with its worst features.

While they held power, the Communist regimes suppressed virtually all public acknowledgment, let alone discussion, of the millions of people they had killed. But even in the absence of public discussion, of monuments to the victims, even of marked graves, what happened was widely known. The fears that these campaigns of oppression, displacement, and murder inspired in those who survived contributed to the political stability that the regimes enjoyed for much of the second half of the twentieth century. The Soviet Union under Stalin, Khrushchev, and Brezhnev enjoyed internal peace; but it was the peace of the graveyard. And the knowledge of what had happened ate away, like termites destroying the foundations of a house, at whatever active, willing popular support Communism had once enjoyed.

Of the two levels of society at which it took place, faith in the system probably eroded more slowly within the elite. Its members were, after all, the beneficiaries of the system, which gave them power and wealth that others did not have the opportunity to acquire. But although Communism was, in effect, their system, ultimately they too turned against it and their rejection delivered the coup de grâce.

The spread of the great religions of the planet often proceeded from the top down. The ruler would embrace the new faith and his subjects would follow. The disintegration of Communism followed this pattern. The departures from orthodoxy of Deng Xiaoping in China and Mikhail Gorbachev in the Soviet Union opened the way to the abandonment of its economic features in the first case and all of it in the second. These two were for international liberalism what Constantine, the Roman emperor who embraced the Christian faith in 313, was for Christianity in Europe.[27]

The metaphor of conversion, because it often produces change from the top down, is at least as useful in understanding the collapse of Communism as the term more frequently employed: revolution. Revolution has come to signify the people rising up, overthrowing an unjust regime, and taking power for themselves. This image served as the subject of dozens of paintings in the nineteenth century and millions of mass-produced posters in the twentieth. All are versions of the Delacroix oil painting paying homage to the Paris uprising of 1830, entitled *Liberty Guiding the People*. It depicts Marianne, the young woman who symbolizes France, holding the tricolor aloft and leading a motley collection of armed citizens forward, across the fallen bodies of their comrades, through the smoke of battle, with the buildings of the capital in the background.[28] Delacroix captured the crucial point in the revolutionary drama, the moment when the people take matters into their own hands: They storm the Bastille, as in Paris in 1789, or the Winter Palace, as in St. Petersburg in 1917. Revolution is war, the people are soldiers, the battle is won through their courage.

That is not exactly how Communism fell.[29] The structure that symbolized the Communist system, the equivalent of the Bastille or the Winter Palace, was the Berlin Wall. When it ceased to divide the city into two hermetically sealed parts, the Cold War had effectively ended. But it was not torn down by a surging crowd.* The guards manning it allowed people to pass through it freely in both directions. It was the gatekeepers who opened the gate.

Having been opened, the Wall was then dismantled, peacefully if often spontaneously. Fragments of the concrete barrier were packaged and sold. Similarly, caps, badges, and even rifles from the Soviet

---

*Two years before, in 1987, the American president Ronald Reagan had stood on the western side, in West Berlin, and issued a clarion call to the Soviet leader: "Mr. Gorbachev, tear

Army turned up for sale in flea markets all over Europe. The transformation of the Berlin Wall and other symbols (and instruments) of Communist oppression into commercial commodities is as vivid an expression of the triumph of liberal economic principles as can be imagined. What was erected as a barrier against capitalism ended as a capitalist product itself. And what had served as a stage for the heroism and tragedy of people trying to escape Communism became a series of souvenirs. What had begun in sacrifice ended in merchandise.

To be sure, in putting an end to Communism the people were not entirely passive. Crowds gathered to express opposition to the Communist regime in several East German cities and in Prague, the capital of Czechoslovakia, in the summer of 1989. And after the attempted coup against Mikhail Gorbachev in August 1991, Boris Yeltsin rallied a crowd of supporters in the heart of Moscow.[30] Those moments were decisive for the fate of Communism but what decided its fate was not the irresistible power of the crowds: It was the decision of the Communist authorities not to fire on them. The authorities certainly could have dispersed the crowds forcibly, as the Chinese regime did in June 1989 in Tiananmen Square in Beijing. Had they done so, European history would have followed a different course. By shooting, the regimes could have prolonged their own lives, as the Communist regime in China surely did. They could have bought time with blood. In Leipzig, Berlin, Prague, and Moscow they chose not to do so.[31]

The decision not to shoot was not entirely selfless and principled. In East Germany it was not really a decision at all. On matters of this sort the local Communist leadership relied in the end on Moscow. It was the Soviet leadership, and above all Gorbachev, that was ultimately responsible for the restraint that was practiced.[32] Nor was the decision by the Communist elite to allow their system to collapse necessarily an act of self-sacrifice. Many high-ranking Communists

---

down this wall." This was telling in two ways: It made explicit what was obvious but not often said: that it was the Soviet Union that had the final say on how and whether Germany would be divided. And Reagan did *not* urge, as someone in his position during the first century and a half after the French Revolution surely would have, that the people of East Berlin rise up and tear it down. It probably never occurred to Reagan or his advisers to say such a thing. That would have been dangerous.

in the Soviet Union, for example, were well positioned to enrich themselves personally—to feast, as it were, on the carcass of the Communist economy. And in some places the collapse of Communism actually enhanced the power of the elites. In Communist Central Asia local leaders doffed their worker's caps with the hammer and sickle emblazoned on the front, put on hats with the new national flag, and continued to rule what had become independent states, but without having to answer to Moscow.

But surely one of the reasons for the decision not to shoot, perhaps the main one, was the loss of faith in the system on behalf of which the bullets would have been fired. As Alexander Solzhenitsyn observed, "The imagination and the spiritual strength of Shakespeare's villains stopped short at a dozen corpses, because they had no *ideology*. . . . Thanks to ideology, the twentieth century was fated to experience evildoing on a scale calculated in the millions."[33] Belief in Marxism-Leninism had become so weak that it could not underwrite the dispatch of the hundreds of people whose deaths would likely have caused active opposition to evaporate or go underground.

The outcome of the Cold War understood as a modern version of religious conversion involves both the loss of faith in Communism and a subsequent leap of faith—the embrace of liberal political and economic principles. While the two are closely related the second does not necessarily follow from the first: Divorce, after all, is not invariably followed by remarriage. Abandoning the faith of Communism did not foreordain allegiance to liberalism and a concerted effort to refashion politics and economics according to liberal precepts. Even after the collapse of Communism, free elections and free markets did not enjoy powerful popular mandates in the parts of Europe where Communism had ruled. Because they were not allowed to leave their countries, it is natural to see the people of the Communist world during the Cold War decades as latter-day versions of Odysseus and his crew, lashed to the mast to prevent them from embracing the siren of liberalism. There is something in that, but another image from the literature of antiquity is equally pertinent to the immediate aftermath of Communism's collapse: Plato's cave, where people were kept in darkness and, after being released, wandered about aimless and disoriented.

Lenin said that in 1917 power in Russia had been "lying in the streets." He and the Bolsheviks seized it, consolidated it in a civil war, and used it to put their illiberal principles into practice across the former empire of the tsars. His successors brought these principles, borne on the bayonets of the Red Army, to the heart of Europe. After the collapse of Communism power once again lay in the streets. Why did those who seized or inherited it—or found themselves, to their surprise, wielding it—decide to use it (or at least feel compelled to say that they would use it) to embark on a liberal path?

For the first time in the modern era, there was no other plausible choice. By the last decade of the century neither fascism nor Communism, nor any other alternative system, appeared to be viable, let alone attractive. Liberalism, by contrast, seemed not only viable but very successful. The analogy to religious conversion points to one of the relevant hallmarks of success. An alien faith has seemed to potential converts worth adopting when many others have already adopted it. The more Christians there were in Europe, the more people who were not Christian were likely to be favorably disposed to the faith. So it was with international liberalism and the end of the Cold War.

Those who inherited the responsibility for guiding the destinies of countries where Communism had held sway were well aware that their former adversaries were devoted to free elections and free markets. But they also knew that liberal practices had made considerable headway over the previous two decades where the contest of systems was not as intense as it had been in Europe and where liberalism had been far less well-established when the Cold War began.

The progress of democracy outside the Communist world was striking. In the 1970s the previously authoritarian countries of southern Europe, Spain, Portugal, and Greece, embraced it. In the next decade, countries in East Asia—Taiwan, South Korea, the Philippines—followed suit. At the outset of the 1970s political liberalism was securely installed in few of the countries of Latin America. By the end of the 1980s, the only one that remained resolutely non-liberal was Cuba.

A similar shift in economic orientation took place. In the 1950s all over the non-Communist world, governments struck a balance in economic affairs between state management and private markets. Four decades later, in almost every country—in North America, Western Europe, Latin America, and East, Southeast, and South Asia—wherever that balance had been initially set it had moved sharply in the direction of the market.[34] In none of these countries was the shift as dramatic as the one that the formerly Communist countries of Europe were to attempt after Communism's collapse there, with one exception. The exception was the world's most populous country. Between 1949 and 1976 under the rule of Mao Zedong, China's economy, like that of the Soviet Union, was subject to state planning and central control. His successor, Deng Xiaoping, largely abandoned Communist economics and embraced the market.

The broad and deep trends toward political and economic liberalism had, by the last decade of the twentieth century, made the Communist world an ideological version of the Galapagos Islands. It was a place where illiberal practices and institutions were preserved in pristine form because its rulers had managed to insulate it from the social and political influences that were strong everywhere else. In this sense the collapse of Communism may be seen as simply a particular stage in a wider, older, more powerful process. And the account of the Cold War to which this observation leads is not an analogy, it is a description. For the competition of liberal and illiberal systems, and particularly the way it ended, can be understood as an example of the oldest and most basic of all historical processes: the diffusion of culture.

CULTURAL DIFFUSION

CULTURE, by the anthropologist's definition, consists of the food, tools, and buildings, the beliefs, ideas, institutions, and practices that make up human civilization. The history of civilization is the history of the creation and the spread of culture. Culture spreads by contacts among different societies. From the Neolithic age to the twenty-first century the hardware and the software that define human civilization have been passed from person to person and from group to group, modified, and then passed along again. And this process has followed a distinctive pattern.

Like minerals on the Earth's crust and the ability to play chess, the capacity for innovation is unevenly distributed across the world's human communities. Cultural innovations take place—new hardware and software are created—in hothouses of innovation, the "cores" of civilization. They then spread beyond their points of origin to neighboring regions and ultimately to distant ones. A cultural gradient slopes, metaphorically, downward from core to periphery. To be sure, the elements of human culture move in two directions between human groups, but the core is the net exporter, the periphery the importer. When India was a British possession it supplied new words—*bungalow, maharajah, thug*—and unfamiliar food—curries—to the metropolis. In return, the British brought to the Asian subcontinent the English language, modern government, and the railroad.[35]

William McNeill, one of the best-known practitioners in the field of the history of human civilization, has summarized this fundamental and age-old historical process:

Through the larger part of recorded history the main drive wheel of historical change was contacts among strangers, causing men on both sides of such encounters to reconsider and in some cases alter their familiar ways of behaving. Such contacts and the reactions to them generated civilizations. Within such civilizations, like a volcano in eruption, there arose specially active "metropolitan centers" of innovation. The emergence of such centers in turn created cultural slopes. From time to time metropolitan centers shifted location, or a quite new center asserted itself; with such changes came changes in direction and velocity of cultural flows, that is, alterations in the alignment of cultural slopes. Such alterations, in turn, may be taken as defining major periods of eras of history.[36]

Culture diffuses by voluntary means: exchange, example, imitation. It also spreads coercively, by conquest and imposition. The two can coincide. The British imposed the Western practice of the rule of law on India; but Indians absorbed it and retained it when the British left.

Just how and why the clusters of innovations come into being, and why the location of the world's cores has shifted over the centuries, are questions to which the contemporary study of social, economic, and cultural history has devoted considerable attention. Clearly geography matters, as do the conditions that arise from it: climate and biology. They help to explain why innovations have rarely come from the tropics and why Europe surged ahead of the rest of the world five hundred years ago.[37] Social and political practices have also been important, accounting for two great and much-studied historical developments: China's failure to capitalize on its many advantages and lead the world into the modern age, and Great Britain's singular ability to do so, at least in economic terms.[38]

The location of the world's civilizational cores has shifted over the centuries. In the first half of the last millennium, for example, from approximately 1000 to 1500, what is now known as Europe consisted of a series of poor and relatively backward political communities grouped near the eastern coast of the Atlantic Ocean. The dynamic societies of the planet were the Islamic communities of the Middle East and above all the great civilization of imperial China. Europe took food, treasure, and technology from them; they got very little in return from Europe. Beginning in the sixteenth century, however, the global initiative shifted to what the rest of the world had previously had good reason to regard as "the poor, parochial, monochrome culture of Christian Europe."[39] The theme of the history of the last five hundred years was born: the rise of the West.[40]

Over the centuries, the core of the West itself shifted location. In the seventeenth century, for example, the principal center of wealth, power, and cultural creativity moved north from Italy and Spain to France, Great Britain, and the Netherlands. In the course of the twentieth century it migrated westward across the Atlantic Ocean.[41] The West's ascendancy initially rested on military superiority. Europe launched its age of discovery, making contact with distant civilizations and conquering the weakest of them, notably in the Americas, by virtue of its "warlikeness, naval technology, and comparatively high levels of resistance to disease."[42]

In the nineteenth century, the West vastly increased its margin of superiority over the rest of the world. The terms of cultural trade tilted even more sharply than before. The flow of cultural innovation moving outward in all directions from Europe grew in volume and accelerated in tempo. For it was at this time that the two clusters of innovations that would define and shape the modern world, the industrial revolution and the French Revolution, appeared in the West. They swept over Europe, and Europe carried them to the rest of the world, creating the first truly global civilization. The dual revolutions created the modern world in the West and, in so doing, made the West, in the nineteenth and twentieth centuries, the most powerful and influential cultural core in the history of human civilization.[43]

Within the core, the French and industrial revolutions created the "long nineteenth century" (1789–1914), when the forces of tradition and liberal modernity clashed mainly within sovereign states, and then the "short twentieth century" (1914–1991), when, traditional institutions and values having been vanquished, the forces of liberalism battled against those of illiberalism.

The diffusion of the fruits of the two revolutions from core to periphery followed a different pattern than its course within the core. Chronologically it is more convenient to divide the modern age in the periphery into two uneven parts: the hundred years from the middle of the nineteenth century to the middle of the twentieth, and then the fifty years from the mid-twentieth century to its end. The initial period was an age of empire; the second the post-imperial, or post-colonial, age.[44]

In the periphery in the first of these periods, as in the core, there was a contest between the forces of tradition and of modernity. But unlike the pattern in the core, it was not an internal struggle. Modernity came to the traditional societies of the periphery in the form of assaults by the core countries. In the second, shorter, post-colonial era, which coincided with the Cold War, while the central conflict pitted liberalism against illiberalism, this conflict was almost everywhere a domestic struggle within countries. Governments in what was known as the Third World adopted both liberal and illiberal practices and institutions, in different combinations from one country to another.

From the sixteenth century to the middle of the nineteenth, Europeans had conquered the Americas and planted their flags on the fringes of the empires of Japan, China, and India while pressing against the traditional Islamic monarchies on the Balkan peninsula and in Central Asia. But traditional non-Western political authorities had managed, with increasing discomfort, to coexist with Western power. The industrial revolution, well underway by the middle of the nineteenth century, extended Europe's reach and expanded its strength. It so widened Europe's margin of military superiority that the Europeans were able to assault, conquer, occupy, and govern most of the planet.[45]

The weaknesses of traditional societies were exposed as the second half of the nineteenth century began. In the decade of the 1850s the imperial government of China, already humiliated by the Europeans in the Opium Wars of 1839–42, came under pressure from the greatest internal uprising in its history. The Taiping rebellion was a quasi-religious movement, led by a charismatic figure named Hong Xiuquian, that sought, in a muddled way, to make use of Western ideas and military techniques, attracted millions of followers, and controlled much of China from 1853 to 1864.[46] The Crimean War of 1854–1856 laid bare the severe shortcomings of the Russian empire, which was defeated by the British and the French. And although the Ottoman Empire was on the winning side, the outcome of the war did not arrest the ongoing decline in its power. In 1854 the United States compelled imperial Japan to agree to open itself, after more than two centuries of isolation, to Western commerce. And the great Indian Mutiny of 1857–1858 triggered the imposition of direct British rule over most of the Asian subcontinent. These diverse events had a common theme: They demonstrated that the traditional methods of political and economic organization, practiced outside the West for centuries, could not resist the surging projection of Western power.

The traditional authorities in the world's periphery responded in a characteristic way. They tried to blend the sources of Western strength with their indigenous political and social practices. They sought to distill the essence of Western power and use this elixir to revitalize their own traditional political structures.

In the nineteenth century the Russian tsars, following the example of their seventeenth-century predecessor, Peter the Great, sought to borrow Western technology—railroads and steel mills—for the purpose of fortifying their imperial, autocratic rule. Similarly, in China the Tung-chih restoration of the 1860s and 1870s attempted to enlist Western administrative methods and military techniques in the service of strengthening the traditional regime.[47] The Turkish sultans tried to strengthen their armies while preserving their throne.[48]

In the world's periphery, as in its core, the old regimes did not succeed in preserving themselves. By the middle of the twentieth century the modern state and the industrial economy, Western innovations both, had diffused throughout the world. Except in the Arab Middle East, traditional monarchs other than mere figureheads were almost all gone.* Those who succeeded them ruled in the name, if not with the actual consent, of the people. The new rulers all tried, with varying degrees of success, to make industry and economic growth part of the life of their societies. They aspired to establish powerful government bureaucracies, effective armed forces, and school systems with a standard, government-approved curriculum. The economic and political modernity created in the West had, by the middle of the twentieth century, triumphed virtually everywhere.[49]

Even what might seem to be the exception to this pattern turns out, upon closer inspection, to conform to it. The mass movement for Indian independence was led by Mohandas K. Gandhi, who relied on traditional symbols to mobilize his countrymen against British rule. He subsisted on the spare diet of a Hindu holy man. He took a spinning wheel wherever he traveled and made a point of producing homespun cloth regularly. He dressed traditionally, favoring a simple loincloth and a shawl.

---

*Monarchs were dethroned in Egypt, Iraq, and Libya but survived in power in Jordan, Morocco, and the oil sheikhdoms of the Persian Gulf, the largest of which was Saudi Arabia. The Gulf monarchies used the windfall they earned from the oil within their borders to support their populations in what, by the standards of the periphery, was a comfortable style. Perhaps bribery is not quite the right word for the governing strategy they employed, but their oil wealth did enable them to make what proved to be productive investments in political stability. In addition, all the hereditary rulers enjoyed the patronage, for a variety of reasons, of the United States, and the Jordanian monarchy also received tacit but vital support from Israel, its western neighbor and, for most of this period, its ostensible enemy.

While Gandhi's wardrobe would have been out of place at West-minster or on Capitol Hill, in all other important ways he was a thoroughly modern figure. He traveled by rail. He spread his message through radio broadcasts. He himself was a cosmopolitan, a lawyer trained in Great Britain who had practiced in South Africa and been influenced by the writings of Westerners, notably Henry David Thoreau. Indeed, the idea of a mass political movement, of the peaceful coexistence of different faiths, and of democratic governance within an independent state—in fact, the idea of India itself—were all distinctly modern and Western.[50]

Gandhi's career epitomizes a signal twentieth-century accomplishment of the societies of the world's periphery. The movement he led secured India's independence from Great Britain. While traditional authorities were not able to preserve their power or the way of life on which it rested, the societies they had ruled did manage, drawing on the French and industrial revolutions, to evict their foreign rulers. They adopted Western military techniques and made use of the weapons the industrial revolution had created. Even more important, especially in the Indian case, they used the idea of nationalism, to which the French Revolution had given rise, to mobilize their populations against their imperial governors. This, combined with the weakness of the main imperial powers—Great Britain, France, and Japan—in the wake of the Second World War, and the growing belief in the core that governing people against their will unacceptably transgressed liberal political norms, put an end to the European empires.[51] In historical perspective latter-day imperialism may be seen as a method both for imposing foreign rule on, and for spreading the techniques of modernity to, the world's periphery. It thus carried within itself the seeds of its own destruction.

With formal independence came the right to choose between liberal and illiberal principles of political and economic organization. The many countries of the periphery chose between them in different combinations, but their choices exhibited, at mid-century, a certain bias in favor of the institutions and practices of the Communist bloc, which had several attractions. Politically, they offered the new indigenous leaders of these countries a formula for holding on to power indefinitely. Economically, they seemed to provide the shortest route to wealth and economic strength. Historically, the new rulers were inclined to reject the politics and economics of their former masters, which had more often than not been the core powers that had practiced liberalism at home. But over the course of the second half of the twentieth century the countries of the periphery gravitated increasingly toward the liberalism that Woodrow Wilson had unveiled in Paris, and for the same reason that the countries once ruled by Communism adopted it: its success.

Another reason for the drift toward liberal practices in the countries of the periphery is worth noting: the end of empire itself. The influence of the liberal core actually increased after its direct military and political control over the periphery had receded. When the countries of the periphery ceased to have to concern themselves with the defense of their territory against Western encroachment, they were freed to adopt political and economic systems, and sometimes even security policies, for purposes other than self-defense. As in the process of evolution, the environment changed and liberal traits became more adaptive and illiberal ones less so. The end of direct Western control made its liberal principles more attractive because they were no longer seen as part of an assault on the rest of the world. They had become, instead, viable solutions to pressing problems.[52]

The era of the Cold War may thus be understood as an episode in the age-old process of cultural transmission and adoption and, in particular, as a variation on the dominant theme of that process over the last five hundred years: the diffusion of artifacts and ideas, of cultural hardware and software, from a shifting, expanding, increasingly powerful and culturally fecund core located along the shores of the Atlantic Ocean to the rest of the world. The result was the creation of a genuinely global civilization, one in which democratic politics and market economics came to occupy a special, privileged, hegemonic status.

As for most of human history, in the last half of the twentieth century ideas as well as products moved from the core to the periphery, but in contrast to the imperial era, during the Cold War the principal method of transmission was voluntary rather than coerced acceptance.[53] And unlike the first half of the twentieth century, the political and economic institutions originating in the West and

embraced the world over were not only modern, they were also liberal. The end of the Cold War thus completed a particular chapter
in world history. The last outpost, the defended bastion of illiberalism, increasingly besieged during the Cold War, finally surrendered.
It surrendered not to a superior military force but to the force of history, history of a certain kind, the kind that pervades the world of the
twenty-first century.

TWO-TRACK HISTORY

H ISTORY PROCEEDS at two levels: the level of events, which the
French social historian Fernand Braudel called *l'histoire évene-
mentielle*, and the level of trends, in his terminology *la longue durée*.[54]
The time scales are different. The first is made up of what counts as
news; the second level is measured in years, decades, even centuries.

Two different sectors of the scholarly community monitor,
record, and analyze the two levels of history. Political, diplomatic,
and military historians study the first, social and economic historians
the second.[55] And in fact their subjects are different. Political historians study the rise and fall of kings and ministers, war and peace,
treaties and battles, coups and elections, legislation and constitutions. Social historians study institutions, habits, tools, technologies,
rituals and beliefs. Change occurs more slowly at the second level of
history than at the first, so that while political historians tend to concern themselves with change, social historians are more interested in
continuity.[56]

There is another and, for the purposes of understanding the outcome and legacy of the Cold War, more important difference
between the two levels of history. The history of events is the realm
of human agency. It is the record of what societies, governments,
and individuals *do*. It is the story of great men and women, of great
deeds, of calculation and miscalculation, of deliberate designs that
succeed or falter. The chroniclers of events describe them with
active verbs: people fight, defend, win, lose, overthrow, decide,
achieve, and fail. By contrast, *la longue durée* is the realm of impersonal forces, of social processes that cannot easily be controlled or

manipulated by governments. Here history happens. The second level constrains and shapes the first. "Men make their own history," Marx wrote, "but they do not make it just as they please; they do not make it under circumstances chosen by themselves, but under circumstances directly encountered, given, and transmitted from the past."[57] The history of events is the history that men and women make; the historian of the *longue durée* studies the forces that circumscribe their choices.

The Cold War proceeded on both levels, but the emphasis in describing and analyzing it fell on the first. The designation of the East-West rivalry as a war biased the discussion sharply in this direction. War is the preeminent activity in the history of events. It is the arena of human action, of purpose and organization, of skill and will. The outcome of war depends on what men and women do, individually and collectively, and how well they do it. In the second half of the twentieth century war became a metaphor for organized, strenuous human agency, for coordinated assaults not on opposing armies but on social problems. Thus the American government declared war on poverty, on crime, on illegal narcotics, even on cancer.[58]

The use of the term "war" to characterize the international history of the second half of the twentieth century was appropriate. The Cold War, as noted, in basic ways *was* a war. The outcome was certainly affected by the constant threat of force, if not, in the end, by its actual use. But referring to the second half of the twentieth century as the era of the Cold War also misleads. Its outcome must also be understood as the product of the impersonal force of global trends, of the transmission of cultural hardware and especially software. It was the forces that operate over the long term, the artillery of the *longue durée*, that brought down the fortress of Communist illiberalism and set the world on the path it followed in the wake of its collapse.

For Braudel, the *longue durée* was very long indeed. His history, *Capitalism and Material Life*, covered four centuries, from 1400 to 1800. The Cold War spanned only four decades. But it is not unreasonable to suppose that the kinds of forces that Braudel charted, and that were also crucial in producing the Cold War's outcome, moved, in the second half of the twentieth century, at ten or more times the speed of the pre-modern period. After all, if the motor of this second level of history is, as McNeill posited, contact among strangers, the volume of contacts was surely at least ten times as great—and probably much greater—in 1990 as it was in 1490 or 1790.[59]

The channels for cultural transmission were much broader and far more numerous. For most of recorded history they were confined to the few routes along which trade in goods and ideas were carried. From the mid-nineteenth century industrial innovations in transportation—the steamship and the railroad above all—accelerated the pace and increased the carrying capacity of the world's contacts among strangers.[60] In the twentieth century, especially its second half, the relevant innovations were in the methods of communication;[61] this was the century of the telephone, the television, and, at its end, the Internet.[62] The revolutions in communication accelerated the diffusion of international liberalism in the second half of the century because what spread all over the world were not only goods and products but also ideas. And for ideas, communication *is* transportation.

The volume of contacts expanded far beyond anything experienced before the modern age not only by virtue of the multiplication of channels but also because of the growth in the number of receptors. As important a development for the transmission of liberalism as radio, television, and the Internet was mass literacy, which tended to precede them.

Understanding the Cold War as the product of the trends of the second level of history as well as of the events of the first explains what otherwise seems puzzling: how the West could have achieved its political goals in the absence of anything resembling a military victory. It also suggests that there is a division of labor between the two levels that is relevant to the post-Cold War world.

History at the level of events can prevent bad things from happening. It can protect liberal practices and institutions. But it cannot create them. Creation takes place at the second, longer, slower, impersonal level of history. War is more an exercise in destruction than in construction.[63] Rome, as the saying goes, was not built in a day, but Nero's fire destroyed much of it in just twenty-four hours.[64] Although World War I was fought to make the world safe for democracy, neither that war nor any other could have made the world democratic.

What the West *did* during the Cold War was to protect the liberal world against the forces of illiberalism, the announced goal of which was to destroy them; what *happened* was that liberal ideas and institutions took root where they had been planted and then spread elsewhere. For the diffusion of liberalism what mattered was not only what the West did but also what it was. Its victory in the Cold War was the triumph of the force of example more than the force of arms.

The importance of long-term, impersonal trends not only helps to explain the course and the outcome of the Cold War, it is also indispensable to understanding the post-Cold War world. In each of the four previous major European and global conflicts, one feature of the war turned out to be crucial to the postwar period.[65] In the Wars of the French Revolution the cooperative program on the basis of which the fourth, final, and ultimately successful coalition against Napoleon was formed laid the foundation for the system of international relations, known as the Concert of Europe, that helped keep the peace in Europe for a century.[66] In World War I, the high price in death and destruction incurred by the victorious powers led to a peace settlement that was, in the French phrase, *trop douce pour ce qu'elle a de dureté*—too soft for its harshness. The allies imposed terms on Germany that the Germans considered unfair and that successive German governments sought to reverse. But the terms were not so harsh that the Germans were unable to reverse them. Ultimately Hitler did so, only temporarily but at great cost to Europe and the world. As for World War II, here the deep differences between the Soviet Union and the West, the powers that, in uneasy alliance, won the war, prefigured the conflict between them that followed quickly after 1945.

In retrospect, the crucial feature of the Cold War is the importance of impersonal historical forces, of the diffusion of ideas, of the force of the Western example. For the trends, forces, and developments that determined how the Cold War ended carried over into the post-Cold War period. They were, if anything, more powerful, because they were uncontested, after the collapse of Communism than before.

This is not to say, however, that individuals, governments, policy, and politics have nothing to do with how widespread and how strong the three parts of the Wilsonian triad will come to be. No more than in other historical eras will international politics be a kind of spectator sport, in which the surging force of liberalism will expand—or not expand—according to its own impersonal logic and rhythm. History may proceed at two levels but each affects the other.

The outcome of what is quintessentially an event—a shooting war—often depends on long-term developments. In the great European wars of the last five centuries, victory often went to the side "with the longest purse"—that is, with the capacity to mobilize the resources necessary to keep fighting longer than its adversary.[67] Great Britain's superiority over its continental rivals in public finance, which was a source of British strength, developed over generations.[68]

At the same time, events influence trends. The outcome of battles decides where the great subterranean currents of the historical process will flow.[69] The cease-fire lines of 1945 in Europe, the product of human decision, determined where Western liberalism and Communist illiberalism would hold sway, which in turn had a profound impact on the countries and the people affected.[70] Before the war Finland and Estonia were roughly comparable in economic terms, as were Austria and Czechoslovakia. Fifty years later Finland and Austria were rich, while Estonia and Czechoslovakia, by European standards, were poor. Those economic differences had accumulated over four decades, but they did so because of decisions made in 1945.[71]

The roles of strategy, policy, and agency are not as obvious, not as dramatic, not as potent in a world in which liberal norms and practices are not under direct threat as they were during the Cold War. But they still matter. In the post-Cold War era, as in the Cold War, the prospects for the Wilsonian triad, unprecedentedly favorable as they are, still depend on what governments do to reinforce them as well as on what happens. The international liberalism that Woodrow Wilson advocated in Paris after World War I has become the dominant current of history in the wake of the Cold War. But the political and economic equivalents of dikes, dams, canals, locks, levees and embankments are still needed to maintain it the world over. For all three parts of the Wilsonian triad, they must be constructed.

The construction crews are sovereign states. The agents, the actors, the strategists, the political collectives that make the history that can be made by human agency, are states. So the world of the post-Cold War era, like the world of the Cold War, is a world of sovereign states. After the end of the Cold War, as before, some are more important than others. After the collapse of Communism, as before, especially among the important members of the international system, roles vary. And in the post-Cold War era those roles are different from the ones the major powers played during the era of East-West rivalry.

CHAPTER THREE

A World of Sovereign States

IN ONE OF HIS RASHER moments Lenin predicted that with the triumph of Communism the state would "wither away."[1] Instead, the Bolshevik seizure of power produced the most ambitious and intrusive type of government ever established. It was, in fact, the demise of the Communist system that he founded and the advent of a world shaped by the forces that had subverted it that seemed to bring his prediction close to fulfillment.

The new world's driving force, cultural diffusion, violates the heart of sovereignty, the sanctity of borders. Post-Cold War states could keep out foreign armies but almost everything else—ideas, products, technologies—crossed their frontiers with increasing ease.

Moreover, liberalism in all its aspects developed in opposition to state power. Political liberty is freedom from that power. The French term *laissez-faire* (to leave alone) expresses the liberal approach to economics, which is based on the idea that the government should leave the economy to its own devices. The essence of the liberal prescription for security policy is opposition to war, and war was for centuries the principal activity of the state.

Despite these developments, however, the global triumph of liberalism did not herald the state's disappearance. Its ambitions and duties changed, but in the twenty-first century, as in the past, governments—with their flags and armies, their bureaus and bureaucrats, their taxing and spending—remained at the center of international affairs. And a major fact of the role of sovereign states in international life carried over to the twenty-first century from the centuries preceding: Some were more important than others.

THE PERSISTENCE OF THE STATE

T HE SOVEREIGN STATE, an impersonal territorial unit with no higher power within its borders,[2] is customarily dated from the Treaty of Westphalia in 1648. It was created by the triumph of the monarch over the nobility and the clergy, among which power had been shared in medieval Europe. Some seventeenth-century European rulers, such as Louis XIV of France and Peter the Great of Russia, gathered so much power compared to their predecessors that they came to be called "absolute" monarchs.

In the modern age, sovereign states came to vary along two dimensions: the distribution of power within their borders and the capacity of the government itself. The modern state, with its machines and methods of social control, can penetrate far more deeply into the society it governs than even the most powerful of the absolute but traditional monarchs.[3] Modern government is to traditional government what modern warfare is to the traditional variety: recognizably the same activity, but with a scope and intensity and with consequences that are far greater.

In the nineteenth century in the world's core, the modern state drove out the traditional one, setting the stage for the twentieth-century clash between states of the liberal and illiberal types. The illiberal—totalitarian—governmental machinery of fascism and Communism differed from the absolutism of the traditional world both in capacity and aspiration. The absolutist state was, in Thomas Hobbes's appropriation of a term from the Old Testament story of Jonah and the whale, a Leviathan. The totalitarian state was, by contrast, a boa constrictor. Jonah survived inside the whale, but modern illiberalism aspired not merely to swallow society but to crush, decompose, and digest its parts.

The liberal state, which defeated fascist and then Communist illiberalism, is distinguished by the limits deliberately placed on state power. But having a liberal state is not remotely the same thing as having no state at all. The duties and aspirations of a liberal state are limited but hardly negligible. Nor is an effective liberal state weak by any reasonable definition of the term.

At the outset of the twenty-first century every person on the planet lived within the confines of a sovereign state, and for good reason. The state offers the best available mechanism for performing a series of related tasks that have always been important and became more important in the modern era. The term for what the state provides was introduced into the vocabulary of politics by the discipline of economics: collective, or public, goods.[4] A public good is something the benefits of which no potential "consumer" can be prevented from enjoying. These goods are difficult to provide because, for that very reason, no consumer has an incentive to pay for them. In fact, it can be downright irrational to pay.

The first and most important public good is public safety. The sovereign state was first established, according to Hobbes, in order to provide it. Without a supreme power to keep order by punishing those who violate it, social life becomes unbearable. It is irrational to be a pacifist without a guarantee that others will act peacefully; but if no one is peaceful the result is what Hobbes called "a war of every one against every one."[5] The establishment of government replaces this vicious pattern with civil peace.

The state exists as well to protect its citizens from threats from beyond its borders. The international equivalent of crime is war, and of a police force an army. But armies do not form spontaneously. Governments are required to assemble them. National defense is another public good and one still required in the post-Cold War period when war remains a distinct possibility in much of the world.

While civil order and national defense are the oldest and most basic public goods, they are not the only ones. Clean air is a modern example. The owner of a car has no incentive to invest in a pollution-control device if no one else does, because one cleaner car will not make the air noticeably less noxious for anyone. If, however, all other car owners purchase and install pollution-control devices, the same driver would still have no incentive to get one and for the same reason: The increment of cleanliness that a single car can contribute makes no appreciable difference to the air everyone must breathe. Since all car owners, if they are rational, will calculate in this way, no one will buy a pollution control device. The air all of them breathe will therefore be polluted even if—and this is the paradox at the heart of the public goods problem—it would be worth the price of such a device to every one of them to breathe cleaner air.

What is needed is a mechanism for ensuring that every driver *does* buy a pollution control device. With its monopoly of legitimate power, the state can compel universal purchase. As with civil order and international security, the state supplies what everyone understands is needed but that will not be made available unless a higher power ensures that it is. If there is no conductor to collect fares on a bus, everyone will ride free. But in that case there will be no funds to pay for bus service and ultimately no one will be able to ride at all. Economists have termed this inherent difficulty in the provision of public goods the "free rider" problem.

The three components of Woodrow Wilson's vision—democracy, free markets, and peace—may be understood as public goods in that an effective state is needed to establish each of them. Political liberty requires that the government actively protect (as well as refrain from violating) the rights of its citizens. A market economy requires a sturdy framework that only the state can provide. Free trade requires rules that can only be negotiated by sovereign states. A liberal state is also necessary for a task that became mandatory for liberal societies in the twentieth century, although it had not been so in the nineteenth: the redistribution of wealth for the purpose of social protection. And a sovereign state is necessary to implement the liberal approach to security that was developed at the end of the Cold War, which emphasizes the kinds of limits on armaments that Woodrow Wilson had advocated and that, like international economic rules, governments had to negotiate.[6]

The sovereign state, in sum, held universal sway in the twenty-first century because it was indispensable. It was the equivalent of the operating system for a personal computer, without which no program of any kind can be run.[7]

At the outset of the twenty-first century the world's almost 200 sovereign states, like all states since 1648, were juridically equal. Each was, in theory at least, supreme within its own borders. Each had its own government and its own flag and was entitled to its own seat in the United Nations General Assembly. But of course sovereign political communities were not and never had been equal in size, shape, geography, demography, geology, power, or wealth. The differences that have mattered most in any historical era have been those relevant to the most significant social forces and political issues of the moment. In the seventeenth century the defining division in Europe was religious: States were either Protestant or Catholic. In the nineteenth century the most important distinction rested on military might, which separated the great powers from the lesser ones. To the great powers belonged special prerogatives: Any major diplomatic settlement had to take into account their wishes and interests.[8] During the Cold War, when the great contest of systems dominated international affairs, it was customary to divide the international system into three parts, the differences among which seemed so vast that each was a world unto itself. The first was the Western core, the second the Communist countries, and the Third World consisted of the many countries formally affiliated with neither of the other two. In the post-Cold War era the second world disappeared and the oldest distinction of all came to the fore, the distinction between core and periphery, between the innovators and exporters of the building blocks of global civilization on the one hand and the imitators and importers on the other.

"All the world's a stage," Shakespeare has one of his characters in *As You Like It* say.[9] If post-Cold War history is a drama, then its plot is the diffusion of international liberalism. The players are the world's sovereign states. In a playbill they would be divided into two groups. The numerically fewer and economically and politically more powerful countries of the core were the originators, the bearers, the sponsors, and the mainstays of liberal values, practices, and institutions. The more numerous and weaker sovereign states of the periphery were on the whole less committed to democracy, free markets, and peace. The core was therefore the place *from* which, the periphery the region *to* which, liberalism was in the process of diffusing.

A drama has supporting players and leading actors. In the core, Germany and Japan played the two most important supporting roles while the lead belonged to the United States. In the periphery most of the many countries were destined to have little or no impact on the world beyond their borders. They were comparable to the actors in a film that make up the crowd and are called "extras."[10] The periphery did, however, include two featured players: Russia and China.

THE LATECOMERS

GREAT BRITAIN and France invented the modern world. From France came popular sovereignty, the prevailing principle of political legitimacy. The idea, born in the French Revolution, that the people rather than a monarch should rule formed the basis for popular sovereignty and nationalism. From Britain came almost everything else. From within its borders emerged the idea that limits should be placed on governmental power through the rule of law, which is, along with popular sovereignty, the essence of political liberalism.[11] The market economy first developed fully and was noted, codified, and supported in the British Isles. Great Britain is the country that first embraced the international implications of the liberal approach to economics, free trade. And it is there that the conviction that war is unnatural and avoidable first took hold.*

It was natural for Britain and France to lead the world into the modern age, for they were the two greatest world powers in the period preceding it. France fielded the strongest army in Europe from the seventeenth century to the second half of the nineteenth century. In that period Britain was the leading maritime and financial power, with the largest overseas empire, even after the loss of the American colonies. But in the twentieth century two other countries, which had been only the dimmest of presences at the outset of the modern age, played more important roles: Germany and Japan.

In the nineteenth century Germany and Japan accomplished what all other countries came to attempt: They caught up, in economic and military terms, with the world's leaders, Britain and France. In the first half of the twentieth century the two mounted the initial illiberal challenge to Anglo-American liberalism, which the most

---

*The British and French legacies were present in other ways as well in the twenty-first century. English was the medium of global communication because it was the language of the greatest military and commercial powers of the modern age—in the nineteenth century Great Britain, in the twentieth the United States. While the modern world sounds English, it looks decidedly French. The prevailing styles in graphic arts, architecture, painting, clothing, industrial design, and household objects that make up the global material culture owe more to the artists, craftsmen, and designers working in France in the nineteenth and twentieth centuries than to the creations in and of any other country.

destructive war in all of human history was required to defeat. After suffering defeat Germany and Japan blazed another trail that many others sought to follow. They successfully converted to liberal values, practices, and institutions. In so doing they contributed to the strength of the Western core that, in turn, was responsible for the outcome of the Cold War. That outcome was a victory for the Western example. Germany and Japan, by virtue of their conversions, offered the most potent examples of all.

At the outset of the modern age neither country was a major presence in the international system. The German nation was dispersed among a series of small and medium-sized monarchies in the center of Europe. Japan was isolated. In the 1630s its rulers had expelled European missionaries and traders and permitted only limited, tightly controlled contacts with other countries. In the second half of the nineteenth century, however, both emerged as major powers. Japan's task was the more difficult one and its achievement, for that reason, the more impressive. That task was not, as in the German case, to assemble the preexisting pieces of a great power, but rather to remake a backward country. The Meiji Restoration, which began in 1868—so called because it nominally restored the emperor to supreme power—was in fact a revolution. It transformed a traditional society, the economic and social relations of which resembled those of feudal Europe before the fifteenth century,[12] into a modern state with an industrial economy, a formidable army and navy, and an efficient national bureaucracy; and it did so in the span of a few decades. This is the most remarkable accomplishment by any nation in modern history. Because it represented the first occasion on which a non-Western country mastered the techniques of modernity and so served as an example for the many non-Western societies of the periphery, it is also arguably the most influential modern national accomplishment. Certainly it ranks with the emergence of the United States as the world's most powerful country, and behind only the French and industrial revolutions themselves, as the most important events in modern history.

Both countries became modern powers in response to challenges from without. The French Revolution and its aftermath triggered German nationalism: The German people, living in their various sovereign states, found themselves dominated by the less numerous but politically united French. The equivalent of the French Revolution for Japan was the encroachment of the West, beginning with the unwelcome arrival in Tokyo Bay of an American fleet commanded by Commodore Matthew Perry in 1854. Perry and those who followed him demanded the right to trade, and within a decade Japan had been forced to sign a series of treaties granting special privileges to foreign powers.[13] Japan began its program of modernization for the purpose of resisting this Western encroachment. Conceding that they could no longer ignore the foreigners, the Japanese sought to strengthen themselves so as to deal with the Europeans and North Americans on an equal basis, and in this they succeeded.

Both Germany and Japan pulled themselves into the first rank of the international hierarchy, thereby demonstrating that latecomers to the political and economic revolutions that defined the modern world could catch up with and even overtake the leaders. Germany's victory over France at Sedan in 1871 established it as the strongest military power on the European continent, and in the 1880s it began to assemble an overseas empire. Japan, too, used its military power to acquire possessions beyond its borders. It defeated China in 1895 and acquired the island of Taiwan and predominant influence on the Korean peninsula. In 1904–1905 the Japanese won an astonishing victory over Russia, the first time in the modern age that a non-European power had defeated a European one.[14]

In the twentieth century both sought to conquer more territory. The two world wars were provoked by the German and Japanese efforts to expand their imperial holdings in what each regarded as its natural, rightful, geographic sphere. Germany launched two campaigns of conquest in Central and Eastern Europe. The second coincided with the Japanese effort to establish an imperial sphere in China, in Indochina (ruled by the French), in Malaya (ruled by the British), in Indonesia (ruled by the Dutch), and in the Philippines (ruled by the Americans). Both efforts came close to success. At the beginning of 1942 Nazi Germany was the master of Europe from the Atlantic Ocean to the Baltic and Black Seas. At the same time Japan had conquered much of China and Southeast Asia.

The challenge the two mounted was not merely a military one, nor was it simply a bid for more power, wealth, and territory. It was as well a challenge to the political and economic systems of Western Europe and the United States. Germany and Japan embodied a distinctive form of illiberalism, one that was, in its way, more potent than the Communist variety with which the liberal powers would struggle during the Cold War.[15]

In politics, both Nazi Germany and Imperial Japan stressed the nation rather than, as does liberalism, the individual. Both considered the divisions and quarrels that are normal in democratic politics to be contemptible and dangerous. Each therefore moved to suppress them: Political parties were banned, information tightly controlled, and independent political activity punished. Each society exalted the leader as the embodiment of the nation. In the German case it was the actual leader, Adolf Hitler; in Japan it was the emperor,[16] who, while exercising some authority, was principally a symbolic figure in whose name officials governed the country.

Unlike under Communism, private property was permitted in both countries. But both, heavily influenced by the economic trauma of the Great Depression of the 1930s, preferred self-sufficiency to the interdependence that international economic liberalism prescribes. Neither regime was devoted to free trade. In both countries the state prevented workers from organizing or striking and intervened more often and more extensively than in the liberal West to coordinate economic activity to serve its own purposes. In the course of World War II each country exploited the foreign territories acquired by conquest in similar fashion, confiscating raw materials and forcing local people to work in conditions that amounted to slave labor.

For both Nazi Germany and Imperial Japan, the organization of politics at home and of economics abroad were designed to serve the regime's supreme goal: military conquest. That goal followed from a particular, and distinctly illiberal, view of the world. They saw international politics as a struggle for survival in which the operative principle of conduct was kill or be killed, subjugate or be subjugated. Violence, brutality, oppression, and war against those they considered their racial inferiors were the essence of the German and Japanese version of illiberalism in the 1930s and 1940s, and they led to the widest, fiercest, bloodiest war the world had ever seen.*

The German and Japanese people fought to the bitter end. In World War I the dynastic empires of the Habsburgs and the Romanovs disintegrated under military pressure. In the Cold War Communism collapsed from within, without a shot being fired. In World War II one of the leading liberal powers, France, lost on the battlefield, surrendered, and installed a pro-German government all in the space of six weeks. Nazi Germany and Imperial Japan, by contrast, had to be beaten into submission. It took the occupation of the German capital and the devastation of two major Japanese cities by atomic bombs to compel their surrender.

In the end, both countries were crushed, occupied, and forced to cede territory.[17] The totality of their defeat was crucial for the course of the Cold War and ultimately for the character of the post-Cold War era. It paved the way for their conversion, in the postwar period, to liberal politics and economics. Germany and Japan became key components of the liberal core, having taken to liberalism with the zeal of the convert. On the ruins of an all-powerful illiberal regime, each assembled a democratic political system in which power was exercised through an elected parliament. Far from being suppressed, the different factions and interests were well represented in both countries, each of which was governed by broad, carefully constructed coalitions.[18]

While their illiberal economic policies had emphasized exploitation and autarky, postwar Germany and Japan relied heavily on

*Germany and Japan lost their wars in part because, like the other great conqueror of the modern period, Napoleon, they overextended their forces. Each found itself bogged down in the vast spaces of the neighbor it had invaded: Germany in the Soviet Union, Japan in China. They lost as well because each called into existence a powerful countervailing coalition that, over time, was able to wear it down. The war plan of each called for a surprise attack leading to a quick victory. Each executed such an attack, with sweeping initial success. But contrary to German expectations, Britain did not sue for peace in 1940 and the Soviet Union was not knocked out of the war in 1941. Contrary to Japanese hopes, the United States did not seek terms after Pearl Harbor.

Germany and Japan also alienated, by their brutal treatment, peoples who might otherwise have joined them. Their brutality followed ineluctably from their view of the world, which held that other nations were their inferiors. Thus what gives, in retrospect, greatest offense about German and Japanese illiberalism—their common, virulent, murderous racism—turns out to have helped to defeat them.

trade, so heavily that Japan in particular inspired the creation of a new political category: the trading state.[19] The category was defined both by their predilection for international commerce and, in military affairs, a degree of self-abnegation never before seen in sovereign states as potentially powerful as they. They adopted novel national strategies, seeking security, prestige, and influence through economic cooperation, political modesty, and military quiescence. The two were transformed from highly aggressive, militarized states into countries with deep popular aversions to, and constitutional prohibitions against, waging war.[20]

Both made a fateful political decision in the early postwar years in favor of an alliance with the United States. Equally important were their initial postwar economic policies—Ludwig Erhard's stabilization measures in Germany in the late 1940s and the decision in the early 1950s by Japan's government, especially its Ministry of Trade and Industry, to build up heavy industry.

In neither case was the conversion entirely voluntary. Both countries were occupied by the powers that had defeated them, Germany by both the Western liberal powers and by the Soviet Union. In the sector where Soviet troops held sway the German conversion took an illiberal form. Rather than religious conversion, the rehabilitation of a convicted felon under close supervision is perhaps the appropriate metaphor for postwar Germany and Japan; but the rehabilitation was an unqualified success.

Moreover, the two benefited from the Cold War. Their Western conquerors needed them as allies and adopted policies to strengthen them in order to assure their loyalty and economic success. The United States furnished economic assistance to Europe in the form of the Marshall Plan, in which the Western-occupied zone of Germany shared. While there was no Marshall Plan for Japan, the outbreak of war in Korea in 1950 led to extensive American procurement in that country for the war effort, which gave a boost to the Japanese economy.

Through a combination of compulsion and persuasion, the Wilsonian triad took root in both countries. Ideas and institutions that before the war had been illegal, alien, and threatening, and in its immediate aftermath were imposed on them, came over time to seem to Germans and Japanese comfortable, normal, and ultimately integral to their national lives. The postwar liberalism of Germany and Japan was like an arranged marriage that turns into a love match.

The national histories of Germany and Japan in the second half of the nineteenth century demonstrated the possibility of doing what all societies in the modern era ultimately attempted to do. The two countries caught up with the international leaders, climbing to the upper tier of the international system. Their parallel histories in the second half of the twentieth century also showed the possibility of doing what most countries were at least rhetorically committed to doing as the twenty-first century began: adopting liberal politics, economics, and security policies. And their experiences demonstrated the benefits of conversion. Germany and Japan were more stable politically, more affluent economically, and more secure internationally after than before World War II. While the German bid for conquest in the east led to shattering defeat, the policy of integration with the West brought international respect and domestic prosperity. So it was with Japan as well. Its quest for an imperial economic sphere in Asia led to the worst disaster in its history. But in the wake of that disaster the opportunities for trade and investment to its south and east became available on a larger scale than ever before. From the 1950s to the 1980s those opportunities helped to trigger a boom so robust that it became widely known as the Japanese economic miracle.[21]

Germany and Japan were integral to the Western core. Their membership made it more powerful and more attractive than it would otherwise have been. In the second half of the twentieth century, although every part of the planet could be in touch with every other part, location still mattered. The diffusion of international liberalism in that period can be mapped in the same way that epidemiologists track the spread of a disease. The countries of western Europe exercised powerful influence over the southern and ultimately the eastern part of the European continent. The cultural gradient in Europe ran, as it had since before the beginning of the modern period, from northwest to southeast.[22] Liberal ideas and institutions were carried from north to south in the Americas: Latin America was heavily influenced by the United States and Canada.[23]

Geography mattered somewhat less in Asia, where the United States, although situated on the far side of the world's largest ocean, had a powerful impact by virtue of its military presence; but even there the diffusion of Western hardware and especially software had a geographic dimension. Japan, by dint of proximity and cultural similarity, served as an example to the islands to its south and to the Asian mainland to its west.

Germany and Japan enhanced the attractive power of the core by contributing to the diversity of its economic systems. In the free market capitalism of the United States the role of the government was more modest in redistributing output than it was in the Western European "social market" systems, and more restrained in directing investment than in Japan's "Confucian" system. Like General Motors with automobiles, therefore, the liberal core offered a variety of political and economic models and thus appealed to societies with different tastes, different needs, different locations, and different backgrounds.

Germany was a crucial part of the liberal security order that was established in Europe at the end of the Cold War. Japan's role in the security affairs of East Asia was similar to Germany's in Europe and, should formal security arrangements similar to those in Europe some day be created in Asia, Japan would be central to them. As for the liberal systems of trade and international finance, Germany and Japan were, after the United States, the most important participants in them.

The two were pillars of the post-Cold War liberal order both at home and abroad, important pieces of the foundation on which international liberalism stood. The prospects for the Wilsonian triad in the twenty-first century thus depended heavily on Germany and Japan playing the roles, and carrying out the policies, that they had adopted in the second half of the twentieth century.

Important though Germany and Japan were, however, and as crucial a premise of the post-Cold War era as the presumption of their liberal sturdiness was, the central pillar, the crucial piece of the foundation, was the United States.

THE LEADER

IN THE NINETEENTH CENTURY the United States followed roughly the same path as Germany and Japan. Like Japan, for the first half of the century it was removed by geography and its own policies from the quarrels of the great powers. Like Germany, it emerged from a war of national unification in the 1860s as a potentially formidable nation-state. Like both, it rapidly built an industrial economy, one that, by the end of the nineteenth century, was the largest in the world.[24]

In the course of that century the original thirteen states along the Atlantic seaboard expanded westward and by 1850 the United States stretched from the Atlantic Ocean to the Pacific. The American Civil War of 1861–1865, in which the northern states thwarted the efforts of the southern ones to secede and form a separate country, determined that there would be but one sovereign between Canada and Mexico.[25]

The outcome of the Civil War also affirmed that the United States would be a country committed to political and economic liberty, a commitment crucial to the history of the twentieth century. To be sure, in the nineteenth century the United States was not entirely liberal in either its domestic or its foreign policies. The institution of chattel slavery in the Southern states meant that people of African descent were considered property, not citizens. The indigenous people of North America were treated as obstacles and enemies. But in the course of the twentieth century the United States, like other Western countries, became more fully liberal, offering full citizenship to people denied it in the nineteenth. The United States was also an imperial power, its victory over Spain bringing effective control of Cuba and outright possession of the Philippines. But the American empire, too, was given up in the twentieth century.

Throughout the history of the United States, these illiberal currents notwithstanding, the liberal principles brought to North America from the British Isles formed the bedrock of American political culture, the American political system, and American economic practices. The colonists viewed their successful rebellion against British rule in liberal terms. They were asserting the "rights of Englishmen."

Despite the pervasive influence of the older country, for most of the nineteenth century relations between the United States and Great Britain were uneasy. Americans regarded Great Britain as posing the greatest threat to their security, a view that was not entirely unfounded. In 1814 British troops burned the American capital. During the Civil War the Union suspected the British government of sympathizing with the Confederacy.[26] In the early years of the twentieth century, however, the two achieved a rapprochement,[27] forging an Anglo-American partnership that was instrumental in winning the two world wars and crucial to the creation of the Western core during the Cold War.

Like Great Britain before it, the United States became, in the twentieth century, Europe's offshore balancer. Twice it sent military forces to Europe to prevent Germany from establishing dominance there, just as Britain had intervened on the continent to check the power of France in the eighteenth and nineteenth centuries. In the struggle against the Soviet Union, the United States did not come late to the opposing coalition, as it did in the two world wars. Rather, it organized and sustained the Western military and economic systems, each designed to prosecute the contest with Communist illiberalism.

Americans had a term for the role their country had played in the Cold War and that they expected it to play in the post-Cold War era: "leadership."[28] Leadership is one of those words that moves through the world enveloped in a nimbus of approbation. Leaders are generally thought to be people with superior insight, wisdom, and courage who can persuade and inspire others.[29] In fact, the substance of international leadership is more mundane and less glorious, which is why, as the post-Cold War era proceeded, it was more popular with Americans in theory than in practice. American leadership required that Americans pay more than their fair share for what governments are created to provide: public goods.

International public goods are harder to obtain than domestic ones because the usual solution to the free rider problem is not available to sovereign states; there is no world government to provide international public goods. Yet international public goods were secured during the Cold War even in the absence of a world sovereign. All potential victims of Soviet aggression benefited from the Western policy of containment, whether or not they contributed to it.[30] The policies necessary to sustain the liberal international economic order also resemble collective goods, as did the 1991 eviction of Iraq from Kuwait. The benefits of the Gulf War were widely distributed among Iraq's neighbors, above all Saudi Arabia, which could have been Iraq's next victims. Also benefiting were the oil-consuming countries, which might have had to pay more for energy if Saddam Hussein had consolidated his grip on Kuwait and intimidated Saudi Arabia, thereby acquiring the power to dictate the international price of oil.

How was this possible? How was the free rider problem solved? Public goods tend to be provided even in the absence of a supreme authority that can compel the beneficiaries to pay for it under one or more of three conditions.[31] When members of the relevant group are small in number, voluntary cooperation to divide the costs is easiest—or least difficult—because the members can monitor one another's compliance.[32] Second, when power and wealth are unevenly distributed within the group—optimally when one member far surpasses all the others in both—the powerful and the wealthy are more likely to pay all the costs themselves. This is particularly likely under a third condition: when providing the public good in question is believed to be a matter of urgency.[33]

All three conditions were fulfilled during the Cold War. The number of sovereign states was small, fewer than 200, and the relevant group for the provision of liberal international public goods was smaller still. Power and wealth were unevenly distributed, especially at the end of World War II when the security and economic orders were organized. The United States, unlike the other prewar great powers, had not suffered extensive damage from the fighting and so towered over all the others in wealth as well as military might. Most important, the United States had an urgent reason to pay the costs of founding and keeping these systems in good working order: the Cold War itself.

Americans considered sustaining military alliances in Europe and East Asia, and maintaining an international economic order in which the military allies would be stronger and more reliable because more prosperous, to be necessary for their own security. World War II had stemmed, in the retrospective American view, from the failure to oppose aggression by means of firm alliances and to prevent the Great Depression through policies of economic liberalism. With the Soviet Union an all-too-plausible candidate to follow in the footsteps of Nazi Germany and Imperial Japan, Americans believed that another war would be even more costly. It was therefore worth paying a high price to prevent World War III, even if that meant assuming a disproportionate share of the costs of doing so.[34] That is what Americans understood themselves to be doing. They considered paying for international public goods to be a wise investment in self-defense.[35]

For almost all of the second half of the twentieth century the American political system was configured to do the things that international leadership requires, because for the United States this was a wartime and not a postwar period. The assumptions, procedures, and institutions for the conduct of foreign policy in the Cold War were largely carried over from World War II.

The international public goods furnished during the Cold War, or modified versions of them, continued to be needed in the post-Cold War period. The American-led international economic order had become global in scope, with virtually every sovereign state seeking to participate in it. The alliances the United States had made and sustained were crucial for the liberal security orders, actual and prospective, of the post-Cold War period. But the three conditions for providing international public goods had all weakened.

The number of sovereign states had grown, and power was more widely dispersed among them. The United States remained the most powerful of all of them, but its margin of economic superiority had declined from the artificial height it had reached at the end of World War II.[36] Most important, the Cold War was over. Paying to maintain the security arrangements and liberal international economic orders had lost its urgency. Leading the world was no longer heroic. Leadership involved not so much marching gloriously at the head of the parade as paying quietly for the parade permit and for the cleanup afterwards. Because the world after the Cold War was less like a jungle than it had been, the leading power was less the king of beasts than a beast of burden. Leading the world meant acting not as its commander in chief but as its concierge.

Whether and to what extent the United States would provide international leadership would depend on circumstances, and these were certain to vary from one occasion to the next. But it was possible, after the first post-Cold War decade, to discern the contending forces that would determine how far the country would continue its Cold War role.

Favoring continuity was the fact that the price of playing that role had decreased. It was no longer necessary to gird for a global conflict against a powerful adversary. Liberal principles and institutions had become easier to defend because opposition to them had weakened dramatically. The attacks of September 11, 2001, did not alter this calculus. Moreover, those attacks partially recreated the Cold War basis for American military operations abroad.

In the years following World War II, Americans had become convinced that the failure to check Adolf Hitler earlier had paved the way for an avoidable and tragic war. It thus became a cardinal principle of American foreign policy during the Cold War to avoid the great mistake of the 1930s by fighting Communism wherever it threatened to dominate rather than allowing the Soviet Union and its allies to gain strength through unopposed military victories. This was the rationale for the American military interventions in Korea in 1950 and in Indochina in the 1960s.

The attacks on New York and Washington created a similar rationale for forceful preemptive attacks against terrorists. Thereafter the argument that a military operation was designed to avoid a repetition of those terrible events would be a powerful one, which American commanders in chief would be able to employ to win public support for such operations.[37]

Also favoring continuity between Cold War and post-Cold War American foreign policy were habits ingrained over the second half of the twentieth century. Americans had become accustomed to the duties and burdens as well as the prerogatives of international leadership. Or rather, some Americans were accustomed to them, for the habits were concentrated in one sector of American society.

In the United States at the dawn of the new century, as in other countries, foreign policy was the preoccupation of only a small part of the population. But to carry out any foreign policy in the American democratic political system requires the support of the wider public. While for the foreign policy elite the need for American leadership in the world was a matter of settled conviction, in the general public the commitment to global leadership was weaker. This was not surprising. The commitment to international leadership depended on a view of its effects on the rest of the world and the likely consequences of its absence. These were views for which most Americans, like most people in most countries, lacked the relevant information because they were not ordinarily interested enough to gather it.[38]

The politics of American foreign policy resembled a firm in which the management—the foreign policy elite—has to persuade the shareholders—the public—to authorize expenditures. This had been true during the Cold War, but in its wake, the willingness to authorize such spending requests had diminished, even though they were smaller than in the past. And if there were reasons to expect the public to be forthcoming with the support needed for American global leadership, there were also post-Cold War currents pushing in the other direction.

The term often used to refer to public reluctance to support international initiatives was "isolationism." This was an attitude to which, by some accounts, Americans were predisposed. They were, after all, a people who, other than African Americans and Native Americans, were immigrants or descended from immigrants who sought to escape the travails of the places from which they had come. Within the foreign policy elite of the United States (and of other friendly countries as well), American isolationism was regarded as a dangerous virus, the equivalent of a disease that was in remission but might recur at any time and for signs of which it was necessary to be ever vigilant.

In fact, there was, strictly speaking, no such thing as American isolationism. No significant figure in American history had ever thought it feasible or desirable for the United States to divorce itself entirely from the rest of the world.[39] To the contrary, from the founding of the country Americans aspired to disseminate their values and institutions across the globe. The missionary impulse was prominent in American history from the eighteenth century to the twenty-first.[40] During the first hundred years of that history, when the United States was comparatively weak, the hopes for spreading the blessings of American-style liberty rested on the mechanism that, in the second half of the twentieth century, did in fact carry it to the four corners of the Earth: the power of example.[41]

A pattern of international conduct sometimes mistaken for isolationism did carry into the post-Cold War period: American unilateralism.[42] This was the tradition of seeking the maximum possible freedom of maneuver. It was hardly unique to the United States. Independence is, after all, the essence of sovereignty. But historically America was freer than other countries to practice unilateralism, in the nineteenth century because of its distance from the European center of the international system, in the twentieth and twenty-first because of its considerable power.

The obstacle to an American international role as expansive as the country's elite thought necessary stemmed not from what was unique about the country—its geography and its history—but rather from what it had in common with others. The United States had the same incentive to be a free rider as all other countries. It was the circumstances that had suppressed that incentive during the second half of the twentieth century that were exceptional. To the extent that Americans were reluctant to pay for international public goods, they were no different from any other people.[43]

A disinclination to pay the costs of international leadership also arises from the essence of liberalism, which places a higher value on individual wishes than on collective aspirations and greater emphasis on domestic goals than on international objectives. Democratic governance is conducted for the people, after all, and for most people most of the time self-interest trumps self-sacrifice. The well-being of its individual citizens is the supreme goal of American public life. The Declaration of Independence, the founding document of the American republic, asserts the right to "life, liberty, and the pursuit of happiness"—presumably individual happiness—not the right to earn military glory or provide foreign tutelage or international stability.

However lofty Americans' hopes for the diffusion of Wilsonian values and institutions, it has never been easy to get them to pay for this. In wartime every American commander in chief has labored to sustain domestic support for the military effort, and the task has almost always proved frustrating. The aversion to expending American blood or treasure overseas becomes all the more pronounced in peacetime and was evident in the first post-Cold War decade in the American public's extreme reluctance to incur any casualties in military operations outside the United States,[44] except after the direct attacks of September 11, 2001. The reluctance to pay was evident as well in the opposition to lowering trade barriers and to using American money to rescue financially distressed countries, even Mexico, America's immediate neighbor.[45]

Thus the post-Cold War international role of the United States revolved around two paradoxes. One was that the same development that lowered the cost of American international leadership—the end of the Cold War—made the American public less willing to pay it.[46] The other was that the features of liberalism that made it globally attractive—above all its emphasis on individual preferences rather than collective goals—also created difficulties in sustaining international institutions that embodied those very features. The institutions and practices developed by the Western core were a club that more and more sovereign states sought to join; but the members were more reluctant to pay for its upkeep than they had been when it was less popular.[47]

The columnist Walter Lippmann once identified the central problem of foreign policy as "solvency."[48] For the United States in the wake of the Cold War, the problem was rather one of "liquidity." The country had the resources to do virtually anything—although not to do *everything*. What was scarce was neither economic nor military resources but rather the political will, in the form of domestic political support, to use them.

The attacks of September 11 expanded the pool of support available for military operations to combat terrorism. But this was only part, and not the largest part, of the post-Cold War international obligations that the consolidation and expansion of Western institutions and practices would require of the United States. Just how much public support for this wider role the American political leadership would be able to mobilize would depend on, among other things, the costs of doing so. And those costs emanated from the world's periphery.

THE PERIPHERY

OF THE ALMOST two hundred sovereign states of the international system, at least three-quarters could reasonably be classified, at the outset of the twenty-first century, as belonging to the periphery. They were consumers rather than producers, importers rather than exporters, of ideas, institutions, and products. They were imitators, not innovators. Chinese students went to the United States to study engineering, or computer programming, or medicine; American students went to China to study China.

Diverse though these peripheral countries were, they did have one thing in common: a commitment to conform to the world's sole surviving political and economic standard, international liberalism. The depth and the sincerity of that commitment varied considerably. In many cases it was purely rhetorical. And even with the will to do so, the capacity to adopt liberal institutions and practices also varied. There was noticeable geographic variation on both counts. If, at the end of the first post-Cold War decade, the countries of the periphery were depicted on a graph measuring political and economic liberalism, they would cluster according to region. East Asia had forged ahead economically, and, to a lesser extent, politically; Latin America was somewhat behind on both axes; India (but not the rest of South Asia) came next, with the Middle East, Central Asia, and Africa lagging behind.

The theme of the post-Cold War histories of the countries of the periphery in the first decade after the end of the East-West conflict was the effort to adopt political and economic liberalism. In few of them was this a smooth process; some were afflicted with terrible violence. But while the post-Cold War trials of the states of the periphery were often local tragedies and regional problems, on the whole they were not genuinely international issues. The core mattered to the periphery; the periphery did not matter to the core.

In economic terms this had almost always been so. And while the economic significance of the periphery for the core probably increased somewhat in the second half of the twentieth century, in matters of security the reverse was true. With the end of the Cold War the salience of the periphery for the core declined sharply.

During the Cold War, the two opposing coalitions saw the world as a great chessboard, with all parts of it connected to the central struggle. The pawns of the world—Vietnam, Korea, Afghanistan—were bitterly contested because their fates were connected to the security of the kings, the United States and the Soviet Union. Each superpower believed that the loss of a pawn would weaken its overall position: lose enough pawns and other lesser pieces, they feared, and the king, the homeland itself, would be threatened.

The significance of the world's pawns predated the Cold War. Great powers have traditionally worried that a defeat on the periphery would start an adverse chain reaction that would ultimately reach the core. The Athenians invaded Corcyra in the fifth century B.C., according to Thucydides' account, to prevent it from coming under the control of their rivals, the Spartans. The ancient Romans expanded their imperial sway to create buffers between their territories and those of rival empires. The British empire in Africa grew in the same way. To protect the Suez Canal, the lifeline to India, the British took control of adjacent territories, and then territories adjacent to the adjacent territories, to deny them to others. Even the creation of the American empire at the end of the nineteenth century was partly motivated by wariness of the ambitions of other powers.[49] For the United States after 1945 this impulse was particularly powerful. It was known as the "domino theory," according to which American security depended on preventing political and military defeats far away lest they begin a chain reaction of setbacks, like a row of falling dominoes, that would ultimately reach the United States.[50]

But in the wake of the Cold War, great-power rivalry, if not necessarily extinct for all time, was at least in abeyance. The core and the periphery, once tightly connected in the eyes of the great powers, were decoupled. In security affairs, unlike economics, the world moved toward separation rather than interdependence. No longer squares on a single chessboard, the core and periphery became, in the wake of the Cold War, like different neighborhoods in the same large American city in which the turbulence and poverty that afflicts some had all too little bearing on the calm and the affluence of others. To the general rule that the periphery did not matter to the core there were, however, three major exceptions.

The exceptions were a mineral—oil, a type of armament—nuclear weapons, and a familiar practice—terrorism. All three combined the timeless with the modern. The Earth's ancient deposits of petroleum replaced coal during the late nineteenth and early twentieth centuries as the principal source of the energy that powered industrial economies and became for the societies of the core what water and oxygen are for human life: a necessity. Nuclear weapons emerged from the application of modern scientific discoveries about the structure of matter to the age-old process of increasing the lethality of the weapons of war. Terrorism—attacks on civilians for political purposes—goes back at least to the Assassins of Mesopotamia in the eleventh century, and became a familiar feature of European politics in the nineteenth and twentieth centuries.[51] The attackers of September 11 communicated with one another via cell phones and the Internet and used as weapons not the daggers with which the Assassins murdered their victims but modern commercial airliners.

All three had the potential profoundly to affect the core, no economy of which could function without oil, no part of which could escape grave damage from a nuclear attack, and no country of which was immune from terrorist attacks. Where oil, nuclear weapons, and terrorism were concerned, therefore, the world's core and its periphery were closely connected. The effort of the core countries to assure a continuing supply of oil and to prevent the spread of nuclear weapons was the equivalent, for the international system, of the public health measures infectious diseases provoke. And those efforts concentrated, in the wake of the Cold War, on one region: the Middle East.

Like other parts of the periphery, the Middle East consumed rather than produced cultural innovations.[52] As in other parts of the periphery, the encounter with the West dominated the history of the region from the middle of the nineteenth century to the end of the twentieth. The local societies followed the familiar sequence: ignoring the great powers of the Western core, resisting them, eventually succumbing to and finally escaping from their formal tutelage. Like other parts of the periphery, it suffered from border disputes and difficulties in constructing modern states.

The Middle East differed from other parts of the periphery in that it was home to the largest readily accessible deposits of petroleum on the planet and to sovereign states that lacked, but wished to acquire, nuclear weapons and that gave financial and logistical support and safe haven to terrorist organizations, which drew their members from their populations. Oil and nuclear weapons were the stakes in the only significant war fought by any of the core powers in the first post-Cold War decade. The aim of the Gulf War of 1991, which was successfully accomplished, was to evict the armed forces of Iraq from tiny, neighboring, oil-producing Kuwait, which the Iraqis had occupied in August 1990. The Gulf War put the main features of post-Cold War relations between the core and the periphery on vivid display. It was ostensibly waged to uphold a basic principle of international law—to affirm the sanctity of sovereign borders, which the Iraqi invasion had violated. But the core powers were roused to military action more by the fear that, if unresisted, the Iraqi dictator Saddam Hussein would take control not only of Kuwait but also of Saudi Arabia, the site of the world's largest deposits of oil. They were motivated in particular by the belief, which proved correct, that Saddam Hussein had launched a crash program to equip himself with nuclear weapons.

The United States led the campaign to evict Iraq from Kuwait, assembling a broad international coalition to oppose Saddam Hussein, although American armed forces did most of the fighting. The Gulf War was emblematic of post-Cold War core-periphery relations in another way. It was the only such conflict in the first post-Cold War decade. There were many other wars but in none were the political and economic stakes sufficiently high for the United States, or any of the other core powers, to conduct military operations that risked casualties.

The war did not settle the issues over which it was fought. Despite the decisive military defeat of the Iraqi army, which was routed from Kuwait in one hundred hours, and despite the damage to the Iraqi nuclear weapons program inflicted by American bombardment in the weeks preceding the land assault, the outcome of the war did not assure, once and for all, Western access to Middle Eastern oil, nor did it prevent, once and for all, nuclear weapons from reaching the hands of Middle Eastern leaders intent on wielding them against the West.

From the Middle East a decade after the Gulf War came the attacks on New York and Washington, which were related to the two other sources of the core countries' interest in the Middle East. It was money that poured into the region from the sale of its oil that made the attacks possible. From Saudi Arabia, the country with the world's largest oil reserves, came the leader of the terrorist group responsible, Osama bin Laden, and most of the hijackers who seized control of the airplanes that were flown into the World Trade Center and the Pentagon, as well as the funds that supported the group's base in Afghanistan and its cells in other countries. The greatest danger that twenty-first century terrorism posed arose from the possibility that such groups would acquire and use a weapon of mass destruction.

Important and volatile as it was, however, the Middle East was not the part of the world's periphery with the greatest capacity to inflict damage on the core. That distinction belonged to the two large formerly orthodox Communist countries that had been liberalism's major antagonists during the Cold War—Russia and China.

THE OUTLIERS

LIKE GERMANY and Japan, Russia and China are countries that had parallel historical experiences in the modern era and played comparable roles in the post-Cold War world. Before the modern age both were traditional autocracies and, on the whole, successful ones. From the time of Peter the Great at the end of the seventeenth century, Russia counted as one of the great powers of Europe. Over the next two centuries the tsarist regime expanded steadily to the south and east while more than holding its own in war and diplomacy to its west. China had an even longer and more glorious premodern history. The oldest continuous political community in the world, China can trace its origins to the third millennium B.C. For much of that time China ranked, by most standards, as the leading state in the world: the largest, the most populous, the richest, the most sophisticated artistically and advanced technologically, and intermittently the most powerful militarily. From the eleventh to the fifteenth centuries China was the world's core, the source of innovations—material and cultural—that others, including Europeans, adopted.

Responding to the challenge that the French and industrial revolutions posed to all traditional societies, Russia and China followed parallel courses. Both autocracies tried to modernize to defend and preserve themselves. Both failed, although the patterns of their failures differed. The traditional Chinese regime disintegrated steadily from the first part of the nineteenth century, when the Europeans established enclaves on its coast from which to conduct trade with the interior, to the consolidation of Communist power in 1949. The formal end of the last Chinese imperial dynasty, the Qing, in 1911, was but one chapter in this long and, for the Chinese, painful decline. By contrast, the Russian autocracy collapsed suddenly, crushed by the weight of defeat on the battlefield, in 1917.

In both cases the Communist brand of illiberalism filled the political vacuum created by the demise of the traditional autocracy. Starting as tiny, secretive, persecuted minorities, the Communist forces, led by dynamic, imaginative, tactically adroit and entirely ruthless leaders—Lenin and Mao—managed to win bloody civil wars and to consolidate power. Once in power, each regime set about implementing a program of radical social and economic transformation.[53]

By some standards, and for some time, Communism in Russia and China achieved success. Communist parties seized and held power. With that power they destroyed all vestiges of the old order. By means of persecution and execution they suppressed dissent, driving into exile actual or potential opponents. They implemented the heart of the Communist economic program, the abolition of private property. They built what they took to be both the essence of economic modernity and the sinews of military strength: an economy emphasizing heavy industry.

All this came at a staggering cost to the Russian and Chinese societies. The cost was especially high for the rural sector in each country, against which the Communist regimes waged war for the purpose of dispossessing property owners and extracting a surplus to support their intensive programs of industrialization. Despite their cost, these programs did achieve their common goal. They enabled Communist governments to succeed where their imperial predecessors had failed, in protecting the territorial integrity of their countries against their predatory and economically more advanced neighbors. When Mao Zedong mounted the Gate of Heavenly Peace at the center of Beijing to proclaim the People's Republic of China on October 1, 1949, he said, "China has stood up."

The Soviet success was even more dramatic. The country withstood a massive German invasion during World War II, paying by far the highest price in blood of the several members of the anti-Nazi coalition. At the end of the war the Red Army had marched westward all the way to the heart of Germany.

In both cases the regime's military success seemed to vindicate, if not the harshness of its rule, then at least the economic measures that had produced the industrial output and the technological developments, including the production of nuclear weaponry, on which the military performance rested. Such legitimacy as the two regimes enjoyed during the second half of the twentieth century derived in no small part from their success in defending their borders.

Over the long term, however, the Communist approach to economic management failed. It could match the liberal core in guns but not in butter.[54] This failure, combined with the disaffection caused by the brutality and mendacity of Communist illiberalism, eroded the foundations of Communist rule in both countries. Orthodox Communism met the same fate as traditional autocracy, and in the same distinctive way. In China it disintegrated gradually and piecemeal. At the outset of the twenty-first century, Communist economics had been largely set aside and Communist ideology was a dead letter but the Communist party retained a political monopoly in the country. By contrast, the Soviet Union collapsed suddenly and completely at the end of 1991. The political system, the economic system, and the state itself all disappeared.

In the wake of the Cold War it was easier to say what these two countries were not than what they were. Both had abandoned orthodox Marxism-Leninism (in the Chinese case Marxism-Leninism-Maoism) but neither was a liberal, modern, industrial democracy. While not fully parts of the world's core, neither did Russia and China belong in all respects to its periphery. In matters of security they continued to carry considerable weight, as they had during the Cold War. In matters of trade and investment they were minor—in the Russian case almost negligible—presences, although China's impact on the global economy was growing at an impressive rate.

While these regimes were not seeking to overturn the post-Cold War order, neither were they fully or irrevocably committed to liberal politics, to market economics, or, and above all, to liberal security policies. And to the extent that they were committed, their capacity to establish liberal institutions and follow liberal practices was questionable. What the American Secretary of State Dean Acheson had said of Great Britain in the years following World War II—that it had lost an empire and had yet to find a role—was true of post-Cold War Russia and China. Their political and economic systems, their foreign policies, their places in the international hierarchy—in short, all the ingredients of that slippery but essential feature of every sovereign state, its national identity—were in flux.[55]

From the point of view of international liberalism, the optimal post-Cold War category for Russia and China was the one pioneered by Germany and Japan after World War II: the challenger-turned-pillar. If the central task for the liberal core during the Cold War had been to block the advance of Communist illiberalism, the highest goal in the post-Cold War period was the transformation and incorporation of its former opponents, in a reprise of what had occurred after World War II. But the circumstances were different, and less favorable, at the end of the Cold War than they had been in 1945, for Russia and China had less previous experience with democratic politics and far less experience with market economics than Germany and Japan had had.[56]

Moreover, Germany's and Japan's paths to core membership were smoothed, unintentionally and even perversely, by their crushing defeats in World War II and by the onset of the Cold War. In 1945 they were shattered and occupied and thus in no position to resist the preferences of their conquerors. Russia and China were deformed by decades of Communism, but their factories were not destroyed by bombs during the Cold War and their post-Cold War institutions would not be fashioned under Western supervision. Moreover, in the aftermath of World War II, the United States in particular made it a high priority to restart the engines of economic growth in Germany and Japan, the better to confront the Soviet Union. At the same time, their alliances with the United States relieved Germany and Japan of the need to rearm swiftly or to pursue independent security policies. This, in turn, provided a more favorable setting for liberal politics and economics than would otherwise have been the case, and underwrote the liberal, self-abnegating security policies that both countries adopted. In the wake of the Cold War, Russia and China received no comparable economic assistance or military protection and in neither country was the setting for liberalism altogether favorable.

One particularly unfavorable feature was the oppressive psychological burden that orthodox Communism bequeathed. Each country was doubly afflicted, a victim of both varieties of murderous twentieth-century illiberalism. The heart of both fascism and Communism was war. For Germany and Japan the main struggle was against other, and, as they saw them, lesser peoples. They waged this struggle with particular savagery against their largest neighbors, Russia and China. For Communist illiberalism the enemy was not different nations but members of what the Communist Party designated as the wrong domestic social groups, people who opposed, or might oppose, Communist rule. The suspect categories turned out to include almost everybody. Communism in power in Russia and China, like the German and Japanese occupation of the countries, was in essence a war against the Russian and Chinese people. In the twentieth century, therefore, and not only in its first half, it was an unhappy fate to be born in either country. The damage inevitably distorted and retarded Russian and Chinese efforts to conduct what qualified by liberal standards as a normal national existence, just as abused children and tortured prisoners have difficulty pursuing normal social lives.

Like other countries of the world's periphery, the history of the first post-Cold War decade in Russia and China was marked by an effort to establish a liberal economic system and, with less conviction (and none at all on the part of the government of China) a liberal political system. Like the others, both Russia and China were intensely interested in joining the liberal international economic order. But where security was concerned, these two countries had a unique status.

In the wake of the Cold War a liberal security order, descended from Woodrow Wilson's advocacy of limits on armaments, was in place—but only in Europe, and there it was new, fragile, and reversible. To the existing liberal security order in Europe, and to the potential comparable set of arrangements in the other part of the world's core where they were conceivable, Russia and China were indispensable. In fact, for the purposes of international security these two countries were part of the core and not the periphery. While the international trade and monetary systems could flourish without them, to establish and maintain a liberal security order in the two regions where great wars were fought in the twentieth century and could be fought in the twenty-first—Europe and East Asia—Russian and Chinese participation was indispensable. Upon them depended the twenty-first century's prospects for peace.

II

THE INVENTION OF PEACE

"We believe that armaments should be reduced to the level of reasonable sufficiency, that is, a level necessary for strictly defensive purposes. It is time the two military alliances amended their strategic concepts to gear them more to the aims of defense. Every apartment in the 'European home' has the right to protect itself against burglars, but it must do so without destroying its neighbors' property."

MIKHAIL GORBACHEV, 1987[1]

*

CHAPTER FOUR

The Cure for Cancer

WITH THE FORTUNE he acquired through his invention of dyna-
mite, the Swedish businessman Alfred Nobel established a
trust to fund annual prizes for great achievement in physics, chem-
istry, medicine, literature, and peace. First awarded in 1901, the
Nobel Prizes turned out to be particularly appropriate in the twentieth century. For whatever the quality of the literary works that
appeared during that hundred-year span, it was without doubt a
great age of scientific advance. And because the achievements of science were routinely incorporated by the world's armed forces, making warfare deadlier and more destructive than ever before, the
search for peace became more urgent than in centuries past.

The prizes for science and peace recognized different types of
achievement. Science involves discovering what has always existed,
whereas peacemaking is an exercise in creating something that does
not exist. What scientists discover are regularities, the laws of the
physical universe. The scientists who earned Nobel Prizes worked
out formulas for understanding and, where their discoveries could
be applied, for changing the world. Peacemakers did no such
thing—until the end of the twentieth century. At the close of that
war-ravaged century there emerged, by a process of trial and error,
out of a complex mixture of motives, something resembling the
work of science—a formula for avoiding the scourge of armed conflict. From Europe, the birthplace of the ideas and institutions that
made the modern world, came an innovation to be compared with
the most important of them: the invention of peace.[2]

COMMON SECURITY IN EUROPE

E UROPE ENTERED the twenty-first century with a system of common security. The parties to it carried out similar and coordinated policies of self-defense, based on the understanding that
security was a problem best solved through common efforts. The
common security order has at its heart a series of negotiated limits
on armaments, all but one concluded near the end of the Cold War
and all but one governing nuclear armaments: the Anti-Ballistic
Missile (ABM) Treaty of 1972, the Intermediate-range Nuclear
Forces (INF) Treaty of 1987, the START I Treaty of 1991, the
START II Treaty of 1993, the reciprocal unilateral reductions by the
Soviet Union and the United States in short-range nuclear weapons
of 1991, and the comprehensive treaty limiting and restructuring
non-nuclear forces, the Treaty on Conventional Forces in Europe
(CFE) of 1990. Together these agreements reshaped the armed
forces of the opposing sides in the Cold War according to two principles that together define common security. The first principle is
defense dominance, according to which armed forces are organized
and deployed for defending territory but not for attacking and seizing it. The second principle is transparency, meaning that all countries are able to see for themselves just what armed forces all others
have and how and where they are deployed.

This common security order is for war and peace what democracy
is for politics and the free market is for economics: a formula for
achieving a universally desired goal. The liberal approaches to politics and economics are vehicles for freedom and prosperity; common
security is a mechanism for securing peace. Like democracy and free
markets it is a system of voluntary association, albeit of sovereign
states rather than individuals. Like democracy and free markets it
places limits on the powers of states through impersonal rules. Like
democracy and free markets, its origins are Anglo-American and it is
a distinctly modern creation, unimaginable at any time before the
nineteenth century and impossible before the end of the Cold War.

But common security was scarcely as well known as democracy
and free markets. It was not widely acknowledged as the liberal

approach to the problem of international security.[3] There was no classic statement of its principles and practices, the equivalent of Hobbes on the state, Locke on rights, or Adam Smith on the market. In one sense this was not surprising. States, rights, and markets were relatively well established when Hobbes, Locke, and Smith wrote about them. At the outset of the twenty-first century the common security order in Europe had only recently come into being. Indeed, the problem to which it emerged as the liberal solution was itself relatively new. While war is an ancient practice, the idea that war is something that can be abolished came to the fore only in the modern era.

Still, common security's relative newness as an idea does not fully account for its obscurity. Cancer, after all, is a relatively new disease, far more common in the modern era than previously because of longer lives and transformed lifestyles. But the discovery of a cure for cancer would command the world's attention. And in fact a comparison between the medical efforts to eradicate cancer and the political efforts to abolish war points to some of the reasons that the advent of common security did not seize the imagination of the international community after the end of the Cold War.

The fight against cancer advances in small steps rather than great leaps. Research produces new therapies by modifying existing ones. So it was with common security. The treaties at its heart took years to conclude, they were not the first treaties ever signed, and in important ways they resembled others already in place. Advances in cancer therapy, moreover, have generally brought some improvement in the treatment of one of the many forms of the disease but they have not abolished any one, let alone all of them. Similarly, common security arrangements were fully established in only one place—Europe—and there they were fragile and reversible.

Reducing the incidence of cancer in a population involves not only the devising of new medical techniques but also broader changes in social behavior: less smoking, healthier diets, the elimination of environmental pollutants. The first approach is the stuff of newspaper headlines; the second is not. Similarly, the two levels of history combined to create common security, which was the product of specific events, the negotiations that yielded the treaties, together with a particular trend—the growing aversion to war in the societies of the world's core.[4] Events are dramatic, trends are not.

There is a final reason that the emergence of a common security order in Europe was little noted. It was overshadowed by more dramatic developments: the downfall of Communism and the effort to build liberal politics and economics on its ruins.[5] In 1990 the world's attention was fixed on the unification of Germany, not on the signing of the long-negotiated, exceedingly complicated treaty governing non-nuclear forces in Europe.

The transformation of the politics and economics of formerly Communist Europe was riveting in a way that the equally momentous changes in security arrangements were not. The rise of democracy and free markets in the wake of the Cold War differed from the emergence of common security in yet another way. Liberal politics and economics replaced totalitarian governments and centrally planned economies; common security's triumph, on the other hand, was not over the illiberal approach to security but over the traditional approach, which remained the international orthodoxy well into the modern age.

The illiberal version of international relations, embraced by the fascists and Communists, made war the supreme national purpose. In the traditional view, war is not necessarily desirable but it is all but inevitable, owing to the anarchic structure of the international system. With no common power to prevent it, war is a constant possibility and states must therefore prepare for it. To eschew such preparations risks playing the chicken in a world of foxes. Anarchy, like gravity, is pervasive. It shapes the conduct of sovereign states whether or not they recognize its effects. Technically, when a glass falls to the floor and breaks there are two causes: a precipitating cause—someone brushing against it and knocking it over—and an enabling cause—gravity itself. Similarly, every war has two causes. "State-level" causes consist of the large category of goals, aspirations, and ideologies over which sovereign states have traditionally gone to war.[6] But war always has another cause as well, although it is seldom noted. This second cause is the underlying anarchy of the international system, the "system-level" cause. While sovereign states fight for the motives that recur in international history, they

are free to fight because of anarchy—because there is nothing to
stop them. State-level causes of war are offensive, based on what sovereign states want. The system-level cause is defensive, based on
what they fear. Because they dwell in an anarchical universe, sovereign states live on, or near, the brink of war, waiting for one of the
many state-level causes with which human history has been generous to push them over it into outright conflict.

It was the Greek general Thucydides, in his account of the war
between his native city-state Athens and its rival Sparta in the fifth
century B.C., who first drew attention to the anarchic structure of
the system of sovereign states and its powerful effects on their conduct. Anarchy, he noted, breeds insecurity: "among neighbors," he
wrote, "antagonism is ever a condition of independence."[7] He recognized that underlying the specific political quarrels that had triggered the Peloponnesian War was the perpetual, pervasive,
system-level cause of conflict: "What made war inevitable was the
growth of Athenian power and the fear which this caused in
Sparta."[8]

Thucydides is to the study of war and peace what Adam Smith is
to economics: the codifier of the fundamental conditions that
endured from his own day through the twentieth century. He was
the first to record the underlying realities of relations among sovereign states, and the school of analysis that descends from him is
known as "realism."[9]

The realist approach does not presume that armed conflict is a
constant feature of international relations; the history of international relations is not a history of war without end. War has been
avoided through a balance of power. A working balance of power is
in effect when the distribution of military power among sovereign
states is such that none is tempted to attack any other because none
believes that it can prevail, at least not at an acceptable cost. Such a
stable balance prevailed during the Cold War. Two heavily armed
coalitions confronted each other. Each was perpetually ready to fight
and each embraced the kinds of political goals for which states had
fought in the past, but there was no war in Europe. The two held
back for reasons of prudence. It was not so much peace as an armed
truce that obtained in Cold War Europe. Indeed, relations between

the two military and ideological blocs were almost never said to be peaceful; they were, instead, described as "stable."

While a balance of power can avoid outright fighting, it places sovereign states on the brink of war. The history of international relations is therefore the history of the unending possibility, and the consequences for diplomacy, of armed conflict.[10] And historically states did not remain on the brink of war indefinitely. Sooner or later a state-level cause tipped them over.

It is not only state-level causes that push countries into war. What students of international relations call the "security dilemma" also plays a part. It stems from the fact that threats and preparations to meet them are interrelated in unpredictable ways. State A may take what it intends to be a defensive measure that State B, however, interprets as offensive and responds accordingly. The sequence of events moves both, unintentionally, closer to war. The security dilemma means that sovereign states can behave like Shakespeare's Othello, driven to tragically unnecessary acts by unfounded suspicions. Because state-level causes of war have always been abundant, and because the security dilemma is a persistent feature of relations among sovereign states, war, in the realist perspective, is like winter in the northern climes: It may come late, it may be mild, but sooner or later, in one form or another, it will always come.[11]

The great achievement of the common security order in Europe is to have modified these fundamental realities of international relations, enabling sovereign states to draw back further than ever before from the brink of armed conflict.

The foundation on which common security rests is a large and historically unprecedented presumption: that the familiar and previously omnipresent state-level causes of war have disappeared, or at least are in abeyance. This was not true in any period before the end of the twentieth century. For almost all of its recorded history Europe was a veritable cornucopia of state-level causes of war. The lures of gold, land, and glory were always present in some combination as incentives to fight. They continued, in the wake of the Cold War, to be present in most places outside Europe. But in the Western core, the end of the Cold War combined with broad social changes that had taken place over the course of the twentieth century to render the panoply of state-level causes of war far less potent than ever before. This, in turn, changed the relationship between arms and war.

Woodrow Wilson favored limiting arms because he believed that by their very existence arms caused war. When state-level causes exist, this is not so. Then it is true, as the old saying has it, that states are not adversaries because they are armed but rather are armed because they are adversaries. Arms are instruments to achieve the political goals for which their possessors are willing to fight. But when state-level causes have shriveled, anarchy-induced insecurity is the remaining cause of war and it is then true that arms cause insecurity. The common security order in place in Europe at the end of the Cold War reduced arms-induced insecurity through negotiated agreements on weapons, agreements that had two important features.

First, the treaties reconfigured the armed forces in Europe to make them suitable for defending territory but not for attacking, conquering, and occupying it. The sovereign states of Europe thus voluntarily adopted the strategy of the porcupine, equipping themselves for self-protection but not for molesting others. They established "defense dominance" as the governing principle of their armed forces.

To be sure, it is not always easy to distinguish offensive from defensive armaments. Sometimes the difference is straightforward: In pre-modern times fortifications were defensive, cannon to breach them offensive. But in the modern age weapons have often served both purposes. By the latter stages of the Cold War, however, nuclear weapons lent themselves to an unusually clear distinction between offense and defense. The nuclear weapons of both sides were so powerful that each could inflict devastating punishment on the other even after absorbing the mightiest attack the other could mount. Thus neither side dared attack, which is exactly the outcome that defense dominance produces.

The governments of Europe and North America applied the principle of defense dominance to non-nuclear armaments in a more straightforward way, by placing limits on military equipment useful for attack—tanks, airplanes, artillery and troops—and by making the two sides numerically equal in these weapons. Equality favors the defensive side because in war a successful offensive campaign ordinarily requires numerical superiority: an often-cited rule of thumb holds that in order to succeed an attacker needs a three-to-one advantage.

The reshaping of armed forces in Europe to conform to the principle of defense dominance thus provided simultaneously the self-protective ferocity of the lion and the inoffensiveness of the lamb. It turned the European powers into the sturdiest and most secure of all creatures, a vegetarian lion.

For defense dominance to ease the insecurity endemic to international society, each country must be able to satisfy itself that others pose no threat. This is the basis for the second defining feature of the common security order, transparency, which makes it possible for each country to know which weapons all the others have and what they are doing with them. A technical innovation from the first half of the Cold War was crucial: reconnaissance satellites, orbiting the Earth in outer space and equipped with high-resolution cameras that could photograph the terrain below. As the resolution of the cameras improved, it became possible to track and count weapons with increasing accuracy.

Satellites made negotiated limits on armaments politically possible. The United States worried that the Soviet Union would cheat on any accord it signed. It was, after all, a closed society, in which even the most innocent public matters were deliberately concealed—and nuclear weapons were not innocent. So the United States would not accept any agreement unless it could independently verify Soviet compliance with its terms. Satellites made verification possible and a rule for arms control was established. Whatever weapons could be accurately tracked and counted by satellite could be included in an agreement. Conversely, weapons that were too small or too readily concealed to be monitored—and for most of the Cold War this included all but the largest nuclear weapons on both sides—could not be limited by treaty.[12] In the closing years of the Cold War the Soviet government decided to permit what it had previously prohibited, the admission of Western inspectors to its territory to assist in the task of verifying Soviet compliance with arms agreements. This considerably broadened the range of armaments that could acceptably be included in such agreements and thus paved the way for the European common security order.

Like defense dominance, the principle of transparency was written into formal treaties governing Europe's military affairs. This gave the two principles a weight that they would not have had if they had been part of only informal arrangements. They became matters of international law. By signing the treaties, countries acknowledged the need to take steps to reduce the insecurity of others.

If the effects of anarchy on international relations are akin to the force of gravity, the common security order can be compared to the techniques of manned flight. The discovery of the principles of aerodynamics and the development of engines powerful enough to lift machines off the ground and carry them through the air did not abolish gravity but did make it possible for humans to overcome its effects under certain conditions. So it was with common security and anarchy.

As a method for avoiding war, the principles of common security represented an improvement on the balance of power. For although it was intermittently effective, the strategy of peace through military equilibrium took a toll—economically, through the constant preparations for war that it required, and psychologically, because of the insecurity and suspicion involved. It required constant vigilance and the continuous exploration of new military technologies lest others develop an advantage. Common security eased the burden of both. It was not based on the fear of losing a war but rather on a lack of interest in winning one. The common security order placed the sovereign states of Europe farther away from the brink of war than a balance of power could.[13]

It did not place them so far from it that war was no longer imaginable. Nor did the common security order provide a vehicle for policing Europe, a fire brigade that could be called upon to extinguish outbreaks of violence all over the continent. Rather, the consensus underpinning it was a negative one. The countries involved agreed on what they would *not* do: They would not fight each other.

The common security order had the same features as a transaction in a market economy. Both were voluntary, contractual, transparent,

and based on the recognition that the arrangement would be mutually advantageous.[14] The logic of common security is the same as the
logic of market economics (and for that matter the logic of public
goods): Cooperation can make all parties better off. While the
underlying logic is clear in retrospect, however, the common security order was not constructed in logical, deliberate fashion, like a
building from an architect's blueprint. Its establishment was, rather,
the unintended product of a series of technical trends and political
choices that had their roots in the major military innovation of the
twentieth century, the atomic bomb.

THE CREATION OF COMMON SECURITY

WHEN THE nuclear age began in August 1945, with the American
attacks on the Japanese cities of Hiroshima and Nagasaki, it was
obvious that the new weapon would profoundly affect international
politics. The appearance of this man-made source of unprecedented
destructive power led almost immediately to two developments, one
military, the other diplomatic. The merger of the two created the
common security order.

The military development was the emergence of deterrence—
preventing an attack by threatening effective resistance, in this case
through retaliation—as the main principle of nuclear strategy. The
United States concluded that this was virtually the only use to which
the new weapon could be put. For much of the nuclear age the
Soviet Union seemed less persuaded of this, but, if only because its
American rival had been the first to acquire them, the Soviet government had to take steps to ensure that its nuclear weapons provided
effective deterrence as well.[15]

Even as they began to accumulate nuclear weapons to deter each
other, the United States and the Soviet Union commenced negotiations to place limits on these weapons. Both were moved by the
impulse to do something about the danger that they posed. In the
early years of the nuclear age both offered plans for "general and
complete disarmament"—the abolition of all nuclear arms and ultimately weapons of every kind. But neither seriously expected the

other to accept. The proposals were part of each government's efforts to convince the world that it was devoted to reducing the nuclear danger.

In 1963 the two did conclude an accord on nuclear weapons, but the Limited Test Ban Treaty, which banned nuclear explosions under water, in the Earth's atmosphere, and in outer space (although not underground, where nuclear testing continued), was effective chiefly as an environmental protection measure. It did not affect the force levels on either side.[16]

In 1972, however, the two reached an agreement that did affect the weapons they could deploy. Nuclear strategy merged with nuclear diplomacy in the ABM Treaty, which effectively prohibited each side from constructing defenses against the offensive weapons of the other. (At the same time they signed an accord putting a cap on some of these offensive weapons.) The ABM Treaty formally committed both the United States and the Soviet Union, for the first time, to the principle of defense dominance.

The treaty was the unintended product of the arms competition between the two sides during the first quarter century of the nuclear age. Nuclear weapons were so powerful that any defense against them had to work perfectly to qualify as even minimally adequate. If one side were to launch one hundred nuclear charges at the other and the other were to deflect or destroy ninety-nine of them, the result would still be a disaster for the defender since the one unchecked explosive could crush a major city and kill millions of people. By 1972 each side had thousands of nuclear explosives, which could be delivered to targets on the other side of the world in a matter of minutes by intercontinental ballistic missiles. Because no piece of military equipment could be expected to perform perfectly the first time it was used, a nuclear attack of any size could easily defeat any system of defense.

So constructing effective defenses against nuclear attack came to seem a hopeless task. Worse still, the two sides concluded, it was dangerous even to try to construct them, for this would leave each of them poorer and less secure. But the fear that the other might somehow succeed would drive each to try to construct defenses in the absence of a joint agreement not to do so. Defense dominance through mutual assured destruction, abbreviated by the appropriately grotesque acronym "MAD," thus emerged as an inevitable fact of life in the nuclear age. The ABM Treaty expressed mutual resignation to that fact.

Ronald Reagan, the American president from 1981 to 1989, was particularly unhappy with the ABM Treaty, believing it to be morally unacceptable because it based the security of the United States on a threat—to kill millions of people—that it would be immoral to carry out. He also regarded the treaty as technically misconceived because it was based on an underestimation of the capacity of the American scientific and technical ingenuity to build effective defenses. In 1983 he announced the Strategic Defense Initiative. Its aim, which was not achieved in his presidency, was to develop and construct the defensive system that the ABM Treaty prohibited. Yet it was Reagan who, along with his Soviet counterpart, Mikhail Gorbachev, built on that treaty to create the common security order with which Europe entered the post-Cold War period.

Reagan and Gorbachev were an odd couple. The mighty nuclear forces they controlled made the two of them, in effect, the joint custodians of a doomsday machine that could destroy each other's country and the world. As a pair they were inevitably oddly matched because the political systems from which they came differed so sharply and because their goals were opposed in every way save one. They shared an interest in what nuclear weapons had put in jeopardy: survival. Their relationship thus resembled a familiar cinematic plot in which two people with nothing in common and no great liking for each other are thrown together by circumstance and forced to cooperate.[17] The Soviet-American partnership, by contrast, almost always ended in grief. Franklin Roosevelt labored under the mistaken belief that he could charm his wartime ally, Josef Stalin, into more accommodating policies in Europe. John Kennedy's only direct meeting with Nikita Khrushchev in Vienna in 1961 concluded in recriminations and the next year the two countries found themselves close to war over Moscow's dispatch of nuclear-capable missiles to Cuba. Richard Nixon and Leonid Brezhnev sought to forge a new relationship in the 1970s, which they called detente, which collapsed in mutual recriminations.

Yet the partnership of Reagan and Gorbachev had a happy ending. Together the two built the common security order in Europe. But that was not what either intended.

After he left office Reagan's admirers saw him as the hero of the contest with the Soviet Union, the man who had won the Cold War without firing a shot. The verdict exaggerated his contribution to the outcome of the conflict.[18] In fact, Reagan is more appropriately understood as a postwar figure, a Harry Truman rather than a Franklin Roosevelt, who helped put in place the security arrangements that Europe carried into the post-Cold War era despite having entered office dubious about the heart of those arrangements, which were the negotiated limits on armaments.

Reagan came to the presidency convinced that the agreements that his predecessors had negotiated with the Soviet Union had been, for the United States, useless at best and damaging at worst. As president he insisted that the American positions in the arms negotiations be redrawn to reflect not what the other side might be willing to accept but rather what it was in the interest of the United States to get.[19] The new positions, translated into treaties covering both nuclear and non-nuclear weapons, formed the heart of the common security order. But Reagan's major purpose in putting forward these positions was not to establish defense dominance as a governing principle but to reduce what American officials regarded as potentially dangerous Soviet military advantages.

Soviet land-based missiles were larger than the American ones and could therefore carry more warheads. By some calculations they might have had the capacity to destroy all the American land-based long-range missiles in a surprise attack. American strategists feared that this Soviet capacity, while it could not entirely eliminate the means for nuclear retaliation, might be converted to a Soviet political advantage. They feared a nuclear version of America's great military shock of World War II, the Japanese surprise attack on Pearl Harbor. For non-nuclear weapons, the Reagan proposals were designed to prevent a recurrence of the Germans' successful lightning strike against France in 1940. The necessary condition for such an attack was widely thought to be a numerical advantage for the attacker, at least at the point of attack, in tanks, troops, and aircraft.

The Soviet-dominated Warsaw Pact armies had more of each than did the NATO forces. The American proposals called for equality in the relevant categories of weaponry at far lower levels than the Communist side had already deployed.

Because these proposals required that the Soviet side give up many more weapons than the United States and its allies, when they were put forward they seemed extremely unlikely to be accepted. Certainly none of the first six leaders of the Soviet Union would have accepted them. But in 1985 the seventh came to power and reached conclusions about international security radically different from those that had guided his predecessors.

Mikhail Gorbachev is one of the great figures of twentieth century history. He was more responsible than any other single person for perhaps the happiest and most surprising event (the word miraculous is not too strong) in a century filled with unhappy surprises: the end of the Cold War, of the Soviet empire, and of the Soviet Union itself, all in an almost entirely peaceful manner.[20] For that reason his career as the last leader of the USSR will always be of interest. Of particular interest will be the question of how a person so committed to change could have emerged from a political system suffocatingly adept at enforcing conformity and suppressing initiative. Of equal interest will be the way in which his personal qualities contributed to the historic outcome over which he presided: his arrogance in believing that he knew how to reform Communism, his ignorance of the country and empire he governed and thus of the disruption that his policies were almost bound to produce, and his decency in refraining from using force to stop the consequences of those policies as they unfolded. Putting an end to the Communist era in European history, which is what he did, was, however, very far from what Gorbachev set out to do.

His initial aim was to reform the Soviet Union. Arms control attracted him as a way of securing some breathing space in the military competition with the West, the better to marshal his country's resources for internal reconstruction, an enterprise he called *perestroika*. Gorbachev did come, however, to grasp and to embrace the logic of common security. He articulated its principles more clearly and explicitly than any other world leader.

Gorbachev asserted that security had to be achieved in common, rather than unilaterally. Security, he said, "can only be mutual."[21] It involved "the recognition of others' interests."[22] The imperative of the age was that "adversaries must become partners and start looking jointly for a way to achieve universal security."[23] This reasoning implied that military doctrines "should be strictly doctrines of defense. And this is connected with such new or comparatively new notions as the reasonable sufficiency of armaments, non-aggressive defense, the elimination of disbalance and asymmetries in various types of armed forces."[24] Gorbachev conceded that this would require changes in the military forces in Europe, including those on the Communist side: "There are imbalances and asymmetries in some kinds of armaments and armed forces on both sides in Europe. . . . We stand for eliminating the inequality existing in some areas, but not through a build-up by those who lag behind but through a reduction by those who are ahead."[25]

All this made for a double irony. The clearest statement of the liberal approach to international security came from the leader of the world's leading illiberal power; and the great political innovation of a would-be Communist reformer was not part of Marxism-Leninism at all but of its ideological opposite, Anglo-American Wilsonian liberalism. Gorbachev received the Nobel Peace Prize, the most deserving recipient in the history of the award. He adopted the liberal approach because, unlike previous Soviet leaders, he did not seek to spread Communism by force. The idea that the use of force, except in self-defense, is illegitimate is integral to common security; and like the other ideas and practices that define the modern world, it originated in the West.

WARLESSNESS

T HE ROMAN saying *sine moribus legae vanae*—without morals, laws are in vain—applies to common security. Attitudes underpin institutions; practices are anchored in values. The treaties embodying the principles of defense dominance and transparency rested on something less tangible but just as important: an increasingly powerful disinclination within the countries of the Western core to go to war.

This growing Western "warlessness" was a product of the twentieth century. For traditional rulers, going to war was always an option, subject to the calculation of costs and benefits. For the core countries in the second half of the twentieth century, that calculation tilted sharply in a negative direction. The costs rose sharply. At the same time, the benefits for which sovereign states had gone to war for millennia came to seem less desirable.

Self-defense remained a universally accepted reason to fight, but with the demise of Communism the countries of the core no longer faced a serious threat. Meanwhile, the other aims of war had also lost much of their appeal. Important among them was the hope of material gain.[26] Traditional monarchs sought to expand their territory, the better to increase their wealth through taxes and tribute and to enhance their power by using their new wealth to hire larger armies. The illiberal regimes regarded territorial expansion as a condition of their survival and Germany and Japan used their conquests as sources of raw materials and cheap (sometimes even slave) labor.

By contrast, the liberal countries of the core came, in the twentieth century, to agree with what Adam Smith had said in the eighteenth: that empire was not a paying proposition. He had opposed his government's war to retain the American colonies on the grounds that Great Britain would be better served if the Americans became independent: Britain could then reap the benefits of trade with them while avoiding the costs of governing them.

The industrial revolution contributed to the devaluation of offensive war by revoking the status of land as the major source of wealth and power. In pre-industrial times wealth came chiefly from agriculture conducted on the land and precious metals extracted from beneath it. The more territory a monarch controlled, the wealthier and more powerful he or she was. With the coming of the industrial revolution, other sources of wealth and military might became available. Territory did not become irrelevant, but by the end of the twentieth century it was widely accepted that to gain wealth a sovereign state was better advised to invest and to trade. In the twenty-first century the tiny city-state of Singapore and the crowded, resource-poor Japanese archipelago produced wealth far more efficiently than did the vast territories of Russia and China.

Wars were often waged for non-material goals as well. Monarchs fought for prestige and to advance the cause of their religious faiths. Illiberal states waged war on behalf of their own secular versions of religious creeds: ideology. Liberal societies were also ideological. They were committed to liberal principles and for a time could justify conquering and governing others as a way to spread them. In the nineteenth century liberal imperialism did not strike the Americans, the British, or the French as a contradiction. They considered it virtuous to bring Christianity to unbelievers, and a service to bring railroads to people who had previously traveled on foot or by animal-drawn carts and the rule of law to those subject to the arbitrary caprice of traditional authorities. But in the twentieth century, liberal societies abandoned the belief, previously axiomatic, in the natural superiority of the core countries and their consequent right to rule the people of the periphery.[27] With the state-level, offensive causes of war in disrepute, the countries of the core had no war aims except peace; and unlike the panoply of war aims of the past, this one could be achieved without fighting.

A steep rise in the costs of war also contributed to the precipitous drop in enthusiasm for its practice. The costs rose in part because the gap in military power between the core and the periphery had narrowed. In the nineteenth century the Western monopoly of industrial weapons—the gunboat, for example, and the machine gun—turned battles between core and periphery into one-sided massacres. In the twentieth century the societies of the periphery acquired modern armaments and learned how to use them. The diffusion of the Western ways of war did not entirely reverse the balance of strength: Communist Vietnam could not conquer the United States, but the Vietnamese could inflict enough damage on American forces to convince the American public that victory in Indochina would cost more than it was worth.

As for war within the core, here the costs soared. In the twentieth century the application of the industrial revolution to economic tasks led to mass production. Clothing, housing, methods of transportation and communication became cheaper, more numerous, and thus far more widely available than ever before. The application of the industrial revolution to warfare led to the mass production of death. This was what made World War I so terrible.

For the first time battlefield casualties far exceeded the toll taken by disease and the lack of medical attention to treatable injuries.[28] For the first time, entire societies were mobilized for warfare. Men were conscripted into the ranks of the armed forces and those not in uniform, along with civilian women and children, were subject to bombardment by airplanes. So intense was the experience of battle, with its non-stop artillery salvos and heavy machine-gun barrages, that it proved psychologically disorienting. World War I even produced a new war-induced psychiatric illness: shell shock.[29]

World War I also began the devaluation of the martial virtues, above all individual courage. The four bloody years did not lack for examples of heroism but it became increasingly difficult to believe that individual valor could ever again be decisive to the outcome of such a conflict. The war demonstrated that Napoleon had been right when he said that God is invariably on the side of the bigger battalions.[30]

After 1918 liberal societies could no longer regard major war as a great and glorious adventure.[31] The liberal democracies did not want to fight another such war and they went to some lengths to avoid one. Unfortunately, the illiberal powers had a different view of the matter, and the determination of the liberal governments in the 1930s to spare their societies a repetition of the horrors of 1914–1918 made the next war even more costly when it came.

The death and destruction of World War II was even greater than the toll taken by World War I, especially for noncombatants. The cost of the Second World War might alone have sufficed to keep the major powers of the international system from fighting one another again.[32] But the revolutionary military innovation that appeared at the very end of that conflict—the atomic bomb—made the disinclination toward war in the West even more pronounced.

If the application of the techniques of the industrial revolution to warfare inflated the costs of war, the advent of nuclear weapons produced hyperinflation. The firepower carried by a single submarine equipped with nuclear-tipped ballistic missiles could inflict more damage on an adversary than all the destruction that any country suffered during the course of World War II—which, especially in the case of Germany, Japan, and the Soviet Union, was vast indeed. A nuclear exchange between the two great nuclear-armed powers of the Cold War would not have been a war at all, in the sense that it would not have been compatible with the ends or the means of war as it had evolved through the centuries. The nineteenth century Prussian military officer Karl von Clausewitz defined war as the continuation of politics by other—more violent—means.[33] A nuclear war between the United States and the Soviet Union could have achieved no plausible political goal for either side. Neither could have hoped to escape grave damage from even a few nuclear strikes, so neither could have expected to "win" a nuclear war.

As for the means of war, from the time of the ancient Greeks through World War II the heart of the enterprise was the battle: armed men in direct combat with one another for control of a piece of territory, fighting until one or the other side fled, surrendered, or was overcome. Battles generally decided wars. A Soviet-American nuclear conflict would have been a grotesque kind of impersonal, hours-long artillery duel that might well have annihilated them both.

After 1945, as before, wars were waged without recourse to nuclear weapons. These, too, were increasingly unacceptable within the Western core, not only because their costs had risen but also because it had become less acceptable to pay any costs at all. The price of war had come to be counted in individual lives lost, and liberal societies were increasingly reluctant to lose even a single one. To this attitude, which flourished in the second half of the twentieth century, several trends contributed.

The decline in religious faith deprived combatants and their families of the consolation of an anticipated afterlife. The decline of social deference increased the reluctance both to issue and to carry out orders the fulfillment of which ran the risk of death. The decline in rates of fertility made families smaller so that each child became more precious and less dispensable.[34] At the same time, the rise in the emphasis on human rights made each individual life seem more valuable, and the rise in wealth and life expectancy within the core meant that every soldier had, in material terms, far more to lose by dying young than in the past.

The broad "debellicization"[35] of Western societies in the twentieth century, the sea change in attitudes toward war, is difficult to document precisely. It involves what French social historians have called *mentalités*, widely held beliefs and assumptions that can be so deeply embedded in a society that they are seldom explicitly stated but that exert a powerful influence on the direction of events, like the effect of the ocean's current on ships. Difficult to fix though it is, there can be no doubt that at the outset of the twenty-first century debellicization was a social fact of consequence within the Western core.[36] What happened to the status and legitimacy of war in Western society is comparable to the fate of religious faith and the acceptance of political and social inequality. These were the pillars of traditional society. They were still robust at the beginning of the twentieth century.[37] By its end they all had been dramatically eroded.

The most dramatic change in the status of war took place in Germany and Japan. In the traditional era the military occupied a central and respected place in both societies, which carried over into their illiberal periods when their armed forces were considered the instruments of national destiny. What had been exalted before 1945 was anathematized and all but forbidden afterward. Although both countries had armed forces, the constitutions each adopted all but prohibited using them. German and Japanese attitudes toward war verged on pacifism.

In the most consistently liberal countries, Great Britain and the United States, the shift in attitudes was less pronounced. War and the armed forces had never been as important to the national life of either country as they were to Germany's and Japan's; neither felt compelled to renounce it as emphatically as did the defeated powers after 1945. But by the close of the twentieth century debellicization had made considerable headway in each country. Where war had once been considered a normal instrument of statecraft, it was now deemed suspect at best. Military service was once seen as integral to citizenship, but by the century's end it had become a highly specialized, technical, and narrow occupation. In some ways the armed forces had come to be as segregated from the mainstream of society as the mercenaries of Europe had been before the advent of mass armies.

The British and American publics became almost as dubious about armed conflict as their German and Japanese counterparts. When Britain went to war in South Africa in 1899, a professor at the University of London said: "War is the supreme act in the life of the State, and it is the motives which impel, the ideal which is pursued, that determine the greatness or insignificance of that act . . . The War in South Africa . . . is the first conspicuous expression of this ideal in the world of action—of heroic action, which now as always implies heroic suffering." In 1998, a young Englishwoman, born seventy years after the Boer War began, expressed a view of armed conflict that captured the extraordinary change in attitude: "Of course our national character has changed, profoundly and not least in our attitude towards war. Culturally, the very notion of being will-ing sacrifice for King and country is anathema to most of my genera-tion. It's class-ridden, mawkish, the stuff of costume drama and [high school level] poetry. I can't imagine any of my male friends accepting the kind of 'duty' which our grandfathers once accepted without protest."[38]

The comparable change in the United States was almost as pro-nounced. It was illustrated by the contrast between the country's chief executives at the beginning and the end of the same century. At the outset the president was Theodore Roosevelt, a passionate impe-rialist who had left his post as assistant secretary of the Navy to lead a regiment in Cuba in the Spanish-American War and whose favored leisure activities included the hunting, shooting, and stuffing of wild animals. As the century ended, in Roosevelt's place was Bill Clinton, the patron of humanitarian intervention who had avoided military service during the Vietnam War and one of whose chief political causes was the control of firearms. Each figure was repre-sentative of his age, as those whose livelihood depends on public approbation must be.

The way wars were officially remembered also denoted the chang-ing American attitude. The style of war memorials from the nine-teenth century through 1945 tended to the heroic: statues of commanders on horseback or, in the case of one such monument near the nation's capital, fighting men engaged in the heroic and symbolically powerful act of planting the American flag on the Pacific island of Iwo Jima. By contrast, the Vietnam Memorial, located less than a mile from the Iwo Jima monument, consisted of a series of stark slabs of black marble with the names of all the American war dead engraved on them. It represented the soldier not as hero but as innocent and literally faceless victim.

The widespread aversion to war within the countries of the Western core formed the foundation for common security, which in turn expressed the spirit of warlessness. To be sure, the rise of common security in Europe did not abolish war in other parts of the world and could not guarantee its permanent abolition even on the European continent. Neither, however, was it a flukish, transient product of an odd combination of post-Cold War circumstances in Europe nor an approach to the problem of war and peace necessarily destined to be confined to that region. The European common security order did have historical precedents, and its principal features began to appear in other parts of the world.

PRECEDENTS FOR COMMON SECURITY

THE SECURITY arrangements in Europe at the dawn of the twenty-first century incorporated features of three different periods of the modern age: the nineteenth century, the interwar period, and the Cold War.

The end of the Cold War was not the first time in European history that the major powers had sought a cooperative solution to the general problem of security. This had also occurred in 1815 in the wake of the Napoleonic Wars. Then a set of procedures was established on the basis of which the great powers agreed to manage their relations with one another for much of the nineteenth century. These were known collectively as the Concert of Europe. The Concert's principal rule was that disputes that had the potential to provoke a great power conflict should be settled by consensus and compromise. In this spirit, a series of conferences was convened in the years following Napoleon's defeat to resolve contentious political questions.[39] For all the differences between them, there are important similarities between the security orders of the early nineteenth century and the early twenty-first.

The first and most important similarity is a recognition that the problem of security is a systemic one. In each case, the major powers concluded that they could improve on unilateral measures for protecting themselves. Security came to be seen as a public good most effectively achieved through cooperation. Second, cooperation had as its purpose in both cases avoiding a major war. Neither system aspired to settle all political quarrels everywhere or even all quarrels in Europe. Third, as in the case of common security, the foundation for the Concert of Europe had been laid during the war that preceded it. In both cases, the establishment of rules for the postwar world helped make possible the end of the war itself. Finally, like the common security order the Concert of Europe was not expressed in a single document or organization. Each was the sum of several ideas, institutions and practices. Each was, in part, an informal arrangement.[40]

If the common security order was not the first occasion on which the European powers adopted cooperative approaches to security, neither were the arms treaties at the heart of that order the first ever concluded or even the first designed to reshape military forces to ease insecurity. The agreements in place in the wake of the Cold War bore a resemblance to the Washington Naval Treaty of 1922. By its terms, four naval powers—the United States, Great Britain, Japan, and France—agreed to limit the tonnage of their Pacific fleets. Like the agreements on nuclear weapons, therefore, the Washington Treaty limited but did not abolish an important category of weaponry. As with the Cold War agreements to restrict armaments, the United States conceived and advocated the Washington Treaty. Most important, like the late Cold War arms limitation measures, the Washington Treaty embodied one of the two principles of common security: defense dominance. It was designed to reshape the naval forces in the Pacific to make them suitable for maintaining but not for upsetting the political status quo. "With the acceptance of this plan," said its chief sponsor, the American Secretary of State Charles Evans Hughes, "preparation for offensive naval war will stop now." [41]

The third familiar feature of the common security order is the

American role. A military balance in Europe marked by defense dominance and transparency did not require an American presence. The two principles could be established among any group of countries. But the American presence was familiar and safe. For Europe as a whole it served a purpose that had been central to the military arrangements within the Western core during the Cold War.

The organization that became NATO began as a Western European grouping to guard against a renewal of German aggression.[42] Even when it assumed the task of counterbalancing Communist military power in Europe, NATO was an instrument of "dual containment," keeping the Soviet Union at arm's length and Germany in a restraining embrace, and for the same purpose: to prevent either from overturning the existing political order on the continent. In the words of Lord Ismay, NATO's first secretary-general, the alliance had three goals: to "keep the Americans in, the Russians out, and the Germans down."

At first West Germany had no choice in the matter, being occupied by the troops of its new allies. But the Germans came to accept and appreciate the arrangement. It relieved them of the burden of defending themselves while at the same time dissipating the cloud of suspicion that would otherwise have enveloped them. Within the Atlantic Alliance, therefore, the United States functioned as a buffer among parties with no cause for conflict but with historical reasons for mistrust. The American presence reassured each that the others harbored no aggressive intentions, which is precisely the purpose of the principle of defense dominance in military matters.[43]

With the end of the Cold War, the American presence on the European continent came to play this role for *all* Europeans, in the east as well as in the west. It reassured Germany that it was not going to be left alone to face a potential threat while at the same time reassuring other countries about Germany. It also reassured the Western Europeans that, if Russia should revert to a menacing foreign policy, the United States would help to keep it in check, as it had during the Cold War. It was especially important in reassuring the Russians that their experience with the German armies in the first half of the twentieth century would not be repeated.[44] This was one reason that Soviet authorities permitted a reunified Germany to remain within the Western alliance.[45]

During the Cold War, while the principal purpose of the American presence in Europe was to deter the Soviet Union, a secondary aim was to reassure its allies about Germany. In the post-Cold War period its purpose was to reassure everyone. Shifting from a deterrence-based balance of power to common security moved Europe from relying on the fear that a change in the status quo would be worse for everyone to relying on confidence that the status quo would not change because no one wanted to change it. If reassurance is the aim of common security, confidence is the product of reassurance.

A number of agreements reached in the 1980s for the purpose of promoting military transparency in Europe came to be known as "confidence-building measures."[46] They furnished information that supplemented what satellites could collect, imposing limits on the movements of forces, requiring advance notice of military maneuvers, and stipulating that foreign inspectors be admitted to the territory of all signatories for the purpose of verification.

The common security system as a whole was a confidence-building measure, its aim to engender confidence in each European country that the intentions of all the others were benign. Such confidence is built not only on the principles of defense dominance and transparency but on something else as well: time.

Time reinforced confidence in two ways. First, a would-be European aggressor would need time to overcome the restrictions on the forces necessary for attack imposed by the rules of common security. Once having accepted and incorporated the restrictions, a country bent on overturning the European status quo could not hope to mount a successful attack without extensive preparations, which would be readily detected and would plainly violate the treaties it had signed. Common security therefore extended the warning time for an attack in Europe from minutes, as it was during the Cold War, to the years that would be required in the post-Cold War era to organize an effective offense.

Second, as common security arrangements persist over time, they become more familiar, reliable, and credible, which in turn engenders confidence in their durability. The fact that limits and restrictions have held in the past becomes evidence that they will hold in the future. Like a personal reputation or a credit rating, confidence rests on past performance: the better the performance and the longer the past, the greater the confidence. The solidifying, validating effect of the passage of time is a feature that common security has in common with democracy and the market. But at the dawn of the twenty-first century, democracy and free markets had had more than two hundred years to establish themselves. Common security had not.

Yet there were signs that its establishment was under way. While nowhere outside Europe could its principles be said to be fully established, elements of common security had begun to appear in other parts of the world.

One notable example was the relationship between Russia and China. The two countries had been bitter adversaries, with large armies poised on either side of their common border, during the second half of the Cold War. By the year 2000 that border was governed by agreements consistent with the principles of common security. The border's location had been fixed to the satisfaction of both countries. Their military forces were configured for defense. In 1996 they agreed to a one-thousand-kilometer (six-hundred-mile) zone on either side of the border free of any military forces at all. They also agreed on measures to promote transparency.[47]

A second example outside Europe was the 1979 peace treaty between Israel and Egypt, which included provisions for transparency. Each side received information on the size and movements of the other's military forces. The terms of the treaty also made it easier for each to defend itself against an attack by the other. The demilitarization of the Sinai desert between them meant that each would have time to mobilize its forces against an overland assault by the other. In its negotiations with its northern neighbor Syria during the 1990s, Israel sought comparable provisions. It insisted on measures to monitor Syrian military activities and wanted Syrian military forces configured and deployed to make it difficult to launch an attack southward.

In South Asia, too, where India and Pakistan both tested nuclear explosives in 1998, proposals were made to lessen the chance that either would be tempted to launch, or would fear that the other would launch, a surprise attack. In the spirit of common security, these proposals were directed at the system-level cause of war, the insecurity that anarchy engenders.

While in each case actual or proposed agreements included measures to promote transparency and defense dominance, in none was the necessary condition for an enduring common security order, warlessness, firmly established. In none of these cases had both sides firmly relinquished all claims on the other, or renounced the use of force to vindicate claims that remained outstanding. Russia, China, and the new states of Central Asia, despite the agreements they had all signed, remained wary of one another. Even in Europe, the common security order was not so firmly anchored that its continuation was guaranteed.

THREATS TO COMMON SECURITY

THE POST-COLD War role of the United States in European security affairs, maintaining a military presence in order to reassure the Europeans, east as well as west, was an example of American international leadership. It was necessary for the common security order and therefore important for the peace of the continent where the United States had taken part in two world wars and the Cold War. But it was not self-evidently an urgent task, nor one that was necessary to protect North America, as deterring the Soviet Union had been during the Cold War.

And in carrying out that task the United States committed a foreign policy blunder by promoting the expansion of the North Atlantic Treaty Organization to include Poland, Hungary, and the Czech Republic. This measure struck a blow, although not necessarily a fatal one, at the common security order. In so doing, it illustrated one of the obstacles to a successful American role as the world's leader—that is, as the chief custodian of the liberal international order of the twenty-first century.

The expansion of NATO, proposed in 1994 and ratified in 1998, violated the spirit of common security because it was not a common undertaking. It was the first change in the security arrangements of Europe since Mikhail Gorbachev's accession to power that was not carefully negotiated with Moscow; Russian opposition meant that it was not acceptable to, and not accepted by, all the countries of Europe. NATO expansion violated the Russian understanding of the terms on which the Cold War had ended. In return for allowing a reunified Germany to join NATO, Gorbachev believed that he had received assurances that the Western alliance would expand no farther east. NATO expansion violated, finally, the one lesson widely thought to have emerged from the great wars of the modern period: that the chance for an enduring postwar settlement is enhanced by fully integrating the vanquished party into the new order, as occurred after the Napoleonic Wars and World War II but not after World War I. Taken at face value, NATO expansion made Russia a second-class citizen of Europe, since two of expansion's premises, the first explicit, the second implicit, were that NATO would be the most important post-Cold War European security organization and that Russia would not have the opportunity to join. For these reasons George Kennan, the venerable American diplomat and diplomatic historian, called NATO expansion "the most fateful error of American foreign policy in the entire post-Cold War era."[48]

It had the effect of alienating Russia. In concert with the American-led NATO war against Yugoslavia in 1999, it produced a sullen, resentful, suspicious Russian attitude toward the United States and made the country's political leadership reflexively inclined to oppose American international initiatives. In the worst case, NATO expansion had the potential to shift the Atlantic Alliance's military mission back to the deterrence of the Cold War, subvert the arms limitation agreements that formed the heart of the common security order, and recreate the military division of Europe—albeit with the line of division well to the east of where it had been from 1945 to 1989.[49] At best, it needlessly imposed on the United States the tricky task of reconciling the expanded NATO with what was genuinely important for European security—Russian adherence to the norms, practices, and institutions of common security.

NATO expansion was an example of the post-Cold War triumph, in the United States, of domestic over international considerations. President Bill Clinton adopted the policy in order to please American citizens with ancestral ties to the new member states, with an eye toward winning their votes in the 1996 presidential election.[50] This was normal in the American political system, in which interest groups routinely press parochial claims. Although the lobby for NATO expansion was not a particularly powerful one, it nonetheless succeeded because the opposition it faced was politically even weaker. During the Cold War the measure it was promoting would have been treated with the utmost seriousness. It would have received intense scrutiny and been the subject of extensive debate because, as a sharp departure from American security policy, the stakes involved would have been very high indeed. But with the Cold War at an end, domestic considerations were paramount and they argued in favor of expansion. When the time for voting on expansion came, it seemed to the Congress an easy request to grant because it imposed no direct, tangible cost on the United States and would gratify one bloc of voters of modest size while offending no other organized interest.[51] The European members of the alliance assented to it because they wanted to accommodate the Americans and because they assumed that the United States would pay any costs involved.

NATO expansion was a needless mistake, the equivalent, for the conduct of American relations with the rest of the world, of an unforced error in tennis. It did not mean, however, that the general aversion to war in the countries of the Western core was fading. Warlessness, and the consequent commitment to common security, could be counted on to remain robust in North America, Western Europe, and Japan. This could not be said with equal confidence about post-Cold War Russia.

On the Russian side the initial commitment to common security was not the expression of values widely shared or deeply rooted—which was why NATO expansion had the potential to subvert that commitment. Common security represented the preference of only one man, Mikhail Gorbachev. As he concluded one arms accord after another, and as he allowed the previously Communist-ruled countries of Eastern Europe to assert their political independence, the Soviet military was consistently dubious and often opposed. The citizens of the Soviet Union were not consulted. With the disappearance of the Soviet Union, the person most committed to the liberal approach to security fell from power. Even so, the end of the Communist era was, on balance, a favorable development for the long-term prospects for the common security order because the Soviet Union's governing ideology was incompatible with that order.[52]

Gorbachev himself was not an orthodox Communist. In matters of security, by the end of his tenure, he was not a Communist at all. And only in a political system as centralized as the one over which he presided could one person effect so radical a change in his country's relations with the rest of the world. The new Russia was free of the principled commitment to international conflict that had defined the Soviet Union. But the social forces promoting debellicization were far weaker in Russia than in the West. Many had been suppressed or excluded over the long decades of Soviet rule.

The new Russia's foreign policy rhetoric asserted the country's continuing importance in Europe and the world, and its right to primacy on the territory of the former Soviet Union. In practice, Russia, like other countries in the post-Cold War period, was preoccupied with its internal affairs to the exclusion of most of what happened beyond its borders. And its relations with the rest of the world, such as they were, were dominated in the first post-Cold War decade by a single overriding factor: its own weakness. Russia could bring less power to bear in the international arena than at any time since the beginning of the eighteenth century, which was why, despite its opposition, the Russian government did nothing in response to NATO expansion except protest it. The country's economic prowess was negligible. By the end of the first post-Cold War decade Russia's output was roughly comparable to that of the Netherlands, a country with one-tenth its population and 0.2 percent of its geographic size.

In the Soviet period (and in the tsarist era as well) the Russian state's place in the world had depended on military rather than economic strength. Here the decline was dramatic. The great military machine that Communism had built, that had won a civil war, that had defeated Hitler's armies, that had occupied Europe to the middle of Germany, and that had more than matched the Western coalition of the world's wealthiest industrial democracies missile for missile and tank for tank while supporting a string of clients around the world, simply crumbled. The number of men in the armed forces fell by about three-quarters. The weapons at their disposal were neither maintained nor replaced. The many factories that had produced these weapons, some located in what became, after the Soviet collapse, foreign countries, largely ceased to function.[53] The new Russian state lacked the requisites for mustering great military power. It could not collect taxes to support a military establishment. It could neither persuade nor coerce young Russians in adequate numbers to serve in the armed forces. By the dawn of the twenty-first century the Russian military was a shadow of what it had been only ten years earlier. The new Russia was in no position to send its armed forces on a conquering mission westward and was too poor to risk restarting the arms competition with its former adversaries.

As the twentieth century ended, therefore, Russian participation in the common security order rested less on conviction than on weakness. Over the long term this was not a promising basis for continued Russian allegiance to common security's principles and tenets, for it required that Russia continue to be weak. But it was possible that Russia would continue to comply with the letter and the spirit of the post-Cold War European security order even as the reasons for compliance shifted. West Germany had at first accepted the post-1945 political and military arrangements because it had no choice, then over time came to see them as serving German interests. So might it be with Russia and common security. The currents of opinion and social trends that made war less and less attractive in the West were at large within Russia as well, although they were weaker there, having had a later start.

Even a Russian trend toward debellicization, however, would not necessarily assure that Russian fidelity to the spirit and the letter of common security would match that of the West. For all apart from its post-Cold War weakness, Russia's circumstances differed from those of the members of the Western core. Western borders were firmly and finally settled. Russia's were not, and unsettled borders were a major cause of large-scale post-Cold War violence. In particular, changes of borders that made groups of people suddenly and involuntarily minorities in new countries, people who had been part of the majority in places where they had lived for decades, even centuries, triggered armed efforts to change those borders. Such was the cause of the Balkan wars of the 1990s, which were waged by and on behalf of Serbs who had been part of the largest national group in Yugoslavia but found themselves with minority status in the new sovereign states of Croatia and Bosnia and in a tenuous position in the Yugoslav province of Kosovo when the Yugoslav Federation, against their wishes, broke apart.[54]

The end of the Soviet Union left millions of Russians in this position. It created new Russian minority populations in Ukraine, in the three Baltic countries (Estonia, Latvia, and Lithuania), and in Kazakhstan.[55] Of these, the last four held less potential for war than the first.

Russia's relations with the Baltic countries were scarcely free of friction in the first post-Cold War decade. The Russian government was unhappy about the prospect of NATO membership for them and complained about their treatment of ethnic Russians living in their countries, not all of whom enjoyed full rights of citizenship. But Russians generally accepted Baltic independence as legitimate and irreversible. Estonia, Latvia, and Lithuania were seen as part of Europe rather than part of Russia. Regarding Kazakhstan, most Russians considered the border dividing it from the new post-Communist Russia to be artificial and arbitrary, and a Russian effort to re-annex the northern part of Kazakhstan was not entirely out of the question. But Kazakhstan was located far from Europe, and any conflict to which irredentist sentiments gave rise there would have only modest effects on the Western powers.

The new independent Ukraine, by contrast, was situated between Russia and the West. Its immediate western neighbor was Poland, a member of NATO. And the border between Russia and Ukraine, which left 18 million ethnic Russians concentrated in the eastern part of Ukraine, seemed as arbitrary and unnatural to most Russians in the wake of the Cold War as the one dividing Russia from Kazakhstan.[56]

Of all the issues involving Russia and Ukraine, the status of the Crimean peninsula evoked the strongest feelings. Russians felt a special attachment to the Crimea—Catherine the Great had conquered it from the Turks in the eighteenth century and Russians had then settled it—but the Soviet leader Nikita Khrushchev had given it to Ukraine in 1954, a time when transfer from one jurisdiction to another within the Soviet Union was a meaningless gesture. The most acute Russian sense of ownership centered on the Crimean city of Sevastopol, the home port of the Russian Black Sea fleet. An epic and costly defense of the city in World War II had invested it with an emotional significance comparable to those attached to Leningrad and Stalingrad.

In the first post-Cold War decade the Russian and Ukrainian governments managed their relationship with some finesse. They largely resisted the temptation to enhance their standing with their own countrymen by making an adversary of the other. Although relations between them were not free of difficulty, they did agree on a transfer of the Soviet nuclear weapons in Ukraine to Russia in 1994 and on a treaty in 1998 under which the naval base at Sevastopol was leased to Russia for twenty years.

Unlike the ethnic Germans who found themselves living involuntarily in Poland and Czechoslovakia after World War I, the ethnic Russians in Ukraine had a weak sense of themselves as Russian nationals and in any case the distinction between Russians and Ukrainians had never been as sharp as the one between Germans and Poles. Russians in Ukraine felt an allegiance to the places where they lived and to the ethnic Russian nation but not to the newly created Russian state.[57] They did not organize themselves to voice grievances against or seek redress from the central Ukrainian government in Kiev. They did not feel especially aggrieved. The Ukrainian government treated them gingerly, generally refraining from heavy-handed insistence, for example, on the use of the Ukrainian language.

Still, the possibility of post-Yugoslav-style conflict in Ukraine remained. Clumsy treatment of ethnic Russians by the Ukrainian government, or radically better economic conditions on the Russian side of the border, had the potential to produce secessionist sentiment. If conflict between Ukraine and Russia did erupt, its unsettling effects would ripple across Europe to North America, imperiling the accords on which common security rested. The Ukrainian-Russian border was one of the potential flashpoints of the post-Cold War world.

Russia's circumstances differed from those of the core countries in another way that bore on Russian security policies. A common security order must be, above all, common. The public goods problem applies: All the relevant countries must subscribe to its tenets. And whereas the international neighborhood in which the countries of the West resided was a quiet, peaceful one, Russia was not so fortunate.

Moscow confronted political turbulence along its southern borders with the former Soviet republics of the Caucasus region and Central Asia.[58] As weak as it was in comparison with the countries of the Western core, Russia was far stronger than these new, struggling, politically incoherent and economically feeble states; and Russia did deploy troops within their borders, in places it had recently governed and in some cases had never left.

A variety of motives had sent or kept Russian forces there: requests from local governments; fear that turbulence would spread northward into Russia proper; the desire for political influence that would bring economic benefits in the form of a share of oil revenues. While Russians occasionally waxed nostalgic for the Soviet Union and spoke of reintegrating its former constituent parts in some form, their government neither adopted nor even seriously proposed measures to achieve this; and what Russia did in the Caucasus and Central Asia did not bear directly on the post-Cold War security order in Europe.

In the first post-Cold War decade Russia fought two southern wars, both in the province of Chechnya within the borders of Russia itself, the first beginning in 1994, the second in 1999. They seemed at first glance an ominous reprise of the brutal wars of conquest waged on the same territory and against the same people by the armies of the tsars in the nineteenth century and of the Communists in the twentieth.

Brutal they certainly were, but the Chechen wars did not in fact herald a resurgence of the imperial habits incompatible with membership in good standing in the security system that Reagan and Gorbachev had created. For one thing, a feature of post-Cold War Russia clearly on display in Chechnya presented a formidable obstacle to imperial revival: the country's weakness. In the first war the

Russian armed forces, badly trained, badly equipped, and badly led, were defeated by a far smaller band of Chechens skilled at guerrilla warfare and above all far more determined to resist than were the Russians to prevail.[59] Moreover, neither conflict was, in legal terms, a war of imperial conquest. The international community recognized Chechnya as a part of Russia. It was the Chechens seeking independence who were in violation of international norms. On the second occasion, if not on the first, Russia had legitimate cause for conducting military operations of some kind (although not the kind of military operations, with indiscriminate bombardment and a heavy civilian death toll, that it did conduct). In the chaotic conditions in the province that the first war had fostered, armed gangs flourished, frequently venturing into Russian areas to the north to launch criminal raids. The second war was precipitated by an attack by Islamic radicals, based in Chechnya, against the multiethnic Russian province of Dagestan to the east in August 1999.

The brutality of the Russian assault, finally, stemmed in part from one of the principal aspects of Western warlessness that Russia had come partly to share: an aversion to casualties. Loath to risk their troops, the Russian commanders bombarded Chechen targets from afar, killing thousands of civilians in the process. The Russians were especially leery of urban warfare. After an abortive and costly assault on Grozny, the Chechen capital, in the first war, the Russian forces pulverized the city by artillery and aerial bombardment. This was, perversely, a sign of debellicization. During World War II Russian troops had fought bravely, taking heavy casualties, in order to capture or recapture from the German army cities from Stalingrad to Berlin. Fifty years later their successors were unwilling to follow suit, even on a far smaller scale, on their own territory. The government adopted its military tactics in response to public sensitivity to the loss of Russian lives. In fact, antiwar sentiment forced the Russian government to make a temporary settlement with the Chechens in 1996, the same kind of antiwar sentiment endemic in the liberal West in the final decades of the twentieth century.

The European common security order faced a final post-Cold War challenge. It was subject to disruptions from other regions. Chief among these potential disruptions was nuclear proliferation.

Countries outside Europe with no stake in the common security order could acquire nuclear weapons and the means to strike Europe or North America. In response to this danger, in the first post-Cold War decade the American government actively explored deploying a system of defense against ballistic missile attacks launched from beyond the boundaries of the common security order. In December 2001, the Bush Administration announced that the United States was withdrawing from the 1972 ABM Treaty in order to develop and deploy missile defenses. But this would not, the administration insisted, subvert the principle of defense dominance where military relations with Russia were concerned, because the United States would not attempt to negate Russia's capacity for assured destruction.

The United States was seeking to design a system of ballistic missile defense sophisticated enough to stop a small-scale attack from a country of the periphery but not so powerful that it placed in jeopardy Russia's capacity to retaliate against a nuclear attack, which could spur Russia to acquire more missiles and abandon other treaty commitments, thereby destroying the common security order. The aim was to deter a would-be nuclear proliferator that did not subscribe to the principles of common security[60] while reassuring Russia, which did.*

One region from which such a nuclear threat seemed likely to come was the Middle East.[61] Another was East Asia, which was also important for European security for a different reason. The two largest and most important parties to the European common security order were both Asian powers as well, Russia by virtue of geography and the United States courtesy of technology and treaties.

*To be effective, an American system of ballistic missile defense had to pass two tests. One was technical. It had to be able to defend successfully against the kind of small-scale attack that a country of the periphery might be able to mount. Even this was a formidable technological feat and at the beginning of the new century, despite decades of research and development costing tens of billions of dollars, the American Department of Defense had not produced a system that commanded confidence. The second test was political. The deployment of a missile shield had to avoid setting in motion responses by other countries that would leave the United States in a weaker position. One such response would be a decision by Russia or China or both to enhance the military capacities, through the sale of bombs and missiles, of the very countries against which the system was being deployed. In order to be useful, that is, an American system of ballistic missile defense required at least tacit approval and cooperation from other countries.

Russia had borders with China, Korea, and, in effect, Japan.[62] The United States was itself a Pacific power, its naval and air forces central to East Asian security calculations, its economy integral to trade and investment in the region, and with a security treaty with Japan.

East Asia was an important part of the world apart from its connection to Europe. It was, along with Europe and North America, one of the three most dynamic centers of economic output. The two largest wars of the Cold War period had been fought there, in Korea and Indochina. The countries with the world's second-largest economy, Japan, and its largest army and third largest collection of nuclear weapons, China, were both located in the region. For both security and economics, therefore, East Asia qualified as part of the world's core, and, as such, was destined to affect the fortunes of the entire planet in the twenty-first century.

CHAPTER FIVE

The Most Dangerous Place on the Planet

COMPELLING PLOTS in drama and literature are rare, so the best of them are recycled. Shakespeare's *Romeo and Juliet* is an example. This sixteenth-century tale of young love tragically thwarted by the hostility of the lovers' families was taken up by the Americans Jerome Robbins, Leonard Bernstein, Arthur Laurents, and Stephen Sondheim 350 years later. They transferred the setting from Renaissance Italy to modern New York City, turned Shakespeare's feuding Montagues and Capulets into rival Manhattan street gangs, added music and choreography, and produced a drama as successful as *Romeo and Juliet* had been: *West Side Story*.

In matters of security, Europe and East Asia may be seen as two versions of the same plot. Their twentieth-century histories followed parallel courses, and at the outset of the twenty-first century the alignments of the leading powers in the two regions were similar. In each the United States was allied with a country that had been its enemy in World War II and then a friend during the Cold War— Germany in Europe and Japan in East Asia. Each region also included a large country that had abandoned its twentieth-century adherence to the tenets of orthodox Communism, including its principled commitment to warfare, but had not fully embraced any of the three parts of the liberal Wilsonian triad. In Europe, that part was played by Russia; in East Asia, by China.

The parallel between drama and geopolitics can be taken a step further. Drama is divided by convention into comedies, which culminate in marriage, and tragedies, which end in death. In matters of international security the parallel outcomes are reconciliation and war. Here the two regions of the world's core differed. While the countries of Europe had taken significant steps toward the establishment of common security, the geopolitical equivalent of tragedy remained more likely (although far from certain) in East Asia.

EUROPE AND ASIA

I N THE NINETEENTH century Europe was the world's core and Asia—poor, weak, and traditional—part of its periphery. In the twentieth century this changed. The political and economic revolutions that solidified the West's standing at the center of world civilization came late to Asia, but come they eventually did, as democracy and free markets put down roots there. While not a center of cultural innovation on a par with the West, parts of Asia did produce concentrations of power and wealth to compare with Europe and North America.

The words "Europe" and "Asia," familiar though they are, require elucidation. In strictly geographical terms there are no such discrete and separate places. There is, instead, a large land mass north of the equator that stretches from the Atlantic to the Pacific Ocean, with the British isles anchored off the western edge and the Japanese archipelago lying to the east. The name for this 5,600-mile stretch of territory, which includes thirty-six percent of the land on the planet and seventy-three percent of the world's population, is Eurasia. In the modern period, it came to be divided by convention into six sub-regions. Two of them, but not the other four, were part of the world's core. The divisions were based not only on geography but also on politics, culture, and history. Like virtually all modern political concepts and conventions they originated in the West but came to be accepted by the peoples of the region themselves. The modern age was born in the political communities along the northwest edge of the Eurasian land mass known, collectively, as Europe. Historically Europe extended eastward to the Ural mountains, the frontier of European Russia. The European peoples so defined have a common Greco-Roman and Judeo-Christian cultural heritage and a history of ongoing political and economic contact with one another.

The other part of Eurasia belonging to the world's core at the turn of the twenty-first century was the cluster of countries at its eastern edge, which borders on the Pacific Ocean. East Asia—or, more precisely, Northeast Asia—includes China, Korea, and Japan. As in Europe, their peoples are ethnically similar and have interacted for centuries.*

East Asia is where the modern era transcended its European origins. It is where Japan, a society without historical ties to Europe, made itself, in a matter of decades, a formidable modern state. In the second half of the twentieth century East Asia became a global center of wealth creation led by Japan, which had the world's second largest economy and accounted for fully seventy percent of the region's total output for much of that period. But just as, in the latter part of the nineteenth century, Japan caught up with the West, so, in

---

*Of the other four sub-regions of Eurasia, South Asia is the most clearly set apart in geographic terms. The Asian subcontinent is bounded on the north by the world's highest mountain range, the Himalayas, and to the east, west, and south by oceans. For the first century and a half of the modern era it was politically distinctive as well, being dominated by Great Britain.

Southeast Asia, which includes Indochina and Thailand on the Asian mainland, the island chains of Indonesia and the Philippines, and the Malay peninsula, received its name from its location between two places that were more important to Europe: it is the region south of China and east of India. The initial designation of Southeast Asia as a distinct region was purely arbitrary; the countries had little in common and were not even close to one another geographically. (Vientiane, the capital of Laos, is 1,700 miles from Jakarta, Indonesia's capital, which is 1,700 miles from the capital of the Philippines, Manila.) But in the second half of the twentieth century they developed a modest sense of cohesion. The regional grouping they founded, the Association of Southeast Asian Nations (ASEAN), acquired a degree of prestige and legitimacy.

Similarly, the lands of the great Islamic civilizations, Arab, Persian, and Turkish, came to be known as the Middle East because they lie between Europe and East Asia. They are also known as the Near East, being nearer to Europe than are China and Japan. (They are farther, of course, from California and British Columbia.)

The interior of the Eurasian landmass, inner Asia, is a region in and of—and virtually unto—itself. It consists of the western, non-Han parts of what is now China—Xinjiang and Tibet—Afghanistan, and the sovereign states of Central Asia that were, for most of the twentieth century, provinces of the Soviet Union. Inner Asia played an important role in global affairs during the period known to Europeans as the Middle Ages. Through it ran the great trading route between China and Europe called the Silk Road. It was the home base of the Mongols, the greatest of all overland conquerors. But in the modern era it has been a backwater. For much of the period it was largely inaccessible to the Europeans, who reached most of the rest of the world by sea. For Europe it had no economic and, notwithstanding the spirited nineteenth-century rivalry in the region between Russia and Great Britain known as "The Great Game," very little strategic value.

the latter part of the twentieth century, other Asian countries began to catch up with Japan.

Beginning in the 1960s four Asian economies, those of South Korea, Taiwan, Hong Kong, and Singapore, recorded growth rates impressive enough to earn them the unofficial title of the Asian "tigers." In the 1980s many of the countries of Southeast Asia, notably the largest of them, Indonesia, also achieved high rates of growth. And during that same decade China, the world's largest country by population, began two decades of double-digit economic growth that made it, by the dawn of the twenty-first century, the third-largest economy in the world. By the third decade of the new century, by some estimates, Asia was likely to be producing fully one-half of the world's goods and services and to contain six of the eight largest economies.[1]

Well before it came into its own economically, East Asia was important in political and military terms. It was home to a great imperial and naval power, which is what Japan had made itself by the end of the nineteenth century. World War II was not only a massive European land war, fought most bitterly and at greatest cost by Germany and Russia; it was also the greatest of all maritime conflicts, featuring naval battles and amphibious assaults—a war between imperial Japan and the United States that stretched across the Pacific Ocean from the Hawaiian islands to the Japanese archipelago. The two bloodiest Cold War conflicts were fought in Asia, on the Korean peninsula in the 1950s and in Indochina in the 1960s and 1970s.[2]

In the second half of the twentieth century China became a military power of consequence. While not a match for the two nuclear superpowers, the People's Republic established itself in the second rank of the global military hierarchy. It fielded the largest army and its stockpile of nuclear weapons, although a distant third to those of the United States and the Soviet Union (and later Russia), was nonetheless a potent force.

Because East Asia, too, harbored the ingredients of a major war, in the post-Cold War period the security arrangements in the region were as consequential as those in Europe, but here they were more fragile. Indeed, East Asia experienced closer brushes with large, dangerous armed conflict than did Europe. Military operations in the waters surrounding the island of Taiwan in March 1996 by two nuclear-armed powers, the United States and China, vividly demonstrated the potential for a major war. At the outset of the twenty-first century the Taiwan Strait was the single most dangerous place on the planet. And in June 1994 on the Korean peninsula, the United States and North Korea came even closer to a lesser but still dangerously violent confrontation.

The need for the liberal approach to war and peace, common security, was, if anything, more acute in East Asia than in Europe, but the region lacked common security's formal, visible features: negotiated limits on armaments embodying the principles of defense dominance and transparency. There were, in fact, fewer formal ordinances governing military forces in the Asia-Pacific region than there had been in the 1920s. Nor was the aversion to war that anchored these arrangements in Europe as deeply rooted in East Asia.

Still, the region was not entirely bereft of the elements of common security and there were precedents for the adoption of liberal security policies there. Over the course of the twentieth century, especially in its second half, some of the countries of East Asia had imported liberal political and economic institutions and practices. And the twentieth-century histories of Europe and East Asia exhibited striking parallels. They proceeded along similar lines, like dramas set in different locales but with the same basic plot.

THE UNITED STATES AND JAPAN

I N EAST ASIA AND IN Europe, twentieth-century history unfolded within the same framework: the uneven diffusion of the techniques of modernity leading to violent consequences. Uneven development underlay both world wars. In both regions, a large, tradition-bound, multinational state with a long history of international primacy, which lagged in incorporating the institutions and practices of the French and the industrial revolutions (Russia and China), suffered an assault by an upstart nation-state (Germany and

Japan) that had adopted these innovations more successfully. Germany and Japan launched these assaults as part of their quests to build empires on the territory of their less advanced neighbors.

Just as Germany attacked Russia in the two world wars, so, at the other end of Eurasia, Japan twice assaulted and defeated China, on both occasions gaining control of territory that had been governed from Beijing. In the Sino-Japanese War of 1895 the Japanese seized control of Taiwan and in 1931 extended their sway to Manchuria. In 1937 their attack on northern China marked the beginning of World War II in Asia.

Coinciding with the two world wars was another of the defining political trends of the twentieth century: the assumption of a global role by the United States. American policies in both Europe and East Asia followed a traditional pattern. The United States aligned itself, following the logic of the balance of power, first with one side and then with the other, depending on which posed the greater threat to American interests.

In Europe, the United States first sided with Russia (as an ally of Great Britain and France) against Germany in World War I, then turned against the Communist regime that supplanted the tsar in 1917; Washington did not establish diplomatic relations with the Soviet Union until 1933. America forged an alliance with Moscow against Nazi Germany from 1941 to 1945, then shifted its allegiance once again to form an anti-Soviet alliance with West Germany and other Western European countries during the Cold War.

The United States pursued a similar course in East Asia.[3] At the beginning of the twentieth century American sentiments favored the Japanese. The United States was sympathetic to Japan in its successful wars against China in 1895 and against Russia in 1905. The American Open Door policy of the 1890s sought to achieve privileges in China for the United States and for Japan equal to those already enjoyed by the European powers. As Japanese strength increased, however, the United States grew wary. Washington came to oppose Japanese imperial designs, which meant supporting the object of those designs: China. Tensions with Japan led, ultimately, to Pearl Harbor and World War II in the Pacific. During that conflict the United States tried to assist China's nominal ruler, Chiang

Kai-shek, in his struggle with Japan, sending arms and other supplies as well as providing military advice.[4] After World War II, and especially after the Communist victory in the Chinese civil war, the United States switched sides again, making common cause with Japan to oppose Communism in Asia.

East Asia differed from Europe in that for most of the modern period a second outside power took part in its political and military affairs. Tsarist Russia occasionally cooperated with China, but more often exploited it, in the nineteenth century acquiring more Chinese territory than any other foreign power. For much of the twentieth century Russia's and then the Soviet Union's principal adversary in East Asia was Japan. Russia fought a losing war with Japan in 1905 and Soviet troops skirmished with Japanese forces on the border between Siberia and Manchuria in 1939.[5] Moscow ignored Western importunings to declare war on Japan, however, until the final days of World War II, when Soviet forces entered Manchuria and Korea and seized several islands in the Kurile chain.

At the outset of the Cold War the politics of security in the region were simplified by the Communist victory in the Chinese civil war and the Sino-Soviet Friendship Treaty of 1950. This made allies of the two large Communist countries. In response Washington organized a countervailing coalition.

As in Europe, the United States placed a formidable array of military forces in the Asia-Pacific region to deter Communist aggression. In Europe the American military presence took the form of a large contingent of armed forces stationed in Germany. In East Asia the United States deployed largely, although not exclusively, naval forces. It established a series of bases in the Pacific, a kind of "floating chain-link fence"[6] around the eastern edge of Eurasia, including the eastern maritime borders of the Soviet Union and China.

Unlike in Europe, the American military commitment in Asia was not based on a single, multinational military alliance; there was no Asian NATO. There was, instead, a series of bilateral military agreements between the United States and several non-Communist countries of the region, of which the most important was the Japanese-American Security Treaty of 1951.

While the form the American commitment to East Asia took was different, it had the same explicit purpose as in Europe: to prevent a military assault by the Communist bloc. But the two regions differed in an important way. As part of the strategy of containment the United States actually fought two wars in Asia, in Korea and Vietnam. In both cases, it was opposed by China—on the first occasion directly, when Mao ordered Chinese troops across the Yalu River that separates China from Korea, on the second indirectly, with Beijing sending arms to North Vietnam and stationing troops on its territory.[7]

The American presence in both regions also enveloped in a restraining embrace the illiberal power that had been defeated in World War II. The American forces in Asia thus insured against a resumption of Japan's disastrous policies of the 1930s just as NATO was a mechanism for preventing a repetition of the German policies that had provoked European wars in 1870, 1914, and 1939. And just as the non-Communist countries of Europe preferred that Germany not conduct a fully independent security policy, so too were the non-Communist Asian countries happy to see their erstwhile conqueror under the protective wing of a more powerful country. The American presence thus provided insurance against a recurrence of the dangers of the past as well as protection against the present-day threat from the Communist powers—what was called "double containment."

Japan, like Germany, did forgo an independent foreign policy and chose not to acquire nuclear weapons. Japan went so far as formally to renounce war altogether through Article 9 of the constitution that it adopted, under American sponsorship, in 1946.[8] In Japan, as in Germany, the traumas of war, defeat, and occupation inculcated a deeply felt and widely held aversion to waging war. The two were more thoroughly permeated with the sentiment of warlessness, and consequently more debellicized, than any other countries. To be sure, Japan equipped itself with an army and a navy, which were known as the "Self-Defense Forces," but for most of the Cold War period, spending on these forces did not exceed one percent of the nation's gross domestic product. One percent of the world's second largest economic output purchased an impressive array of military hardware, but the Japanese were loath to use it. Even more than

Germany, during the Cold War Japan pursued an almost pacifist foreign policy, made possible by American protection.

The policy of double containment had similar political and economic consequences in Europe and East Asia. It underwrote normal
political relations between Germany and Japan, on the one hand,
and their former adversaries, which in turn made possible the economic reintegration of Germany into Europe and of Japan into East
Asia. That triggered an economic boom of historic proportions in
both regions, which proved decisive to the outcome of the Cold
War.[9] Double containment, by providing both a ticket of admission
for Germany and Japan into the Western economic community and
a barrier to a Communist assault against that community, created a
framework for the extraordinary economic growth of the second half
of the twentieth century.[10]

In the wake of the Cold War, Russia came to regard keeping Germany in NATO as reassuring, just as the Western Europeans had felt
reassured during the East-West conflict. In East Asia, the Japanese-
American alliance reassured as well as deterred the major Communist power, the People's Republic of China, even as the Cold War
was still under way. This was because, in 1972, China aligned itself
with the United States in opposition to the Soviet Union and thus
became associated with, although not formally part of, the Ameri-
can-centered system of bilateral alliances in East Asia.

When the Cold War ended, what had been a formidable Soviet
military presence all but disappeared. Much of the large army on the
Chinese border was withdrawn and the Soviet Pacific fleet disintegrated. In the first post-Cold War decade, therefore, in both East
Asia and Europe the American military presence served the purpose
of reassurance. In East Asia, the Japanese-American Security Treaty,
the foundation of that presence, reassured the other Asian countries
that Japan would not conduct an independent security policy while
simultaneously reassuring the Japanese that they would not have to
do so.

The deployment of American forces in the Western Pacific, like
the residual American garrisons in Western Europe, acted as a hedge
against uncertainty, a buffer between and among countries that otherwise would have felt more suspicious and uneasy about one

another. American officials said this explicitly: "While the tensions of the Cold War have subsided, many Asian nations harbor apprehensions about their closest neighbors. An American withdrawal would magnify those concerns. And so America must stay engaged."[11]

The need for a buffer in the form of an American military presence was, in one way, less urgent in East Asia than in Europe. Nature had already supplied, in the form of the Pacific Ocean, a liquid buffer between the Japanese archipelago and all other countries of the region. Military operations, especially the seizure of territory, are more difficult across water than across land. The terrain to be crossed is less stable, transport moves more slowly, and there is no place to hide.[12]

In another sense, however, the American security cocoon in which Japan was wrapped during the Cold War was more valuable in the post-Cold War era than the analogous protection of Germany. For unlike Germany, Japan was not integrated into a larger, formal, region-wide organization such as NATO or the European Union. Germany's reputation for neighborliness, moreover, stood higher in Europe than did Japan's in Asia: Japan had made fewer, weaker, and therefore less convincing declarations of remorse about its wartime assaults on its neighbors.[13]

In the twenty-first century the case against keeping American military forces in the Pacific was the same as the case against keeping them in Europe: The Japanese, like the Europeans, were free riders, and the time had come for them to assume responsibility for their own security, including its costs.[14] If threats to security persisted in East Asia, with the collapse of the Soviet Union and the end of the Cold War these were not, as they had been during that conflict, mortal threats to the United States. The existence of such threats therefore could not justify continuing the military deployments on which the policy of containment had been based. To the extent that American allies were themselves threatened, they could defend themselves without the American army, navy, and air force. From this point of view, the post-Cold War American presence was an exercise in unremunerative babysitting for people who were fully grown.[15]

The case in favor of continuing the American military presence was in one way easier to make for East Asia than for Europe, for it was primarily a naval presence and Americans traditionally preferred navies to armies. Navies are mobile and thus useful all over the world; they incorporate advanced technology, a particular American national strength; they can stay out of harm's way and are therefore less likely to sustain casualties; and they are associated with the economic benefits of trade. But if technology made the American military presence in East Asia potentially more palatable to the people who had, ultimately, to pay for it, politics, economics, and history made it less so.

For the last two decades of the Cold War the United States was at odds with Japan over trade between the two countries. Not only did Japan consistently run a trade surplus with the United States, but the level of foreign direct investment in Japan was considerably lower than in virtually every other industrial democracy. These economic facts gave rise to a view of Japan as an economic predator, a view that an increasing number of Americans came to hold in the 1980s.

Japan's allegedly devious and sinister approach to international economic matters was the theme of *Rising Sun*, a best-selling novel by Michael Crichton that achieved the apotheosis of popular literature when it was made into a Hollywood film. Its message was expressed in a phrase attributed to the Japanese: "business is war." The assault by Japanese business on the United States was a war that, readers of the book and viewers of the film were left in no doubt, the American side was losing.[16] To the extent that these ideas penetrated public opinion (and books generally become best-sellers because they *reflect* public opinion), they undercut the American public's disposition to devote blood and treasure to Japan's defense.

Resentment of Japan in the United States was counterbalanced by the conviction that the dangers of the Cold War required political solidarity between the two countries, however justified America's economic grievances might be. But as the Cold War wound down, Japan seemed a candidate to displace the fading Soviet Union as the chief threat (although not a military threat) to the United States, which would surely have put the Security Treaty in jeopardy.

In the first post-Cold War decade this did not happen. To the contrary, in the 1990s the two economies reversed course. While the

American economy soared, the Japanese economy slumped. Over the course of the decade American resentment of Japan faded. Still, in the middle of the decade the political underpinnings of the alliance seemed shaky enough to require shoring up by adjusting the balance of military responsibilities between Japan and the United States. Accordingly, Japan agreed to provide more support to American forces in the Pacific and to provide it over a wider part of the region than during the Cold War.*

A potentially greater threat to the alliance was the emerging discontent within Japan regarding its subordinate role in its own region and a corresponding desire for all of the prerogatives, including the military ones, of a great power. Such sentiments were present at the outset of the twenty-first century, and while they did not command anything like majority support, they had the potential to do so. However, the chief threat to the post-Cold War peace in East Asia came not from Japan but from China.

CHINA

THE MILITARY FORCES on the European continent had two features that lent themselves to a common security order that those in East Asia lacked: symmetry and equality. The Soviet and American military blocs equipped themselves with the same kinds of weapons, in roughly (although not exactly) equal numbers. Devising a set of limits on military forces that could be applied equally to both sides was therefore not particularly difficult. The Communist side had to relinquish more than the West, but the end point was equality, a status more acceptable than inferiority.

In the security affairs of East Asia, China assumed the role Russia

*Whether American public support for the alliance with Japan could survive a shooting war in Asia—on the Korean peninsula, for instance—in which American troops fought and Japanese troops did not was very much an open question. The Japanese decision in 1991 to send money but not soldiers to fight in the Persian Gulf, the oil from which was if anything more important for the Japanese than for the American economy, was not well received in the United States, but it did not end the partnership between the two countries. The same question for the American alliance in Europe was almost put to the test in the war over Kosovo in 1999. Had NATO launched a ground war to remove Yugoslav troops from Kosovo, the bulk of the fighting would have been done by the Americans and none at all by the wealthiest and most powerful European member of the alliance: Germany.

had played in Europe: the major power least committed to liberal
norms at home and abroad, on whose willingness to adopt its defining principles the prospects for a common security order depended.
But the military forces of China and the United States, the other significant power in the region, were neither symmetrical nor equal.
China was a land power, with very modest air and naval forces. The
United States, by contrast, was the greatest naval and air power in
the history of the world but with a militarily underdeveloped and
politically inhibited capacity for waging a military campaign on the
Asian mainland. Even where the two countries' armed forces were
similar, they were not equal. Both deployed nuclear weapons. But
the American nuclear arsenal was the largest on the planet, boasting
a full complement of platforms—missiles, manned aircraft, and sub-
marines—capable of striking targets anywhere in the world. China's
was smaller, less varied, and included only a few missiles that could
reach the United States.[17]

The American and Chinese military forces were therefore different creatures, at home in different habitats. China was an elephant,
slow and not particularly agile but by reason of bulk formidable on
land, yet no match for American naval and air forces at any distance
beyond its own coast. The United States, in East Asia at least, was a
whale and an eagle, powerful on the high seas and in the air, weaker
on dry land. These differences built a measure of stability into the
Sino-American military relationship. Geography itself served as a
kind of buffer between them. Nature rather than diplomacy imposed
a pattern of defense dominance on the two. Neither posed a mortal
threat to the other on its own terrain.

Still, throughout history other pairs of sovereign states with comparably dissimilar forces found ways to fight each other: seaborne
Athens and land-bound Sparta in ancient Greece, maritime Great
Britain and continental France in the eighteenth and nineteenth
centuries. Indeed, the Cold War rivals, the United States and the
Soviet Union, overcame geographic obstacles to wage an intense
geopolitical rivalry. At the dawn of the twenty-first century geography alone could not guarantee that offensive military initiatives by
either China or the United States against the other would fail, but
other features of the history and politics of the two countries

reinforced the geographically based disposition to avoid armed conflict.[18]

Insurmountable material shortcomings did not compel the United States and Japan to adopt a defensive military strategy in East Asia. The two countries could, if they chose, assemble the military forces necessary for attacking, defeating, and occupying the Chinese mainland. For this there was, of course, historical precedent. The European great powers, the United States, and Japan had all occupied parts of China from the early decades of the nineteenth century to the middle of the twentieth.

But it was not remotely likely that they would seek to repeat the experience in the first decades of the twenty-first. Empire was out of fashion. The aversion to war had deep roots in Japan and was, where wars of conquest were concerned, almost as powerful in the United States. Nor had the twentieth-century military experiences of either country in China, or in other parts of the Asian mainland for that matter, been rewarding ones. Japan had become bogged down in North China in the 1940s, where it found itself overextended, bedeviled by Chinese guerrillas, and unable to release troops to fight the Pacific War against the United States. Neither of the two more recent wars that the United States waged in Asia had come to an entirely satisfactory conclusion. Korea was a stalemate, Vietnam a defeat. A repetition of either the Japanese imperialism of the 1930s and 1940s or the American anti-Communist wars of the 1950s and 1960s held no appeal for either country.[19] For the United States and Japan an offensive military strategy against China was what major war in general had, under the influence of the social trends that underwrote warlessness, increasingly become: not altogether impossible, perhaps, but certainly unthinkable.

If the United States and Japan would not, China on the whole and with an important exception could not launch a war of conquest in the twenty-first century. The United States and Japan were barred by disinclination, China by incapacity. The industrial revolution came so late to China, which therefore fell so far behind the world leaders technologically, that no Chinese government during the twentieth century could realistically aspire to a military force that could challenge the West's strongest power, the United States, beyond the edge of the Eurasian landmass. Here China differed from Russia. The tsarist and Soviet regimes were, by many measures, the most backward of the great powers, but each was nonetheless a great power. Each had to struggle to keep up militarily with its more advanced neighbors and rivals and each ultimately failed. But the hope of keeping up was not a vain one; for decades each did manage to hold its own in an ongoing military competition.

China never harbored such a hope. Under Mao it pursued a military strategy not of equality but of weakness.[20] This was a strategy designed to compensate for the technical superiority of China's potential adversaries in ways that would secure the country against encroachment by them. It was therefore a defensive strategy, both because China felt genuinely threatened and because an offensive strategy, no matter how attractive ideologically, was not within the realm of possibility.[21]

Mao proclaimed China's adherence to the doctrine of "People's War," which called for guerrilla resistance to an invasion by poorly armed but presumably highly motivated Chinese fighters.[22] Under Mao, China did acquire nuclear weapons, but only a handful, which the Chinese leader calculated would suffice to give more powerful adversaries pause before invading China.[23]

To be sure, Chinese foreign policy during the first three decades of the People's Republic did not *look* defensive. During that time China was frequently at war, at one time or another fighting with each of its largest neighbors: the United States, a neighbor by virtue of its Pacific fleet, in Korea in 1950; India in 1962; the Soviet Union in 1969; and Vietnam in 1979. In each case, moreover, it was China that initiated the fighting.

Appearances to the contrary notwithstanding, China's purpose in each case was indeed defensive. The Chinese military operations—in the last three cases strictly limited ones—were calculated to deter what the leadership in Beijing believed were the aggressive designs of other powers by demonstrating that a direct attack on China would be costly.[24] In Korea, Mao feared that the United States would carry its military campaign across the Yalu River into China and attempt to reverse the Communist victory in the recently concluded civil war. A similar motive animated the skirmishes with India in 1962 and even more so the clashes with the Soviet Union seven years later: The Chinese suspected the Soviet leadership of seeking to extend to their country the recently proclaimed Brezhnev Doctrine, which arrogated to Moscow the right to impose its will on wayward Communist countries and had been used to justify the Soviet invasion of Czechoslovakia in August 1968. Moreover, in both cases, beyond being intended to warn against assaulting China, the wars were fought over disputed borders. China did not try to capture territory to which it did not have at least an arguable claim. The Vietnam campaign was designed to punish China's southern neighbor for what Beijing regarded as aggressive conduct. Chinese troops invaded, briefly occupied, then withdrew from the northern part of the country.

In the Maoist period and under Deng Xiaoping as well, the expansion of China's military strength was not the regime's highest priority. Of the "four modernizations" to which Deng had committed China in the late 1970s, military modernization was the fourth—after industry, science and technology, and agriculture.[25] After Mao's death in 1976 China upgraded its armed forces and shifted its strategy, from people's war to the defense of the country at its borders. But it did not acquire, nor did it seriously seek, the capacity to project power beyond them.[26] In the first post-Cold War decade China did not qualify as a military power of the first rank.[27]

For China, as for Russia, the fact of weakness substituted for the conviction of warlessness. But China was not destined to remain weak. By the end of the twentieth century the country was in fact far stronger than it had been at the beginning. Acutely conscious of its weakness, China's overriding twentieth-century goal, through war and revolution, was to overcome it. In the century's third quarter the effort to do so produced results. In its third quarter, under Mao, the country was pacified militarily and unified politically. In the century's last quarter, largely under the leadership of Deng Xiaoping, it enjoyed a surge of economic growth. The combination made China, at the outset of the twenty-first century, a rising power.

Historically, the means at the disposal of sovereign states often determine the ends they pursue: Ambition has a tendency to grow with strength. So it was with Germany in the latter part of the nineteenth century, when political unification and rapid industrialization made it the most formidable power on the European continent. Early twenty-first century China resembled early twentieth century Germany both in its economic advances and its declarations of dissatisfaction with its place in an international order designed and controlled by others.[28] The historical parallel had a worrisome implication: Germany's aspirations and resentments led to World War I.

The differences between pre-World War I Germany and post-Mao China, however, were more telling than the similarities. Germany already exceeded its neighbors and rivals in military strength at the outset of the twentieth century. It had won a decisive victory over the country that had been the greatest European power, France, in 1871. It fielded the most powerful army in Europe. None of this was true of China in its relationship with the principal defender of the East Asian status quo, the United States, at the beginning of the twenty-first century.

At the outset of the twentieth century the mark of international primacy was the possession of an empire, acquired by military conquest. By the beginning of the twenty-first century the age of empire had ended. It was no longer politically legitimate, militarily feasible, or economically profitable to set out on a campaign to conquer and govern other peoples. Finally, when Germany embarked on World War I its leaders envisioned a difficult, costly conflict, but reasonably believed that they would win it. In the age of nuclear weapons a Chinese leadership initiating a comparable conflict could harbor no such expectation.

Surging economic growth, military modernization, and harsh rhetoric about international inequality were all features of Chinese foreign policy in the first post-Cold War decade, but, even in the absence of formal measures for common security, they did not, singly or together, make China a serious threat to seek to overthrow the existing political arrangements in its region as Napoleonic France, Wilhelmine Germany, Nazi Germany, and Imperial Japan had done.

If twenty-first-century China was not about to duplicate the experience of pre-World War I Germany, however, neither was it likely to follow the example of the altogether more liberal Germany of the post-World War II period. Like Russia, and unlike the countries of the Western core, China was not imbued with the spirit of warlessness, and the social trends that had debellicized the core countries were much newer and weaker there. The forces of modernity had made little headway in both societies when they had been governed by traditional autocracies and in the Communist period liberal ideas and practices were actively discouraged.

Like Russia, China inhabited a more difficult and dangerous neighborhood than the democracies of Western Europe and North America. It had land borders with fourteen different countries and maritime frontiers with six more;[29] and with virtually none of them were sources of conflict entirely absent.

But one thing that set China apart from Russia was that it remained committed to a practice the discrediting of which had been crucial for the growth of warlessness in the West. Beijing continued to govern, against their will, non-Han Chinese peoples—Tibetan Buddhists and Muslim Central Asians in the vast western regions of the People's Republic. China was a multinational empire and thus susceptible to unrest, which evoked the use of force, where Chinese rule was resented.

Moreover, post-Cold War China was still ruled by Communists, who had cast aside Marxist-Leninist orthodoxy in economic affairs but retained it in matters of politics. For them the essence of politics was not negotiation and compromise but brutal struggle. If their outlook on the world had a Western counterpart it was the traditional one. China's leaders were realists, not liberals.

China, like Russia, had suffered assaults by more modern neighbors. Russia incurred a series of defeats in the nineteenth and twentieth centuries: in the Crimea at the hands of Britain and France in 1854–56; by Japan in 1905; by Germany in World War I; and by Nazi Germany in 1941–42. But tsarist and later Communist Russia always managed to reverse, usually in short order, the setbacks it suffered.

The Chinese did not. Between the first Opium War in 1839–1842 and the Communist conquest of power in 1949 they experienced eleven decades of decline, retreat, and humiliation. Here China resembled the societies of the periphery that were conquered, occupied, disrupted, and generally harassed by the West. By the end of the twentieth century the consequences of the Western onslaught for almost all of them had been eliminated. Foreign occupation had long since ended. For China this was not so.

In the first decade of the twenty-first century one humiliation remained, in Chinese eyes, unreversed. Towering over the sociological, geographical, and historical reasons that the policies of common security did not commend themselves to the Communist regime in China even as they were being practiced in Europe was what was emphatically inconsistent with a common security order. There was a political issue over which China preferred fighting to giving way or compromising: the status of Taiwan.

TAIWAN

Taiwan was for East Asia in the first post-Cold War decade what Ukraine was for Europe: a place where disputes over sovereignty and borders had the potential to provoke a war involving one of the two large, unpredictable, formerly orthodox Communist giants of Eurasia. Both Taiwan and Ukraine were effectively independent, with flags, armies, national currencies, and elected governments. Of the two, Taiwan's claim to independence was in most ways the stronger. It had a longer history of effective independence. While Ukraine had been ruled from Moscow or St. Petersburg almost uninterruptedly from the mid-seventeenth century until 1991, Taiwan was declared a province of China relatively late in Chinese history, in 1885. At no time during the twentieth century was it governed from Beijing. Japan ruled the island from 1895 to 1945. In 1949 the losing side in the Chinese civil war, Chiang Kai-shek's Kuomintang, decamped to Taiwan and took control of the island. The self-declared Republic of China on Taiwan was a far more imposing international presence than independent Ukraine. It had the world's eighteenth-largest GNP, thirteenth-highest volume of foreign trade, and one of the highest totals of monetary reserves.[30]

The central difference between the two was, however, crucial:

Ukraine's giant neighbor and former master, Russia, accepted in principle its independence within the borders of what had been the Soviet republic of Ukraine. Beijing, by contrast, so emphatically denied that Taiwan had the right to elevate its de facto sovereignty to legal, de jure status that it declared itself willing, indeed determined, to go to war to prevent this.

Ukraine and Taiwan had something else in common. They illustrated one of the truths of the post-Cold War era, namely that while the end of the Cold War may have been a blessing, it was a mixed blessing. As always in history, pain accompanied gain. From the standpoint of the great liberal values the world had become a better place, freer, more prosperous, and more secure. But this was not the case everywhere. In some places things were worse. Some parts of the planet were less orderly and more dangerous after than before the collapse of European Communism.[31] The Cold War's end resolved the most dangerous late-twentieth century problems, the European and global conflict between Western liberalism and Communist illiberalism that had the potential to trigger a devastating nuclear war. But it created other problems. Before 1991 there was not the slightest chance that issues involving Russia and Ukraine, then part of the same country, would lead to armed conflict. And the end of the great East-West rivalry also aggravated existing problems, such as the relationship between China and Taiwan.

For the first two decades of the Cold War Taiwan was protected by the hostility between the United States and the People's Republic of China, itself a subset of the larger conflict between liberalism and Communist illiberalism. From his island stronghold, one hundred miles from the Chinese mainland, Chiang Kai-shek declared his regime to be the legitimate government of all China and vowed to reconquer it. The American government supported his claim. For the United States, the Taiwan Strait was another battle line in the Cold War, like the one that divided East from West Germany. Taiwan, like West Berlin, was an outpost of the free world, to be defended at almost any cost.

The Maoist regime proclaimed its determination to gain control over what it regarded as a renegade province. In the 1950s, Taiwan and China skirmished over control of a number of tiny islands lying between them in the Taiwan Strait. Beijing regularly shelled some that Taiwan controlled. The United States issued veiled nuclear threats in an effort to dissuade the Communist side from launching an assault across the Strait; and, despite its bellicose rhetoric and occasional artillery salvos, Beijing never seriously tried to capture (or, in its own view, recapture) the island.[32]

From 1972 to the end of the Cold War, by contrast, the Sino-American rapprochement protected Taiwan. The United States and the People's Republic came together to oppose the Soviet Union, which both regarded as a threat. For the sake of this common cause they put aside the issues that divided them, including the status of Taiwan. In the Shanghai Communique of 1972, the charter of the Sino-American Cold War partnership, the United States abandoned its explicit support of Chiang's claim to govern all of China without endorsing the competing claim of the Communist government in Beijing. Washington did disavow Taiwanese independence, which the Taiwanese government was not then seeking: "The United States acknowledges that all Chinese on either side of the Taiwan Strait maintain there is but one China and that Taiwan is part of China. The United States government does not challenge that position."[33]

The government of the People's Republic placed a higher value, in the 1970s and 1980s, on maintaining solidarity with the United States against the Soviet Union than on exerting control over Taiwan. But the Sino-American alignment met the same fate as other wartime partnerships. With the war ended and the common adversary defeated, the differences suppressed during the conflict rose to the surface as had happened between the United States and the Soviet Union after World War II. The fact of the Cold War's end, and the forces that its end set in motion, made it more difficult for each of the three parties to the conflict—Taiwan, China, and the United States—to accommodate the other two.

China had concrete military reasons for seeking control of Taiwan. In unfriendly hands the island posed a clear threat to the mainland. For the United States in the 1950s Taiwan had functioned as an "unsinkable aircraft carrier" from which punishing air strikes and even an invasion of China could have been mounted. If Taiwan presented only a prospective military problem for China, however, limitations on the armaments permitted on the island, in the spirit of common security, would have solved it. The mainland's objection to an independent Taiwan was not primarily military. It was political, and it had deep roots.

The Taiwan question was for Beijing a matter of national sovereignty and historical justice. Winning control of the island would be the final step in regaining the sovereignty that foreign gunboats and armies had violated. Taiwan was a piece of unfinished business from the nineteenth century, the last outpost of foreign control in China. It had, after all, been separated from the mainland by foreign military power—first Japanese, then American. After the return of Hong Kong from the British and Macao from the Portuguese, Taiwan was the last vestige of foreign aggression and Chinese humiliation.

This aggression and humiliation continued to rankle, indeed sometimes enrage, the Chinese—even in the twenty-first century. This was perhaps the most powerful and certainly the most explosive current of Chinese political opinion. The two best-known popular Chinese uprisings early in the twentieth century, the Boxer Rebellion of 1898–1900 and the May the Fourth Movement of 1919, both honored by the Communist regime as expressions of anti-imperial patriotism, were triggered by anger at foreign encroachment on Chinese territory.[34] Although its principal allegiance was to the internationalist principles of Marxism-Leninism, as adapted to Chinese circumstances by Mao and his colleagues, the Communist regime also fostered and sought to profit politically from the powerful current of nationalist feeling in China. The end of the Cold War aggravated matters. Catering to this sentiment became even more important to the Chinese government than before.

Although the Chinese government was explicitly undemocratic, it still sought popular acceptance, and nationalism was the most promising source of it. The Communists' claim to rule in China had two components. The party promised both to transform the society and to defend the nation. By the end of the Cold War the Communist prescription for transformation was as thoroughly discredited in China as it was everywhere else. Mao's economic formulas had failed to make the country a modern industrial society. His political whims had brought disaster: famine during the Great Leap Forward of the

1950s, anarchy during the Cultural Revolution of the 1960s, and mass murder during the recurrent campaigns against those he designated enemies of the revolution from the 1930s almost to the moment of his death in 1976. This left the regime's claim to being the defender of China's national territory, along with its success in promoting economic growth, as the bases for its legitimacy, and the commitment to regaining Taiwan was integral to that claim. That commitment appeared to enjoy wide support in the Chinese populace, even among people not enthusiastic about other features of Communist rule.[35] To discard it, to concede to the people of Taiwan the right to govern themselves, would have overturned one of the central tenets of the first fifty years of Communist governance.

Great and sudden reversals had, in fact, punctuated the first Communist half-century. Mao broke with China's Communist senior partner, the Soviet Union, and aligned with the arch-imperialist United States. Deng threw out the Communist approach to economic management in favor of what could only be called capitalism. But as with Mikhail Gorbachev's embrace of common security, Mao and Deng were able to change course dramatically because of their enormous personal authority, the kind of authority that none of their successors could reasonably expect to enjoy and that Deng's immediate successor, Jiang Zemin, certainly lacked. Chinese leaders in the twenty-first century were bound to be weaker because more restrained by the opinions and wishes of other officials and groups, which made it more difficult to modify China's claim on Taiwan.[36]

Modifying that claim, let alone abandoning it, was all the more difficult because Taiwan was not the only part of China where Beijing's claim to rule was contested. The vast western provinces of the People's Republic, Tibet and Xinjiang, which constituted almost 40 percent of the country's territory, were populated by non-Han Chinese who deemed Chinese rule illegitimate. Their compelled inclusion in the People's Republic was for them what the Western treaty ports of the nineteenth century had been for the Chinese: a forcibly imposed form of imperial domination.[37] Contributing to the Communist leaders' adamant insistence that Taiwan was properly a part of China was the lurking anxiety that retreating from this position would give encouragement to the widespread secessionist sentiment in the western part of their domain.[38]

If the end of the Cold War made the recovery of Taiwan more important to Beijing, it made Taiwan less willing to contemplate being ruled from the mainland and more determined to resist. At the beginning of the new century the island had enjoyed effective independence for fifty years. Over the decades a distinctive Taiwanese identity had evolved among its people. They did not think of themselves as belonging to the mainland[39] and, indeed, Taiwan was a very different kind of place from China. For all its extraordinary economic growth in the last two decades of the twentieth century, China remained predominantly poor and rural. Taiwan was neither. By the world's standards it was wealthy, with a per capita income of $16,000, compared with $3,800 in China.

As dramatic and telling as the economic differences were the political ones. For the first quarter-century after Chiang's 1949 flight to Taiwan, he governed the island autocratically and occasionally brutally. His Kuomintang (KMT) Party, dominated by mainland refugees, monopolized political power to the exclusion of the local Taiwanese. Beginning in the 1980s, however, Chiang's son and successor, Chiang Ching-kuo, relaxed the KMT's grip. The political system became more open and liberal. By the mid-1990s, Taiwan was a full-fledged democracy, whose people did not wish to submit to the rule of a regime that did not, as its suppression of the demonstrations in Tiananmen Square in June 1989 confirmed, permit political freedom. For the Taiwanese the central conflict of the Cold War, between liberty and oppression, was still very much alive.

The process of Taiwanese democratization aggravated relations with the mainland. As part of that process, the Taiwan authorities abandoned their claim to be the legitimate government of all of China. The premise of the 1972 Shanghai Communique was thereby voided. No longer did Chinese on both sides of the Taiwan Strait maintain that there was but one China. Taiwan's renunciation of its claim to the mainland implied that the government of the mainland had no legitimate claim on the island, a claim that Beijing refused to relinquish. Since Taiwan was in effect declaring that the Chinese civil war had finally ended and that the Communists had won, this was surely one of the few instances in history in which the concession of defeat by the losing side in a conflict was taken as a serious provocation by the victor.

Moreover, in Taiwan's free elections, candidates were at pains to demonstrate their devotion to what the people of Taiwan most wanted: the maintenance of the island's de facto independence and the acquisition of as many of the trappings of formal sovereignty as possible. President Lee Teng-hui, the first native Taiwanese president and in 1996 the first to be freely elected, outraged Beijing by paying a quasi-formal visit to the United States to receive an honorary degree from his alma mater, Cornell University, in 1995, and by describing Taiwan's international status in language that all but proclaimed the island a sovereign country. One of his motives was to protect the political interests of his party, the reformed KMT, against its rival, the Democratic Progressive Party (DPP), which threatened to outflank the ruling group in enthusiasm for independence. But in the second presidential election, in 2000, the DPP candidate, Chen Shui-bian, was the winner.

East Asia in general and Taiwan in particular could not help but be affected by the end of the Cold War. The collapse of the Soviet Union and Yugoslavia, the Communist multinational empires of Europe, and the attainment of full sovereignty by their constituent provinces could scarcely have gone unnoticed by the inhabitants of the Communist multinational empire in Asia, China. Independence was in the air in the 1990s and none of the peoples in Europe who received it had the history of effective self-government or the record of democratization or the list of economic achievements of which Taiwan could boast. If sovereignty were to be awarded on the basis of merit or logic Taiwan would surely be at the head of the line to receive it. If, in the spirit of Wilsonian self-determination, it were to be awarded on the basis of what the people within a particular jurisdiction wanted, the Taiwanese claim would be just as strong.

At the turn of the twenty-first century the dispute between Taiwan and China was fifty years old. It had not yielded to a cooperative solution because the differences between the parties were too wide for them to strike a compromise. Taiwan was never willing to accept a status that was also acceptable to the Communist government of the mainland. Nor was the dispute susceptible to settlement by unilateral measures, and the reason for this was geography.

Because the island was separated from the mainland by one hundred miles, China was not able to mount a successful invasion. In the early decades of the Cold War American military power prevented this; by its latter stages Taiwan had become strong enough to defend itself. Had Taiwan been attached to the mainland its fate would likely have been that of the Portuguese enclave of Goa on India's west coast, which the Indian army easily overran in 1960, or of Hong Kong, the 1997 return of which to China was negotiated by Great Britain. On the other hand, if the island had been situated, say, 250 miles from the Chinese coast, it could probably have detached itself completely from the affairs of the mainland, as the British and French overseas possessions did when the European empires ended. But one hundred miles was not enough distance for this. It put Taiwan well within range of the aircraft and ballistic missiles of the mainland.

While politics and geography made the Taiwan question all but insoluble, it was the involvement of the United States that made it the most dangerous of all post-Cold War political disputes. The United States had been the midwife of Taiwanese autonomy. When the Korean War erupted in June 1950, President Harry Truman ordered the Seventh Fleet into the Taiwan Strait. Had he not done so the Chinese Communists might well have carried out their plan to seize the island, in which case the question of Taiwanese independence would never have arisen. Instead, American military power protected the island from the mainland. In 1979, in conjunction with the establishment of formal diplomatic relations with Beijing, Washington abrogated the security treaty that had been signed with Taiwan in 1954 and replaced it with the less binding Taiwan Relations Act. The Shanghai Communique represented a tacit agreement between the United States and China to put aside the Taiwan question indefinitely.

The end of the Cold War worsened relations between the United States and the People's Republic and changed the way Americans saw China's government. Beijing had once been seen as a fellow soldier on the front lines against a common threat, but in the wake of Tiananmen came to seem an unapologetic opponent of democracy and violator of human rights on a massive scale. During the Cold War it had in fact been both, but with the end of the conflict it ceased to be the first and, if only by default, the second became more important in American eyes.[40]

The transformation of the American image of the Beijing regime gave the conflict between China and Taiwan a moral dimension that had been common during the Cold War but was far less so in its aftermath: A free people was resisting a Communist takeover. Under such circumstances, the American public felt a moral obligation if not necessarily to guarantee Taiwanese democracy then certainly to refrain from contributing to its demise. For its part the American government recognized a strategic interest in the continuation of Taiwan's de facto independence, or at least in preventing it from being forcibly revoked. The general credibility of American commitments was important in East Asia for the solidity of the alliance with Japan and the effectiveness of the American-supported deterrence of North Korea. And while the Taiwan Relations Act did not include a binding American commitment to protect Taiwan,[41] it was not something from which the United States could easily walk away.[42]

A Chinese attack on Taiwan would immediately make East Asia seem a more perilous place. If the attack succeeded, American commitments would come into question and the consequence, it was reasonable to believe, could well be the chain reaction of distrust, arms competition, nuclear proliferation, and conceivably region-wide conflict. In most of the world the fear that a local setback would set off an adverse chain reaction, which had governed the security policies of most great powers most of the time, was in abeyance. For the Taiwan question this kind of "domino thinking" continued to be a part of the security calculations of the countries of the region, especially the United States.

The United States had a substantial interest in deterring a military assault by Beijing on Taiwan, and a policy of deterrence ordinarily gains in strength from being clearly stated. This suggested reinstating, in the wake of the Cold War, the explicit guarantee of American protection that Taiwan had enjoyed for a quarter century. But in the first post-Cold War decade the government of the United States did no such thing. It had no wish to resume the hostile relationship with China of the period between the Korean War and the

Nixon-Mao rapprochement of 1972. Nor, for the same reason, would the other countries of the region have joined in such a policy. All hoped that the dispute over Taiwan's status could be resolved peacefully. Nor would a firm guarantee necessarily have served the cause of military stability in East Asia. Here the security dilemma operated: what would be intended by the United States as a defensive measure risked being taken by China as a provocation, especially if an American security guarantee inspired a formal Taiwanese declaration of independence.

The Taiwan question obstructed the creation of a common security order for East Asia like the one that Ronald Reagan and Mikhail Gorbachev had fashioned for Europe at the end of the Cold War. It alienated China from the American policies that were designed to reassure all the other countries of the region. The Chinese authorities saw the value of continuing the Japanese-American Security Treaty even after the Cold War had ended[43] but objected to the modification of Japan's defense guidelines that the Americans believed necessary to sustain domestic public support for the Treaty, because it seemed to bring Taiwan within the alliance's defensive perimeter.[44] The Chinese wanted the American armed forces to remain in the Asia-Pacific region for purposes with which they agreed but not for those of which they disapproved.[45]

Because of China's claim on Taiwan, the idea of structuring its military forces so that they lacked the capacity to attack held little appeal for Beijing. For the same reason, the Chinese were not attracted to formal accords limiting their armed forces. The Taiwan question was an obstacle to another feature of common security, transparency. The United States pressed for broad military-to-military contacts with China but the Chinese were reluctant and guarded, no doubt bearing in mind that their forces might come into conflict with those of the United States in the Taiwan Strait.[46]

Without the opportunity to keep the peace in East Asia through common security, the United States was forced, in the first post-Cold War decade, to practice a policy of "double deterrence."[47] It aimed at keeping China from attacking Taiwan while at the same time keeping Taiwan from formally declaring itself independent, which the Communist government in Beijing had announced would trigger an attack. In the matter of Taiwan, the United States had to steer between the twin dangers of weakening its commitment to the point of abandoning Taiwan, thereby encouraging more aggressive tactics by the mainland, and of strengthening that commitment to the point that Taiwan felt confident enough to declare independence, thereby also provoking a Chinese attack in which the United States would be entrapped.[48]

In the first post-Cold War decade the combination of American, Chinese, and Taiwanese policies produced an anxious stability that two sources of volatility, one political, the other technological, put at risk.

The domestic politics of all three countries pushed their governments to do things that made war more likely. Taiwanese officials repeatedly sought ways to assert the island's independence and gain international recognition of it.[49] The Communist leaders of the mainland, who had little popular legitimacy, had to assume the role of uncompromising defenders of China's territorial integrity, which emphatically included the island of Taiwan.[50] In the United States the Taiwanese cause had influential allies, particularly in the American Congress.[51] The combination produced two provocative Chinese military exercises in the 1990s that were designed to warn and restrain Taiwan. On the second occasion the United States became involved.

The 1995 visit of Taiwanese president Lee Teng-hui to Cornell University came as a rude shock to Beijing, which had received assurances from the American government that it would not admit him to the country. The Clinton administration reneged on this assurance under pressure from the American Congress, which the opposition Republican party controlled. In response, China conducted military exercises that involved firing ballistic missiles from the mainland that landed near Taiwan.

The next year came the first fully democratic election for the presidency of the island, which Lee Teng-hui won. The Communist government of the mainland regarded this, too, as provocative, and once again the Chinese military conducted a missile exercise, with the missiles again landing close to Taiwan. On this occasion the United States responded with a military maneuver of its own, moving two aircraft carrier task forces into the waters around the island. Neither China nor the United States intended to go to war. Each was sending a signal: China that it would not tolerate further movement by Taiwan toward independence, the United States that it would not necessarily remain aloof if China attempted to bully Taiwan militarily. The episode illustrated the potential for war.

In such a war, control of the airspace between the island and the mainland would hold the key to success. In the first post-Cold War decade air superiority there belonged to Taiwan.[52] If China were to send an armed flotilla across the Taiwan Strait to seize the island, the Taiwanese air force had the capacity to sink it. But this did not give Taiwan the military basis for declaring itself fully independent. With its growing fleet of ballistic missiles China could inflict serious damage on the island without conquering it. The military relationship between the two was therefore one of mutual deterrence.

The Taiwanese aerial advantage was not necessarily permanent, however. The two sides both sought to improve their air forces, making the military balance over the Taiwan Strait the subject of an arms race, one of the few actively under way at the dawn of the twenty-first century. Unlike the Soviet-American nuclear competition during the Cold War, in which neither the United States nor the Soviet Union could reasonably have hoped to gain a militarily decisive advantage over the other, China and Taiwan competed to achieve just that. Taiwan had the advantage, and so retained de facto independence. If China were to achieve air superiority, Taiwanese independence would be placed in jeopardy; and because the relevant technology changed rapidly, and China, with its size, could devote superior resources to perfecting it, over time the reversal of the air balance was entirely conceivable. To match China, Taiwan had to rely on access to American technology, notably high-performance aircraft and battle-management radar. This was yet another way in which the United States was entangled in the cross-strait dispute.[53]

Even with air superiority Taiwan was menaced by China's ballistic missiles, and as these became increasingly accurate they could threaten not only Taiwan's population but also its air bases and thus Taiwanese control of the air. The island's government therefore had an interest in defending itself against a missile attack as well as against an amphibious assault. In the first post-Cold War decade the United States sought ways both to defend its own population from missile attack from long range and to protect military forces from missiles launched from shorter distances. The second type, "theater missile defense," fit Taiwan's military requirements. Not surprisingly, the Chinese government objected strenuously to the prospect of including Taiwan in any system of theater missile defense.[54] At the end of the first post-Cold War decade the United States did not have a working system of missile defense of any kind. But theater defenses were an attractive prospect as a way of fulfilling an American commitment in another part of Northeast Asia, where the United States came even closer to war than in the Taiwan Strait in the first post-Cold War decade: the Korean peninsula.

KOREA

L IKE RELATIONS between China and Taiwan, the political status of the Korean peninsula was an issue with roots in the Cold War that the end of that conflict aggravated. Korea was a divided country. Its division, which was the cause of the closest brush with war in East Asia in the first post-Cold War decade and made it one of the major flashpoints of the post-Cold War world, came about almost by accident.

With a culture shaped by Chinese influence and a continuous existence as a united independent political community for almost thirteen centuries, Korea's modern history began when it came under Japanese domination in 1905. Having declared war on Japan in the final days of World War II, the Soviet Union moved troops into Manchuria, also controlled by the Japanese, and into the northern part of Korea. Without giving the matter much thought, the American government decided that it, too, should have a zone of occupation on the peninsula and arbitrarily designated the thirty-eighth parallel as the zone's northern boundary.[55] A Communist regime headed by Kim Il-sung established itself in the north with the Soviet Union as its patron. In the south a non-Communist government was formed under Syngman Rhee.

On June 25, 1950, with Stalin's assent, Kim launched an attack on the south with the aim of reunifying the peninsula under his rule. Under United Nations auspices, the United States sent troops to repulse the attack. In response to a successful American counterattack, the newly installed Communist regime in China dispatched an army that ultimately numbered 1.2 million men across the Yalu River, which separated China from Korea, to do battle with the Americans. The Korean War ended with an armistice in 1953, establishing a demilitarized strip two and one-half miles wide cutting across the thirty-eighth parallel as the line of separation between the two Koreas.

Up to a point relations between North and South Korea followed the same pattern as relations between the two Germanys.[56] Each side claimed to be the legitimate government of the entire Korean peninsula. Neither accorded diplomatic recognition to the other. Large armies were assembled on either side of the border between them. Each was part of, and drew support from, one of the two contending camps in the Cold War. But unlike the two Germanys in the 1970s, the two Koreas effected no diplomatic reconciliation during the Cold War. They had almost no contacts and there was no dilution of the mutual rhetorical vituperation, especially from the north.

North Korea was the Communist country most isolated from the rest of the world. Its government claimed to follow the tenets of its own, home-grown ideology, "juche," a kind of self-reliance intended to justify its self-imposed isolation. It was heavily militarized and the cult of the leader was particularly pervasive and grotesque. Public homage to Kim Il-sung outdid in intensity even the tributes paid to Stalin and Mao in their lifetimes.[57]

Like the two Germanys, indeed like the Western and Communist camps as a whole during the Cold War, the rivalry between the two Koreas had an economic dimension as well as military and political aspects. In the Korean case, as in the others, the performance of the liberal system proved decisively superior. In 1960, a decade after the outbreak of the Korean War, the two states were more or less equal economically. Thereafter the economy of the south soared. In four decades its per capita yearly income rose from $100 to $10,000. The North's economy sputtered. By the end of the century the South had enormous advantages in industrial production, exports, and overall standard of living. By one estimate, its output was twenty-four times greater than that of the North.[58] So pronounced was the North Korean failure that the country could not feed itself. In the final years of the twentieth century it was beset by famine.[59]

As in the other theaters of the Cold War, economic performance, good and bad, had political consequences. South Korea became so powerful economically that the two formerly Communist giants of Eurasia, the Soviet Union and the People's Republic of China, put aside the politics of the Cold War era in favor of the gains available from trade with the South. Formal diplomatic relations followed the establishment of economic contacts in both cases, with the Soviet Union in 1990, with China in 1992. These were political blows to the North and were followed by an economic shock. Its two former patrons decided to reduce their economic subsidies to North Korea. For all its rhetoric of self-reliance, the government in the North Korean capital of Pyongyang had depended heavily on these, especially in securing supplies of energy.[60] This brought the North to the brink of economic collapse. By one estimate, by 1998 its industrial sector, in which the regime had invested heavily, was operating at ten percent of capacity.[61]

All this called into question the viability of a separate, Communist, Korean state. It evoked the specter of the fate of East Germany once its border with the liberal, non-Communist, economically successful German Federal Republic was opened. Collapse and absorption into South Korea did not appeal to the North Korean regime, which, after Kim Il-sung's death in 1994, was ruled by his son Kim Jong-il. Apparently untroubled by any concern for the well-being of the people it governed, the regime's overriding concern was its own survival. Unlike the Communist regime of East Germany, North Korea managed to resist, into the twenty-first century, the tide of history that threatened to sweep it away.

The North Korean leadership was more determined to survive in power than had been the East German government. It was more determined because it was more independent. Like the founders of East Germany, Kim Il-sung had been put in place after World War II by the Soviet Union, but his regime, unlike theirs, did not depend on Soviet or Chinese troops to keep it in power.[62] North Korea had fought a war without direct Soviet participation (although in alliance with Chinese forces) against not only the non-Communist South but also the mighty United States.

The Communist North Korean government was in a better position to resist the forces that had destroyed East Germany for two other reasons. One was the tight control it exercised over the society it governed. The loans, the visitors, the broadcasts from the outside world that the East German government welcomed in increasing numbers in the latter years of the Cold War were not permitted by North Korea's rulers.[63]

The other reason for the effective North Korean resistance was geography. By the end of 1989 East Germany was surrounded by countries that were either non-Communist and liberal or formerly Communist and in the process of liberalization. North Korea had only one common border with a non-Communist country, and across the heavily militarized line of demarcation with South Korea the two-way traffic was minimal. Its northern neighbor, China, while far from North Korea in its economic practices and less rigid politically, was still governed by Communists who did not wish to see it collapse. To the east and west of North Korea was water—the Sea of Japan and the Yellow Sea. In this way it resembled the other truculent post-Cold War Communist holdout against the trends of global liberalism, the Caribbean island of Cuba.

Still, the prospects for the North Korean regime at the end of the first post-Cold War decade were not rosy. To survive it needed resources that it could not generate internally, and so faced a dilemma. To stem the economic collapse required loosening its grip on the society and opening the country to foreign trade and investment, but such measures threatened to undercut the political basis of Communist rule.[64] The Communist elite was like a man stranded on a desert island who could either stay where he was and risk starvation or venture into the surrounding shark-infested waters at the peril of being eaten alive or drowning.

In these circumstances, the Northern regime adopted the strategy of extracting through blackmail enough assistance from the West, particularly the United States, to keep itself afloat. North Korea demanded payment to refrain from acquiring nuclear weapons. In August 1998, the regime launched a ballistic missile that flew over the Japanese archipelago, raising the prospect that it was determined to acquire the means to send a warhead all the way to North America. Even without using a nuclear bomb, moreover, the mere possession of one would give Pyongyang leverage not only to assure its own survival but also to extract concessions from others. As such, a North Korean nuclear weapon had the potential to set in motion a destabilizing chain reaction of nuclear acquisition in East Asia.

So dangerous was the prospect of a North Korean bomb that the United States was prepared to go to war to stop it, and for a nerve-wracking moment in 1994, even before the missile test, war on the Korean peninsula did seem imminent. The issue that precipitated the 1994 crisis was the North Korean decision to remove irradiated fuel rods, from which material for a bomb could be extracted, from an existing nuclear reactor without international inspectors present. This could have led to UN sanctions, which North Korea had announced would be cause for war. The crisis was settled when North Korea agreed to freeze its nuclear program in return for Western-supplied nuclear power-generating reactors.[65]

A war with North Korea loomed as more costly than the Gulf War had been. An army of 1.1 million North Koreans was massed just north of the thirty-eighth parallel, only thirty-five miles from the South Korean capital of Seoul. In comparison with the South Korean and American forces that faced it—numbering 660,000 and 37,000 respectively—the North Korean army was neither well-trained nor well equipped, and by the second half of the 1990s it was unlikely to have been adequately fed. It had no chance of winning a second Korean War, in which, unlike the first one, it could not count on receiving assistance from either Russia or China. But in losing it could do considerable damage to South Korea. The American military estimated that in a war 52,000 Americans and 490,000 South Koreans would be killed or wounded in the first ninety days and that the cost of the damage inflicted would reach $61 billion.[66]

The Communist regime could not expect to survive such a war. Starting one would therefore be an act of political suicide. But the North Korean leaders had, over the years, earned a reputation as the

kind of people who were sufficiently fanatical, unstable, or discon- nected from reality—or all three—to embark on a suicidal military campaign. They had dug vast tunnels across the border into South Korean territory. They had planned and sponsored the assassination of several members of the South Korean cabinet during an official South Korean visit to Burma in October 1983. Even as they were seeking aid from the West they had sent a small submarine to the South Korean coast that had either landed deliberately or run aground. Its crew had hidden out in the countryside until spotted and hunted down by the South Korean authorities.[67] In a reversal of the logic of the confrontation during the Cold War, when the United States and South Korea feared that North Korea would attack if it became too strong, in the post-Cold War period North Korean weakness enhanced the credibility of its threat to fight. Like the Biblical Samson, who pulled down the temple and killed himself along with his enemies after having been deprived of the source of his strength, the North Korean regime was assumed to have fewer reservations about starting a war that would lead to its demise if it were on the point of expiring anyway. In the eyes of the countries that had to deal with it, the regime was like a wild animal flushed from its habitat, deprived of food, and desperate enough to attack anything in its path.[68]

A resolution of the Korean question would require something like the Concert of Europe. All of the interested powers—South Korea, the United States, Japan, China, and Russia—would have to sub- scribe to it. In recognition of this, in 1991 the South Korean govern- ment, after consultation with all of them, proposed four-power talks, to include the two Koreas, China, and the United States, to achieve a permanent peace agreement on the peninsula.[69] By the beginning of the twenty-first century all the parties involved, with the conspicu- ous exception of North Korea, agreed on some general points. None wanted a war in Korea. None wanted nuclear weapons in the hands of a Korean government, North or South.[70] And none favored the immediate reunification of the Korean peninsula following the Ger- man precedent.[71] China and Japan preferred that Korea not be united at all. Two Koreas would be weaker and more easily managed than a single one.[72]

South Korea did not share this view. To the contrary, since the peninsula had been united for the fourteen centuries before the Cold War divided it, the impulse for reunification was powerful on both sides of the thirty-eighth parallel. But in the first post-Cold War decade the South Korean leadership recognized that, because of the immense economic disparity between North and South, the forging of a single Korea, even if it could be accomplished peacefully, would encumber the South with an enormous social and economic burden.[73] Thus South Korea favored neither war, which would be costly even though it would be won, nor the collapse of the North Korean regime, which would also be costly and would thrust responsibility for the destitute people of the North upon the government of the South. Seoul came to prefer a gradual, peaceful liberalization of the North.[74] This was the course that the North Korean government sought, at all costs, to obstruct. For the purpose of bringing it about, the United States and South Korea adopted a particular strategy.

They began negotiations with North Korea with the goal of opening the country to the political, social, and economic forces beyond its border that the regime had assiduously kept out. Breaking the seal on the society and exposing it to the political equivalent of oxygen and sunlight would, the two countries hoped, erode the calcified structures of Communist politics and economics. The approach yielded results that, in the first year of the new millennium, set the two Koreas on a course that looked like the detente on which the two Germanys had embarked three decades earlier.

In June 2000, the leaders of the two Korean states held an unprecedented meeting in Pyongyang, the capital of North Korea. Lower-level official meetings followed, and North Korea began to set aside its policy of isolation and self-reliance, joining several international organizations and establishing or resuming diplomatic relations with a number of countries. At the same time, the faltering economy of the North was coming increasingly to depend upon economic assistance from abroad. All this seemed to increase the chances that the conflict on the Korean peninsula would be settled by gradual change in North Korea and a rapprochement with the South, rather than through the complete collapse of the Communist regime or by war.

Such a war, like a war over the status of Taiwan, would have involved the United States. Unlike the case of China and Taiwan, there was little risk that, in a Korean war, nuclear weapons would be employed. In this and other ways the Korean dispute resembled the many post-Cold War conflicts in the world's periphery. Like most of them, at its heart was a dispute over the location of borders. The governments of both North and South objected to the division of the peninsula, although they disagreed on which of them should preside over it once it was reunited.

As with many of the post-Cold War conflicts beyond the world's core, the immediate effect of the end of the Cold War was to aggravate the Korean problem. Unlike Korea, however, in most of these other post-Cold War conflicts the United States was not directly involved. Also unlike the Korean conflict in the first post-Cold War decade, many of the other conflicts actually did erupt into open warfare, and so gave the post-Cold War period one of its most noticeable and least attractive features: widespread violent disorder.

CHAPTER SIX

Post-Cold War Disorders

C HESS IS OFTEN used as a metaphor for international relations.
Both are strategic activities, in that each party acts in response
to what the other does or is expected to do. Both are competitive,
and a gain for one party is a loss for the other. But neither invariably
comes to a definitive conclusion. Just as a chess match can end in a
draw, so wars are not necessarily decisive, and sovereign states are
not continuously at war with one another.

Each has inequality built into it. In chess, some pieces are more
valuable than others, with the king having the highest value of all. In
international politics, the sovereign states of the core have more
power and greater wealth than those of the periphery. Since every
chess piece is part of the same game, however, and is moved about on
the same sixty-four-square board, all are important. The shrewd
player will take care to protect his or her pawns, the loss of which
puts rooks and knights and ultimately the queen and the king in
jeopardy.

So it is with international politics. The powers of the core intervene regularly in the periphery to forestall adverse developments
that if unchecked would, they fear, bring danger to their doorsteps.
Or rather, so it was in international politics for most of recorded history until the end of the Cold War. For the end of that conflict did a
great deal to disconnect the fates of the sovereign states of the
world's core from the destinies of the countries of the periphery,
with profound and not entirely happy consequences for the poor and
the weak of the planet.

FRAGILE STATES

I F THE END of the Cold War was in general a mixed blessing, in some parts of the world's periphery the blessings were not in evidence at all. Although free of ideologically inspired tyranny, many of the countries there did not enjoy the blessings of liberty. Nor had they achieved prosperity, which the industrial revolution brought to the countries of the world's core. As for peace, the third great liberal and modern goal, at the beginning of the twenty-first century this was even more conspicuous by its absence than were liberty and prosperity.

The proverbial man from Mars, set down during the first post-Cold War decade in almost any country in Africa south of the Sahara desert, or in the independent countries of the Caucasus and Central Asia that had emerged from the Soviet Union, or in Indonesia, Cambodia, Haiti, or the Balkans, would have concluded that the defining feature of the post-Cold War era was not the ascendance of liberal values but rather the prevalence of violent disorder. The inhabitants of these places were living in a Hobbesian state of nature rather than the liberal Wilsonian world of the world's core countries.

The various disorders were not entirely the result of the end of the Cold War. Modernity itself had a great deal to do with them. The political and economic revolutions that made the modern age disrupted traditional patterns, toppling old authorities, smashing old ways of life, and creating new sources of wealth and power as well as new groups that aspired to both. Nowhere was it easy to accommodate these developments peacefully. The modern era has been an age of revolution on the world's periphery as at its core, and for the same reasons.

The Cold War sometimes aggravated the violence that the modern age brought to the world's periphery. The great global antagonists took opposing sides in local quarrels in Korea, Vietnam, Afghanistan, and southern Africa, making them deadlier than they would otherwise have been. But the Cold War also had a stabilizing effect. It was a source of order, and its end was therefore one of the causes of the violence it left in its wake.

During the Cold War the many countries of the periphery were legally the equal of those of the core. They were all sovereign states. But in social composition they differed, and from one such difference many of their post-Cold War troubles arose. In the nineteenth century the contest between the forces of tradition and modernity was, among other things, a contest between two kinds of state: the traditional multinational empire, which dominated the planet, and the modern nation-state. In the twentieth century the modern form triumphed. After World War I the empires of the Turkish Ottomans, the Austrian Habsburgs, and the Russian Romanovs dissolved. After World War II the British, French, and Japanese empires were liquidated. The multinational Communist states that survived, the Soviet Union and Yugoslavia, made concessions to nationalist sentiment. Local nationals who were also members of the Communist party dominated local governments. Croatia, Slovenia, and Serbia were administered by Croat, Slovene, and Serb Communists respectively; in the non-Russian parts of the Soviet Union, Communist Party members of the "titular nationality" predominated in local governments—Georgians in Georgia, Uzbeks in Uzbekistan, and so on—although ultimate power resided in Moscow. But at the end of the Cold War the multinational Communist empires (except for China) also perished.

In deference to the triumph of the national principle as the widely accepted basis for sovereignty, the independent countries that emerged from the ruins of the old empires were called "new nations." For many, however, the term was a misnomer. They were "empires in miniature,"[1] composed of different national groups involuntarily placed within a single jurisdiction. Unlike in the core countries, the power of the government did not, in these mini-empires, derive from the consent of the governed. Instead, one group was strong enough to keep the others in check, producing the peace of effective repression.

The Cold War helped make it effective. In the era of the East-West rivalry, borders were widely regarded as unchangeable. Precisely because the borders of so many countries had been arbitrarily drawn, often by colonial administrators, and lacked legitimacy in the eyes of the governed, the new post-colonial regimes were eager to keep them from being challenged. The United States and the Soviet Union had their own reasons for sharing that preference. If borders were actively contested, the two great nuclear powers themselves might be drawn into the contest on opposing sides. In the age of nuclear weapons, this was a particularly daunting prospect. At the same time, each of the two opposing coalitions supplied money and guns to regimes in the periphery that supported it in the global struggle.

The arbitrarily governed sovereign states of the world's periphery with their arbitrarily drawn borders were often politically unstable. They experienced frequent changes of government. But these changes were generally swift and often bloodless exchanges of one elite for another. The preferred method was the coup. And while the question of who would govern was often at issue, the question of who was to *be* governed was not. Borders remained intact. When the eastern region of Nigeria sought to secede in 1967 and become the sovereign state of Biafra, only five countries accorded it diplomatic recognition.[2] It received no international support, and it was crushed.[3] The political map of the globe, which recorded the distribution of sovereignty, was like a grid fixed in place by a series of adhesions all of which were associated with the Cold War. When that conflict ended, the geopolitical glue dissolved and the grid loosened. The dissolution of Yugoslavia and the Soviet Union and the emergence of their constituent provinces as independent, internationally recognized sovereign states severely weakened the principle that borders could not be changed. At the same time, the resources once supplied by the great global rivals, which the governments of the periphery had used to keep order, ceased to be available. The Soviet Union, which no longer existed, could not, and the United States therefore would not, distribute the guns and money on which so many regimes had come to depend. Deprived of the political equivalent of tranquilizers, much of the periphery ceased to be tranquil.

The point is illustrated by three of the countries where revolts against the regime in power came to command the world's attention and ultimately to provoke Western military intervention. The leaders of all three had managed, during the Cold War, to gather assistance from *both* sides. Mohammed Siad Barre of Somalia, Saddam Hussein of Iraq, and Josef Broz Tito (and his successors) in Yugoslavia had made themselves clients, at one time or another, of both the Communist and the Western blocs.[4] When the Cold War ended, the largesse stopped and the grip of their regimes on power loosened. Across much of the great periphery of the international system this produced political turmoil, often leading to deadly violence.[5]

Whether the disorder of the post-Cold War era was worse than the upheavals, violence, and human suffering during the Cold War is a matter for debate.[6] Measured by the scale of destruction none matched the wars in Vietnam or Afghanistan. Measured by the loss of life none was the equal of the Chinese famine of the late 1950s. What is beyond doubt is that the post-Cold War disorders had a different cause. That cause was the weakness of many states of the world's periphery, a weakness that took two forms.

In some places the authorities simply could not keep order. In what came to be known as "failed states" the government could not discharge its most basic duty. Large parts of Africa but also patches of Eurasia—Albania and Chechnya, for example—fell into anarchy.[7] In other places governments were challenged by secessionist movements, groups that sought to leave the existing state and establish their own or join another. Anarchy flouted the sovereignty of the state in practice; secession challenged it in principle. This second challenge to state authority was more purposeful, and often well enough organized on both sides to qualify as war.[8]

The disorders in the world's periphery were local tragedies and, because of television, international spectacles. The spectators in the core countries responded to them with one of the two emotions that Aristotle said a tragic drama must evoke: pity. The pictures of violence and suffering did not, however, produce the other emotion that he had identified: fear. For the governments and people of the core, the pathologies of the periphery came in two distinct types: the ghastly, in which terrible things were happening to others, and the dangerous, which had the potential to harm them.

What was ghastly—massacres in Bosnia and Rwanda, for example—evoked pity, which inspired international efforts at charity. The core powers were distressed by what they saw and wished to do something to stop it, but they would no more invest heavily in the task than the average person would give all of his or her money to the needy. What was dangerous—the prospect of the interruption of the flow of oil from the Persian Gulf and the spread of nuclear weapons—evoked fear, which led to a more serious commitment, a commitment to obtain the geopolitical equivalent of insurance.[9]

There was little overlap between the two. The areas of worst local suffering were not the places of greatest importance beyond their borders. The ghastliest regions of the planet produced sound and fury—the fury of violence on the ground and the sound of the core countries deploring it from afar. Where the disorder was at its worst the powerful did the least, but they did not do nothing.

BORDER PROBLEMS

A T THE HEART of many of the conflicts of the first post-Cold War decade was the question of where borders should be located. Russia's potential conflicts with its neighbors and China's actual conflict with Taiwan, the division of the Korean peninsula, the wars in the Balkans, the Arab-Israeli conflict, the Iraqi invasion of Kuwait, and the tension between India and Pakistan over the Indian state of Kashmir were all, in one way or another, border disputes. A single universal standard for deciding border demarcation could therefore be expected to contribute to peace, and it was reasonable to look to the countries of the world's core to provide one. It was, after all, from Europe that the political ideas and norms that pervaded the modern world, including the concept of sovereignty itself, had emerged.

The core seemed, in fact, already to have furnished a standard for setting borders, the one upon which Woodrow Wilson had insisted at Paris in 1919. This was national self-determination, the principle that every nation is entitled to its own sovereign state, from which it follows that sovereignty ought to be divided among independent nation-states.

The principle is a modern one. Nationalism is the product of the two great revolutions that together shaped the modern age. The French Revolution was made in the name of the people—the French nation—and gave the world the revolutionary idea that it is the people and not the monarch who have the right to rule. The industrial revolution resulted in mass literacy and large urban concentrations, the conditions for widespread nationalist sentiment.[10] Nationalism, like the modern state, began in the West and, in the course of the two centuries of the modern age, diffused to every corner of the planet.

The national principle for determining borders is also a liberal one. It stands in contrast to the traditional method, whereby hereditary rulers drew lines arbitrarily, heedless of the wishes of the people affected. The national principle responds to what are, in most cases, popular wishes since people ordinarily prefer to be grouped with others like themselves. National self-determination may be seen as democracy applied to the task of allocating sovereignty.[11]

The history of the twentieth century provides evidence that vindicates the primacy of the national principle. At the outset of the twenty-first century, the most successful political communities on the planet, the stable, prosperous, and powerful states of the Western liberal core, were nation-states. In the United States, Germany, Japan, Great Britain, and France, with minor exceptions a single nationality dominated the state and the state recognized only one nationality.[12]

The national principle does have a serious drawback, however, which Wilson and the other peacemakers at Paris quickly discovered. It cannot be consistently applied.[13] There is, in the first place, no clear definition of a nation, no universally accepted way of deciding which group deserves its own state and which does not.[14] The number of groups that could, in theory, claim to be nations has no limit. It would scarcely be possible to honor all such claims: The result would be international chaos, the specter of which offered a powerful argument in favor of keeping existing borders intact.

Even when the definition of national groups is uncontroversial, it is not always possible to draw clear lines of division between and among them. Sometimes nations are intermingled. In Bosnia, one of the flashpoints of post-Cold War violence, the pattern of settlement was not that of a neatly tiled floor, with definable, delimitable, homogeneous clusters clearly separated from one another; it was more like a tossed salad.[15]

Attempting to apply the principle of national self-determination to ethnic and national tossed salads provoked violence. The democratic method for determining borders became a cause of war. Since national self-determination is feasible where territory is dominated by a single nation, in the former Yugoslavia some nations moved to create this condition by expelling the others, an odious practice that became known as "ethnic cleansing."[16]

In the post-Cold War period, as before, it was not possible to divide the world neatly into nation-states. In the post-Cold War world some sovereign jurisdictions, probably the majority, were fated to have more than one nation within their borders.[17] Neither, however, was the Cold War formula for border-determination, the inviolability of all existing frontiers, universally tenable. Once the Soviet Union and Yugoslavia were allowed, indeed encouraged, to break apart and sovereignty was bestowed upon their constituent republics,[18] it became more difficult to deny in principle the same opportunity to other self-defined nations that sought it. And the end of the Cold War reduced the international incentives to intervene to stop them from seizing it.

Thus neither the principle of the sanctity of all existing frontiers nor the principle of national self-determination could be either fully embraced or entirely discarded. The Clinton administration offered a vivid example of the impossibility of holding fast to one or the other principle. Two of its favored diplomatic projects were the Arab-Israeli peace process and the conflict in Bosnia. In the first it exerted itself to promote, in the second to prevent, the partition of a former Ottoman province. What then was to be done about the problem of borders? A formula for compromise was available that was easy to define in theory but difficult to apply in practice.

The compromise formula was this: If it is not possible to give distinctive groups sovereign independence by partitioning territory, the next-best solution is to give them some of the attributes of independence by dividing sovereignty, allowing these groups a measure of independent control over the political matters that affect them. The commonest term for the result is autonomy. It is the ubiquitous, indeed the all-but-inevitable proposal for resolving disputes over borders.[19]

The idea of dividing sovereignty is not new.[20] When it became clear to Woodrow Wilson and the other peacemakers in Paris that they could not give each self-proclaimed nation in the collapsed continental empires its own state, that some sovereign states would inevitably have more than one nation, and that relations among the different and sometimes unwilling inhabitants of the same state could lead to violence, they devised a series of treaties to guarantee national minorities a measure of autonomy. The provisions of these minority treaties were not, on the whole, carried out, foreshadowing a difficulty of the post-Cold War period.[21]

Autonomy was an attractive solution to the conflict between the two principles of border-setting because any set of arrangements on which different national groups within a single state can agree is by definition adequate. But autonomy has proven not to be a panacea in the post-Cold War period because in many parts of the periphery different national groups could not agree, or, if they could agree in principle, did not observe the terms of their agreement in practice,[22] turning instead to violence. Moreover, where the post-Cold War epidemic of state failure led not to organized wars of secession between identifiable political and military forces but rather to murderous anarchy, autonomy did not offer even a theoretical antidote to violence.[23] In both cases, for the violence to stop other countries would have to stop it, which brought to the fore one of the oldest of all international political issues, the forcible intervention by one sovereign state in the internal affairs of another.

INTERVENTION:
INTERNATIONAL LAW

INTERVENTION TO put an end to violence and suffering had one serious drawback. It was illegal under international law. The Treaty of Westphalia of 1648, from which the concept of state sovereignty is commonly dated, inaugurated a strong bias in principle in favor of the right of governments to act within their own borders free of interference from beyond them. This rule has a clear advantage. International order would be impossible if every sovereign state considered itself entitled to rearrange the internal affairs of every other. But it has a disadvantage as well. In pure form, it obliges the international community to turn a blind eye to anything, no matter how awful, that a government does within its borders.*

The end of the Cold War weakened the presumption against intervention. The hegemony of liberal values conferred broader international acceptance on the proposition that every government ought to respect these values and that the international community had the right to demand, and do more than demand, that all do so. At the same time, the end (or the suspension) of great power rivalry markedly reduced the chance that intervention would lead to a confrontation between the strongest members of the international system. The end of the Cold War thus made the world safe, if not for the reversal, then at least for the modification of the verdict of 1648.

Each of the three United Nations secretaries-general to serve in the last decade of the twentieth century contested the long-held international presumption against infringing on sovereignty.[24] After NATO's 1999 war against Yugoslavia over the Belgrade government's treatment of the people of Kosovo, which NATO recognized as a Yugoslav province and therefore within Belgrade's sovereign jurisdiction, President Bill Clinton said: "I think there's an important principle here that I hope will be now upheld in the future . . . And that is that while there may well be a great deal of ethnic and religious conflict in the world . . . that whether within or beyond the borders of the country, if the world community has the power to stop it, we ought to stop genocide and ethnic cleansing."[25]

The phrasing was inelegant, the precise conditions in which such interventions were justified far from clear, but the general message was plain. While he did not speak for all of the members of the international community, and indeed while some of the most prominent of them—Russia, China, India—strongly objected to the NATO

*The principle did not go unchallenged. In the twentieth century prominent international proclamations—the United Nations Charter of 1945, the Universal Declaration of Rights issued three years later, Basket Three of the Helsinki Final Act of 1975—specified internal norms that governments were expected to respect. The norms came to be known as human rights. Like other modern political innovations, these originated in the core of the international system and diffused unevenly elsewhere. But expecting governments to treat their citizens according to certain standards was one thing, compelling them to do so, or according other governments the right to compel them to do so, was another.

action, the leader of the planet's most powerful country was putting the world on notice that, in the post-Cold War era, sovereignty would not have the same inviolate legal status as in centuries past.

Changes in international practice accompanied the modification of long-standing principle. Intervention in the internal affairs of sovereign states, frequently under the auspices of the United Nations, became routine in the first post-Cold War decade. Cambodia, the Kurdish zone of Iraq, Somalia, Haiti, Bosnia, Kosovo, East Timor— these were the most visible recipients of the kind of international attention that for three and one half centuries was consistently illegal and sometimes uncommon.[26] If a twentieth-century Rip Van Winkle had fallen asleep in 1920 and awakened, say, in 1998, he might initially have concluded that the vision that Woodrow Wilson had brought to Paris after World War I had been fulfilled to the letter, with Wilson's prized League of Nations growing into a powerful international organization for coping with conflict the world over. But such an impression would have been wrong.

Three different kinds of operations took place under UN sponsorship. The first and least difficult of them was called peacekeeping, in which lightly armed or unarmed forces were inserted between warring parties that wished to cease fire but did not trust the other side to reciprocate. The international presence served as a neutral, passive buffer. The other two were more taxing. Historically more common than peacekeeping, they were known by different names than the ones the United Nations gave them. One of them was peace-enforcement, or, in plain English, war. The full-scale military operations conducted under the UN banner in Korea in the 1950s and in the Persian Gulf in the 1990s were instances of peace-enforcement. In Cambodia the UN practiced "peace-building," defined as "support for the transformation of deficient national structures and capabilities, and for the strengthening of democratic institutions."[27] This was state-building, of the kind often undertaken in the world's periphery by imperial and colonial powers.

War and imperial governance were historically the province of sovereign states rather than of international organizations, and this was also the case in the first post-Cold War decade. The UN was prominent but not powerful. It was a trade association of sovereign states that could pass resolutions but could no more carry them out than a trade association of hospitals could perform heart surgery. For implementing its resolutions it had to rely on its members, in particular the most powerful ones, the industrial democracies of the world's core.

The UN-sponsored operations of the post-Cold War period did differ from the wars and empires of history in one important way. They were undertaken for different motives. In the past, the powerful had intervened beyond their borders for strategic or economic reasons or both; some large interest was always at stake. In the post-Cold War interventions, by contrast, the countries carrying them out did so for minimal profit or protection. The United States had little to gain from changing the course of events in the Balkans and little to lose by their continuation. The dispatch of military forces to southern Europe was purely for the benefit of the people of the region. (Whether Western policies did in the end benefit them was a different question.)* It was an act of altruism, an example of humanitarian intervention.[28] The change of motive was important, for it affected the way the post-Cold War interventions were carried out and the results—or lack of them—that they achieved.

INTERVENTION: POST-COLD WAR PRACTICE

T HE PATTERN of post-Cold War intervention exhibited three telling features. The first was a regional bias. The powerful tended to involve themselves in the affairs of peripheral countries close to them. While continuing to observe the Cold War proscrip-

---

*The principal goal of the interventions in the Balkans, which were spearheaded by the United States, was not peace, which would have involved separating the warring national groups, but rather justice, which the Americans defined as the peaceful coexistence of these groups in a single, united, multiethnic political jurisdiction. None of the groups in Bosnia and Kosovo accepted the principle of multiethnicity, however, which meant that the interventions failed to bring about a just settlement as the United States defined it. The peace that intervention made possible was in both places a tenuous one. At the end of the first post-Cold War decade the formerly warring parties were kept apart by NATO garrisons, the departures of which from the region were deemed certain to lead to renewed fighting.

tion against sending armed forces to other countries, Japan did make a substantial economic contribution to the UN operation in Cambodia in the early 1990s. At the end of that decade Australia led the UN contingent to East Timor after the Indonesian army went on a violent rampage there in response to a Timorese vote in favor of independence. Russia sent or kept troops in the former Soviet republics turned independent countries to its south, in the Caucasus and Central Asia. For the Western Europeans, intervention in the Balkans was a way of trying to stem the flow of refugees from that region to their countries. And it was American forces that landed in Haiti to replace a government that had contributed to economic and political conditions in which thousands of Haitians left the Caribbean island for Florida. The American government wanted to keep them at home.[29]

The second characteristic feature of the post-Cold War interventions was a particular kind of inconsistency: The worst outrages did not receive the most attention.[30] The death tolls in the two Russian assaults on Chechnya exceeded 100,000 but neither the international community in general nor the United States in particular contemplated intervening there. Similarly, the United Nations Security Council declined to act to stop the wholesale slaughter of ethnic Tutsis by Hutus in Rwanda. The inattention to the slaughter of the innocents extended to other African countries as well.[31]

Third, the interventions that were launched did not, on the whole, achieve the goals announced for them. The government established in Cambodia was not democratic or even particularly effective. Somalia was not pacified. Despite the promises of the occupiers to reverse the conditions that they found, Haiti remained impoverished, Bosnia effectively partitioned,[32] and Kosovo a crucible of ethnic strife in which ethnic cleansing continued, with the Serbs and Albanians exchanging the roles of persecutor and victim.

These three features of the post-Cold War interventions had a common cause. In each case effort was tied to interest. Where geography created an interest, where poisonous conditions threatened to spill across borders, the powerful of the international system were willing to intervene. Where there was no interest there was no intervention. But even where there was an interest, it was so modest that outside powers were willing to make only minimal investments even when they did intervene.

The post-Cold War interventions were, on the whole, noble but half-hearted; they were half-hearted *because* they were noble. The growing warlessness of Western societies inhibited good deeds as well as bad ones, making the core countries not only reluctant to kill for causes that had come to be seen as unworthy, but also hesitant to die even for goals deemed highly desirable. Where the expenditure of blood and treasure for international goals was concerned, squalid, narrow, parochial self-interest carried greater weight than lofty and virtuous altruism. Perhaps the chief victims of this fact of international life in the first post-Cold War decade were the people of Africa. They were unlucky in that their distress neither affected nor could plausibly threaten to affect anyone beyond their own continent, and so outsiders were not willing to relieve it.[33]

The limits to humanitarian intervention were evident in the policies of the country that assumed the most prominent role in them, the United States. It was natural that the United States take the initiative in promoting post-Cold War interventions. It saw itself as the international leader. It had more disposable military power than any other country. Within the United States there was a constituency for humanitarian intervention. The protection of human rights was more important to Americans (judging, at least, from their political rhetoric) than to other people. And the country had a long tradition of criticizing the non-liberal practices of others. Beginning in the nineteenth century, Americans regularly denounced European persecutions of one kind or another.[34] In the nineteenth century the United States was not strong enough to do anything about abuses of human rights; in the twentieth it was, and did—or at least tried to.

Americans as well as others were exposed to human rights violations, mayhem, bloodshed, and suffering through television, which created a constituency to act to stop them.[35] Contrary to what was believed within the American government, however, this constituency was not all-powerful. Public officials were not pushed into dispatching armed forces abroad for humanitarian purposes by an irresistible tide of public opinion.[36] For none of the post-Cold War American humanitarian interventions did there exist majority support in the United States. To the contrary, it was not possible to mobilize public support for the exertions necessary to meet the goals that these same officials proclaimed for the interventions they launched. So the goals were not met.

Heart-rending though the television pictures were, the American public and its elected representatives displayed no enthusiasm for spending anything beyond very modest sums of money to rescue beleaguered peoples in the world's periphery. After the deaths of eighteen American soldiers in Somalia in 1993 triggered a public backlash against the mission that compelled its termination, the American government operated according to an unwritten but clearly established rule for the shedding of blood in humanitarian missions. The maximum number of politically allowable American deaths was zero.[37]

The language of foreign policy discourse in the United States was revealing. Values-based interventions were distinguished from the Cold War military operations launched on behalf of interests. "Interests" involved whatever affected Americans; "vital" interests were matters of life and death. "Values" affected other people. Not surprisingly, Americans were willing to do more and pay more to assure their own safety than the safety of others. In 1796, Charles Cotesworth Pinckney, the American ambassador to France, faced with French demands for payment as compensation for the signing of a treaty with Great Britain, which the French considered a renunciation of an American diplomatic commitment to Paris, uttered the words taught to schoolchildren thereafter as the essence of American international principle: "Millions for defense but not one cent for tribute." On the evidence of the Cold War, and then of the first post-Cold War decade, Americans were prepared to spend billions for security but very little money and no blood at all for good deeds.[38]

This preference conformed to what seems to be a more or less universal principle of moral economy, according to which social distance and the willingness to pay costs are inversely related: The greater the first, the more modest the second. Virtually everywhere human beings are willing to do more for themselves than for others, more for their families than for their communities, more for their communities than for their countries, and more for their own countries than for other ones.[39]

Since the policies of liberal political communities tend to reflect the preferences of their citizens, the American reluctance to intervene, and, when it did intervene, the reluctance to act forcefully enough to achieve the goals that its government had proclaimed, could be counted a consequence of ordinary political liberalism. During the Cold War the United States was no less liberal politically but had nonetheless been willing to pay substantial costs for military interventions far from home. Then, however, the distant places to which troops were sent seemed connected to the well-being of the American homeland itself, and the interventions were deemed acts of self-defense. The end of the Cold War disconnected the core from most of the periphery.

The point may be illustrated by comparing two Caribbean invasions, ten years apart, in which the United States sought to remove an unfriendly government: the Reagan administration's dispatch of forces to Grenada in 1983 and the Clinton administration's efforts to intervene in Haiti in 1994. By most criteria Haiti qualifies as the more important of the two to the United States. It was larger, closer, and, unlike Grenada, a source of refugees as well as a country the United States had occupied and governed from 1915 to 1934. Yet the invasion of Grenada enjoyed more public support: Nineteen Americans died securing the tiny island. The Clinton administration conducted the Haiti operation so as to insure that not a single American was killed.

The reason for the difference is that the first invasion was part of the Cold War. The radical Grenadan government was aligned with Cuba, an ally of the Soviet Union, with which the United States was locked in a mortal struggle. The intervention in Grenada could thus be portrayed as an act of self-defense, albeit at several removes. The invasion of Haiti could not be so defined. Grenada affected American interests. Haiti transgressed American values.[40]

Americans proved willing, in the first post-Cold War decade, to pay the costs of reassurance in Europe and East Asia and of deterrence in the Taiwan Strait and on the Korean peninsula. But they would not pay the costs of bringing stability to Africa, democracy to Haiti, or political pluralism to the Balkans—nor would anyone else.[41]

THE GREAT DISCONNECTION

T HE NEW RELATIONSHIP between the world's core and its periphery made for an ironic feature of the post-Cold War world. The ancient but not honorable practice of intervention in the internal affairs of other sovereign states became easier in theory but more difficult in practice. A broad loophole was opened in international law to make intervention more legitimate, but at the same time the countries with the power to intervene became less willing to march through it. While the demand for intervention rose, the supply fell. It was as if the hunting of deer in a game preserve, once considered poaching, had been made legal but the hunters had meanwhile become vegetarians and had put away their guns.

The cause of these offsetting reversals in theory and practice was the same as the cause of the instability that had put the question of intervention high on the international agenda in the first place: the end of the Cold War. The disappearance of the global ideological conflict that had dominated the second half of the twentieth century made violations of Westphalian sovereignty less dangerous internationally, but also less appealing domestically.[42] The end of the Cold War thus dealt a double blow to the afflicted regions of the periphery. It contributed both to the outbreaks of disorder there and to the reluctance of the core countries to extinguish the violence.

In the post-Cold War era, when the world was more closely and tightly connected in economic terms than in the past, when cultural innovations in the core—both products and ideas, hardware and software—diffused farther and faster than ever before, in matters of security the planet was more *dis*connected than it had been during the Cold War. In this sense the post-Cold War world was a larger version of the Mediterranean region: peaceful, prosperous Europe to the north, impoverished, chaotic Africa to the south, and a large body of water between them shielding the fortunate Europeans from most of the effects of Africa's internal disorders.

The picture of the world's peaceful, prosperous core entirely aloof from and wholly uninterested in the planet's wretched and turbulent periphery needs to be qualified in two important ways. First, the post-Cold War disconnection did not mean that the post-Cold War disorders in the world's periphery were destined to grow in number, or that where they had broken out they would continue indefinitely. While in theory the number of groups eligible to demand their own sovereign states was enormous, in practice the number likely to do so was limited. The number of conflicts arising from such efforts actually *decreased* in the second half of the 1990s. Whether through exhaustion, or a willingness to compromise, or a process of learning from the experience of others, or all three, conflicts were settled without the large-scale injection of foreign military forces.[43] Second, when the core did turn its attention to the periphery the dominant attitude was not exclusively pity. One region continued to provoke fear. The fear stemmed from three dangers to the well-being of the core countries, each of them evoked by the attacks on New York and Washington of September 11, 2001: an interruption in the world's supply of oil; the spread of nuclear weapons; and the practice of terrorism. The region from which these threats emanate is the Middle East.

CHAPTER SEVEN

The Dragons' Lair

T HE TERRIBLE EVENTS of September 11, 2001, evoked memories of another deadly assault on the United States sixty years earlier: the Japanese attack on the American fleet at Pearl Harbor, Hawaii, on December 7, 1941. In the magnitude of their historical impact the two events differed dramatically. The first was part of the bloodiest and most destructive war in human history, the outcome of which reordered the world and altered America's place in it. The consequences of the second were far more modest, but did bear some resemblance to those of the first: The American public rallied in support of a foreign war—this one in Afghanistan.

There is another instructive parallel between December 7, 1941, and September 11, 2001. Both attacks shocked the United States and the world, yet forewarnings were abundant in each case. The United States was sharply at odds with Japan over Japanese policies in Asia, and Tokyo had made plain that it regarded the oil embargo that Washington had imposed earlier that year, in response to the continuing Japanese occupation of China, as a severe provocation.

Similarly, the terrorist group responsible for the September 11 attacks, Al Qaeda, had claimed responsibility for three previous attacks on Americans outside the United States: against American soldiers in Somalia in October 1993; against American embassies in Kenya and Tanzania on August 7, 1998; and against the USS *Cole*, an American naval vessel anchored outside Aden, the capital of Yemen, on October 12, 2000.

The attacks of September 11 should not have shocked the world as they did for yet another reason. The personnel, the resources, and the motivation for them all came from a part of the world well recognized as the source of the greatest post-Cold War threats to the world's core: the largely Muslim part of Eurasia stretching from the eastern Mediterranean to the Indian Ocean.

On early European maps, unexplored parts of the world thought to be dangerous were marked by the Latin warning "*Cave, hic dragones*"—Beware, here there are dragons. At the outset of the twenty-first century, the region deserving of that phrase was the Middle East. But unlike the European mariners of centuries before, the countries of the core knew precisely what dangers lurked there, though they could not easily avoid them.

OIL

A s the post-Cold War era began, the countries of the Middle East exhibited the familiar features of the world's periphery. Weaker than the states of the core, the societies there faced the prospect of becoming increasingly poor as well, squeezed as they were between high rates of birth and low rates of economic growth. In the post-Cold War period, as throughout the modern era, the region was a net importer of political and economic innovations.[1] For parts of the modern period the Western core had controlled much of the region, through imperial rule or mandates established by international bodies such as the League of Nations. Borders were often drawn arbitrarily, laying the basis for the familiar kind of post-Cold War instability in which dissatisfied minorities chafe at the political arrangements with which they have been saddled. But the Middle East was different from the rest of the periphery in one immensely consequential way. What made it important was its oil. Two-thirds of the world's proven petroleum reserves were to be found in countries with borders on the Persian Gulf.[2] Oil made the Middle East the one region that combined the importance of the core with the volatility of the periphery.

During the Cold War, oil gave the countries of the Middle East a measure of independence from and indeed leverage against the

United States and the Soviet Union, despite the intervention of both superpowers in the political and military affairs of the region. It gave Middle Eastern rulers the means to appease or repress discontented groups without having to rely on the generosity of the core powers, and it made the Middle East more significant to the core than any other region in the world's periphery, so significant that the core powers were prepared to go to war to protect their interests there.

The significance of oil was very much a feature of the modern age. It owed its value to the industrial revolution. At the heart of that great change in the economic life of the planet was the harnessing of inanimate sources of power. Of these oil was, for most of the twentieth century (and into the twenty-first), the most prominent. The modern age was the machine age and the world's machines ran on oil, the importance of which for the economic activity of the planet could therefore scarcely be overstated. Oil came to be known as "black gold" and like gold it was a kind of universal currency, exchangeable almost anywhere for almost anything. Oil was also known as "the blood of the earth," and it was almost as vital to the arteries of industrial economies as is blood to the human body. A better comparison of this kind, however, was with oxygen, something just as important but externally supplied. Oil, like oxygen, could be cut off, imposing the economic equivalent of suffocation. Economic strangulation, the withholding of supplies of oil from the Persian Gulf region, was a great strategic danger to the Western liberal core during the Cold War;[3] it remained a danger, although a less acute one, after the Cold War's end.

The West faced two associated dangers: that these reserves would come under the control of people who would place unacceptable conditions on their continued flow to the West, thereby subjecting the West to blackmail; and that those who controlled the oil would accumulate great wealth from its sale that would underwrite political and military power that they would turn against the West itself. So important was the oil of the Persian Gulf that during the Cold War the Western powers declared themselves ready to fight to assure access to it; at the end of the Cold War they actually did go to war for this purpose.[4] Oil made the Middle East, in strategic terms, effectively *part* of the core, like a reservoir supplying a city's drinking water. Separated from the world's centers of wealth, power, and innovation by geography, the region was connected by economics, and the connection was on vivid display during the 1970s.

Twice in that decade sudden decreases in the production of oil triggered sharp increases in the world price, which rose twelvefold in ten years.[5] This in turn led to the world's worst economic downturn since the great depression of the 1930s. The two oil shocks, the first occasioned by a partial embargo imposed by the Arab oil-exporting states in response to the Arab-Israeli war of October 1973, the second by the collapse of Iranian production brought about by the overthrow of that country's pro-Western ruler, the Shah, in 1979, introduced to the world the unanticipated and unwelcome economic syndrome known as "stagflation": Output dropped while prices rose. The oil shocks also produced a large transfer of wealth from the oil-consuming to the oil-producing countries.[6]

The conditions that had made the oil shocks possible eased in the 1980s and 1990s. The supply of oil increased and demand for it weakened, less by virtue of the policies adopted by governments than through social and economic developments that operated over the longer term, and in particular the normal workings of the free market. The rise in the price of oil created economic incentives to find more of it and technology improved the techniques of both discovery and recovery. At the same time, more expensive oil gave consumers an incentive to use less of it.

As supplies expanded and the rate of growth of consumption declined, the price of oil drifted downward, a trend reinforced by the members of the oil cartel, the Organization of Petroleum Exporting Countries (OPEC), who began to exceed the production limits to which they had previously agreed, limits that restricted the world's supply and thus propped up the price.

A change in the character of industrial production in Western Europe, the United States, and Japan also eased the pressure on the price of oil. In the 1980s and 1990s new products and new processes based on new technologies came into being, making Western industry less dependent on energy than it had been for the previous half-century.[7] Even so, the core countries could not dispense with it altogether. Indeed, as output rose, so too did oil imports, although not as rapidly as in the past.[8] And economic growth in other parts of the world—especially in East Asia and Southeast Asia—required increasing supplies of oil, which could most readily come from the Middle East.[9] So the region retained its status as part of the core geopolitically. The chief danger to Western interests in and from the Middle East also changed after the 1970s, from sharply escalating prices to the kind of threat historically familiar in Europe.

INTERNATIONAL CONFLICT

TWO LOCAL POWERS made bids to dominate the Middle East in the waning years of the Cold War. Each of these challenges—by Iran at the beginning of the 1980s and by Iraq at the outset of the 1990s—led to a major war in which the challenger was battered. As with the would-be European hegemons of the modern era, each of the two bids for mastery of the Middle East had an ideological basis. Iran sought to export its Islamic revolution to the other countries of the region. Iraq tried to rally support for its confrontation with the West, triggered by its seizure of neighboring Kuwait, by claiming to be defending the cause of Arab nationalism.

Like the militant creeds that fueled the French, German, and Soviet efforts to dominate Europe, these two sets of ideas had revolutionary implications. They challenged the existing systems of government within sovereign states and the distribution of power in the region. Like Europe's revolutionary ideologies, the countries propounding them intended to use them to establish their own political dominance. But if the two ideologies were Western in form, they were non-Western in content. At the center of both was Islam, explicitly in the case of Iran, implicitly in the Iraqi case because what the various Arab states had in common, what made binding them together in a single, powerful political community seem a plausible goal, was their common Islamic faith.[10]

If the ideologies on which Iran and Iraq based their claims to primacy in the Middle East were Western in form and non-Western in content, they were *anti*-Western in aspiration. Among their aims was to reduce Western power and, if possible, to eliminate the Western presence in the Middle East. The Iranian and Iraqi ideological offensives targeted local regimes closely associated with the West and, above all, with the United States. Both Iran's Islamic revolution and the Arab nationalism on which Iraq sought to capitalize drew much of their popularity from local resentment of the liberal core powers, a sentiment that had its roots in the modern encounter between the Middle East and the West.

The Middle East is home to three great non-Western civilizations: the Persian, the Arab, and the Turkish. Each flourished before the modern era. Between the eleventh and the sixteenth centuries they made the region, along with China, the most advanced in the world. It was there, not in Europe, that great military power resided, that great wealth was generated, that great innovations were created for other, less sophisticated peoples to adopt. In the modern era the West caught up with the Middle East and then surpassed it. In the twentieth century, between the two world wars, Great Britain and France governed much of the Arab world directly.[11] After 1945 the European empires receded but the United States emerged as a major regional presence, the patron of the monarchies that controlled so much of the world's oil.

To the rise of the West the three great civilizations reacted, in the twentieth century, in different ways. Turkey, a powerful antagonist of Christian Europe from the fifteenth century to the nineteenth, concluded, after World War I, that it could neither overcome nor resist the West and so decided to join it. From the ruins of the Ottoman empire there emerged in Anatolia a secular Turkish republic. After World War II Turkey was intermittently democratic, an integral part of NATO, and an aspiring member of the European economic community.

The impulse for accommodation with and assimilation to the West was powerful in the Persian and Arab worlds as well, but so, too, was the opposite political current, the determination to resist. That determination gave impetus to the Iranian revolution and to the pan-Arab movement, the heyday of which lasted from 1956 to 1967 under the leadership of Egypt's Gamal Abdel Nasser and that Saddam Hussein sought to revive for his own purposes in the 1990s.[12]

The Iranian ruler overthrown by the Islamic revolution, Shah Mohammed Reza Pahlavi, was a figure familiar from the first century of the modern period: a modernizing monarch. He attempted to build a modern economy within the framework of traditional political authority. The revolution that removed him was led by Islamic clerics who resembled another familiar historical type from the modern age. They were revolutionaries, like the men who made the French and Russian revolutions. They aspired to construct an entirely different social and political order, although in the Iranian case the basis of that order was to be the essence of tradition: religion. The clerics' revolutionary Islamic principles could, they confidently believed, be applied to the Muslim countries throughout the Middle East. They considered the regimes governing these countries, many of them pro-Western and none of them committed to the principles of Islam in the manner the Iranians thought appropriate, to be illegitimate. The new Iranian regime therefore threatened all the other countries of the region.

One of these countries confronted the Iranian revolution directly. Iraq had reason to feel threatened. It shared a border with Iran and part of its population adhered to the Shia branch of Islam, which predominated in Iran and the traditions of which formed the basis of the Islamic republic there. Iraq was big enough, powerful enough, and wealthy enough to believe that it could stand up to its more populous neighbor. Its ruler, Saddam Hussein, considered the mission of opposing the Iranian revolution to be in keeping with what he deemed his rightful status as the leader of the Arab world.

When Iraq attacked Iran in September 1980, Saddam expected a quick, cheap victory. Instead, the war dragged on for eight years and claimed between 150,000 and 350,000 Iraqi lives and 450,000 to 750,000 Iranian lives. Caught off guard at first, Iran recovered its bearings, took the initiative, and for most of the conflict had the upper hand; but the Iranian forces, although numerous and in the beginning highly motivated, were unable to win a decisive victory. The war ended in stalemate, with both sides exhausted. The Islamic revolution remained in power in Iran but its example no longer attracted or threatened its neighbors. The war had drained it of its expansive energy. The monarchs of the region, with their subterranean oil wealth, no longer felt vulnerable to it. But this was not the end of challenges to the political arrangements of the Middle East. On the heels of the Iran-Iraq war came another, pitting an international coalition against Iraq itself.

The origins of the Gulf War of 1991 lay in the heavy costs Iraq had had to pay for its war with Iran, as well as in the psyche of Saddam Hussein. He ordered the invasion of Kuwait in August 1990 because he needed money to rebuild his country and Kuwait, with its oil wealth, was the equivalent of an unguarded bank.[13] The immediate motive for the invasion was thus as old as organized social life. It was a raid for plunder of the kind launched by the strong and the greedy from time immemorial. The invasion was also in keeping with Saddam's ambition to lead the Arab world, dominate the Middle East, and defy the powers of the world's liberal core. The personality of the Iraqi dictator was composed of megalomania, cruelty, and cunning, a combination that proved deadly for the people of Iraq and dangerous for the region as a whole.*

The platform for his bid for regional dominance was pan-Arabism, the idea that the Arab people constitute a single nation, that they rightfully belong within a single political jurisdiction, and that their division into different sovereign states came about through a nefarious Western scheme to weaken them. The leading twentieth-century champion of the cause of pan-Arabism was Nasser, an army colonel who seized power in Egypt in 1952 and ruled the country

---

*Like Fidel Castro of Cuba and Kim Jong-il of North Korea, Saddam perpetuated a particularly grotesque kind of regime into the post-Cold War period. Having once professed an ideology, all three governments came to rest on a cult of personality, with power residing in a single man and his family. All were examples, in Bernard Lewis's phrase, of a political oxymoron: "hereditary revolutionary leadership" (Lewis, *The Multiple Identities of the Middle East*, New York: Schocken Books, 1968, p. 97). In all three, the disappearance of the Cold War facade of ideology left sheer repression as the basis for their rule. All three were international pariahs and a common consequence of their rule was deprivation: chronic shortages in Cuba, hunger in Iraq, actual starvation in North Korea. Of interest to connoisseurs of political exotica, they seemed, in the wake of the first post-Cold War decade, on their way to extinction—although when it would arrive and whether the arrival would be peaceful was uncertain in each case. Iraq lacked one asset that enabled the other two regimes to stay in power. It was neither wholly nor partly surrounded by water. It had, however, a different asset, relevant to survival, that they lacked: oil. Saddam's regime managed to sell enough petroleum to keep itself in power despite the limits imposed on its sale by the UN in the wake of the Gulf War, which were in place during the first post-Cold War decade.

until his death in 1970. The issue that he used to generate enthusiasm for the pan-Arab cause and his own leadership of it, which ultimately brought an end to his regional ambitions but that Saddam, too, tried to exploit in the 1990s, was the Arab-Israeli conflict.

That conflict began, after World War I, as a communal struggle between Arabs and Jews in the British-controlled former Ottoman province of Palestine. From 1967 onward it was a dispute about the disposition of the territories that Israel had captured from Egypt, Syria, and Jordan in the war of June of that year. The two phases were connected by the crucial event in the conflict, the war of 1948. For Israel this was a war of independence. The United Nations had voted to establish a Jewish state (alongside an Arab one) in what had been British Palestine, but Israel was attacked by its Arab neighbors immediately after it declared independence. In the wake of the Arab defeat, steadfast opposition to Israel became integral to such legitimacy as the Arab governments enjoyed among the people they governed.

The Arab regimes portrayed Israel's very existence as another chapter in the Western assault on, and humiliation of, the Arab peoples of the Middle East.* The Jewish state came to have something like the symbolic resonance in Arab societies that Beijing's claim on Taiwan had in China. It was the obligation of the Arabs to remove it, even as they had forced the end of the Crusader kingdoms in the Middle Ages. To this project, Nasser in particular emphasized, Arab unity (not surprisingly under his leadership) was indispensable. The anti-Israel sentiment that Nasser helped to arouse pushed him into a war in 1967 that he lost decisively. That defeat put an end to his larger aspirations in the same way that the outcome of the Iran-Iraq conflict blunted the ideological drive of Iran's Islamic republic.

*In fact Israel was arguably the most successful of all the "new nations" that emerged from imperial rule to independence in the wake of World War II. It forged a powerful national identity and maintained an impressively democratic political system while organizing successful resistance to the assaults of its neighbors. Amid all this Israel had achieved, by the dawn of the twenty-first century, a standard of living comparable to that of the countries of the Western liberal core despite the absence of natural resources and the obligation to absorb immigrants numbering several times its original population. It was thus a standing reproach to its neighbors because it was a living reminder of their far more modest accomplishments in absorbing and making use of the fruits of the two great modern revolutions.

Pan-Arab sentiment was weaker but not entirely extinct by the 1990s and Saddam tried to use it for his own ends. He claimed that his assault on Kuwait was part of a program to liberate Palestine from the Jews. But Saddam's bid for mastery of the Middle East failed. A broad multinational coalition was assembled to oppose the Iraqi occupation of Kuwait, spearheaded by the military power of the United States, and it routed the Iraqi army in March 1991— although Saddam himself survived the defeat to remain in power.

The Gulf War was a textbook case of an international public good provided chiefly through the leadership of the most powerful member of the international community. The United States saw a major interest in reversing the invasion of Kuwait and reducing Saddam's power. Had his gambit succeeded he would have controlled directly the considerable oil reserves of Iraq and Kuwait and indirectly, through intimidation, the even larger petroleum deposits of Kuwait's neighbor Saudi Arabia. It was Saudi oil, above all, that the United States went to war to protect.[14] This goal was compelling enough to justify investing the diplomatic capital needed to assemble a broad coalition and to risk American lives by putting troops into combat.

The rest of the world was willing to join the coalition for a variety of reasons. For oil-consuming countries an economic interest was at stake. For countries of the periphery it was prudent to join an undertaking sponsored by the most powerful members of the international community. For the rulers of the Middle East it was a way to ensure that they would not live in a region dominated by Iraq. And for those who viewed foreign policy in moral terms, the invasion, occupation, and despoiling of an internationally recognized sovereign state was as clear a violation of international law as could be imagined.

Saddam's timing could not have been worse. He attacked Kuwait just as the Cold War was ending, which meant that the Soviet Union did not reflexively oppose the United States, as it might previously have been expected to do. To the contrary, Moscow ultimately joined the anti-Saddam coalition.[15] The war was close enough in time to the Cold War, however, that the forces the United States had built to wage that conflict were still at the ready,[16] and the habits and political arguments that made it possible to use them still resonated with the American public.

In the first post-Cold War decade the principal aim of Western policy in the Middle East was the same as Great Britain's traditional goal on the European continent: to prevent any one state from achieving political and military dominance. For most of the period between the sixteenth and the twentieth centuries the British were able to achieve their goal at a distance. The European powers balanced each other, with the help of judiciously placed diplomatic and financial assistance from Great Britain. Only occasionally did British troops fight on the continent.[17]

In the post-Cold War Middle East a full-fledged version of the policy of offshore balancing was not entirely feasible. The West could not depend on local powers to arrive by themselves at a military equilibrium that would safeguard the outward flow of oil. Iran and Iraq had been weakened by the wars of the 1980s and 1990s and remained hostile to each other, but both were also hostile to the West. Moreover, as weak as Iran and Iraq were, the monarchies of the Gulf, on which the industrial economies relied so heavily for oil, were weaker still. These regimes required support from the outside, as Western Europe had required protection from the Soviet Union during the Cold War.

Post-Cold War Western policy in the Gulf was, like Western policy in Europe during the Cold War, one of containment. Because it was aimed at two states simultaneously—Iraq and Iran—it came to be known as the policy of "dual containment."[18] The responsibility for carrying out the policy fell to the United States. It was another of the tasks of post-Cold War leadership for which there was no other plausible contender.

In Europe in the wake of the Cold War, deterrence had given way to reassurance; containment had been replaced by common security. But in the Middle East, the end of the Cold War did not change the American military mission, which remained deterrence for the purpose of containment. In this region the elements of common security were all but nonexistent. While neither Iran nor Iraq had the strength to launch another bid for mastery of the region, both retained, at least rhetorically, the ambition to do so and thus had to be deterred. But the signal feature of Cold War deterrence in Europe, the stationing of American troops in large numbers on a continuing basis in the territories of the countries to be protected, was politically awkward for the largest and most important of the regimes that needed protection, that of Saudi Arabia. So the United States built a large air base in the country, deployed a small American force far from the populated areas,[19] and maintained the capacity to intervene should the need arise.

As with all the other post-Cold War security tasks the United States undertook, protection of the Gulf oil had to meet another test. It had to be acceptable to an American public often skeptical of overseas commitments. The countries being protected did not qualify, by American standards, as models of admirable domestic governance. But in the wake of the Gulf War the American commitment to the oil monarchies of the Middle East aroused little public opposition at home because Americans seldom if ever heard about it.[20]

This instance of American international leadership also brought with it the familiar free-rider problem. Americans could wonder why the allies in the Gulf did not do more to defend themselves. Those countries were less populous than Iraq and Iran but considerably wealthier.[21] And Israel, heavily outnumbered by its adversaries, managed to survive and prosper without the assistance of any foreign troops.[22]

Americans might equally wonder why the countries of Western Europe and Japan, which depended more heavily on oil from the Gulf than did the United States and that had contributed personnel and financial and logistical support to the war against Saddam Hussein, did not bear a share of the burden of safeguarding that oil proportional to their interest in doing so.[23] In some cases, in fact, they pursued policies contrary to those the United States considered necessary for the security of the West's oil supplies. During the 1990s many European countries were more willing than the Americans to do business with the Islamic republic of Iran and to ease international pressure on Saddam Hussein.

The perpetuation of the post-Cold War arrangements for assuring the continuing stream of petroleum depended on these questions remaining unimportant to public opinion in the United States. Or, to the extent that the questions became important, it depended on their not undermining public acquiescence in the arrangements that marked the first post-Cold War decade. That, in turn, was likely to the extent that the costs, in blood and treasure, remained relatively modest, as they were in the first post-Cold War decade.

Iran and Iraq still threatened Western interests, but the form of the threat was not ideological subversion or direct military assault. It was, instead, the acquisition of a weapon the diffusion of which the countries of the core were anxious to prevent. The most pressing problem in the Middle East was one that, while not confined to the region, was particularly acute there: nuclear proliferation.

NUCLEAR PROLIFERATION

I F OIL WAS insignificant before the modern age, nuclear weapons were inconceivable. The atomic bomb harnessed, for military purposes, the ultimate source of power in the material world, the energy locked in the heart of matter itself, thereby producing a dramatic increase in the destructive power at the disposal of governments. A single nuclear weapon, detonated in a populated area, would wreak destruction on a scale exceeding virtually any flood, fire or earthquake in all of recorded history.

Nuclear weapons played what could be called a dialectical role in the international politics of the twentieth century, alternately disrupting and pacifying politics within the core. The only two nuclear shots fired in anger in the twentieth century, against the Japanese cities of Hiroshima and Nagasaki in August 1945, helped end World War II, the first round of the great global struggle between liberalism and illiberalism. In the second round, the Cold War, the accumulation of large stockpiles of these arms by the United States and the Soviet Union made their conflict initially more dangerous than it would have been without them, because each side could destroy the other, but ultimately more stable, because the understanding that this was so imposed caution on them both. Nuclear weapons prolonged the Cold War, since neither could afford to resolve it by force; but they also helped to end it by providing the basis for common security. But if nuclear weapons in the world's core contributed to the settlement of the political conflict there, the spread of these weapons beyond the core threatened both that settlement and the security of the core countries themselves, as in the plot of a Raymond Chandler novel in which a crime long forgotten or a scandal long suppressed surfaces to ruin the lives of people who believe they have left it far behind them.

Stopping the spread of nuclear weapons to the periphery was as important a goal for the Western liberal core in the post-Cold War period as assuring the flow of oil in the opposite direction. So powerful were these weapons that even a small number conferred a particularly vivid kind of power. Nuclear weapons were like the magic potion in Alice in Wonderland that made the heroine suddenly grow much larger. They put the possessor on a par with the most powerful members of the international system, for they made it possible to inflict the kind of damage on a society that had previously required the defeat of its army to achieve. With the appropriate means of delivery, the possessor of nuclear weapons became part of the security calculations of the countries it could reach.

To put it differently, nuclear weapons separated military might from what had always been its necessary underpinning: national strength. They allowed countries to skip all the stages previously necessary for amassing great military power. If the end of the Cold War disconnected the world's core from its periphery, the possession of nuclear weapons by peripheral governments reestablished that connection.

In the second half of the twentieth century, in the wake of the obliteration of Hiroshima and Nagasaki, the terrible radiation-induced physical debilities many of the survivors suffered, and the accumulation of enough weapons to destroy all human life on the planet, nuclear arms came to evoke widespread horror and revulsion. A taboo attached to them. Their use came to be regarded, by the century's end, as unthinkable, inhuman. Like cannibalism, it seemed unjustifiable in almost any circumstance or for almost any purpose. And in the fifty-five years from the end of World War II to the end of the twentieth century nuclear weapons were not used. To mark them as different from other instruments of warfare they received a special designation: "weapons of mass destruction."

Two other types of armaments were often included in this category: chemical and biological weapons.[24] Like nuclear arms, chemical weapons were the subject of a taboo,[25] although they had been used in combat, first during World War I and occasionally there-after.[26] But they were far less destructive than nuclear weapons. One reason they were little used in the wars of the twentieth century was that militarily they were not especially effective.

Biological weapons, which draw their toxic effects from live agents like viruses or bacteria, are more plausible weapons of mass destruction. Released into the air or infiltrated into a water supply, such agents are capable of killing hundreds of thousands of people. While they have the potential to wreak mass destruction, however, historically such attacks have done relatively little damage.[27]

Networks of rules, customs, and organizations were created during the Cold War to govern each of the three types of arms. The aim in each case was to restrict their distribution and, to the extent that this failed, to prevent their use. But only the spread of nuclear weapons had a special name, which made it seem a type of infectious disease: nuclear proliferation. Because nuclear proliferation had the unwelcome potential to reattach the core to the periphery, nuclear *non*proliferation ranked high on the post-Cold War agendas of the world's industrial democracies.

Like the rules and procedures for humanitarian intervention, which evolved in response to a new and disturbing international problem in the first post-Cold War decade, the nonproliferation system came into being during the Cold War in response to a new and pressing international challenge of that period. The heart of the system during the second half of the Cold War and afterward was the Nonproliferation Treaty (NPT) of 1968. Its aim was expressed in its name, and 186 countries had joined it by the turn of the new century. The NPT created the International Atomic Energy Agency (IAEA), which was charged with inspecting the nuclear power-generating facilities of the countries that were signatories, to make certain that these facilities were not being used for bomb-making. For the same purpose, countries that manufactured technology for nuclear power-generation that could also be used for fabricating weapons formed the Nuclear Suppliers' Group to monitor the diffusion of this "dual-use" equipment.[28] Roughly the same group of countries established the Missile Technology Control Regime in 1987, which set rules for the dissemination of the most effective and thus the most dangerous means for delivering nuclear weapons to distant targets.[29]

The NPT applied some of the principles of common security to nuclear weapons, and on a global rather than a regional basis. The renunciation of nuclear weapons that the Treaty mandated embodied the spirit of defense dominance: No one can be threatened by nonexistent nuclear weapons. And the IAEA was an agent of transparency, its mission to assure the world that the signatories to the NPT were fulfilling the promise they had made by signing it. The NPT resembled the late Cold War European arms control accords in yet another way. A change in attitude ordinarily preceded adherence to it. Its signatories did not renounce nuclear weapons because they signed the NPT; they signed the treaty because, for their own reasons, they had already decided to forgo these arms. Adhering to the NPT was a way of getting the benefits of nuclear abstinence by credibly assuring others of this decision.

In one important way the Nonproliferation Treaty did not, however, conform to the canons of common security. Its proscription against the possession of nuclear weapons was not universal. It included two classes of signatories: countries without nuclear weapons that promised not to acquire them and countries already possessing these weapons that were permitted, by the terms of the treaty, to keep them. Initially the United States, the Soviet Union, and Great Britain belonged to the second, privileged category, joined later by France and China.

The NPT was an unequal treaty, a mechanism by which the United States and the Soviet Union, its co-architects, sought to keep others from acquiring the bomb. The Americans, at least, were persuaded that this served the interest of the entire planet, believing that the more independent centers of nuclear control there were, the greater would be the chances that one of them would launch, deliberately or accidentally, a nuclear attack. It followed that the fewer nuclear-weapon states there were, the safer the world would be.[30]

Restricting the number of nuclear-armed states also enhanced the political and military advantages of those that already possessed these weapons, and during the Cold War the owners of the world's largest stockpiles of nuclear weapons were the United States and the Soviet Union. Whether or not nuclear proliferation would make the world less safe, it would certainly make the two of them less powerful, which was an important reason, if not the only one, that they

were willing to cooperate to try to stem it.[31] To meet the objection
that the NPT was a hypocritical exercise in perpetuating what the
government of India called "nuclear apartheid," the Treaty included
a promise that the nuclear-weapon states would work toward the
ultimate goal of eliminating their own weapons. But this was a cos-
metic rather than a binding part of the nonproliferation system.

For the purpose of restricting proliferation, potential proliferants
were divided informally into three categories:[32] those for which the
anti-proliferation policies of the core were designed to alleviate the
demand for nuclear weapons; those for which the emphasis was on
denying the supply of these weapons; and a third category, toward
the countries in which the Western liberal states adopted both
approaches but where the stakes for the West were lower than for
either of the other two.

The first category consisted of American allies. These were countries that had both the motive—a threat from a nuclear-armed
adversary—and the opportunity—the requisite technical competence—to acquire their own nuclear weapons but chose not to do so
because they received nuclear protection from the United States.
NATO and the Japanese-American Security Treaty were (and to a
lesser extent the Soviet-centered Communist coalition during the
Cold War had been) instruments of nonproliferation. While one of
the two aims of the American Cold War policy of double containment in Europe and Asia was to keep the Soviet Union from using
nuclear weapons, the other was to prevent Germany and Japan from
acquiring—or even from wanting—these weapons. The West Germans and the Japanese were willing to adhere to the NPT because
their need for nuclear protection was met by the United States.

The Cold War effort to promote nuclear abstinence by offering
alliance guarantees as a substitute for the weapons themselves did
not achieve universal success. China was not satisfied to take shelter
under the Soviet nuclear umbrella. Beijing wanted its own nuclear
weapons, and when the Soviet leadership reneged on a commitment
to provide one, the Chinese built a bomb themselves. Within the
Western camp the French also acquired their own nuclear weapons.
Their rationale was that they could not count on American nuclear
protection because, once the Soviet Union acquired the means to

strike the United States, defending France required risking a terrible retaliatory bombardment of North America. It was unreasonable, the French said, to expect Washington to risk the annihilation of New York in order to protect Paris.

But American guarantees did keep Germany and Japan non-nuclear, which was important for their full integration into the post-war core of Western liberal states, the strength of which, in turn, had a great deal to do with the outcome of the Cold War. Because the American alliances with Germany and Japan were justified by the Cold War, the end of that conflict put them in jeopardy, which threatened the major barrier to their acquisition of nuclear weapons. A major theme of the politics of security in Europe and East Asia in the first post-Cold War decade was therefore the effort, not always explicitly described as such, to keep in place the arrangements that relieved Germany and Japan of the nuclear temptation.

At the Cold War's end, the Soviet Union did not have the equivalents of Germany and Japan, genuine allies that, but for its protection, might well have felt compelled to acquire their own nuclear weapons and, if they had done so, would have rivaled the two major nuclear weapon states in power. But the collapse of the Soviet Union did aggravate, and complicate, the post-Cold War task of preventing the spread of nuclear weapons. It led to the weakening of the Soviet-era control on the nuclear material that had accumulated within the former Soviet borders and to the reduction of Moscow's leverage on the countries the nuclear ambitions of which were most worrisome to the West.

In the first post-Cold War decade, however, despite their ambitions, none of the nuclear undesirables succeeded in equipping itself with these armaments. The countries that did join the "nuclear club" belonged to a different category and were the objects of a different set of policies. That category was the orphans, and it included India, Pakistan, Israel, South Korea, Taiwan, Ukraine, and South Africa. They had several things in common.

All except Ukraine had had reason, during the Cold War, to contemplate seriously the acquisition of nuclear weapons, for they confronted threats for which nuclear weapons would be helpful, if not indispensable, to keep in check. In the wake of the Cold War, all had

some connection with the United States but none could feel confident of the degree of American nuclear protection that the NATO
allies and Japan enjoyed. Germany and Japan had been, in effect,
adopted by the United States. They were, for strategic purposes,
members of the family. Their territories enjoyed the same guarantee of
protection, according to what the American government said, as any
one of the fifty American states. The orphans, by contrast, had to
rely ultimately on their own resources to meet the threats they faced.

Their nuclear policies varied widely. By the beginning of the
1990s India and Pakistan had advanced nuclear weapon programs
but neither had explicitly tested a bomb.[33] In 1998 both did so. Israel
was widely believed to have a stockpile of bombs, which its government did not publicly acknowledge.[34] South Korea and Taiwan
began nuclear weapons programs in the 1970s but abandoned them
under American pressure.[35] Ukraine inherited part of the Soviet
Union's huge nuclear stockpile upon achieving independence in
1991 but ultimately returned the weapons to Russia, the Soviet successor state designated the legitimate repository of all such arms.
South Africa made a few bombs but, when a radical change occurred
in its internal politics with the abandonment of the policy of racial
apartheid, its government destroyed them.[36]

The United States opposed the acquisition of nuclear weapons by
each of the orphans. It provided military assistance and political support to each of them at one time or another but in no instance was
Washington willing to go so far as to offer an unconditional guarantee against the threat on which that interest was based.[37]

The United States did not ignore the orphans' strategic concerns.
Washington sought to help resolve, by diplomacy, the political issues
that gave rise to their nuclear ambitions. It maintained an ongoing
effort to broker a settlement between Israel and its Arab neighbors
and intermittently tried to mediate between India and Pakistan. It
convened negotiations with Ukraine and Russia that led to the transfer of Soviet-era nuclear weapons from one to the other. American
policies toward China and Korea, although they relied heavily on
deterrence, had as their ultimate aim the ending of the conflicts
between the mainland and Taiwan and between North and South
Korea. But while not offering the ultimate incentive, neither did the

United States resort to the most powerful sanction. It was not willing to use or threaten to use force to deny nuclear weapons to the orphans, as it was in the case of the third category of nuclear aspirants—the rogues.

In the case of the orphans, the denial of a nuclear arsenal was a less urgent matter because nuclear possession was less threatening than it was for either allies or rogues. The important difference between the orphans and the allies was geographic. The allies were located in the world's core, at the heart of the international system. Their acquisition of nuclear weapons would have changed the balance of military power where the stakes were highest. Like rearranging the foundations of a building, this risked sending the entire structure crashing to the ground and was therefore something to be avoided if at all possible.[38]

In the age of ballistic missiles, of course, distance could be overcome by technology. Any of the orphans could reach North America with a nuclear weapon if equipped with ballistic missiles of a suitable range, and several of these countries had active programs of ballistic missile development.[39] What set them apart from the rogues, what made their nuclear ambitions less disturbing to the countries of the core, was politics. It was the political uses to which they wished to put the nuclear arms they sought that distinguished, indeed defined, the third post-Cold War category of nuclear aspirants.

The idea of a "rogue state" comes, presumably, from the term "rogue elephant"—referring to an elephant that is no longer part of the herd and has adopted savage or destructive behavior. The political rogues were, similarly, both politically isolated and militarily dangerous.

The category of rogue states, which, like other political distinctions, was established by the liberal Western core, was not a large one. It included Iran, Iraq, North Korea, and, by some lights, Syria and Libya as well.[40] All but Iran had had a Cold War connection of some kind to the Soviet Union, which had once given Moscow a measure of influence over their governments that could be enlisted in the cause of nuclear restraint. With the collapse of the Soviet Union that influence, such as it was, evaporated: The rogues were the orphans of the losing side of the Cold War.

From the Western and particularly the American point of view, the major purpose of the nonproliferation system was to deny nuclear weapons to this small group. As with the allies and orphans, and as with the other post-Cold War international public goods, the United States assumed the largest share of this task. And nonproliferation was one international public good for which the American public displayed no ambivalence about cost. It paid for the eyes and ears of the nonproliferation system. The vast American intelligence-gathering apparatus, constructed during the Cold War to monitor the Soviet Union, was, in the wake of the Soviet collapse, increasingly trained on the nuclear activities of the rogues. It was the United States that sounded the alarm about the North Korean nuclear weapon program in the 1990s and kept track of the nuclear progress of Saddam Hussein's Iraq. Insofar as the system had teeth, these, too, were supplied mainly by the United States. In the war against Iraq in 1991, waged officially to oust its army from Kuwait, the coalition forces, led by the United States, took the opportunity to inflict severe damage on Baghdad's nuclear weapon program.[41] And the United States was prepared to go to war on the Korean peninsula in 1994 over the nuclear weapon program of North Korea.

In the first three decades of its existence, the nonproliferation system performed remarkably well. In 1963, five years before the NPT was signed, President John F. Kennedy predicted that there would be fifteen to twenty nuclear weapon states by 1975. Twenty-five years *after* the date he chose there were only seven overt nuclear powers, fewer than half the lower end of his estimate. None of the rogues had managed to obtain the bomb.

In the post-Cold War era, however, the same degree of success was not guaranteed. The forces in favor of the diffusion of nuclear armaments were persistent and far from feeble. Like the tide crashing regularly against a seawall, these forces might well, over time, erode the barriers erected against them no matter how scrupulously these were maintained.

Working against the man-made barriers to nuclear proliferation, after all, was the oldest and most relentless of social processes, indeed the motor of human history itself: the diffusion of innovations from the core to the periphery. Nuclear proliferation was only the most dramatic instance of one of the major trends of the twentieth century, the spread of innovations that narrowed the gap in power between core and periphery. The once-traditional peoples of the world beyond Western Europe adopted the modern state and the instruments of modern warfare in order to regain their sovereign independence. Nuclear weapons were simply the most powerful of these instruments.

They were not as readily copied or purchased as the tank or the machine gun. But although not simple, neither were the relevant technologies particularly new. By the dawn of the twenty-first century, the bomb was fifty-five years old, the ballistic missile only slightly younger. The physical principles on which the bomb was based were well known. Making one was a feat of engineering—difficult, but not impossible. Any country wishing to do so could learn a great deal of what it needed to know from open scientific literature. The same was true of ballistic missiles. It was an American habit to say, of a task not requiring much ingenuity or training, that it was "not rocket science." By the twenty-first century, even rocket science was no longer rocket science.

As with the political conflicts between China and Taiwan and between the two Koreas, the end of the Cold War aggravated the problem of nuclear proliferation. The collapse of the Soviet Union loosened what had been tight controls on an abundance of weapons and fissionable materials, and of personnel with the scientific and technical expertise to produce them. Not only were they free of the kinds of restrictions that only a totalitarian government could impose, but nuclear materials were also increasingly subject to international circulation for political and especially commercial purposes. China assisted the Pakistani nuclear weapon program for the oldest of geopolitical reasons: to oppose their common rival, India. But North Korea trafficked in ballistic missiles simply to earn money. For post-Soviet Russia, the export of missile technology and nuclear power plants was a source of income for a country that manufactured very few goods that others wanted to buy. The nonproliferation system was designed to prevent such transfers and had a respectable record on this score. But an instructive perspective on its long-term prospects was provided by the strenuous but at best incompletely successful effort to stop the cross-border transfer of another illegal commodity, narcotics. The Western war against illegal drugs demonstrated a near-universal rule of human affairs: Where there is a demand there will be a supply. No doubt governments could more readily monitor and suppress the supply of nuclear materials than the passage of cocaine from Latin America to the United States, but the general point was relevant.

Those countries that had successfully defied the nonproliferation system and acquired nuclear arms, moreover, had suffered no real penalty for having done so. None was made an international outcast. None found itself markedly less secure than before. To the contrary, the strategic goals for which the proliferators of the Cold War era sought and acquired the bomb were largely achieved. The destruction of Hiroshima and Nagasaki did help to persuade Japan to surrender in 1945. Nuclear weapons also helped the Soviet Union to become the military equal of the United States. They helped China avoid a military assault by either of the two superpowers. Their unacknowledged possession conferred advantages on Israel.[42] The threat to join the nuclear club brought North Korea political attention and economic assistance. Absent that threat, the regime of Kim Il-sung and his son might well have joined most of the world's other Marxist-Leninist regimes in the dustbin of history in the twentieth century.[43]

From the rogues' point of view, their quest for nuclear weapons was entirely rational. Saddam Hussein could well have reflected that, had he been in possession of a bomb before ordering the 1990 invasion of Kuwait, he might have been more successful. The decision by the United States and its coalition partners to evict his troops forcibly would have been more difficult to make if they had had to reckon with the possibility of a nuclear attack on their own forces. The Iraqi case bears on the most enduring argument in favor of becoming a nuclear power, that nuclear weapons empower the weak by permitting a country that has them to skip the normal stages in the accumulation of military power. They provide quick and easy access to something that is widely desired, which accounts both for their appeal and for the determination of the strong to prevent their spread. After all, of the almost 200 sovereign states of the international system, many more are weak than are strong.

Thus, in the wake of the Cold War, the countries of the liberal core—above all the United States—could not be certain of avoiding the occasional failure of the nonproliferation system, to which three broad responses were available. One was deterrence, a tried and true method of dealing with hostile nuclear-armed states. The second way of coping with nuclear-armed rogues was defense against their nuclear weapons. The United States and the Soviet Union had forsworn defense against the other's ballistic missiles through the 1972 ABM Treaty because each came to regard such defense as technically impossible and strategically unnecessary. The revival of American interest in ballistic missile defense in the wake of the Cold War and the December 2001 announcement that the United States was withdrawing from the ABM Treaty arose from the presumption that defending against rogues was both possible and necessary. It was considered possible because their nuclear arsenals were or would be small enough that effective defenses against them could be built, and necessary because the governments of these countries were erratic, unpredictable, and rash enough that deterrence might not restrain them as it had the Soviet Union. The third method of coping with the nuclear ambitions of rogue states was the preemptive use of force against their weapons. This would not be easy. Simply bombing the nuclear facilities of the target country might not suffice. Conquest and occupation might well be necessary. Whether the required political support for such an undertaking would be available in the international community, or within the Western core, or even in the United States, could not be predicted. But the American government served notice that it was prepared to contemplate preemption. In his State of the Union Address on January 29, 2002, President George W. Bush referred to three rogue states with nuclear aspirations, Iran, Iraq, and North Korea, as an "axis of evil," the governments of which "pose a grave and growing danger." In dealing with them, he said,

America will do what is necessary to ensure our nation's security. We'll be deliberate, yet time is not on our side. I will not wait on events, while dangers gather. I will not stand by, as peril draws closer and closer. The United States of America will not permit the world's most dangerous regimes to threaten us with the world's most destructive weapons.

Just how the nonproliferation system would operate when confronted with a nuclear-armed rogue was one of the questions that only the experience itself could answer. So was another, related question: What would be the impact of the actual military use of nuclear weapons (which the world managed to avoid for all of the twentieth century after the American raid on Nagasaki on August 9, 1945)? If this occurred outside the core, if there were a nuclear exchange between India and Pakistan, for example, it might be treated by the core in the same fashion as most of the post-Cold War disorders in the world's periphery. It might have the same impact as a typhoon in Bangladesh or a brutal war in Africa—appalling, indeed horrifying to the rest of the world, prompting offers of medical assistance or international mediation, or both, but not leading to basic changes in the security policies of the core powers. Such was the political and emotional resonance of nuclear weapons by the end of the twentieth century, however, that the use of even one had the potential to compel the recalculation of precisely these policies in ways that could not be foreseen.

The attacks of September 11, 2001, deadly though they were, did not involve weapons of mass destruction. Nor did they fundamentally alter the world of the twenty-first century. The United States treated them as acts of war, as indeed they were. But they were also examples of an age-old practice that, like oil and nuclear weapons, connected the world's periphery to its core. They were acts of terrorism.

TERRORISM

TERRORISTS DELIBERATELY attack non-combatants for political purposes. Although they are waging a form of armed conflict, they do not expect to achieve the traditional military aim of controlling territory. Instead, the goals they seek to achieve are psychological.

They wish to announce their presence and publicize their larger political aims. Acts of terror are "propaganda by deed."[44] In so doing they hope to rally people to their cause, whatever it is, and encourage those who have already embraced it. At the same time, they seek to demoralize their adversaries by causing them to experience fright, panic, and horror—that is, terror. Terrorists often wish to provoke a harsh reaction to their attacks, believing that this will expose their adversaries (usually governments) as brutal and thus polarize public sentiment, bringing people previously indifferent or hostile to them into their camp.[45]

The practice of terrorism is a very old one.[46] In the modern age the most common targets of terrorist attacks have been individual political leaders. Terrorists assassinated a Russian tsar, a French president, an Austrian empress, a Spanish prime minister, an Italian king, and an American president between 1881 and 1901. In the twentieth century the practice became even more common. In its final four decades more than sixty national leaders were killed.[47] Terrorism at the outset of the twenty-first century, however, differed from its earlier versions in two related and ominous ways.

First, terrorist attacks aimed at, and succeeded in, killing people in far larger numbers than previously. The attacks on New York and Washington, D.C., of September 11, 2001, which claimed almost 3,000 lives, qualified as the deadliest individual acts of terrorism ever committed. But in the preceding decade terrorist attacks, and the counter-terrorism campaigns they provoked, had killed tens of thousands of people in Kashmir, Algeria, and Sri Lanka.[48] Moreover, the moral considerations that had concerned earlier generations of terrorists had disappeared. In attacking officials of the tsarist regime, nineteenth-century Russian radicals had tried to avoid injuring innocent people.[49] By contrast, Osama bin Laden, the head of the Al Qaeda network that was responsible for the September 11 attacks, declared it not only permissible but a religious obligation to kill Americans wherever and whenever possible.[50]

Terrorists have operated in every part of the world but at the beginning of the twenty-first century much of the terrorist activity came from the Middle East. It was there that the September 11 attacks on the United States originated. Although the home base of Al Qaeda was Afghanistan, its leaders, its money, and the people who carried out the attacks all came from the Arab world. The rise of Al Qaeda was part of a larger trend, which went beyond the Middle East: an association between militant Islam and violence.

A disproportionate share of the world's conflicts at the outset of the twenty-first century involved Muslims.[51] The roots of this association lie in that faith's unhappy encounter with the modern world, especially in the Middle East. The people of the region had failed to master the great world-changing political and economic developments, the French Revolution and the industrial revolution, that have defined the modern period. In the words of the eminent scholar Bernard Lewis, "For vast numbers of Middle Easterners, Western-style economic methods brought poverty, Western-style political institutions brought tyranny, even Western-style warfare brought defeat."[52] These failures placed Middle Eastern societies far behind those of Europe and North America in wealth and power, a humiliating reversal of what the people of the region believed to be the natural, indeed the divinely ordained order of things. For the first millennium of its existence Islam had been a conquering faith. Starting with a handful of adherents on the Arabian peninsula in the seventh century, it came to dominate the Middle East and southern Europe and spread to Central, East and Southeast Asia as well as to Africa. But beginning in the seventeenth century, and accelerating in the nineteenth, Islam lost ground to the Christian West. To add insult to injury, from the West came ideas and practices that many Muslims found alien, threatening, and even blasphemous, including the separation of religious from political affairs and the insistence that women be accorded civil equality with men.

The attacks of September 11, 2001, thus shared with the Iraqi and Iranian bids for dominance in the region in the 1980s and 1990s a common motive: resentment of Western power and influence. From this followed a common aim: the expulsion from the Middle East of Western power and influence, especially that of the United States.[53] Bin Laden declared the principal *casus belli* of his war against the United States to be the presence of a small American military force on the Arabian peninsula.[54]

While Arab nationalist regimes like those of Saddam Hussein and Gamal Abdel Nasser governed according to secular principles (insofar as they had any principles at all), Al Qaeda drew its inspiration from a particular variant of Islam called Wahhabism, the tenets of which had long been championed by the rulers of Saudi Arabia.

The origins of the Saudi regime lie in an eighteenth-century alliance in the Arabian peninsula between the al-Saud clan and a religious crusader named Ibn Abd al-Wahhab. Al-Wahhab preached an uncompromising form of Islam that hearkened back to the form the faith had taken when it was founded in the seventh century. He considered subsequent additions and changes to be heretical and those who advocated them enemies of the faith.[55] By assuming responsibility for adopting and spreading the Wahhabi version of Islam the al-Saud clan could claim a basis for ruling the entire Arabian peninsula, over which it finally secured control in the 1920s. This version of Islam lent itself to hostility to the West.

Wahhabi Islam came to exert powerful global influence in the twentieth century for two reasons. First, it derived prestige throughout the Muslim world from the fact that the tribe that had embraced it controlled the sacred cities of Mecca and Medina: the Saudi monarch styled himself as the "custodian of the two holy shrines." Second, the ruling family came to dispose of fabulous wealth by virtue of the royalties it received from the oil beneath its sands. The Saudi monarchy used this money to propagate the Wahhabi brand of Islam.

Saudi money supported the religious schools in northwest Pakistan that trained many of the officials of the Taliban regime in Afghanistan that practiced religious repression throughout the country and offered its hospitality to the leaders of the Al Qaeda terrorist network. Saudi money also supported the mosques in Western Europe where Al Qaeda recruited Muslims for terrorist missions, including the attacks of September 11, 2001.

If the Saudi regime depended on the United States to protect it against foreign enemies, it relied upon its proclaimed fidelity to Wahhabi principles to justify its existence to a potentially more dangerous audience, the people it ruled. The need for such justification increased in the last decades of the twentieth century. The regime acquired a reputation, both at home and abroad, for personal corruption and economic incompetence. The five thousand princes of the house of Saud diverted much of the wealth from the steep rise in oil prices in the 1970s to their own personal uses and failed to launch the country on a path of economic growth. From the mid-1980s to the end of the century per capita income in the kingdom, while still comfortable by the standards of the Arab world, fell by forty percent. To compensate for, and to divert attention from, its own failings the regime emphasized its support for Wahhabism and militant Islam, the status of which was enhanced in some sectors of the Muslim world by its perceived role in the eviction of the Soviet Union from Afghanistan in the 1980s. Both encouraged the anti-Western passions that animated Al Qaeda.

Thus at the outset of the twenty-first century, the countries of the world's core relied for their economic lifeblood on a regime whose grip on power depended on the promotion of a set of religious principles that bred deep hostility to, and occasionally murderous assaults on, these same core countries. Nor were there good prospects in the short term either for ending Western dependence on Middle Eastern oil or for bringing a regime more devoted to liberal precepts to power in Arabia.

Throughout its history terrorism, while always threatening to its potential victims and sometimes shocking to the whole world, has seldom achieved its political aims. This was likewise true of the September 11, 2001, attacks, which provoked a determined counterattack by the United States that removed the Taliban government from power in Afghanistan and severely damaged the Al Qaeda network. Yet terrorism presented a greater threat in the twenty-first century than ever before. This was because of the availability of increasingly destructive methods of attack, which made possible assaults that could well claim many times the number of victims of September 11.

Of the three types of armaments conventionally designated "weapons of mass destruction"—nuclear, chemical, and biological— terrorist groups could reasonably aspire to acquire and use the latter two. Both could do enormous damage, especially biological agents; over the course of human history epidemics have killed more people than warfare. Terrorist groups were likely to be less inhibited in the use of these weapons than governments had proven to be in the twentieth century because terrorists would find less daunting their drawbacks: the difficulty of directing them with precision, the danger that those launching the attacks as well as their intended victims will succumb to them, and the likelihood of retaliation by the country being attacked. Terrorist groups such as Al Qaeda seek to kill as many people as possible, the deaths of their own members count as an acceptable price for doing so, and they present difficult targets for reprisals.

On March 20, 1995, the Japanese Aum Shinrikyo cult did launch a terrorist attack using chemical weapons, releasing deadly sarin gas on five trains in the Tokyo subway. Given the toxicity of the chemical compound, the toll was more modest than it might have been: twelve were killed and forty injured. In the camps and offices that Al Qaeda abandoned in Afghanistan when its Taliban protectors were ousted from power documents were found indicating an active interest in obtaining and using chemical weapons.

Nuclear weapons are more difficult to obtain than biological and especially chemical armaments. Fabricating a nuclear explosive is likely beyond the capacity of terrorist organizations—although purchasing one would not be.[56] But if nuclear proliferation is not necessarily a central part of the problem of terrorism, it is in important ways similar to it. The two pose similar twenty-first century challenges to the countries of the world's core.

Both are weapons of the weak, methods by which the inhabitants of the periphery can inflict damage on the distant and more powerful core. Both incorporate the spirit of ju-jitsu, employing the strengths of the core against it. Nuclear proliferation and twenty-first century terrorism make use of the products of scientific research and technological development, which have given the core countries their striking advantages in wealth and power over the rest of the world.[57]

Neither threat can be entirely abolished. Nuclear weapons cannot be disinvented. As for terrorism, insofar as it is rooted in social and political discontent, its causes are limitless; insofar as it is the expression of particular versions of the human personality, these are probably eternal. While the possibility of nuclear proliferation and terrorism cannot be entirely eliminated, however, these two threats can be substantially suppressed. The key to doing so in both cases is that familiar unit of international politics, the sovereign state.

It is a particular group of sovereign states—the rogues—that make the spread of nuclear weapons a potentially ominous development. It is consequently these states that the countries of the core, led by the United States, have exerted themselves to deprive of such armaments. Terrorist organizations need not be sovereign states. But they do need bases from which to operate, and such bases will be located within the borders of states, the governments of which will therefore be crucial to ending their activities.

Al Qaeda was reported to have cells operating in as many as fifty countries.[58] In most of them these cells operated without the knowledge, and against the wishes, of the local government, which could be enlisted to track down and eliminate them. A handful of governments, by contrast, knowingly and actively sponsored the terrorist organizations they harbored. It is no surprise that, at the outset of the twenty-first century, the list of rogue states and the list of terrorist-harboring states displayed considerable overlap.[59]

It was these countries (the majority of them—Iraq, Iran, Syria, and Libya—located in the Middle East) that posed the greatest problems of security to the world's core in the wake of the Cold War. The obvious solution to this general problem is to replace the governments of the countries in question with regimes opposed to launching or assisting attacks on others—that is, with regimes committed to the precepts of common security. This solution in principle raises two questions in practice: What form of government is most likely to embrace the norms of common security? And how can governments of this type be fostered? To those two questions, crucial for twenty-first-century security, the countries of the world's core had ready answers.

THE LIBERAL THEORY OF HISTORY

THE APPLICATION of the principles of common security would ameliorate the most serious post-Cold War security problems. Common security could assure that Russia and China did not molest their neighbors, it could dampen the conflicts in the Middle East and on the Korean peninsula, and it could reduce the threats posed by would-be nuclear rogues and terrorist-harboring governments.

Common security would not settle all of the lesser conflicts in the world's periphery because it assumes what was often lacking there: distinct, universally recognized sovereign states capable of negotiating agreements with one another. But even for conflicts over sovereignty, one feature of common security would enhance the chance of a settlement: the willingness to strike compromises politically, based on an aversion to settling conflicts militarily. There was no conflict anywhere for which the liberal approach to security was not at least potentially helpful.

Common security rests on a commitment to warlessness, which is related to the internal politics of the world's sovereign states. Domestic politics is the seedbed of common security in the sense that a common security order is created by a series of decisions by governments to adopt policies to overcome the force of international anarchy to which all are subject. And it is from liberal political systems that the demand for a liberal security policy first arises. This leads back to the apostle of the liberal approach to relations among sovereign states, Woodrow Wilson.

Wilson's vision had three parts: popular government, free trade, and restraints on arms. By the end of the Cold War the three parts of the Wilsonian triad had been modified and expanded. Popular government had become democracy, which, the world had learned, was not assured simply by ending imperial rule. Free trade had expanded to encompass market relations within as well as among sovereign states. Arms restraints had become the specific aims—the promotion of defense and transparency—at the heart of common security. Insofar as Wilson had a view of their relationship to one another he seems to have seen them as a kind of triptych, like the three-paneled icons of the Holy Family popular in Orthodox Christianity—closely related but detached and separable. For Wilson they were important above all in that each helped to promote the major purpose of the Paris Conference of 1919: peace. Wilson's approach was that of the man who wears both a belt and suspenders. The three parts of the triad made independent contributions to the same supreme goal. But the advent of all three, and the rise to a position of international dominance of democracy and free markets, raises these questions: Are liberal approaches to politics, economics, and security entirely independent of one another? Are they to be understood metaphorically as separate parts of a triptych, or instead as three legs of a tripod, with each reinforcing the other two? Or are the three even more closely connected than that? Does one lead to another?

These questions bear on the prospects for resolving post-Cold War conflicts through the establishment of common security arrangements. If one part of the triad did lead to, or at least encourage, another, this was a good omen for common security. At the outset of the twenty-first century the institutions of democracy and especially the practices of market economics were well-known, firmly established, and widely welcomed throughout the planet. Common security was none of these things. But its prospects were bright to the extent that democracy and market economics create the soil in which common security grows. And for this there was historical precedent.

Before the modern age the characteristically traditional approaches to politics, economics, and security—hereditary rule, mercantilist economics, and balance-of-power strategies—appeared at the same times and in the same places. Similarly, illiberal approaches clustered together in the twentieth century: Communism in power featured total control of political activity, central planning of economic activity, and an approach to international security that put war at its center. International liberalism has followed the same pattern. The countries where warlessness was most deeply ingrained, where the practice of common security was most legitimate, were the democratic market economies of the Western core.

In the Western core in the wake of the Cold War it was something like an article of faith that this affinity of the three parts of the Wilsonian triad was not an accident. Ironically, the prevailing view of the relationship among the liberal approaches resembled not the speeches of Woodrow Wilson but the writings of the man who inspired a great illiberal movement, Karl Marx.

Where Wilson had proposed policies for shaping the future, Marx offered a theory of how the march of historical events, over the course of the *longue durée*, was bound to shape it. Wilson had preferences, Marx made predictions. Wilson had a vision of how the world ought to be, Marx a theory of how it had to be and therefore would be. Marx's writings had the defining property of a theory—falsifiability. His forecasts were specific enough to be tested against subsequent events.

They turned out to be false. Marx asserted that the necessary workings of the market economies of Europe—that is, of capitalism—would inevitably destroy the capitalist system itself. There was, he said, an irreconcilable conflict between the two social classes that the industrial revolution had created, the bourgeoisie, the owners of capital, and the proletariat, the workers they hired. The all-important rate of profit would fall, causing the capitalists to squeeze the workers harder and harder. This would produce a large, oppressed, self-conscious, revolutionary proletariat. Ultimately the vast, angry, powerful army of oppressed workers would rise up and overthrow the system that had impoverished them.

Things did not work out that way. To the contrary, over the long term, albeit with periodic interruptions and an especially acute one in the 1930s, capitalism proved capable both of producing economic growth and of distributing its fruits broadly enough to underwrite political stability. Rather than a great grindstone pulverizing all within its scope, the market system turned out to be the rising tide that lifted the boats of almost everyone who rode on it. Whatever else may be said of them, none of the Communist regimes of the twentieth century came to power through the uprising of an impoverished, mobilized, ideologically committed working class.[60]

While the predictions of Marx the scientist of history were wrong, the observations of Marx the historian of nineteenth-century politics and economics were not inaccurate and one of them is particularly relevant to the post-Cold War period. Marx observed that the ongoing industrial revolution, in its different stages, was the powerful driving force in history, affecting not only the economic life of sovereign states but also the politics within and among these states.

In the wake of the Cold War there came to be, in the Western core, a widespread belief that history does indeed have a pattern, a shape, a direction, that rests on powerful connections among the three parts of the Wilsonian triad. Like Moliere's bourgeois gentleman, who did not realize until it was pointed out to him that he had been speaking prose all his life, the political classes of the Western liberal core did not think of themselves, as the new millennium began, as the adherents of a coherent view of the relationship among the past, the present, and the future. But they harbored, and professed, a series of beliefs that added up to what can best be described as a liberal theory of history.

It did not take the form familiar to Marx, nor was it an official ideology, a set of precepts that everyone was expected at least to profess to believe. It had the status of what the economist John Kenneth Galbraith termed "the conventional wisdom," a set of beliefs that are comfortable, widely accepted, virtually axiomatic, and thus not ordinarily subject to major challenge.[61] They recurred in official speeches in Western democracies, which are not occasions for stepping outside the bounds of the familiar. Public rhetoric in the liberal core is an exercise in saying what it is safe to say.

Nor, of course, was its content Marxist. It was liberal. The liberal theory of history held that the great liberal institutions and practices that had developed in the nineteenth century, to which Woodrow Wilson gave authoritative voice after World War I and that occupied a hegemonic position at the end of the Cold War, were organically connected, one to the other. Its origins lie in the ideas that influenced Wilson, in particular the prediction of the eighteenth-century German philosopher Immanuel Kant that peace would arrive when the political systems of sovereign states changed from monarchical to republican[62] and the conviction of influential nineteenth-century British liberals that free trade fostered peace. The twenty-first-century liberal theory was both more complicated and more confident than its intellectual ancestors. Indeed, it raised to new heights the optimism about the course of history to which the Anglo-American world was periodically subject.

The liberal theory of history began with a revised version of Kant's proposition that democracies are disposed to conduct their relations with other countries in a peaceful manner. If the key to peace is democracy, what makes sovereign states democratic? Here the contemporary version of liberal optimism included an innovation, a proposition not in wide currency until the end of the twentieth century: that political liberalism is the product of economic liberalism, that a market economy leads to democracy. Under what circumstances, then, do sovereign states adopt market practices and institutions? The answer to that question was the source of the kind of confidence that the liberal theory of history shared with the Marxist one. All sovereign states seek to install market economies because all seek to become prosperous. At the outset of the twenty-first century, the market was universally acknowledged to be the one true path to prosperity. The irresistible attraction to the market set in motion a virtuous chain reaction. Liberal economics begets liberal politics, which begets liberal security policies.

So confident was Marx that history was moving in the direction that he had specified (and that he favored) that the logical answer to the political question his Russian disciple Lenin posed—what is to be done?—was: nothing. The revolution would come by itself, unaided. But Marx and Lenin were impatient. They wished to hasten its arrival. Both founded political parties for this purpose and Lenin's seized power in Russia in 1917.

The comparably confident liberal theory of history also inspired an effort to help history along its foreordained path. The core's most powerful country sought to encourage and assist in the formation and functioning of free markets wherever possible, and especially in countries the international aspirations of which were not necessarily benign. In the first post-Cold War decade the United States devoted considerable political capital and financial resources to the task of establishing a market economy in newly non-Communist Russia.[63] Over the same period the thrust of the American approach to China shifted from harsh words of condemnation for its government's denial of political rights to warm words of support for its progress in installing market practices and institutions. Washington buttressed its encouraging words by keeping the American market open to Chinese products and paving the way for China's entry into the World Trade Organization. Rogue states suspected of troublesome nuclear aspirations received the same treatment. The United States opened negotiations for economic contacts with North Korea, tried to do the same with Iran, moved in the direction of a similar policy toward Cuba, and made it clear that Iraq could expect a similar opportunity once the regime of Saddam Hussein had ended. The Western Europeans and Japanese were, if anything, more disposed than the Amer-

icans to policies of economic "engagement" with potentially dangerous countries.

To be sure, the post-Cold War Western approach to China,
North Korea, and Iran did not consist solely of praise for free markets and invitations to trade. These countries were the objects of
more conventional policies of deterrence as well. During most of the
Cold War, however, the Western approach to its principal adversaries had been confined to deterrence. The goal was to balance the
opposing military power. In the post-Cold War period, in keeping
with the liberal theory of history, a more desirable goal had come to
seem feasible, a goal that, if achieved, would remove the need for
deterrence. That goal was conversion.

For its adherents the liberal theory of history implied that the
world was moving implacably in the direction they favored. Even
better, it opened the inviting prospect of doing well by doing good.
If trade with and investment in other countries promoted democracy
and peace abroad this was, after all, a bonus. The purpose of trade
and investment abroad was to generate wealth at home. The liberal
theory of history posited a heartening congruence between the values and the interests of the countries of the liberal core: Make
money and the world will be peaceful. Such a world could not help
but be powerfully attractive to those who believed in it, and it is a
well-known feature of human psychology that people tend to believe
what they wish to believe. The propositions that comprise the liberal
theory of history, the view that good things go together—that they
in fact engender one another—may seem too good to be true. But
that does not make them false.

Just as Marxism was born of the effort to make sense of the revolutionary changes that swept over nineteenth-century Europe, the
liberal theory of history was similarly an interpretation and an
extrapolation of the dramatic events of the last decade of the twentieth century. For the first of its propositions, the global popularity of
the market as the organizing principle of economic activity, there
was considerable evidence. Almost no country rejected the liberal
approach to economic management. Where a properly functioning
market economy was lacking, as was the case in much of the world's
periphery, this was almost always because the government could not,

rather than because it would not, sustain one. The broad interest in constructing markets meant that the second proposition of the liberal theory of history, the affinity between liberal economics and liberal politics, would be widely tested.

As for the third, the affinity between liberal domestic politics and liberal security policies, this was, in the final decades of the twentieth century, a subject of interest to a group in the core countries with something in common with Marx himself, who was one of the earliest and most influential systematic students of modern society. A century later social scientists with similar interests subjected the liberal theory of history's third part to rigorous scrutiny and produced a series of studies of the proposition that democracy is the engine driving the train of peace.

III

THE LIBERAL THEORY OF HISTORY

"Our country has not been lucky. Indeed, it was decided to carry out this Marxist experiment on us—fate pushed us precisely in this direction. In the end we proved that there is no place for this idea. It has simply pushed us off the path the world's civilized countries have taken."[1]

BORIS YELTSIN, 1991

*

The Democratic Peace

THE SYSTEMATIC STUDY of society began in the nineteenth century and by the twenty-first century thousands of people, the
majority of them in academic settings, were engaged in it. Social scientists aspire to accomplish for the social world what natural scientists have achieved for the natural world: to find regular, law-like
patterns, as basic science has done, and, on the basis of those patterns, make discoveries that contribute to human betterment in the
fashion of applied science.

Two fundamental differences between the social and the natural
worlds make this task difficult for social scientists. First, the units
they study exhibit far greater variety than the building blocks of
nature. Societies, political systems, and human beings are far more
different from one another than are atoms and molecules, genes and
chromosomes. Moreover, the units of the social world have minds of
their own. Unlike the work of natural scientists, therefore, theories
of human behavior can affect that behavior.

Despite these obstacles, in the last decade of the twentieth century
social scientists found a strong relationship between democratic politics at home and peaceful conduct abroad. For the politicians and
citizens of the democratic Western core this finding had a double
attraction. It was flattering, for it meant that the more the world
reproduced their own political arrangements the more tranquil it
would be; and it posited that their form of government, which they
valued and promoted for its own sake, had an additional, unexpected
benefit—as if cherry-topped cheesecake had turned out to be not
only tasty but nutritious.

Like the liberal theory of history, of which it was an integral part, the theory of the "democratic peace" seemed too good to be true. But the world at the beginning of the twenty-first century provided considerable evidence in favor of its validity.

ELECTIONS AND CONSTITUTIONS

IN THE SECOND HALF of the twentieth century the members of the world's core, the countries of Western Europe, North America, and Japan, came to identify themselves above all as democracies.[2] This was their common brand name, the banner under which they marched, and indeed, the defense of political freedom was an increasingly important war aim of the winning side in the three great conflicts of the twentieth century.[3] The Cold War may have been won on economic grounds but it was waged for political purposes. The liberal core opposed Communism to protect and promote democracy at home and abroad. The core countries called themselves, collectively, the free world, not the rich world.

Democracy was supremely important for the largest and strongest of these countries. While Great Britain and France had been sovereign states long before they became democracies, the United States had democratic features from its beginning. In fact, political liberalism provided the basis for establishing an independent republic in North America. The American nation was not made up of people who had lived together with a common language and a common faith for centuries. The citizens of the United States (or their forebears), with the conspicuous exceptions of North America's original inhabitants and people of African descent, arrived in the New World voluntarily from elsewhere for the purpose of taking advantage of its freedoms. Nothing had greater importance for American public life, and the American national identity, than democracy's supreme political value, liberty: The word appears on every American coin.

As the post–Cold War era began, the members of the world's core identified themselves not only as freedom-loving but also as peace-loving. This was a more recent development. For most of the twentieth century the democracies had been at war, usually with illiberal

CHAPTER EIGHT

powers, and they had histories of armed conflict going back centuries. By the dawn of the twenty-first century, however, the association of democratic governance at home with peaceful conduct abroad was a settled, central feature of the liberal theory of history, buttressed by academic scholarship that found the relationship between democracy and peace to be a strong one. Democratic countries, a series of empirical studies concluded, seldom if ever go to war with one another.[4]

The association between democracy and peace is plausible, if only in the negative sense that liberal governments are more likely, all other things being equal, to value peaceful conduct than fascist or Communist ones. To democracies war has seemed occasionally necessary but almost always regrettable and distasteful. Traditional regimes, by contrast, considered warfare to be a normal and acceptable instrument of statecraft, to be employed in order to enhance the power, prestige, and wealth of the monarch.[5] For the fascist and Communist regimes of the twentieth century, war was more than a convenience, more than merely one option among several in the conduct of statecraft: War was central to their purposes.

A pronounced and principled aversion to war is hardly a necessary consequence of liberal politics. The two oldest democracies, the United States and the United Kingdom, have long, often bloody, and largely successful military histories. But democracy is plainly the form of government most conducive to warlessness. Democracies are more receptive than others to the idea that war is worse than an inconvenience and more avoidable than a natural disaster, that it is a barbaric custom like slavery that can and should be abolished; or, alternatively, that it is a kind of public health problem that can be contained and eventually eradicated. It was in the wealthy democracies of the world's core that this sentiment gained broad acceptance in the second half of the twentieth century. It was in the core that it took root and from which it spread elsewhere—to the extent that, by the end of the first decade of the post-Cold War era, it had spread at all.

Plausible though it is, the connection between democracy and peace has two troubling gaps. First, the positive association between the two is clustered in the Cold War period, raising the possibility that the democratic peace is an artifact of the East-West rivalry rather than the expression of something fundamental to democracy. Democracies may have refrained from fighting each other in the second half of the twentieth century for a familiar reason that has nothing to do with political liberalism—because they were allied with each other against the greater Communist threat.[6] There is a second difficulty in equating democracy with peace. In the post-Cold War era, political liberalization in several parts of the world, notably on the territory of the former Yugoslavia, coincided with an upsurge in large-scale violence.[7]

These two gaps in the democratic peace theory can be closed by refining the definitions of both democracy and peace. In the Cold War, when the conflict with illiberalism dominated global political affairs, their meanings seemed perfectly straightforward: Democracy was the opposite, and the adversary, of Communism; peace was the absence of war. In the post-Cold War period the definitions came to be more complicated. Both liberal politics and the liberal approach to security can usefully be divided into two distinct parts. In the case of peace the relevant distinction is a product of the last decades of the twentieth century; in the case of democracy the division involves the recovery of a much older distinction.

Peace, at the outset of the twentieth century, came in two varieties. One was the traditional form, the absence of conflict due to an equilibrium of power. This was the principal basis for the respites from state-sponsored international violence that the world enjoyed from ancient times onward. The other was the liberal peace that the application of the precepts of common security produced. Unlike the first kind of peace, this second variety was not a byproduct of the normal workings of power politics. It arose instead from the deliberate substitution of liberal principles of international conduct for traditional ones. Traditional peace was based on prudence about the dangers of war, liberal peace on convictions concerning the virtues of peace. The first is a cease-fire; the second emerges from a permanent political settlement. Traditional peace arises from the calculation that war cannot be won, at least not at an acceptable cost; liberal peace stems from the belief that the fruits of victory are not worth having.

A truce based on military equilibrium scarcely requires democracy. Many such truces have been struck between undemocratic governments. For the post-Cold War era, therefore, the question at the heart of the democratic peace theory is this: Does democracy lend itself to the liberal kind of peace?[8] More specifically, are there features of liberal politics that particularly lend themselves to the principles and practices of common security? But the question requires further modification, for the liberal political systems of the Western core in the post-Cold War era combined *two* political values, which are not only separate but were regarded, for most of the modern era, as incompatible.

Democracy is the rule of the *demos*, the Greek word for the people. It is popular sovereignty. The people choose the government. Its origins lie in ancient Greece, in particular in the city-state of Athens in the fifth and fourth centuries before the common era, where the people not only chose but actually formed the government. The principle disappeared for more than twenty centuries until it was revived by the French Revolution,[9] and from that time and place it spread all over the world.

The mainstay of the liberal political tradition before the French Revolution was not, however, popular sovereignty. It was a different idea, the idea that the power of the ruler should be limited. This is the principle of constitutionalism, with the related concept of rights, which it is the purpose of constitutions to protect. The principle's origins lie in the ancient Roman republic. It was revived and carried into the modern world by Great Britain.

The crucial period in the rise of constitutionalism in Britain was the seventeenth century, when, after a civil war, a regicide, a protectorate, a restoration, and the eviction of one royal house and the establishment of another, it was finally settled that the Parliament had certain prerogatives that the monarch had to accept.[10] Liberty in the Anglo-American world came to be defined as constitutional restraints on the exercise of power and not, at least until the nineteenth century, as ever-wider popular participation in selecting the government.

The two principles address different questions. For popular sovereignty the question is: Who selects the rulers? For constitutionalism

it is: What can the rulers do (and what must they not do) once chosen? The first concerns politics, the second government. The two
are not mutually exclusive but until the twentieth century they were
considered incompatible in practice. Mass democracy, in fact, was
widely regarded as a threat to liberty. Greek democracy, it was commonly believed, had degenerated into tyranny, due in no small part
to the baleful influence of demagogues—eloquent, unscrupulous
orators who ignited the baser passions of the populace and led it
astray. Democracy would lead to mob rule, ending in dictatorship,
which would stamp out liberty.[11] The most influential liberal political writings of the nineteenth century, John Stuart Mill's anxious
essay *On Liberty* and Alexis de Tocqueville's travelogue-cum-political
sociology text *Democracy in America*, were devoted, each in its own
way, to exploring the political threat to liberty posed by the prospect of
widening political participation beyond the small circle of educated,
propertied males.[12]

In the nineteenth century, constitutionalism without democracy
was common and was in fact the political system of the world's two
leading liberal countries. In Great Britain, even after the second
major franchise-broadening Reform Act of 1867, only 7.7 percent of
the adult population had the right to vote.[13] In the United States, not
until after World War I were women eligible to vote and not until
the last third of the twentieth century were Americans of African
descent readily able to participate in elections.

In the twentieth century, contrary to the widespread fears of an
earlier age, liberty and political equality proved to be compatible in
Britain and the United States and throughout the Western core.[14]
Because they flourished simultaneously, and because liberalism's
great political opponent, Communist illiberalism, suppressed both,
the two ceased to be regarded as distinct, let alone opposed. By the
end of the twentieth century the word *democracy* connoted both.

But in the wake of the Cold War, the distinction was all too apparent in the world's periphery. The post-Cold War period was rich in
examples of countries that practiced popular sovereignty by holding
free elections but lacked constitutional restraints on the governments so elected. Post-Communist Russia was but one example
among many.[15] In the light of this distinction, the question at the

heart of the democratic peace theory may be rephrased yet again: What contributions do popular sovereignty and constitutional practices make to peace in its traditional and liberal forms?

CONSTITUTIONALISM AND PEACE

IN THE EARLY VERSIONS of the democratic peace theory it was popular sovereignty that prevented war. This was Immanuel Kant's view[16] and also Woodrow Wilson's. The mechanism of prevention was straightforward: The people would refuse to vote themselves into war. The reason for this was also straightforward: While the rulers reaped the gains from warfare, it was the people who invariably paid the price. If they were allowed to vote, therefore, they would reject what was, for them, invariably a losing proposition.[17]

The belief that the people could be counted on to oppose war became more plausible with the passage of time, for in the twentieth century the costs of warfare soared as the circle of those directly affected by it widened. In World War II more than half of the nearly fifty million people who died were noncombatants. In a nuclear war fought on an appreciable scale the ratio of civilian to military deaths would be even more grotesquely skewed toward the civilians. It was not accidental that, in the post-Cold War world, the countries considered by the core powers to be the most dangerously bellicose— the rogue states—were all ruled by dictators. One of them, Saddam Hussein, started the biggest wars of two different decades, the Iran-Iraq war of the 1980s and the Gulf War of the 1990s. In both cases he apparently made a personal decision to launch an attack that did not have to be approved and could not be blocked by anyone else.[18]

Popular sentiment is not always pacific. The American public was aroused in support of military action at the outbreak of the Spanish-American War in 1898. The Social Democratic members of the German parliament abandoned their anti-war principles and voted in favor of war in 1914. While these episodes occurred before the immense costs of twentieth-century warfare were apparent, in the wake of the Cold War public enthusiasm could be—and was— enlisted in support of war, albeit war of a particular type.

The impact of political liberalism on the propensity to fight depended on the motive for fighting, and on this count armed conflict came in two varieties, wars of aggression and wars of secession. The first, war as defined by international law, challenged the integrity of borders: One sovereign state attacked another, as Germany did in the two world wars and as Iraq attacked Kuwait in 1990. In the second case what was in dispute was where, precisely, borders should be located. Wars of secession, all too familiar in the post-Cold War period, belong to the modern period of history because their common goal was born with the modern age. While the two world wars and the Iraqi assault on Kuwait had motives that had been present at all stages of recorded history, the aims of the Balkan conflicts of the 1990s, like the purpose of the Greek war of independence against Ottoman Turkey in the 1820s, were unthinkable before the French Revolution.

Indeed, the second type of war qualified as something that, by the lights of the theory of the democratic peace, was not only unlikely but positively oxymoronic: a *liberal* war. It is liberal in that the cause of war is the national principle—the idea that nations should have their own states and that sovereign borders should therefore conform to the distribution of national populations, which is, in effect, the democratic formula for border determination. While compatible with political liberalism, the national principle is alien to the political traditions with which liberalism has competed in the modern age. Traditional states waged war to augment the power and wealth of the monarchy, illiberal regimes to bring more of the planet under the authority of fascism or Communism. It was the defeats the non-liberal ideologies suffered in the twentieth century that triggered many "liberal" wars by dissolving the multinational empires that were based on these ideologies. Wars of secession are even arguably compatible with a general aversion to war itself, since their aim, in the minds of those seeking to secede, is the one that even societies firmly in the grip of warlessness deem legitimate: self-defense. The United States had no compunction about waging war in Afghanistan in response to an attack on two of its cities. Secessionists are seeking to acquire or restore the sovereignty that they believe is rightfully theirs but has been wrongfully taken from or denied to them.

In the post-Cold War period political liberalism aggravated some national conflicts. On the territories of the collapsed Communist empires, and elsewhere in the post-Cold War world, nationalism proved a potent political force and thus an attractive basis for political appeals. Shaky new regimes reached for sources of political legitimacy. Politicians faced with the need to win elections searched for sources of popularity. In the competition for votes, office-seekers in more than one newly sovereign state strove to outbid one another in invoking nationalist claims. In this way some elections encouraged violence.*

In these circumstances democracy, defined as popular sovereignty, had the opposite effect of the one that Kant and Wilson had expected. Instead, the age-old critique of rule by the *demos* was borne out as demagogy led the manipulable mob in dangerous, destructive directions. But if one part of the political system widely known as democracy was a cause of war in the wake of the Cold War, the other part of the liberal political tradition provided an antidote to such conflicts.

If popular sovereignty can worsen the problem of war, constitutionalism, its partner in liberal government, can help to solve it. The letter and the spirit of constitutionalism, applied to relations among groups, is a source of peace. The principle of constitutionalism places limits on the power of governments, which in turn protects individuals. In practice such protection matters most to those who differ from, or are unpopular with, the majority of their fellow citizens: in other words, constitutionalism protects minorities. What is generally required to forestall or resolve a conflict over the location of borders—that is, over the distribution of sovereignty—is the

*This is a major theme of Jack Snyder, *From Voting to Violence: Democratization and Nationalist Conflict*, New York: W. W. Norton, 2000, which argues that in the former Yugoslavia and elsewhere unscrupulous elites from the old regime sought to keep power by arousing public hostility at other national groups, thereby deflecting attention from their own privileges and predations. The Communist elite of Serbia, led by Slobodan Milosevic, is perhaps the most egregious but by no means the only example.

When civil rights demonstrations began in the American South in the early 1960s, defenders of the system of racial segregation insisted that the local African-American population was satisfied with existing laws and customs but had been demagogically stirred up by people from other parts of the United States, whom they termed "outside agitators." Snyder places the blame for the nationalist violence of the post-Cold War period on *inside* agitators.

guarantee of protection for minority groups. One cause of conflict is the minority's fear that it will receive worse treatment than the members of the majority. This fear can be assuaged by constitutional guarantees to the contrary. Another source of unrest is a minority's demand for special treatment, which can be fulfilled by clearing political space within which the central government may not intrude, space reserved not simply for individuals but for the group as a whole: that is, by providing for group autonomy of some kind.[19]

Transposing the spirit and practice of constitutionalism from the individual to the group is the basis for the kind of political compromise that has regularly been proposed, beginning with the minority treaties at the Paris Peace Conference of 1919, to resolve the conflicts over borders to which the national principle has given rise. Sometimes constitutionalism has resolved such conflicts.[20]

More generally, the constitutional feature of liberal governments provides an antidote to wars of both aggression and secession by fostering habits of political conduct within sovereign states that, if carried over to relations among them, favor non-belligerence. Just as adults unconsciously reproduce the patterns of conduct first learned as children in their dealings with others, so too, according to the more recent, "cultural" explanation of the tendency of democracies to maintain peaceful relations with others, habits of conduct developed within liberal political systems are carried into the international arena, with pacific consequences.[21]

The hypothesis is sensible on its face. The two realms, the domestic and the international, are not, after all, hermetically sealed from one another. Political leaders operate simultaneously in both. Democratic norms and procedures can be expected to spill over, or to leak, from one to the other. Cultural diffusion, which accounts for so much historical change, occurs within as well as between societies. Indeed, the first is probably easier, more common, and more rapid than the second.

Two democratic habits are of particular relevance to peace, especially to its liberal, late-twentieth century form, common security. One is the presumption of compromise. Democracy does not abolish differences. Rather, it provides a framework for resolving or managing them without violence. A crucial feature of the liberal political system is the widely held and therefore often self-fulfilling belief that political differences will be resolved peacefully. The presumption of amicable resolution stands at the heart of the attitude on which common security rests, namely warlessness—the pervasive and principled aversion to the use of force for all but defensive purposes.

A second democratic habit feeds directly into common security: transparency. Liberal politics are conducted in the open. The public is deemed to have the right to know. Concealment in all but the rarest of circumstances is considered illegitimate. Transparency of military forces is one of the two pillars—defense dominance being the other—of common security.

To be sure, democracy, even constitutional democracy, does not guarantee peace wherever it exists. The association between the two is not a law of history—if only because there are no laws of history comparable in rigor to the laws of the physical world. What can be said, though, is that democracy carries with it a predisposition for peaceful conduct. If war is a kind of disease, as twenty-first-century liberalism on the whole considered it to be, democracy does not qualify as a vaccination against it. It is more like a robust immune system, countries possessing it being better able to resist the virus of bellicosity than those lacking it. On the whole, therefore, the progress of democratic governance augured well for the prospects for peace and especially for the liberal version of peace, common security. What, then, could be said, after the first post-Cold War decade, about the global prospects for democracy?

THE RISE OF DEMOCRACY

D URING THE SECOND half of the twentieth century, and especially in its final quarter, the world became markedly more democratic. The trend was unmistakable, powerful and global. There was a "democratic wave."[22] This is true if democracy is considered a dichotomous property, that is, if a sovereign state either is or is not democratic. By that standard there were many more democracies in the year 2000 than there had been in 1950, or 1970.[23] It is also true if democracy is taken to be a matter of degree. Most countries became more liberal in the final decades of the twentieth century, even if they did not all have fully liberal political systems. China, for example, had a much less oppressive although still far from popularly elected or constitutionally circumscribed government. While in the first post-Cold War decade the whole world had not become democratic, and in some of its regions liberal institutions and practices were rare, nowhere were they absent altogether.[24]

The spread of liberal political practices and institutions had three related causes: democracy was the political system of the world's most powerful states; the political systems that had opposed liberalism in the modern era were discredited; and the features of social life historically conducive to democratic politics spread.

Democracy, like other innovations, diffused from its point of origin to other places because it appeared successful, was therefore attractive, and so was voluntarily adopted.[25] The spread of democracy is a striking but not unusual instance of cultural diffusion. Its aura of success came from the fact that the sovereign states highest on the widely accepted indices of success—wealth and power—all, without exception, had, at the end of the twentieth century, fully liberal political systems.[26]

The conditions conducive to the spread of democracy were different, and far less exacting, than the conditions necessary for its creation. As with any innovation, the first instance was the hardest, requiring an unlikely, difficult-to-arrange, and in some cases fortuitous set of circumstances. Constitutionalism emerged in Great Britain out of a combination of geography, land tenure patterns, economic development, religion, history, and the personalities of a series of monarchs and their opponents. Without any of these, British political history might well have proceeded differently.[27] Democracy might not have flourished as it did in the United States, to take another example, without the layer of protection from Europe that the Atlantic Ocean provided.[28]

While hothouse conditions were necessary to nurture the first tender shoots of liberal politics on the planet, once the plant was hardy and well-established it could spread to almost any climate. While innovations are rare, difficult, and to some extent matters of chance, imitation, by contrast, is common, easy, and within limits predictable. The conditions that made democracy possible in the British Isles and North America do not all have to be reproduced in Africa for it to take root there. Democracy in America, Great Britain, and many other places was itself, by the end of the twentieth century, a condition—necessary although obviously not sufficient— for democracy in Africa.

The post-Cold War dominance of democracy was not necessarily permanent. The rise of liberal politics had been interrupted, even reversed, earlier in the modern era.[29] But on those previous occasions political liberalism confronted problems that it seemed unable to solve, and other, seemingly viable forms of political organization were available. In the post-Cold War era there was, at least temporarily, no full-fledged and plausible alternative to political liberalism. Indeed, the success of democracy cannot, in historical terms, be disentangled from the failure of its opponents.

Traditional political systems were challenged by the French Revolution, were put on the defensive throughout the nineteenth century, and were swept from the European continent by World War I. In the first half of the twentieth century the fascist form of illiberalism was defeated militarily. In the second half, illiberalism's Communist variant faltered economically. Liberalism's two rivals were not only defeated, they were also discredited. Every political system is based, at least implicitly, on an argument about the proper distribution of political power. Liberalism's traditional and illiberal rivals rested on claims in favor of particular forms of political inequality. The political history of the modern era's first two centuries is, among other things, the history of the weakening and ultimately the virtual disappearance of those claims.

Traditional political systems allocated political power by birth. The divine right of kings and the natural superiority of the aristocracy were taken for granted in Europe until the late eighteenth century. By the beginning of the twenty-first, belief in these principles had all but vanished. In the twentieth century the claims to power of the illiberal regimes rested on the presumed superiority of the self-selected members of particular political parties. In the first post-Cold War decade the claim on which Lenin and Hitler had based the governments they established commanded little credibility any-where.

In the nineteenth century two kinds of inequality were integral even to the liberal political tradition. Inequality on the basis of social class was one: Only propertied males were eligible to vote. Inequal-ity on the basis of race and nationality was the other: Both the United States and Great Britain maintained empires—Britain's the largest in population and territory in the world—in which the indigenous peoples lacked political power. By the end of the twenti-eth century both kinds of inequality were inconceivable in the liberal core and lacked substantial support anywhere else.[30] In the post-Cold War era in the many countries where liberal democracy was absent this was usually explained as a failure of implementation rather than a matter of principle. To be sure, there were exceptions. Vestiges of the principled arguments for political inequality that had once dominated the social life of the planet persisted in the first decade of the post-Cold War period. But these half-hearted defenses of departures from political liberalism were not robust.

In two parts of the world, the Arab Middle East and East Asia, arguments against political equality could still be heard, if faintly. The arguments emphasized the presence of cultural differences between these two regions and the Western cradle of political liber-alism.[31] In each region one important country grounded its political system in the kind of inequality familiar in the past but incompatible with the tenets of twenty-first century political liberalism. Saudi Arabia was ruled by a traditional regime, a hereditary monarchy; China was governed by a Communist Party.[32]

Both the Islamic political culture of the Middle East and the Con-fucian political culture of East Asia included non-liberal elements.[33] They emphasized group cohesion and solidarity rather than individ-ual liberty,[34] and they favored the enforcement of orthodoxy over free inquiry and discussion. Moreover, the ruler was more like an authoritarian parent presiding over a family than a fellow citizen chosen to perform certain limited duties by a sovereign public. The ruled could petition the rulers in both the Islamic and Confucian traditions but did not elect them. The rulers were constrained by a moral commitment to proper conduct but not by constitutional lim-its on their power.

In the modern era, moreover, both the Islamic Middle East and China experienced the Western liberal countries as dangerous, aggressive, intrusive adversaries and were therefore inclined to resist Western political values as part of their struggle against Western domination.

Still, the two traditions, although certainly not Western, were not monolithically anti-liberal. Islam had gained converts at the expense of Christianity in its early years because it was a more egalitarian faith. Confucius taught that the ruler must not govern arbitrarily but must respect customs and moral rules.[35] Nor were the Islamic or Confucian traditions immutable or immune to the political currents of the modern age.[36]

The enormous increases in the volume and the speed of the process of cultural diffusion made possible by the great technical advances in transportation and communication in the second half of the twentieth century, which contributed so much to the disappearance of orthodox Communism, brought liberal ideas to every part of the planet. They were so widespread and so powerful in the wake of the Cold War that no country could evade or ignore them entirely. Some countries, to be sure, were more susceptible than others. It was not accidental that political liberalism took root earliest and most firmly outside the Western core in places that had been part of the British Empire. The British exported their political traditions to India and, as a result, they became part of the Indian tradition as well.[37]

By the outset of the twenty-first century, liberal political ideas pervaded the world, even where they had few indigenous roots and where they had never been deliberately transplanted. If a country's history consists of the features of the past that make up the agenda of the present, then the Glorious Revolution of 1688, which is usually taken to mark the triumph of constitutionalism in England, had, three centuries later, effectively become part of Chinese and Arab history as well, in the sense that neither could ignore the ideas associated with it.[38] At the end of the twentieth century both the Arab Middle East and Confucian East Asia harbored liberal political systems, or at least elements of them. There were several full-fledged democracies in East Asia, including a Chinese one on the island of Taiwan. Partly free elections and legislatures with some authority had appeared in the political life of the Arab world. In the 1990s the partly liberal exemplars were Jordan, Kuwait, and Qatar, in each of which, however, the monarch retained ultimate power.

Moreover, the Saudi and the Chinese regimes did not claim in their own defense, as the traditional and illiberal opponents of democracy had asserted in the nineteenth and twentieth centuries, that political liberalism was undesirable in principle and thus ill-advised everywhere. They asserted, rather, that, whatever its advantages elsewhere, it was unsuitable for *them*. Nor did either follow the political principles it professed with perfect fidelity. The Saudi kingdom's most important asset, its oil, was managed by modern, Western-educated technocrats.[39] The Chinese Communist Party allowed much of the country's economic life to be governed by the principles of the free market, the heart of liberalism in economics.

Nor, ultimately, did either government rely on the voluntary acceptance of political inequality to remain in power. Both practiced selective repression. Both relied on bribery as well as coercion. The Saudi royal family, while keeping a generous share for itself, distributed the country's oil wealth widely enough to provide a relatively comfortable, although sharply declining, standard of living for the inhabitants of the kingdom, which reduced the potential for unrest. Similarly, the Chinese Communist regime relied on the surging economic growth achieved in the 1980s and 1990s to persuade the Chinese people to accept its rule.

Both regimes could draw, moreover, on yet another source if not of legitimacy then at least of tolerance on the part of those they ruled: the fear of something worse. The Saudi monarchy asserted that the alternative to its rule was not Western liberal democracy but rather Islamic fundamentalism of the type that had established itself in Iran, provoked a bloody civil war in Algeria, gained adherents throughout the Middle East, and fueled terrorist attacks against the United States (and that the monarchy tried to keep at bay at home by appeasing it). The Chinese Communists claimed that without their rule the country would fall into the kind of violent chaos from which it had suffered in the first half of the twentieth century.[40]

Liberal politics are portable. But not all regions were, in the wake of the Cold War, equally hospitable to popular sovereignty and constitutionalism because not all had the conditions conducive to political liberalism. Still, the correlates of democracy were on the rise in the post-Cold War world.[41]

The most prominent of them, the condition with which liberal politics was most strongly associated, was rising per capita income. The wealthier the populace of a country, all other things being equal, the more likely it was to have liberal institutions and practices. The association was a plausible one: Income tends to breed independence, curiosity, time to participate in public affairs, and a sense of responsibility for them.[42]

In East Asia in the last two decades of the twentieth century the association between income and democracy was close. The countries of the region demonstrated an impressively regular practice of adopting liberal political systems once a certain level of personal wealth was attained.[43] The sequence was reminiscent of American home ownership patterns in the second half of the century in which families, once their incomes rose to a certain level, regularly moved from cities to suburbs. Higher levels of education and literacy are associated with liberal politics as well. Better educated people are more likely to be active politically and to reject doctrines that relegate them to an inferior political status. Educational levels, too, tend to rise over time, albeit at widely varying rates, the world over. The migration from the countryside to the city, a demographic hallmark of the modern age because a consequence of the industrial revolution, also tends on the whole to promote liberal politics, in particular popular participation. The medieval phrase *"stadtluft macht frei"*— city air promotes freedom—has some basis in modern experience.[44]

Finally, the late-twentieth-century technologies of communication made popular sovereignty and constitutionalism more likely to the extent that these technologies themselves spread. To be sure, history demonstrates no simple, one-way relationship between technological progress and the expansion of liberty. The printing press proved compatible with centuries of traditional rule. The telegraph, telephone, and television were widespread in the illiberal political systems of the second half of the twentieth century.[45]

But the inventions of the last part of that century—the facsimile machine, the audiocassette, and above all the Internet—seem inherently subversive of non-democratic rule. They cannot readily be censored or used as exclusive channels for the transmission of official opinion. The information they carry can evade the control of the authorities, and central control of information was one of the hallmarks of non-democratic rule in the twentieth century.[46] In the Soviet Union the practice of *samizdat*—the self-publishing of unauthorized manuscripts—was a precarious undertaking with a limited audience. A few typescripts of forbidden books or articles expressing independent views were made in secret and circulated clandestinely. The Internet is *samizdat* on a far larger scale—every owner of a computer is potentially both a publisher and a reader—and it is far more difficult, and perhaps ultimately impossible, to control.[47]

The association of liberal politics with economic success, urban life, literacy and education, and the innovations in information technology of the end of the twentieth century is, like the association between democratic governance and peaceful international conduct, a tendency, a predisposition, not an invariable law of politics. There are exceptions to the pattern: At the outset of the twenty-first century India, with a low per capita income, chose its leaders in relatively free elections; Singapore, with a far higher standard of living, did not. But an association nonetheless existed, and the spread of the features of social life with which democracy was associated, combined with the victory of the liberal core in the Cold War, raised democracy to hegemonic status in the post-Cold War world. However, although it was hegemonic—powerful, widespread, and without major challengers—democracy was not universal.

Not all of the nearly two hundred members of the community of sovereign states were fully liberal; a good number were not liberal at all. In part this could be explained by the wide differences in the extent to which countries possessed the social correlates of liberal politics. In part it was a matter of timing. Liberal democracy cannot be established overnight and many countries had made a late start. The United States began its trek toward full popular sovereignty and constitutionalism in the eighteenth century, Great Britain even earlier. At the dawn of the new millennium Russia had been embarked on this path for less than a decade. The late developers were bound to lag behind the countries of the democratic core.

But this was not the whole story. The uneven spread of democratic governance in the wake of the Cold War had two other causes, which were illustrated by the experiences of the two most important countries outside the liberal core, Russia and China.

DEMOCRACY AND INSTITUTIONS

A T THE BEGINNING of the twenty-first century Russia and China were the two places in the world where the consolidation of liberal politics had the potential to have the widest international effects. They were the two countries the policies of which could most easily lead to a major war. In each case the sources of conflict would be eased to the extent that political liberalism took hold. Each would be less likely to fight with its neighbors insofar as the public chose the government charged with making the decision for war. The spirit of constitutionalism and the democratic presumption and habit of compromise had the potential to help resolve the political issues over which Russians had gone to war—Chechnya—and over which the Chinese threatened to fight—Taiwan. The prospects for peace in the post-Cold War world could thus be said to depend in part on the prospects for political liberalism in these two countries.

Their political systems shared certain features. Orthodox Communism was extinct in both. It would have been difficult to find even a Party official in China who believed that the political deeds of Mao Zedong were beyond reproach and not even the Communist Party of the Russian Federation aspired to return to a Stalinist political and economic system.

As the new century began neither Russia nor China had had much direct experience with political liberalism. Both had been governed, until early in the twentieth century, by traditional autocracies.[48] In the nineteenth century most of Europe's absolute monarchs made some concessions to constitutionalism, accepting restraints—often minor ones, to be sure—on their authority. The Romanov and Qing dynasties did not. Their power remained absolute.

In both countries liberal practices came late, were installed grudgingly, failed to sink deep roots, and were soon swept away by the conquering forces of Communist illiberalism. Only after 1895 did anyone not officially part of the court have any opportunity to influence official Chinese policy.[49] Only in 1905 did Russia establish a parliament.[50] And Russian and Chinese liberalism, partial and tentative as it was, was overthrown by Communist Parties that replaced it with the two great illiberal regimes of the second half of the twentieth century.

If democracy is an either-or proposition, if the world is divided into democracies and non-democracies, then post-Cold War Russia qualified—barely—as democratic. Public officials were chosen by elections in which all adult citizens could vote. Russian elections were not models of propriety: Electoral rules were not faithfully followed, money of dubious origin played a large role in their outcomes, and the final tallies were not always scrupulously accurate.[51] But the campaigns were reasonably open, voting more or less free, and for general fairness the Russian elections of the 1990s did not necessarily suffer by comparison with every election ever held anywhere else in the twentieth century, including in the Western core.

As well as popular sovereignty, post-Cold War Russia practiced constitutionalism, at least on paper. Power was divided among the federal president, the parliament, and the regional governments. But the legislature, the Duma, had little effective power. Russia's first elected president, Boris Yeltsin, ruled more by issuing decrees than through the laborious process of steering legislation through a fractious parliament. The regional governors more often than not acted in corrupt and arbitrary fashion. At no level of the Russian government were officials effectively responsive to the wishes of the voters.

By the either-or standard China was not a democracy. The Communist Party retained a monopoly of political power and dealt severely with any person who openly questioned its monopoly and any group that tried to operate independently, even, as in the case of the quasi-religious sect Falun Gong, for non-political purposes. The government crackdown on demonstrators in Tiananmen Square in Beijing and in other cities in June 1989 made the same point as the Soviet military interventions in Hungary in 1956 and Czechoslovakia in 1968 and the assault on the free trade union movement Solidarity in Poland in 1981: No challenge to the monolithic authority of the Communist Party would be tolerated.

Still, post-Cold War China did exhibit, in embryonic form, some of the features of liberal politics. The government staged partly contested local elections in many of the country's villages. The parliament, the National People's Congress, while not freely elected, displayed occasional signs of preferences different from those of the supreme Communist leaders.[52] The flowering of a market economy had created different economic interests that had to be reconciled in the formation of public policy, and institutions for doing so had begun to develop.[53] The social features associated with liberal politics—wealth, education, an urban population—were all rising briskly in China in the wake of the Cold War.[54]

If Russia had the forms of political liberalism without all of the substance, China had some of the substance without much in the way of the forms. Neither met the standards of political liberalism established in Western Europe, North America, and Japan, but the chief obstacle was different in each of the two countries.

In China it was the resistance of the political elite, something that, in the second half of the twentieth century, was the most common barrier to political liberalism. As long as elites stood in the way of democracy they could usually manage to block it. Conversely, the transition to democracy most often took place when the political elite, or part of it, came to favor it and permitted, encouraged, or even helped it to take place. This is generally what happened in Communist Europe in 1989 and 1991.[55]

In Russia the obstacle to putting into practice the principles of constitutional democracy was different: The government did not have the capacity to carry out the public tasks that political liberalism requires. In this shortcoming it was not alone; in the post-Cold War era, state weakness was a widespread and virulent malady.[56]

The state in Russia was not as weak as in many countries of the world's periphery—in much of sub-Saharan Africa, for example—where it had failed completely and where as a consequence anarchy reigned. The Russian state had not failed at the fundamental task of government, keeping order—although post-Communist Russia was not a particularly orderly place. State weakness was not the same thing as state collapse. The Russian government was strong enough to keep social life from descending into war but not sufficiently strong to sustain a liberal political system or a liberal economy. A

working state of the kind Russia lacked is indispensable for both features of a liberal political system. Only the state can organize and
carry out elections, ensuring that they are free and fair. A state is
necessary for constitutional government as well. Restrictions on the
power of the authorities create an autonomous zone of individual
conduct. The common term for these zones is rights, and rights
must be protected. Someone or something must build and maintain
fences around these reserved areas and step in when they are
breached. That something is, inevitably, the state. Rights, like environmental protection and national defense, are a species of public
good. They are secured not by individuals acting alone but through
collective action, and the most effective agent of collective action is
the state.[57]

During the Cold War the world's sovereign states could be divided
into three categories: the liberal—free—world; the Communist
world; and the Third World, the countries of which could choose to
affiliate themselves with one or the other.[58] Political orientation was
taken to be a matter of choice, with unaffiliated countries like consumers with a choice between rival products. A shift from one brand
to the other, while not frequent, was always a possibility. As with religious conversion—leaving one faith and joining another—it might be
psychologically difficult to decide to transfer loyalties but, once
made, the decision to do so was thought easy enough to carry out.

A shift of foreign policy, like China's shift from the Soviet to the
Western camp in the 1970s, was relatively simple, like a member of
the British parliament changing partisan allegiance by crossing the
aisle of the House of Commons from the benches of one party to
those of the other. It was a matter of pointing the guns in a different
direction. But changing domestic political systems, in particular
making the transition from Communist illiberalism to liberalism,
proved anything but easy. The presumption that this could be readily accomplished turned out to be mistaken because it rested on an
error about the character of the state.

It was assumed, without the matter being seriously considered,
that late-twentieth century states were compatible with both liberal
and illiberal political institutions and practices and that the switch
from illiberal to liberal politics would be like shifting from basketball

played in the United States to the same game played under international rules. There are minor differences between the two: the length of the game, for example, and the distance from the goal at which a successful shot counts for three rather than two points. But the two versions are basically similar and a player accustomed to one can quickly adjust to the other. In fact, the difference between liberal and illiberal politics turned out to be akin to the difference between basketball and an entirely different sport, such as baseball, which requires another set of skills that take years to master, a point that was vividly illustrated in the 1990s when the world's most accomplished basketball player, Michael Jordan, tried his hand at baseball and failed to achieve with a bat and glove anything like the level of proficiency that he had displayed on the basketball court.

Although no straightforward answer to the question of how a suitable state can be constructed became apparent in the first post-Cold War decade, two relevant points did emerge. One was that it could not be done quickly or easily. A working, liberal, rights-protecting state was the result not only of deliberate policies but also of the habits, skills, and experience that accumulate over the course of the *longue durée*. One of the defining features of Western state-formation was captured in the story begun by Gina Lollabrigida and completed by Humphrey Bogart in the 1954 film *Beat the Devil*, about the Americans who ask an English gardener how his country has produced such wonderful lawns. The secret, he replies, is to "get some good grass and roll it every day for six hundred years."[59]

The second point is that to build a modern, liberal, rights-protecting state encounters a frustrating circularity—the difficulty of building one without having one in the first place.

At the heart of the problem stands taxation. Revenues are necessary to pay the elected and appointed officials, the bureaucrats, the police, and the judicial personnel needed to operate a state in liberal fashion. But for this a revenue-collecting agency is needed and its personnel, too, must be paid—with money that will not be available unless and until they collect it. In liberal political systems most revenue is collected voluntarily but this, too, encounters a chicken-egg problem. Citizens will be disposed to pay voluntarily if they see that they are thereby purchasing services that are of value to them; but these services will not be provided unless and until the citizens already have paid, so that those who provide the services can be hired.[60]

Difficult though it undoubtedly is, the task of state-building is not impossible. The wealthy, stable, successful states of the core all, over time, managed it. But two of the most prominent historical patterns of state-development were of limited relevance in the post-Cold War world. In the first instance, state institutions have been implanted by an occupier. Thus did Roman practices spread throughout Europe in ancient times, and British institutions around the world in the modern age. The pattern was highly unlikely to be repeated in the post-Cold War era. For the purposes of building a liberal state it may be that, contrary to Russia's and China's common national ethos, which glorifies resistance to and above all the eventual eviction of conquerors from the West, it was the historical misfortune of both countries not to have been conquered, occupied, and governed as was India.

The second pattern of state-building occurred in response to the requirements of defense and warfare.[61] The saying that "war made the state and the state made war" is a roughly accurate capsule summary of the history of many western countries, but it was not a promising formula for the post-Cold War period. It was unpromising because states that prepare for wars often fight them. It was unpromising as well because, in the wake of the Cold War, war suffered a sharp decline in status. Preparations to wage it no longer offered as attractive a basis as they once did for organizing or mobilizing a society.

Logically, the origins of the state lie in the need for a minimal level of order, and the symptom of state failure of the worst kind in the post-Cold War world was the murderous disorder that was found in all too many places. Russian and Chinese state weakness, by contrast, was more conspicuous in a different sector of social life, which assumed a place of unprecedented importance in the lives of almost all sovereign states in the twenty-first century: the economy.

For most of its history the main task of the state was to keep order within its borders. For most of the modern era its defining preoccupation was war. In the post-Cold War period, in the liberal core above all but elsewhere as well, the bulk of the state's resources have been devoted to economic matters, as governments have sought to increase, and to redistribute, the economic output of the societies they governed. The nineteenth century, with its ongoing assault on traditional structures of political authority, was an era of revolution. The twentieth century was above all a time of war, actual and potential, between liberal and illiberal forms of modern political and economic organization. The twenty-first century began as the age of the market.

Economics and markets preoccupied post-Cold War Russia and China. The government of each country was convinced that the key to power beyond its borders and stability within them was economic success. Each was further convinced that the key to economic success was the third part of the Wilsonian triad, the liberal approach to the organization of economic activity—the free market. Ambivalent at best about liberal politics, the Russian and Chinese authorities in the first post-Cold War decade displayed genuine enthusiasm for free markets because of what they had seen markets achieve.

The countries of the Western core, above all the United States, encouraged this enthusiasm and promoted measures to assist the establishment of functioning market economies in Russia and China because they, too, wanted the two formerly orthodox Communist giants to be successful economically. The principal reason for this Western emphasis, however, was the belief that economic liberalism promoted political liberalism. The guiding principle of post-Cold War Western policy toward Russia and China, as well as toward the countries of the periphery, was one of the precepts of the liberal view of history: Free markets make free men.

DEMOCRACY AND MARKETS

THE CONVICTION that economic liberalism has beneficial non-economic effects originated in the nineteenth-century belief in a connection between unfettered international commerce—free trade—and peace. Cross-border economic ties, it was reasoned, would breed familiarity and sympathy among the countries involved, creating what came in the twentieth century to be known as "inter-dependence," which in turn would foster peace.[62] By definition those who participate in trade gain from it; otherwise they would keep their goods at home. If trade were disrupted by war they would lose their gains. So they would not wish to make war.

But in the twentieth century they did. Sovereign states with appreciable cross-border flows of goods and capital nonetheless fought against each other in World War I. Trade does not guarantee peace[63] but the experience of World War I does not prove that international commerce can never exert a pacifying influence anywhere. The forfeiture of the benefits of trade is not the only loss from war, but it can be a substantial one, and a country contemplating armed conflict will likely consider its impact on commerce.

The risk of provoking international economic isolation is certainly one reason that China refrained, in the first post-Cold War decade, from carrying out its threat to seize control of Taiwan.[64] Post-Communist Russia's relations with other countries were influenced by the political weight of people who profited from the economic access to the rest of the world that the Communist regime had prohibited.[65]

Peace is also the consequence, by some accounts, of liberal economic practices within sovereign states. The twentieth-century Austrian-American economist Joseph Schumpeter considered capitalist countries to be inherently peaceful because they were dedicated to economic rationality defined as the maximization of wealth; war, an exercise in the destruction of wealth, is economically irrational. (World War I came about, it followed, because European societies were incompletely capitalist.)[66] The liberal theory of history posits yet a third connection between liberal economics and peace, an indirect one via liberal politics: The market leads to democracy, and democracy leads to peace.

The core countries did try to promote democracy directly. In the last decade of the twentieth century they adopted, in the words of the American Secretary of State James Baker, a "new mission . . . the promotion and consolidation of democracy,"[67] and they established agencies that mounted programs for this purpose.[68] These were, however, more exercises in expressing their own intentions than in transforming the political structures of other countries. The budgets in question were modest and there was no evidence that the activities to which those budgets were devoted—the conferences organized, the fellowships provided, the missions dispatched to monitor elections, the many reports that were published—had any significant effect on the internal political arrangements of the target countries.[69] They could do little to overcome the two principal twenty-first-century obstacles to the establishment of political liberalism: powerful internal opposition, as in China, and the absence of the required institutions, as in Russia.

Thus the principal strategy of the core countries for the promotion of democracy was an indirect one: encouraging liberal politics by supporting liberal economics. The heart of the Western policy toward post-Communist Russia was a mixture of loans, grants, technical assistance, and high-level exhortation, all mobilized in support of the transition, initiated after the collapse of the Soviet Union, from a centrally planned economy to a market economy.

Western policy toward China also emphasized the promotion of economic liberalism. The principal instruments in the Chinese case were private investment and trade. In the leading core country, the United States, the domestic politics of China policy in the first post-Cold War decade revolved around the question of whether to grant normal trading status to the People's Republic or instead to withhold it as punishment for Beijing's non-liberal domestic political practices.

In both cases, the ultimate rationale of the Western approach was as much political as economic. The Russian government was attempting to establish democracy. Without economic success, it was feared, this effort would fail and democracy would be discredited in Russian eyes just as the economic failures in the interwar period had undermined the first German exercise in political liberalism, the Weimar Republic. The Chinese government, by contrast, was not trying to establish democracy. The Communist rulers were instead trying to block it. The West believed that economic liberalization would promote democracy despite the Communists' efforts to the contrary.[70] In the Russian case, support for the market was the equivalent of training wheels for the bicycle of democracy, intended to ensure that the inexperienced Russian rider did not fall off; in

China it was a Trojan Horse, to be wheeled inside the walls the Chinese Communists had erected against political liberalism.

Was the premise of Western policy correct? As with democracy and peace, there was no simple, direct causal link between economic and political liberalism. Sovereign states with economies operating according to market rules did not automatically become functioning democracies with regular popular elections and effective constitutions. As with democracy and peace, however, both logic and the evidence of history suggested a connection between them.

Historically, a market economy is a necessary but not a sufficient condition for democratic politics. Not all countries with market economies have been democracies, but all modern democracies, without exception, have had market economies.[71] Moreover, modern countries with market economies have found it easier than countries without liberal economic systems to adopt democratic practices. The countries of southern Europe in the 1970s and of Latin America in the 1980s, which combined market economies with undemocratic governance, made the transition to political democracy more easily than did the formerly Communist countries of Eastern Europe and Central Asia in the 1990s, in all of which the economy had been centrally planned for at least four decades.

Liberal economics and liberal politics were also connected through economic growth. A rising standard of living is associated with democracy and, at the end of the twentieth century, liberal economic institutions and practices were closely associated with increases in a society's total and per capita wealth.[72] But the connection between the two is broader and deeper than economic growth, important though that is. There is both an affinity and an overlap between the design and the procedures of liberal economics on the one hand and those of liberal politics on the other.

Market economies and liberal political systems are separate realms: The free market is by definition at least partly independent of political control.[73] But two defining features of liberal politics have counterparts in market economies. First, individual choices are paramount. The popular sovereignty by which governments are selected in democracies corresponds to the principle of consumer sovereignty in the market, by which individual preferences determine what gets produced and the prices at which products are sold.[74]

Second, the reach of the state is limited, with certain areas—political rights in the case of democracy, private property in a market economy—fenced off from government control.

While they are distinct, moreover, the two realms are not unconnected. As with domestic politics and foreign policy, the barrier between politics and economics is less an iron wall than a permeable membrane. Ideas and habits from one seep into the other. Someone accustomed to making his or her own economic decisions would not find it strange to make political ones. When governments are fenced off from large tracts of economic activity it does not seem extraordinary to build similar fences around political activity. In this sense, liberal politics and liberal economics are like the United States and Canada: separate and distinct, with clearly marked borders between them, but closely enough connected that they borrow from one another and similar enough that a person passing from one to the other does not feel out of place.

But politics and economics are more than closely connected. They overlap in a crucial way. A market economy is the basis for one of the main features of modern liberal political systems—civil society. Civil society consists of the independent social organizations—religious and professional groups, labor unions, civic associations—that stand between society's basic unit, the family, and the state.[75] Countries under the sway of illiberal rule lacked all of them. It was the aim of the Nazi and Soviet states to eliminate all social groupings that the ruling party did not control. Civil society contributes to both parts of liberal politics. It gives weight to constitutional restrictions by providing a counterbalancing force to the state. A private economic sector is a base from which to criticize and oppose what the government does.[76] And it is the locus for much of the political activity associated with popular sovereignty. In the core democracies electoral competition takes place between and among political parties, important institutions of civil society. Parties are organized to represent interests and the most important interests they represent are economic ones.[77] At the outset of the twenty-first century it was the private economy that gave rise to the most powerful and influential intermediate organizations.[78]

Market economics and democratic political systems merge in yet another and even more consequential way. They have a common underpinning, one so important that it is often regarded as an integral part of the liberal political system itself: the rule of law. The term refers to the impartial, consistent, and equal application of clear and well-known rules across a society. If democracy is an invention of the Greeks of antiquity and constitutionalism an innovation of Great Britain in the age of absolutism, the rule of law has its origins in ancient Rome. The practice was lost for centuries, then revived in medieval Europe and in particular in the British Isles.[79]

It is separate from the other two components of a liberal political system. Just as it is possible to have free elections without constitutionalism or the rule of law—there were many such "illiberal democracies" in the wake of the Cold War—so history offers many examples of societies in which the rule of law obtained, where norms were consistently and impartially enforced, but where the public had no say in how the rules were made, or by whom, and no protected sphere in which individuals could exercise political rights. British colonies such as the last important one, Hong Kong, are examples. The largest of them, India, became a democracy in 1947 by adding popular sovereignty and constitutionalism to the rule of law that the British had already established.

But it is hard to find, in the sweep of history, a sovereign state in which rights were protected but that lacked the rule of law.[80] In fact, they are two sides of the same coin. Constitutionalism applies the rule of law to the public sphere; it concerns politics and government. What is commonly designated the rule of law, from Roman times to the present, has applied to private, personal matters. It encompasses a society's criminal and civil codes, and civil law pertains principally to economic affairs. These fraternal twins, constitutionalism and the rule of law, converge on the concept of property.[81]

Property is, of course, an economic concept. It is also a right. Property rights are individual rights that involve things that can be bought and sold. The rule of law came into being largely to protect them. Among the most often-quoted lines in the entire history of political philosophy is Jeremy Bentham's assertion that "property and law are born together and die together. Before the laws there was no property; take away the laws, all property ceases."[82]

Property was the spawning ground not only of the rule of law but also of constitutionalism itself. It was the protection of property that gave birth, historically, to political rights. The watershed events in the modern emergence of liberty in the West were, essentially, struggles over the sanctity of property. The seventeenth-century English disputes between crown and Parliament concerned whether the king could appropriate revenues—that is, the property of others—without the consent of those who owned it as expressed through the legislature. The outcome of the struggle was that he could not. The American Revolution was sparked by a comparable dispute. The slogan of the rebellious colonists—"no taxation without representation"—asserted the same principle: A person's property could not be taken by the state without his consent. It was not accidental that the most influential philosopher of Anglo-American liberty, the thinker most closely associated with the English and American revolutions, John Locke, put the right to property at the center of his thought. Similarly, the French Revolution began with the monarch's efforts to extract more revenue and the insistence of the legislature on its rights in the matter.

At the heart of both property and liberty, therefore, and underpinning both economic and political rights, is the rule of law. Historically, the three parts of what the twenty-first century has defined as liberal politics were established in a particular order: first the rule of law in the economy (property rights); next the rule of law in the public sphere (constitutionalism); and finally the extension of the franchise to all adult citizens.[83]

Applying the rule of law publicly and privately is the task of, indeed is impossible without, the state.[84] And a rights- and property-protecting state is precisely what Russia, China, and many other sovereign political communities lacked in the wake of the Cold War. Its creation was their most important piece of post-Cold War business and this was the case for many other sovereign states as well. The key was a market economy. Logically and historically, the rights-protecting state, without which functional democracy is not possible, comes into being to protect property, and property is the sine qua non of a market economy.

While property rights are indispensable to the operating of the modern, wealth-generating market economies of the Western core, they are *not* indispensable to markets per se. Limited, local markets in which exchange is self-enforcing are found all over the world in the absence of rights-protecting states. They have existed since the beginning of recorded history, and no doubt before that. In such markets trade, often conducted by barter, is self-enforcing: Two parties meet, exchange the goods they have brought, and depart. But market *economies*, which produced the historically unprecedented and, before the modern age, undreamed of wealth of the West, operate across space and time. They extend far beyond the places where and the moments when tangible products actually change hands. To participate in a market economy, to be willing to ship goods to distant destinations and to invest in projects that will come to fruition or pay dividends only in the future, requires confidence, the confidence that ownership is secure and payment dependable. That is, the confidence necessary for a wealth-generating market economy is the confidence that property rights will be respected. The importance of the presence or absence of this confidence can scarcely be overstated. The difference between local, self-enforcing exchange and the broader, globe-girdling, decade-spanning exchanges that confidence in property rights makes possible is the difference between the modest huts in which those engaged in strictly local trade live and the spacious, lavishly furnished, technologically equipped domiciles, sometimes in towering apartment buildings, created by the affluence that expansive markets make possible. It is the difference between poverty and wealth.

The confidence indispensable for wealth-creating market economies is provided by the property-protecting state.[85] The state protects property by enforcing the contracts that form the basis of market transactions. A market system rests on a legal system and a legal system rests on a state.[86] Most exchanges in a market economy do not have to be enforced. Compliance is voluntary. But each party to the millions of daily transactions in a state-supported market economy can proceed with confidence, knowing that if the other reneges the state will step in to safeguard the property involved. The state is to a market economy what a safety net is to a high-wire circus acrobat: a guarantee of protection in case something goes wrong.

The confidence that holds a market economy together is also indispensable to the liberal approach to security relations among sovereign states, common security, and it is produced in similar ways. Transparency is common to both, as well as to liberal politics. Potential purchasers of products and financial assets ordinarily require all relevant information about what they are buying before parting with their money. Similarly, sovereign states are willing to place limits on their armaments if, but only if, they can be certain that other countries are observing similar limits on theirs. The equivalent for liberal economics of the principle of defense dominance in common security is the existence of the state. Both provide assurances against harm, the first by diminishing the capacity to inflict it, the second by offering protection against it.[87]

The contract-enforcing state is a state of a particular kind. It is a liberal state, strong enough to protect property—and liberty—but not so powerful or ambitious or intrusive as to suppress liberty or expropriate property. It is a state able and willing to enforce the law but not disposed to violate it. The liberal state, which upholds the rule of law in both the public and private spheres, which safeguards both political and property rights, and that is, not coincidentally, also the kind of state likely to enter into and observe military and political arrangements for common security, occupies the middle ground between the extremes of anarchy and tyranny.

It is the presence of a market-enhancing, property-protecting state that distinguishes the experiences of the two defeated illiberal powers in the aftermath of World War II from the fate of Russia and China in the first post-Cold War decade. Germany and Japan had constructed thriving market economies and states that enforced the rule of law that underpinned these economies before being taken over by the illiberal ideologies that led them, and the world, into a ruinous war. For much of the modern era Germany was in fact the prototype of a political system with the rule of law but without full popular sovereignty or constitutionalism. From German comes the term used to describe such a system: *Rechtsstaat* (rights-state).[88] Eighteenth-century Prussia, the core of modern Germany, was an orderly and, by the standards of the age, an intellectually lively place.[89] The code of laws promulgated by the Prussian King Frederick in the second half of the century remained in force until 1900 and provided the legal framework within which Germany emerged as a great industrial economy in the second half of the next century. But under neither Frederick nor his monarchical successors did Germans have full power to choose their government, nor were their political rights comprehensively protected. As for Japan, one of the most impressive features of its astonishing transformation in the second half of the nineteenth century from a traditional to a modern state was the installation, in short order and largely by decree from above, of a property-protecting state.[90]

After 1945 Germany and Japan were able swiftly to reconstruct their property-protecting states, which then underpinned their rapid economic recoveries. At the same time, it was a relatively easy matter to adapt these states to the protection of political as well as property rights. With the foundation of a liberal state in place in the economic sphere, the transition to a liberal political system was not formidably difficult.

In the wake of the Cold War, however, Russia and China lacked such foundations. Having moved almost directly from absolutism to Communism, neither had ever had a liberal political structure of any strength or durability. In neither country was the rule of law ever securely established: Communism in practice was a form of principled lawlessness, with the interests and wishes of the Communist Party, as defined by its leaders, taking precedence over formal, impersonal rules. In neither country were the qualities of character and habits of behavior associated with political liberalism—trust and compromise foremost among them—at all widespread. In the Communist era it was often fatal to exhibit either. Nor had the institution of private property struck deep roots. Its absence distinguished Russia from the rest of Europe.[91] In the 1980s the Soviet Union was scornfully called "Burkina Faso [a small African country] with missiles." The characterization was accurate, and remained accurate in the post-Communist period, in that, where the basis of a liberal state was concerned, Russia was closer to most African countries than to most Western European nations. For this reason, the Russian and Chinese transitions to liberal institutions and practice were bound to be, at best, longer and rockier than Germany's and Japan's had been a half century earlier.

The first post-Cold War decade provided evidence that, despite the lack of relevant historical experience in Russia and in the face of the opposition to political liberalism on the part of China's rulers, both were embarked on that transition. There was reason to believe, that is, that the course of events envisioned by the liberal theory of history was under way, and not only in the two most important non-liberal countries but elsewhere, indeed—provisionally, reversibly, and at different rates, to be sure—the world over.

The third of the liberal theory of history's three constituent propositions was that democracies are peaceful, and the non-belligerent tendencies of countries with liberal political systems had a basis in historical experience and logic. Its second proposition posited an affinity between democratic politics and market economics. Here, too, historically and logically, a number of connections between the two were apparent, not the least of them the fact that both rested on a liberal state enforcing the rule of law.

As for the first proposition, the universal appeal of the market, this was the most important of all. The engine of the liberal theory, its independent variable, the motor force of the liberal current at large in the world in the wake of the Cold War, was economic liberalism. So the prospects for peace, the great liberal goal that Woodrow Wilson had sought at Paris in 1919 but that had proven elusive then and throughout the twentieth century, and for democracy, which several generations of citizens of the core countries had defended over the course of that same century, rested heavily on the prospects for the liberal economic system first authoritatively described by Adam Smith in the last quarter of the eighteenth. Whereas in Marx's scheme of history the market—capitalism—was the villain and the loser, in its twenty-first century liberal counterpart the market assumed the role of hero and victor. And 225 years after the publication of *The Wealth of Nations*, its prospects had never been brighter.

For while the liberal approach to international relations, common security, was new and fragile, and the liberal approach to governance, democracy, was neither practiced nor even preached everywhere, the liberal approach to economic organization, the free market, was all but universally admired. At the beginning of the new millennium, only an eccentric handful of the two hundred or so sovereign states rejected economic liberalism. It had almost no principled opponents, not even secret ones. For this impressively broad acceptance there was a powerful reason. The history of the previous hundred years was widely considered to have rendered at least one unambiguous verdict. If the nineteenth century had established the irresistible force of the economic growth that the industrial revolution made possible, the twentieth century had demonstrated that there was a single optimal method of achieving it. The market was the path to wealth. In their own eyes the core states' defining feature was democracy: They were the free world. To others what was salient, impressive, and worthy of emulation was their common economic system. They were the rich world and, because the acquisition of wealth was a mandatory goal for Russia, China, and virtually every other organized political community, this was a world they all wanted to join.

The popularity of the market among governments had its roots in the rise of economic prosperity as an important basis for political legitimacy. Here the consequences of the two great revolutions that defined the modern world ran on parallel tracks. In the wake of the French Revolution it became increasingly difficult to justify endowing some members of society with political power because of their lineage. By the twentieth century it was accepted that government had to express the will of the people, and the great international schism concerned whether this should be accomplished by liberal or illiberal methods. Similarly, once the industrial revolution occurred it became increasingly difficult to maintain that the prosperity it brought to the world's core was impossible or undesirable or irrelevant elsewhere. By the middle of the twentieth century it was a settled task of government everywhere to achieve, or at least not to inhibit the achievement of, the universally desired goal of material well-being. The great question at the heart of twentieth century economic history was which formula for prosperity, the liberal or the illiberal one, was the more effective. And to that question, by the dawn of the twenty-first century, the answer was clear.

CHAPTER NINE

The Triumph of the Market

I N MEDIEVAL Europe alchemists searched for a formula to turn base metals into gold. In the modern era the formula was found. Alchemy is a metaphor for the industrial process, the process of transforming raw materials into products with a higher value. It is in fact superior to alchemy, which aimed, in the terms of modern economics, simply to create more purchasing power without producing more things to purchase.

The industrial revolution did create, and in remarkable profusion, more things for people to purchase[1] and in so doing became the most influential development in human history since the invention of agriculture ten thousand years earlier.

At the outset of the twentieth century, a little more than a hundred years after the industrial revolution began, the capacity to produce wealth through economic growth, once the subject of myths, had become an established fact of life. This set the stage for the twentieth-century competition to determine the most appropriate political framework for industrial economies, which pitted the centralized planned system of the Communist world against the decentralized free markets of the West.

Its outcome was decisive. By the last decades of the twentieth century, as the market economies of Western societies lifted their inhabitants to ever higher standards of living, the giant Communist economies of the Soviet Union and China had come to practice a kind of reverse alchemy: The raw materials they used to create products had a greater value on the world market than the manufactured goods that were made out of them. Of all the legacies of the twentieth century, this sweeping triumph of the free market is the one most widely accepted, and therefore most important, for the world of the twenty-first century.

TWENTIETH-CENTURY ECONOMICS

IN THE FIRST decade of the post-Cold War era the market reigned supreme. Most sovereign states were indifferent to common security, the liberal approach to international relations. Many were hypocritical about democracy, the liberal method of governance. Yet virtually all embraced the liberal formula for organizing economic activity. The market's commanding status derived in no small part from the outcome of the Cold War, which was, among other things, a contest of economic systems. Indeed, the pattern of the economic contest more closely resembled the two world wars of the twentieth century than did the Soviet-American military rivalry.

In military terms, the Cold War was a stalemate. Dangerous at the outset, by its end it had settled into a stable and almost comfortable standoff, like a chess match in which the two contestants agree to a draw. The collapse of Communism was not the result of military victory.

As in the two world wars, in the first phase of the economic competition, which spanned the middle third of the century, the illiberal forces were in the ascendant and the West was in retreat. The Communist economic system, in which all economic activity was planned and controlled by the government, seemed more dynamic and successful than the market system.[2] The Soviet Union, where the command system was first established, appeared to escape the effects of the Great Depression of the 1930s that paralyzed world capitalism. It generated the military resources that enabled the Soviet Union to withstand and repel a massive invasion by Nazi Germany in World War II, and both before the war and in the two decades thereafter it produced impressive economic growth.

In the middle third of the twentieth century it was the command system, not the market, that inspired admiration and imitation.

Where Communist parties monopolized political power, in Eastern Europe, China, Vietnam, and Cuba, they established replicas of the Soviet economy. Even where orthodox Communism did not take hold, some features of its economic system were adopted. In much of what was known as the Third World, governments owned and managed much of the economy. The state did not plan everything, but it did plan a great deal.

In the Cold War economic contest between East and West, as in the two world wars, the tide eventually turned. In the last three decades of the century Communist economic principles were in retreat. By the century's end they were as thoroughly defeated as Germany had been in 1918 and 1945. The command system was all but extinct.

On the Western side, moreover, the economic competition, unlike the military contest, was waged by a genuine coalition, just as the two world wars had been. While in Cold War military affairs Germany and Japan played largely passive roles, in the economic arena they made crucial and independent contributions to the Western triumph.

Theirs were the largest economies in the two regions where the economic contest was most important. Europe and East Asia were both part of the world's core, where wealth and power were clustered and from which cultural innovations emerged. In both regions the contest was directly joined. Each contained both market and command economies and sometimes they were installed in different parts of the same divided nation: East and West Germany, North and South Korea, China and Taiwan.[3] In every case market principles proved superior. Western Europe in the third quarter of the century and East Asia in the fourth recorded the most impressive sustained growth on the planet.

Germany and Japan both rose from the ruins of military defeat to make themselves among the most powerful economies in the world.[4] Both promoted economic development in their home regions by exporting capital to their poorer neighbors.[5] In Europe, Germany was a partner to its western neighbors, a founding member of the economic and political association that had become, by the outset of the twenty-first century, the fifteen-member European Union. In

Asia, however, Japan was less a partner than a model, as other East Asian countries adopted features of its economic system with impressive results. South Korea, Taiwan, Singapore, Hong Kong, and several countries in Southeast Asia followed Japan's lead in achieving high rates of growth. Their collective experience came to be known as the Asian economic miracle.[6]

It is important to recognize that the late-twentieth-century triumph of the market was not only an outcome of the Cold War but also the culmination of the economic history of the twentieth century, the major theme of which was the expansion and then the contraction of the role of the state in economic affairs.

THE RISE AND FALL
OF STATE MANAGEMENT

FOR MOST of the twentieth century the role of the government in economic affairs expanded. In the last three decades the trend reversed itself and the state retreated from the major tasks of economic activity: investment, production, and distribution. At the start of the century, in the countries of the world's core, it had been widely accepted that the government had, at best, a very modest part to play in each of the three. Government intervention in economic affairs came to be thought a relic of the pre-industrial, undemocratic world of tradition, which had been in full retreat during the course of the nineteenth century and was swept away, in Europe, by World War I. But that war also overturned the consensus on the proper balance, in economic activity, between state and the market.

In World War I the governments of the warring countries assumed far more economic responsibility than ever before. They took control of industrial production, they directed the allocation of capital and labor, and they rationed a host of commodities, all in order to enhance their military efforts. For the first time, all of society's resources were mobilized for a particular purpose, and it was the state that mobilized them.[7] The war demonstrated what government intervention could accomplish, and in the half century between 1920 and 1970 the economic role of the state expanded—in some countries more than in others.

In the world's core—North America, Western Europe, and Japan—the market remained the principal economic mechanism but, breaking with the pattern of the years before World War I, the state's role grew. Investment remained largely but not exclusively the preserve of the private sector, but the government influenced the allocation of capital, notably in Japan. Most firms and factories were owned and managed privately but some came under the jurisdiction of the state, often transferred to government control by the process known as nationalization. As for distribution, core governments redirected an increasing percentage of the national output to those deemed needy and deserving, such as the elderly and the indigent, or to those with sufficient political power, or both. The Western state in the twentieth century became a combination vacuum cleaner and sprinkler system, taking in wealth through taxation and recirculating it through transfer payments.

In illiberal Soviet-style economies the state took responsibility for everything. Lenin had been impressed by the German war economy and made it the model for Communist economics.[8] Government planning determined investment. Production took place in farms and factories owned and managed by the state. Communist regimes nationalized industry and agriculture across the board.[9] Decisions about distribution were also the preserve of the party-run state. Whereas in the core, and in most of the rest of the world, prices and wages were largely determined by market forces, in Communist countries the authorities set them by administrative fiat.

In much of what was known during the Cold War as the Third World—in Latin America, the Middle East, and especially South Asia—a hybrid economic system developed. The government exercised more control over investment than in the core, although not the total control characteristic of command economies. A larger state-owned industrial sector was created, but, unlike in Communist systems, it operated alongside privately owned industrial enterprises. The government also assumed considerable responsibility for distribution.

In this third approach to economic management, the government's role was undertaken in support of a particular strategy of economic development, one heavily influenced by the Communist example. That strategy aimed at developing heavy industry, which, for most of the twentieth century, was considered the hallmark of economic modernity and the route to national wealth as well as the basis of national military strength. This strategy was known as state-led industrialization. It also went by the name of import-substitution, which was one of its principal policies: The countries following it aimed to make their own steel rather than being obliged to import it. In pursuit of this strategy Third World governments adopted a practice anathema to economic liberalism but central to the economics of Communism: discouraging trade with, and investment from, the rest of the world.

From the Bolshevik consolidation of power in Russia to the end of the 1960s, the prevailing economic trend in the world's core, in the Communist bloc, and in the Third World was not a liberal one. Some students of economic and political affairs predicted that, over the long run, the economic practices of Communism and the West would converge, with the economic role of the state everywhere becoming increasingly expansive and intrusive.[10]

At the end of the century a different type of convergence had become a reality. The world's economies were more alike in their institutions, practices and policies than at any time since World War I, but the economic model on which they were converging was not the one toward which they had seemed to be moving during the century's middle decades. In the century's last three decades, each of the three economic types encountered problems to which the market came to seem the only solution.

In the 1970s the core countries experienced, simultaneously, rapid rises in prices and dismaying declines in their rates of economic growth. In response to this distressing combination, which came to be known as "stagflation," market-oriented governments came to power in Great Britain in 1979, the United States in 1981, and Germany in 1982. Led by Margaret Thatcher, Ronald Reagan, and Helmut Kohl respectively, each country took steps to reduce the economic role of the state. Reagan and Thatcher practiced privatization, selling state-owned enterprises to private investors and managers, and deregulation, subjecting the previously regulated economic activities to market rules.[11]

The reversal of the trend toward greater government control over the economy occurred even where self-styled conservatives did not hold sway. In 1981 Francois Mitterrand became the president of France and formed that country's first socialist government in twenty-five years, which proceeded to implement economic policies that French socialists had always favored: nationalization, increased government spending, and more regulation. The result was a currency crisis. Capital fled the country and the value of the French franc fell sharply. In response, Mitterrand executed an economic reversal, putting in place policies that resembled the ones being carried out in northern Europe and North America. Of the various episodes of economic liberalization in the core, the French case was perhaps the most telling. Thatcher, Reagan, and Kohl carried out policies in which they believed. Mitterrand, by contrast, found himself sponsoring the kind of economic policies that his party had opposed. The British, American, and German leaders were liberalizers by conviction. Mitterrand's socialist government embraced the market because there was no alternative.[12]

The economic pathology that led to a reversal of course in the import-substituting Third World was a crisis of debt. In the early 1980s a number of Latin American countries could no longer pay the interest charges on the loans they had received from major Western banks. They applied for relief. The banks, Western governments, and international financial institutions insisted that, in order to receive it, these countries adopt liberal economic measures: selling off state-owned assets, reducing government oversight and direction of economic activity, and opening their countries to goods and capital from abroad.[13] Although this meant repudiating the principles on which they had based their economic policies, the debtors agreed.

A decade later India found itself in comparable circumstances. It was by far the largest of the import-substituting countries and perhaps the most committed of any of them to that particular economic strategy. In the four decades after independence India had built a large state-owned industrial sector and had entangled its economy in a maze of regulations so intricate that a government permit was required for activities ranging from hiring and firing employees to opening and relocating factories to importing virtually anything from abroad. So pervasive were these regulations that, while the imperial government of the first half of the century had been called the British raj, its successor came to be known as the "license raj."[14]

In June 1991, the Indian government found itself in a balance-of-payments crisis, with enough hard currency on hand for only two weeks of imports. It applied to the International Monetary Fund for a loan, which came with conditions similar to those the Latin American debtors had been obliged to accept a decade earlier.[15] India agreed in principle to open its economy, to cut back on its regulations, and to pare its state-owned industrial sector.[16]

The end of the third distinctive approach to economic management, the Communist command economy, took place in two stages. In 1978 China began a program of economic reform that led in short order to private property in agriculture, a quasi-private industrial sector alongside the state-owned enterprises created in the Maoist era, prices set by the market, and trade with and investment from the rest of the world.[17] By the 1990s the Chinese government had abandoned even a rhetorical commitment to a planned economy.

China underwent gradual economic reform. A decade later the Communist countries of Eurasia experienced sudden political collapse. The end of Communist rule left in its wake twenty-seven post-Communist countries stretching from the eastern border of Germany to the western border of China. In the first post-Cold War decade, in order to make the transition from central planning to free markets, all committed themselves to a more ambitious and difficult version of the package of measures pressed upon the import-substituting debtor countries of the Third World. The measures involved freeing prices from government control, shifting ownership from the state to private hands, and building the institutions that a functioning market economy requires.[18] By the beginning of the twenty-first century, success in making these changes varied widely among the twenty-seven, but all had embarked, at least tentatively, on the transition. None had tried to retain the Communist economic system.*

*The economic problems of the core countries in the 1970s, and of the Third World debtors in the 1980s, were bound up with the price of energy. The two oil shocks of 1974 and 1979, the first associated with the Arab-Israeli War of October 1973, the second with

The final chapter in the late-twentieth-century retreat of the state was triggered by the Asian financial crisis of the late 1990s, which affected the Third World countries that had, in the last three decades of the century, enjoyed the greatest economic success. The economic strategy of the East Asian countries differed from the one pursued in Latin America, the Middle East, and South Asia. It was more liberal. It relied for growth on exports rather than producing for a protected home market. This exposed the East Asian countries to the essence of market economics, vigorous competition, especially in the United States, which bought more of their products than any other country. Although the East Asians eschewed many of the illiberal economic practices of other Third World countries, they did embrace two of them. Their governments played major roles in channeling investment, through the control of foreign exchange and influence on large banks that served as the main conduits for capital. And although they depended on access to the markets of other countries, the East Asian countries did not reciprocate by opening their own to imports. When their currencies plunged, they, too, sought loans. As with Latin America and India, the loans came with conditions. Those conditions were familiar, involving a commitment to reducing the role of the state in economic activities.

What took place in the last three decades of the twentieth century is clear: The economic role of the state, having expanded for the preceding half century, began to contract the world over. How this happened is also clear enough: In the world's liberal core, in the partly

---

the Iranian revolution of 1979, imposed the equivalent of a tax on the West and contributed to economic sluggishness. These same price increases drove Third World countries to borrow heavily to maintain the inflow of oil on which their economies depended. But when the core countries, especially the United States, went into recession in the late 1970s and early 1980s—a slump caused by the rise in interest rates designed to eradicate the inflation that the oil shocks had triggered when governments printed money to replace the purchasing power the surge in oil prices had removed—the debtors were not able to export to the markets in sufficient volume to earn the hard currency needed to service their debts.

The oil shocks also affected the Communist economies. The price increases gave Russia, an oil exporter, an economic windfall, which postponed, or at least disguised, its economic difficulties. The price spikes prompted both conservation in the consuming countries and the discovery of new sources of supply, which led to a decline in the price of oil in the 1980s. This penalized the Soviet Union and its clients by reducing their major source of hard currency.

liberal Third World, and in the entirely illiberal Communist countries economic problems, or crises, arose to which the solution was economic liberalization.

But *why* did this happen? Why did the state shift from hero to villain, from the key to economic growth to an obstacle to it? Why, in particular, did the most extreme version of government management, the Communist command economy, which had seemed, for much of the twentieth century, one of history's great successes, fail so emphatically that by the end of the century it had been entirely abandoned? Its failure can be understood by putting the economic history of the final decades of the twentieth century into the broader context in which it belongs, the two centuries of the modern era, which also happens to cover most of the history of the industrial revolution.

ECONOMIC GROWTH
AND POLITICAL LEGITIMACY

THE DEFINING FEATURE of the industrial revolution is economic growth. Beginning in the last decades of the eighteenth century and continuing to the beginning of the twenty-first, it yielded a steadily expanding volume of products for human use. Growth has three sources: increases in capital from investment; increases in labor through population increase, immigration, or the inclusion of a greater proportion of the society in the workforce; and increases in the output that a particular amount of inputs—capital and labor—can produce, an increase in what is known as productivity. At different points in the industrial revolution the way that these three ingredients have combined has varied.

The initial stage was made possible by the invention of the first significant machines driven by inanimate power: the steam engine, the spinning jenny, the early techniques for mining coal and smelting iron. Once these were available two developments enabled Great Britain, the pioneer in the industrial revolution, and then other Western countries, to take advantage of them. One was the accumulation of capital. Britain had, in the eighteenth and nineteenth cen turies, the most sophisticated and powerful financial system in the world. The other was the movement of people in large numbers from the village to the city and from farms to factories, where they could operate the new machines. This counted as an increase in productivity as labor was transferred from a less to a more productive economic sector.

The first phase of the industrial revolution made traditional society obsolete because it was incompatible with the basic requirements of an industrial economy. Among these requirements was the commercialization of agriculture. Land had to be treated as a commodity that could be bought and sold in order to produce enough food to feed a growing urban population and to make some rural labor redundant so that people would move to the cities to work in the new factories. Traditional societies varied widely across the globe but everywhere they were based on the land and nowhere was land simply a commodity. It was, instead, the basis of a complicated network of obligations and privileges, a social structure binding owner to field worker, lord to peasant. It was these traditional institutions, these social worlds, that the industrial revolution threatened and that it ultimately swept away.[19]

Unlike the world of tradition, for this first phase the Communist system proved adequate. Indeed, for a time it seemed optimal.[20] The command economy could not have produced the machines on which the first stage of the industrial revolution depended.[21] Once they had been invented, however, and the initial pattern of industrialization established, the command system proved serviceable. The enormous power of the state gave the government the means to squeeze savings out of the agrarian sector and to direct it to industry on a large scale. Communist countries typically had higher rates of investment than countries with market economies,[22] and the governments of Third World countries attempting state-led industrialization also devoted themselves to mobilizing and directing investment. Communist governments could also compel rural laborers to move to cities and work in factories.

In fact, the Communist command system, first developed by the Soviet Union in the 1920s, was simply the most extreme version of a common pattern of industrialization in which the later the industrial revolution came to a country, the more extensive the role of the government in promoting it was likely to be, above all in mobilizing capital for investment.[23] To be sure, the guiding hand of the state was not necessarily superior to the invisible hand of the market in promoting the initial stage of the industrial revolution. In retrospect, it is not clear that Russian economic growth even accelerated under the system the Bolsheviks put in place. Imperial Russia had set out on a more conventional path of industrialization (although one in which the Russian government played an important role) before World War I. Had it continued on that path it might have grown just as rapidly and more efficiently, and the price of growth paid in blood by the Russian and the other peoples of the Soviet Union would certainly have been much lower.[24]

But if not necessarily superior to the market, the command system did work. The Soviet Union, the countries of Eastern Europe in which the USSR installed ideologically similar governments after World War II, and China after 1949 did acquire industrial economies under Communist auspices. People migrated in large numbers from the countryside to the cities. Governments built, owned, and managed huge industrial complexes.

Third World countries committed to state-led industrialization also achieved economic advances, particularly in heavy industry. The average annual rate of economic growth in India after independence was 3.5 percent. This was hardly spectacular, and because the Indian population also increased, per capita growth was low.[25] But that rate was an improvement on the estimated rate of 1.3 percent for the period of formal British rule from the mid-nineteenth to the mid-twentieth century.

The major products of the initial stage of the industrial revolution were capital goods, which were themselves used for production rather than sold to individual consumers. As Karl Marx and Friedrich Engels observed in *The Communist Manifesto*, written in 1848, the bourgeoisie, as the promoter and beneficiary of industrialism,

> has created more massive and more colossal productive forces than have all preceding generations together. Subjection of nature's forces to man, machinery, application of chemistry to

industry and agriculture, steam navigation, railways, electric telegraphs, clearing of whole continents for cultivation, canalization of Rivers, whole populations conjured out of the ground.[26]

These were enormous and momentous changes, but they differed from the changes in social life brought about by the next stage of industrial revolution. These subsequent changes were in what was produced, and above all in what people could own and use themselves. The next stage brought to human life something that Marx and Engels did not live to see: the age of mass consumption. For the first time people in large numbers gained access to what once had been either luxuries reserved for the very few or unavailable to anyone because they did not exist.[27] The great beneficiaries of this stage of economic advance were members of the general population. It was they who were the main purchasers of goods produced on a mass scale. They had to be: There were not enough people of great wealth to buy them.

In 1964 the sociologist David Riesman published a collection of essays on American life entitled *Abundance for What?*[28] The title would have been unthinkable at any other time and in any other place. An abundance of material goods had never existed in any society anywhere prior to the twentieth century. But by the middle of that century in the wealthiest country of the Western core, and in the ensuing decades in other core countries, abundance had become a fact of everyday life. Mass consumption was indispensable for economic growth in the twentieth century as it had not been in the nineteenth, and the failure to sustain it was at the heart of the Great Depression of the 1930s.

As important as it was in economic terms, in the twentieth century mass consumption turned out to be just as significant politically. It was something in which everyone, everywhere, wished to participate. Marx had called religion the "opiate of the masses." Its mysterious allure had, he lamented, bewitched the people of the capitalist countries and so diverted them from the militant pursuit of their true interest—the overthrow of capitalism. In the twentieth century the opiate of the masses was consumer products, the failure to make adequate provision for which subverted the political systems that had been established in Marx's name.* The term economists used for what people consumed, "goods and services," was revealing. Goods implied things universally acknowledged to be positive and desirable. Services are what were available, before the twentieth century, only to those wealthy or privileged enough to employ servants. In the twentieth century goods and services were what people the world over wanted, were determined to get, and increasingly demanded that their governments help them acquire.

Mass consumption was another innovation of the Western core. Here the pioneer was the United States and it was a significant American contribution to human civilization. Like other innovations, once it was made and it was clear that it could be made, the demonstration effect of mass consumption turned out to be powerful. With travel and communication possible on an ever-widening scale in the twentieth century, more and more people could see that abundance was available; once they saw it they wanted it for themselves.[29]

This development had political consequences. In the Western core, national elections often turned on economic conditions. Growth favored the incumbents, its absence gave the advantage to challengers.[30] While the core had entered the age of mass consumption,[31] many of the countries of the world's periphery had not, which endowed with even greater significance the capacity to nurture and sustain an economy that could provide consumer goods on an appreciable scale. That capacity became a test of the worthiness not of a particular political party but of the political system itself. The Chinese economic reforms testified to this. The Communist Party gave up most of its ideological pretension and much of its control over Chinese society in order to foster the economic advances on which, it came to believe, depended its chances of remaining in power at all,

---

*The parallel could be taken further. In traditional society the most familiar images, the ones that dominated the man-made landscape, were religious: churches, icons, works of art depicting Biblical scenes. In consumer society what were visually ubiquitous were images of, and thus both reminders of and tributes to, consumer products—that is, advertising. The singer John Lennon once caused offense by asserting that his group, the Beatles, was "more popular than Jesus." The statement was dubious even at the time it was made, but the image of, say, a bottle of Coca-Cola was certainly as familiar in the second half of the twentieth century as the depiction of Christianity's central figure.

even in a role much diminished from what it had been at the Maoist zenith.[32]

For most of the modern age the test of political legitimacy was the capacity to protect sovereign borders. By the end of the twentieth century another test had equal, if not greater, importance: the capacity to "deliver the goods." This was a test on which the state-led industrializers of the periphery did badly and on which the command economic systems of the Communist world did even worse. The evidence of Communism's failure had a profound effect on Russia's first post-Communist president, Boris Yeltsin.

A turning point in Yeltsin's intellectual development occurred during his first visit to the United States in September 1989, more specifically his first visit to an American supermarket, in Houston, Texas. The sight of aisle after aisle of shelves neatly stacked with every conceivable type of foodstuff and household item, each in a dozen varieties, both amazed and depressed him. For Yeltsin, like many other first-time Russian visitors to America, this was infinitely more impressive than tourist attractions like the Statue of Liberty and the Lincoln Memorial. It was impressive precisely because of its ordinariness . . . On the plane traveling from Houston to Miami, Yeltsin seemed lost in his thoughts for a long time. He clutched his head in his hands. Eventually he broke his silence. "They had to fool the people" [he said.] "It is now clear why they made it so difficult for the average Soviet citizen to go abroad. They were afraid that people's eyes would open."[33]

Even in the Soviet Union before the Gorbachev era, a country entirely without political freedom, the rulers felt the need to make some concessions to the wishes of those they ruled. In the latter stages of its existence there was an unofficial, tacit "social contract" between the two, in which the populace gave up any claim to political participation in exchange for a steadily rising standard of living. But the Communist system did not maintain its side of the bargain. In its early years the command system was a mechanism for catching up with the advanced industrial economies of the core; at the end it had become a way of falling further behind. The reason that it did not pass the test of delivering the goods was that it could not do so. It was, unintentionally, designed to fail.

Passing the test required shifting from one pattern of economic advance, extensive growth, to another, intensive growth. The first approach increased output by increasing inputs, the second by making more efficient use of existing inputs. The first growth pattern is investment-led, the second driven by advances in productivity. Advances in productivity were an important part of the first phase of the industrial revolution, but they were achieved in no small part by transferring labor from the agrarian to the industrial sector. In the next stage, which was also the stage of production for mass consumption, with surplus labor no longer available, improvements in productivity had to take place *within* sectors, by the more effective use of a steady stream of resources. This the command economy proved unable to do: The kind of productivity upon which growth in the twentieth century depended was beyond its capacity to deliver.

Productivity in the twentieth century core economies was something of surpassing importance—growth depended on it—but also curious and even mysterious.[34] Economists could track and measure it but they did not know how to generate it.[35] But if the precise way to engender improvements in productivity was not known, the circumstances in which improvements were likely to occur, the features of an economic system conducive to them, were evident. And these happened to be features integral to market economies and impermissible in command systems.

Competition among firms is important for productivity. It puts pressure on each enterprise to make better, less expensive products lest its rivals do so and thus drive it out of business. Command economies did away with competition and outlawed the standard by which market competition is waged—profitability.[36] Firms must be autonomous so that they are free to experiment with different ways of doing things, which is how better ways are discovered. In the Communist system firms were completely controlled by government planners and in many of the Cold War economies of the periphery—India's, for example—they were tightly circumscribed by government regulations. But to promote advances in productivity private ownership is indispensable because it gives owners a powerful incentive to find ways to increase profits: The profits accrue to them. In state-owned enterprises none of the personnel stood to benefit from a better performance and none stood to sustain a comparable loss—of personal assets—from a bad one.[37]

The market system can enlist one of the most powerful of human motivations, the pursuit of self-interest, in the quest for economic growth. On this score the less liberal economies of the periphery were less successful, and the command economies of the Communist world entirely unsuccessful. The institutions and practices necessary for economic growth in the latter part of the twentieth century were not only missing from the planned economies, they were also antithetical to the economic and political principles that these systems embodied.

Just as the traditional social, economic, and political order was incompatible with the initial needs of the industrial revolution, so at the end of the twentieth century the Communist economic system proved incompatible with the requirements of the next stage. It, too, was consequently rejected and discarded. Marx was stood on his head. He had asserted that capitalism was a transitional stage between traditional society and Communism. Instead, Communism proved to be a way station between the peasant societies in which it took power and the mass-consumption society that only the liberal approach to economic management could provide. In the vocabulary of natural evolution, the market system proved to be adaptive, while the command system (and its less rigorously controlled imitators) failed to meet the acid test of adaptation, the equivalent of evolution's capacity for reproduction—the provision of consumer abundance.

Yet the traditional and Communist orders that the market eclipsed have had a kind of posthumous revenge.

OPPOSITION TO THE MARKET

FOR ALL THE wonders that it produced, the free market has had a consistently unsavory reputation. The human qualities necessary for the successful operation of the market have seldom been highly valued, least of all in the ways that artists have depicted Western society.[38]

In feudal Europe, in the caste system of India, and in imperial China, merchants never stood at the top of the social hierarchy. In modern times the calculation, the compromise, and the determined pursuit of self-interest that fuel the system that created abundance have more often been denigrated than exalted. Selflessness is a term of approbation; selfishness is not. Yet the market system, which is explicitly based on selfishness, did more for those living in societies where it operated than did the system of planning, which was, ostensibly, the expression of selflessness.[39] Philanthropists earn praise for giving away their money, not for making it.[40]

Modern literature has not been kind to men whose working lives were spent in the marketplace. Balzac's bankers and proprietors are not admirable characters, and perhaps the best-known fictional American businessman of the first part of the twentieth century, Sinclair Lewis's Babbitt, is not an advertisement for the life of commerce.

One notable twentieth-century contribution to the understanding of the dynamics of economic growth did define an heroic role arising from the modern market. In attempting to explain how the innovations that make economic growth possible come to pass, the economist Joseph Schumpeter assigned a crucial part to the individual he called the entrepreneur, the person who launches a new way of doing things. The entrepreneur is an heroic leader who, against the odds, without the guidance of precedent, and at risk to his fortune creates an enterprise that is new, vital, and profitable.[41]

The entrepreneur, and the executive who directs the enterprise the entrepreneur has established, found an admiring constituency in the twentieth century in the United States. A conspicuous vehicle for celebrating their virtues was the nation's largest general interest weekly magazine, *Time*. Especially during the boom decades of the 1920s, 1950s, and 1990s, captains of industry regularly graced the magazine's cover, which functioned as a kind of nationwide billboard and gave the person so depicted, for a week, the kind of public visibility usually available only to figures from politics, entertainment, and sports.[42] But even in the United States, the market and the people who worked in it were not universally admired. In the vivid cinematic depiction of the heart of the American financial system, Oliver Stone's *Wall Street*, the central figure, Gordon Gekko, takes his name from a lizard and displays a reptilian character as well.

The mixed reputation that commerce and industry enjoyed in the Western core even as they were producing riches previously un- dreamed of was hardly a fatal hindrance to recruiting people into their ranks.[43] But beginning in the nineteenth century the market was subjected to criticisms beyond its alleged complicity in fostering undesirable patterns of conduct, and these had deeper political con- sequences.

One such criticism was that the market was not, and could not be, the most effective way of organizing economic activity. The market was deemed contrary to the spirit of the modern age and to the cen- tral precept of the European Enlightenment that helped pave the way for it: the power of the human intellect to comprehend and manage the world. In this sense, Communist central planning, the application of human reason to one of society's most important tasks, was the quintessential Enlightenment project. Economic plan- ning by the government seemed, on its face, a more promising approach to economic management than depending for food, cloth- ing, and shelter on the haphazard, uncoordinated, and apparently random workings of the free market.

In fact, the market does not work haphazardly. Like central plan- ning it is a system of coordination, but one that operates through the decentralized pursuit of self-interest on the basis of impersonal rules rather than by hierarchically administered commands given by gov- ernment officials.[44] It is a liberal system of coordination, based on individual desires and voluntary transactions in the context of uni- versal rules rather than an illiberal one in which the few exercise arbitrary power over the many. Adam Smith called it "a system of natural liberty"[45] and it turned out to be effective in promoting eco- nomic growth. In economies as complex as those of the twenty-first century, an enormous amount of information must be transmitted, processed, and acted upon; this is far more effectively accomplished in a decentralized than in a centralized manner.[46]

A more telling criticism of the market indicted it for dizzying and economically painful oscillations between boom and bust. This criticism was well-founded. From the early decades of the nineteenth century the economies of the core were prone to slumps, in which decreases in production destroyed businesses and deprived people of their jobs. The worst of them, in the 1930s, was so severe that it shook faith in the market throughout the West. Central planning won converts because it seemed able to avoid such downturns.

It was the achievement of John Maynard Keynes, the most influential economist of the twentieth century, to discover how to moderate, if not abolish, Western capitalism's downward swings. Before Keynes, the market was understood as a self-regulating mechanism, with downturns that could not be prevented but that would ultimately correct themselves. Keynes had a different vision. He saw the market economy as a machine powered by the battery of consumer spending. Occasionally the battery would run down, causing the machine to falter; this was what had happened in the 1930s. The machine could be restarted by recharging the battery, which spending by the government could accomplish.[47] With Keynes the profession of economics came into its own. By the end of the twentieth century it had become the priesthood of economic life, its authority recognized, its advice sought, its members fully integrated into the governance of modern states.

Like the industrial revolution itself, and like the liberal approach to international relations, common security, and the liberal approach to political order, democracy, the study of the liberal method of economic organization—the market—had its origins in the Anglo-American world. The founder of modern economics was a leading figure of the eighteenth-century Scottish Enlightenment, Adam Smith. It was he who, in *The Wealth of Nations*, published in 1776, first described in detail the workings of the market. Most of his prominent successors, Keynes foremost among them, were either British or American by birth, training, or residence—or all three.[48] All of neoclassical (that is, non-Marxist) economics is descended from Adam Smith in the sense that all neoclassical economists have taken the market as their subject and virtually all have believed in its virtues as a way of coordinating economic activity.[49]

In the twentieth century economics came to resemble another

field of inquiry and practice for which a Nobel Prize was awarded: medicine. Both were applied sciences devoted to the enhancement of human welfare. Both proceeded by experimentation through trial and error. Both were far more sophisticated at the end of the century than at the beginning. Economists, like medical practitioners, knew more, and knew what they knew with greater precision. Both relied on exact measurement. Greater knowledge made both more useful. People were richer and lived longer in 2000 than in 1900, in no small part because of advances in economics and medicine.[50]

The findings of both medical science and economics, moreover, are universally applicable. No two human bodies are exactly alike, of course, and the treatment of the same disease will vary from case to case, but some basic medical principles are true for everyone. Similarly, while national economies differ widely in important ways, some economic principles are relevant to them all. Perhaps the most important of these are the principles of growth. There was, at the end of the twentieth century, a consensus among economists on what is required for economic growth everywhere: a liberal, market-enhancing state that protects property rights and encourages investment; freedom for firms to enter and compete in markets; openness to trade with and investment from the rest of the world; sound monetary and fiscal policies with modest deficits and low inflation; and measures to enhance the health and levels of education of the population.

This meant that the rapid growth of the East Asian economies in the last three decades of the twentieth century was not the result of a singular local form of political management but rather of diligent attention to the fundamentals, especially investment financed by high rates of saving.[51] It also meant that Africa was not poor for any uniquely African reason but because the countries of the region had not put in place the institutions and practices that would lift them out of poverty. Poor countries had no need to invent the machines and technologies of industrial production, which were well known and widely available. They had simply to create the conditions in which these could be effectively utilized.[52]

It was not, however, a magic formula, one that every country could easily adopt. If it had been, the gap between the richest and the poorest countries would have narrowed steadily in the years following the end of the Cold War, with the least wealthy following, smoothly and rapidly, the path that the leaders, with far greater effort, had blazed. Instead, the gap grew wider because the two hundred-odd sovereign states of the international system varied greatly in their capacities to put in place the conditions for economic growth.[53] The failure to do so, in Africa and elsewhere, had its roots in local history, culture, and politics, and here economics resembled not so much medicine as public health.

Eradicating cancer, for which no cure was known at the outset of the twenty-first century, depended on advances at the frontiers of medical science. Eradicating cholera, by contrast, for which a vaccine was available but outbreaks of which still occurred in poor countries, was a problem of public health. What was missing in the case of cholera was not the scientific understanding of the disease but rather the administrative and ultimately the political capacity to put into practice the measures that followed from scientific understanding.

To extend the average life expectancy in rich countries, to take another example, from seventy-five to one hundred years is a scientific problem; to extend it from fifty to seventy-five in poor countries is a political one. Similarly, to raise the long-term rate of economic growth in the United States, which has the world's most advanced economy, is a problem in economic research; it requires a breakthrough in the understanding of the nature of productivity. Slow growth in poor countries is a political problem, requiring for its solution the political capacity and the political will to create the conditions known to make economic advancement possible.

At the outset of the twenty-first century, economists did not believe that the market, remarkable instrument for the generation of material abundance though it was, could perform all the functions that an economy requires. To the contrary, one of the major subjects of economic research was how and why markets fail. It is market failure, when the pursuit of individual interest does not lead to optimal outcomes, that creates the need for public goods. An important part of the study of economics is deciding what markets can and cannot do and how best to compensate for their deficiencies. In the modern age the ongoing challenge to the market system, however, and one that prompted basic alterations in the nineteenth century model of industrial capitalism, came not from the market's failures but from its successes. Historically, the chief threat to the political viability of the liberal economic system was not what it could *not* do, but rather what it did well.

THE PROBLEMS OF SUCCESS

THE WORKINGS of the market when harnessed to the industrial revolution disrupted the long-established routines of millions of people. The market produced spiritual and physical impairment on a scale that before the modern age even wars seldom did. Marx and Engels were especially eloquent on the psychological dislocation:

> The bourgeoisie . . . has put an end to all feudal, patriarchal, idyllic relations. It has pitilessly torn asunder the motley feudal ties that bound man to his "natural superiors," and has left remaining no other nexus between man and man than naked self-interest, than callous "cash payment." It has drowned the most heavenly ecstasies of religious fervor, of chivalrous enthusiasm, of philistine sentimentalism, in the icy water of egotistical calculation. It has resolved personal worth into exchange value, and in place of the numberless indefeasible chartered freedoms, has set up that single, unconscionable freedom—free trade.[54]

In traditional society, people led the same lives, in the same places, as had their parents and grandparents. In the modern society the industrial revolution made, the world was new for every generation. This created unprecedented opportunities for betterment, to be sure, but it also produced many unfamiliar pitfalls. In traditional society life was a process of repetition, in modern society one of adaptation. A migrant from the traditional countryside to the modern city moved from security to insecurity, which made for disorientation and discomfort. It was not accidental that one of the medical innovations of the modern age, which was born at the end of the nineteenth century and grew rapidly in the twentieth, was psychiatry, and that one of the widespread ills it addressed was anxiety.

Industrial life took a physical toll as well. Crowded into unsanitary dwellings, toiling in unsafe mines and factories, workers were prey to diseases and accidents that their peasant forbears had never had to encounter. Nineteenth century urban poverty was not necessarily worse than the life of chronic shortages and occasional epidemics of traditional rural society but it was more visible and painful because it festered within sight and within reach of the rising affluence that economic growth produced. In traditional society poverty was the natural, unavoidable lot of the vast majority. In modern society everyone came to aspire to, and ultimately to expect, something better. The costs of modern urban life were noticed, and captured, in literature. The industrial revolution inspired the nineteenth century novel of realism, with its (sometimes) implicit theme of social protest, as practiced by writers such as Charles Dickens in England, Theodore Dreiser in the United States, and Emile Zola in France. On the whole, the combination of the market and the industrial revolution increased human welfare; neither would have been sustained over two centuries otherwise. But the advance in welfare came at a price. And this had to be so.

Schumpeter called economic growth a process of "creative destruction."[55] By its nature it both created and destroyed: indeed, it created *by* destroying. Economic growth depends chiefly on increases in productivity. Productivity involves doing things differently: making new things, or old things in a new way, or the same things in the same way but by different people in new places. The essence of productivity is change and change is usually disorienting and often painful. It requires adaptation and penalizes those who cannot adapt.

The mechanism by which the market produces growth is expressed in a story some version of which is a standard feature of introductory economics. If steel can be made more cheaply elsewhere, under free-market conditions local steelworkers will lose their jobs. Labor and capital will thereby be released so that they can be redeployed to a more efficient and thus more profitable use. In theory, the newly unemployed steelworker puts down his tools, changes from his heavy work clothes to a more comfortable outfit, walks across the street to a newly constructed office building and takes one of the jobs available there as a computer programmer. The story is, at some level, true, and it has a happy ending. Under the pressure of the market, steel industries do shrink and computer-programming firms do expand, making both steel and computer programs less costly to consumers everywhere. Society is better off. Consumers are winners.

But within this happy story there is an unhappy subplot. Unemployed steelworkers are losers. Few if any will be reemployed as computer programmers, many will have to take jobs paying less than the ones they have lost, and some will find no new job at all. In rural, traditional society virtually every person made some contribution to scraping a living from the soil. Unemployment is an artifact of the modern age. So, too, is poverty among the elderly. In rural, traditional society few people lived longer than they were able to work and their families cared for those who did. The combination of medical advances leading to longer life and the strain of industrial labor produced, in the twentieth century, a growing number of people unable to continue to support themselves but lacking the dense family networks that would have supported them in the traditional countryside.

Not surprisingly, the social costs of the industrial revolution gave rise to the impulse to prevent, cope with, and compensate for them, which, in the second half of the nineteenth century, took a political form. The name commonly given to the political movement with these goals is socialism.[56] In the twentieth century socialism split into two camps. The Marxist-Leninist wing took power in the former tsarist empire, created the international Communist movement that gained control of Central Europe, and carried the banner of illiberalism in the contest with the liberal West in the second half of the twentieth century.

In the Western core the socialist movements generally accepted as axiomatic political democracy and the economic primacy of the market. They sought, by democratic means, to moderate the market's destructive effects. European social democrats were attracted, for much of the twentieth century, to an expanded role for the government in investment, through planning, and in production, through state ownership. This enthusiasm died away in the last decades of the century. But the social democrats' principal interest, which they shared with similar political forces in North America, was to enhance the role of the state in the distribution of what society produced in a way that mitigated the harsh consequences of industrial civilization. Here the Western branch of the socialist movement succeeded. It created the welfare state.

Political pressure encouraged the creation of the welfare state. The forces demanding government-supplied padding for the shocks of the industrial revolution grew in strength from the middle of the nineteenth century to the middle of the twentieth, overcoming the resistance of the partisans of strict laissez-faire. As its advocates grew in strength (and its beneficiaries grew in number), the welfare state expanded in scope, from old-age pensions to unemployment insurance to health care. Within each category throughout the Western core, the scope of the services on which each citizen could count, and the sums the government spent on them, also grew steadily, as, in consequence, did the level of taxation needed to pay for them.

The welfare state came into being and expanded not only because its proponents were increasingly powerful, but also because of the growing legitimacy of the idea that society owed its members some form of social protection. Behind the idea lay three related arguments. One was that the victims of the industrial revolution deserved support. They were the casualties of a struggle that brought wide benefits to the society that waged it. Economic progress was like a war that had been worth waging and had ended successfully but that had also produced wounded people who were therefore owed compensation for their sacrifices.[57]

Another was that compensation for the risks of the industrial revolution was necessary to induce people to take part in it in the first place. The welfare state provided a "social safety net," a term suggesting that participation in the modern economy resembles walking across a high wire: No reasonable person would attempt it, and no one would have the confidence to do it successfully, without knowing that society was supplying something to break a possible fall. A third motive for yielding to the demands for social welfare was fear: Without some protection from the costs of the market system, those who benefited from it had reason to worry, its victims and potential victims would rise up and overthrow it. The ambitions and, after

1917, the achievements of the revolutionary wing of socialism served as a powerful incentive for the propertied classes to accede to the demands of its social democratic wing. This was a way of buying the internal peace and stability without which free markets cannot function, and it was not coincidental that a large upsurge in social spending in the West occurred in the years following 1945. From the onset of the Great Depression to the end of World War II all the countries of the Western core were riven by social conflict, which was aggravated, if not always created, by economic stress. In many cases the conflict approached, and in some cases it crossed, the threshold of civil war.

The growth of the welfare state substantially modified the nineteenth-century model of economic liberalism. In the early decades of the industrial revolution the liberal orthodoxy held that the proper economic role of the government was a minimal one. The ideal was the "night-watchman state," with the government standing guard at the factory gate to prevent theft but keeping resolutely clear of anything to do with the factory's operation. In the twentieth century, in the Western core, the state acquired an ever-larger role in redirecting the fruits of economic growth, a role that Adam Smith had never imagined and that the most powerful political forces of the nineteenth century had opposed.

The rise of the welfare state reconciled the two strands of political liberalism—popular participation and constitutionalism—which in the nineteenth century had seemed to be at odds with each other. It made popular sovereignty through universal suffrage compatible with the protection of private property by giving every citizen property in the form of an entitlement to benefits from the state. The liberal state of the twentieth century guaranteed the social protection of the poor just as it did the estates and businesses of the rich, thereby giving the first group as well as the second a stake in maintaining it.

For a hundred years, starting in the middle of the nineteenth century, one question at the heart of the politics of the liberal Western core was whether the state should compensate the public for the displacements and injuries caused by the industrial revolution. By the middle of the twentieth century the argument had been settled. For the second half of the twentieth century the domestic politics of the countries of the core were concerned with how extensive government welfare benefits should be.[58]

Due to advances in medicine more people were living longer lives, thereby increasing the costs of the benefits promised to everyone after the age of retirement. Virtually every public benefit in every Western country was financed on a "pay-as-you-go" basis, meaning that they were financed out of current revenues rather than with existing savings. But in the first decades of the twenty-first century the ratio of the working-age populations that generated the revenues to the sector of the population eligible to receive them was destined to fall, the result of a reduction in fertility rates in all of these countries.[59]

Thus, while public life in the core in the second half of the twentieth century revolved around how far to raise and extend benefits, the politics of the first half of the twenty-first century seemed likely to have at their center the issue of how far and how fast to reduce benefits.[60] The politics of generosity are easier and more pleasant to conduct than the politics of restraint. It is better—in any event it is easier—to give than to take away. But even if the less agreeable of the two should dominate the political debates and elections of Western Europe, the United States, and Japan in the first half of the twenty-first century, this would still make for an easier set of tasks and choices than the ones that most of the countries of the world's periphery faced.

CHAPTER TEN

The Invisible Construction Site

Wᴴᴇɴ ʜᴇ ᴊᴏɪɴᴇᴅ Lenin's revolutionary Bolshevik party, the Georgian ex-seminarian who would succeed him as the supreme leader of the Soviet Union, Josef Djugashvili, decided to call himself "Stalin"—man of steel. It was the perfect Communist name, for steel was the essence of Communist economic policy. Workers toiled in mines and steel mills to produce it, and out of what they produced were fashioned the factories, the skyscrapers, and the tanks that the Stalinist planned economy in the Soviet Union was devoted to making. Communism and steel turned both the Soviet Union and Maoist China into vast construction sites, and in the second half of the twentieth century many Third World governments sought to follow their example.

By the century's end, however, a gargantuan output of steel had become a sign of economic backwardness, not strength, and the central planning system that had produced it in the Soviet Union and China had become an obstacle to economic progress. At the outset of the twenty-first century, therefore, Russia and China and many of the countries in the world's periphery had once again become vast construction sites, but what was under construction was invisible, not tangible: the institutions of a market economy, which were everywhere considered the indispensable vehicle for achieving wealth.

This second construction project proved harder than the first. It was bound to take longer. Factories, buildings, and tanks could be produced in large quantities within the compass of a five-year project, but to amass the habits, practices, and skills needed for operating a market economy is the work of a generation. If time posed one obstacle, politics presented another.

The second modern exercise in large-scale construction involved the demolition of the obsolete structures of the old economy, and this encountered political resistance. Albert Einstein, when asked why mankind had had the wit to make bombs of unimagined power but had not been able to order human affairs in such a way that these weapons could not be used, is supposed to have replied that the answer was simple: Politics is more difficult than physics.[1] The difficulties that so many of the world's two hundred sovereign states encountered in constructing working free markets demonstrated that, in the twenty-first century, politics is also more difficult than economics.

ECONOMIC STRATEGIES

THE TWENTY-FIRST-CENTURY task of the countries of the core was to keep well-established market economies functioning smoothly. The countries of the periphery had embarked on a more difficult enterprise, building market economies. Among the countries in which market-construction dominated the public agenda of the first part of the new century were Russia and China.

Both had considerable economic potential. Russia was rich in natural resources and skilled people; China was endowed with the largest population of any country in the world, an increasing percentage of which was well educated. But the political stakes in their post-Cold War economic trajectories were, if anything, higher than the economic ones. Because they were potentially the most disruptive members of the international system, Russia and China were the countries where the liberal theory of history, if it proved accurate—if economic liberalism led to political liberalism, which underpinned a liberal foreign policy—would have the deepest and most salutary impact on the international politics of the twenty-first century.

The economic differences between the two in the first post-Cold War decade were striking. In the 1980s and 1990s China advanced economically as rapidly as any country in history, sustaining an average rate of eight percent annual growth over two decades. Russia had the opposite experience, recording the steepest decline in production of any industrial country ever, including during the Great Depression. Even allowing for the likelihood that Chinese growth was officially overstated and Russian production underreported, on the spectrum of economic performance the two countries were situated at opposite ends.

These contrasting performances, moreover, had come after, and as a result of, parallel efforts, launched a decade apart, to shift from central planning to the market. This naturally led to the question of why, when attempting the same thing, China had done so well and Russia so badly. The answers to that question fell into two categories: those emphasizing the conditions prevailing in the two countries when they began their transitions,[2] and those emphasizing the different economic strategies Russia and China adopted.

The first explanation was the more persuasive. Communism had a weaker grip on China at the end of the 1970s than on Russia at the outset of the 1990s. The political upheaval of the 1960s and 1970s known as the Cultural Revolution had undercut Communist control of China and the party was especially weak in the Chinese countryside, where the market reforms first flourished. Rural Russia, by contrast, could not serve as the incubator for the market. The agricultural sector was a far smaller part of the economy and society and was thoroughly dominated by the Communist system.

Moreover, much of China's late-twentieth century economic growth, like the growth experienced by every other country in the first phase of the industrial revolution, came from the transfer of people from less productive agricultural work to more productive industrial employment, a route that was closed to Russia in the 1990s. While China had an enormous reservoir of peasants on which to draw, Russia did not. It was already an urban country. Economic growth in Russia required improvements within the industrial sector.

If the Communist system was weaker, the economic environment in which reform began was more stable in China than in Russia. The end of the Soviet Union divided what had been a unified economic space into fifteen separate sovereign states, inhibiting access to

familiar markets and so administering a severe economic shock to
Russia just at the time that it was struggling to establish free markets.

Two other differences between Russia and China contributed to
their differing economic performances. Russia began its transition
with serious inflation, the result of the excessive printing of money
in the last years of Communism. To prevent hyperinflation, austerity
measures were required, which came to be known as "shock therapy." China confronted economic difficulties—it was in response to
them that the government authorized the changes that triggered
reform—but not that particular problem. And in the 1980s and
1990s Chinese society had a high rate of savings, which facilitated
investment; post-Communist Russia did not.[3]

China also followed a different, more gradual strategy of economic reform than did Russia, which is the basis for the second
explanation for their sharply differing economic performances.[4]
China began with the easing of state controls in the rural sector.
Chinese farmers took advantage of the greater scope for independent initiative that this permitted, went further than the government
had intended, and created private enterprise and private property in
agriculture.[5] At the same time, the relaxation of central government
oversight gave rise to new, quasi-private enterprises engaged in
manufacturing, construction, and trade, under the sponsorship and
management of local Chinese authorities. These "township and village enterprises" were perhaps the most important economic innovation of the Chinese experience. They were not exactly private
concerns, and China's Communist government did not establish the
formal property rights that made possible economic expansion elsewhere; but they existed outside the dictates of the plan and were
conducted in many ways like private businesses.[6]

As a result, China evolved a dual-track economy. Down one track
lumbered the old state-operated economy, with its Communist
emphasis on heavy industry. On a parallel track moved the smaller,
faster, private and semi-private economic sector, which expanded
steadily following the beginning of reform in 1978 and from which
most of China's remarkable growth came.

Critics of post-Communist Russian economic policy asserted that
Moscow should have followed a Chinese-style gradualist course of

economic change after the collapse of Communism.[7] Even had Russia done so, the differences in initial conditions would have made Russia's economic course rockier than China's. But Russia was not in a position to follow it. The essence of the gradualist strategy was the maintenance of a Communist as well as a free-market economic sector. To manage a Communist economy required a Communist government. In December 1991, Russia ceased to have one. The transformation of its economic system was forced upon Russia by the revolution in its politics. Russians could not have waded slowly into the waters of the market as did the Chinese. They found themselves abruptly hurled by political events into the middle of the lake, where they were forced to sink or swim.

For all their differences, Russia and China exhibited important economic similarities. Like other countries of the periphery at the end of the first post-Cold War decade, neither had a fully functioning market economy, and the struggle to build and operate a market was destined to be central to their post-Cold War public affairs. Here Russia and China were both typical and atypical of the sovereign states of the world's periphery. They were typical in that the three principal obstacles they faced were the ones confronted by other countries that lagged behind the economic leaders of the world's core. All lacked the proper political and economic institutions; all were plagued by corruption; and all had to cope with economic distortions resulting from the decades-long and systematic direction of resources to unprofitable uses. The two were atypical in that their common Communist background made each problem more serious than it was for many of the other countries of the periphery.

Russia and China lacked the institutions associated with market economics and necessary for economic growth. The great lesson of the 1990s in formerly Communist Eurasia was that economic policies, no matter how well considered and skillfully designed, will fail without the appropriate institutions to implement them. This is why the prescriptions of the international financial community did so little for the economies of many of the former Communist countries. The measures recommended were like computer programs without the necessary underlying operating system. Foremost among the missing institutions was a market-enhancing state—a government that enforced the rules of the market, protecting property and securing economic transactions against fraud, theft, and non-compliance while leaving economic decisions to private individuals operating according to market rules.

Here the Communist legacy was worse than useless, for the Communists had built their system on contrary principles. It was governed not by rules, and certainly not by rules protecting private property, but by the decisions involving all facets of economic life of those who wielded political power.[8]

And because they had been ruled by Communists, Russia and China had had no opportunity to establish the other crucial market institution, a financial system, which, like political institutions, takes time to develop.[9] The financial system is both the circulatory system and the brain of the economy, directing capital from those who have it to those who can use it productively, thus enabling investor, producer, and intermediary all to benefit.

A financial system must rest on an appropriate political system. No one will lend or invest money without the assurance of repayment that a liberal state provides. But a financial system is more than a collection of institutions—banks and stock and bond markets—crucial though these are. It is also a collection of skills—assessing investment opportunities, evaluating risk—and like the human brain these can neither be transplanted nor created instantly.

In many countries of the periphery following the end of the Cold War, few people had the relevant skills. When they broke with orthodox Communism, Russia and China had virtually none. In the Communist era, investment had been determined by government fiat according to the wishes of the planners, not on the basis of prospective profitability. Rather than furnishing opportunities for developing these skills, orthodox Communism had made them illegal. At the height of Mao's power in China, and Stalin's in the Soviet Union, suspicion of following the "capitalist" road was cause for imprisonment, or worse. It was the absence of the relevant institutions and the impossibility of acquiring them rapidly that, more than anything else, made the transition from plan to market on the territory of the former Soviet Union so difficult in the first post-Cold War decade.

CORRUPTION

THE ABSENCE of institutions was related to another typical obstacle to the establishment and operation of a market economy, which loomed particularly large in Russia and China: corruption. Corruption is the misuse of public power for private gain. It occurs when a private person bribes a public official to acquire an economic privilege worth far more than the bribe, or a public official uses his or her position for illicit personal enrichment.[10] The temptation to corruption is inherent in government itself, with its monopoly of legal power. Corruption is therefore eternal and universal.[11]

It is also inversely related to the rule of law. When one is strong, the other will be weak. In economic terms, corruption is a tax. Because it is found in some form everywhere, including the wealthiest countries, the tax obviously is not necessarily economically crippling. Corruption per se does not pose an insurmountable barrier to economic growth. Some countries are more corrupt than others. At the dawn of the twenty-first century the core countries were, on the whole, almost certainly less corrupt than those of the periphery and probably less corrupt than they had been in the past.[12] The more extensive the corruption, the higher the tax, and thus the greater the drain on productive activity will be. In the worst cases, government itself becomes an exercise in predation, without any pretense of providing public goods, including public safety. Public office in such cases becomes a license to loot.

Whatever its direct economic effects, corruption has adverse *political* consequences, which bear, indirectly, on economic performance. The beneficiaries of corruption have a vested interest in blocking the establishment of the rule of law, which would threaten their gains. They can be expected to form a lobby against this central feature of political liberalism, which is also one of the conditions for efficient markets. The chief obstacle to liberal politics in much of the world where it did not exist in the first post-Cold War decade was not a principled allegiance to non-liberal forms of government, or even a desire for arbitrary power per se, but rather the felt need to monopolize power to preserve and protect corruptly acquired wealth. The more corruption there is in a society, the more powerful will be the forces arrayed against political liberalism and the more difficult it will be to establish the rule of law.[13]

In post-Cold War Russia and China corruption was rampant. Russia was particularly susceptible because it was rich in raw materials, which create a powerful temptation to behave corruptly wherever they are found. Possession alone guarantees wealth. No breakthroughs in technology, no innovations in management, no skill in marketing are needed to make a fortune from oil, or diamonds, or nickel, or timber. All that is needed is title to them, and this can be conferred by political authority. Power therefore leads directly and easily to wealth. Paying an official to gain control of valuable raw materials, or using an official position to seize them, is a sure route to riches and one that many have taken.[14]

Their common Communist background also made Russia and China vulnerable to corruption. The essence of the Communist economy fits the basic definition of corruption: the allocation of resources by political power rather than market rules. In Communist societies market-based activity was confined to the underground economy—the black market—which the government tried to suppress. If the free market is a system of natural liberty, the command economy was a system of natural corruption.[15] When market reforms began in Russia and China, what had been the property of the state suddenly became available for private ownership. The most valuable assets were acquired by those best placed to seize them by virtue of being in or close to power. The temptation was powerful and, in the absence of a well-established and firmly entrenched liberal state, there was nothing and no one to stop it.[16]

As distasteful to the Russian and Chinese people as the appropriation of wealth by the politically well-connected undoubtedly was, and as debilitating as it was for the reputation of the market, which millions of Russians and Chinese came to identify with thievery, it was also probably partly responsible for the bloodlessness of the movement away from Communist economic practices in both countries and from the Communist political system in Russia. Through corruption those with the greatest stakes in the old system acquired major interests in the new one. Communist officials in both countries, who had powerful reasons to resist the dismantling of the planned system, were bought off by valuable shares in the new market enterprises.[17] This was a case of bribery in the service of peace, a golden parachute for people who would otherwise have had both the motive and the opportunity to cause trouble.

It helps to account for one of the striking ways in which what were, after all, revolutionary changes in Russia and China in the last decades of the twentieth century differed from the other great revolutions of the modern era. In the previous upheavals the old elite resisted, was defeated, and went into exile: after the French Revolution to Austria, after the Russian Revolution to Germany, in the wake of the Communist victory in the Chinese civil war to Taiwan, and after the revolutions in Cuba in the 1960s and Iran in the 1970s to Miami and Los Angeles respectively. In the second modern Russian and Chinese revolutions, the economic system and, in the Russian case, the political system changed radically but the old Communist elites adapted and remained rather than fighting and fleeing.

DISTORTION

I N ADDITION to the absence of the proper institutions and the presence of widespread corruption, Russia, China, and most of the other countries in the world's periphery faced, in the post–Cold War era, a third obstacle to the construction and successful operation of a market economy: the results of policies of economic distortion. The line between corruption and distortion is a blurry one. Like corruption, distortion involves the allocation of resources by political decisions rather than market rules. Like corruption, distortion is a form of "rent-seeking," rent being the economist's term for the difference between free-market prices and the higher prices made possible by political restraints on competition. But there are also important differences between the two.

Although distortion, like corruption, is sometimes undertaken for personal gain, it usually has a wider purpose—to confer benefits on a favored group rather than on a particular individual, or on society as a whole. Corruption diverts resources for the purpose of consumption. It is a form of scavenging. Distortion typically involves investment. It is an exercise in building and usually takes place on a larger scale than corruption. Thus, while corruption is as old as organized social life, distortion, the diversion of resources on a large scale to economically unproductive uses, required the capacities of the modern state to come into its own.

Corruption is contrary to, and subversive of, liberal politics. For distortion, this is not always so. Economically irrational it may be, but distortion is not necessarily illegal. Democratic governments have routinely practiced it. Indeed, as the twenty-first century began, the major problems of two large democracies—Japan and India—stemmed from economic distortion on a large scale over a long period of time.

The Japanese economy was divided into two parts. One, devoted to exports and operated according to market principles, was a model of efficiency. The other, prominently including energy, retail distribution, transportation, and construction, was inefficient, the creation of distortion accomplished by competition-restricting measures such as tariffs, cartels, and subsidies provided directly by the government and indirectly through government-encouraged loans.[18] This second part of the Japanese economy employed far more people, at higher wages, with lower output, than would have been the case had it been subject to the full discipline of the market.

Similarly, in India the license raj served as an instrument of economic distortion, as did the extensive government subsidies for power and water, which set their prices lower and thereby encouraged higher consumption than would otherwise have been the case. Policies of economic distortion had also produced the large sector of state-owned and operated industries in the Indian economy.[19]

At the end of the first post-Cold War decade, distortion dominated economic life in the Middle East as well. Democratic Turkey, partly democratic Iran, non-democratic Egypt, and illiberal Syria all had large state-owned sectors and provided government subsidies to a variety of economic activities.[20] This was true, as well, of countries in Latin America.[21]

Distortion invariably has an unwanted economic consequence: It retards growth. Economic activity resulting from distortion eats up resources that could otherwise be put to productive use, weighing down the economy, making it sluggish. The protected sectors in Japan, the products of economic distortion in India, the parts of the economies of the countries of the Middle East and Latin America that distortion built all had the effect on these economies of a tapeworm on the human body. The burden of the protected sector lay at the heart of the deep and prolonged Japanese recession of the 1990s.[22] Distortions kept India, until the 1990s, at a growth rate of 3.5 percent, which lagged behind the Chinese performance of the 1980s and 1990s and was not high enough to lift the mass of Indians out of poverty.

Another common, although indirect, consequence of distortion was the most familiar and, at its worst, the most damaging of all market pathologies: inflation. Prices rise when too much money is available for too few goods. Governments print too much money when they can neither reduce their obligations nor raise enough revenue to pay for them. Inflation is a method of taxation without representation, as the government arbitrarily creates purchasing power for its own use.[23] The classic occasion for inflation is wartime, when demands for spending are urgent but governments cannot tax the population at the levels necessary to meet them.

Policies of economic distortion occasioned inflation in the same way that wars did. Especially, although not exclusively, in the countries of the periphery,[24] governments lacked the strength to collect enough in taxes to support unproductive activities. The tax revenues available were depressed by the drag distortions exerted on economic growth, and so these governments resorted to the profligate printing of money. The result was high inflation—even, in seventeen of the post-Communist countries of Eurasia, hyperinflation[25]—and often a currency crisis, as holders of local money rushed to convert it to more stable currencies.

While all governments have a powerful economic interest in reducing distortions, reductions are almost invariably politically difficult to accomplish. Many people benefit from policies of distortion. They stand to lose a great deal—income, privileges, jobs—if these policies end. In smoothly functioning market economies such losses are normal. Firms fail, people lose their jobs, labor shifts from one sector to another with regularity. But in a smoothly functioning market economy all this occurs more gradually than when policies of economic distortion are abruptly terminated. The difference between normal market attrition and the wholesale correction of policies of distortion is the difference between seeking regular dental care, involving frequent cleaning and the occasional filling of a cavity, on the one hand, and on the other ignoring the matter until all the teeth require root canal or extraction. The first can be unpleasant and annoying; the second is usually painful and disruptive.

The words commonly used to describe what the correction of distortions required were anodyne: "adjustment" and "restructuring." But these were euphemisms for upheaval, dislocation, and deprivation in the lives of millions of people. The universally embraced social safety net also qualifies as a kind of economic distortion, for it, too, is the product of political rather than economic decisions. Often distortions serve the same purpose: Japan's protected sectors were a kind of welfare system for the people employed in them.[26]

Because they injure the beneficiaries, measures designed to end distortions invariably encounter political resistance, which can be more effective in democratic than in non-democratic political systems. The Japanese Liberal Democratic Party (LDP), in power almost continuously from the aftermath of World War II to the turn of the century, built its political dominance on government support for economic distortions. Those who benefited gave the LDP their votes in return.[27] In India, unions that gained from government-imposed hiring and firing, and rural landowners enriched by government subsidies for power and water, organized voting blocs that they delivered to politicians who promised to continue these distortions.

Democratic politicians who retract benefits risk being voted out of office. Leaders in political systems that are not democratic do not have to concern themselves with elections but run the risk of violent protest and even overthrow. Both are caught between the Scylla of inflation and slow growth and the Charybdis of mass unemployment. Where economic distortions are concerned, the logic of economics runs counter to the imperatives of politics. No doubt in the long run a society that removes its distortions will be better off economically, which will redound to the credit of its political leaders. But politicians live in and for the short term.

When the inability to sustain distorted economic policies drove governments to the International Monetary Fund, the conditions for loans invariably involved ending the policies and practices that had caused the problems. The beleaguered governments invariably accepted the conditions in principle but were not always able to fulfill them. In the last decades of the twentieth century Turkey contracted sixteen agreements with the fund but successfully completed only two.[28]

At the end of the first post-Cold War decade, the conflict between the irresistible force of economic rationality and the immovable object of political self-interest dominated the political agenda of many of the 150 or so sovereign states of the world's periphery. Of all of them, Russia and China were among the most severely afflicted by economic distortions, which they had inherited from the orthodox Communist past. The overriding purpose of Communist economic policy was to build precisely the kind of industrial structure that was obsolete in the twenty-first century. Soviet planners specialized in enormous steel mills, vast coal mines, and giant tank factories. All operated under a "soft budget constraint," receiving all the funds they needed from the government without regard for efficiency, let alone profitability. Firing workers was unknown, bankruptcy unthinkable. The legacy was a rust-belt archipelago stretching across Russia from the Baltic Sea to the Ural Mountains, which employed millions of people turning out products for which there was no demand.

Communist authorities in China had followed the Soviet example. Even after fifty years of Communist rule the country remained predominantly rural, but the Chinese population was so large that even the relatively modest fraction of the Chinese economy that consisted of Communist-built industrial white elephants employed millions of people.

Many of the massive industries in both countries fit the definition of economic irrationality. They were net subtractors of value.[29] This meant that privatization could not solve the economic and political problems these industries posed, for they were not economically viable. Private owners would not be willing or able to continue to employ the people who worked in them. Shutting down these industrial dinosaurs was all the more difficult because in Russia, although not in China, there was no thriving private economy into which unemployed workers could be absorbed. Shutting them down was also difficult because of a feature of the Communist economic system common to both.

Under Communism basic benefits and services—health care, housing, education, even food—were tied to employment. A place to live and enough to eat came with the job and thus would be forfeited if the job were lost. Unemployment is nowhere a pleasant experience but in formerly orthodox Communist countries it could be catastrophic. Even Russian and Chinese firms with good prospects for profitable private management could not survive in the market while encumbered with these Communist-era social welfare obligations. A well-functioning market economy in both countries therefore required divesting these obligations from employment.

But that, in turn, required a private housing market, a new health care system, and the reconstruction of the system of primary and secondary education. These were not minor undertakings. They all required time to accomplish, as well as money that neither the Russian nor the Chinese government had the administrative capacity to raise. Both governments were far less effective at revenue collection than the sovereign states of the core.[30] Without access to housing, health care, and education, however, ending the economic distortions from which Russia and China suffered risked leaving millions of people stranded, destitute, and angry—a risk that any government would avoid if possible.[31] In the first post-Cold War decade, therefore, Russia and China devised, or stumbled into, strategies for avoiding massive unemployment that, although averting a social and political explosion, aggravated their underlying economic problems.

ECONOMIC REMEDIES

THE INITIAL RESPONSE of the post-Communist Russian government to the problem of sustaining obsolete industries without adequate revenues was to print more money. The result, inevitably, was high inflation, which the Russian government managed, in the second half of the 1990s, to bring under control. It then attempted to fill the gap between income and obligations by borrowing. It floated loans and issued bonds. But the ensuing cost of paying the interest and the premiums outran the government's capacity to meet them and, in August 1998, it defaulted on its obligations and devalued its currency, dealing a severe blow to an already weakened economy.[32] Meanwhile, in the course of the 1990s the deadly combination of the political incapacity to close or substantially reduce the rust-belt archipelago with the economic incapacity to support it caused the Russian economy to develop in a peculiar way. By a combination of deferring wages and bills and, when payment had to be made to creditors or to the government, supplying products rather than money, Russian industrial concerns managed to continue to function, albeit at a very low level. This mixture of IOUs and barter—Russia's "virtual economy"[33]—served as a life support system for the great floundering behemoth enterprises that Communism had created.

China also experienced bouts of inflation but found another way to sustain its unprofitable state-owned enterprises. The Chinese populace saved at a high rate. Its savings went by and large to state banks—there were no others—which paid modest interest on them. The banks channeled them to the state enterprises, which were able to continue to function and employ large numbers of workers. This postponed paying the costs of liquidating the distortions in the Chinese economy[34] but did not eliminate them. In fact, it increased them. During the two decades of economic reform the state-owned sector grew rather than shrank.

As more Chinese savings flowed into unprofitable economic activities, less was available for the healthy private sector, and this held down the rate of growth.[35] Because concerns receiving capital were not profitable, they were unable to repay their loans, which meant that the banks would fail if savers in large numbers demanded their deposits.[36] That, in turn, was an obstacle to establishing a modern financial system with institutions that could compete with the state banks for national savings.

At the center of Russian and Chinese political affairs in the wake of the Cold War was the need to reduce the parasitic sector of the economy and the difficulty of doing so. It was difficult not only for these two governments but for governments all across the world's periphery, which raised the question of whether those that were not democratically chosen and democratically accountable were better placed to take the necessary steps because less susceptible to public pressure than those governed according to liberal principles.

The liberal theory of history holds that free markets encourage the establishment of liberal political systems. But it is a matter of debate whether democratic politics, once established, have a tendency to inhibit the effective workings of the market.[37] The beneficiaries of economic distortion can and do seek to preserve them and a democratic political system gives them the opportunity to do this openly, legitimately, legally, and often successfully. Over time, democratic societies tend to accumulate such groups, like barnacles on the hull of a ship that reduce its speed.[38]

The evidence concerning the association between democratic and economic growth is inconclusive.[39] But there is no logical reason to believe that non-liberal governments are better at whittling down economic distortions than liberal ones. Non-democratic regimes do not have flawless records of fidelity to market principles and the illiberal Communist regimes of the twentieth century were, because they suppressed the market entirely, the world's worst offenders in practicing policies of economic distortion.[40] Moreover, if the lack of accountability may liberate the economic policies of non-democratic governments, the lack of legitimacy may well have the opposite effect. In an effort to win public tolerance the Communist governments of Central and Eastern Europe constructed more generous social safety nets than those of the West, with which their liberal successors were saddled after 1989.[41]

In post-Communist Europe, where economic success involved coping with the distortions of the Communist period, the most successful countries were also the most democratic. It may be that people are more willing to accept the social pain of "adjustment" if it is, in effect, self-inflicted—that is, imposed by a government that they have chosen and can, by democratic means, remove.[42] And even if non-democratic governments can, on occasion, do better than democratic ones at dealing with economic distortion, liberal political systems are far more effective at overcoming the other two major obstacles to a well-made market: the absence of the relevant institutions[43] and the presence of corruption.

In the nineteenth century in the world's European core, traditional and even partly liberal regimes came under pressure for being illegitimate because they were insufficiently liberal, governed as they were in the east by monarchs and in the west by parliaments selected by a small fraction of the adult population. In the twenty-first century in the world's periphery, political legitimacy had come to depend, indirectly, on economic liberalism. It depended directly on the production of prosperity, which meant expanding access to consumer goods and a rising standard of living. In the wake of the Cold War prosperity seemed to be available only through a well-functioning market economy. A market economy was therefore what most of the sovereign states of the periphery were attempting to build.

This was nowhere a painless enterprise but it was everywhere, in the first instance, a solitary one. Building institutions, controlling corruption, and reducing distortions fell within the competence and responsibility of individual governments. But the construction of free markets, the beginning of the virtuous chain reaction posited by the liberal theory of history, had an international dimension as well.

THE GOLDEN STRAITJACKET

THE WORLD affected the economic policies and practices of individual countries in the time-honored way: by example. In the design of economic systems in the twenty-first century the process of cultural transmission was at work. The people and governments of the periphery observed the market economies of the core, were favorably impressed, and sought to replicate what they saw. But there was another, more direct kind of influence at work as well. Economic affairs, like security but unlike domestic governance, are by nature international as well as domestic in scope.

In the second half of the twentieth century the core countries established not only a series of liberal economic structures within their sovereign borders but also an overarching liberal international economic order binding them together, participation in which

reinforced the tendency toward liberal economic policies and practices at home. And in the wake of the Cold War, integration into the
liberal global economy was something that virtually every country of
the periphery sought.

This represented a change. For most of the twentieth century the
prevailing attitude in the periphery toward the Western-dominated
international economic order, and to economic engagement with
the core countries, had ranged from ambivalence to outright hostility. The Communist countries for the most part shut themselves off
from the rest of the world. Other countries outside the core were not
so categorical. But many erected barriers against products made
elsewhere and made foreign capital unwelcome, regarding it as an
instrument of subversion and control—the continuation of imperialist exploitation by other means. By the end of the century the prevailing sentiment had reversed itself. The market economy had
come to be seen as the key to the prosperity that was both desirable
for its own sake and necessary for political stability, and participation
in international markets for goods and capital[44] had come to be
regarded as part and parcel of the adoption of the market system.

Foreign-made products were desirable because local consumers
wanted them. Foreign capital was indispensable for the investment
that fueled economic growth in countries with low indigenous rates
of saving. Even where savings were high, foreign investment brought
technology and managerial techniques not available locally.

The widespread wish in the countries of the periphery to participate in the Western-dominated trade and monetary orders had consequences for their foreign policies. It created a disincentive for
policies that would hinder access to the international economy, just
as a household will go to some lengths to avoid having its electricity
cut off.[45] Russia and China were restrained—although not categori-
cally prevented—from attacking their neighbors by concern for the
international economic consequences of doing so. Fear of being cut
off from global trade and capital markets was one reason that the
Chinese government conducted a generally circumspect policy
toward Taiwan. Any leader in Beijing contemplating seizing control
of the island by force would have had to assess the impact of war in
the Taiwan Strait on economic relations with the core countries and

on the prospects for China's economic growth, on which the political stability of the country and the political legitimacy of the Communist Party had come very heavily to depend.[46] This had not been a consideration in Mao's day.

It also had consequences for the effort to build the market. To tap into the global utility required the proper kind of plug. Liberal economic institutions and practices at home were necessary to take advantage of the liberal global economic order. The desire to take part in that order, and exposure to it, thus acted as forces for the construction of a liberal economic system at home.

Trade, one of the oldest human activities, is also the longest-standing and, before the modern age, perhaps the most influential method of cultural transmission. It is also a powerful solvent of inefficient practices and a force for the adoption of the most advanced ones, as Marx and Engels noted:

> The bourgeoisie, by the rapid improvement of all instruments of production, by the immensely facilitated means of communication, draws all, even the most barbarian, nations into civilization. The cheap prices of its commodities are the heavy artillery with which it batters down all Chinese walls, with which it forces the barbarians' intensely obstinate hatred of foreigners to capitulate. It compels all nations, on pain of extinction, to adopt the bourgeois mode of production; it compels them to introduce what it calls civilization into their midst, i.e., to become bourgeois themselves. In one word, it creates a world after its own image.[47]

The words apply to the twenty-first century as much as to the nineteenth. Trade brings competition and competition is a force for economic efficiency. It raises productivity by forcing local firms to adopt the most efficient practices available, which is the key to productivity. Locally made products either match imports in price and quality or fail to find buyers, forcing their producers out of business. Trade therefore counteracts, and compels corrections to, economic distortion.[48] For this reason governments sometimes sign trade agreements mandating the removal of import barriers precisely in order to bring pressure on inefficient industries and illiberal practices.

Mexico's membership in the North American Free Trade Association and China's decision to join the World Trade Organization (WTO) may be understood as efforts by their governments, or liberal-minded officials within their governments, to ally themselves with the international forces of economic liberalism. Both sought to enlist foreign artillery to batter down the obstacles to an effective market economy that could not be removed by strictly local political forces. WTO rules required the lowering of barriers China had erected to protect agriculture, manufacturing, and finance; competition would force Chinese firms to become more efficient and increase pressure to end government support for inefficient ones.* WTO membership also had the potential to affect China's internal political arrangements, since it required that trade be regulated by tariffs overseen by an institution the People's Republic lacked: an independent judiciary.

The import of capital also exercises a liberalizing effect. Banks can wield considerable power over borrowers. When firms need loans to survive, banks generally insist that they take steps to make themselves more profitable. The IMF, functioning as a bank for financially strapped countries, often insisted on changes in a country's domestic economic policies as the conditions for loans. Frequently these involved lower budget deficits, which in turn required reducing the distortions in the economy.[49] Occasionally the IMF went further, insisting on changes that addressed other obstacles to a

*David M. Lampton, *Same Bed Different Dreams: Managing U.S.-China Relations, 1989–2000*, Berkeley: The University of California Press, 2000, pp. 178–184. See also pp. 121, 129–130. In the core, the European Union had a similarly liberalizing effect. The rules for participating in the common currency, the euro, forced governments to reduce their budget deficits, which economic distortions often caused. Italy was an example. Perhaps the most dramatic instance of the EU's liberalizing effect was the French reversal of economic policy in the early 1980s. French officials concluded that the continuation of the policies that Francois Mitterrand had launched would force the country out of the European Monetary System, the predecessor of the euro, membership in which was a hallmark of fidelity to the project of constructing a united Europe. Mitterrand thus had to choose between socialism and Europe. He chose Europe.

EU membership arguably had the most profound impact on Spain and Ireland, two countries at the extremes of Western Europe that were noted, for the first two-thirds of the twentieth century, principally for economic backwardness, emigration, great literature, and civil war. As EU members they transformed themselves, in the century's last three decades, into prosperous, peaceful, modern European nation-states.

smoothly functioning market economy. The Fund refused to extend a loan to Kenya until the Kenyan government enacted an anti-corruption law written according to IMF specifications.[50]

In the first post-Cold War decade, the flow of private capital from the core to the periphery considerably exceeded the volume of loans and grants from governments and international financial institutions, and the countries of the periphery competed with one another to attract this private capital. The competition for private investment focused attention on the foremost obstacle to a functioning market, the absence of a law-enforcing government. Foreigners were reluctant to put money in countries where they could not be sure that it would be secure; that assurance required a government willing and able to protect property rights. Nor were foreigners likely to invest in firms without transparent procedures for internal governance and honest accounting practices, which made foreign investment from core countries a counterweight to corruption.[51] The competition for capital also created pressure for restrained fiscal policies, which required attacking economic distortions; the obligation to support these distortions gave rise to the temptation to inflate the local currency, and inflation in turn eroded the value of foreign investments.

Adopting the economic policies and practices needed to attract money from abroad was tantamount to putting on, in a phrase coined by Thomas L. Friedman, a "golden straitjacket." Together these measures offered little room for maneuver in economic policy. Discarding or modifying them would make governments freer to act, but would also make those they governed poorer, since foreign capital would be redirected toward the countries willing to live with the constraints.[52]

The golden straitjacket was also necessary to attract foreign direct investment—investment in and ownership of land, plants, and equipment rather than simply equity shares. Direct investment attacked distortions by promoting competition. In addition, it affected the very culture of the countries in which it took place. Western-owned and operated plants became islands of modernity and efficiency. They transplanted economic practices. The wages and labor standards in the American-owned factories in northern

Mexico were higher than those in locally owned plants elsewhere in the country.[53]

The ubiquitous McDonald's hamburger restaurants, the late-twentieth century symbols of the American economic presence the world over, were, appropriately, bearers of Western cultural and political norms in the tradition of missionaries and even imperial rule. With its clean, safe restaurants where people could pass the time, and its courteous, efficient personnel, McDonald's did a great deal to bring the Western concept of service to China.[54] The restaurant chain introduced the idea of celebrating a child's birthday with a restaurant meal replete with gifts, thus insinuating into Chinese culture two values at the heart of liberal politics and economics: individualism—the holiday honored one person rather than the nation or the Party—and consumption.*

One of the most striking properties of the liberal theory of history, and one it shared with Marxism, is inevitability. Not only is history moving in a liberal direction, not only do good things go together, but this is happening in the world's periphery without any conscious effort on the part of liberalism's practitioners in the core. Governments will strive to build market economies because such economies, and they alone, make possible prosperity; prosperity is the post-Cold War condition for political legitimacy; legitimacy is necessary for survival; and every government, like every species in the scheme of natural evolution, seeks to survive. Liberal economic practices contribute to, in some ways require, liberal political ones.

---

*McDonald's joined Coca-Cola as the most visible American brand around the world. As such, both were the objects of protest: Coca-Cola was banned by the Indian government in the 1970s, McDonald's picketed and assaulted in France in the 1990s. There were, however, differences between the two. Coke was a mildly narcotic beverage that often replaced local sources of refreshment. McDonald's hamburgers provided a more nutritious meal than had previously been available to most people in most countries of the periphery, and the service that the restaurants offered was largely unknown. Coca-Cola was first spread around the world by the American army in World War II. The global growth of McDonald's coincided with the retrenchment of the American military presence. Coke varied the formula for its syrup from one locale to another, but McDonald's was an even more decentralized and flexible organization. In the Indian city of Bombay, for instance, the basic McDonald's fare was vegetarian. It would no doubt be an exaggeration to call Coke an illiberal product and McDonald's a liberal one, but it is the case that China before the reforms welcomed Coke, and the Soviet Union admitted its rival, Pepsi-Cola, during the Brezhnev era, while McDonald's entered Russia and China only after reforms had begun in both places.

The market begets—and is begotten by—democracy. Democracies are more inclined than non-democracies to practice peaceful foreign policies, and in particular to embrace the principles of common security. Eight decades after the end of World War I, therefore, the world was moving toward the kinds of economics, politics, and security policies that had formed the basis of the program of international reform that Woodrow Wilson had presented in Paris.

But even if this chain of reasoning was sound, even if all the propositions that comprise it were true—or at least plausible and widely applicable—there was a problem with the first of them, one that required a concerted effort by the countries of the core to address. All governments might wish to build market economies, and might try to build them, but most, even with the best will in the world, faced formidable difficulties in doing so. A major resource for overcoming them was the liberal international economic order; and it was here that the burden of sustaining the global liberal agenda fell on the countries of the core. For the international economic order was the creation, and maintaining it was the responsibility, of the liberal, prosperous, powerful countries of the core, in particular the most powerful of them, the United States.

CHAPTER ELEVEN

The Global Utility

WHILE THE settlement after World War I was a personal failure for Woodrow Wilson, who could not even persuade his own country to join the League of Nations he had worked to organize, it was also a disaster for the world as a whole, for it sowed the seeds of an even more destructive world war two decades later.

John Maynard Keynes, who attended the Paris peace conference as part of the British delegation, diagnosed the settlement's fatal flaw. It was designed to punish the losing powers rather than to foster the conditions of economic cooperation in which all of Europe could prosper. A key to prosperity was the free movement of goods across borders, something that the peacemakers did not seriously attempt to establish. In his scathing indictment of the settlement in *The Economic Consequences of the Peace*, published in 1920, Keynes wrote: "In a regime of Free Trade and free economic intercourse it would be of little consequence that iron lay on one side of a political frontier and labour, coal, and blast furnaces on the other. But as it is, men have devised ways to impoverish themselves and one another; and prefer collective animosities to individual happiness."[1]

Twenty-five years later, at the end of World War II—an even more savage outbreak of collective animosity—the winning powers had a second chance to lay the basis for prosperity and therefore peace. This time they followed Keynes's counsel, in no small part because he himself took part in the crucial negotiations.[2] They created an international economic order based on liberal principles that functioned successfully for the rest of the twentieth century and into the twenty-first. These liberal rules and institutions, and the remarkable economic growth they fostered, played a major role in the Western victory in the Cold War. In the wake of that conflict observing those rules and participating in those institutions stood at the top of the public agenda of virtually every sovereign state on the planet. To the countries of the periphery the world trading system and international capital markets, both organized and dominated by the core, loomed as a kind of global utility that, if they could tap into it, could power their own economies.

A GLOBAL ECONOMY

THE MARKET ECONOMY, according to Adam Smith, springs from human nature. Humankind has a natural propensity to "truck, barter, and exchange one thing for another,"[3] which leads directly to the basis for the wealth that the market creates: the division of labor. Each person finds it in his interest to specialize in making one particular thing so that he has more to exchange and thus can get more of everything for himself.[4] By that logic economic activity is naturally, optimally, international in scope.[5] The more extensive is the division of labor, the greater will be the number of people who participate in it and the wider the range of specialization, which will thus maximize the wealth produced. It is one of the central tasks of government, according to Smith, to overcome the physical barriers to exchange by improving the methods of transporting goods from one place to another through the building of roads, canals, and harbors.[6] Whatever public works governments provide, however, on no account should they do anything to *hinder* exchange.

But of course governments do hinder international trade, and always have. They impose tariffs and other obstacles to cross-border commerce. In Adam Smith's day, as at the beginning of the twenty-first century, for the purposes of the liberal approach to economics the distribution of sovereignty in the world was the opposite of what was desirable. On the one hand, the multiple jurisdictions into which the planet was divided made it possible for the various governments to interrupt exchange across their borders. On the other, because economic activity thrives on predictability, which is best provided by a market-enhancing government that enforces the contracts upon which large-scale exchange depends, and because, optimally, the division of labor should encompass the entire planet, there ought to be a government for the whole world. But at the dawn of the twenty-first century, as at the end of World War I when Woodrow Wilson placed the liberal vision of world order at the top of the international agenda, and as in 1776, the year when Smith's great work *The Wealth of Nations* was published, there was no world government.

Nonetheless, there was an international economy, and, at the outset of the twenty-first century, it was busy, bustling, and growing. The volume of international exchange had become so large and so important to the sovereign states that engaged in it that it supplied the word frequently used to characterize the post-Cold War era itself: globalization.

The term referred to the substantial and ever-increasing economic integration of the entire planet. The most important unit of economic activity was no longer the street, the village, the principality, the nation-state, or even the continent. It was, or was fast becoming, the planet itself.[7]

The common usage of the term globalization in the first post-Cold War decade denoted not only the growth of international economic activity but also its importance as the defining feature of the post-Cold War era. International economic integration had become a supreme goal of, and an inescapable influence on, all the sovereign states of the international system. While the second half of the twentieth century was the era of the Cold War because the East-West rivalry dominated international affairs, turning the world into a single chessboard, at the outset of the post-Cold War period the primacy of international economic affairs transformed the planet into the equivalent of a single switchboard, with each part connected to all the others.

The forces of globalization in the wake of the Cold War were not geographically symmetrical. The economic flows were greater within the world's core than between the core and the periphery, although the volume of core-periphery transactions was expanding rapidly.[8] Nor was the economic integration of the post-Cold War era unprecedented. It was, in fact, the second, not the first, era of globalization.

The first began in the middle of the nineteenth century, when the industrial revolution was well under way in Europe,[9] and continued to 1914, when it was halted by the outbreak of World War I.[10] By some measures the world was more integrated in the first era than it was for most of the second.[11] Strictly speaking, the post-Cold War era is the second part of the second era of globalization. For the trend toward international economic integration resumed after 1945, at first principally within the western core and then increasingly in the world's periphery as well.

In the first era, agricultural commodities and people moved across national borders in increasing volume: The earlier period of globalization was a great age of migration. In the second, the principal transborder flows involved manufactured products and capital. Technological change created the initial era of globalization. The steamship and the railroad made possible far swifter transportation across much greater distances than ever before in history. Grain grown in the middle of North America could be sent in quantity to the middle of Europe; people born in the middle of Europe could relocate, in large numbers, to the Western Hemisphere. At the same time, the telegraph made communication over long distances far more rapid.

Technological change was part of the second post-1945 era of globalization as well. Jet airplanes transported people from one continent to another faster than steamships could. With the invention of the microchip, millions of dollars could be moved around the world with a single keystroke. More important in breaking down barriers to international economic integration in the second period, however, was politics. It was the failure of the alternatives to the liberal approach to economics that led, after World War II in the world's core and in the 1980s and 1990s in the periphery, to the reduction of the man-made barriers to global trade and investment that had been erected in the twentieth century. In that century's latter decades the barriers in the periphery began to come down because the economic rationales on the basis of which Communist and Third World governments had erected them had been discredited.[12]

The use of the term globalization sometimes implied that the process was all but inevitable. This was not so. The political decisions that created the conditions in which international economic integration flourished could be reversed. The sense of inevitability, however, was in keeping with the spirit of the liberal theory of history, which assumed that prosperity was a mandatory goal for every government and that a market economy was the only mechanism for achieving it. Integration into the global economy was one of the ways that the market produced prosperity. International integration was therefore part of the mechanism by which the liberal method of economic organization produced the twenty-first century basis for political legitimacy.[13] The aura surrounding globalization implied that every country had to organize its economy so as to be able to plug itself into the great global utility that the world economy had become. Each country had, to vary the metaphor, to build access roads to the global economy's two main arteries: the international trading system and the international monetary order.

Unlike the liberal approach to war and peace, the international trading system and the international monetary order were well established when the Berlin Wall fell in 1989. Each had been constructed at the end of World War II and had been successfully sustained, while being modified and expanded, for almost half a century. At the heart of each stood the basic liberal practice of free exchange. And each had a familiar pedigree. Like the other elements of the liberal order—popular sovereignty, constitutionalism, the rule of law, and the norms and practices of common security—the liberal international trading system and the liberal international monetary order were Anglo-American innovations that had spread to other countries during the first two centuries of the modern era. In the first age of globalization, Great Britain supplied the rules for international trade and the cross-border flow of money. Shattered by the two world wars and the Great Depression, the two systems were reconstituted under the leadership of the United States after World War II. It was these American-sponsored sets of rules, practices, and institutions that the post-Cold War world inherited.

Trade is simply the exchange at the heart of the free market, conducted across sovereign borders. The basis of the world trading system is the straightforward idea that international exchange should proceed freely, without government-imposed inhibitions, and the idea of free trade had considerable political importance in nineteenth-century Britain. It was closely associated with the cause of political liberty. The political struggles to expand the franchise and to dismantle barriers to trade were similar and, in the eyes of some of those who waged them, connected, since both reduced the power of government and expanded the range of human choice. Free trade was also associated with peace in the eyes of its partisans, who elevated it to a principle of statecraft.[14] Trade was freed in Britain in the second half of the nineteenth century, and by dint of the British example and the British arguments for its merits, the practice spread, unevenly, to Europe and North America.

Britain was economically the most powerful country in the world in the mid-nineteenth century. A hundred years later the United States held that position and, like Britain before it, took up the cause of free trade. Taking their cue from the United States, the governments of other countries began to remove the obstacles they had placed in the way of international commerce, first within the Western core and then, at century's end, increasingly in the world's periphery as well.[15]

Money plays a supporting role in international economic affairs: It supports exchange. Money serves as a common denominator, a universal unit of account that can be exchanged for anything and so is a far more efficient mechanism of payment than barter.[16] Money is like a system of canals along which goods are transported from sellers to buyers. It is also the medium of investment. A financial system, international or domestic, is like a system of irrigation, in which purchasing power moves from those who have it in surplus to those who need it to create wealth.

The nineteenth-century international monetary system, the gold standard, grew out of the British practice of using gold for international transactions. When it came time to reconstruct a monetary order near the end of World War II, the United States, with Great Britain as its junior partner, did not try to repeat the post-World War I effort to revive the gold standard but instead devised, at a conference at Bretton Woods, New Hampshire, in 1944, similar but more complicated monetary arrangements, with stable exchange rates and the American dollar performing some of the tasks previously assigned to gold.

Both the trade and monetary systems changed considerably in the decades following World War II. But at the outset of the twenty-first century both were still in existence, recognizable versions of what had begun near the end of World War II, functioning as the main arteries of the post-Cold War forces of globalization. Whereas market economies within many of the sovereign states of the periphery had to be constructed from scratch, the international trade and monetary systems had only to be kept in working order and adapted to the increase in the number of participants that the triumph of the market produced.

But maintenance was neither simple nor easy. Both the trade and monetary systems were subject to difficulties that carried over from the Cold War. The artery of world trade was vulnerable to accidents and traffic jams, and required constant and well-organized efforts at road clearance for traffic to flow smoothly. For international monetary affairs, precise rules of the road proved, over the course of the twentieth century, impossible to establish. Traffic had to proceed without the equivalent of stop signs and traffic lights. Improvisation, caution, and cooperation were required to keep the monetary artery open and even then it was subject to snarls and accidents.

Whereas the burden of constructing working markets in the periphery rested with the governments and people of the countries involved, the responsibility for unblocking and unsnarling these thoroughfares, for keeping the international economic order in good working condition for the benefit of all the world's subscribers to it, fell mainly to the wealthy democracies of the world's core, foremost among which was the United States.

FREE TRADE

THE BENEFITS of free trade are a matter of logic, the same logic that underpins the division of labor. As Adam Smith put it:

> All commerce that is carried on betwixt any two countries must necessarily be advantageous to both ... when two men trade between themselves it is undoubtedly for the advance of both ... The case is exactly the same betwixt any two nations. The goods

which the English merchants want to import from France are certainly more valuable to them than what they give for them."[17]

Trade's benefits are also a matter of objectively established fact. The proof of its worth rests on the principle of comparative advantage, the best known demonstration of which was provided, early in the nineteenth century, by the British economist David Ricardo. He showed that even if one country can produce all goods more cheaply than another, each will still benefit from trade with the other. Trade will make each better off than if there were no trade at all when the more efficient producer concentrates on goods in which its margin of advantage in efficiency—its comparative advantage—is greater. The principle of comparative advantage has, in economics, the status of a law of physics. With minor exceptions it is true always and everywhere.[18]

Free trade enhances a society's total wealth. Barriers to trade reduce it. Yet free trade has not always been practiced everywhere. At most times, in most places, it has been the exception, not the rule. One reason for this is that in few if any pre-modern states did the government have as its supreme goal maximizing the welfare of the population. In traditional Europe the chief aim was to enhance the power, prestige, and wealth of the monarch—often by waging war. War required armies, which were raised and supported in the field through the disbursement of precious metals. These were obtained, when not indigenous, as payments for exports.[19] A traditional monarch therefore sought to contrive a trade surplus, which would produce a net influx of the needed precious metals. This was the system of mercantilism.[20]

Mercantilism was a European practice. In Asia free trade was unpopular for much of the modern era for a different reason. In both Japan and China it acquired an unsavory political reputation as a result of its inauspicious debut. Commerce with the West was brought to both countries by Western military force and so they experienced it as an assault on their sovereignty. American gunboats opened Japan to trade in 1854. The British opened China in the same way and, to add injury to insult, one of the commodities to which China was thereby opened was opium. Once it became available its use spread rapidly among the Chinese people, with debilitating consequences.

The illiberal regimes of the twentieth century, Nazi Germany, imperial Japan, and Communist Russia and China, while they differed in important ways from the traditional governments they replaced, shared with their predecessors an aversion to international commerce—and for the same reason. Their common goal was to increase the strength of the state, not the welfare of the people, and they calculated that controls on what entered and left the country could achieve this.[21]

Free trade is a liberal practice, championed in the modern era by the liberal powers. It is logical to expect it to flourish to the extent that members of the international system organize their internal politics and economics along liberal lines. So it has proven—up to a point. But even liberal countries such as Great Britain and the United States have erected barriers to international commerce. The ordinary meaning of the term used to refer to this practice—protection—is telling. It has a positive connotation. It suggests safeguarding something valuable; and what the proponents of protectionism in trade sought to protect usually was of considerable value to them.

The spirit of mercantilism lived on even in liberal societies at the end of the twentieth century, where the widespread if unfocused sentiment persisted that exports are good and imports bad. Sovereign states were seen as being in economic competition with one another, although a country's economic well-being is determined by its own efforts, endowments, and policies and not by what others do.[22] A country's trade balance was taken as the measure of its national prowess, and a higher level of imports than of exports was considered a troubling sign of weakness, whereas in fact such an imbalance indicates nothing per se about a country's political or economic health and can even be desirable.[23] The bias against trade deficits is often accompanied by a related myth: that trade policies determine whether a country is in surplus, with more exports than imports, or in deficit, when the reverse is true. In fact, this depends on domestic considerations—the ratio of savings to investment.[24]

The enduring sentiment in liberal societies for erecting barriers to products made abroad resulted not only from a residual attachment to the basic premise of mercantilism but also from an ignorance of the workings of market economies.[25] This included ignorance of the principle of comparative advantage, leading to the erroneous belief that without an absolute advantage in the production of something, international commerce is not worthwhile. It included, as well, the misapprehension that trade between a core and a peripheral country, because it is trade between one with high wages and one where pay is low, *must* result in the richer country losing jobs to the poorer one. The American businessman and politician H. Ross Perot summarized this mistaken belief when he opposed the creation of a free trade area in North America on the grounds that it would generate "a giant sucking sound" as employment in the United States was transferred to Mexico. In fact, the aggregate level of employment in any country is the result of domestic forces.[26] A related belief perpetuating protectionist sentiment even in wealthy, liberal societies of the core was that trade with low-wage countries would drag down wage levels across the board in wealthier societies. This, too, was erroneous: Wages are set by productivity, which is higher in the core because it is the result of capital investment and training, which are more abundant there.[27]

Since the middle of the nineteenth century, however, there have been sophisticated as well as naive and uninformed arguments in favor of restricting imports—or at least arguments made by sophisticated people, including professional economists. The most influential of them has been the "infant industry" argument, first brought to prominence by a nineteenth-century German, Friedrich List. The metaphor contains the argument: Industries are like children. In their early years they must be protected because, weak and unformed as they are, if exposed to the normal forms of competition to which mature industries are routinely subject they will be stunted, or perish entirely. Tariff walls are like cocoons in which vulnerable, earth-bound caterpillars are transformed into soaring butterflies. Once grown to full size, and having learned the secrets of survival that their competitors have mastered, the protection can, and according to List should, be removed, leaving them to survive the normal pressures of the market just as adults must confront the vicissitudes of life that children, if they are fortunate, are spared.

Germany did shelter some of its industry in the nineteenth century, keeping out the industrial products made in the world's economic leader, Great Britain. Another protectionist country of that era was the United States, and List was influenced by the American example.[28] In the twentieth century tariffs based on the infant-industry rationale were erected in many countries, especially, after World War II, in the world's periphery.

At the end of the twentieth century the United States itself, the citadel of international economic liberalism, spawned a particular version of the case for assisting infant industries. It called not for restricting imports but for providing government support to certain industries to improve their prospects for exporting. This was the doctrine of "strategic trade."

Strategic trade was initially inspired by the discovery by economists that competitive advantage is not always the result of acts of God or nature. Sometimes the vagaries of history are responsible. The state of Georgia became a center of carpet manufacture because a few carpet-making businesses happened to start there and others followed. So it was with the motion picture industry and southern California. The United States had a large aircraft industry because, among other things, of the demand for military aircraft first in World War II and then during the Cold War. The doctrine was also based on the finding of professional economists that, in industries characterized by imperfect competition in which a few firms are dominant (the aircraft industry is an example), governments can in theory improve the chances of indigenous firms to be among the select few by providing subsidies, protection, and other forms of encouragement. Strategic trade doctrine had a third ingredient: the conviction that some industries were more valuable than others. This echoed the original infant-industry argument, which had asserted that industry was more valuable than agriculture.[29] In the late-twentieth-century version, industries making products involving high technology were deemed the most valuable of all.

The doctrine held that the American government should promote such industries for the sake of the nation's long-term economic prospects. Its proponents believed that Japan owed its post-1945 economic success to precisely the practices that they were urging on

the United States. A farsighted and adept government had selected the most important products and put in place policies that enabled Japanese firms to gain a foothold, and in some cases a commanding position, in the global markets for these products.

The various challenges to free trade were debated and tested within the ranks of the economics profession, which expanded steadily in the course of the twentieth century. The challenges did not, on the whole, emerge with their claims confirmed.[30] New firms in promising industries, after all, can ordinarily secure commercial loans to sustain them until they become profitable.[31] Industries throughout the world did receive tariff protection from the middle of the nineteenth century to the end of the twentieth. Some of them thrived. But there was little conclusive evidence that those that thrived did so because of the protection they received and would have withered without it. Some studies found that the Japanese government's role in trying to promote various industrial sectors either had produced no effect or had made the country modestly less well off.[32]

As for strategic trade policy, its critics noted that the fact that competitive advantage was sometimes the product of the complicated and unpredictable forces of history did not mean that it could actually be created by the often-clumsy hand of government. Even the most skillful and successful industrial policy was not likely to raise national income significantly. And most government policies in this area were not skillful. For all their virtues, liberal governments were unlikely to be sufficiently perspicacious or politically independent to select the most economically promising (rather than the politically best connected) enterprises and give them just the assistance they needed to succeed in the international marketplace. Nor could it be shown that "high-tech" industries were indispensable for the national well-being in the twenty-first century. It proved difficult even to say which industries would belong to this category.[33] As the Japanese economy, the inspiration and model for the doctrine of strategic trade, slumped in the last decade of the twentieth century, the North American enthusiasm for the idea, and the policies it suggested, waned as well.[34]

PROTECTIONISM

THE EBBING of the late-twentieth-century challenge to the doctrine of free trade did not lead to the crumbling of all barriers to
it. For as Adam Smith recognized, the most powerful force behind
policies of protection had little to do with any doctrine or theory.
Free trade was obstructed by commercial and personal interests.[35]
Trade is, after all, the normal market activity of exchange carried on
across sovereign borders, and normal market activity, especially in
the age of the industrial revolution, is inherently disruptive. Substituting cheaper foreign goods for more expensive domestic-made
ones is the essence of commerce. But domestic producers are
thereby injured. By substituting cheaper for more expensive goods,
trade promotes economic growth, but growth is a process of creative
destruction and those whom the destruction adversely affects are
prone to try to prevent or minimize it. In the case of trade this means
keeping out foreign products. Policies of protection are designed to
protect those injured by free international exchange.

Trade is simply an advance in productivity, a cheaper method of
producing something.[36] Advances in productivity that originate
abroad, however, are easier to oppose than productivity advances
that are homegrown. When the source of the disruption is foreign,
the cause of protection can ally itself with the most powerful political sentiment in the modern era: nationalism. Someone who resists
an improvement in productivity at home is widely considered a reactionary, a Luddite, but one who resists such an improvement from
abroad can pose as a patriot, standing against harm inflicted by a foreign country.[37]

Trade can be made to seem a form of external aggression because
in both trade and warfare fellow citizens are injured by foreigners.
Of course citizens also benefit from international trade, and the beneficiaries vastly outnumber those suffering losses. But the distribution of gains and losses from trade does not ordinarily translate into
a political advantage for the cause of liberalization. In fact, the political arithmetic weighs in the opposite direction.

The total gains from trade are invariably greater than the total losses, as economists since Ricardo have demonstrated, and the winners outnumber the losers. But for each of the many winners the benefits are modest: a slightly lower price for an imported good—a shirt, for example—than what one made domestically would cost. The gains are thus diffuse. The losses, by contrast, are concentrated. Only a few shirtmakers lose their jobs but each of them thereby loses a great deal more than any one of the benefiting consumers gains. The losers are acutely aware of what they have lost while the winners are generally oblivious to what they have gained.

Winners therefore have little incentive to organize themselves to lobby for free trade. Time is money, and the value of the time they would have to spend in political activity outstrips the minor losses they suffer if shirt prices are slightly higher. The losers, by contrast, have a powerful incentive to organize themselves in opposition to unrestricted trade. For them, the price of political activism is worth paying.[38] The issue of free trade thus characteristically pits one side for which the stakes are very high against another that is scarcely aware that a contest is under way.

To be sure, when the losers from trade prevail, society pays a price.[39] But if economic analysis leads to the conclusion that, from the standpoint of overall social welfare, restrictions on international commerce are virtually never justified, an assessment of the politics of trade raises the question of how it can ever be possible for trade to be free.

The great historical breakthrough for free trade, the equivalent for liberal international economic policy of 1688 for the rule of law and 1789 for popular sovereignty, was the repeal of the Corn Laws, the system of agricultural protection in Great Britain, in 1846. The Corn Laws were overturned for economic reasons. A majority of the British Parliament was persuaded of the virtues of cheap grain from abroad, virtues publicized by an organization formed for this purpose, the Anti-Corn Law League. But opponents of protection were able to prevail because theirs was part of a larger political struggle. The cause of free trade in agriculture came to be associated with the advance of political liberty (some who benefited from cheaper food had been enfranchised by the Reform Act of 1832) and with the struggle for political power between the merchants and manufacturers who made the industrial revolution, on the one hand, and the landed aristocracy, which had dominated the Parliament and the country before the nineteenth century and whose economic interests the Corn Laws served, on the other.[40]

Like all innovations, the first exercise in trade liberalization faced an obstacle with which its successors did not have to cope: the lack of a precedent. As epochal as it was, however, the repeal of the Corn Laws was in one important way not a precedent for the trade liberalization of the twentieth century. It was a unilateral act. The Parliament did not insist that the grain-exporting countries lift their tariffs on British manufactures.[41] In purely economic terms this was sensible. A country gains from accepting imports from others even if the others refuse to accept its exports.[42] But the dominant pattern of trade liberalization of the next century and a half was different.

It was marked by the evolution of a series of procedures for the reciprocal, multilateral lowering of barriers to trade. The Cobden-Chevalier Treaty of 1860 between Great Britain and France introduced the principle of "Most Favored Nation," according to which each party to a trade agreement promises to give to the other parties any trading opportunities it has already granted to a third party. Widely adopted in subsequent decades, this practice proved an effective instrument of trade liberalization.[43]

In the years after World War II, reciprocity and multilateralism were embodied in a series of ever-more complicated and protracted negotiations, in which an increasing number of countries participated and that yielded a series of elaborate, overlapping, and reinforcing bargains on many issues and products. Under the auspices of trade rules codified in the General Agreement on Tariffs and Trade (GATT),[44] four negotiating rounds were held between 1946 and 1960. After 1960 came the Kennedy Round, named for the American president who called for it, from 1962 to 1967, followed by the Tokyo Round, begun in the Japanese capital, from 1973 to 1979. The last and most complicated set of negotiations, the Uruguay Round, the first meeting of which was held in that South American country, stretched from 1986 to 1994.

There were economic reasons to proceed multilaterally. In a few restricted circumstances unilateral tariffs can increase the welfare of the country imposing them—while also decreasing the aggregate welfare of all countries. The advantage disappears, however, if others reciprocate with tariffs of their own, in which case all countries are worse off than they would be without any tariffs at all. Multilateral agreements therefore remove the temptation to try unilaterally to create such "optimal tariffs."[45]

The principal reason that trade liberalization proceeded multilaterally rather than, as with the repeal of the Corn Laws, on a unilateral basis, however, was political.[46] Economists may demonstrate that unilateral reductions in obstacles to trade are beneficial but, in the twentieth century, governments were seldom willing to act on the basis of economists' theories. The public insisted on reciprocity. The language of trade politics was again telling. The reduction in a barrier to trade came to be called a "concession" to other parties, implying that it was something that favored only the recipient and with which the country offering it was parting only reluctantly. In fact, in economic terms, such a "concession" is actually a benefit to the people of the country making it. But the political realities of trade negotiations made free trade, like common security, a species of public good, something achievable only by collective action, when all parties to it can be persuaded simultaneously to "pay" for it—with tariff reductions in the first case, arms limitations in the second.[47]

Ongoing multilateral negotiations came to be seen, in the second half of the twentieth century, as indispensable for trade liberalization. The successive trade rounds were the motor powering the fragile craft of free trade against the powerful political tide of protection. Negotiations provided a necessary counterweight to the constant pressure for protection arising from the resistance of those injured by imports and the general prejudice against unilateral liberalization. Freeing trade, to use another metaphor in common currency, was the equivalent of riding a bicycle: Without constant forward movement the enterprise would not merely stop, it would tip over.

After 1945 it did move forward. Indeed, like a cyclist peddling downhill, it gained momentum. The sources of protectionism—the political arithmetic of trade and the almost universal aversion to unilateral action—also contributed to its opposite, liberalization. They did so because they turned exporters into active advocates for free trade[48] who were likely to suffer from protectionist measures taken by their own country because other countries would retaliate, closing the markets in which they sold their products. Like those subject to competition from imports, exporters were well aware that the stakes for them were high. Like those whose jobs are threatened by imports, but unlike consumers who benefit from them, exporters' incentive to lobby for trade policies favorable to themselves was considerable.[49]

The post-1945 negotiations for trade liberalization were successfully concluded and world trade expanded steadily, promoting economic growth. And just as trade promoted growth, growth facilitated trade. The greater the volume of economic activity, the better even import-competing companies could expect to do.[50] Economic growth, to which trade contributed, meant that displaced workers could find jobs more readily, and government programs to support, compensate, and retrain the victims of the disruption wrought by trade could be more generous. The volume of international trade, its value, and its ratio to total output all grew in the second half of the twentieth century, at first largely within the Western core but then, increasingly, in the world's periphery as well. The second era of globalization was, like the first, a great age of trade, and therefore, like the first, required support from an international monetary system.

SOUND MONEY

MONEY WITHIN sovereign states serves two purposes: It is a unit of account, to simplify exchange, and it is a store of value, so that people can keep their wealth in readily usable—liquid—form. In the international economy, both tasks are complicated by the existence of multiple sovereignties, most of which issue their own money. An international monetary order must make it possible for those within one country, with its own money, to buy from places where the official currency is different. This is the task of convertibility. International monetary arrangements must also include some method for balancing a country's receipts and expenditures of money over time, lest it run out of currency that others will accept.

This is the problem of equilibrium: Achieving it is the task of adjustment. The first modern international monetary system, the British-led gold standard of the latter part of the nineteenth century and the early years of the twentieth, made possible both convertibility and adjustment.

In simplest terms, the gold standard worked because gold was accepted as a common currency by each of the participants in the system. When country A made a purchase from country B it transferred gold to B in payment. This gave A less money but at the same time set in motion a process by which equilibrium was restored. With less gold both the purchasing power and the price level in country A declined, restricting what it could buy abroad while making its goods cheaper for foreigners. As a consequence, imports declined and exports increased, offsetting the initial loss of gold. In country B the opposite process occurred: Purchasing power and price levels both rose, stimulating imports and depressing exports, thus eliminating the initial surplus of gold.

In practice the gold standard did not function in quite such a neat, straightforward way. Some countries used silver as well as gold as money. Often gold was transferred between banks rather than shipped across borders. Most important, rather than shifting gold, adjustment was often achieved by changing banks' discount rates. This raised or lowered interest rates, which lowered or raised—whichever was appropriate—the demand for imports. Much of all this took place in London. Great Britain was such a large participant in the international trade and payments systems of the nineteenth century that it could, in effect, unilaterally manage the workings of the gold standard.[51]

The gold-based system that was the vehicle for international payments in the first age of globalization was as close to a purely liberal monetary system as has ever functioned. It was liberal in that money flowed freely across borders and so, therefore, could trade. Governments did not manipulate the value of their currencies, which were fixed, thus ensuring that they would remain reliable stores of value and so upholding another liberal principle: the rule of law in monetary affairs. Finally, the gold standard was a liberal system in that governments did not, on the whole, interfere with the process of adjustment to restore equilibrium. This, however, proved the system's undoing. For the process of adjustment, like the normal workings of the market within countries, had disruptive effects. And as with the normal workings of the market in the core countries, in the twentieth century those disruptions proved politically impossible to sustain.

Under the gold standard, payments deficits were eliminated by lowering the level of economic activity in the deficit country. Prices fell when there was less money available, interest rates rose when banks increased their rates to regain gold, and the aggregate level of employment was often adversely affected. This meant that some people suffered economic injury from the process of adjustment. Businesses ceased to be profitable, workers lost their jobs, farmers had to pay more for the credit on which they depended. For most of the nineteenth century, however, the injured parties could not alter the policies and mechanisms that inflicted the injuries. With the franchise strictly limited (or governments entirely unaccountable to the public) political power belonged, throughout the world's core, to those unaffected by the disruptions caused by adjustment. By the twentieth century this had changed. With the rise and spread of popular democracy, those injured by what were, under the gold standard, the normal processes of adjustment gained the vote and so were in a position to demand that the government prevent these injuries, just as they demanded that the government supply a social safety net to cushion the shocks administered by the normal workings of the market. The gold standard as it operated in its heyday ceased to be viable; the same social and political developments that had made the nineteenth century laissez-faire version of the market economy untenable in the twentieth brought about its demise.[52]

In the first half of the twentieth century two other drawbacks to the gold standard came to light. The rise of fractional-reserve banking, a practice in which banks kept on deposit funds worth only a fraction of their outstanding obligations, increased economic activity but made these institutions susceptible to sudden, large, panic-driven demands for repayment by depositors, which could ruin banks that were fundamentally solvent but temporarily illiquid. Preventing the destruction of banks in this way required the government to act as the "lender of last resort," supplying credit to banks so that they were in a position to pay, thereby calming the panic-stricken demands for immediate payment. But this required creating— printing—money, which violated the rules of the gold standard.[53]

The second drawback stemmed from Keynes's diagnosis of the Great Depression. It had been caused, he argued, by inadequate private spending. It could be cured by governments replacing the missing spending with expenditures of their own. But this, too, required money-creation. In fact, fidelity to the norms of the gold standard was one reason that the governments of the core countries initially failed to respond to the slump of the 1930s in a way that would have mitigated it. Government spending sufficient to end the downturn altogether had to await the one occasion on which governments are usually willing to put aside all normal rules: wartime.[54]

THE GREAT TRILEMMA

B Y THE END of World War II the rules of the gold standard could no longer be followed. Governments in the core countries of the West felt obliged to avoid as far as possible the social dislocations that adjustment under those rules caused. In extraordinary circumstances they also felt obliged to create and spend money. This presented them with a vexing set of choices. Three features are desirable in any monetary system. One, the result of the evolution of political liberalism in the course of the nineteenth century, is the capacity for each government to conduct an independent monetary policy in order to offset the shocks that the normal workings of a market economy deliver. The other two desirable features are fundamental liberal principles: fixed exchange rates so that all money can be a reliable store of value, and the free flow of capital across borders, to underpin free trade and thus maximize economic welfare.

It proved impossible to have all three. Depressing economic activity, changing the value of the national currency, and controlling the inflow of goods and money are the three methods for eliminating a deficit in a country's balance of payments. If none is available—and in a monetary system incorporating all three desirable features none would be—what every set of monetary arrangements must have would be missing: a method of adjustment.[55] The gold standard provided the second and third of the three desirable features by eliminating the first.[56] When, because of the political developments of the first century of the modern era, monetary independence became impossible to forswear, sovereign states confronted a "trilemma," which formed the framework for the politics of international monetary policy thereafter.[57]

The post-1945 monetary system designed at Bretton Woods, like the welfare state of the twentieth century, was an attempt at a compromise between the principles of economic liberalism and the imperatives of mass democracy. (It was also a compromise between the United States, which, because it anticipated having balance-of-payments surpluses and thus no need to adjust, argued for economic liberalism, and Great Britain, represented by Keynes himself, which, anticipating deficits, sought provisions to soften the impact of adjustment.) It was designed to provide the benefits of the gold standard—fixed exchange rates and the free flow of money across borders—without its drawbacks—a single, painful, politically unacceptable method of adjustment.[58] The heart of the Bretton Woods system was a modified version of the gold standard. The British and the Americans created a gold-dollar system, with the dollar pegged to gold at a price of $35 per ounce and other currencies linked to the dollar. Rather than insisting on an inflexible rate of exchange for the non-dollar currencies, Bretton Woods permitted fluctuations in value within specified limits. It also stipulated that countries with balance-of-payments deficits could receive loans to avoid the need for adjustment through the constriction of economic activity, and, in exceptional circumstances, could devalue—that is lower the value of their own currencies against the dollar and gold—thereby reducing the price of all foreign obligations. To make the loans and preside over the devaluations the Bretton Woods conference created the International Monetary Fund (IMF).

The Bretton Woods system did not function as planned.[59] It stipulated that the wartime controls on the movement of capital be lifted soon after the war's end, but this did not happen.[60] The resort to capital controls was a routine feature of the Bretton Woods era, even by the United States.[61] Devaluations were more frequent than the architects of Bretton Woods had intended them to be and governments that lowered the value of their currencies seldom bothered to consult the IMF, let alone receive its permission, before doing so. Countries with balance-of-payments deficits did receive financial assistance but not necessarily from the IMF. The most important assistance at the outset of the postwar period came, in the form of the Marshall Plan, from the United States.

The Achilles heel of the Bretton Woods system proved to be the special role of the dollar. On the one hand, the privileged status of the American currency was indispensable. Dollars were used along with gold as universally accepted reserves with which international transactions could be conducted. This made possible a far higher level of international economic activity than the finite quantity of gold available to the core countries could have supported, and so made the world richer. The post-World War II economic boom depended on treating the dollar as international money that was as good as gold.

On the other hand, this special status created a contradiction. By Bretton Woods rules, dollars could be redeemed for gold by any foreign holder at the price of $35 per ounce. But the more dollars there were in circulation, the more difficult it became for the United States, with its stock of gold growing only slowly, to keep this promise.[62] By the 1960s it was not possible to keep it. The United States did not own enough gold to redeem all the dollars in circulation abroad although in theory it was committed to doing so.

The French government threatened to present its dollars for redemption. It was motivated less by the desire to enhance its own gold stock than by its objection to the privileges the dollar's status conferred on the American government.[63] Because it was the world's reserve currency, the dollar was, and had to be, universally accepted. For other countries to refuse dollars would risk undermining the international monetary order on which they all depended. But the universal and unlimited acceptability of the dollar meant that the United States could pay its foreign bills with money that it printed itself,[64] a prerogative available to no other country and a license, in the French view (and not only in the French view) for fiscal profligacy. The privilege the United States enjoyed penalized others because, by accepting dollars, they increased their own money supplies, which ultimately produced inflation. To avoid inflation they had to take steps to depress their own economic activity, the political difficulty of which was what had put an end to the gold standard. The Americans were, in effect, forcing others to adjust.[65]

While taking advantage of the privileges the dollar's special status conferred, the American government also began to chafe at the restrictions this status imposed. As the anchor of the international monetary system the United States could not, as all other countries could, change the value of its currency.[66] But it was not entirely immune to pressure to adjust, that is to stem the outflow of dollars, and the steps it took to accomplish this had the effect of slowing the American economy, making the government unpopular with the American electorate.[67] In addition, over time the dollar became overvalued in relation to the other core currencies. This was not surprising. The exchange rates had been set in the immediate aftermath of the war when the currencies of America's trading partners, their economies shattered by war, were historically weak. This inflexibility placed an increasingly heavy burden on American exports. Finally, on August 15, 1971, the American government unilaterally severed the link between the dollar and gold and so put an end to the Bretton Woods system.

American officials did not intend to do away with Bretton Woods entirely. Their aim was to devalue the dollar, eliminate the American balance-of-payments deficit, and then reconstruct an exchange rate regime based on this lower value.[68] But the effort to put Bretton Woods back together again failed and the world entered an era in which exchange rates tended to float, with recurrent and not entirely successful efforts by individual countries and, in Europe, regional groupings to fix them. The system established in 1944 was replaced by a non-system in which no universally agreed-on rules governed international currency flows, although in practice even governments with floating rates did try to steer their currencies so as to prevent them from varying too widely or rapidly.[69] This non-system performed the basic tasks of money less well than had its predecessor. Because currency values now fluctuated, from an international standpoint all currencies including the dollar were less reliable both as stores of value and as units of exchange. The non-system was a less liberal monetary order than Bretton Woods, let alone than the nineteenth century gold standard, because governments were freer to manipulate their currencies, and thereby manipulate important global prices.

The fear that the end of Bretton Woods and the advent of floating exchange rates would bring world trade to a halt, however, was not realized. The fear had both a logical and an historical basis. Continual and sometimes considerable fluctuation in the value of currencies discourages international transactions because buyers and sellers cannot be sure of a transaction's ultimate price and uncertainty is the enemy of economic activity. Just as exchange does not take place without the confidence that contracts will be enforced, so it is hampered when the participants cannot be confident of the value of the money that will change hands. In the previous experience of unfixed exchange rates, after the Depression-induced collapse of the gold standard in the interwar period, the volume of trade had plummeted. Governments had used currency manipulation as an instrument of protection, devaluing in order to price other countries' goods out of their home market while making their own products cheaper abroad. These were the infamous "beggar-thy-neighbor" policies that made all who practiced them worse off, policies that Bretton Woods, with its emphasis on exchange-rate stability, was explicitly designed to prevent.

The rate at which global trade expanded did decline after 1971, but this had a number of possible causes: not only the end of fixed exchange rates but also the global recessions of the 1970s triggered by steep increases in the price of oil, the reduction in the rate of economic growth in the core countries because of the little understood decline in the rate of improvement in productivity, and the appearance of new forms of protection known as "non-tariff barriers." Overall world trade did continue to expand after August 15, 1971, albeit at a reduced rate. The world learned to live, if not always entirely comfortably, with floating exchange rates.

But the end of Bretton Woods was not without consequences for the international economy. One important result was the appearance of large pools of capital that were used to hedge against the risks that exchange rate volatility raised.[70] These reservoirs of money were available for currency speculation. And currency speculation turned out to be a major and unsettling feature of the first post-Cold War decade, a sign that, despite the triumph of the market among as well as within sovereign states, the liberal structures of the international economy were not necessarily destined to function smoothly in the twenty-first century.

CHAPTER TWELVE

The Future of
the International Economy

A LITTLE GIRL VISITS her friend's house for dinner. "We're having Brussels sprouts tonight, Susie," her friend's mother says, "do you like them?" "Oh yes," the little girl replies. But when the mother clears the plates away she notices that the girl's Brussels sprouts are untouched. "I thought you said you like Brussels sprouts, Susie," she says. "I do like them," the girl replies, "but not enough to eat them."

So it was for the principles of international economic liberalism for almost every country in the world at the outset of the twenty-first century. All belonged to, or aspired to join, the principal international economic organizations, the World Trade Organization and the International Monetary Fund. All were committed, in principle, to the ideas these organizations embodied: the free flow of goods and capital across international borders. But when it came to permitting unimpeded access to their own markets of other countries' money and especially other countries' exports, virtually all had reservations. For products and money from abroad can disrupt as well as enrich. Disruption imposes political costs, which governments would prefer to avoid.

Like Susie and the Brussels sprouts, therefore, the theme of global international economic affairs in the twenty-first century was the conflict between a principled commitment and a practical aversion to liberal principles.

HOT MONEY

THE 1990s, the first post-Cold War decade, witnessed several major monetary crises. In each of them a government was forced to abandon a currency that it had promised to defend (that is, redeem in exchange for reserves) at a fixed rate; the demands for redemption grew to the point that the government risked running out of reserves altogether unless it reduced the price it was offering for its own money, making redemption much cheaper.

The first of these crises came in Western Europe. There a regional version of the Bretton Woods arrangements called the European Monetary System (EMS) had been established, within which currencies were permitted to fluctuate only within designated limits. In 1992 Great Britain and Italy decided not to defend their currencies at the EMS-mandated rates, withdrew from the system, and devalued their currencies. Two years later the Mexican peso came under attack and the Mexican government ceased to defend it at the rate to which it had committed itself. Then, in 1997, currency crises erupted in Asia. In July of that year Thailand and Malaysia ceased to defend their currencies. In October and November Indonesia and South Korea followed suit. The epidemic spread to Russia the following year. In August, the Russian government not only abandoned its defense of the ruble, allowing it to float downward to a much lower level, but also stopped payment to foreign holders of some Russian securities.[1]

Currency crises of this kind were hardly unique to the post-Cold War period but, like the wave of ethnic violence of the 1990s, each of them had its roots in political developments stemming from the end of the Cold War. Central to the European events was the post-Cold War unification of Germany. Having annexed the formerly Communist German Democratic Republic, the Federal Republic of Germany confronted the prospect of an avalanche of people moving from east to west to take jobs with higher wages and qualify for the more generous western social benefits. To keep their new citizens at home, the German government decided to subsidize wages and benefits in the east.[2] This proved expensive, and because Chancellor

Helmut Kohl had pledged not to raise taxes to pay for unification it was funded by borrowing. As a consequence, German interest rates rose and, by the rules of the EMS, the interest rates in the other member countries rose as well, which proved politically untenable for Britain and Italy.[3]

In Mexico and in Asia the global triumph of the market made countries that were previously exotic and even forbidding seem attractive destinations for Western capital. Whereas during the Cold War they were known as "developing countries," in the post-Cold War period they graduated to the status of "emerging markets" and were transformed, in Western eyes, from candidates for international public assistance to opportunities for private profit.[4] Capital flooded in, only to take flight when the risks of repayment appeared to rise. One reason the perception of risk increased was the integration of China into the Western-led global economic system. With its cheap labor, China was establishing itself as a formidable economic competitor to its Asian neighbors in Western markets, raising concerns in the West that the other Asian countries would be unable to earn enough Western currency to service the Western loans to their banks. These concerns helped to trigger the Asian currency crises. And, of course, an epidemic of currency instability could not have spread to Russia during the Cold War because the Soviet Union did not participate in the liberal international monetary system.

The currency crises bore the stamp of the post-Cold War era in another way: At the heart of each was the effort to maintain both fixed exchange rates and a free flow of capital, in the spirit of the liberal economic principles that stood unchallenged after the collapse of Communism. First in the core and then in the world's periphery, capital controls were steadily dismantled in the second age of globalization.[5] Countries of the periphery such as Mexico came to depend on foreign capital to fuel economic growth and pegged their currencies to the dollar to assure foreign investors that what was put in could also be withdrawn at no loss in currency value.[6]

In each case, however, speculators came to suspect that the countries in question would not be able to defend the exchange rate to which they had committed themselves, and the absence of capital controls meant that enormous sums of money could be moved in and out of local currencies very rapidly. Speculators sold the currency under attack[7] in anticipation of a devaluation. They thereby hastened—and perhaps even, in the fashion of a self-fulfilling prophecy, helped to cause[8]—what they had anticipated. In each case the government initially mobilized its reserves to defend its currency, but the amount of money available for attack, the pools of capital that had collected since the end of the Bretton Woods system, were so large that the government was overwhelmed.[9]

There were important differences among the three outbreaks of currency instability. Unlike in Italy and Great Britain, those in Asia involved private debt rather than government obligations, debt owed mainly by local banks that had borrowed dollars at fixed rates and then loaned the money in local currencies.[10] Unlike the others, the attacks on the Asian currencies were not triggered by the fiscal imbalances of governments. They bore a resemblance to the great financial bubbles of history, the Dutch tulip craze of the seventeenth century or the South Sea Bubble of the early eighteenth.[11] In each case money gravitated to a particular investment, creating the erroneous impression that its price would continue to rise indefinitely. At some point the dominant emotion switched from greed to fear. Holders of the asset—Dutch tulip bulbs, shares in the South Sea company, the Thai baht, the South Korean won—began to sell. This triggered a stampede as investors, anticipating a fall in value, rushed to liquidate their holdings, thereby causing the price to plunge. In such circumstances panic is rational. In a plummeting market, the sooner the investor sells, the more of his investment he can recoup.

The crises in Mexico and Asia proved contagious, and currency instability spread from one country to another. The initial currency difficulty in both cases made neighboring or similar countries look suddenly risky, igniting a rush to sell their currencies as well.[12] And when one country devalued, the currencies of countries that exported to the same markets suddenly seemed fragile, since sustaining the existing value would handicap that country's exporters and deprive it of hard currency. The logical assumption was that they, too, would devalue, and the prudent course was to sell their currencies as well.[13]

For Mexico and the distressed countries of Asia, although not for

Great Britain or Italy, international rescue packages were organized and emergency loans provided, with American prodding, by the IMF. Despite the loans, in the countries of the periphery the currency crises had devastating economic effects. While Great Britain and Italy benefited from their devaluations, with exports rising and unemployment falling,[14] in Mexico and especially in Asia production plummeted. Banks, businesses, and factories closed; jobs disappeared; wages fell; prices rose. In Mexico and in some Asian countries (although not Indonesia) growth did resume in an encouragingly short period of time, but the economic downturn in almost every one of them was worse than any of the periodic recessions in the Western core after 1945.

MONETARY PRECAUTIONS

IN THE WAKE of the currency crises, a consensus formed on one measure to prevent similar mishaps: more extensive reliance, in the afflicted countries, on the fundamental liberal practice of transparency. Asian banks that had received loans from the core countries had not made available the kind of information about their operations, and about the economic viability of the loans they had made with what they had borrowed, that was standard—indeed, legally required—in the West. (Nor had the Mexican government been entirely candid about its fiscal position.) Because bad news was unexpected, when it surfaced in the form of reports of bad loans on the books of the Asian banks, for example, investors rushed to withdraw their funds.[15]

A related, longer-term reform was to decrease reliance on banks and increase the use of equity—stock—markets, which require more information than banks in order to function. Without transparency investors will not part with their money. And markets, unlike banks, cannot ordinarily be manipulated by a small number of people. The system of directing money to economically dubious projects in order to benefit politically well-connected people, which came to be known as "crony capitalism," was far easier to operate if banks rather than markets were the agents of financial intermediation.[16]

Another familiar method of forestalling speculative attacks on currency was the imposition of controls on the international movement of capital, and this also came to the fore in the wake of the currency crises. Such controls serve the same purpose as the controls on an irrigation system: to prevent sudden surges that can cause damaging flooding. Capital controls were more controversial than the practice of transparency.[17] As government-imposed restraints on free international exchange, they departed from liberal orthodoxy[18] and so risked lowering overall economic well-being.

Moreover, in the second age of globalization, with its enormous pools of capital and myriad commercial channels, money was difficult to control. Like water, it had a way of going around or seeping through barriers erected against it. One afflicted Asian country did impose capital controls, with modestly successful short-term results. But this country, Malaysia, was led by the eccentric and offensive Mohammed Mahathir, who evoked an old and ugly stereotype when he blamed Jewish speculators for his country's financial troubles.[19] On the departure from liberal economic principles that capital controls represented, therefore, the cadre of international economic experts was, in a reversal of the Christian injunction, better disposed to the sin than to the sinner.

The role of the IMF was as controversial as capital controls in the wake of the currency crisis. The organization's supporters credited it with preventing even worse economic damage than in fact occurred by providing loans to help stabilize the stricken currencies.[20] Its critics leveled two charges against the Fund. One was that its rescue packages had aggravated the "moral hazard" problem, which is the danger that rescuing investors from the consequences of bad investments will simply encourage imprudent investing.[21] It is, after all, the risk of failure that produces market discipline, compelling the kind of care with investment that channels capital to productive destinations. Where the allocation of capital is concerned, the existence of a safety net can encourage recklessness. (Taken to its logical conclusion this point of view suggests that the IMF should not exist at all.[22]) Other critics charged that the economic policies that the IMF demanded of the Asian countries in return for its loans, especially the raising of interest rates to retain or re-attract foreign capital, had unnecessarily deepened the recessions into which they had fallen.[23]

Perhaps the most striking features of the currency crises of the 1990s in the world's periphery, and the most vivid evidence that they were the products of the post-Cold War era, were the political and economic consequences in the afflicted countries. When economic disaster struck the countries of the core in the 1930s, it discredited liberal politics and economics. It made Communist illiberalism, newly installed in the former tsarist empire, seem promising and led to the consolidation of illiberal regimes in Germany and Japan. All rejected democracy, free trade, and peaceful foreign policies. Six decades later, in the world's periphery, the consequences were different. The lesson the countries involved drew from their experiences was the need for greater liberalism. This extended beyond introducing transparency into the financial system. It included politics as well.

In Mexico seven decades of one-party rule came to an end in 2000, as the opposition candidate for president, Vicente Fox, defeated the nominee of the ruling Institutional Revolutionary Party. This occurred, to be sure, six years after the country's currency crisis, but in Asia the political consequences of the economic shocks came more swiftly and were also liberal. In Indonesia, the thirty-five-year dictatorship of General Suharto was replaced by a democracy, albeit a disorganized and fragile one. In South Korea Kim Dae Jung, a former dissident once imprisoned by the regime, was elected president.

It is difficult to imagine a more persuasive demonstration of the hegemony of liberal ideas than the immediate consequences of the financial crises of the 1990s. The economic difficulties that these countries experienced stemmed, after all, from their integration into an international monetary order organized and dominated by the liberal powers and based on liberal principles. But in the wake of the Cold War, whatever the problem, the solution could only be a liberal one. The first post-Cold War decade thus demonstrated the world's susceptibility to large monetary shocks but it also demonstrated a global commitment to as liberal a monetary order as was feasible, if only for lack of a viable alternative.

THE VICISSITUDES OF TRADE

T HE VERDICT of the first post-Cold War decade on international trade was also a mixed one. The Uruguay Round of trade negotiations, the most elaborate ever undertaken, was successfully completed in 1994. Its completion led to the formation of something that had been proposed at the end of World War II but, largely because of American objections, had never been established: a formal body to preside over international commerce, the World Trade Organization (WTO).[24] But a WTO meeting in Seattle in December 1999, convened to launch a new "millennium round" of trade talks, attracted 50,000 protesters who loudly expressed their displeasure with international commerce. A number of their objections involved trade's effects on the world's poor, although virtually all of those registering such objections were citizens of the wealthy core countries and the actual representatives of the countries of the periphery evinced little sympathy for their views. The demonstrations that the protestors mounted turned violent.[25]

In the country with the world's largest economy, the United States, the fate of trade liberalization was a mixed one. Free trade's champions won important political battles in the United States Congress, which approved not only the treaty that emerged from the Uruguay Round but also the North American Free Trade Agreement (NAFTA) and, in 2000, permanent Most Favored Nation trading status for China, paving the way for the admission of the world's most populous country to the WTO. But the opposition to each of these measures was formidable and all the more telling as an indicator of popular disenchantment with free trade, because NAFTA and "normal" trade status for China were clearly advantageous for the United States in that the American market was far more open than Mexico's or China's.

Mixed as it was, the pattern of the politics of trade in the wake of the Cold War was a familiar one. Political resistance to liberalization was all but inevitable. Because trade disrupts and displaces as it creates wealth, those whose lives are disrupted organize to protect themselves against its effects. The greater the volume of exchange within or among sovereign states—and globalization was defined, after all, by the depth and breadth of economic integration—the more intense the likely resistance.[26] In the first age of globalization the increases in cross-border transactions provoked a backlash in the form of protective tariffs against what was most frequently traded— agricultural products—and laws restricting a cross-border flow of people—immigration—that was, in relative terms, greater in the first era than in the second.[27]

There were additional reasons to expect the multilateral machinery of trade liberalization to make headway only slowly in the wake of the Cold War. One was the increase in the number of sovereign states involved. As a result of the triumph of economic liberalism virtually every country desired to take part in the world trading order and all wanted a say in writing its rules. The greater the number of parties to a negotiation, the harder it is to reach agreement.

In addition, after 1945 new forms of protection were devised even as old ones were reduced. Formal tariffs were lowered but non-tariff barriers that had the same effect, such as voluntary export restraints and anti-dumping laws, were created. Moreover, new trade issues arose on which agreement would not have been easy to reach even with fewer negotiators because they were complicated and touched on sensitive matters of domestic governance. Two in particular aroused controversy: the demand that trade agreements mandate environmental standards and that they incorporate rules governing workers' rights.

These demands were aimed at the countries of the periphery, where both sets of norms, when they existed at all, were more lax and less rigorously enforced than in the core. The poorer countries suspected that those who advocated including these issues in the trade talks were seeking to raise their costs of production and thereby protect the jobs of workers in core country industries that competed with the periphery's exports.[28] The rise of the environment and labor as trade issues stemmed from the central challenge to the post-Cold War trading system: fully integrating the countries of the periphery. Whereas during the Cold War the resistance to their full incorporation had come principally from the peripheral countries themselves, in the post-Cold War period it was the countries of the core that were less than enthusiastic. In one sense this was odd: Most of the core countries' trade was with one another, not with the periphery. But a particular feature of trade within the Western core that softened political opposition was missing in commerce between core and periphery. Trade among core countries tended to be conducted by firms that produced for both the home and foreign markets. This made the core countries reluctant to lobby for protection in the first for fear of losing access, through retaliation, to the second. The industries under pressure from exports from peripheral countries, such as textiles, felt no comparable countervailing pressure because they did not sell to the periphery.[29]

The effort to make trade freer in the post–Cold War era carried one other noteworthy burden: the absence of the Cold War conditions that had assisted the cause of liberalization. Foremost among them was the role of the world's strongest country. In the wake of World War II the United States was powerful enough to do for the international economy something like what governments do for economies within sovereign states. It provided, if not contract enforcement, then security, with the system of alliances that gave the assurance that transactions could be completed without interference from hostile powers. And, as governments do within countries, the United States supplied the currency for international transactions. America did not provide the world with a government, but it did act as the leader of the Western core and, as such, took the initiative in organizing the liberal trade and monetary systems that functioned throughout the Cold War and lived on into the post–Cold War era.[30] The American government offered incentives, in the form of access to its own market, the richest in the world, to persuade other core countries to take part in an open trading system.[31] By furnishing what became a global currency and extending loans and grants that helped promote the financing for trade the United States also, in the early post-war period, laid the foundation for a monetary order in which capital flowed relatively freely and in increasing volume.[32]

The American government also contributed to the establishment of liberal international economic norms by indulging others' departures from them, following liberal rules even when others did not, thus keeping the system alive. In monetary affairs, the Europeans did not achieve the liberal goal of making their currencies fully convertible into dollars and other currencies until 1958. In trade the United States encouraged the formation of the regional trading association in Europe that became the European Union, and tolerated barriers to imports of various sorts in Japan even as it kept its own market open to Japanese exports.[33]

The United States was moved to adopt such policies for the same reason that Great Britain played a comparable role in the liberal economic order of the first era of globalization. As the country with the strongest economy in the world it stood to gain from opportunities to export goods and capital that liberal rules offered. The conviction that trading partners would conduct peaceful foreign policies toward one another, which Woodrow Wilson had taken from the nineteenth-century British proponents of the idea, was very much alive in the United States. Through World War II its chief advocate was Secretary of State Cordell Hull. The conviction was reinforced by what, in its immediate aftermath, the Americans took to be the lessons of World War II. They believed that the interruption of trade and formation of rival, or at least uncooperative, monetary blocs in the interwar period had contributed to the outbreak of armed conflict in Europe in 1939 and the Pacific in 1941. Illiberal economic policies had led to the quintessentially illiberal foreign policy: war.

The most potent American motive for establishing and sustaining a liberal economic order, however, arose from the Cold War. Americans saw the trade and monetary systems as part of that global struggle, bulwarks against Communist illiberalism because they strengthened and united the Western core. The Marshall Plan of 1947, which helped make liberal economic policies (as well as regional economic cooperation) feasible and attractive for the Western Europeans, had an explicitly anti-Communist purpose: to buttress pro-American governments on the continent against the subversion of Moscow's allies and sympathizers within their own borders.

The need for solidarity within the Western alliance was an important reason that the United States indulged European and Japanese departures from liberal international economic practices; and it was a reason that America's allies, in turn, indulged the United States. The American government was spared the need to reduce its expenditures, and thus the outflow of dollars, by the German and Japanese willingness to absorb them even when this was economically disadvantageous to them, and by the allies' contributions to arrangements that shielded the United States from having to keep its promise to exchange them for gold.[34] All parties made economic sacrifices for strategic purposes. The requirements of the Cold War lubricated the international economic machinery of the Western core. In the 1990s that lubricant ceased to be available.

Its absence was evident in American trade policies in the first post-Cold War decade, which stood in sharp contrast to those the country had adopted in the aftermath of World War II. Whereas after 1945 the United States followed liberal rules even when others strayed from them, after the Cold War the United States asserted the right to ignore these same liberal norms. Negotiated multilateral measures were the heart of liberal international economic procedure but the Clinton administration, the first one with the opportunity to define the post-Cold War American approach to the world, insisted on the right to act unilaterally. The essence of the liberal approach to economics is to allow the market—private decisions—to determine the allocation of resources and the outcome of exchanges. The Clinton administration tried to compel Japan to agree to numerical targets for Japanese purchases of products made in the United States.[35] After World War II it was the policy of the American government to sacrifice short-term economic gains for the larger goal of building a liberal international economic order. After the Cold War the priority was reversed. The United States sought short-term economic gain at the expense of the integrity of the system it had been principally responsible for establishing. The prospects for a liberal global economic order in the twenty-first century thus depended on the same uncertainty as the prospects for the liberal approach to security in Europe and East Asia: whether the United States would pay the costs of leadership.

To be sure, American international economic leadership was not entirely absent in the first post-Cold War decade. Washington took the initiative in assembling rescue packages for Mexico and the Asian countries in response to their currency crises. The United States also continued to provide the world's largest and most open market for exports, which was particularly important in the wake of these crises because the employment the afflicted countries had to restore and the reserves they needed to earn would have to come mainly from exports. Here the United States played the role for other countries that Keynes had assigned to the government within a sovereign state. It was the engine of demand, triggering a rise in production in economies with underutilized capacities. The first post-Cold War decade coincided with a great boom in consumption in the United States, which welcomed exports from many other countries in which it thereby fueled economic growth.

The American departures from liberal trade policies in the 1990s did not destroy, or even gravely damage, the world trading system. For one thing, Japan did not accept the American program for "managed trade."[36] For another, the effort to introduce it was not the first American departure from liberal trade orthodoxy. It was, instead, part of a trend that was three decades old. Since the 1970s the United States had sought by various means to reduce or eliminate its trade deficit with Japan. While the preferred method of doing so was to increase American exports rather than the protectionist tactic of restricting Japanese imports, when export-promotion involved unilateral American measures or fixed targets for American products it violated the spirit and the letter of free trade. The 1974 Trade Act included a section that permitted (while the later Trade Act of 1988 required) the American government to impose sanctions on countries with surpluses that the United States deemed to be the result of unfair trade practices. This was a flagrant violation of the norms of free trade.[37]

In the final decades of the twentieth century, the ongoing Japanese-American trade dispute posed the most significant challenge to the open world trading system. American critics charged that Japan systematically and deliberately engaged in unfair trade practices, protecting its home market while subsidizing and encouraging collusion among its exporting firms that permitted them to capture dominant positions in the American market. To Japan's defenders, the critics' diagnosis was inaccurate and the various departures from liberal trade practices proposed as remedies were unwarranted. Japan had, they said, done well without breaking the trading rules, to

the benefit of both Japan and its trading partners. American resentment, in this view, was to be understood as the product of the
"diminished giant syndrome"—alarm at seeing the reduction of an
enormous but transitory margin of economic superiority over other
countries. Alarm led to pressure for ill-advised trade policies, as it
had in Great Britain at the end of the first era of globalization when
the British lead in economic output, which the birth of the industrial
revolution within its borders had made possible, was eliminated by
the rapid economic growth of other countries, notably Germany and
the United States.[38]

During the Cold War the two countries' common commitment to
political solidarity kept the Japanese-American dispute within
bounds, although the restraints on the quarrel were stronger in the
1950s and 1960s than in the 1970s and 1980s. With the end of the
Cold War that particular incentive disappeared, but the first post-
Cold War decade was marked by a severe recession in Japan that
made the Japanese economy seem far less formidable, and thus less
predatory, even to its harshest American critics.

Fortunately, the maintenance of a trading relationship between
the United States and Japan unencumbered by barriers to imports or
quotas for exports did not depend entirely on a poor economic performance by Japan. Over the course of the second half of the twentieth century, the idea of free trade became ever more widely
accepted, at least in principle. No doubt the political tide still flowed
in the opposite direction, but pushing against that tide the world
over was the body of economic studies, the vast majority of them
conducted after World War II, that were virtually unanimous in vin-
dicating Adam Smith: Free trade was integral to making nations
wealthy.

Only a tiny fraction of the world's population had any acquain-
tance with these studies, of course, but a far larger part could observe
the evidence on which they were based. The countries most successful in economic terms conducted liberal trade policies. Free trade
was associated with the enormous expansion of wealth that was as
salient a feature of the twentieth century as its manifold horrors.

The commitment to liberal international economic principles
during the Cold War drew strength from the memories of the poli-

tics and economics in the world's core in the 1930s and 1940s as well
as from the Cold War itself. By the outset of the twenty-first century
the memories were less politically salient and the Cold War had
ended. But in their place, to reinforce that commitment, was the
economic history of the preceding half century. Where once the
reputation of liberal policies had depended on what had happened
politically when they were not followed, now it rested on what had
happened economically when they were. Moreover, what required
political support in the wake of the Cold War was not, as in the aftermath of World War II, the construction of an entire new international economic order out of the rubble of war, but rather the less
taxing task of preserving and extending the existing one.

This is not to say that international economic liberalism faced no
challenges at the outset of the new millennium. Of those it did face,
perhaps the most formidable was a surprising one. The second age
of globalization witnessed a trend toward the organization of the
world's economic affairs not on a global but on a regional basis.

THE EUROPEAN PROJECT

AT THE BEGINNING OF 1999 twelve members of the European
Union began to merge their various national currencies into a
single one. The birth of the euro and other, less prominent movements toward monetary consolidation had their origins in the monetary "trilemma" with which the world had had to wrestle for much of
the twentieth century. Bretton Woods had represented an attempt to
combine all three desirable features: the free flow of capital, the
autonomy of national monetary policies, and steady if not frozen
exchange rates, the last by finding a middle ground between the
fixed exchange rates of the gold standard era and the floating rates of
the interwar period. At the dawn of the twenty-first century this
approach seemed to have failed.

The Asian countries afflicted by currency crises in the 1990s had
tried a version of this compromise. They had pegged their exchange
rates to the dollar but then had been unable to defend them. The lesson of their failure was that rates had to be either firmly fixed, which

meant surrendering either monetary autonomy or the free flow of capital, or freely floating.[39] The countries with the world's largest economies, the United States and Japan, did allow their exchange rates to float. But floating did not suit smaller countries because their economies were more severely buffeted by frequent changes in the international price of their money. The uncertainty of unfixed exchange rates was a further hardship for those, like the members of the EU, that traded extensively with one another. While floating exchange rates were undesirable for the Europeans, so, too, were capital controls, since these countries aspired to create a single market among themselves for capital as well as for traded goods. Committed as they were to fixed exchange rates and capital mobility, by the terms of the trilemma the Europeans had to abandon independent monetary policies. With the creation of the euro that is what they did.

No other group of countries went as far in monetary consolidation as the Western Europeans but a number of countries of the periphery took a step in this direction with a latter-day version of the gold standard known as a currency board, in which the dollar (or, in theory, any "hard" currency) played the role of gold. When the supply of dollars expanded or contracted, so, too, at the designated ratio, did the local currency.[40]

In trade, the trend toward regional integration was more pronounced. In the last three decades of the twentieth century a number of regional trading arrangements were formed.[41] The EU was the oldest and most closely integrated. It was followed by the Association of Southeast Asian Nations (ASEAN) in the Pacific region, NAFTA in North America, Mercosur in South America, and several others.[42] Such arrangements were undesirable in purely economic terms to the extent that they diverted trade from less expensive suppliers outside the bloc to more costly ones within, thereby lowering aggregate wealth, rather than creating trade that would otherwise not have taken place.[43] Regional trade arrangements raised, however, an even more worrisome political specter.

The liberal theory of history holds that good things go together. The experience of the history of the modern age suggests that bad things—illiberal practices across the range of political and economic activity—also go together. The burst of imperial acquisition in the period before World War I was driven in part by the conviction, with its roots in a vulgarized version of Darwin's theory of evolution, that prosperity and even survival would depend on the creation of large, integrated political and economic blocs. Geographically circumscribed economic activity, imperial conquest, and ultimately war among the great powers were all connected.[44] They were even more closely connected in World War II. The moment when the modern world came closest to being organized along regional lines occurred in the early 1940s. At the zenith of their power, Nazi Germany and Imperial Japan treated the huge tracts of Eurasia and the Pacific that they had conquered as exclusive economic zones, arenas for exploitation and plunder.[45] The most extreme form of economic illiberalism went hand in hand with the most extreme political illiberalism, as well as with the most illiberal of all foreign policies—aggressive, brutal, and constant war.

This historical record was the basis for the concern that a drift away from liberal principles in economic affairs, which is what economic regionalism had the potential to promote, could lead to far more serious and dangerous departures from liberal principles and practices.[46] The motives for the formation of regional trade organizations did sometimes echo, albeit faintly, the geopolitical fears and calculations of the interwar period. One of the reasons the United States agreed to form NAFTA—not the only or even the most important reason, to be sure—was the worry that the EU was forsaking liberal trade policies and the fear of Japanese imports to the Western hemisphere. European integration also stimulated the formation of the Asia-Pacific Economic Cooperation Forum (APEC) in 1989.[47] The trend toward regional economic consolidation at the outset of the twenty-first century raised two questions: What were the prospects for organizing the world along regional lines? And how dangerous would this be? The test for both was Europe.

The birthplace of the modern world, where the industrial revolution and the French Revolution took place, and the location of the political innovations that have dominated the modern era, Europe was the site, in the second half of the twentieth century, of another innovation: the wealthy political and economic association of fifteen countries that was the EU.

EU members aspired to more than the creation of a customs

union, which, by the century's end, they had achieved, or even a more closely integrated financial area, which the successful management of the euro would make it. Their aim was ultimately to speak with a single voice and act as a single unit on political and military issues. The Maastricht Treaty of 1991, signed by all EU members, committed them not only to a single currency but also to a common foreign and security policy. While the goal of a federal Europe was by no means unanimously shared among the EU's members, it was implicit in some of the aims to which the member countries had committed themselves and commanded significant, if not majority, support within them.

It was not entirely fanciful to imagine that, in the twenty-first century, an ever-more united Europe would serve as a model for comparable regional blocs in other parts of the world, just as the forms of political and economic organization first developed there had ultimately diffused throughout the planet. In view of the history of the twentieth century it was not an exercise in political hypochondria to worry that such a world would be a less-than-liberal one. The long history of human civilization is replete with ironies. It would not be the least of them if, after vanquishing traditional political and economic institutions in the nineteenth century and overcoming the challenge of illiberalism in its various forms in the twentieth, international liberalism, standing alone as a set of organizing principles for public life at the dawn of the twenty-first century, turned out to contain within itself the seeds, if not of its own destruction then of its substantial and unwelcome modification. The division of the world into distinct, mutually exclusive, and none-too-cordial political and economic blocs as the result of efforts to cope with the problems associated with the operation of a liberal international monetary order would be as perverse an outcome as could be imagined. While this was a course that international history *could* take in the new century, however, there were good reasons to doubt that it was the path the world *would* follow: Europe's future was not entirely certain; the prospects for similar regional blocs elsewhere were shaky; and the power of liberal ideas and institutions was formidable.

The EU was committed to becoming both a deeper and wider association. The main vehicle for deepening—that is, intensifying—

relations among its members was the common currency. But the success of the euro was not guaranteed. It was vulnerable to the same problem that had put an end to the gold standard. The renunciation of independent monetary policies by the adherents to the euro might prove politically difficult to sustain.

The monetary union would inevitably be subject to "asymmetrical shocks," events affecting different countries in different ways. If the level of employment drops in a European country with its own monetary policy, the government can raise it by lowering interest rates, making it easier to borrow money to start businesses that will hire people. When that country is part of the euro, however, it does not have the power to lower its own interest rates. It is for the European Central Bank to lower them and, if employment is high in other European countries, it may well decide not to do so, thereby penalizing the country with high joblessness for its membership in the common currency.

Asymmetrical shocks occurred frequently in the United States, the thirteen original colonies of which formed the world's oldest and most successful currency union. One part of the country might benefit, but others suffer, from lowering interest rates, and the American equivalent of the European Central Bank, the Federal Reserve Board, might choose not to lower them. But the United States had other ways to relieve regional economic distress. The federal government could redirect funds to the afflicted parts of the country. People living where jobs were scarce could find employment in more prosperous regions of what was the same country. These possibilities, which made the United States an "optimal currency area" in which a single currency was both economically useful and politically viable, were lacking in Europe.[48] There was no powerful central government to redistribute resources on an appreciable scale and it was culturally, if not always legally, difficult for the citizens of one country to move to and work in another—language being almost as effective a barrier to immigration as tariffs are to trade.

Whether the euro's member countries would find its benefits sufficient to offset the loss of an effective instrument of national economic policy was a question that only the experience of a common currency could answer.[49] So, too, was the related question of whether, on the basis of economic integration, Europe could conduct a single foreign and security policy.[50]

As for widening, to include the formerly Communist countries of Central and Eastern Europe, this, too, would not be easy. Although not on the scale of the American federal government, the EU had some union-wide funds that came from the richer member countries of the north and could be directed to the poorer ones of the south. Admitting countries from the east that were poorer still threatened to increase the bill for the north while reducing the benefits to the south, a prospect attractive to neither. The expansion of membership to the east would also confront the EU with the problem the world trading system faced in the wake of the Cold War: More members made coherent action of any kind more difficult. The EU's aspirations to speak with a single voice and act decisively in the international arena were in tension with its simultaneous aspiration to encompass as much of Europe as possible.[51]

THE EUROPEAN MODEL

IF, AT THE DAWN of the twenty-first century, the prospects for an ever more united Europe were not unclouded, neither, however, were they hopeless. The history of the European project since its launch after World War II was one of fitful advance toward greater depth and breadth of integration through the process of institutional adaptation and the inevitably messy business of political bargaining and compromise. But even if the European Union were to widen and deepen, countries in other regions would not find it easy to follow the same path. The Europeans were well endowed with the prerequisites for regional integration: a common Roman, Christian, medieval, and modern background; a long history of interaction; and roughly comparable size and level of economic development.

While lacking many of these features, the Western hemisphere also had a plausible basis for economic integration, with the United States in the dominant position, and even for political cohesion, as a result of the spread of democracy in Latin America. But Asia, even only East Asia, was too large, heterogeneous, and disputatious for

any serious effort at integration in the early years of the twenty-first century. In the last decade of the twentieth century, Japan made extensive investments in the poorer countries of the region, as the United States had done in Latin America. Some Japanese envisioned this as the basis for a regional economic bloc, the metaphor for which was the v-shape of a flock of flying geese, with Japan in the lead.[52] But a Japan-centered East Asian bloc was a considerably more remote possibility than a United States-centered economic association of the Americas.

For one thing, Japan, and the other countries of East Asia, would have no more interest in arrangements that shut them out of the American market than the United States would have in economic exclusion from Asia.[53] Globalization was more than a slogan: International economic activity did take place on a global scale and interruptions would impose real economic costs. For another, the other, poorer countries of East Asia would be even less attracted to Japanese regional leadership than the Latin Americans, with their historical wariness of the colossus to the north, would be to lining up behind the United States. This was emphatically the case for China, the most populous country in the region. If East Asia were to have a regional leader, the only candidate acceptable to the Chinese would be China itself.[54] And even if the European model of regional organization did spread to the Western Hemisphere and East Asia in the twenty-first century, large chunks of the planet—the former Soviet Union, the Middle East, South Asia, Africa—would still remain outside any of them.

The unification of Europe, however rapidly it proceeded and whatever its influence on the rest of the world, did not portend a cramped, hostile, illiberal world order in the twenty-first century for yet another reason, the most important one of all. The reason was this: European unity itself was a liberal project. The members of the EU all were, and by statute were required to be, liberal, constitutional democracies.[55] The integration of their economies had expanded trade and investment among them without reducing the flow of goods and capital between Europe and the rest of the world. It is possible to regard regional agreements as the equivalents, for trade, of the welfare state for domestic economies and the Bretton

Woods system for money: a compromise between what is economically desirable and what is politically feasible and thus a stepping stone, rather than a stumbling block, to a more liberal international economic order.[56] And relations among EU members were impeccably peaceful in the second half of the twentieth century, making Western Europe an oasis of non-belligerence on the territory where, in that century's first half, the most violent and destructive wars in all of recorded history were waged. The political and economic history of Western Europe after World War II was the most powerful evidence in favor of the liberal theory of history: There all good things—democracy, prosperity, and peace—*did* go together.

If the European Union is a foretaste of the way the world of the twenty-first century will be organized, therefore, it is more plausibly a harbinger of a liberal international order than an illiberal one, a point that can be reinforced by noting the ways in which the EU was, at the dawn of the new century, similar to the common security order in Europe and the international trading system and international monetary arrangements—the monuments to liberal internationalism that embodied the triad of goals that Woodrow Wilson had unveiled in Paris in 1919.

The premise of each was a world of sovereign states. In the twenty-first century, as in the twentieth, the nineteenth, and all the centuries before, there was no world government to keep order or to act as a global monetary authority, issuing currency and rescuing countries afflicted by monetary crisis.[57] On the most important matters, within the European Union as with common security, trade, and money, ultimate power resided with national political authorities. In each, therefore, the participating countries observed liberal norms voluntarily; the success of each in the second half of the twentieth century demonstrates that international order without international government is possible.

Each involved more than rule-following. Each had first to be launched and then adjusted as goals and circumstances changed. This required negotiation and compromise. It involved, that is, politics rather than simply administration.[58] In the second half of the twentieth century, with varying degrees of difficulty, the members of the EU, the parties to the European common security order, and the participants in the international trade and monetary systems managed enough agreement to establish and sustain them. The ways in which they did so varied. Within the EU and the world trading system, ongoing negotiations produced explicit agreements. For the international monetary system, especially after the end of the Bretton Woods system, there were occasional formal agreements but more often informal coordination, as the countries involved steered their monetary policies so as not to come into dangerous conflict with those of the others.[59]

With no overarching authority, sovereign states hewed to liberal norms not because they were required to but because they wished to do so. The wish was born of a common, broad, and deep commitment to liberal principles, which, in each case, was rooted in the politics and economics of the participating countries themselves. They could build and maintain liberalism abroad cooperatively because they practiced liberalism at home individually. It was not only the European Union but also the common security order and the international trade and monetary systems that validated the liberal theory of history, or at least its major premise—that liberal values and practices are mutually reinforcing across the different sectors of political and economic life.

The establishment and the success of liberal values and practices helped to end the Cold War on Western terms. The end of the Cold War, in turn, created the opportunity for democracy, the market economy, and common security to be established where they were once forbidden, and for international trade and monetary systems to expand to include countries that had stood outside them for most of the second half of the twentieth century. And the extent to which they were established and did expand, the extent to which they followed the pattern, as old as human history, of cultural diffusion, would be the measure, in the twenty-first century, of what the end of the Cold War made possible: a new world order.

Conclusion

I<small>N THE</small> Marx Brothers' film *Duck Soup*, their version of international politics, a scene takes place in the office of Trentino, the ambassador of Sylvania. A telegram arrives and Harpo, the silent brother who embodies the spirit of happy chaos, seizes it and crumples it up. To the puzzled ambassador, Chico, the piano-playing pseudo-Italian brother, helpfully explains: "He gets mad because he can't read."

The scene can stand as an epigraph for the world at the outset of the twenty-first century. The liberal Wilsonian triad—peace, democracy, and free markets—had attained the same status as literacy: widespread although not universal, dominant, unchallenged. The traditional or illiberal methods of organizing political, economic, and international life had no more legitimacy and commanded no more allegiance than did the arguments in favor of illiteracy.

Yet this did not mean that all of the world's sovereign states had put liberal Wilsonian principles fully into practice. Although virtually every country wanted a market economy, not all had successfully installed one. The list of the world's liberal democracies included more sovereign states than ever before, but it did not include all of them. Many of the governments in the world's periphery, behind a facade of constitutionalism and popular sovereignty, held power by force rather than consent and exercised power in an arbitrary manner. As for the liberal approach to international relations, common security, far from being the prevailing pattern the world over, was confined to Europe. It had the same status, at the beginning of the twenty-first century, as democracy and free markets had had at the beginning of the nineteenth: It was new, promising, untried, and fragile.

Moreover, the widespread failure to install the institutions and practices of liberalism, especially the market, produced resentment against the great hegemonic triad and the countries that embodied them. This sentiment in turn fueled attacks, actual and potential, on the liberal order. The most spectacular of them were the assaults on New York and Washington of September 11, 2001; but terrorism was not the only threat to the post-Cold War order. It was not even the most serious one.

THE TYRANNY OF CULTURE

COMPLICATED, dense, and sprawling though it has been, the two-hundred-plus-year history of the modern age, seen from the beginning of the twenty-first century, has a clear theme: the rise to hegemonic status of the liberal approach to politics, economics, and (with qualifications) security that Woodrow Wilson advocated in Paris in 1919, all three of them with roots in the Anglo-American world of the early modern era.

In the nineteenth century liberalism challenged and overcame the traditional ways of doing things. In the twentieth, the liberal approaches defeated, in World War II and the Cold War, the systems of illiberal politics, economics, and foreign policy that the fascist and Communist powers embodied.

Not all countries were equally liberal. Indeed, some were not liberal at all. While their attitudes toward peace and democracy varied, however, virtually all of the world's almost two hundred sovereign states sought to construct, or to maintain, a market economy, a global pattern that stemmed from a major change in international affairs in the second half of the twentieth century.

This change was a shift in the nature of political legitimacy—a government's ultimate source of strength and staying power. From time immemorial the central test of any government's fitness to rule was the capacity to defend its own borders. The modern age brought another test. Governments were required, in one way or another, to represent those they governed, although not, in the case of the illiberal powers of the twentieth century, through freely elected and politically accountable officials. By the end of the twentieth century the borders of most sovereign states commanded broad acceptance and few regimes remained in which rulers came to office by heredity, as almost all had done before the French Revolution. As the importance of defense and representativeness declined, however, a third basis for political legitimacy emerged: prosperity.

In the course of the twentieth century it became clear that material well-being for a country's citizens was possible on a scale previously unimagined. Once available, affluence came to be universally desired. The highest goal of political life was, increasingly, to foster it. The economic history of the twentieth century also demonstrated that the mechanism for delivering prosperity was the market, which placed enormous pressure on those who aspired to govern to equip their societies with wealth-producing liberal economic systems.

The international system thus came to resemble a wagon train or a convoy of ships moving in a single direction. But while the wagons in a wagon train and the ships in a convoy keep close to one another for the sake of safety, in the post-Cold War international system the world's sovereign states were strung out along the route to liberalism. Why did some countries trail so far behind others?

Many got a late start, committed as they had been for most of the modern era to traditional or illiberal politics and economics. Once having made a commitment to liberalism, however, progress was not necessarily destined to be rapid. Would-be liberalizers faced internal opposition to democratic politics from those who held power and did not wish to share it and resistance to the construction of a market economy from the beneficiaries of policies of economic distortion. There was yet another, deeper reason that some sovereign states had gone farther than others in installing the Wilsonian liberal triad: culture, defined as a society's values, attitudes, and beliefs.[1]

At the outset of the twenty-first century culture had a great deal to do with whether a sovereign state had established a market economy. A well-functioning market must be embedded in a set of supporting political and economic institutions and the capacity to develop and operate these institutions depends heavily on whether a society's dominant values equip it for the task.[2] In many cases they did not.[3] So an important step in building a market economy, as well as in making a commitment to peace and democracy, is the acquisition of the appropriate cultural underpinnings.

Changes in values accompanied by changes in patterns of behavior, the consequence of the contact between and among strangers, is the motor force of human history and the modern era is full of examples of cultural change. Germany and Japan, in the first half of the twentieth century among the most bellicose nations on the planet, became, in the century's second half, perhaps the least warlike. The rapid debellicization of these once illiberal powers was the product of a large traumatic event—World War II—and the foreign occupation that followed. Cultural change also takes place at history's other level, the level of trends and developments, in the course of what the historian Fernand Braudel termed the *longue durée*. Cultural change of the kind that affects economic performance is more likely to come from social learning based on millions of discrete individual experiences than on a single national trauma.

Such change does not take place overnight. The pertinent unit of time is the generation, for a shift in a society's prevailing values requires that people whose formative experiences equipped them with one set of norms be replaced by others who embraced, at later times and in other circumstances, different values. Like learning a new language, the acquisition of new values becomes more difficult with age. And the replacement of personnel across a society occurs, in the normal course of events, when one generation succeeds another.

So while cultures do change and have always changed, and while they have changed more rapidly and broadly in the modern period than ever before, they cannot readily *be* changed by acts of official policy. Liberal political systems require the rule of law, liberal economics a financial system and private property, liberal security policies a commitment to warlessness. All involve values and all have evolved, where they exist, over the course of generations. Establishing liberal political and economic institutions and embracing liberal security policies is less like architecture than like horticulture.

This means that, at the outset of the twenty-first century, deliberate, organized collective action had less potential to achieve major political goals than had been the case in the preceding two hundred years. Revolution, the centerpiece of the nineteenth century, was made by people inspired and guided by political leaders. War, the main business of the twentieth, was waged by armies organized, equipped, and directed by governments. The diffusion of liberal values, practices, and institutions, the crucial feature of international life at the outset of the twenty-first century, cannot be summoned and controlled in the same way. It is not readily initiated or targeted. In this case history is not made; it happens.

This created a post-Cold War paradox. The countries of the world's liberal core found themselves both more and less powerful than they had been previously. Their common example carried unprecedented weight. As a political and economic model, liberalism had no competitor. But the instruments of foreign policy that the core powers wielded were comparatively weak. The achievement of their supreme international goal, the creation of a fully liberal world, depended less on what other countries did beyond their borders than on how those countries evolved within them. The traditional tools of foreign policy—guns, money, and words promising or suggesting the use of either or both—were not particularly effective.[4] A version of a venerable American joke illustrates the point: "How many psychiatrists does it take to change a light bulb? None. The light bulb must want to change itself." In inducing the wish to change, the Western example had a powerful effect; in actually bringing about the desired changes Western instruments were at best of modest use.[5]

The vocabulary of foreign policy in the United States reflected this paradox. Members of the American foreign policy establishment were in the habit, in the first post-Cold War decade as before, of urging other countries to do and to be what Americans considered appropriate. They regarded it as their responsibility to take an active role in pushing other countries in desirable directions.[6] But because they had only a limited capacity to effect what was most important beyond the borders of the United States, they sprinkled their discourse with a particular kind of verb, which denoted the earnest intention to act, without, however, conveying any particular action. Americans proclaimed themselves committed, in the first post-Cold War decade, to "promoting," "fostering," "encouraging," and "facilitating" democracy and free markets (not to mention "shaping" the international environment). These fine-sounding words had a metaphorical tendency to dissolve on contact with reality. They meant nothing in particular.[7]

The weakness of post-Cold War government policies did not, however, doom the prospects for the spread of the three parts of the Wilsonian triad. How far and how fast they spread in the twenty-first century would greatly depend on the strength of the associations posited by the liberal theory of history—on the extent to which market economies give birth to political democracies and the extent to which political democracies put the principles of transparency and defense dominance at the center of their security policies.

Those associations do not have the regularity of laws of physics. They are tendencies, predispositions. The presence of a working market economy generates a certain momentum for free elections and constitutional government, although it does not guarantee them. The same is true for democracy and peace. Moreover, the strength of these associations is bound to differ from one country to another, as is the indigenous resistance to political and economic liberalism. Still, liberal institutions and practices were widely enough distributed and deeply enough rooted, and the precepts of the liberal theory of history seemed credible enough, that the world of the new millennium resembled the world of one hundred years earlier.

HISTORICAL OPTIMISM REVISITED

THE TURN of the twentieth century, like the turn of the twenty-first, was a moment when, in the world's core, liberalism was in the ascendant. Products and capital circulated more freely and widely and in greater volume than ever before; this was the first great age of globalization. Across Europe the number of people with the right to vote had steadily expanded and one country after another had adopted constitutions: In 1905 even the autocratic tsar of Russia accepted one. As for international security, the cause of peace seemed to be making progress. In 1899 an international conference at The Hague issued guidelines for limiting armaments and called for the creation of an international court to arbitrate international disputes that might otherwise be settled by war. A book published in 1910 captured the spirit of the time. In *The Great Illusion* the Englishman Norman Angell argued that a European war would so disrupt international credit and commerce that such a conflict would never be allowed to begin, or, if it did begin, would be stopped almost immediately.

Angell turned out to be wrong. The liberal optimism and confidence to which he had given expression perished in the great conflagration of 1914 to 1918, which, in turn, inaugurated the era during which liberalism engaged in a fierce and protracted competition with illiberal approaches to politics, economics, and foreign policy. At the beginning of the twenty-first century, a similar fate for the liberal hegemony of the early post-Cold War period was not beyond the realm of possibility. War on a large scale had not become impossible. Neither, however, was it likely, because of three ways that the beginning of the twenty-first century differed from the beginning of the twentieth.

The status of war had undergone a dramatic transformation. In 1900 the governments and the people of the countries of the world's core considered war, if not exactly normal, at least occasionally necessary and even noble.[8] One hundred years later, in the eyes of their descendants, war had become morally dubious and politically pointless. Moreover, the governments of the later period had to reckon with nuclear weapons, which could wreak devastation on a scale unimagined in 1900. And from the vantage point of the early twenty-first century it was possible to look back on what those living one hundred years before had yet to experience: the horrors of the two world wars. These experiences did not inspire the widespread desire to repeat them. It was the two world wars, combined with the fact of nuclear weapons, that did most to bring the ancient practice of organized warfare into disrepute, at least in the countries of the world's core, in the second half of the twentieth century.

Nor were the other two closely related twentieth-century causes of upheaval, revolution and dictatorship, as potent in the twenty-first. The scope for revolutions, and for revolutionary leadership, had narrowed considerably. The racism that provided Hitler's inspiration for seizing power and his guidance for using it, and the Marxism that served the same purposes for Lenin, Stalin, and Mao, had been discredited and discarded. Human ingenuity is no doubt capable of contriving other ideological alternatives to liberalism but at the outset of the new century there was no sign of any serious effort to do so. Moreover, the radical, murderous twentieth-century ideologies came to power—and could only have come to power—in the disorder created by major wars, the kind of war now less likely. Finally, Lenin, Stalin, and Mao presided over societies composed mainly of illiterate peasants. Such societies were considerably more malleable than those of the twenty-first century, with their large cities, rising rates of literacy, mass media, and burgeoning middle classes.

Still, the shrinkage of the greatest sources of twentieth-century turmoil does not mean that the world of the twenty-first century is destined to be placid and unchanging.

It is possible that the rate of *political* change will ultimately slow. A static political world, one in which all sovereign states have liberal political systems, is conceivable, although the world had not come close to such a condition as the new century began. Even if the basic need for food and shelter of every inhabitant of the planet were satisfied, however, human wants would remain inexhaustible. Since the ongoing progress of science and technology will guarantee an endless supply of things to want, what Adam Smith called the pursuit of opulence will continue. Keynes looked forward to the day when, with material requirements satisfied, humankind could concentrate on esthetic and spiritual pursuits.[9] For the planet as a whole, that day will never come.

The free market will continue to create and destroy wherever it operates, making winners of some people and losers of others. The different interests of the two groups will create political conflict even in the absence of the great clashes of systems that marked the nineteenth and twentieth centuries. In this sense politics, and therefore history, will never end. But there is a difference between steady change within individual countries, which is inevitable, and major changes in their relations with one another and in the international system to which they all belong. This is the difference between change that is the consequence of the liberal project that sat atop the world's agenda in the wake of the Cold War and change that alters that agenda. In the modern era some changes are incremental and normal, others sudden, large, and unwelcome.

While the world-shaping wars and revolutions of the twentieth century were not likely features of the twenty-first, there were other sources of change of the second kind. Political and military conflict could arise from the gap in wealth between the rich and the poor of the world, the uncertainties surrounding the foreign policy of the United States, the ambivalence of Russia and China toward the liberal Wilson triad that dominated the post-Cold War era, and the spread of nuclear weapons.

POLITICAL PERILS

IN THE 1990s the gap in material well-being between the rich and the poor of the international system was an extremely wide one.[10] It provoked moral discomfort in the wealthy precincts of the Western core; private organizations and even government bureaus devoted themselves, without success, to closing it. It also inspired gloomy forecasts that the gap would trigger conflict between the wretched and the fortunate[11] and may have contributed to the growth of anti-Western terrorist networks with their origins in the Middle East. Yet this was one major twenty-first century global problem that the governments of the world's core countries were not likely to mount a concerted effort to address.

The rich countries had surpassed the poor ones economically during the Cold War and this fact had not gone unnoticed by either. The governments of the world's wealthy countries and of its poorer states had deplored the poverty of the second group, to which the core countries had provided financial assistance. But in the wake of the Cold War changes in both economic beliefs and political circumstances had reduced the pressure on the West to heed the economic problems of the periphery.

For most of the second half of the twentieth century the countries of the periphery embraced two economic doctrines. One held that it was proper for the government to take a very large role in economic management. The other deemed their poverty to be at least in part the consequence of the core's wealth, conferring upon the rich countries responsibility for alleviating it.[12] In the wake of the Cold War, however, if a country was doing badly economically the fault was increasingly thought to lie within its own borders.

Capitalism requires capital and the countries of the periphery looked to the core countries to supply it. But they could no longer realistically hope that government-provided foreign aid would deliver it. The foreign aid the rich gave to the poor in the second half of the twentieth century was modest, and the results in creating wealth unimpressive. By some accounts official aid had even produced harmful effects because recipient governments tended to use it for corrupt, or at best inefficient, purposes. Foreign aid was like candy: sweet and addictive, a source of energy in the short run but unhealthy over the long term.[13] Even if foreign aid were used wisely, however, and even if the core made the most expansively generous donations imaginable, it would supply only a small fraction of the resources for investment that the countries of the periphery needed from abroad. The bulk would have to come from privately controlled capital, the transborder flow of which, in the first post-Cold War decade, dwarfed the volume of official aid.

Attracting private capital required having the appropriate institutions and pursuing the appropriate policies. It required, that is, putting on the "golden straitjacket" in order to appear a worthy (that is, potentially profitable) recipient of resources for investment, rather than wearing rags in the hope of inspiring charitable contributions.[14] Reform at home rather than generosity from abroad held the key to economic success.[15]

The peoples of the periphery also needed access to the markets of the core in order to earn money by selling their (often chiefly agricultural) products. To these products the core countries, contrary to the basic liberal economic precept of free trade, did not always open their borders. This reversed a pattern of the Cold War, during which the governments of the core had urged their counterparts in the periphery to install liberal economic institutions themselves. In the post-Cold War era it was the governments of the periphery that complained that the countries of the core were failing to practice the liberal economic principles they had so often preached.

Economic policies are never determined solely by economic theories. During the Cold War economic assistance from the core to the periphery, like military intervention, was motivated as much by fear as by pity and intellectual conviction. The core powers feared that, unless they offered economic assistance, the governments of the periphery would join the opposing ideological camp. With the end of the Cold War that fear disappeared and with it much of the incentive for giving foreign aid (as well as for launching armed interventions). Without the option to defect to the other side the poor lacked effective means to threaten the rich.

No doubt a nuclear weapon or two in the hands of a government in the periphery would serve to concentrate the core countries' attention on its economic requirements. While it is difficult to think of the brutal North Korean Communist dictators Kim Il-sung and his son and successor Kim Jong-il as latter-day versions of the English folk hero Robin Hood, who stole from the rich and gave to the poor, they did use the threat that they would acquire nuclear weapons to extort resources from the United States, Japan, and South Korea—although it is unlikely that the aid ever reached the destitute people they ruled. But other needy countries lacked the wherewithal to follow their example. Iraq and Iran could aspire to nuclear weapon status precisely because the oil deposits within their borders made them rich by the standards of the periphery. Their nuclear ambitions had little to do with extracting money from the core, which they received by selling their oil.[16]

The world's poor did have in abundance one thing with potential leverage on the rich: themselves. The threat of inundation by a tidal wave of immigration from the periphery was, in theory, a way to induce the rich countries to contribute to the well-being of the poor.[17] Immigration from the periphery to the core had for decades been a fact of international life. For the wealthy countries these immigrants were, on the whole, what they had always been: economic assets. Immigration brought needed younger workers to countries in which the aging of the workforce threatened the existing structure of welfare benefits by increasing the ratio of retirees to active workers. As in the past, immigration also proved controversial. In the first period of globalization, the decades leading up to World War I, the objections to immigrants were largely economic in character: Their presence was thought to lower wages. In the first post-Cold War decade, by contrast, immigrants were unpopular because they were considered unable or unwilling to learn the local language (Hispanics in the United States) or adopt the local customs (Muslims in Western Europe). In the twenty-first century the core countries were no doubt destined to receive a steady stream of immigrants, but the prospect that they would be swamped by a tidal wave of desperate people from poor countries was remote.[18]

In the post-Cold War world the country with the largest capacity for perpetrating global disruption was the United States. The United States had more power and bore greater responsibility for sustaining the rules and institutions than any other country. American military forces underpinned common security in Europe as well as military stability in East Asia and served as the guarantor of the core countries' access to the oil of the Persian Gulf. The United States acted as the chief of the constabulary that stood guard against the spread of nuclear weapons to those likely to misuse them. In the global economy, America's was the largest and most open market, upon exports to which the economic health of many others depended. American economic officials led the global financial equivalent of a volunteer fire brigade when it assembled to contain the conflagrations to which free markets are susceptible.

Since the United States was not only the chief sponsor but also the principal architect and a major beneficiary of the world's liberal arrangements, any damage it did to them would be inadvertent. Potential inadvertent American harm took two forms.

Its generous supply of power in all its aspects subjected the United States to the temptation of unilateralism—pressing forward with initiatives such as the expansion of NATO and the withdrawal from the Antiballistic Missile (ABM) Treaty in the face of opposition from other countries. When President George W. Bush branded North Korea, Iraq, and Iran an "axis of evil" in January 2002 and hinted at American military action against them to ensure that they did not acquire nuclear weapons, officials of other countries expressed dismay at what they took to be an American threat to go to war without consulting other governments. The sharpest criticism came from the oldest and closest allies of the United States in Western Europe. If pressed too far, unilateral measures had the potential to call into being an opposing coalition and so produce the kind of political conflict and military rivalry familiar in previous periods of history.

A threat as serious as excessive zeal in pursuit of policies unpopular in the rest of the world was insufficient support from the American public for policies of which other countries did approve. This was the danger that the public would tire of sustaining the country's post-Cold War role as the world's leader. While the costs of American international leadership had fallen since the days of the Cold War, the reasons for the United States to play such a role had, at the same time, become somewhat less compelling. The attacks of September 11, 2001, restored some of the Cold War urgency about engagement with the rest of the world. Rooting out terrorists around the globe became a matter of self-defense, just as opposing Communism had been. But how serious the terrorist threat to the United States would ultimately prove to be, and how far that threat would help to sustain a political consensus within the United States in favor of international leadership, were questions to which only the history of the twenty-first century would provide answers. International leadership certainly imposed a kind of tax on the people of the United States and the normal attitude toward taxation was expressed in a ditty coined by the American legislator Russell Long, who was much concerned with the subject during his career in the United States Senate from 1948 to 1987:

> Don't tax you,
> Don't tax me,
> Tax that man behind the tree.

While the terrorist attacks on New York and Washington gave the American people a new and potent reason for involving themselves heavily with the rest of the world, it was nonetheless conceivable that they would tire of being the man behind the tree, especially if the threat of terrorism faded.

They might conclude that the Europeans and the Japanese no

longer required American troops patrolling their neighborhoods, which were evidently safe and for the protection of which, in any case, the locals were capable of taking responsibility. Americans might decide that the cost of ensuring the flow of oil to the core and preventing nuclear proliferation should be borne by those who would be more directly affected by a failure in either case than Americans would be. They might find attractive the idea of closing their borders to products made elsewhere in order to preserve jobs held by Americans, or rule out any responsibility for coping with economic turmoil in other countries brought about by unwise policies, or faulty institutions, or the whims of the market, or all three.

Overbearing or underperforming American foreign policies could put the post-Cold War order in particular jeopardy to the extent that they alienated or provoked Russia and China. By virtue of size, location, military power, and historical experience these two countries had, in the twenty-first century, the potential to trigger a major war. In the 1990s both had abandoned the tenets of orthodox Marxism-Leninism, including the designation of war as the essence of political relations between and among countries. Neither, however, was as imbued with the spirit of warlessness as the liberal democracies of the Western core, and in the relations of both with their neighbors there lurked the basis for armed conflict.

In the case of China, the most dangerous issue, indeed the most dangerous issue on the planet in the wake of the Cold War, was the status of Taiwan. A resolution of the political conflict over which a war would be fought depends on the changes under way on the Chinese mainland following the path posited by the liberal theory of history, thereby creating conditions in which either the Beijing regime abandons its claim to Taiwan, or Taiwan itself no longer resists close association with the mainland, or a combination of the two.

While the Taiwan question carried over from the Cold War, the basis for Russian dissatisfaction with the liberal approach to international relations stemmed from the events of the 1990s. The danger was that Western initiatives opposed by Russia, such as NATO expansion, the war against Yugoslavia, and the termination of the ABM Treaty, would lead the Russian government to reverse permanently the presumption, with which Russia had begun its post-Communist life, in favor of cooperation with the West on international issues and would persuade the Russian public that in the post-Cold War era, as for so much of recorded history, only military strength could assure respectful treatment by other countries.

One major reason that outright Russian or Chinese opposition to the liberal order of the twenty-first century would threaten that order is that both possess nuclear weapons. Another threat stemmed from the prospect that sovereign states already opposed to the liberal order would acquire such weapons. It is the possession, not the use, of nuclear armaments that the nonproliferation system was created to prevent. The one is, of course, the necessary condition for the other, but it is also the case that having a bomb brings a clearer strategic advantage than actually using it. A country that acquires a nuclear weapon has enhanced its power, while one that has used it has entered a new, uncharted, and dangerous strategic environment.

The twentieth century produced a tried and true method for keeping governments in possession of nuclear weapons from using them: deterrence. Thanks in no small part to deterrence, no nuclear shot was fired in anger in the decades following the American atomic raids on Hiroshima and Nagasaki, even though tens of thousands of nuclear explosives were fabricated and deployed around the world. In the last third of the twentieth century the nonproliferation system proved surprisingly effective, albeit not leakproof. The policy of deterrence, over a longer period, had an even more impressive record—indeed, it had a perfect record—but eternal perfection could not be guaranteed.

The consequences of a failure of deterrence would depend on the circumstances in which history's second nuclear war was fought. If Russia or China or the United States were involved, the conflict would qualify as a major war, with broad effects on international security. If, on the other hand, it involved countries in the world's periphery the consequences might be confined to the place or places that had launched and suffered the nuclear attack.

In 1999 India and Pakistan, both of which had tested nuclear explosives the year before, became the first nuclear powers to fight each other directly since the Sino-Soviet border skirmishes of 1969, when Indian troops battled forces trained, equipped, and supported by Pakistan in the disputed Indian province of Kashmir. If the conflict over Kashmir were to lead to a nuclear attack it is possible that the countries of the core would react as they did to the disorder in the world's periphery in the first post-Cold War decade: that is, with private concern—horror at the destruction and sympathy for the victims—but official disinterest. In that case, the post-Cold War disinclination of the core powers to entangle themselves in the political affairs of the periphery would be strengthened. The core powers might well treat nuclear-infested regions of the planet in the same way—as no-go areas.

Alternatively, a nuclear shot fired in anger might strengthen the trend toward legitimating military intervention in the internal affairs of sovereign states. Preventing the acquisition, or preempting the use, of weapons of mass destruction would join the rescue of a beleaguered population as a legitimate cause for military intervention. New international arrangements to conduct the newly legitimate interventions might accompany such a change in the international norm. Such arrangements would build on the steps the United Nations took after the Gulf War of 1991 to ensure that Saddam Hussein's regime did not acquire weapons of mass destruction. The UN established teams of inspectors to monitor Iraq's activities, but it lacked a standing military force to assure that the inspectors could carry out their duties unhindered. It fell to the United States to perform that task, which it did at first sporadically and then not at all.

As well as political perils, two economic threats hovered over the world of the twenty-first century. One was the danger of economic failure, of the kind that occurred in the 1930s. The other was associated, ironically, with economic success. This was the danger that economic growth would exhaust the planet's capacity to cope with growth's unwanted byproducts.

ECONOMIC PITFALLS

ALTHOUGH TYPICALLY it has been war that has brought about sudden, sweeping international change in the modern era, markets have had comparable effects when they have failed on a large scale.

Two characteristic pitfalls plague them. One is the swift rise in the value of an asset followed by a sudden drop when optimism turns to fear, triggering a panic-stricken stampede to sell. Europe experienced such speculative bubbles well before the modern age. The industrial revolution brought with it a second market pathology: the slump. Once economic growth became possible so, too, did its opposite, economic decline. In the first century and a half of the industrial age the economies of the world's core countries were prone to slumps. The worst of them, in the 1930s, was caused by the bursting of a financial bubble—the American stock market crash of 1929—which infected the rest of the Western economies through the institution that links finance and production, the banking system.

In the second half of the twentieth century the core countries found ways to mitigate the effects of both chronic problems. Government regulations reduced the frequency of speculative bubbles. When bubbles did form and burst, government played the role of "lender of last resort," providing liquidity to stem panic-stricken withdrawals that could have ruined financial institutions. And Keynes's ideas, translated into public policy, showed that governments could counteract economic downturns through the injection of purchasing power into the economy either by creating credit or spending money.

Economic research and economic policy did not abolish the diseases to which free markets are vulnerable in the modern age but they did provide methods of controlling them and limiting their damage. Just as there were many violent conflicts but none using nuclear weapons from 1945 until the end of the century, so, too, during those decades regular economic downturns in the core—recessions—occurred but none matched in severity the Great Depression of the 1930s. The twenty-first century supremacy of the market economy rests on the implicit assumption that while markets are prone to occasional recessions, large, protracted, devastating depressions can be avoided. As with the non-use of nuclear weapons, however, the indefinite continuation of the impressive economic record of the second half of the twentieth century cannot be guaranteed. The pathologies to which markets are subject might, in the twenty-first century, escape the limits that twentieth-century public policy placed upon them in the same ways that contagious diseases sometimes overcome individuals or entire populations, despite the progress of modern medicine and public health.

The patient may refuse the therapy. Economically sensible measures sometimes meet political resistance, which is why so many countries of the periphery suffered from economic distortions. Or, economic distempers may prove too powerful for the antidotes governments have at their disposal. Or, a new strain of economic pathology may appear, one for which countermeasures have not yet been devised. The ongoing processes of creation and destruction change not only firms and industries but entire economies as well, in ways not always immediately understood.

In the worst case, one or more of these syndromes could provoke economic failure in core countries on a scale unseen in the second half of the twentieth century. The near-universal post-Cold War attraction to liberal economics has depended on the demonstrated capacity of free markets to generate rising levels of wealth. An economic slump on the scale of the Great Depression would call into question the value of free markets, as it did in the 1930s, and so shake the foundations of the international system. A slump of that magnitude could only arise from serious and concurrent failures in several of the major economies of the world's core, above all that of the United States. An economic collapse on an international scale would place on the world's agenda the question of how to do for the global economy in the twenty-first century what precautionary and therapeutic government policies had achieved for national economies in the twentieth.

No international regulatory agency exists to curb excessive speculation, although there are internationally recognized (if not enforceable) standards for lending and investing. Nor does the world have an international lender of last resort. The International Monetary Fund has often assumed this role in currency crises but it could not cope with major financial difficulties in several core countries. No global authority has the power to increase international demand in the face of a world-wide recession, although the United States has acted as the engine of the world economy.[19]

To perform, effectively and reliably, the tasks of global regulation, global lending in the last resort, and the provision of demand on a global scale would require something that remained beyond the range of even serious discussion at the outset of the twenty-first century: the creation of a world government. A global sovereign was also the logical response to the worst imaginable version of another potential threat to the liberal world order of the twenty-first century: "global warming" that changes the very climate of the planet.

Here the threat stemmed not from economic failure but from economic success. The more productive the global economy became, and the more fully a basic premise of the liberal theory of history—the wonders that free markets can work—was therefore borne out, the more pressing this particular danger would become. It is a danger of the kind initially described in the second most influential eighteenth-century British tract on economics (after *The Wealth of Nations*), Thomas Malthus's *Essay on Population*, which warned that the number of its human inhabitants would outstrip the planet's capacity to provide food for them.

The development of agriculture started the process, because it permitted homo sapiens to depart from the prevailing pattern of human social life in small bands of hunters and gatherers and to form fixed communities that, over the millennia, became progressively larger and socially more complex. Agriculture made possible the exponential growth in the human population of the planet, about the consequences of which Malthus issued his warning.

The industrial revolution, however, vastly expanded human control of the material world while also helping to expand the planet's food supply, thereby enabling the world to escape the fate Malthus had predicted for it. Agricultural communities had leveled forests to provide themselves with space for living and cultivation as well as with fuel. Industrial societies accelerated the destruction of the Earth's wilderness, which in the twentieth century inspired political movements in the core countries, especially the United States, to conserve it. In the second half of the twentieth century the effects of industrial production on the planet went further. It began to despoil the two elements necessary for human life itself, air and water.[20] This, too, evoked a political response, in the form of movements in the core countries to protect the planet's environment.[21]

Air or water pollution in the second half of the twentieth century were generally local, national, or at most regional problems, addressed by policies undertaken by individual governments. But one potentially dangerous effect of industrial production on the environment involved the whole world: global warming.

Industrial production, especially the burning of fossil fuels, released gases, notably carbon dioxide, that accumulated over the decades and trapped heat within the Earth's atmosphere. The effect was the same as the one produced, for the purpose of growing tropical plants in cooler climates, by greenhouses: hence the name "greenhouse gases." The greenhouse effect makes life on the planet possible. Without it the Earth would be too cold for human life. But a rise in the average temperature of the Earth's surface, which is what scientists were increasingly persuaded the growing volume of man-made greenhouse gases was producing, had the potential to bring to the Earth's social and economic life disruption as great as the major wars of the modern era had inflicted upon the planet's political life.

The gloomiest forecasts sounded like latter-day versions of the plagues that the Bible records were visited upon the ancient Egyptians as punishment for their mistreatment of the Israelites. Global warming could make some parts of the world warmer and drier while others would turn cooler and wetter, interrupting the patterns of cultivation upon which the world's supply of food depends. It could melt the polar ice caps, raising the levels of the Earth's oceans and thereby swamping low-lying coastal regions, some of them densely populated. Global warming could change the planet's weather patterns, provoking more numerous, fiercer, and more destructive storms.

Environmental pollution is an example of what economists call "externalities." It is a form of damage that the normal workings of the market do not correct. An externality of this kind is a "public bad"; preventing or compensating for it is therefore a public good. But with it comes the inevitable free rider problem: how to get sovereign states to pay for the task of coping with global warming in the absence of an overarching authority to compel them to do so. Containing global warming would require reducing the emission of greenhouse gases, which in turn would necessitate reducing the use of fossil fuels. Because of the heavy reliance of virtually every national economy on coal, oil, and natural gas this would be costly, at least in the short term. The question of how to apportion these costs divided the core from the periphery, with each group of countries finding reasons that the other should undertake the major share of the reductions.[22]

From the core countries, the pioneers in the industrial revolution, had come most of the greenhouse gases already concentrated in the atmosphere and these countries continued to be the largest emitters of them, with the United States the leader in both absolute and per capita terms. On the other hand, the countries of the periphery were, for economic and geographic reasons, likely to suffer the severest adverse effects of global warming.[23] Their rate of increase in the consumption of fossil fuels was higher than in the core and, because they used energy less effectively, reducing fuel consumption was cheaper for them: The production foregone per unit of energy unconsumed was lower for them than it was for the core countries.

The treaty on global warming signed in Kyoto, Japan, in 1997 did not settle the question of how to allocate the costs. The core countries did commit themselves to targets for reducing greenhouse gas emissions but the countries of the periphery were not part of the agreement and the United States Senate made clear that it would not ratify the treaty, as it would have to do to make the agreement binding on the United States, unless and until all other countries undertook to share the costs of addressing the problem.[24] On global warming, international leadership in the form of bearing a large share of the costs was not something the United States sought to exercise.[25]

In the first post–Cold War decade global warming provoked considerable discussion among specialists and inspired modest public policies aimed at prevention. Unlike the defection of Russia and China from the general commitment to liberal international relations, but like the detonation of a nuclear weapon or a sharp downturn in the global economy, if a dramatic event triggered by man-made climate change—the equivalent for global warming of a nuclear shot fired in anger—were to galvanize world opinion and generate pressure for a sweeping solution to the problem, the necessary measures would involve effective action at the international level. A method would have to be found for allocating among the world's two hundred countries the costs of reducing greenhouse gases to safe levels and ensuring that those costs were duly paid. If, as would seem likely, even a system-shaking event in the tradition of a major war did not pave the way for the creation of an effective international sovereign body, the world would confront the task, which might come to dominate the international agenda of the twenty-first century, of providing for global governance without a global government.

For this task the liberal model of political organization has better credentials than any other. Liberal political systems permit the open-ended discussion that brings problems to public attention. They permit, as well, the politicking that impels governments to act on these problems. Liberal states have a better record than others on what the solution to such problems requires: international cooperation. They created the forums for such cooperation, the world's international organizations. Indeed, the very idea that international cooperation beyond temporary marriages of convenience for the sake of fighting wars is feasible and desirable is a liberal one.[26] So a world of liberal sovereign states qualifies as the second-best solution, after world government, to the problems of nuclear war, economic collapse, and global climate change. If not the best of all imaginable solutions, it is the best of all feasible ones. Whether it would prove to be good enough to cope with these problems in the twenty-first century is a question to which only the history of that century could furnish an answer. To two other questions concerning the world of the twenty-first century, however, answers were already available: How did it differ from the historical era that immediately preceded it? And is it better or worse than what went before?

THE IDEAS THAT CONQUERED THE WORLD

IN MARCH 2000, twelve-year-old Natalie Friedman of Bethesda, Maryland, entered a National History Day competition for middle school students. The contestants were asked to illustrate an historical turning point of their choice through text and pictures mounted on large boards. Hers, which was judged the best, depicted the Soviet Union's launch of the first Earth-orbiting satellite, Sputnik, in 1957. It was, she explained, a turning point in history because it set in motion the events that ultimately led to the creation of the Internet.[27] Her presentation vividly illustrated the contrast between the epoch of the Cold War and the post-Cold War period, as well as the manner in which one historical era can give way, abruptly and decisively, to another.

To be sure, Sputnik was considered highly significant when it was launched, but its significance then was entirely different from the one Miss Friedman identified because the international context was entirely different. It occurred at the height of the rivalry between the Western liberal countries, led by the United States, and the Communist bloc, led by the Soviet Union. At the time the portents for the West seemed grim and dangerous: Sputnik appeared to confer on the Communist side a decisive military advantage. The Soviet Union, the West feared, had acquired the capacity to unleash a devastating attack from space on North America. In response, the United States increased defense spending and accelerated scientific research and technological development for military purposes. The government encouraged families to store canned food and bottled water in their basements, which would become shelters in the event of such an attack.

Miss Friedman not only had no personal memory of these events, she had no personal memory of the geopolitical circumstances in which they took place. Born in 1988, she had lived virtually her entire life in a world from which the great military, political, and economic rivalry that had dominated most of the second half of the twentieth century had disappeared—almost without a trace.

So it is with the march of history. Aspects of an historical event that are central when it takes place lose their significance in a later era, while what was marginal at the time looms as consequential decades later.* The changing significance of Sputnik in historical perspective demonstrated just how rapidly this kind of transforma-

---

*Another entry in the History Day competition illustrated this point. The Crimean War of 1854–1856 was portrayed as the moment when modern nursing made its debut with the care given to wounded English soldiers by the subsequently celebrated Florence Nightingale. Her role was indeed the most memorable and important feature of that conflict from

tion could occur at the end of the twentieth century. The world in which the launch of Sputnik was an ominous development in a dangerous arms race, although it endured into the decade of the 1980s, was, by the turn of the century, almost as distant to Miss Friedman and her age-mates as the Great Depression or even the American Civil War. To them it was noteworthy as the event that led to the system of communications that suffused their lives and that was in the process of transforming the way commerce was transacted. The changing significance of Sputnik vividly illustrates the shift of the preoccupation of the governments with the end of the great ideological conflict of the second half of the twentieth century from protecting their borders to fostering prosperity.[28]

Natalie Friedman's prize-winning exhibit thus exemplified one undoubted feature of the post-Cold War world: how different it was from the world of the Cold War. It was also relevant to another, perhaps more arguable difference between the two. It provided evidence in favor of the proposition that the world was a better, happier place after the end of the Cold War than before.

To be sure, a decade after the Cold War's conclusion not every part of the world was in the process of living happily ever after. Some regions, some societies, some people were worse off than they had been before. The end of the East-West conflict brought war to the Balkans. It made much of Africa more chaotic. Post-Communist Russia suffered an economic contraction sharper, by some estimates, than the one that befell the core countries in the Great Depression.[29] So the world after the Cold War was not the best of all imaginable worlds. That would be a world in which all political communities were as free, as peaceful, and as prosperous as the industrial democracies of the core. This was an attractive and not impossible state of

the perspective of the twenty-first century. When the war was fought, however, the conflict's significance lay in its impact on one of the great issues of European politics, the fate of the rickety Ottoman Empire. Great Britain and France sought to prop it up lest its collapse, which Russia was promoting, touch off a scramble for its territories among the great powers of Europe that would lead to a major war among them. A century and a half later, all that remained of what had been called the "Eastern Question," which had once loomed so large in the international relations of the world's core, was the ultimate disposition of a few fragments of territory once ruled by the Ottomans that had become, after World War I, part of Yugoslavia. The problems of Bosnia and Kosovo, messy though they were, hardly counted as crucial for the future of the international system.

affairs but not one that had come close to realization at the outset of the twenty-first century.

Moreover, in the liberal scheme of things, with its emphasis on individuals rather than collectives, political and economic systems and security policies do not themselves confer happiness. Markets create opportunities for individual economic fulfillment, while democracy and common security erect barriers to two sources of unhappiness—oppression and war. Furthermore, the satisfaction of even the most intensely felt collective desire does not guarantee the achievement of individual hopes. A two-line poem of the 1930s by William Butler Yeats about Charles Stewart Parnell, a hero of the struggle for Irish independence, made the point that national independence does not necessarily bring upward economic mobility, a lesson learned by millions of inhabitants of countries once ruled by imperial powers:

Parnell came down the road, he said to a cheering man:
'Ireland shall get her freedom and you still break stone.'[30]

Still, about the relationship between the post-Cold War world and human happiness two conclusions may be drawn. The first begins with the fact that happiness, by one definition at least, is a product of modernity. Insofar as it presumes the existence of choice among different life experiences and outcomes, with some being preferable to others, happiness became possible only with the creation, set in motion by the French and industrial revolutions, of alternatives to the tightly circumscribed traditional world in which a person's life was a social and economic replica of the lives of his or her parents.* And in the wake of the Cold War, although not every one of the six billion human inhabitants of the planet was happy,

*It has, of course, frequently been argued that, to the contrary, modernity introduced unhappiness of a new and virulent kind into the world by tearing humankind loose from its familiar, comfortable, traditional social moorings. The unhappy sense of dislocation and disorientation that Durkheim called anomie, that Marx called alienation, and for which Freud and his successors developed an entire vocabulary and medical specialty, appeared only in the modern era. The Garden of Eden was, after all, a rural—and presumably a traditional—setting. But however persuasive this general argument has been in theory, it has had little, and diminishing, practical import. In the nineteenth and twentieth centuries tradition steadily gave way to modernity everywhere.

there was, for the first time in the modern era, a rough consensus on the political, economic, and international conditions best suited for them to be happy. For this purpose liberalism was the sole surviving standard.

The second conclusion is this: While the global triumph of peace, democracy and free markets substituted one set of problems for another, from the standpoint of human happiness the new ones were preferable to the old. War in the traditional age had served as the occasion for the display of some admirable human qualities: courage, social solidarity, and self-sacrifice. But these paled in comparison with the death and destruction that war inflicted upon the modern world. Similarly, democracy has sometimes set loose dangerous passions when first introduced, but the tyrannies of the twentieth century that democracy supplanted caused far more human suffering. As for free markets, their normal workings inevitably bring with them unwelcome side effects. The market destroys and displaces. It assaults the natural environment. It creates material inequality, which breeds envy and anger. But the absence of functioning free markets leads to poverty and its offspring—squalor, disease, and violence. Where happiness is concerned, therefore, two centuries of modern history have demonstrated that for the planet Earth, its two hundred-odd sovereign states, and their six billion inhabitants, the one thing worse than the triumph of the ideas that conquered the world is their defeat.

NOTES

I. WILSON VICTORIOUS

1. Quoted in John Lewis Gaddis, *We Now Know: Rethinking Cold War History*, New York: Oxford University Press, 1997, p. 109.
2. H. G. Wells, *The Shape of Things to Come*, quoted in Thomas J. Knock, *To End All Wars: Woodrow Wilson and the Quest for a New World Order*, Princeton: Princeton University Press, 1995, p.b., p. 1.
3. This term, commonly used to refer to the Cold War, was geographically misleading and politically unstable. "East" referred to the east of Europe, above all the Soviet Union itself, which was, however, as much an Asian as a European country if the Ural Mountains are taken as the dividing line between the two. For part (but not all) of the period in question the East also included China. The West meant the western part of Europe but also North America. Japan was also part of the West in political, military, and economic terms but geographically fit more comfortably into a category created in Europe before the Cold War, which had a more straightforward geographic meaning and to which, in this sense, China also belonged: the Far East.
4. An account of European history as a succession of bids for continental dominance is given in Ludwig Dehio, *The Precarious Balance*, New York: Vintage Books, 1963. The aftermaths of the four major international conflicts of the modern period are compared in G. John Ikenberry, *After Victory: Institutions, Strategic Restraint, and the Rebuilding of Order After Major Wars*, Princeton: Princeton University Press, 2001.
5. "World Wars," *Encyclopedia Britannica*, Fifteenth Edition, Chicago, Encyclopedia Britannica Inc., 1977, Volume 19, p. 966. Some estimates put the total even higher: "Over 10 million men died as a result of direct military action." J. M. Roberts, *Twentieth Century: The History of the World, 1901–2000*, New York: Viking, 1999, p. 266.
6. A valuable account of post-Napoleonic statecraft is Henry Kissinger, *A World Restored*, New York: Grosset and Dunlap, 1964 p.b. (First published, 1954.) The period from the end of the Napoleonic Wars through World War I is covered by two classic works of diplomatic history: Paul Schroeder, *The Transformation of European Politics, 1763–1848*, New York: Oxford University Press, 1992, and A. J. P. Taylor, *The Struggle for Mastery in Europe, 1848–1918*, Oxford: Oxford University Press, 1971 paperback. (First published, 1954.)
7. Winston Churchill, a major figure in the first world war as in the second, wrote of Wilson: "It seems no exaggeration to pronounce that the action of the United States with its repercussions on the history of the world depended, during the awful period of Armageddon, upon the workings of this man's mind and spirit to the exclusion of almost every other factor; and that he played a part in the fate of nations incomparably more direct and personal than any other man." Quoted in Arthur S. Link, *Woodrow Wilson: Revolution, War, and Peace*, Arlington Heights, Ill.: Harland Davidson Inc., 1979, p.20.
8. The wars of the French Revolution had been politically traumatic. The event that had

triggered them, the overthrow of the French monarch, had been unprecedented and unexpected, and the wars themselves had deeply threatened the conservative dynasties that dominated the European continent. World War I was also unexpected and unwelcome, and in its wake the victors were determined to avoid another conflict, but for a different reason: the slaughter involved. For sheer numbers the death toll had no precedent in European warfare. Unlike World War I, during the Napoleonic wars few of the deaths came directly from injuries inflicted in battle. Until the twentieth century "[t]he really frightening risk of war was neglect, filth, poor organization, defective medical services and hygienic ignorance, which massacred the wounded, the prisoners, and in suitable climatic conditions (as in the tropics) practically everybody." Eric Hobsbawm, *The Age of Revolution, 1789–1848*, New York: Barnes and Noble Books, 1996 (first published, 1962), p. 94.

9. The literature on Wilson is considerable and still growing. His most prolific and prominent defender is Arthur S. Link, who edited his papers at Princeton University, of which he had been president before entering political life, and wrote several volumes on Wilson's life and work. A later and on balance favorable assessment of his diplomacy is Knock, op. cit. One of the earliest unfavorable portraits was drawn in the book *The Economic Consequences of the Peace*, New York: Penguin Books, 1971 (first published, 1920), pp. 38–55, by the great English economist John Maynard Keynes, who was present at the Paris peace conference. Sigmund Freud weighed in unfavorably on Wilson's personality, in Freud and William Bullitt, *Thomas Woodrow Wilson: A Psychological Study*, Boston: Houghton Mifflin, 1966, but the standard study of the psychological basis of Wilson's politics is Alexander George and Juliette George, *Woodrow Wilson and Colonel House*, New York: Dover, 1964. For more recent, jaundiced appraisals, see Robert W. Tucker, "Woodrow Wilson and His Advisors," *The National Interest*, 51, Spring 1998, and Walter McDougall, *Promised Land, Crusader State*, Boston: Houghton Mifflin, 1997, Chapter 6.

10. One skeptical senator, William Borah of Idaho, put the problem at the heart of the debate over the League succinctly: "What will your league amount to if it does not contain powers that no one dreams of giving it?" Quoted in William C. Widenor, *Henry Cabot Lodge and the Search for an American Foreign Policy*, Berkeley: University of California Press, 1980, p. 268.

11. Knock, op. cit., p. 259; Widenor, op. cit., p. 338.

12. Wilson spurned any specific commitment to defend Great Britain and France, which the French themselves preferred to the League. The League's American opponents were willing to contemplate such a commitment, which would have addressed head-on what turned out to be the central problem in postwar European security: dealing with Germany. John Milton Cooper, *The Warrior and the Priest: Woodrow Wilson and Theodore Roosevelt*, Cambridge, Mass.: The Belknap Press of Harvard University, 1983, p. 343, and Widenor, op. cit., pp. 274, 286, 297. As proponents of an alliance with Britain and France, Theodore Roosevelt and Henry Cabot Lodge, the chief opponents of the League, have a better claim than Wilson to being the intellectual and political godfathers of the organization that became the core of American policy in Europe after World War II, the North Atlantic Treaty Organization (NATO).

13. The principal public defense was based on an historical inaccuracy: that in rejecting League membership the United States turned its back on Europe and retreated into isolation, which was in turn a cause of World War II. This is a legend propagated at the end of World War II to promote American support for the United Nations (Cooper, op. cit., p. 359). It has had a long life. At the end of the twentieth century

senior officials of the American government repeated it as if it were gospel. "After World War I, America had withdrawn from the world, shunning responsibility and avoiding risk. Others did the same. The result in the heart of Europe was the rise of great evil." Commencement Address by Secretary of State Madeleine K. Albright at Harvard University, June 5, 1997. In fact, the United States did not withdraw from international affairs. In the early postwar period economic questions were as important as military ones; here the American role was central and constructive. The United States was the chief sponsor of the Dawes and the Young Plans, which resolved the contentious question of war debts and, until the advent of the Great Depression, seemed to have put Europe's finances on a sound basis.

14. Roberts, op. cit., pp. 265, 274.
15. On this point, and as an antidote to nostalgia for the Habsburgs and their empire, see Lewis Namier, "The Downfall of the Habsburg Empire," in Namier, *Vanished Supremacies*, New York: Harper and Row, 1963.
16. Mark Mazower, "Minorities and the League of Nations in Interwar Europe," *Daedalus*, Spring 1997; Inis L. Claude, *National Minorities: An International Problem*, New York: Greenwood Press, 1969, Chapters 1 and 2.
17. The speech is summarized in Knock, op. cit., pp. 143–144.
18. The importance of commercial freedom in Wilson's view of the world is a theme of one of the better accounts of the Wilsonian vision, which emphasizes the influence of the Russian Revolution on the deliberations at Paris, N. Gordon Levin, *Woodrow Wilson and World Politics: America's Response to War and Revolution*, New York: Oxford University Press, 1968. See especially pp. 27, 146–147.
19. Robert Dallek, *Franklin D. Roosevelt and American Foreign Policy, 1932–1945*, New York: Oxford University Press, 1995, (first published, 1979), p. 283. Six decades later the first Democrat since Roosevelt to serve two full terms as president, Bill Clinton, listed the goals of his foreign policy as "enhancing security at home and abroad, promoting prosperity, and promoting democracy and human rights." *A National Security Strategy For a Global Age*, Washington, D.C: The White House, December, 2000, p. 1.
20. "War appears to be as old as mankind but peace is a modern invention." Sir Henry Maine, a nineteenth-century British jurist, quoted in Michael Howard, *The Invention of Peace: Reflections on War and International Order*, London: Profile, 2001, frontispiece.
21. While it was impossible to preserve or restore dynastic rule in Europe (the remaining monarchs there lacked effective political power), imperial rule lived on in the French and British possessions outside Europe.
22. Hobsbawm, *The Age of Revolution*, p. 52.
23. On the nineteenth century origins of Wilsonianism, especially in Great Britain, see, inter alia, Martin Ceadel, *The Origins of War Prevention: The British Peace Movement and International Relations, 1730–1854*, Oxford: Oxford University Press, 1996; Michael Howard, *War and the Liberal Conscience*, New Brunswick, N.J., Rutgers University Press, 1978, Chapters II and III; F. H. Hinsley, *Power and the Pursuit of Peace: Theory and Practice in the History of Relations between States*, Cambridge, U.K.: Cambridge University Press, 1967, Chapters 5–7; and A. J. P. Taylor, *The Trouble Makers: Dissent Over Foreign Policy, 1792–1939*, Harmondsworth, U.K.: Penguin Books, 1985 (first published, 1957), Chapters 1 and 2.
24. "Monarchical sovereignty, the enemy of mankind and the source of misery, is abolished, and sovereignty is restored to its natural and original place, the nation. Were this the case throughout Europe the cause of war would be taken away." Thomas Paine, "The Rights of Man," in Paine, *Common Sense and Other Writings*, Indianapolis,

Ind.: Bobbs-Merrill, 1953, p. 109. Thomas Jefferson held this view as well. See Walter McDougall, *Promised Land, Crusader State*, Boston: Houghton Mifflin, 1997, p. 23.

25. A precursor of this feature of the Wilsonian vision was the American "Open Door" policy on China. On the commercial tradition in American foreign policy see Walter Russell Mead, *Special Providence: American Foreign Policy and How It Changed the World*, New York: Knopf, 2001, pp. 105–112.

26. The prospect of a great European war was naturally a more immediate problem on the European continent, where one prominent idea for peace prescribed a federation of all the European powers. That prescription was embodied at the outset of the twenty-first century by the European Union, the ultimate purpose of which for some Europeans was a political union of some kind. The different approach to peace in Great Britain persists in the widespread skepticism there about the political aspect of the European project. See Chapter 12 on the significance of the European Union.

27. Restraint here does not necessarily imply the establishment of a separate body to do the restraining. There is no higher power than the sovereign state, a fact particularly important for matters of international security. Restraint is self-restraint.

28. Adam Smith, *The Wealth of Nations*, New York: The Modern Library, 1994, p. 745. First published, 1776.

29. The differences between a liberal peace and peace through a balance of power are discussed in Chapter 4.

30. Excessive taxation could and sometimes did provoke unrest. Peasant uprisings, sometimes politically serious ones, occurred everywhere in the pre-modern world. It was, after all, a tax revolt of sorts—the summoning of the quasi-parliamentary body the Estates-General to justify new levies—that triggered the French Revolution, the political event that began the modern era.

31. Sigmund Freud, *The Psychopathology of Everyday Life*, New York: W. W. Norton, 1965, pp. 265–268.

32. *Freedom in the World, 1999–2000*, New York: Freedom House, 2000, p. 602.

33. These are exported products, as distinct from services.

34. Some examples: in 1913 the percentage for the United States had been 3.7; in 1992 it was 8.2. For France, 8.2 and 22.9; for Germany, 15.6 and 32.6; for Japan 2.4 and 12.4; for Korea 1.0 and 17.8; for the world as a whole, 8.7 and 13.5. All figures from Martin Wolf, "Wealth of nations," *Financial Times*, May 19, 1998, p. 16. See also *The Economist*, September 20, 1997, "Survey," p. 24.

35. Robert Gilpin, *The Challenge of Global Capitalism: The World Economy in the 21st Century*, Princeton: Princeton University Press, 2000, pp. 21–24. "Turnover on the world's foreign-exchange markets has risen fiftyfold in the past two decades. Foreign direct investment jumped from around $50 billion in 1985 to $644 billion in 1998 and was on track to top $800 billion in 1999." John Micklethwait and Adrian Wooldridge, *A Future Perfect: The Challenge and Hidden Promise of Globalization*, New York: Crown, 2000, p. xxi.

36. "There is today widespread agreement, including among most socialist economists, that whatever form advanced societies may take in the twenty-first century, a market system of some kind will constitute their principal means of coordination. That is a remarkable turnabout from the situation only a generation ago, when the majority of economists believed that the future of economic coordination lay in a diminution of the scope of the market and an increase in some form of centralized planning." Robert Heilbroner, *Twenty-first Century Capitalism*, New York: W. W. Norton, 1993, p. 97. This theme is discussed in Chapter 9.

37. Seth Faison, "Messy Free Market Plunge Rattling China's Businesses," *The New York Times*, October 5, 1997, p. 10.

38. *Annual Report 2000*, Washington, D.C: The International Monetary Fund, 2000, pp. 123–124.

39. Here is an example drawn from a widely read daily chronicle of international economic matters in the post-Cold War world, the *Financial Times*. Edited in London but printed around the world, the newspaper functioned as the unofficial house organ of globalization: "The Congo Brazzaville government, which took power last year after a civil war, said yesterday that it would hold elections within three years and possibly within months. Rodolphe Adada, foreign minister, said the government hoped this month to receive International Monetary Fund approval for a national development programme." "New rulers look for elections and IMF help," July 1, 1998, p. 11.

    Globalization's weekly chronicle was another London-based publication, *The Economist*. Here is a typical item from its pages: "Madagascar is open for business. Five years ago, arrival at Antannarivo's airport was a bureaucratic assault course that could last three hours. It now takes 30 minutes. Visas are no longer required, exchange controls have been abandoned, travel restrictions lifted. What is going on?

    Answer: the 'Bretton Woods' institutions and Didier Reatsiraka. On February 9th, he took over as president of this island-country off East Africa after defeating Albert Zafy with just over half the votes . . . So far, the former dictator has made all the right moves. Visiting the World Bank last week, he secured hefty lending commitments through to 1999." "Bad guy makes good," March 22, 1997, p. 51.

40. Eloquent testimony to the hegemony of liberalism came from its putative rivals. The Islamic republic of Iran was established in 1979 as a theocracy based on the teachings of the Koran. Yet the elected president of the Islamic republic published a book in which he had this to say about the liberal ideas that the government over which he was later to preside was formed to contest and supersede: "Liberalism and its intellectual and practical repercussions are not minor issues which we can easily ignore and dismiss. They have their roots deep in the philosophies and motivations of Western man and are the context of the modern way of life. Today the West is the dominant civilization, and without understanding liberalism we cannot understand the depth of thinking of the political form of Western civilization." This might seem the simple recognition of fact, and not necessarily a fact to be welcomed. But of the content of liberalism, that is, of its major ideas, Mohammed Khatami went on to say, "If we do not regard all these as the greatest single achievement of modern civilization, they are definitely among some of its major achievements." Quoted in Fred Halliday, "Mohammed and Mill," *The New Republic*, October 5, 1998, p. 33.

41. This way of dividing the modern period originated with the historian Eric Hobsbawm. See, for example, Hobsbawm with Antonio Polito, *On the Edge of a New Century*, New York: The New Press, 1999, p. 2.

42. This relationship is a major theme of Chapter 8.

2. THE COLD WAR RECONSIDERED

1. The point is made by John Mueller in the "Introduction" to *Quiet Cataclysm*, New York: HarperCollins, 1995, pp. 1–3.

2. In the course of the Cold War the Soviet hopes for success did not always rest on their armed forces. Stalin believed that the capitalist camp would be weakened by the kind

of intramural imperialist bloodletting that had taken place twice in his lifetime—in the two world wars. Stalin's successor, Nikita Khrushchev, assumed that the Communist bloc would ultimately outstrip its liberal rival in economic terms. In 1961 he designated the year 1970 as the moment when the Soviet Union would overtake the United States in per capita economic output. This belief, like Stalin's, came from personal experience: When Khrushchev was the supreme leader Soviet economic growth rates were, or seemed, impressive. It was Leonid Brezhnev who came to rely on Soviet military power to advance Communist political purposes. See Vojtech Mastny, *The Cold War and Soviet Insecurity*, New York: Oxford University Press, 1996, p. 192.

3. The fear of Western governments that it might happen was one of the reasons Woodrow Wilson felt called upon to put forward his vision of the postwar world. It was, among other things, an alternative to Lenin's program of socialist revolution. This is a theme of N. Gordon Levin, *Wilson Versus Lenin*, New York: Oxford University Press, 1968.

4. Cuba also had something like this status. The Communist rulers there declared themselves in competition with the non-Communist (but not in every case wholly liberal) regimes that governed the other countries of Latin America. The large Cuban community that formed in south Florida created another contest of systems involving a single national group that resided in two different sovereign states.

5. The Communist side did not accept the economic contest as entirely fair. Soviet officials complained that West Germany received support from the United States, which had not been damaged by World War II, while East Germany had to rely on the Soviet Union, which had been devastated by the war and so could do far less for its client. At the end of that war, far from helping East Germany to recover, the Soviet authorities insisted, in the tradition of exacting reparations from the losing side in a war, that the Germans help them. They stripped the Soviet zone in Germany of industrial equipment and sent it back to the Soviet Union. Given the destruction the invading German armies had wrought on the Soviet economy and Soviet society during the war this was perhaps understandable, but it did not assist the Communist side in the contest of economic systems in Europe. In any case, the effects of wartime damage in postwar performance faded over time. Moreover, the Communist countries achieved higher growth rates in the early than in the late postwar period. By the 1980s the shortcomings of the Communist economies could no longer plausibly be blamed on the Nazis.

Similarly, the competition between the People's Republic of China and Taiwan was not an equal one: The mainland's huge population was certainly a drag on its economic performance and American assistance was a spur to Taiwan. Despite these differences, the verdict in favor of liberal economic practices was decisive in the Chinese case because the mainland experienced a momentous surge in economic activity when (and, no one doubted, because) it adopted features of the liberal economic system that Taiwan—and much of the rest of the world—had already embraced.

6. Quoted in Francis Fukuyama, *The End of History and the Last Man*, New York: Avon Books, 1992 paperback, p. 89.

7. Great Britain, which was part of the victorious coalition, was the exception. It was the most liberal of the great powers in the early part of the nineteenth century, although not as liberal as it and other countries would subsequently become. But Britain was disinclined to try to use the victory over Napoleon to spread its political principles on the continent.

8. Thomas Knock, *To End All Wars: Woodrow Wilson and the Quest for a New World Order*,

Princeton: Princeton University Press, paperback, 1995. First published, 1992, p. 248.

9. None sought or received reparations, either. With very modest economic assistance from the Western Europeans and the United States to the formerly Communist countries and the huge subsidies from West Germany to the former German Democratic Republic, it was the winners who paid.

10. The Cold War was scarcely bloodless. The two sides took part in proxy wars, sponsoring opposing forces all over the world. Sometimes their own troops were involved, as in Korea, Vietnam, and Afghanistan, but never directly against the armies of the other.

11. The end of the Cold War was unexpected and occasioned astonishment even—perhaps especially—among those with a professional interest in it, even that tiny minority of specialists who saw what was coming and said so. "While I think I got the basic mechanism for the demise of the Cold War right, I was as flabbergasted as anybody by the speed with which events in East Europe took place. After I presented the paper [predicting what in fact was to happen] at [a] March 1986 meeting, someone asked me when I thought the Soviet Union might decide to leave East Europe. The paper suggests this might happen 'eventually' and 'in the long term,' and I tried to take refuge behind such crafty vapidities. But he kept badgering me, and I finally blurted out, 'maybe by 1995' with what I felt was amazing heroism. If I had heard myself saying '1989' I would have had myself committed." John Mueller, "When Did the Cold War End?," Paper presented at the Annual Conference of the Society for Historians of American Foreign Relations, Princeton University, Princeton, N.J., June 24–26, 1999, p. 10. On this general subject see as well Michael Mandelbaum, "The End of the Cold War," *Foreign Affairs*, Spring 1989.

12. World War I lasted four years, World War II six. The Cold War, depending on the dates chosen for its beginning and its end, continued for at least four decades. (The fact that a choice of dates is available, that the conflict has no clearly defined opening gun and agreed-upon conclusion—no equivalent of the firing on Fort Sumter and the surrender at Appomattox Courthouse in the American Civil War—is itself a sign that this was, as wars go, an unusual one.) Its length makes the Cold War unusual but not unique. The Napoleonic wars were waged almost continuously for twenty-eight years, from 1792 to 1815. The great conflict of the first half of the seventeenth century, which was fought mainly between the armies of Protestant and Catholic monarchs and principally on German lands, is known as the Thirty Years War because it began in 1619 and ended, with the Peace of Westphalia, in 1648.

13. Studies of evolution have offered two different accounts of its pace. One holds it to be gradual and steady, the result of the accumulation of millions of imperceptible changes. The other considers change to be uneven and sudden. (The fossil record does not lend conclusive support to either version. "The process by which a new species is formed is apparently too fast to show up in the fossil record, but too slow to be observed in human experience." Thomas Nagel, "Why so cross?," *The London Review of Books*, April 1, 1999, p.22.) The second pattern, known as "punctuated equilibrium," corresponds to the course of the Cold War: decades of stability then sudden, dramatic, sweeping change.

14. Sometimes one species disappears because it is destroyed—extinguished—by another. But this is not the motor of inter- or intra-specific competition. Indeed, the disappearance of its prey can deal a severe evolutionary setback to the predator.

15. Ken Jowitt, *New World Disorder: The Leninist Extinction*, Berkeley: The University of California Press, 1992. See also John Lewis Gaddis, *We Now Know: Rethinking Cold War*

History, New York: Oxford University Press, 1997, p. 295. It has been argued that cultural forms develop and spread in literally the same way as biological ones, that the evolutionary process is a description of, not simply a metaphor for, social as well as natural history. See Susan Blackmore, *The Meme Maker*, Oxford, England: Oxford University Press, 1999. On evolution as the master concept for the study of society see W. G. Runciman, *The Social Animal*, London: HarperCollins, 1998. While evolution in nature has, on the whole, multiplied the number of species, the consequence of the Cold War was to *reduce* the number of different types of political and economic systems.

16. Chapters 8 and 9 consider the crucial questions of how and why authoritarian politics and centrally planned economies became, in effect, dysfunctional in the latter stages of the Cold War.

17. Some species do, of course, prey on others, but this gives the predator a vital stake in the perpetuation of the species on which it preys.

18. This is not to say that natural history is entirely random and accidental and that "if the evolutionary tape was rerun . . . the evolutionary outcome—homo sapiens and our vertebrate relatives—would have been very different." (Douglas C. Palmer, "Backbone of evolution," *Financial Times*, April 24, 1998, citing the paleontologist Stephen Jay Gould). That is a contested point among students of evolution. What is not contested is that, even if a design can be deduced from the observed pattern of the development of life, it is not the work of a designer, at least not one accessible to the analytical tools of science. On the general issue see Simon Conway Morris, *The Crucible of Creation: The Burgess Shale and the Rise of Animals*, Oxford: Oxford University Press, 1999.

19. Evolution and commercial competition do exhibit marked similarities, which influenced Charles Darwin in the formulation of the theory of evolution through natural selection. Eric Hobsbawm, *The Age of Revolution, 1789–1848*. New York: Barnes and Noble Books, 1996, (First published 1962), p. 293.

20. "It was the half-hearted reform program launched by Gorbachev after 1985 that disrupted the creaky functioning of the planned economy and triggered the dire economic conditions that led to the collapse." Peter Rutland, "Explaining the Soviet Collapse," *Transition*, February 1998, p. 16, citing the argument of Vladimir Kontorovich and Michael Ellman, *The Disintegration of the Soviet Economic System*, London: Routledge, 1992.

21. Historically, fiscal crises have triggered political upheavals. Perhaps the most prominent example is the French Revolution, but there are others. Russian history, for example, is filled with them. See S. Frederick Starr, "The Changing Nature of Change in the U.S.S.R.," in Seweryn Bialer and Michael Mandelbaum, editors, *Gorbachev's Russia and American Foreign Policy*, Boulder: Westview Press, 1988, pp. 14–17. At the end the Soviet government was, as businesses and banks can be, insolvent. That is, it was unable to collect the funds it needed to meet its obligations. See Robert Skidelsky, *The Road from Serfdom*, New York: Penguin Books, 1997, pp. 97 and 109 and Mancur Olson, *Power and Prosperity: Outgrowing Communist and Capitalist Dictatorships*, New York: Basic Books, 2000, pp. 58–59.

22. Boris Yeltsin reportedly experienced such an epiphany in a Texas supermarket. See Michael Dobbs, *Down with Big Brother: The Fall of the Soviet Empire*. New York: Alfred A. Knopf, 1997, pp. 317–318. See also Chapter 9.

23. "By and large [during the latter part of the Brezhnev era] ordinary Soviets had ceased to believe in socialist ideology, but they continued to go through the motions. The whole country was engaged in a mass deceit. In the privacy of their kitchens people

laughed at their doddering leader. In public they kept straight faces." Dobbs, op. cit., p. 86.

24. On the Soviet famine, see Robert Conquest, *Harvest of Sorrow: Soviet Collectivization and the Terror-Famine*, New York: Oxford University Press, 1986. Conquest estimates the total deaths from the famine and the Communist regime's campaign against the peasantry that accompanied it at eleven million. (See p. 301.) On the Chinese famine see Jasper Becker, *Hungry Ghosts: Mao's Secret Famine*, New York: The Free Press, 1996. R. J. Rummel estimates the deaths from that famine, caused by the Great Leap Forward of the 1950s, at 27 million. Rummel, *Death by Government*, New Brunswick, N.J.: Transaction Publishers, 1994, p. 97. The Nazis also produced famines. Mark Mazower, *Dark Continent: Europe's Twentieth Century*, London: Allen Lane, The Penguin Press, 1998, p. 156.

25. Cited in Dobbs, op. cit., p. 188. Rummel estimates the total number of deaths caused by what he calls the "Soviet Gulag State," including the periods before and after Stalin's leadership, at about 62 million. Rummel, op. cit., Chapter 4. For China under Mao the number killed is almost 35 million. Ibid., Chapter 5.

26. Ibid., Chapter 9. Deaths from all causes were even greater. "In proportion to its population, Cambodia underwent a human catastrophe unparalleled in this century. Out of a population of probably nearly 7,100,000 Cambodia probably lost almost 4 million people to war, rebellion, manmade famine, genocide, politicide, and mass murder." Ibid., p. 160.

27. The propagation of Christianity throughout Europe undertaken in the centuries after Constantine was often the work of elites. Because the Communist system was in political terms an absolutist one, and because it was a quasi-religious order with its political leaders functioning as priests, changes initiated at the top had wider and deeper effects throughout the society than in more democratic, less hierarchical societies. A distant but suggestive parallel to the change of heart of the leaders, leading to the collapse of the system itself, is with the Aztec and Inca civilizations. "The higher political and cultural organization of the Aztec and Inca empires disappeared almost overnight when the priests and warriors who had sustained these structures lost faith in their inherited social and cultural systems." McNeill, *The Rise of the West*, Chicago: The University of Chicago Press, 1991 (First published 1963), p. 600. This was true beyond the Communist world. Democracy spread in the second half of the twentieth century when political elites came to believe in it. Samuel P. Huntington, *The Third Wave: Democratization in the Late Twentieth Century*, Norman, Okla.: The University of Oklahoma Press, 1991, p. 36, and John Mueller, *Capitalism, Democracy, and Ralph's Pretty Good Grocery*, Princeton: Princeton University Press, 1999, p. 203.

28. A painting hanging in the room in the Louvre adjacent to the one where *Liberty* is located provides an unintentionally ironic commentary on the reality of the kind of revolution that Delacroix celebrated. It is Jacques-Louis David's stately, adoring portrait of Napoleon crowning himself emperor. In France in 1789, in Russia in 1917, and in China in 1949 the overthrow of the old regime led to the consolidation of power in the hands of a single tyrant.

29. Nor, as Charles Maier has pointed out, does it accurately depict the way all the various events of modern history credited as revolutions have invariably occurred. In modern European history, the Eastern pattern has differed sharply from the Western one. Maier, *Dissolution: The Crisis of Communism and the End of East Germany*, Princeton: Princeton University Press, 1997, pp. 112–114.

30. "In most revolutions the population becomes radicalized and pours into the political

arena. But the Russian population did not. Only a few thousand people, mostly in Moscow, were directly involved in the political activity, while the rest of the country, and indeed most Muscovites, went about their daily business." Thane Gustafson, *Capitalism Russian-Style*, New York: Cambridge University Press, 2000, p. 21.

31. "Perhaps most crucial is that the [East German] Politburo was deeply divided: It takes resolution to carry through with force and only a few of the old guard still had it. Ultimately the leadership no longer possessed the coherence or conviction to impose force successfully." Maier, op. cit., p. 146.

32. Mikhail Gorbachev's part in the downfall of Communism affirms the importance of the role of individuals in great historical episodes. Had someone else—any of his predecessors, for example, or his chief rival Viktor Grishin—occupied the position of supreme Soviet leader in the second half of the 1980s it is unlikely that events would have unfolded as they did. The changes that he set in motion, and his refusal to suppress their unintended conseqences by force, led to Communism's collapse. Gorbachev's central, indispensable personal role in the events of 1985 to 1991 also illustrates the impact of chance on history. He succeeded the feeble Konstantin Chernenko, who had come to power only because kidney failure cut short the life of his predecessor, Yuri Andropov, a far stronger political figure who had won the political battle to succeed the long-serving Leonid Brezhnev. "As Dimitry Shlapentokh has observed, were it not for Andropov's kidney disease, communism would still be around." Vladimir Kontorovich, "The Economic Fallacy," *The National Interest*, Number 31, Spring 1993, p. 44.

    For a useful assessment of Gorbachev in power see Rajan Menon, "The Perils of Perestroika: The Life and Legacy of Mikhail Gorbachev," *The Harriman Review*, Volume 10, Number 1, Spring, 1997. Gorbachev's crucial role in creating the post-Cold War security order in Europe is discussed in Chapter 4.

33. Solzhenitsyn, *The Gulag Archipelago 1918–1956*, Volumes I-II, translated from the Russian by Thomas P. Whitney, New York: Harper and Row, 1973, pp. 173–174. "When the end came, the Communists were too exhausted and too dispirited to fight back ... they had exhausted their own idea, an idea that had moved millions by its grandeur and simplicity, the idea of building paradise upon this earth." Dobbs, op. cit., p. 421.

34. See Chapter 9.

35. "The balance sheet of cultural influence was ... overwhelmingly one-sided. While the teaching of Marx has been a force throughout twentieth-century Asia, the last non-European whose words had any comparable influence in shaping the west was Jesus Christ." J. M. Roberts, *Twentieth Century: The History of the World, 1901–2000*, New York: Viking, 1999, p. 37.

36. William McNeill, *The Shape of European History*, New York: Oxford University Press, 1974, p. 42–43. The book summarizes the main arguments of his longer work *The Rise of the West*.

37. David Landes, *The Wealth and Poverty of Nations*, New York: W. W. Norton, 1998, Chapters 1–3; Jared Diamond, *Guns, Germs and Steel: The Fate of Human Societies*, New York: W. W. Norton, 1999.

38. The literature on both subjects is vast. Good summaries are found in Landes, op. cit., pp. 93–98, 335–345, and 213–230. Chance also undoubtedly played a role. For an interesting argument that historically weighty developments could have been the work of chance, that the rise of Europe, for example, could have been "a complete fluke," see Mark Ridley, "The uselessness of zebras," *TLS*, November 14, 1997, p. 6.

39. Bernard Lewis, *The Middle East: A Brief History of the Last 2000 Years*, New York: Scribner's, 1995, p. 270.

40. The academy has spawned two debates on the great historical development of the last five centuries. One is how, precisely, to define the West and the Western tradition. This is a matter of taste. (On this subject see David Gress, *From Plato to NATO: The Idea of the West and Its Opponents*, New York: The Free Press, 1996.) The second is whether the rise of the West has been a good or a bad thing. This, too, is a matter of judgment. It is not difficult to find aspects of the Western ascendancy that appear, from the perspective of the twenty-first century, highly undesirable. The indigenous peoples of the Americas paid a very heavy price for their encounter with Europeans. The West, as is well known, practiced slavery, especially in North America. But so did the non-West, which, unlike the West, did not produce a successful movement to abolish slavery. Indeed, it is generally more difficult to find things that seem, in retrospect, worth preserving in the civilizations the West displaced than in the civilization of the West itself—but that is another matter.

41. "Since 1950 important cultural trends as well as the new economic abundance have tended first to be observable in the United States, then in Europe and later to spread to other continents." Roberts, op. cit., p. 608.

42. McNeill, *The Rise*, p. 574. The military techniques and instruments on which the Europeans relied—gunpowder, the compass, and printing—originated, as it happened, in China. Ibid., pp. xix, xxviii.

43. "From the perspective of the mid-twentieth century, the career of Western civilization since 1500 appears as a vast explosion, far greater than any comparable phenomenon of the past both in geographic range and in social depth." McNeill, *The Rise*, p. 567.

44. Sometimes used interchangeably, imperialism and colonialism, although often found together, are, properly defined, different practices. The first refers to the rule of one people by another, the second to the establishment of settlements—colonies—abroad. The ancient Greeks established colonies that were not part of empires. British India was part of the British empire but the sparse British population scattered across the subcontinent did not qualify as a colony.

45. The United States, an offshoot of Europe, and Japan, Europe's most successful non-Western imitator (and for a time the only one), also acquired empires. But the two were latecomers to overseas conquests—the crucial date for the United States was 1898, for Japan 1895—and their imperial domains (at least until the 1930s in the Japanese case) were relatively modest.

46. After a decade of fighting the imperial forces finally managed to defeat them with Western assistance. A brief overview of the Taiping movement is in John King Fairbank, *China: A New History*, Cambridge, Mass.: The Belknap Press of Harvard University Press, 1992 p.b. pp. 206–212. A longer history, with an emphasis on the leader, is Jonathan Spence, *God's Chinese Son*, New York: W. W. Norton, 1996.

47. Mary C. Wright, *The Last Stand of Chinese Conservatism: The Tung-chih Restoration, 1862–1874*, Stanford: Stanford University Press, 1957.

48. Lord Kinross, *The Ottoman Centuries: The Rise and Fall of the Turkish Empire*, New York: Morrow, 1979 paperback, Part VI; McNeill, *The Rise*, p. 694. Would-be authoritarian modernizers were found throughout Europe in the nineteenth century. Hobsbawm, *The Age of Revolution*, p. 22. Mikhail Gorbachev may be seen as a late twentieth-century heir to their tradition. They tried to combine modern economics with traditional politics. He tried to combine economic liberalism with at least the vestiges of political illiberalism. Like them, he failed.

49. It is in this sense that the period from the middle of the nineteenth to the middle of the twentieth century, for the non-Western world, can be considered "the era when all past history, however long and distinguished, came to a necessary halt." Eric Hobsbawm, *The Age of Empire 1875–1914*, New York: Pantheon, 1987, p. 338.

50. See Sunil Khilnani, *The Idea of India*, New York: Farrar Straus and Giroux, 1997, especially Chapter 1. The India that Gandhi and his associates sought to wrest from foreign hands had never existed as a single political jurisdiction until the British assembled it in the second half of the nineteenth century. To be sure, Gandhi was dubious about industrialization. He was killed shortly after independence, but had he lived it is unlikely that he would have been able to override the enthusiasm in the independence movement for bringing the industrial revolution to India on a large scale.

51. "The Indian Census Report of 1901 recorded that just under 300 million Indians were governed by about 900 white civil servants. Roughly speaking, there was also about one British soldier in India for every 4,000 Indians." Roberts, op. cit., p. 207. Four decades later India "could not be governed except with the substantial consent of its elites and the practical collaboration of huge numbers of its people"—both of which were withdrawn after World War II. Ibid., p. 470.

52. In the second half of the twentieth century, to use Joseph Nye's terminology, the "hard power" of the West, which they resisted, waned, while the "soft power"—the ideas, institutions, and values—which they were increasingly eager to embrace, waxed. Nye, *Bound to Lead*, New York: Basic Books, 1990.

53. Competitive impulses encouraged voluntary acceptance, however. According to the daughter of Deng Xiaoping, "In the mid-1970s, my father looked around China's periphery, to the small dragon economies [Singapore, Hong Kong, Taiwan, and South Korea]. They were growing at eight to ten percent per year, and these economies had a considerable technological lead over China. If we were to surpass them and resume our rightful place in the region, and ultimately the world, China would have to grow faster than them." David M. Lampton, *Same Bed Different Dreams: Managing U.S.-China Relations, 1989–2000*, Berkeley: The University of California Press, 2001, p. xi. Similar calculations about the Soviet Union's relationship to China affected Mikhail Gorbachev's fateful decision to launch economic and then political reforms.

54. Braudel, *On History*, translated by Sandy Matthews, Chicago: University of Chicago Press, 1980, p. 27.

55. A national difference is relevant. International history at the first level was pioneered by German scholars, notably Leopold von Ranke, in the nineteenth century. They used official archives to chart the rise and fall of states. The avatars of social history were the French members of the *annales* school, which was founded the first half of the twentieth century and of which Braudel was a distinguished member. The school studied the habits and customs of everyday life. It is perhaps not entirely accidental that Germans chose to study the state and Frenchmen to study food.

56. There are, of course, exceptions to this generalization. Social historians have been interested in social movements that produced social and political change. But Braudel wrote about what endured for centuries.

57. He added, "The tradition of all the dead generations weighs like a nightmare on the brain of the living." Karl Marx, "The Eighteenth Brumaire of Louis Napoleon," in Lewis Feuer, editor, *Marx and Engels: Basic Writings on Politics and Philosophy*, New York: Doubleday Anchor Books, 1959, p. 320. To make the point another way: historical figures are often called "actors," but they are actors in two different meanings of the word, each of which is appropriate to one of the levels of history. They are actors in

that they act in and on the world and their actions produce the results that make up the history of events. But they are also actors playing prewritten roles that restrict what they can do on the stage. They have the freedom to interpret their parts—two versions of Hamlet can differ sharply one from the other—but that freedom is not unlimited.

58. It is unlikely that war would, after 1945, have become a generic term in this way, shorn of what is its essence—violence—had the Cold War been as bloody as the three previous major conflicts, filled, like them, with battles causing death and destruction on a large scale.

59. A classic statement of the proposition that history has accelerated in the modern period comes from the American patrician and author Henry Adams, writing at the outset of the twentieth century: *The Education of Henry Adams*, New York: The Modern Library, 1931, first published (privately), 1906, Chapters XXXIII and XXXIV.

60. A major innovation in communication also appeared in the nineteenth century. Samuel F. B. Morse produced his first working telegraph in the 1840s. The speed at which relatively brief messages could be transmitted increased dramatically. "A merchant conducting business with the Far East in 1801 had been obliged to wait at best for four or five months for a question to be answered. His successor in 1901 could have his answer within twenty or thirty minutes, if he needed it." Roberts, op. cit., p. 131.

61. The innovations in transportation in this period were scarcely inconsequential. But the automobile and the airplane were improvements in, not radical changes from, what the railroad and the steamship had already made possible.

62. The digital revolution has multiplied the number of actual transactions almost beyond imagining. "Robert Moore, one of the co-founders of Intel, had already shown that the density of circuits on the chips would double every 18 months. That axiom, enshrined as 'Moore's Law,' has held good throughout the three decades of the microprocessor's existence. The resulting growth in computational power is hard to grasp. In the course of my writing this piece my computer has performed more calculations than have been done by hand in the whole of human history." John Lanchester, "See you in court, pal," *The London Review of Books*, September 30, 1999, p. 5.

"Between 1970 and 1990 the transistor density on a chip went up from 1,000 to 1,000,000 per chip: if aeroplanes had improved so much in the same time . . . a London to New York flight would now take five minutes or so and would cost only a few pence." Roberts, op. cit., p. 563.

63. This is not entirely the case. Social change does take place during wartime, and did so especially during the two world wars of the twentieth century.

64. The difference in time and overall cost required for destruction and construction is particularly pronounced in the creation of one important element of liberal institutions, which economists call human capital. Educating a man is a long and expensive process, killing him is quick and cheap.

65. Locating the fulcrums of history was, Braudel thought, one of the prerogatives of the historian. "Can we not at first sight distinguish the crucial factor as far as the future of a given historical situation is concerned? We know which of all the conflicting forces will prevail. We can see in advance which events are important, which ones will have consequences, which ones will affect the future. What an immense privilege!" Braudel, *On History*, p. 84.

66. This is a major theme of Paul Schroeder, *The Transformation of European Politics, 1763–1848*, Oxford: Oxford University Press, 1996 p.b. (first published 1994), especially Chapters 10–12.

67. This is the theme of Paul Kennedy, *The Rise and Fall of the Great Powers*, New York: Random House, 1988.
68. Ibid., pp. 80–82, 98. See also Landes, op. cit., p. 234.
69. This is the overarching theme of Edward S. Creasey, *Fifteen Decisive Battles of the World*, Harrisburg, Pa.: The Military Service Publishing Company, 1943. First published, 1851.
70. The combination of political calculation and military strategy on the American side that contributed to the location of these borders is the subject of David Eisenhower, *Eisenhower: At War, 1943–45*, New York: Random House, 1986.
71. "Between 1950 and 1980, the four poorer countries of western Europe [Greece, Portugal, Spain and Ireland] grew twice as fast as the communist countries. Czechoslovakia, Hungary and Poland, only slightly behind Austria in 1937, were far behind it by 1980." Samuel Brittan, "Time to buck up," *Financial Times*, September 17, 1998, p. 14.

3. A WORLD OF SOVEREIGN STATES

1. V. I. Lenin, *The State and Revolution*, New York: International Publishers, 1974, pp. 15–20. First published, 1917.
2. This definition comes from Martin van Creveld, *The Rise and Decline of the State*, Cambridge, England: Cambridge University Press, 1999, especially Chapter 2. A slightly different definition may be found in S. E. Finer, *The History of Government From the Earliest Times: Volume I, Ancient Monarchies and Empires*, Oxford, England: Oxford University Press, 1997, p. 2.
3. S. E. Finer, *The History of Government From the Earliest Times: Volume III: Empires, Monarchies, and the Modern State*, Oxford: Oxford University Press, 1997, p. 1611. "The most elementary functions of the liberal state, such as the efficient assessment and collection of taxes by a body of salaried officials or the maintenance of a regular nationally organized rural constabulary, would have seemed beyond the wildest dreams of most pre-revolutionary absolutisms." Eric Hobsbawm, *The Age of Revolution, 1789–1848*, New York: Barnes and Noble Books, 1996. First published, 1962, p. 193. "Up until the nineteenth century, no state was capable of carrying out an accurate census . . . It [was] even difficult to know the precise positions of the territorial borders of national sovereignty." Hobsbawm, with Antonio Polito, *On the Edge of the New Century*, New York: The New Press, 2000, p. 32
4. Robert Skidelsky, *The Road from Serfdom*, New York: Penguin Books, 1995, pp. 21–22, 72.
5. Thomas Hobbes, *Leviathan*, New York: Collier Books, 1962, p. 100. First published, 1651.
6. "The state not only makes war possible: it also makes peace possible. Peace is the order, however imperfect, that results from agreement between states, and can only be sustained by that agreement. It is not clear what alternative creators and guarantors of peaceful order could or would take the place of the state in a wholly globalized world." Michael Howard, *The Invention of Peace*, London: Profile, 2001, p. 103.
7. In the second half of the twentieth century there was a strong preference for a particular type of state: a nation-state. People tended to prefer that the mechanism for providing public goods—government—be controlled by people like them. This was one reason for the proliferation of sovereign states, some of them quite small, over the course of the twentieth century. "At the outbreak of the first world war, only 62 independent countries existed in the entire globe. The past half-century has seen the num-

ber grow from 74 in 1946 to 193 today. The upshot has been the creation of many more small states . . . 87 countries have populations of under 5m; 58 have fewer than 2.5m people; and 35 have fewer than 500,000." "Small but perfectly formed," *The Economist,* January 3, 1998, p. 65.

8. J. M. Roberts, *Twentieth Century: The History of the World, 1901–2000,* New York: Viking, 1999, p. 78. The distinction carried over into the twentieth century in the composition of the United Nations Security Council. Its five permanent members—the United States, the United Kingdom, France, China, and Russia—each had the power of veto over any resolution in the Council. At the outset of the twenty-first century a closer approximation of the great European powers of the nineteenth was perhaps the G–8, the group of the six most important industrial economies plus Russia and a representative of the European Union. This group staged economic conferences annually and occasionally exercised, informally, something like the kind of influence on international economic affairs that the nineteenth century great powers had had on political matters.

9. Act II, Scene vii.

10. The role of the extra is to look on as the major characters act out the plot. Members of a crowd can be extremely powerful, but only if all act together.

11. See Chapter 8.

12. W. G. Beasley, *The Rise of Modern Japan: Political, Economic, and Social Change Since 1850,* second edition, New York: St. Martin's Press, 1995 paperback, pp. 2–8.

13. "Foreigners were to be permitted to trade at the specified ports free of official interference, save for the imposition of a low level of customs dues, which were fixed by treaty; they could establish commercial and residential premises in designated foreign settlements in those ports; and they were to live there under the laws of their own countries, administered, if at all, through consular courts." Beasley, op. cit., p. 34.

14. This was "the first defeat of a European power by non-Europeans in a major war since the Middle Ages." Roberts, op. cit., p. 213. The Japanese victory foreshadowed one of the great trends of the first half of the twentieth century, the decline in the advantage in power that the West had enjoyed over the rest of the world for a hundred years, leading to the end of the overseas empires that had rested on that advantage. It foreshadowed as well two other major twentieth-century developments. It triggered a revolution in Russia, an upheaval on a smaller scale than the one touched off by an even more sweeping Russian military defeat in 1917. And the Russo-Japanese War drew the United States onto center stage in international politics. President Theodore Roosevelt brokered a settlement at Portsmouth, New Hampshire, for which he received the Nobel Prize for Peace.

15. Whether the similarities between Nazi Germany and Imperial Japan were pronounced enough to justify grouping them together under the heading "fascism" is, in the end, a matter of judgment. Roberts, op. cit., p. 316. The differences between them are at least as striking as the similarities in historical tradition and early twentieth-century political and economic experience. Among the differences was the degree of military control over the society. During World War II it was far more extensive in Japan than in Germany. Whatever else may be said of the Nazi regime, civilians did control the military. The military predominance in Japan was closer to the pattern of German governance in the second half of World War I.

Communism is more clearly a single category because all countries belonging to it either were controlled by, or consciously modeled themselves after, or took instruction from, the Soviet Union.

16. In theory the Japanese leader, as a super-human descendant of the sun god, was even

more exalted. On the role of the Japanese emperor in World War II see Herbert Bix, *Hirohito and the Making of Modern Japan*, New York: HarperCollins, 2000.

17. Germany was divided into two sovereign states: the German Federal Republic in the west and the German Democratic Republic in the east. The Soviet Union occupied several small islands in the Kurile chain that had belonged to Japan, an occupation that continued into the twenty-first century.

18. In Japan, the Liberal Democratic Party formed the national government for almost the entire Cold War period. But the party was a loose collection of personal fiefdoms representing many regions and economic sectors of the country.

19. Richard Rosecrance, *The Rise of The Trading State: Commerce and Conquest in the Modern World*, New York: Basic Books, 1986.

20. Their postwar pacifism followed from the lessons each nation had learned from the war, but the lessons were different. The Germans shunned war because they saw themselves as having been the aggressors, the Japanese because they considered themselves to have been the victims. Germans had to confront Auschwitz and the Holocaust. For the Japanese, the defining moral event of the war was not the terrible Japanese assault on China's second most important city, known to the world as the rape of Nanjing, but rather the American atomic raids on Hiroshima and Nagasaki. The story of how the two countries came to understand the war and their respective roles in it is told in Ian Buruma, *The Wages of Guilt*, New York: Farrar, Straus and Giroux, 1994.

21. The postwar West German economic performance was also often referred to as a miracle (*wirtschaftwunder*.) The Japanese economy prospered despite the fact that, through the 1960s, Japan did not have access to China, the country that it had considered, during the first half of the century, to be crucial to its economic well-being. In effect, in economic terms Japan traded Chinese labor for American consumers. The bargain proved a profitable one for the Japanese.

22. One of the crucial events in the collapse of Communism in Central Europe in 1989 was the decision of the Communist government of Hungary to allow East Germans vacationing in their country to go to West Germany through neighboring Austria. The Communist foreign minister of Hungary, Gyula Horn, described this decision as Hungary's "choosing Europe," by which he meant conforming to the political norms of *western* Europe. Charles Maier, *Dissolution: The Crisis of Communism and the End of East Germany*, Princeton: Princeton University Press, 1997, p. 129.

23. Ironically, the closest southern neighbors of the United States, the countries of Central America in which the American government had historically intervened extensively and often, were less democratic and less prosperous than the larger Spanish- (and Portuguese-) speaking countries to their south.

24. "In 1870, the United States had the largest economy in the world, and its best years still lay ahead. By 1913 American output was two and a half times that of the United Kingdom or Germany, four times that of France. Measured per person, American GDP surpassed that of the United Kingdom by 20 percent, France by 77, Germany by 86." David Landes, *The Wealth and Poverty of Nations*, New York: W. W. Norton, 1998, p. 307. On the assumption by the United States of the policies and prerogatives of a great power see Fareed Zakaria, *From Wealth to Power: The Unusual Origins of America's World Role*, Princeton: Princeton University Press, 1998.

25. The outcome of this conflict was momentous for European and world history in the twentieth century, in which the United States played a central role, a role that it might well not have assumed had it been one of two (or more) sovereign states between

Canada and Mexico, which a successful Southern secession would have created. (A whimsical but thought-provoking essay on this theme is Lexington, "The voice of the victorious Confederate States," *The Economist*, December 31, 1999, p. 52. Former president Harry Truman had addressed the same subject four decades earlier. See Arthur M. Schlesinger Jr., *A Life in the Twentieth Century: Innocent Beginnings, 1917–1950*, Boston: Houghton Mifflin, 2001, p. 452.) But the American war between the states had little direct effect on European affairs at the time it was waged. By this standard the most important North American conflict was the French and Indian War of 1756 to 1763, waged by Britain and France, the two great rivals for European (and global) primacy in the eighteenth century, on North American soil. The British victory had major reverberations on the European continent, as the Northern victory did not. The earlier war had long-term effects as well. Its outcome made English the dominant European language in North America, a fact that, in the second half of the twentieth century, formed the basis for its rise to the status of the global language.

26. Bradford Perkins, *The Creation of a Republican Empire, 1776–1865*, New York: Cambridge University Press, 1993, pp. 217–229.

27. The turning point was the Hay-Pauncefote Accord of 1905, in which Great Britain conceded what it had previously contested—the right of the United States to build a canal connecting the Atlantic and Pacific Oceans across the Panamanian isthmus in Central America. This was one of several British diplomatic initiatives that together marked the abandonment of the late-nineteenth century policy of splendid isolation in favor of understandings with other actually or potentially hostile powers: the treaty with Japan in 1902, the *entente cordiale* with France in 1904, the understanding with Russia in 1907. Each of the last three had greater immediate importance than the transformation of relations with the United States, which, however, dwarfed them all in long-term significance.

28. Warren Christopher, secretary of state from 1993 to 1997, designated as "the first principle" of his administration's international strategy "the imperative of American leadership." Christopher, "Principles and Opportunities for American Foreign Policy," Address before the John F. Kennedy School of Government, Harvard University, Cambridge, Massachusetts, January 20, 1995. In his farewell address President Bill Clinton said that "America's security and prosperity require us to lead in the world." Quoted in *The New York Times*, January 19, 2001, p. A16.

29. "We are the indispensable nation," Madeleine Albright, secretary of state from 1997 to 2001, once declared. "We stand tall. We see further into the future." Quoted in Bob Herbert, "War Games," *The New York Times News of the Week in Review*, February 22, 1998, p. 16.

30. During the Cold War all the members of the principal instrument for containment, NATO, contributed something to it, but the member that was, in geographic terms, the least threatened—the United States—contributed most. And some countries that did not formally belong—the European neutrals—also benefited from NATO's existence. Michael Mandelbaum, *The Fate of Nations: The Search for National Security in the 19th and 20th Centuries*, New York: Cambridge University Press, 1988, pp. 228–240. Since Switzerland, Sweden, and Yugoslavia contributed to their own defense, where deterring the Soviet Union was concerned they were not, strictly speaking, free riders.

31. The *locus classicus* for the discussion of this issue is Mancur Olson, *The Logic of Collective Action: Public Goods and the Theory of Groups*, Cambridge, Mass.: Harvard University Press, 1965, especially Chapter 1.

32. A major theme in the literature of international relations in the last quarter of the

twentieth century is the exploration of the conditions in which international coopera-tion could and did take place. Among the prominent contributions to this literature are Robert Axelrod, *The Evolution of Cooperation*, New York: Basic Books, 1984, Robert O. Keohane, *After Hegemony: Cooperation and Discord in the World Economy*, Princeton, N.J.: Princeton University Press, 1986, and Kenneth A. Oye, editor, *Cooperation Under Anarchy*, Princeton, N.J.: Princeton University Press, 1986.

33. "Realists maintain that international public goods are produced, if at all, by the lead-ing power, a so-called 'hegemon,' that is willing to bear an undue part of the short-run costs of these goods, either because it regards itself as gaining in the long run, because it is paid in a different coin such as prestige, glory, immortality, or some combination of the two." Charles P. Kindleberger, "International Public Goods Without Interna-tional Government, *The American Economic Review*, 76:1, March, 1986, p. 8. This means that, in these cases, there is "a tendency for the exploitation of the great by the small." Olson, op. cit., p. 4.

34. Charles Kindleberger has argued that the Depression occurred because the task of stabilizing the international economy—providing a market of last resort for exports and acting as the banker of last resort to maintain liquidity—could not be performed by Great Britain, the hegemon of the nineteenth century, and was not performed by the United States, the hegemon of the second half of the twentieth. Kindleberger, *The World in Depression*, Berkeley: The University of California Press, 1973, p. 28.

35. So powerful was the impact of the threat of war that it justified non-military projects, and even domestic public goods, the contribution of which to the struggle against Communism was not immediately apparent: the interstate highway system, for instance, or funds to teach foreign languages to post-graduate students that were fur-nished under the "National Defense Education Act."

36. In the immediate aftermath of World War II, the United States had been responsible for fully forty percent of the world's output. At the end of the Cold War the figure was around twenty percent. But it had been at that level since the 1970s. (Samuel P. Hunt-ington, "The U.S.—Decline or Renewal?" *Foreign Affairs*, Winter 1988/89, p. 81). It was the natural consequence of the recovery of production in the rest of the world, particularly in the Western core, which the United States had done so much to foster and which, if it had made the country relatively less powerful, had made individual Americans absolutely richer.

37. The two preceding paragraphs are drawn from Michael Mandelbaum, "Diplomacy in Wartime: New Priorities and Alignments," in James F. Hoge Jr. and Gideon Rose, editors, *How Did This Happen? Terrorism and the New War*, New York: PublicAffairs, 2001, p. 257.

38. There was another reason. For the public, international leadership was a cost—per-haps worthwhile but a cost all the same. For members of the foreign policy elite it was, or could be, a benefit. "To be Number One . . . provides foreign policy elites—the people who orchestrate the security alliances, staff the embassies, negotiate the treaties, attend the innumerable conferences, churn out policy papers at think tanks, devise scenarios and compose theoretical essays at universities, and write dispatches for the media—not only with prestigious jobs but also with the sense that they are doing important work." Ronald Steel, *The Internationalist Temptation*, Washington, D.C., Division of International Studies, The Woodrow Wilson International Center for Scholars, August 1996, p. 3.

39. Walter McDougall, *Promised Land, Crusader State: The American Encounter with the World Since 1776*, Boston: Houghton Mifflin, 1997, pp. 39–40.

40. Walter Russell Mead, *Special Providence: How American Foreign Policy Changed the World*, New York: Knopf, 2001, Chapter 5.

41. The American tradition of "exemplarism" is discussed in H. W. Brands, *What America Owes the World: The Struggle for the Soul of Foreign Policy*, New York: Cambridge University Press, 1998, Chapter 1. Also relevant is Walter McDougall's distinction between foreign policy in the nineteenth century, which he terms the "Old Testament," evoking the people of Israel's exemplarist mission of serving as a "light unto the nations," and the interventions of the twentieth century, the "New Testament," closer in spirit to the Christian practice of converting unbelievers. McDougall, op. cit.

42. McDougall, op. cit.

43. The logic of free riding found pithy expression in Joseph Heller's novel of World War II, *Catch–22*. Yossarian, the hero of the story, tells a major on the airbase in Italy from which bombing attacks are launched that he does not want to fly any more missions because he is afraid of being killed. "But suppose everybody on our side felt that way," the major says, to which Yossarian replies, "Then I'd certainly be a damned fool to feel any other way. Wouldn't I?" Joseph Heller, *Catch–22*, New York: Simon and Schuster, 1961, p. 104.

44. This reluctance was a safeguard against another fear about post-Cold War American foreign policy: that, where military intervention was concerned, the United States would behave less like a teetotaler and more like a binge drinker, roaring off on ill-advised international crusades. On this point see Robert W. Tucker and David C. Hendrickson, *The Imperial Temptation: The New World Order and America's Purpose*, New York: The Council on Foreign Relations, 1992. While the rhetoric of American foreign policy has regularly evoked higher purposes, both secular and religious, there has just as frequently been a gap between rhetoric and reality. Americans have historically been reluctant to pay heavily in blood and treasure to close this gap.

45. The opposition to free trade is discussed in Chapter 12. Accepting cheaper products from abroad is not a cost to a country; but many Americans erroneously regarded it as such.

46. Two features of American foreign policy in the 1990s provided evidence of the gap between the goals of the foreign policy elite (or at least part of it) and the willingness of the public to pay to achieve them. One was the increasing resort to economic sanctions to punish countries pursuing policies of which the United States disapproved. The tactic gave concrete expression to that disapproval while costing the public virtually nothing. The other was the habit of exaggerating rhetorically the dangers or crimes that members of the foreign policy establishment wished to combat. Thus those seeking a more robust policy of opposing China commonly referred to the Beijing government as "totalitarian," although the extent of official repression was far smaller, and the scope of individual freedom correspondingly vastly wider, in twenty-first century China than these had been in the third quarter of the twentieth century under Mao and than they had been in the Soviet Union under Stalin and his successors. Similarly, the proponents of military intervention against Serbia in Bosnia and Kosovo compared Belgrade's policies in both places to Hitler's by terming it "genocide," although the Serbs killed far fewer people and did not seek, as had the Nazis with the Jews, to kill all Bosnian Muslims or all Albanian Kosovars. A closer parallel to the Nazi crimes was the slaughter of Tutsi by Hutu in Rwanda in Africa. Because the Clinton administration did not wish to intervene, however, in describing the atrocities there it scrupulously avoided using the term genocide.

    "In our time," George Orwell wrote in 1946, "political writing and speech are largely the defense of the indefensible." ("Politics and the English Language," in Sonia Orwell and Ian Angus, editors, *The Collected Essays, Journalism and Letters of George Orwell: Volume 4: In Front of Your Nose, 1945–1950*, New York: Harcourt Brace and World, 1968, p. 136.) In the post-Cold War, United States rhetoric came to have the opposite aim: to make the bad seem worse in order to arouse rather than to pacify the public.

47. To make the point differently, the sometimes unsteady quality of American leadership helped make that leadership acceptable to others. "It was an accident of history that left the United States as the world's only superpower. If its potential economic leverage . . . cultural influence, and military superiority were employed coherently, in a disciplined, power-maximizing way, its weight in world affairs would be such that all political entities desirous of retaining their independence would coalesce against it, to oppose, resist, sabotage and undermine all its initiatives." Edward Luttwak, "American Power—For What?" *Commentary*, January, 2000, pp. 38–39.

48. "For nations as for families the level may vary at which a solvent balance is struck. If its expenditures are safely within its assured means, a family is solvent when it is poor, or is well-to-do, or is rich. The same principle holds true of nations. The statesman . . . must bring his ends and means into balance. If he does not, he will follow a course that leads to disaster." Quoted in James Chace, *Solvency: The Price of Survival: An Essay on American Foreign Policy*, New York: Random House, 1981, pp. 52–53.

49. The United States annexed the Philippines in part to deny access to the Luzon harbor to others. Americans also feared European encroachment in Central America. The Monroe Doctrine of 1823 declared the hemisphere off limits to European powers although claiming no explicit imperial prerogatives for the United States. Bradford Perkins, *The Creation of a Republican Empire, 1776–1865*, New York: Cambridge University Press, 1993, pp. 165–169; McDougall, op. cit., Chapter 3.

50. The ideology and the foreign policies of America's chief adversary reinforced the premise. The Soviet Union was the hub of a worldwide movement, united by a common, aggressive, expansionist ideology. It sponsored Communist governments, Communist parties, and Communist insurgencies the world over. All were opposed to the United States, its interests, and its allies. Through Soviet patronage, trouble spots, actual and potential, around the world were connected to one another, even if they were not geographically contiguous. Dominoes could topple through the force of inflammatory example. Mandelbaum, *The Fate of Nations*, Chapter 3.

51. Walter Laqueur, *The New Terrorism: Fanaticism and the Arms of Mass Destruction*, New York: Oxford University Press, 1999, Chapter 1.

52. Bernard Lewis, *The Middle East: A Brief History of the Last 2,000 Years*, New York: Scribner, 1995, pp. 1–18.

53. Why Communism triumphed in these countries is a much-debated question. Part of the answer is to be found in the singular and contingent features of the two countries in the twentieth century. Their histories would surely have been different, perhaps radically different, if Lenin had remained in exile in Zurich in 1917 or if Mao had never left his native Changsha, in Sichuan province, for Beijing. An explanation of the two greatest of twentieth century revolutions must also draw on the second level of history, the level of long-term trends and developments. It may be that the economic and political backwardness, in the face of the power of the core countries that had already successfully modernized, produced Communist regimes claiming vast, indeed total, power because only total power could mobilize the resources needed to resist, let alone catch up with, the leaders. Different versions of a comparative and sequential

explanation are found in Barrington Moore, *The Social Origins of Democracy and Dictatorship: Lord and Peasant in the Making of the Modern World*, London: Penguin Books, 1968, and Alexander Gerschenkron, "Economic Backwardness in Comparative Perspective," in Gerschenkron, *Economic Backwardness in Comparative Perspective: A Book of Essays*, Cambridge, Mass.: Harvard University Press, 1962.

54. On the reasons for Communism's economic failure, see Chapter 10.

55. "[It is] useful to think of Russia and China as analogous to unruly adolescents . . . In the adolescent stage of development, individuals, like post-Cold War Russia and China, are in the midst of a rapid, bewildering transition from one status to another: no longer what they were but not yet what they will eventually become. They are outgrowing old habits and attitudes without yet settling into new ones." Michael Mandelbaum, "Westernizing Russia and China," *Foreign Affairs*, May/June 1997, pp. 93–94.

56. A prominent theme of histories of Russia is the various ways in which it has differed from Western Europe: its lack of feudal social relations, private property, and the fainter impact of the Renaissance, the Reformation, and the Enlightenment. Histories of China generally do not feature such themes because, unlike Russia, China was so far removed from the main currents of Western, European, liberal civilization that no explanation for the absence of liberal institutions and practices was deemed necessary.

4. THE CURE FOR CANCER

1. Mikhail Gorbachev, *Perestroika: New Thinking for Our Country and the World*, New York: Harper and Row, 1987, p. 204.

2. This phrase is also the title of a book by Michael Howard, London: Profile, 2001.

3. Essays that do emphasize features of the liberal approach to security are in Janne E. Nolan, editor, *Global Engagement: Cooperation and Security in the 21st Century*, Washington, D.C.: The Brookings Institution, 1994. The subject also receives extensive treatment in Leon V. Sigal, *Hang Separately: Cooperative Security Between the United States and Russia, 1985–1994*, New York: The Century Foundation, 2000.

4. The growth of "warlessness" is discussed in Section III.

5. These developments were directly relevant to the invention of peace. Orthodox Communism was a cause of conflict; democracy and free markets, where they exist, tend to contribute to peace. On this last point, see Chapter 8.

6. This passage, and others in this chapter, are drawn from Michael Mandelbaum, *The Dawn of Peace in Europe*, New York: The Twentieth Century Fund Press, 1996, Chapters 4–6.

7. Cited in Kenneth N. Waltz, *Man, the State, and War*, New York: Columbia University Press, 1954, pp. 10–11.

8. Thucydides, *The Peloponnesian War*, translated by Rex Warner, Harmondsworth, England: Penguin Books, 1972, p. 49.

9. Because the basic structure persists, in international relations patterns recur over time. While the politics of the ancient Greeks bear only a passing resemblance to the politics of the twenty-first century, and the economic life of fifth century B.C. Athens none at all to the economic concerns of the contemporary age, the relations between and among the tiny Greek city-states of that era are familiar to anyone acquainted with the history of the twentieth century. The issues, the calculations, and the strategies are similar, making Thucydides' account, in the realist view, a text for all time. In the literature of international relations such comparisons are familiar. See, for

example, Michael Mandelbaum, *The Nuclear Revolution: International Politics Before and After Hiroshima*, New York: Cambridge University Press, 1981. A powerful statement of the realist perspective on international affairs is John Mearsheimer, *The Tragedy of Great Power Politics*, New York: W. W. Norton, 2001.

10. "Cooperation among states has its limits, mainly because it is constrained by the dominating logic of security competition, which no amount of cooperation can eliminate. Genuine peace, or a world where states do not compete for power, is not likely, according to realism." John Mearsheimer, "The False Promise of International Institutions," *International Security*, Winter, 1994/5, Vol. 19: No. 3, p. 9.

11. This passage and others in this section are drawn from Michael Mandelbaum, "Is Modern War Obsolete?" *Survival*, Winter, 1998–1999.

12. Satellites made the world less dangerous well before the creation of the common security order by giving each side basic information about the military establishment of the other. This information reduced the chance that either could launch an unseen military buildup, develop a new secret weapon, or successfully prepare a surprise attack. In strategic matters, ignorance is not bliss. Satellites thus reduced the chance that either side would believe that the other was doing any such thing and act accordingly. In the late 1950s, without the benefit of satellite photographs of all of the territory of the Soviet Union, the United States vastly overestimated the number of ballistic missiles the Soviet Union was deploying and geared its own missile-building program to this erroneous estimate. On the expansion of the American missile force in the early 1960s see Desmond Ball, *Politics and Force Levels: The Strategic Missile Program of the Kennedy Administration*, Berkeley: University of California Press, 1980.

13. In a balance of power world the distribution of military power has crucial importance. The dynamics of a world of several major powers differs from the workings of the international system of the Cold War, in which there were only two. (This is a theme of Kenneth N. Waltz, *Theory of International Politics*, Reading, Mass.: Addison-Wesley, 1979.) The post-Cold War international system seemed, at first glance, to be "unipolar," with the United States towering over all other countries. To the extent that the rules of common security apply, however, the distribution of military power becomes less important—although not entirely unimportant.

14. For almost all of recorded history sovereign states saw their interests, where security was concerned, as opposed. This was so because all sought to maximize power and power is finite; more for one country means less for others. They sought to maximize power because power was the vehicle for the achievement of the state-level goals for which wars were fought as well as for self-defense, the need for which anarchy imposes on all members of the international system. But with the first set of goals gone, common security emerged as a method of obtaining the second cooperatively. More security for one country could mean more for others as well.

15. The evolution of American nuclear strategy is described in Michael Mandelbaum, *The Nuclear Question: The United States and Nuclear Weapons, 1945–1976*, New York: Cambridge University Press, 1979, Chapters 3–5.

16. The Test Ban Treaty was also a nonproliferation measure, designed to make it more difficult for other countries to acquire nuclear weapons. Ibid., Chapter 7.

17. Popular films being what they are, the story almost invariably ends with joint experience forging mutual respect, as in *The Defiant Ones* (1958), in which Tony Curtis and Sidney Poitier play two escaped prisoners who are manacled together. In the best films of this genre, Alfred Hitchcock's *The Thirty-Nine Steps* made in 1935 and *The Lady Vanishes* of 1938, the oddly matched couples are a man and a woman and the con-

sequence of their intense, involuntary association is more than respect. In the first of them, Robert Donat and Madeleine Carroll are handcuffed together; in the second, Michael Redgrave and Margaret Lockwood are passengers on the same train. In both, initial distaste is transformed, through adversity and triumph, into love.

18. Reagan's admirers assign a decisive role in ending the Cold War to the Strategic Defense Initiative. Demoralized by the impossibility of matching the United States in what would have been a contest in the development and deployment of the most complicated and advanced technology, according to this explanation, the leaders of the Soviet Union gave up. (The thesis has received some support from former Soviet officials. See Robert Conquest, *Reflections on a Ravaged Century*, New York: W. W. Norton, p. 184.) While the Soviet leaders were indeed alarmed by the prospect of American strategic defenses when Reagan launched his initiative, they became progressively less concerned as it became increasingly clear that the United States was making little headway in designing a system capable enough to be worth deploying. Mikhail Gorbachev, a relevant if not entirely disinterested witness, denied that the prospect of an American missile defense system played any appreciable role in the events that led to the collapse of the Soviet Union. A useful brief discussion of this issue is in Thomas Powers, "The Great Contest," *The New York Review of Books*, June 20, 1996, p. 24. The history of the Strategic Defense Initiative is recounted in William J. Broad, *Teller's War: The Secret Story Behind the Star Wars Deception*, New York: Simon and Schuster, 1992, and Frances Fitzgerald, *Way Out There in the Blue: Reagan, Star Wars, and the End of the Cold War*, New York: Simon and Schuster, 2000.

19. He insisted as well that the name of the negotiations on long-range nuclear weapons be changed from Strategic Arms Limitation Talks to Strategic Arms Reduction Talks. The shift from SALT to START as the reigning acronym reflected Reagan's belief that agreements were not worth having unless they lowered the overall total of nuclear weapons.

20. See Chapter 2.

21. Quoted in Raymond Garthoff, *Deterrence and Revolution in Soviet Military Doctrine*, Washington, D.C.: The Brookings Institution, 1990, p. 35.

22. Mikhail Gorbachev, *Perestroika: New Thinking for Our Country and the World*, New York: Harper and Row, 1987, p. 142.

23. Ibid.

24. Ibid., pp. 142–143.

25. Ibid., p. 203.

26. War may have begun as a contest for resources, with settled agricultural communities organizing the first armed forces to defend themselves against nomadic raiders. John Keegan, *War and Our World*, London: Hutchinson, 1998, p. xii.

27. Political inequality within these societies was discredited, leading to the extension of the franchise. (See Chapter 8.) Political inequality among different societies was similarly cast into disrepute. The result was the end of empire.

28. Keegan, *War and Our World*, p. 24. Before World War I "the soldier's work in western countries was, by and large, considerably less dangerous than that of certain groups of civilian workers such as those in transport (especially by sea) and the mines . . . The greatest risks to life and limb were not run in uniform." Eric Hobsbawm, *The Age of Empire, 1875–1914*, New York: Pantheon, 1987, p. 306.

29. John Keegan, *The Face of Battle: A Study of Agincourt, Waterloo and the Somme*, New York: Vintage Books, 1977, pp. 329–334. See also Ben Shepherd, *A War of Nerves: Soldiers and Psychiatrists, 1914–1994*, London: Cape, 2001.

30. This was the reason for the postwar celebrity of T. E. Lawrence, who had encouraged and assisted the Arab uprising against the Turks in the last years of the war and became known to history as Lawrence of Arabia. His own talent and bravery seemed to have made a major contribution to victory, although in what was a secondary theater of the conflict, the Middle East. Whether the legend that grew around him had a basis in fact is another matter. The most extensive assessment is John Mack, *A Prince of Our Disorder*, Boston: Houghton Mifflin, 1976.

31. The theme of Paul Fussell's *The Great War and Modern Memory* (New York: Oxford University Press, 1975) is that the experience of the war made irony a dominant theme in the subsequent literature of Great Britain.

32. The point is argued in John Mueller, *Retreat from Doomsday: The Obsolescence of Modern War*, New York: Basic Books, 1989.

33. On non-Western forms of war, with different purposes, see John Keegan, *A History of Warfare*, New York: Knopf, 1993.

34. Edward Luttwak, "Toward Post-Heroic Warfare," *Foreign Affairs*, 74:3, May/June, 1995, pp. 109–122.

35. The term originates in Martin van Creveld, *The Transformation of War*, New York: The Free Press, 1991. The exact word used is "debellicized."

36. "The lasting peace [since 1945] has created a large and placid majority in wealthy countries, for whom the idea of dying for a cause isn't a concept that they would ever contemplate. With the decline of general conscription, this attitude is destined to take root. It is not easy to imagine how this could change, or whether there could be a return to the reality of the twentieth century in which wars made every individual face up to the question of death, either at home under the bombs or at the front." Eric Hobsbawm with Antonio Polito, *On the Edge of a New Century*, New York: The New Press, 2000, p. 127.

37. At the end of the nineteenth century "there existed in governing elites, military circles, and imperialist organizations a prevailing view of the world order which stressed struggle, change, competition, the use of force, and the organization of national resources to enhance state power." Paul Kennedy, *The Rise and Fall of the Great Powers: Economic Change and Military Conflict from 1500 to 2000*, New York: Random House, 1988, p. 196.

38. The first quotation is from Michael Howard, *The Lessons of History*, New Haven: Yale University Press, 1991, p. 75; the second is from Peter Hitchens, *The Abolition of Britain: From Lady Chatterley to Tony Blair*, London: Quartet Books, 1999, p. 35.

39. The standard work in English on the Concert of Europe, its antecedents, its founding, and its operation, is Paul W. Schroeder's magisterial diplomatic history, *The Transformation of European Politics, 1763–1848*, New York: Oxford University Press, 1996 paperback. Also valuable is Henry Kissinger, *A World Restored*, New York: Grosset and Dunlap, 1964.

40. As well as similarities there were important differences between the two. The forces that debellicized the societies of the West in the second half of the twentieth century had barely appeared at the beginning of the nineteenth. The nineteenth-century great powers did not respect the territorial integrity of existing states. To the contrary, they moved territory from one sovereign jurisdiction to another as a matter of course. They also competed to acquire territory outside Europe. Underlying the Concert of Europe was a commitment to a fair division of the spoils of war in Europe. Common security rests on a disavowal of any spoils. And while the ultimate aim of the Concert was to preserve in power the traditional regimes of the continent, common security grew out of the triumph of the old regime's nineteenth-century adversary, liberalism.

41. Quoted in Walter A. McDougall, *Let the Sea Make a Noise: Four Hundred Years of Cataclysm, Conquest, War and Folly in the North Pacific*, New York: Avon Books, 1994, paperback, p. 528. The Naval Treaty did not stand on a foundation of warlessness. Each party to it accepted it out of a combination of domestic pressure and strategic calculation. These pressures and calculations are discussed in Roger Dingman, *Power in the Pacific: The Origins of Naval Arms Limitation, 1914–1922*, Chicago: The University of Chicago Press, 1976. When Japan's calculations changed, it withdrew from the Treaty.

42. This was a typical purpose of alliances in the nineteenth century. See Schroeder, op. cit., p. 42.

43. It is also the purpose of United Nations peacekeeping forces, such as the one deployed on the Sinai peninsula between Israel and Egypt, which are inserted between parties neither of which seeks to attack the other but both of which have reason to doubt that the other's intentions are benign.

44. It was not only Russia that needed reassuring. France and Great Britain harbored doubts about the wisdom of German reunification, doubts strong enough to be raised publicly in 1989 by their leaders, Francois Mitterrand and Margaret Thatcher.

45. "The idea of Europe without frontiers opposed to the US is unrealistic and not in Russian interests. The united Germany is instead a problem: and the American presence in Europe for quite a considerable period of time yet is a factor that is beneficial to Europe and a factor that is beneficial to Russia." Vladimir Lukin, member of the Russian parliament and former ambassador to the United States, *Radiostantsiia Ekho Moskvy*, October 10, 1997. Quoted in Maurizio Massari, "Russia and Europe after the Cold War," unpublished paper, Harvard University, June, 1998, p. 62.

46. They grew out of a series of East-West negotiations between 1986 and 1992. The first of them was concluded during the Cold War, in 1975, as part of the Helsinki Accords signed that year. A more comprehensive set of confidence-building measures than Helsinki produced was authorized in Stockholm in 1986, paving the way for further measures agreed to at Paris in 1990 and Vienna in 1992.

47. Kazakhstan, Kyrgyzstan, and Tajikistan, the three successor states to the Soviet Union that, like Russia, had borders with China, were also party to the Sino-Russian accords. These were described in a semi-official Chinese publication in the language of common security (a term explicitly used to characterize them): "The first agreement stipulates that troops of both sides stationed in the border areas shall not attack each other, nor hold military exercises targeting the other side and should invite observers from the other side for actual fighting exercises. The second agreement demands that both sides reduce their border force to the lowest level consummate [sic] with good neighborliness and on the defensive only. It further forbids mutual use of force or the threat of the use of force, pursuit of unilateral military supremacy and requires the exchange of information on border military force. Such kind of confidence building and mutual commitment is a rarity in human history. It delineates for the first time areas of transparency and mutual trust along a 7000-plus kilometer-long border, with military activities predictable and subject to supervision." Chen Mingshan and He Xiquan, "The 'Shanghai Five' Mechanism for Regional Security," *Contemporary International Relations*, China Institute of Contemporary International Relations, Volume 10, Number 8, August, 2000, pp. 3–4. On this see also Rajan Menon, "The Strategic Convergence Between Russia and China," *Survival*, 39:2, Summer, 1997, especially pp. 107–109.

48. George F. Kennan, "A Fateful Error," *The New York Times*, February 5, 1997.

49. In September and October 1991 Mikhail Gorbachev and U.S. President George Bush

removed, through reciprocal unilateral measures, the short-range nuclear weapons that each side had deployed in Europe by the thousands during the Cold War. Baltic membership in NATO would confront Russia with a powerful military coalition on its border from which it was excluded, thereby tempting the Russian government to compensate for the weakness of its non-nuclear forces by redeploying these short-range "tactical" nuclear weapons.

50. The official rationale for expansion—to solidify the status of liberal political systems and market economies in the three new member countries—was not plausible. There was no evidence that belonging to a military alliance had any appreciable effect on the prospects for democracy and free markets. If such a connection did exist, moreover, the wrong countries were being admitted to NATO. Democracy and free markets were not in jeopardy in Poland, Hungary, and the Czech Republic. Russia and Ukraine, where they *were* in jeopardy and where their success or failure would affect the West, were not invited to join NATO. The case against NATO expansion is presented in Michael Mandelbaum, *NATO Expansion: A Bridge to the Nineteenth Century*, Chevy Chase, Md.: The Center for Political and Strategic Studies, 1997.

51. The American Congress treated Russia less well than it treated China. Although Beijing retained a Communist government and threatened an American ally, Taiwan (see Chapter 5), Congress consistently overrode efforts to deny it normal trading status with the United States. One reason for this was that powerful interests in the United States, firms that did business on the Chinese mainland, mobilized politically on its behalf. Had Russia had a comparable lobby, NATO would not have been expanded.

52. This was the central message of George Kennan's 1947 article "The Source of Soviet Conduct," often credited with laying the conceptual basis for the American Cold War policy of containing the Soviet Union. "The first of these [fundamental Communist] concepts is that of the innate antagonism between capitalism and Socialism. . . . It has profound implications for Russian conduct as a member of international society. It means that there can never be on Moscow's side any sincere assumption of a community of aims between the Soviet Union and powers which are regarded as capitalist. It must invariably be assumed in Moscow that the aims of the capitalist world are antagonistic to the Soviet regime." *Foreign Affairs*, vol. 23, July, 1947, p. 572.

53. The decline of the Soviet and Russian armed forces is chronicled in William E. Odom, *The Collapse of the Soviet Military*, New Haven: Yale University Press, 1999.

54. It was also a cause of World War II. The Treaty of Versailles created German minorities in the new sovereign states of Poland and Czechoslovakia. This occasioned German resentment and a determination to overturn the Treaty, on which Hitler capitalized.

55. The new Russian diasporas, along with three other cases of divided nations in Central and Eastern Europe, are discussed in Michael Mandelbaum, editor, *The New European Diasporas: National Minorities and Conflict in Eastern Europe*, New York: The Council on Foreign Relations, 2000.

56. Overviews and analyses of Russian-Ukrainian relations are in Anatol Lieven, *Ukraine and Russia: A Fraternal Rivalry*, Washington, D.C.: U.S. Institute of Peace, 1999, and Aurel Braun, "All Quiet on the Russian Front? Russia, Its Neighbors, and the Russian Diaspora," in Mandelbaum, editor, *Europe's New Diasporas*.

57. Lieven, *Ukraine and Russia*, pp. 49, 143. Their allegiance to the new Ukrainian state was also less than fervent. Studies of Russian speakers living outside post-Soviet Russia are reported in David Laitin, *Identity in Formation: The Russian-Speaking Populations in the Near Abroad*, Ithaca: Cornell University Press, 1998.

58. Post-Soviet Russia had a common border with only one Central Asian country, Kazakhstan, but Moscow considered the southern borders of the other four Central Asian states—Uzbekistan, Turkmenistan, Tajikistan, and Kyrgyzstan—to be its own de facto frontiers.

59. The first Chechen war is described in Anatol Lieven, *Tombstone of Russian Power*, New Haven: Yale University Press, 1998.

60. The post-Cold War term for countries that posed, or might pose, this threat was "rogue states." See Chapter 6.

61. This is discussed in Chapter 7.

62. Russia controlled the northern islands of the Kurile chain, which the Japanese claimed as their own; Japan controlled the southern ones.

5. THE MOST DANGEROUS PLACE ON THE PLANET

1. Cited in Aaron L. Friedberg, *Europe's Past, Asia's Future?* Washington, D.C.: The Johns Hopkins University School of Advanced International Studies, SAIS Policy Forum Series, Report Number Three, October 1998, p. 1.

2. American military planning at the height of the Cold War put Asia on a par with Europe, envisioning the need to conduct, simultaneously, "two and one half wars"—major conflicts in Europe and Asia and a lesser one elsewhere.

3. The standard work in English on Japanese-American relations from the middle of the nineteenth century is Walter LaFeber, *The Clash: U.S.-Japanese Relations Throughout History*, New York: W. W. Norton, 1997.

4. American aid to China began in 1935. (Ibid, p. 172.) The partnership with Chiang was not a happy or successful experience for the United States. His army did little effective fighting against the Japanese. The American frustration is described in Barbara Tuchman, *Stillwell and the American Experience in China, 1911–45*, New York: Macmillan, 1970.

5. A good description of this little-known battle is in Walter A. McDougall, *Let the Sea Make a Noise: Four Hundred Years of Cataclysm, Conquest, War and Folly in the North Pacific*, New York: Avon Books, paperback, 1994, pp. 590–599.

6. The phrase is from Andrew J. Nathan and Robert S. Ross, *The Great Wall and the Empty Fortress: China's Search for Security*, New York: W. W. Norton, 1997, p. 60.

7. Allen Whiting, *The Chinese Calculus of Deterrence*, Ann Arbor, Mich.: University of Michigan Press, 1975, p. 170. Ironically, although adversaries in each war, both the Americans and the Chinese did better in the first than in the second. In Korea the United States preserved an independent non-Communist state in the southern part of the peninsula while the newly established Communist regime in China saved the Communist government of the north and established its capacity for self-defense. In Vietnam, the United States lost the war but the victorious Vietnamese Communists fell out with their Chinese comrades. Only four years after the expulsion of the Americans, Vietnam and China were themselves at war.

8. The relevant language is as follows: "The Japanese people forever renounce war as a sovereign right of the nation . . . In order to accomplish [this] aim . . . land, sea, and air forces, as well as other war potential, will never be maintained."

9. Cold War exigencies prompted the United States to help finance the economic take-off in both regions. In Western Europe, the Marshall Plan was designed to spur economic recovery so that local governments could better resist Communist forces

within and without. In East Asia, the outbreak of the Korean War created the need for purchases to sustain the American war effort. Largely made in Japan, these served as a tonic for the war-damaged Japanese economy.

10. In East Asia the United States was committed to defend, and thus guarantee Japanese economic access to, all of Asia except China. In World War II the United States had gone to war to contest the Japanese campaign of conquest and occupation of the same countries, a campaign undertaken explicitly for the purpose of ensuring economic access—albeit by a different kind of Japanese government.

11. Warren Christopher, "America's Pacific Future," Address presented at the University of Washington, Seattle, Washington, November 17, 1993.

12. Such difficulties did not, of course, prevent Japan and the United States from mounting successful amphibious assaults in the Pacific on an impressively large scale in the first half of the twentieth century, nor did it prevent the greatest amphibious operation of all, the Allied landing in northern France on June 6, 1944.

13. The differing German and Japanese experiences in coming to terms with World War II are described in Ian Buruma, *The Wages of Guilt*, New York: Farrar, Straus and Giroux, 1994. The Japanese sometimes contended that the Pacific War had been fought to oust Western imperialism from Asia, which was true but not the whole truth since what replaced it was a hardly less oppressive Japanese rule, and that Hiroshima and Nagasaki had made the Japanese the victims of the war, which overlooked the Japanese attacks on China and on Pearl Harbor that had begun it.

14. Japan was not literally a free rider. It paid 70 percent of the American military costs in Japan. South Korea and Taiwan, also the beneficiaries of American military protection, spent a substantial proportion of their respective economic outputs on defense. But the fact that they were able to defray much of the costs of their own defense without undue economic strain reinforced the argument that they could easily afford to pay all of these costs. Nor did the Japanese financial contribution erase the American suspicion that no matter how much money the Japanese contributed to the common defense effort in East Asia, in an actual shooting war Japan would not put its troops into battle.

15. The case against perpetuating Cold War-era security guarantees in East Asia was forcefully made in a series of publications from the Cato Institute of Washington, D.C. Among these were Ted Galen Carpenter, "Paternalism and Dependence: The U.S.-Japanese Security Relationship," Cato Policy Analysis No. 244, November 1, 1995; Doug Bandow, "Free Rider: South Korea's Dual Dependence on America," Cato Policy Analysis No. 308, May 19, 1998; Ted Galen Carpenter, "Let Taiwan Defend Itself," Policy Analysis No. 313, August 24, 1998; and Doug Bandow, "Old Wine in New Bottles: The Pentagon's East Asia Security Strategy Report," Policy Analysis No. 344, May 18, 1999. See also Ted Galen Carpenter, editor, *A Search for Enemies*, Washington, D.C.: Cato, 1992, and Doug Bandow, *Tripwire*, Washington, D.C.: Cato, 1996.

16. The theme that Japan was different in ways the United States was well-advised either to imitate or resist, or both, was advanced in the writings of several authors during the 1980s: the journalists Karel van Wolferen and James Fallows, the economist Clyde Prestowitz, and the political scientist Chalmers Johnson. Some of their writings were cited at the end of Michael Crichton's *Rising Sun* (New York: Ballantine Books, 1992), making it perhaps the only best-selling novel to offer its readers, in addition to suspense, romance, and drama, a scholarly bibliography. The question of whether the post-1945 Japanese economy did in fact operate according to different principles, and was successful for that reason, is discussed in Chapter 11.

17. The modest size of its nuclear arsenal in comparison with those of the United States and Russia was the reason the Chinese government gave for its refusal to take part in the negotiations to place limits on offensive nuclear forces.

18. China had land borders with other Asian countries, with which negotiated security arrangements like those in Europe *were* feasible. In the Chinese relationship with neighboring Russia, elements of common security were in place after the first post-Cold War decade. (See Chapter 4.) With Indochina, "Beijing seeks neither control . . . nor bases there for its military forces. Its interests are served when Indochina is divided and free of outside military influence. As long as Vietnam does not lend its territory to a great power, its animosity is only an annoyance" (Nathan and Ross, op. cit., p. 106). This was an approach that combined elements of the traditional attitudes of the United States to Latin America and of Great Britain to the European continent. With India, the Chinese relationship was one of deterrence—after India's 1998 nuclear tests, one of nuclear deterrence—made easier for both sides by the fact that the two countries were divided by the highest mountain range in the world. An overland invasion from either direction was hardly feasible logistically, let alone attractive politically. In dealing with India the Chinese also employed a hoary balance-of-power tactic by supporting its adversary Pakistan.

19. The unpromising prospect of even a militarily successful campaign against China was captured by a joke that was current when the Sino-Soviet rivalry was most intense. War breaks out between the two countries and on the first day Soviet forces advance twenty-five miles into China and capture 15 million Chinese. On the second day they advance fifty miles further and capture 30 million more Chinese. On the third day the Soviet troops advance another seventy-five miles and capture an additional 100 million Chinese. On the fourth day the Soviet Union surrenders.

20. This is the theme of Michael Mandelbaum, *The Fate of Nations: The Search for National Security in the Nineteenth and Twentieth Centuries*, New York: Cambridge University Press, 1988, Chapter 5.

21. The principal task of the People's Liberation army was to control China, in particular to resist internal opposition to the regime, a recurrent feature of Chinese history.

22. The Communists survived campaigns by their rival nationalists, and fought them and the Japanese, as a guerrilla army in the 1930s and early 1940s. But the final victory over the rival Kuomintang was achieved by infantry formations; and it was a conventional army, not a guerrilla force, that crossed the Yalu to fight American troops in Korea in November 1950.

23. Mao is reported to have said in 1965: "All I want are six atom bombs. With those bombs I know that neither side will attack me." Quoted in Mandelbaum, op. cit., p. 248.

24. The theme is developed in two books by Allen Whiting: *China Crosses the Yalu*, New York: Macmillan, 1960, and *The Chinese Calculus of Deterrence*, Ann Arbor, Mich.: The University of Michigan Press, 1975.

25. Jonathan Spence, *The Gate of Heavenly Peace: The Chinese and Their Revolution, 1895–1980*, New York: Viking, 1981, p. 358.

26. Tim Huxley and Susan Willett, *Arming East Asia*, Adelphi Paper 329, London: International Institute for Strategic Studies, 1999, p. 67.

27. "There is little disagreement that the People's Liberation Army (PLA), a generic designation for all the Chinese armed forces, remains a threadbare force, well below Western standards. Pockets of excellence notwithstanding, most personnel are poorly educated and trained. Weapons systems are old, and even those acquired most recently are inferior to those in Western arsenals. Many units spend a good deal of

time in non-military activities; staffs do not practice complex, large-scale operations; exercises and training regiments are limited; and equipment is not well maintained." Richard K. Betts and Thomas J. Christensen, "China: Getting the Questions Right," *The National Interest*, 62, Winter 2000/01, p. 18.

28. The comparison became a commonplace in the first post-Cold War decade. See, for example, Fareed Zakaria, "Speak Softly, Carry a Veiled Threat," *The New York Times Magazine*, February 18, 1996, p. 36; Arthur Waldron, "Deterring China," *Commentary*, October, 1995, p. 18; and Betts and Christensen, op. cit., p. 23.

29. "China's immediate territorial interests overlap with those of twenty-four other governments." Nathan and Ross, op. cit., p. 9.

30. Ibid,., op. cit., p. 213. Another difference was relevant. The sentiment in Ukraine for rejoining Russia, while not widespread or strong, was not nonexistent; on Taiwan the commitment to independence and aversion to "reunification" with the mainland was both widespread and strong.

31. This is a subject of Chapter 6.

32. Nathan and Ross, op. cit., pp. 63, 214.

33. Quoted in James Mann, *About Face: A History of America's Curious Relationship With China, From Nixon to Clinton*, New York: Knopf, 1999, p. 48. The circumstances surrounding the Shanghai Communique are discussed on pp. 46–49.

34. The Boxers were members of a Chinese secret society who attacked missionaries and foreign enterprises and besieged the capital of Peking in 1900. The siege was lifted by a foreign, multinational expeditionary force. The May the Fourth Movement was a protest, prominently including students, against the awarding to Japan of the German treaty rights in Shandong, in north China, by the victorious powers at the Paris Peace Conference.

35. "A recent opinion poll of nearly 2,000 Chinese respondents . . . indicated that 87% would approve of the government's decision to invade Taiwan if the ROC declared independence." Denny Roy, "Tensions in the Taiwan Strait," *Survival*, 42:1, Spring 2000, p. 95. In 1996, political activists in Hong Kong, then still a British crown colony, staged demonstrations in favor of military action to reinforce China's claim to the tiny Diaoyu Islands north of Taiwan, which were also claimed by Japan under the name Senkaku Islands. "The Hong Kong actions reverberated in China, where students and intellectuals of different political stripes were galvanized into signing petitions and calling for their own demonstrations against Japan." Steven Mufson, "Island Dispute Offers Option to Chinese Seeking Forum for Dissent," *The Washington Post*, September 23, 1996, p. A12. More evidence that liberalism and nationalism were not mutually exclusive in China came from the Internet: "The need for political reform is a common topic in Chinese [Internet] chat rooms, but so are demands that China stand up to the United States . . . Since NATO's bombing of the Chinese Embassy in Belgrade on May 7 [1999], much of the chat has taken on a strong nationalist bent. A campaign launched on the Web blasted President Jiang Zemin for not reacting more strongly to NATO's attack." John Pomfret, "Chinese Web Opens Portals to New Way of Life," *The Washington Post*, February 13, 2000, p. A26. Similar nationalist sentiments were expressed when an American airplane performing a reconnaissance mission was forced to land on Chinese-controlled Hainan island off the south China coast in April 2001.

36. David M. Lampton, *Same Bed Different Dreams: Managing U.S.-China Relations, 1989–2000*, Berkeley: The University of California Press, 2001, p. 287.

37. To Tibet, Chinese rule brought an assault on the traditional culture, the persecution

of the Buddhist monks who had played a leading role in that culture, the expulsion of the religious leader, the Dalai Lama, the destruction of venerable and hallowed manuscripts, monasteries, and temples, and the importation of Han Chinese settlers to strengthen Beijing's grip on a territory that China had seldom ruled directly before 1950.

38. Concern for sovereignty was the reason for China's assertive policies toward the Spratly islands in the South China Sea, to which Beijing and four other countries (plus Taiwan) asserted claims of one sort or another. Nathan and Ross, op. cit., pp. 115–117.

39. On the distinctive Taiwanese identity, see David M. Lampton and Gregory C. May, *Managing U.S.-China Relations in the Twenty-first Century*, Washington, D.C.: The Nixon Center, 1999, pp. 47–48. Taiwanese attitudes toward the mainland were not static. In a poll taken in 2001, "While those who favor one country, two systems [as proposed by Beijing] are still a minority, the number has almost doubled, to 33 percent, since the last polls in 1999." Mark Landler, "Taiwan's Hard Times Rekindle 'One China' Debate," *The New York Times*, July 8, 2001, p. 3.

40. Popular trust in Beijing in the United States was not enhanced by revelations that Chinese officials had funneled money to the Democratic Party in the 1996 presidential campaign, or by accusations, which were not proved, that a scientist in an American weapons laboratory had passed classified designs for nuclear warheads to the Chinese.

41. "Efforts to determine the future of Taiwan by other than peaceful means, including by boycotts or embargoes, would be a threat to the peace and security of the Western Pacific area and of grave concern to the United States." Quoted in Carpenter, *Taiwan*, p. 11. The Act also obliges the United States "to make available to Taiwan such defense articles and defense services in such quantity as may be necessary to enable Taiwan to maintain a sufficient self-defense capacity." Quoted in Lampton, op. cit., p. 175.

42. "We have a legal and moral obligation to provide for Taiwan's security, and if Taiwan feels secure there's more likelihood for a real cross-straits dialogue between Beijing and Taipei about the future." Winston Lord, former assistant secretary of state for East Asia and former ambassador to China, quoted in *The New York Times*, June 26, 1998, p. A9. In April 2001, President George W. Bush, in answer to the question of whether the United States would defend Taiwan in the event of an attack from the mainland, answered in the affirmative.

43. Nathan and Ross, op. cit., p. 79.

44. Japanese officials said that the geographic scope of the alliance, referred to in the defense guidelines simply as the "areas surrounding Japan," did include Taiwan. Lampton and May, *op. cit.*, p. 56.

45. In a conference on Sino-American relations held in Beijing, "in response to a US participant's question as to whether China wants the United States to remove its troops from the region, a Chinese delegate stated the following: 'If the United States needed $5 to support all US troops in Asia and asked China to cover the costs, China would have to break the money into five parts and evaluate how each dollar is spent.' He said that China would pay the first dollar for Japan, as Japan must be restrained militarily. China would also pay the second dollar for Korea, as China does not want to be responsible for the Korean peninsula. The third dollar, however, is for the protection of Taiwan, and for that the Chinese would not pay. China would not pay the fourth dollar either, as it would be for the South China sea, which China views as an internal or bilateral matter. Finally, the fifth dollar is for the Middle East, which Chinese would most likely pay because it is necessary for stability in that region." "Summary

Report," Conference on U.S.-China Relations and Geopolitical Trends, Sponsored by the John F. Kennedy School of Government, Harvard University, March 26–28, Beijing, China, p. 6. See also Lampton, op. cit, p. 234–240.

46. The subject is discussed in David Shambaugh, "Sino-American Strategic Relations: From Partners to Competitors," *Survival*, 42:1, Spring, 2000, pp. 107–110. See also Lampton, op. cit., pp. 79–80. The United States sought to foster some of the elements of common security in the Asia-Pacific region. The commander of the American forces in the Pacific, Admiral Dennis Blair, "has been promoting the notion of 'security communities' in Asia in which balance-of-power politics is replaced by constant diplomacy, negotiation, communication, and cooperation." Richard McGregor, "Observer role for China at Asia drill," *Financial Times*, March 19, 2001, p. 4. And China occasionally adopted the rhetoric of common security. Lampton, op. cit., p. 170–171.

47. The phrase is from Lampton and May, op. cit., p. 54.

48. On the abandonment-entrapment dilemma see Michael Mandelbaum, *The Nuclear Revolution: International Politics Before and After Hiroshima*, New York: Cambridge University Press, 1981, pp. 151–152.

49. These included paying poor countries to accord Taiwan diplomatic recognition, pressing for admission to the United Nations, and asserting that talks with the mainland had to be conducted on a "state-to-state" basis.

50. David M. Lampton, *Same Bed Different Dreams: Managing U.S.-China Relations, 1989–2000*, Berkeley: University of California Press, 2001, p. 106.

51. "Approximately 25 pieces of legislation, including ten stand-alone bills and resolutions, dealing with Taiwan (counting both House and Senate versions) were introduced in the first seven months of the 106th Congress." Lampton and May, op. cit., p. 51.

52. China "has far more planes than Taiwan, but most are out-of-date blowflies compared with Taiwan's jets. The 72 SU–27 fighters that China has bought from Russia could outmaneuver Taiwan's aging F–5s but probably not the island's 150 F–16s, 60 French Mirage 2000's or air defenses, which include advanced Patriot missiles." Craig S. Smith, "Behind China's Threats," *New York Times*, March 7, 2000, p. A10. China faced other obstacles to invading Taiwan: Few places on the islands were suitable for amphibious landings; the PLA lacked adequate sea transport; a Chinese attack would not have the advantage of surprise. Denny Roy, "Tensions in the Taiwan Strait," *Survival*, 42:1, Spring 2000, p. 82–84.

53. The China-Taiwan arms race resembled the Anglo-German competition in the construction of battleships before World War I. At stake in the early years of the twentieth century, as at the outset of the twenty-first, was a politically decisive military advantage. Both Britain and Germany sought command of the sea in their common home waters, the North Sea, which, like control of the air over the Taiwan strait, one or the other but not both could secure. Command of the sea was vital for Britain, a maritime power, but not for Germany, which was why the German challenge so alarmed the British. Similarly, Taiwanese control of the air space between them did not threaten China, but a reversal of the balance would threaten Taiwan. On the earlier arms race see Mandelbaum, *The Nuclear Revolution*, Chapter 4.

54. Among the reasons for its objection was that, whether or not such a system actually worked, integrating Taiwan into a complicated American missile system would accord the island a de facto American military guarantee. Any military action involving Taiwan and China would automatically draw in the United States. Lampton and May, op. cit., pp. 51–52.

55. "No division of a nation in the present world is so astonishing in its origin as the division of Korea; none is so unrelated to conditions or sentiment within the nation itself at the time the division was effected; none is to this day so unexplained; in none does blunder and planning oversight appear to have played so large a role." Korea scholar Gregory Henderson in 1974, quoted in Don Oberdorfer, *The Two Koreas: A Contemporary History*, Reading, Mass.: Addison-Wesley, 1997, p. 7.

56. In historical perspective Korea also resembled another European country: Poland. Both were victims of their location, between two more powerful neighbors—Germany and Russia in the Polish case, China and Japan for Korea—in relations between which each became something of a pawn. Both were divided by their more powerful neighbors, but each was animated by a tenacious, powerful nationalism.

57. "In the late 1980s, according to one count, there were at least 34,000 monuments to Kim in North Korea, not including benches where he once sat, which were protected with glass coverings, and other memorabilia of his many visits throughout the country." Oberdorfer, op. cit., p. 20.

58. International Institute for Strategic Studies, *The Military Balance: 1997–98*, Oxford, England: Oxford University Press, 1997, pp. 183–184.

59. "No one knows exactly how many people have died in the current North Korean famine. Most guesses are around two million, or nearly 10 percent of the pre-crisis population—though no one is certain what that was, either." Marcus Noland, "Stumbling Toward Apocalypse: The Economics of Korean Unification," *The Milken Institute Review*, Second Quarter, 1999, p. 36. According to relief officials working in North Korea, 50 to 80 percent of its children suffered from malnutrition. Oberdorfer, op. cit., p. 399. To underscore the contrast between the two Koreas, at the same time that famine was ravaging the North it was reported that one-third of the people of the South had placed themselves on diets. Ibid., p. 386.

60. David Reese, *The Prospects for North Korea's Survival*, Adelphi Paper 323, Oxford: International Institute for Strategic Studies, 1998, pp. 27–28.

61. Ibid., p. 25.

62. East Germany had 560,000 Soviet troops within its borders, North Korea had none. Without the massive Chinese intervention in late 1950, however, it is doubtful that North Korea would have survived the Korean War as an independent state.

63. The East German government wired the part of the country that could not receive broadcasts from the West for cable, so that it, too, could watch western television programs. By contrast, the radios in North Korea were capable of receiving only the government-controlled station.

64. Noland, op. cit., pp. 40–42.

65. The events are described in Oberdorfer, op. cit., Chapter 13. A history of the diplomatic dealings between the United States and North Korea over nuclear weapons is Leon V. Sigal, *Disarming Strangers: Nuclear Diplomacy With North Korea*, Princeton: Princeton University Press, 1998.

66. The figures are cited in Oberdorfer, op. cit., p. 315. "Any North Korean offensive might involve strategies against which the South cannot be effectively defended. . . . preemptive attack by *Frog* and *Scud* missiles armed with chemical, biological and, possibly, nuclear warheads. Multiple-rocket launchers and artillery could be used to direct massive volumes of high-explosive and chemical weapons against South Korean and US forces south of the DMZ." Tim Huxley and Susan Willett, *Arming East Asia*, Adelphi Paper 329, p. 70.

67. A partial list of North Korean provocations is in Reese, op. cit., pp. 39–40.

68. The United States and its allies sought to deny nuclear weapons to North Korea because possessing the weapons would give it unacceptable military leverage and thus political power. But they were constrained in using the most effective method of keeping North Korea non-nuclear—military force—because, with its enormous army and reputation for being willing to use it no matter what the consequences, North Korea already *had* considerable military leverage and political power.

69. The precedent was the "two plus four talks" that led to German unification. They are described in George Bush and Brent Scowcroft, *A World Transformed*, New York: Knopf, 1998, Chapters 10 and 11, and Philip Zelikow and Condoleezza Rice, *Germany Unified and Europe Transformed*, Cambridge, Mass.: Harvard University Press, 1995, Chapter 5.

70. In the 1970s South Korea began a nuclear weapons program. The United States exerted pressure to put a stop to it. Oberdorfer, op. cit., pp. 68–74.

71. One other possible feature of a settlement between the two Koreas commanded surprisingly broad support: the continuing presence of American troops. At the summit meeting of the two Korean leaders, in June 2000, the Northern leader, Kim Jong-il, was reported to have endorsed the continuation of an American presence on the Korean peninsula.

72. For China, having a friendly regime in power on the other side of the Yalu was valuable to enough to justify the resumption of modest aid to Pyongyang in 1995, to keep it from complete collapse. Beijing was also helpful in persuading the North Koreans to accept the terms on which the crisis of 1994 was settled. Reese, op. cit., pp. 13, 30; Oberdorfer, op. cit., p. 320.

73. Martin Wolf, "Korea's German lesson," *Financial Times*, May 28, 1996, p. 20. An extensive discussion of the costs of Korean unification is in Marcus Noland, editor, *Economic Integration of the Korean Peninsula*, Washington, D.C.: Institute for International Economics, 1998, Part III.

74. Reese, op. cit., p. 60.

6. POST-COLD WAR DISORDERS

1. Michael Howard, *The Lessons of History*, New Haven: Yale University Press, 1991, p. 33.

2. The five were Tanzania, Gabon, Ivory Coast, Zambia, and Haiti.

3. The exception to this pattern was Bangladesh, but it was an exception that proved the rule. What had been the eastern part of Pakistan was able to secede from the western part because the two were separated by a thousand miles and because the most powerful local state, India, intervened militarily on its behalf.

4. Siad Barre, the leader of one of several competing Somali clans, was initially the recipient of aid from the Soviet Union and then, after 1974, from the United States. Saddam, a Sunni Muslim in a country in which Shia Muslims and Kurds outnumbered Sunnis, also attracted support from both camps. His army was largely equipped by the Communist bloc but he bought additional arms from France and received credits from the United States. Tito was the dictator of a federation that recognized six distinct official nations. After Nikita Khrushchev repaired Stalin's breach with the Yugoslav Communist Party, the Soviet Union sold weapons to the Yugoslav Army. But because Tito's state was seen as a bulwark against Soviet expansion southward, the West furnished dollars to the Yugoslav treasury.

5. The conflict in the Congo, in geographic terms the largest in the first post-Cold War

decade, had a similar cause. The rule of its dictator, Mobutu Sese Seko (originally Joseph Mobutu), had attracted a number of challenges during the Cold War. "But then [his regime's] failings had been compensated by outside forces, as the US, Belgium, France, Morocco, and the United Nations leapt to the rescue of a country regarded as a bulwark against Communism. By 1996, the end of the cold war finally registered. The US and Belgium, Zaire's former colonial master, were sick of Mr. Mobutu. And after the criticism poured on France for its 1994 intervention in Rwanda, Paris no longer dared to launch a solo rescue operation." Michela Wrong, "End of an era in Africa's mineral treasure house," *Financial Times*, May 5, 1997, p. 4.

6. "Of the 86 violent conflicts recorded by the UN between 1989 and 1997 only three involved war between states: the rest were wars within states and were usually caused by inter-ethnic and inter-communal conflict." Dominic Lieven, *Empire: The Russian Empire and Its Rivals*, New Haven: Yale University Press, 2000, p. 368.

7. "Africans are not fighting over boundaries. Wars are raging because many states have become hollow entities. Governments cannot exercise basic control over their territories, let alone carry out other functions of a modern state. There are 15 active conflicts in Africa today, but only that between Ethiopia and Eritrea can be properly described as a border conflict. The problem is not boundaries but state failure." Marina Ottaway, "Keep out of Africa," *Financial Times*, February 25, 1999, p. 14.

8. The distinction between anarchy and war was not always clear-cut. The wars of secession on the territory of the former Yugoslavia were waged not by trained, disciplined soldiers but by loosely organized bands of armed thugs bent on mayhem and plunder. They were not much different from the groups that terrorized much of Africa. (See John Mueller, "The Banality of Ethnic War," Paper presented to the 2000 annual meeting of the American Political Science Association, Washington, D.C., July 26.) All over the world an amorphous kind of "low-intensity conflict" appeared more frequently than formal modern warfare. Martin van Creveld, *The Transformation of War*, Cambridge, England: Cambridge University Press, 1999, p. 20.

9. See Chapter 7.

10. One of the most prominent theories of nationalism, that of Ernest Gellner, considers it to be the product of the mass literacy in a single standardized language that the nineteenth century European state sought to impose on its population through universal schooling in order to create the kind of workforce necessary for an industrial economy. Gellner, *Nations and Nationalism*, Oxford, England: Blackwell, 1983.

11. There is certainly an affinity, if not a necessary connection, between democracy and nationally or ethnically homogeneous states. Democracy requires the willingness to be outvoted. People are willing to be outvoted if they believe they will not suffer while in the minority. They are more likely to believe this to the extent that the majority is like them.

12. The exceptions were Germany and Japan, where there were permanent residents—Turks in Germany, Koreans in Japan—who were not eligible for full citizenship. People who were not American or British or French did, of course, immigrate to the United States, Britain, and France, but they were then invited, indeed expected, to assume the relevant national identity through assimilation.

13. Here the traditional method of border delineation had an advantage. It was simple to practice. Borders were placed where monarchs said they should be. Monarchical regimes enforced them. The populace had no say in the matter. Paul Schroeder, *The Transformation of European Politics, 1763–1848*, New York: Oxford University Press, 1992, pp. 17–18.

14. A brief overview of the history of the international norms for border determination is in Michael Mandelbaum, "Introduction" to Mandelbaum, editor, *The New European Diasporas: National Minorities and Conflict in Eastern Europe*, New York: The Council on Foreign Relations, 2000, pp. 10–14.

15. Not coincidentally, the French term for such a salad is "macedoine," after the heterogeneous former Yugoslav republic of Macedonia.

16. While the term originated in the 1990s, the practice was considerably older, dating back at least to the nineteenth century. (See Lieven, op. cit., pp. 183, 213.) It became an all-too-familiar feature of the dissolution of multinational empires in the twentieth century. The first instance was the exchange of populations between Greece and Turkey in the early 1920s. In numerical terms, the ethnic cleansings on the territory of the former Yugoslavia were not history's worst. More people were killed or uprooted in the wake of the partition of the British empire in South Asia into India and Pakistan in 1947. Probably the worst of the twentieth century episodes was the expulsion of ethnic Germans from Eastern Europe after World War II. As many as 12 million people were driven out of their homes; one million may have died (Mark Mazower, *Dark Continent: Europe's Twentieth Century*, London: Allen Lane the Penguin Press, 1998, p. 220). Terrible though the practice is, it can also contribute to political stability over the long term, as it apparently did in Poland. See Mandelbaum, "Conclusion" to Mandelbaum, op. cit., p. 294–295.

17. By one count fewer than ten percent of sovereign states consist predominantly of a single nation. Walker Connor, *Ethnonationalism*, Princeton: Princeton University Press, 1994, p. 96.

18. The decision to bestow sovereignty on the largest constituent units of the Soviet Union and Yugoslavia can be seen as "a compromise between the impossibility, and from many points of view the undesirability, of retaining the communist multinational states, on the one hand, and the need, on the other, for as consistent and readily applicable a principle of sovereignty as possible in order to minimize the disruption and violence that making legitimate the revision of borders would inevitably provoke." Mandelbaum, "Introduction" to Mandelbaum, editor, op. cit., p. 13.

19. One example, among the many that could be cited, was the conflict in Sri Lanka between the majority Sinhalese Buddhists and minority Tamil Hindus and Christians. The country's president "has recognized that a return to a unitary state controlled by Sinhala political parties will not succeed. She has offered to devolve powers to regions. But which powers and how many, and to what regions?" Robert I. Rotberg, editor, *Creating Peace in Sir Lanka: Civil War and Reconciliation*, Washington, D.C.: The Brookings Institution, 1999, p. 12. An overview of the issue is provided by Ted Robert Gurr, *People versus States: Minorities at Risk in the New Century*, Washington, D.C.: United States Institute of Peace Press, 2000, Chapters 1, 5, 6, and 8.

20. Some features of nineteenth-century governance in the multinational Ottoman and Habsburg empires anticipate twentieth-century schemes for autonomy. Lieven, op. cit., pp. 150–151, 160–161, 184–185.

21. Mazower, op. cit., pp. 54–55; C. A. Macartney, *National States and National Minorities*, New York: Russell and Russell, 1934; reprinted, 1968.

22. Such was the case, for example, in Ethiopia. "By dangling the right to secede in front of the provinces, [the government in] Addis [Ababa] hoped to defuse regional tensions and keep Ethiopia together. But critics say the scheme proved a sham, as locally stationed [government] cadres maintained rigid central control." Michela Wrong, "Eritrea conflict puts Ethiopian prime minister in firing line," *Financial Times*, July 17,

1998, p. 10. "There are some obvious and nonobvious reasons for the unpopularity of parceling out sovereign power in divided societies . . . those who have all of state power within their reach have no incentive to take a large fraction of it and give it away. The most likely motive advanced, the awareness by leaders of the risk of mutual destruction, is based on a time horizon not generally employed in the calculations of political leaders . . ." Donald Horowitz, "Self-Determination: Politics, Philosophy, and Law," in Ian Shapiro and Will Kymlicka, editors, *Ethnicity and Group Rights*, New York: New York University Press, 1997, p. 439.

23. Post-Cold War state failure and the violence to which it led occasioned a burst of scholarly inquiry into causes and cures, the most comprehensive example of which was the work of the Carnegie Commission on Preventing Deadly Conflict, sponsored by the Carnegie Corporation of New York. Its final report, *Preventing Deadly Conflict*, was issued in 1997.

24. Javier Perez de Cuellar: "We are clearly witnessing what is probably an irresistible shift in public attitudes toward the belief that the defense of the oppressed in the name of morality should prevail over frontiers and legal documents." "Secretary-General's Address at the University of Bordeaux," Bordeaux, France, April 24, 1991, United Nations Press Release SG/SM 4560, p. 6. Boutros Boutros-Ghali: "The time of absolute and exclusive sovereignty has passed." Boutros Boutros-Ghali, *An Agenda for Peace: Preventive Diplomacy, Peace-making, and Peace-keeping*, New York: United Nations, 1992, p. 9. Kofi Annan: "Even national sovereignty can be set aside if it stands in the way of the [UN] Security Council's overriding duty to preserve international peace and security." "The Secretary General Reflects on 'Intervention' in Thirty-Fifty Annual Ditchley Foundation Lecture," UN Press Release SG/SM 6613, June 26, 1998, p. 2.

25. Quoted in "The Clinton Doctrine," *The Weekly Standard*, July 5/July 12, 1999, p. 2.

26. "The United Nations launched more peacekeeping operations between 1989 and 1994 than it had in its first forty-three years." Terrence Lyons and Ahmad I. Samatar, *State Collapse: Multilateral Intervention and Strategies for Political Reconciliation*, Washington, D.C: The Brookings Institution, Brookings Occasional Papers, 1995, p. 4.

27. UN Secretary-General Boutros Boutros-Ghali, cited in Michael Mandelbaum, "The Reluctance to Intervene," *Foreign Policy* 95, Summer, 1994, p. 11.

28. The disinterested military operations were given appropriately therapeutic titles: "Provide Comfort" in Northern Iraq, "Restore Hope" in Somalia.

29. The most important American intervention in the post-Cold War era occurred in Mexico. But the threat against which it was launched, and the method of intervention, were economic rather than political or military. In 1994 the American Treasury Department provided funds to prop up the tottering Mexican currency, the peso. Washington acted both to protect investors north of the border and to prevent an economic collapse in Mexico that could have sent thousands of impoverished Mexicans across it.

30. ". . . it turns out in practice that the new universal dispensation [for humanitarian intervention] can only apply to Serbia and a mere handful of other states that meet very exacting requirements; they must be sufficiently weak to be easily defeated, yet sufficiently advanced to present worthwhile targets for no-casualty bombardment . . . It can hardly be argued that Serbia was attacked [by NATO in 1999 for the violations of human rights in Kosovo] because it was the world's foremost violator of human rights. In that competition, Serbia is far down the list." Edward Luttwak, "No-score war," *TLS*, July 14, 2000, p. 11.

31. "In Africa, an estimated 1.5 million people have died in Sudan; 1m in Rwanda; over 500,000 in Angola; 150,000 in Liberia; 80,000 in Algeria; and 15,000 in Sierra Leone. In Ethiopia and Eritrea, some 40,000 have been slaughtered since the beginning of this year." Quentin Peel, "Forgotten wars," *Financial Times*, May 6, 1999, p. 14.

32. "The country still lacks nearly all the markings of a normal state. It has no national customs authority, no national border police, no working supreme court . . . The few central institutions Bosnia does have, like the presidency, are themselves divided along ethnic lines." Neil King Jr., "An Army of Outsiders Tries to Piece Bosnia Back Together Again," *Wall Street Journal Europe*, August 26, 1998, p. 8.

33. France did maintain a consistently high level of interest in Africa during the Cold War, managing a sphere of influence of former French colonies on the continent. French officials advised local governments, none of them a democracy, and French troops enforced order where necessary. French firms enjoyed special economic status and the French government provided economic assistance and guaranteed the local currency, the African franc. But in the wake of the Cold War the French commitment flagged. In 1994 the French government devalued the African franc, a sign that it was no longer willing to pay to prop it up. And France did not stop the chaos and bloodshed that enveloped Rwanda in 1994 and the Congo in 1997.

34. The inconsistency that marked the post-Cold War practice of intervention was not unprecedented. When, in 1850, one member of the United States Senate criticized the Habsburg empire for suppressing Hungary, another Senator took the critic to task for sparing a worse but more powerful offender against national freedom, Russia. (Arthur Schlesinger, Jr., "Human Rights and the American Tradition," *Foreign Affairs*, 56:3, 1979, p. 506–7.) The same thing could have been said (and indeed was said: see note 31 above) of the American government 150 years later when it unleashed a campaign of aerial bombardment against the hapless, although scarcely innocent, government of Serbia in retaliation for its mistreatment of Albanians in the province of Kosovo while saying nothing about the far more powerful government of Russia's devastation of one of its provinces, Chechnya.

35. "Values are stirred up when people get upset by what they see on CNN: They say, 'We have to do something, we must do something about this ethnic cleansing, we must do something about this starvation, we must do something to bring peace here, we've got to do something.' And 'something' means using U.S. military forces. But decisions are driven by what is on television in a way that interests and security protection are not." Former U.S. Secretary of Defense Les Aspin, "Challenges to Values-based Military Intervention," Washington, D.C.: U.S. Institute of Peace, February, 1995, p. 3.

36. Johanna Neuman, *Lights, Camera, War*, New York: St. Martin's Press, 1996, p. 14. John Mueller, "The Common Sense," *The National Interest*, 47, Spring 1997.

37. The American military deployments in the Balkans were designed first and foremost to protect the troops, a priority at odds with what is generally the purpose of deploying military forces in the first place. Care with the lives of soldiers is, of course, important for any commander but to make this the highest, indeed the absolute, priority is, to say the least, unusual.

38. A survey of American opinion taken in 1995 found that "Self-interest has consistently dominated the public's assessment of foreign policy priorities over the past decade. But support for many of the more humanitarian goals among both the public and leaders has declined to the lowest level in two decades." John Rielly, "The Public Mood at Mid-Decade," *Foreign Policy*, Spring 1995, p. 81. That is, American public

support for humanitarian intervention was actually *lower* in the post-Cold War period than during the Cold War.

39. This is true for combat. Surveys taken in World War II showed that considerations of group solidarity—"sticking together, loyalty to comrades, pride in outfit, etc."—were more important motives for fighting than "idealistic motives—patriotism and concern about war aims." Samuel Stouffer, et al., *The American Soldier: Volume II: Combat and Its Aftermath*, Princeton: Princeton University Press, 1949, pp. 110–111. The exceptions to the rule of social distance stand out. They are often considered admirable, even heroic. But most people are not heroic.

40. Michael Mandelbaum, "Foreign Policy as Social Work," *Foreign Affairs*, January/February 1996, pp. 19–20.

41. In the post-Cold War era order in the world's periphery had the properties of an international collective good. The important members of the international system favored it in principle. It was usually possible, although not always easy, to find a basis for settling conflicts there on which they could agree. But it was not possible to agree on how to enforce the agreed-on settlement. The vexing question was not what to do but how to do it, not who would govern but who would pay. "The most important obstacle to preventing deadly conflict today is the deficit of collective and individual preventive action, not an excess of illegitimate actions. The democracies have pursued collective abstinence as often as collective action." Graham Allison and Hisashi Owada, *The Responsibilities of Democracies in Preventing Deadly Conflict: Reflections and Recommendations*. Discussion Paper of the Carnegie Commission on Preventing Deadly Conflict, New York: The Carnegie Corporation of New York, July, 1999, p. 3.

42. The Clinton administration, the first confined entirely to the post-Cold War era, was populated by people for whom humanitarian intervention had the highest priority. One of them, W. Anthony Lake, lamented, "When I wake up every morning and look at the headlines and the stories and the images on television of these conflicts, I want to work to end every conflict, I want to work to save every child out there." (Quoted in Elaine Sciolino, "New U.S. Peacekeeping Policy De-emphasizes Role of the U.N.," *The New York Times*, May 6, 1994, p. A1.) During Lake's time in office the United States did not work to end every conflict and save every child. The obstacle to a serious effort to do so was not a lack of material resources but rather the absence of the requisite public support. The obstacle to Lake's vision of American foreign policy was democracy in America.

43. Ted Robert Gurr, *People versus States: Minorities at Risk in the New Century*, Washington, D.C.: United States Institute of Peace Press, 2000, Chapters 2, 8.

7. THE DRAGONS' LAIR

1. The point is elegantly made in Bernard Lewis, *The Middle East: A Brief History of the Last 2,000 Years*, New York: Scribner, 1995, pp. 1–18.

2. The three largest were Iran, Iraq, and Saudi Arabia, the last of them possessing fully twenty-five percent of the world's total. The others were the tiny oil monarchies of Kuwait, Bahrain, Qatar, the United Arab Emirates, and Oman.

3. It was not a threat to the Soviet Union, which harbored considerable reserves of oil beneath its own territory. Many of the oil-producing parts of the Soviet Union were located outside the Russian Federation, however, in what became, after 1991, independent states.

4. The official aim of the Gulf War of 1991, which was successfully achieved, was to vindicate the first principle of international law, the principle of sovereignty itself. Iraq had invaded, occupied, and announced the annexation of Kuwait, an internationally recognized sovereign state. But had tiny Kuwait not sat on a pool of oil, and had it not been located next to Saudi Arabia, a country even richer in oil deposits, Iraq's invasion would probably not have triggered the formation of a broad international coalition that sent an expeditionary force to the region to evict the Iraqi troops. Of course, had Kuwait not been a treasure trove of oil the Iraqi dictator Saddam Hussein might not have considered it worth seizing.

5. Robert Lieber, *The Oil Decade: Conflict and Cooperation in the West*, New York: Praeger, 1983, p. 4.

6. Although hailed at the time as a great victory for the "developing" countries, this was not precisely a transfer from rich to poor. Some of the oil states already had per capita incomes that were high by the world's standards, while some of the countries hardest hit, because least able to afford oil at the higher prices, were located in the world's periphery, not its core. The oil shock contributed to the Third World debt crisis of the 1980s.

7. Robert Manning and Amy Meyers Jaffe, *Foreign Affairs*, p. 20. In 1980 the United States spent approximately nine percent of its gross domestic product on oil; in 1998 the figure was three percent. "Oil Price Surge Raises Fears of Inflation Spike," *The New York Times*, February 21, 2000, p. A16.

8. "In 1970, North America consumed 16m barrels of petroleum a day. Today it consumes 22m barrels. In 1970 the western European nations got through 12m barrels a day. This year they will consume 15m. In 1970 Japan consumed 4m barrels. Today it is 6m. . . . Moreover, to obtain oil, the western nations as a group rely more on imports than in the 1970s.

   What is meant, I suspect, by the commonly repeated assertions about our lower reliance on petroleum, is that now, in 2000, we obtain more units of gross domestic product per unit of petroleum . . . [I]f we had the income and lifestyle of our parents' generation then we would today be less dependent on petroleum. We do not, of course." Andrew Oswald, "West more dependent than ever on oil," *Financial Times*, November 1, 2000, p. 18.

9. An assessment of the possible consequences of rising Asian energy consumption is in Robert Manning, *The Asian Energy Factor: Myths and Dilemmas of Energy, Security, and the Pacific Future*, A Council on Foreign Relations Book, New York: Palgrave, 2000.

10. Because it did not separate church and state, because religious faith and secular power were fused throughout its history, Islam could serve as the basis for political mobilization in a way that Christianity could not. On this point see Bernard Lewis, *The Multiple Identities of the Middle East*, New York: Schocken Books, 1998, pp., 27–28, 39.

11. Western political intrusion predated World War I. France established an imperial presence in North Africa and Britain came to dominate Egypt in the second half of the nineteenth century.

12. The standard work on the subject is Fouad Ajami, *The Arab Predicament: Arab Political Thought and Practice Since 1967*, New York: Cambridge University Press, 1981.

13. Lawrence Freedman and Efraim Karsh, *The Gulf Conflict, 1990–1991: Diplomacy and War in the New World Order*. Princeton: Princeton University Press, pp. 37–41.

14. The coalition forces attacked the Iraqi nuclear weapon program as well, the goal of destroying which was a more important source of public support in the United States for the war than the liberation of Kuwait.

15. During the Cold War Moscow's ties with Baghdad, which had shriveled by 1990, might have given the Soviet leadership the leverage, and the fear of triggering a confrontation with the West might have supplied the incentive, to prevent Iraq from invading a neighboring country. True, the Soviet leadership had done no such thing a decade earlier when Saddam had attacked Iran. By that time, however, the Islamic revolution had already put Iran at odds with the West. The attack on Kuwait, by contrast, threatened a crucial American ally, Saudi Arabia.

16. The war was fought principally by American armed forces using, for the first time on an appreciable scale, "smart weapons" that incorporated the advanced information-processing technology of the last part of the twentieth century. These were the result of an unintentional collaboration, and unplanned division of labor, among three successive American presidential administrations. The weapons were designed by the technology-conscious Pentagon of the Carter administration in the 1970s, purchased with the increases in defense spending in the early part of the Reagan presidency in the 1980s, and used by Reagan's successor, George Bush, who presided over the end of the conflict for which they were designed and built in the first place. The contribution of each administration was indispensable and it is unlikely that any one of them would have done what the other two did.

17. Michael Howard, *The Continental Commitment*, London: Temple Smith, 1972.

18. This was not to be confused with the "double containment" practiced in Europe during the Cold War, which embraced both an adversary, the Soviet Union, and an ally, West Germany. Iran and Iraq were both adversaries.

19. The small force that the United States did keep in Saudi Arabia after the 1991 Gulf War became the object of a terrorist attack. On June 15, 1996, a truck bomb exploded at an apartment complex for American military personnel in the Saudi city of Dahran, killing nineteen Americans and injuring 372. Moreover, evicting this token presence was one of the expressed aims of Al Qaeda, the terrorist organization responsible for the attacks on New York and Washington of September 11, 2001.

20. The attacks of September 11, 2001, threatened to change this. Fourteen of the nineteen men who hijacked four American airplanes on that day were Saudis. Osama bin Laden, the head of the Al-Qaeda network that recruited, trained, and sponsored them, was born, raised, and educated in the Saudi kingdom. The Saudi government had revoked his citizenship but he had continued to receive generous support from Saudi citizens. The uproar in the United States caused by the attacks cast a harsh light on the American alliance with the Saudi monarchy and generated a measure of public opposition to it for the first time.

21. "The combined economies of the six states (of the Gulf Cooperation Council) are over 15 times that of Iraq. (Saudi Arabia and Kuwait alone have a combined economic output that is almost 11 times that of Iraq.)" Ivan Eland, *Tilting at Windmills: Post-Cold War Military Threats to U.S. Security*, Washington, D.C.: The Cato Institute, Policy Analysis No. 332, February 8, 1999, p. 12.

22. The casual observer might find this comparison all the more powerful on the grounds that the Gulf monarchies, with their massive oil revenues, were far wealthier than Israel. Once this had been so. But by the beginning of the twenty-first century, due to the combination of Israel's extraordinary economic success and the steady decline in the price of oil, it was no longer true. On a per capita basis Israelis were considerably wealthier than Saudis.

23. "The Pentagon pays out between $30 billion and $60 billion a year for defense of the Gulf (depending on how you cost it), a formidable sum for protecting the import into

the United States of some $30 billion worth of oil. Thus Americans pay what amounts to a substantial hidden gasoline tax that Europeans and Japanese, benefiting from American willingness to 'carry the burden,' largely escape." Graham E. Fuller and Ian O. Lesser, "Persian Gulf Myths," *Foreign Affairs*, May-June 1997, p. 43. According to another estimate, the gap between what the United States paid for defense and what it received in oil was even wider: "We import almost nothing except oil from the gulf, but what we pay for imports—about $11 billion a year—is about one-fifth of the cost of our military presence there." Shibley Telhami and Michael O'Hanlon, "Europe's Oil, Our Troops," *The New York Times*, December 30, 1995, p. 27. In response the Europeans and Japanese could note that the United States was by far the biggest and most profligate consumer of energy, in 1999 consuming 20 million of the 75 million barrel daily worldwide consumption of oil. Robert Corzine and Hillary Durgin, "Running on empty," *Financial Times*, February 26/27, 2000, p. 8.

24. The case that these, particularly biological weapons, pose serious post-Cold War threats, especially to the United States, is made in Richard K. Betts, "The New Threat of Mass Destruction," *Foreign Affairs*, January/February, 1998. A different, more skeptical, view is offered in John Mueller, "Weapons of Mass Destruction and the Escalation of Language," Department of Political Science, University of Rochester, December 2, 1998, and Jonathan B. Tucker and Amy Sands, "An Unlikely Threat," *The Bulletin of the Atomic Scientists*, 55:4, July/August, 1999.

25. See Michael Mandelbaum, *The Nuclear Revolution: International Politics Before and After Hiroshima*, New York: Cambridge University Press, 1981, Chapter 2, and Leonard Cole, "The Poison Weapons Taboo: Biology, Culture and Policy," *Politics and the Life Sciences*, September 1998.

26. Saddam Hussein enhanced his reputation as a particularly vile dictator by launching a chemical attack against the Kurdish village of Halabja in March 1988. The village was located in the northern part of what the world recognized as Iraq, giving Saddam the distinction of having gassed citizens of the country that he himself ruled.

27. Clive Cookson, "Deadly concerns," *Financial Times*, August 27, 1999, p. 14; Tucker and Sands, *op. cit.*, pp. 47–49.

28. Supplementing the work of the Nuclear Suppliers' Group was the Zangger Committee, which was "made up of 33 nuclear-exporting countries and provides a list to the IAEA of items which, if exported to an NPT member, should trigger the application of IAEA safeguards; the group also exchanges information on exports that are outside the treaty." "The desperate efforts to block the road to doomsday," *The Economist*, June 6, 1998, p. 22.

29. George Perkovich, *India's Nuclear Bomb: The Impact on Global Proliferation*, Berkeley: The University of California Press, 1999, p. 300.

30. The opposite case—the more the better—also had a basis in logic and history. The diffusion of nuclear weapons, according to what was distinctly a minority view in the West, would impose on adversaries the world over the prudence and caution that marked the nuclear-influenced Soviet-American rivalry of the Cold War. This point is argued and rebutted in Scott D. Sagan and Kenneth N. Waltz, *The Spread of Nuclear Weapons: A Debate*, New York: W. W. Norton, 1995.

31. A high-level committee within the American government convened in 1965 to consider how to deal with the prospect of proliferation, the report of which was influential in laying the basis for the NPT, concluded: "as additional nations obtained nuclear weapons, our diplomatic and military influence would wane, and strong pressures would arise to retreat to isolation to avoid the risk of involvement in nuclear war." Quoted in Perkovich, op. cit., p. 102.

32. Michael Mandelbaum, "Lessons of the Next Nuclear War," *Foreign Affairs*, March/April 1995.
33. India had detonated a nuclear explosion in 1974 but had claimed that this was for peaceful purposes. In physical terms the 1974 blast was identical to a bomb test.
34. The history of the Israeli nuclear program to 1970 is the subject of Avner Cohen, *Israel and the Bomb*, New York: Columbia University Press, 1998.
35. Don Oberdorfer, *The Two Koreas: A Contemporary History*, Reading, Mass.: Addison-Wesley, 1997, pp. 69–72, and David M. Lampton, *Same Bed Different Dreams: Managing U.S.-China Relations, 1989–2000*, Berkeley: The University of California Press, 2001, p. 210.
36. Mitchell Reiss, *Bridled Ambition: Why Countries Constrain Their Nuclear Capabilities*, Washington, D.C.: The Woodrow Wilson Center Press, 1995, Chapters 2, 4. Argentina and Brazil also abandoned nuclear weapon programs after changes of regime. Neither had actually produced a bomb. Ibid., Chapter 3.
37. India differed from the others in that its motives for crossing the nuclear threshold in 1998 were more domestic than strategic. The Indian government justified its nuclear tests as a response to the nuclear arsenal of its neighbor and sometime adversary China. But China had become a nuclear power in 1964, a full thirty-four years before India did. In fact, the national nuclear history India's most closely resembled was that of France, which also joined the nuclear club as much for reasons of domestic pride and international prestige as for calculations concerning security. For the last two decades of the Cold War India was aligned with the Soviet Union. But at different points in the second half of the twentieth century Indian officials did suggest that an American security guarantee would dissuade them from pursuing nuclear weapons. Perkovich, op. cit., p. 86–8, 119.
38. Taiwan and South Korea were located in the East Asian wing of the world's core, making their acquisition of nuclear weapons more disruptive than in the case of the other orphans. For this reason the American commitment to their security was stronger than it was for other "orphans," approaching the intensity of the commitment inherent in NATO and the Japanese-American Security Treaty.
39. The list included India, Pakistan, and Israel. Taiwan and South Korea were capable of developing missiles.
40. Cuba qualified in all respects save one. The United States would not permit even the beginnings of a nuclear weapon program there. The most extensive assessment of the concept of rogue states, which finds it unhelpful as a guide to policymaking, is Robert S. Litwack, *Rogue States and U.S. Foreign Policy*, Washington, D.C.: The Woodrow Wilson Center Press, 2000.
41. Without Iraq's invasion of Kuwait it is doubtful that the United States would have attacked that program. The only military operation of the twentieth century devoted exclusively to the prevention of nuclear proliferation was the Israeli air raid on Iraq's nuclear reactor in 1983.
42. Shlomo Aronson, "The Nuclear Dimension of the Arab-Israeli Conflict: The Case of the Yom Kippur War," *Jerusalem Journal of International Relations*, 7, no. 2, 1984.
43. It was possible that India would turn out, in the twenty-first century, to be the exception to this pattern. By testing a bomb and thereby pushing Pakistan to do the same, India reduced its margin of military superiority over its South Asian neighbor and rival, which was wider when neither country had nuclear weapons than when both did. Nuclearization had the potential to hurt Pakistan as well if it forced that country into an economically ruinous arms competition with its larger, richer adversary. And if the course of events in South Asia in the twenty-first century led to a nuclear war

between them, the verdict on India's decision to acquire the bomb would, to understate the matter, be decisively negative.

44. The phrase comes from the nineteenth century. Walter Laqueur, *The New Terrorism: Fanaticism and the Arms of Mass Destruction*, New York: Oxford University Press, 2000 paperback, p. 140.

45. The nineteenth century European and North American anarchists and other radicals who attacked public officials sought to provoke a harsh response that would expose what they considered to be the essential repressiveness of the political systems they served. Similarly, Yasir Arafat sponsored acts of Palestinian terrorism against Israeli civilians, even as Israel offered to negotiate the establishment of a Palestinian state, hoping that the inevitable Israeli response would trigger a regional war, or the intervention of Western countries, or both, scenarios in which he believed he could make territorial and political gains.

46. Laqueur, op. cit., pp. 10–11. The willingness of terrorists to give up their own lives to carry out attacks also has a long history, dating at least to medieval times. Laqueur, op. cit., p. 140.

47. Ibid., p. 46.

48. Ibid., pp. 130–131, 150.

49. Ibid., p. 39.

50. Bin Laden "called on Muslims to kill 'Americans and their allies . . . in any country in which it is possible to do so.'" Fouad Ajami, "The Uneasy Imperium," in James F. Hoge Jr. and Gideon Rose, editors, *How Did This Happen? Terrorism and the New War*, New York: PublicAffairs, 2001, p. 20.

51. "In twenty armed conflicts proceeding at present in the world, Islam is involved in sixteen, or 80 percent. Of the thirteen United Nations peace missions in action at the present time, nine concern Muslim countries or interests. The proportion of Muslim involvement in terrorism could well be of a similar magnitude." Laqueur, op. cit., p. 129.

52. Bernard Lewis, "The Roots of Muslim Rage," *The Atlantic Monthly*, September 1990, p. 59.

53. Iraq and Iran also sponsored terrorist attacks against Americans: Iraq was implicated in the first attack on New York's World Trade Center, in 1993; Iran sponsored terrorists who took Americans hostage in Lebanon in the 1980s.

54. Ajami, "The Uneasy Imperium", p. 20.

55. Nadav Safran, *Saudi Arabia: The Ceaseless Quest for Security*, Cambridge, Mass.: Harvard University Press, 1985, Chapters 1 and 2.

56. More feasible for a terrorist organization would be to obtain fissionable material and find a way to release it in a populated area without making it explode. Such a "radiological" weapon would have the same poisonous effects as a chemical weapon.

57. "The extremists acquired modern means: frequent flyer miles, aviation and computer skills, ease in Western cities." Ajami, "The Uneasy Imperium", p. 17. Both also rely on the openness of Western societies, terrorist groups to infiltrate people to carry out acts of terrorism, would-be nuclear weapon states to glean the information and acquire the materials necessary to acquire a bomb.

58. Mark Huband and John Willman, "Holy war on the world," *Financial Times*, November 28, 2001, p. 6.

59. Some countries that offered sanctuary to terrorists, such as Taliban Afghanistan, Somalia, and Sudan, did not qualify as rogue states because they were too poor and disorganized to acquire nuclear weapons.

60. Lenin's Bolshevik Party, which seized power in the Russian capital in 1917 and consolidated it in a bloody civil war, did have some working class support. The relationship of Marx's theory to Marxism (or more properly Marxism-Leninism) in practice is a contentious one. At the least it may be said in Marx's defense that the second was not a perfectly faithful translation of the first. Nor, however, were the two entirely unrelated. Lenin's violent antipathy to his political enemies, and his conviction that he alone possessed the truth, also characterized the intellectual father of his movement.

61. These beliefs were to be found in the pronouncements of public officials, which, in Western democracies, are ordinarily exercises in stating what is unchallengeable. "After these four decades, then, there stands before the entire world one great and inescapable conclusion: Freedom leads to prosperity. Freedom replaces the ancient hatreds among nations with comity and peace." President Ronald Reagan, Address at the Brandenburg Gate in West Berlin, June 12, 1987.

    "Democracies create free markets that . . . make for far more reliable trading partners and are less likely to wage war on one another." President Bill Clinton, *A National Security Strategy of Engagement and Enlargement*, Washington, D.C.: U.S. Government Printing Office, 1996, p. 2.

    "Liberal economics and liberal democracy go hand in hand. Freedom, democracy, the rule of law, stability and prosperity are found most frequently in one another's company." Chris Patten (British Member of Parliament, Governor of Hong Kong, and Commissioner for Foreign Affairs of the European Union), *East and West*, London: Pan Books, 1999, p. 4.

62. Kant's definition of a republic was not precisely the same thing as the twenty-first century concept of democracy. See Chapter 8.

63. The task turned out to be formidably and unanticipatedly difficult, a point discussed in Chapter 10.

8. THE DEMOCRATIC PEACE

1. Quoted in Francis Fukuyama, *The End of History and the Last Man*, New York: Avon Books, 1992 paperback, p. 89.

2. The idea of an association of democracies, like so much else, had its origins in the Anglo-American world. At the end of the nineteenth century Great Britain, seeing its own power declining and that of the United States rising, sought to forge a partnership with its former colony, with which relations had been tense throughout the nineteenth century. (Dominic Lieven, *Empire: The Russian Empire and Its Rivals*, New Haven: Yale University Press, 2000, pp. 110–111.) The British effort began by emphasizing the biological affinity between the two countries: references to the "Anglo-Saxon race" were common. Kipling's poem urging his audience to take up "The White Man's Burden" was addressed to Americans. (Christopher Hitchens, *Blood, Class and Nostalgia: Anglo-American Ironies*, New York: Farrar, Straus and Giroux, 1989, Chapter 3.) As the twentieth century wore on, appeals to racial solidarity lost popularity and the emphasis shifted to common political values, which Churchill, in particular, emphasized.

3. World War I was billed in Great Britain and France as a war "against German militarism" and in the United States as a war "to make the world safe for democracy."

4. An early study is Rudolf J. Rummel, *Understanding Conflict and War. Volume 4. War, Power, Peace*, New York: Russell Sage, 1979. Perhaps the most widely read is Bruce M.

Russett, *Grasping the Democratic Peace*, Princeton: Princeton University Press, 1993. Also important is Spencer Weart, *Never At War: Why Democracies Will Not Fight One Another*, New Haven: Yale University Press, 1998. The literature is summarized in James Lee Ray, *Democracy and International Conflict*, Columbia, S.C.: University of South Carolina Press, 1995.

5. The doctrine of enlightened absolutism in eighteenth-century Europe "was a doctrine and method for increasing the power of the ruler and his bureaucratic servants over the state machine, his subjects, the economy, and the social groups resisting central authority. As such, enlightened absolutism directly increased the war-making potential of states (often its explicit purpose) and indirectly weakened traditional norms and restraints in international politics. It is no accident that enlightened absolutists ruled the most expansionist, aggressive great powers in the latter half of the eighteenth century." Paul W. Schroeder, *The Transformation of European Politics, 1763–1848*, New York: Oxford University Press, 1996 p.b. (first published, 1994), p. 50.

6. This is the argument of Joanne Gowa, *Ballots and Bullets: The Elusive Democratic Peace*, Princeton: Princeton University Press, 1999. See also Ray, op. cit., pp. 26, 203–204.

   The question at the heart of the critique is a technical, statistical one. Is the sample of democracies large enough, and are there enough cases of democratic non-belligerency before the Cold War, to conclude, on the basis of the laws of probability (the substitute, in the social sciences, for the experimental method by which the natural sciences arrive at their conclusions), that the association is not coincidental, that it is, to use the term of art, statistically significant?

   There is another potential difficulty with the statistical finding of a connection between democracy and peace. The statistical method of investigation presumes that different cases are comparable, that democracies in the nineteenth century are, for purposes of peaceful conduct, the same as democracies in the twentieth. To the extent that warlessness was a major factor in the peaceful conduct of democracies this assumption is not justified, since this cluster of attitudes and beliefs came to prominence only in the second half of the twentieth century. In Great Britain the prevailing attitude toward war at the end of the twentieth century was sharply different from what it had been at the end of the nineteenth. To the extent that warlessness is important, the statistical case covering two centuries linking democracy and peace is weakened. On the other hand, warlessness strengthens the case for the democratic peace even if the association holds only for the Cold War period. For it means that democratic nonbelligerency has at least two causes specific to that era. One, the Cold War itself, has disappeared. But the other, warlessness, persists, and so is a continuing source of peaceful conduct.

7. Jack Snyder, *From Voting to Violence: Democratization and Nationalist Conflict*, New York: W. W. Norton, 2000, p. 28.

8. The question cannot be addressed statistically; there are too few cases of common security. The connection can only be demonstrated "mechanically," by logical, empirical observations of the connections between the two.

9. The French "Declaration of the Rights of Man and the Citizen," issued on August 26, 1789, declared that the "basis of all sovereignty lies, essentially, in the Nation" and that "legislation is the expression of the general will in which all citizens have a right to participate." The significance is noted in S. E. Finer, *The History of Government from the Earliest Times: Volume III, Empires, Monarchies and the Modern State*, Oxford, England: Oxford University Press, 1997, pp. 1538–1542. The American Revolution also involved the principle of popular sovereignty. The Declaration of Independence was issued in the name of "the people of the United States."

10. The principle received its fullest elaboration in the world's most famous constitution, the one written in the United States at the end of the eighteenth century that has been in effect, with a few modifications, ever since. The American constitution imposed on the executive both procedural limits, through the separation of powers, and substantive limits, by means of the Bill of Rights.

11. This was the basis of James Madison's verdict in Federalist 10: "A pure democracy—by which I mean a society consisting of a small number of citizens, who assemble and administer the government in person, can admit no cure for the mischiefs of faction . . . hence it is that such democracies have ever been found incompatible with personal security or the rights of property." According to S. E. Finer, the prevailing pre-twentieth century view of the fate of Greek democracy had no basis in fact. Finer, op. cit., *Volume I, Ancient Monarchies and Empires*, p. 362. In the twenty-first century the term *democracy* had passed beyond reproach in the West. But the old negative association lived on the aura surrounding the term *populist*, which connoted, or could connote, the mindless, dangerous power of uninformed and unchecked public sentiment.

12. Both Mill and Benjamin Constant, the well-known French liberal of the early nineteenth century, were wary of universal suffrage. Finer, op. cit., Volume III, p. 1575. Practicing politicians were of the same view: "If you establish a democracy . . . you will in due season have great impatience of the public burdens, combined in due season with great increase of the public expenditures . . . wars entered into from passion and not from reason. You will in due season find your property is less valuable and your freedom less complete." Walter Russell Mead, *Special Providence: American Foreign Policy and How It Changed the World*, New York: Knopf, 2001, pp. 46–47, quoting Benjamin Disraeli in 1830.

13. Finer, op. cit., Volume III, p. 1638.

14. "In the years between 1880 and 1914 ruling classes discovered that parliamentary democracy, despite their fears, proved itself to be quite compatible with the political and economic stability of capitalist regimes." Eric Hobsbawm, *The Age of Empire: 1875–1914*, New York: Pantheon, 1987, p. 110. The point is cleverly made by John Mueller in what he calls a "fanciful dialogue between a pair of citizens in a prospective democracy."

    "How many voters really know what's going on?"

    "Beats me, not many probably."

    "Wouldn't it be better to keep the ignorant and the incompetent from voting?"

    "Tried that. Doesn't seem to make all that much difference so they just let everybody vote." Mueller, *Capitalism, Democracy, and Ralph's Pretty Good Grocery*, Princeton: Princeton University Press, 1999, p. 193–194.

15. Fareed Zakaria called such countries "illiberal democracies." "The Rise of Illiberal Democracy," *Foreign Affairs*, 76:6, November/December 1997, especially p. 28.

16. "If the consent of the citizens is required in order to decide that war should be declared . . . nothing is more natural than that they would be very cautious in commencing such a poor game, decreeing for themselves all the calamities of war. Among the latter would be: having to fight, having to pay the costs of war from their own resources, having painfully to repair the devastation war leaves behind, and, to fill up the measure of evils, load themselves with a heavy national debt that would embitter peace itself and that can never be liquidated on account of constant wars in the future." Immanuel Kant, *Perpetual Peace*, Indianapolis: Bobbs-Merrill, 1957, pp. 12–13.

17. This came to be known as the "structural" version of the democratic theory, and was initially set out by Kant. See ibid. See also Weart, op. cit., pp. 5–6.

18. Thus the view of Israeli Prime Minister Benjamin Netanyahu: "In the Middle East,

peace is based on security and the ability to deter war. The aspects of peace that we are all so enamored of—the idea of normalization, economic exchanges, people-to-people contacts, cultural contacts and so on—those are an added bonus. They can be taken away at any time because of the nature of the regimes around us. They are not built into a process that is irreversible. They can be reversed at any time by the whim of a ruler." "Special Policy Forum Report: Israeli Prime Minister Benjamin Netanyahu," *Peacewatch* Number 165, Washington, D.C.: The Washington Institute for Near East Policy, May 18, 1998, p. 1.

19. The two solutions are in an important way opposites. The first ratifies a "civic" definition of nationalism, according to which all citizens are politically equal. The second accepts that ethnic or national differences are pronounced, pervasive, and divisive enough to warrant constitutional acknowledgment. The first seeks, that is, to overcome, bypass, or ignore group differences, the second recognizes, accommodates, and builds on them. The difference is explored in Rogers Brubaker, *Citizenship and Nationhood in France and Germany*, Cambridge: Mass.: Harvard University Press, 1992.

20. It is to the presence of constitutional norms and practices that Snyder seems to be referring when he asserts that "well-established" or "consolidated" democracies are less likely to breed national conflict than democracies that are not well-established. Snyder, *op. cit.*, pp. 20, 26, 195.

21. Important statements of this version of the democratic peace argument are in Weart, op. cit., and John M. Owen, *Liberal Peace, Liberal War: American Politics and International Security*. Ithaca: Cornell University Press, 1998. "Americans managed to retain the multilateral conception of security that they had developed in World War II . . . because Truman's foreign policy, like Roosevelt's military strategy, reflected the habits of domestic democratic politics. Negotiation, compromise, and consensus-building abroad came naturally to statesmen steeped in the uses of such practices at home." John Lewis Gaddis, *We Now Know: Rethinking Cold War History*. New York: Oxford University Press, 1997, p. 50. The same point is made, for other Cold War episodes, on pp. 288–289.

22. The term is from Samuel P. Huntington, *The Third Wave: Democratization in the Late Twentieth Century*, Norman, Okla.: The University of Oklahoma Press, 1991.

23. In 1970 there were forty-four democracies; in 1980, fifty-six; in 1991, ninety-one. Cited in Snyder, op cit., p. 313. A graphic depiction of the progress of democracy in the modern era is provided in Huntington, op. cit., p. 14.

24. In the 1990s in sub-Saharan Africa, for example, forty-two out of fifty countries held elections, although few met the standards for liberal politics normal in the Western core. "Africa's democratic joys and tribulations," *The Economist*, June 15, 1999, p. 43.

25. Democracy was also imposed, by liberal colonial powers in India, for example, or liberal occupiers, as in Japan. But Indian and Japanese democracy count as voluntary because, once the British and the Americans left, the two countries were free to reject, but instead retained, the political system they had brought. Other countries—Nigeria, Pakistan, the Philippines—did not consistently retain it.

26. "By the 1970s and 1980s . . . not to be democratic was to be benighted and obsolete . . . Democratization emerged as the only acceptable political agenda in Europe and the Americas." Charles S. Maier, *Dissolution: The Crisis of Communism and the End of East Germany*, Princeton: Princeton University Press, 1997, p. 57.

27. "But this grand future for English parliamentarism was not due to its superior techniques or wisdom in medieval times compared to very many of the *Cortes*, or *paral-*

menti, or the *Riksdag* and the like. Its peculiar formation, its survival and supremacy over the executive and then, by historical accident, its export to the thirteen American colonies were, none of them, foreordained. Very much the reverse." Finer, op. cit., *Volume II, The Intermediate Ages,* p. 1051.

28. "The American revolutionaries were ... successful [in establishing a stable democracy] thanks to a peculiarly favorable conjunction of factors—a mature political culture, good leadership, luck and the willingness ruthlessly to root out potential causes of disorder." Mark Falcoff, "The poison in the cup of novelty," *TLS,* June 13, 1997, p. 8.

29. Huntington reckons the latest one to be the third democratic wave since the eighteenth century, with the previous two followed by reversals—"counter-waves." Huntington, op. cit., pp. 13–26.

30. Democratization in the United Kingdom and the United States involved not so much the overthrowing of inegalitarian principles, as in the case of traditional and illiberal systems, as the diffusion, the "trickling down," of political equality from the apex of society to its base and from the imperial metropolis to the provinces.

31. The leader of Singapore, Lee Kuan Yew, asserted in the 1990s that "Asian values" were inherently less liberal than those of the West. The term was misleading in at least one way: Asia was a vast and immensely heterogeneous place to which few political generalizations, and certainly not the imputation of a single set of values, comfortably applied.

32. Neither was an isolated relic of the traditional and illiberal period of history. The Saudi monarchy was not the only one in the region. The other, smaller oil states of the Persian Gulf were also ruled in this way. And Communist parties remained in power in East Asia in North Korea and Vietnam.

33. On Islam, Bernard Lewis, *The Middle East: A Brief History of the Last 2000 Years,* New York: Scribner, 1995, p. 371, and Elie Kedourie, *Democracy and Arab Political Culture,* Washington, D.C.: The Washington Institute for Near East Policy,, 1992, pp., 2–10, 103. On China, William Theodore de Bary and Tu Weiming, editors, *Confucianism and Human Rights,* New York: Columbia University Press, 1999, and *The Analects of Confucius,* translated by Simon Leys, New York: W. W. Norton, 1997.

34. "The historian of classical antiquity Moses Finley notes 'that it is impossible to translate the word "freedom" into any ancient Near East language, including Hebrew, or any Far Eastern language either, for that matter.'" Finley, *The Ancient Economy,* Berkeley: The University of California Press, 1973, p. 28. Cited in Richard Pipes, *Property and Freedom,* New York: Knopf, 2000, p. 118.

35. "Imperial Confucianism only extolled those statements from the Master that prescribed submission to the established authorities, whereas more essential notions were conveniently ignored—such as the precepts of social justice, political dissent, and the moral duty for intellectuals to criticize the ruler (even at the risk of their lives) when he was abusing his power, or when he oppressed the people." Simon Leys, "Introduction" to *The Analects of Confucius,* p. xvi.

36. China, after all, was governed by something distinctly modern: a Communist Party. Much of the Arab world had governments that, while not liberal, were scarcely traditional and could not be considered Islamic. Moreover, while the teachings of Confucius continued to exert an influence on post-Cold War China, those twenty-five centuries-old writings were not necessarily more widely read than the American Constitution, which was available in Chinese translation and the ideas of which were part of political (although not necessarily public) discussions in early twenty-first century China.

37. They included parts of the liberal tradition, such as the right to vote, that the imperial British government was not, in the early decades of the twentieth century, anxious for the Indians to adopt.

38. On liberalism as part of the Chinese agenda, Arthur Waldron, "China's Coming Constitutional Challenges," *Orbis*, Winter, 1995, pp. 19–35; on political liberalism as part of the agenda of the Arab Middle East, Bernard Lewis, *The Multiple Identities of the Middle East*, New York: Schocken Books, 1998, p. 137.

39. Nawaf E. Obaid, *The Oil Kingdom at 100: Petroleum Policymaking in Saudi Arabia*, Washington, D.C.: The Washington Institute for Near East Policy, 2000, pp. xi–xii.

40. "The [Communist] regime's support today comes primarily from only four groups: the bureaucracy, the military, the security forces, and the rapidly increasing urban middle-class that will have much to lose (such as the value of their stocks and real estate) in the event of political instability." Minxin Pei, "Is China Unstable?" *Wire*, volume 7, number 8, July 1999, Philadelphia: Foreign Policy Research Institute, p. 2. The argument that Communist rule stood between China and something worse persuaded at least a few Westerners, as well. See, for example, Robert Kaplan, "Sometimes, Autocracy Breeds Freedom," *The New York Times*, News of the Week in Review, June 28, 1998, p. 17.

41. The correlates of democracy are discussed in Huntington, op. cit., Chapter 2, and Mueller, op. cit., pp. 197–202.

42. On the connection between economic development and democratic politics see Seymour Martin Lipset, *Political Man: The Social Basis of Politics*, New York: Anchor Books, 1963 p.b., Chapter 2, and Huntington, op. cit., pp. 59–72.

43. The point is made in Henry S. Rowen, "The Short March: China's Road to Democracy," *The National Interest*, Fall 1996. Of particular interest is the graph representing the way freedom varies with income in East and Southeast Asia, on p. 68. On the basis of the regularity in the variation the author felt able to state that China would become a democracy "around the year 2015" (p. 61).

44. One explanation for the reforms that Mikhail Gorbachev attempted in the Soviet Union in the latter half of the 1980s is that, because of rising levels of education and urbanization, the modified Stalinist system he inherited was no longer effective and had to be changed. On the changes in the Soviet Union, see Moshe Lewin, *The Gorbachev Phenomenon*, Berkeley: The University of California Press, 1985. On Gorbachev's initial response see Thane Gustafson, "The Crisis of the Soviet System of Power and Mikhail Gorbachev's Political Strategy," in Seweryn Bialer and Michael Mandelbaum, editors, *Gorbachev's Russia and American Foreign Policy*, Boulder: Westview Press, 1988.

45. In George Orwell's dystopian fantasy *1984*, published in 1949, technology is used to extinguish liberty. The Communist government of East Germany could not prevent most of its citizens from receiving Western television, but ultimately decided that access to it had a pacifying rather than an agitating effect on East Germans. It served, they came to believe, as a kind of vaccination, with a controlled dosage of Western culture, vicariously experienced, restraining the appetite for more. They therefore went to the trouble of wiring for cable reception the easternmost parts of the G.D.R., which were outside the range of West German broadcast signals.

   Moreover, modern mass media have often been associated with nationalist violence, from Hitler's Nuremberg rallies, which were broadcast by radio all over Germany, to Serb television and Rwandan radio in the 1990s, both of which spurred their audiences to murderous rampages.

lished, or at least can most readily be explained and justified, and the public good for which that justification is, in liberal terms, most powerful, is constitutional liberty. After enumerating the rights in defense of which the colonists were proclaiming themselves separate from Great Britain, the American Declaration of Independence states, "it is to secure these rights that governments are instituted among men."

8. In practice Third World governments did not necessarily regard themselves as obliged to choose, nor did they necessarily see any advantage in choosing between the two rival camps. Indeed, many joined together to form the Non-aligned Movement, which accomplished almost nothing, but the existence of which underscored the disinclination to affiliate with either side.

9. Two studies that emphasize the major role of historical time in the formation of institutions are Douglass C. North, *Institutions, Institutional Change, and Economic Performance*, New York: Cambridge University Press, 1990, and Robert D. Putnam et al., *Making Democracy Work: Civic Traditions in Modern Italy*, Princeton: Princeton University Press, 1993.

60. "We are faced here with a vicious circle: Russian authorities cannot improve government performance (in law enforcement and elsewhere) without more trust and cooperation from society; but society will neither trust the government nor cooperate with it unless the authorities perform more effectively (in law enforcement and elsewhere.)" Stephen Holmes, "Can Foreign Aid Promote the Rule of Law?" *East European Constitutional Review*, Fall, 1999, p. 70. ". . . at the heart of the Russian fiscal crisis was massive and ubiquitous tax evasion. The arcane system of more than 200 overlapping federal and local taxes arbitrarily interpreted and enforced by corrupt federal and local authorities resulted in an unbearable tax burden often amounting to more than 100 percent of entrepreneurs' profit. The predictable result was a vast off-the-books underground economy of unrecorded cash deals, barter, and second jobs estimated at 25–40 percent of the country's official GDP." Leon Aron, "Crisis of Confidence," *Russian Outlook*, Summer, 1998, Washington, D.C.: The American Enterprise Institute, p. 3.

61. This is the subject of Bruce Porter, *War and the Rise of the State: The Military Foundations of Modern Politics*, New York: The Free Press, 1994. Two influential early essays on this subject are Otto Hintze, "The Formation of States and Constitutional Development: A Study in History and Politics," and Hintze, "Military Organization and the Organization of the State," in Felix Gilbert, editor, *The Historical Essays of Otto Hintze*, New York: Oxford University Press, 1975, Chapters 4 and 5.

62. The leading proponent of free trade as a vehicle for international peace was the English businessman and Member of Parliament Richard Cobden. A. J. P. Taylor, *The Trouble Makers: Dissent Over Foreign Policy, 1792–1939*, Harmondsworth, England: Penguin Books, 1985 (first published 1957), Chapter II; Anthony Howe, *Free Trade and Liberal England, 1846–1946*, Oxford, England: The Clarendon Press, 1997, Chapter 3.

63. Economic interdependence was a *cause* of World War II. The United States tried to change Japanese policy in China by cutting off the oil that Japan needed. Tokyo responded by attacking Pearl Harbor.

64. The mainland's trade with and investment from Taiwan was itself appreciable. The Taiwanese government worried that this made the island dependent on the mainland and so susceptible to pressure and manipulation even in the absence of an armed attack. Thus the Taiwanese policy was one of "maintaining a vigorous business relationship with the PRC so that Beijing will be reluctant to forego the benefits of Taiwanese investments but not permitting economic dependence on the mainland to

46. By some accounts these technologies helped to overthrow Com
    Michael Dobbs, *Down With Big Brother: The Fall of the Soviet*
    Knopf, 1997, p. 197.

47. The contest between the Internet and government control was b
    the dawn of the twenty-first century, not in Russia but in China
    favor the government. The authorities in Beijing were "doing
    power to stop ordinary Chinese from becoming citizens of Cyber
    what could the authorities reasonably hope to achieve? "How ca
    make sure that millions of people limit themselves only to what
    know? The point of the World Wide Web, after all, is that it is oper
    answer is that the government cannot." In fact, "anyone who speal
    afford an expensive local call and a cup of coffee can get all the nev
    an Internet cafe]." Ian Buruma, "China in Cyberspace," *New Yor*
    November 4, 1999, pp. 10–11. On the rapid growth in Chinese a
    media free of government control see David M. Lampton, *Same Bed*
    Managing US-China Relations, 1989–2000, Berkeley: The Univer
    Press, 2001, p. 266.

48. By one account, authoritarian rule in both places had its roots in g
    mate. The distribution of political authority, according to this accor
    determined by the availability of the one resource that is indispensab
    water. When the water supply was centralized, in rivers, the resul
    authority. If water was available in decentralized fashion, through
    authority was—or could be—decentralized. Russia and China were
    eties. David Landes, *The Wealth and Poverty of Nations*, New York:
    1998, pp. 18–19. The idea originated with Karl A. Wittfogel, *Orie*
    Comparative Study of Total Power, New Haven: Yale University Pre
    developed the concept of "hydraulic societies."

49. Andrew J. Nathan, *Chinese Democracy*, New York: Knopf, 1995, p. x.

50. "The Russian tsar's power was unconstrained by a constitution, by l
    sentative institutions. This was the case in 1550: it remained so in 18
    considerable degree, down to 1917." Dominic Lieven, *Empire: The Ru*
    Its Rivals, New Haven: Yale University Press, 2000, p. 251.

51. On Russian electoral irregularities in the 1990s, see Lilia Shevtsova
    Myths and Reality, Washington, D.C.: The Carnegie Endowment fo
    Peace, 1999, pp. 96–97, 190.

52. According to Qiao Shi, at the time chairman of the People's Congres
    of the Chinese Communist Party was not supreme: "The party sho
    activities within the limits permitted by the constitution." At the tin
    statement the party did not conduct its activities in this way nor had
    should do so been endorsed by either Mao or Deng Xiaoping. Trudy
    ing China Under the rule of law," *The Philadelphia Inquirer*, December

53. Lampton, op. cit., Chapter 4.

54. This was the basis of the assertion by Henry S. Rowen that China w
    democracy around the year 2015. Cited in note 43, above.

55. On the general pattern see Huntington, op. cit., Chapters 3 and 4.

56. The Russian version of state weakness is a principal theme of Thane G
    talism Russian-Style, New York: Cambridge University Press, 2000.

57. Stephen Holmes and Cass R. Sunstein, *The Cost of Rights: Why Liber*
    Taxes, New York: Norton, 1999, p. 48. It is to secure public goods that st

46. By some accounts these technologies helped to overthrow Communism in Europe. Michael Dobbs, *Down With Big Brother: The Fall of the Soviet Empire*, New York: Knopf, 1997, p. 197.

47. The contest between the Internet and government control was being played out, at the dawn of the twenty-first century, not in Russia but in China. The odds did not favor the government. The authorities in Beijing were "doing everything in their power to stop ordinary Chinese from becoming citizens of Cyberspace China." But what could the authorities reasonably hope to achieve? "How can the government make sure that millions of people limit themselves only to what it wants them to know? The point of the World Wide Web, after all, is that it is open to everyone. The answer is that the government cannot." In fact, "anyone who speaks English and can afford an expensive local call and a cup of coffee can get all the news in the world [in an Internet cafe]." Ian Buruma, "China in Cyberspace," *New York Review of Books*, November 4, 1999, pp. 10–11. On the rapid growth in Chinese access to electronic media free of government control see David M. Lampton, *Same Bed Different Dreams: Managing US-China Relations, 1989–2000*, Berkeley: The University of California Press, 2001, p. 266.

48. By one account, authoritarian rule in both places had its roots in geography and climate. The distribution of political authority, according to this account, is historically determined by the availability of the one resource that is indispensable for human life: water. When the water supply was centralized, in rivers, the result was centralized authority. If water was available in decentralized fashion, through rainfall, political authority was—or could be—decentralized. Russia and China were "riverine" societies. David Landes, *The Wealth and Poverty of Nations*, New York: W. W. Norton, 1998, pp. 18–19. The idea originated with Karl A. Wittfogel, *Oriental Despotism: A Comparative Study of Total Power*, New Haven: Yale University Press, 1957, which developed the concept of "hydraulic societies."

49. Andrew J. Nathan, *Chinese Democracy*, New York: Knopf, 1995, p. x.

50. "The Russian tsar's power was unconstrained by a constitution, by laws or by representative institutions. This was the case in 1550: it remained so in 1850 and even, to a considerable degree, down to 1917." Dominic Lieven, *Empire: The Russian Empire and Its Rivals*, New Haven: Yale University Press, 2000, p. 251.

51. On Russian electoral irregularities in the 1990s, see Lilia Shevtsova, *Yeltsin's Russia: Myths and Reality*, Washington, D.C.: The Carnegie Endowment for International Peace, 1999, pp. 96–97, 190.

52. According to Qiao Shi, at the time chairman of the People's Congress, the authority of the Chinese Communist Party was not supreme: "The party should conduct its activities within the limits permitted by the constitution." At the time he made the statement the party did not conduct its activities in this way nor had the idea that it should do so been endorsed by either Mao or Deng Xiaoping. Trudy Rubin, "Bringing China Under the rule of law," *The Philadelphia Inquirer*, December 18, 1996.

53. Lampton, op. cit., Chapter 4.

54. This was the basis of the assertion by Henry S. Rowen that China would become a democracy around the year 2015. Cited in note 43, above.

55. On the general pattern see Huntington, op. cit., Chapters 3 and 4.

56. The Russian version of state weakness is a principal theme of Thane Gustafson, *Capitalism Russian-Style*, New York: Cambridge University Press, 2000.

57. Stephen Holmes and Cass R. Sunstein, *The Cost of Rights: Why Liberty Depends on Taxes*, New York: Norton, 1999, p. 48. It is to secure public goods that states are estab-

lished, or at least can most readily be explained and justified, and the public good for which that justification is, in liberal terms, most powerful, is constitutional liberty. After enumerating the rights in defense of which the colonists were proclaiming themselves separate from Great Britain, the American Declaration of Independence states, "it is to secure these rights that governments are instituted among men."

58. In practice Third World governments did not necessarily regard themselves as obliged to choose, nor did they necessarily see any advantage in choosing between the two rival camps. Indeed, many joined together to form the Non-aligned Movement, which accomplished almost nothing, but the existence of which underscored the disinclination to affiliate with either side.

59. Two studies that emphasize the major role of historical time in the formation of institutions are Douglass C. North, *Institutions, Institutional Change, and Economic Performance*, New York: Cambridge University Press, 1990, and Robert D. Putnam et al., *Making Democracy Work: Civic Traditions in Modern Italy*, Princeton: Princeton University Press, 1993.

60. "We are faced here with a vicious circle: Russian authorities cannot improve government performance (in law enforcement and elsewhere) without more trust and cooperation from society; but society will neither trust the government nor cooperate with it unless the authorities perform more effectively (in law enforcement and elsewhere.)" Stephen Holmes, "Can Foreign Aid Promote the Rule of Law?" *East European Constitutional Review*, Fall, 1999, p. 70. ". . . at the heart of the Russian fiscal crisis was massive and ubiquitous tax evasion. The arcane system of more than 200 overlapping federal and local taxes arbitrarily interpreted and enforced by corrupt federal and local authorities resulted in an unbearable tax burden often amounting to more than 100 percent of entrepreneurs' profit. The predictable result was a vast off-the-books underground economy of unrecorded cash deals, barter, and second jobs estimated at 25–40 percent of the country's official GDP." Leon Aron, "Crisis of Confidence," *Russian Outlook*, Summer, 1998, Washington, D.C.: The American Enterprise Institute, p. 3.

61. This is the subject of Bruce Porter, *War and the Rise of the State: The Military Foundations of Modern Politics*, New York: The Free Press, 1994. Two influential early essays on this subject are Otto Hintze, "The Formation of States and Constitutional Development: A Study in History and Politics," and Hintze, "Military Organization and the Organization of the State," in Felix Gilbert, editor, *The Historical Essays of Otto Hintze*, New York: Oxford University Press, 1975, Chapters 4 and 5.

62. The leading proponent of free trade as a vehicle for international peace was the English businessman and Member of Parliament Richard Cobden. A. J. P. Taylor, *The Trouble Makers: Dissent Over Foreign Policy, 1792–1939*, Harmondsworth, England: Penguin Books, 1985 (first published 1957), Chapter II; Anthony Howe, *Free Trade and Liberal England, 1846–1946*, Oxford, England: The Clarendon Press, 1997, Chapter 3.

63. Economic interdependence was a *cause* of World War II. The United States tried to change Japanese policy in China by cutting off the oil that Japan needed. Tokyo responded by attacking Pearl Harbor.

64. The mainland's trade with and investment from Taiwan was itself appreciable. The Taiwanese government worried that this made the island dependent on the mainland and so susceptible to pressure and manipulation even in the absence of an armed attack. Thus the Taiwanese policy was one of "maintaining a vigorous business relationship with the PRC so that Beijing will be reluctant to forego the benefits of Taiwanese investments but not permitting economic dependence on the mainland to

become so substantial that one's own freedom of maneuver is greatly diminished." David M. Lampton, "Recent U.S. Perspectives on Cross-Strait Relations," *American Foreign Policy Interests*, Volume 21, Number 2, New York, National Committee on American Foreign Policy, April, 1999, p. 6.

65. Michael McFaul, "A Precarious Peace: Domestic Politics in the Making of Russian Foreign Policy," *International Security*, 22:3, Winter, 1997/98, p. 21. Anatol Lieven, *Chechnya: Tombstone of Russian Power*. New Haven, Connecticut: Yale University Press, 1998, p. 184.

66. Schumpeter, "The Sociology of Imperialisms," in Schumpeter, *Imperialism and Social Classes*, Cleveland: Meridian Books, 1955. It was also suggested, in the nineteenth century, that international bankers had the power to prevent war in Europe, which could not be waged without loans from them, and the incentive to prevent it, since war was generally bad for business. Niall Ferguson, *The House of Rothschild: Money's Prophets*, New York: Penguin Books, 1999, p. 231.

67. Secretary of State James A. Baker, speaking in April 1990, quoted in Huntington, op. cit., p. 284.

68. Democracy-promotion was a continuation of, but also a departure from, the missionary tradition of the nineteenth century. Then representatives of the West eager to spread Western ideas went to live among those they sought to convert. The latter-day democracy-promoters dropped in for short visits, often staying in expensive local hotels. In general, the missionaries learned as much about the indigenous peoples as those they were proselytizing learned about Christianity—if not more. This was true as well of the missionaries' secular descendants in the second half of the twentieth century, the American Peace Corps volunteers. Whether it was also the case for the agents of democracy promotion is doubtful.

69. The most careful and authoritative study of the democracy assistance programs, *The Learning Curve* by Thomas Carothers, Washington, D.C.: The Carnegie Endowment for International Peace, 2000, although contending that those programs are worthy, provides evidence of the limits to their effectiveness.

70. This was a recurrent theme in American officials' public pronouncements on China. "By joining the World Trade Organization, China is not simply agreeing to import more of our products. It is agreeing to import one of democracy's most cherished values, economic freedom. The more China liberalizes its economy, the more fully it will liberate the potential of its people . . . And when individuals have the power, not just to dream, but to realize their dreams, they will demand a greater say." President Bill Clinton, Speech at the Paul H. Nitze School of Advanced International Studies of the Johns Hopkins University, March 8, 2000, quoted in *The New York Times*, March 9, 2000, p. A10.

71. Mueller, *Democracy*, p. 232; Robert Dahl, *On Democracy*, New Haven: Yale University Press, 1998, Chapter 13.

72. According to the president of the Chinese Economists Society, an association of Chinese-born economists at North American universities, "It is a very promising sign for China to establish a market economy. I think maybe five years down the line, the private sector will play a more dominant role in China's economy. And when the people have a better standard of living, they will want to protect their private interests and want to elect representatives to speak on their behalf." *Democracy*, The National Endowment for Democracy, Washington, D.C.: fall 1997, p. 3. Zhao Zhiyang, the Communist Party leader ousted after the crackdown on demonstrations in Tiananmen Square in June 1989, made the same point: "After living standards and cultural

levels have been raised, the people's sense of democracy and sense of political participation will grow stronger." Quoted in Chris Patten, *East and West*, London: Pan,
1998, p. 141.

73. "Capitalism is the first society to place its overall guidance under two authorities, one
public, one private, each with its powers and its boundaries to power. The public
authority—government—wields force and establishes law, but does not set itself up to
carry on the everyday tasks of production and distribution." Robert Heilbroner, *The
Worldly Philosophers: The Lives, Times and Ideas of the Great Economic Thinkers*, New
York: Simon and Schuster/Touchstone, revised seventh edition, 1995, p. 313.

74. Individuals are also free to sell their labor in a market system. In traditional society
they were bound by inherited social obligations, in Communist economic systems by
the dictates of the party.

75. A good brief discussion of the concept, its history, and its several meanings is in
Charles S. Maier, *Dissolution: The Crisis of Communism and the End of East Germany*,
Princeton: Princeton University Press, 1997, pp. 187–195.

76. It is also a place to which to retire from office. Communist officials were loath to give
up power because, unlike their counterparts in the West, there was no private sector
to which to retire. Former presidents of the United States could look forward to
wealth, influence, and honors. The one supreme leader of the Soviet Union to leave
office alive, Nikita Khrushchev, although given a villa comfortable by Soviet standards, was reduced to the role of state pensioner, with limited economic opportunities
and none at all in political life.

77. The property qualification for the franchise, common in the West into the twentieth
century, was based on a particular conception of the relationship between the private
economy and democracy. Only those with a stake in society were thought deserving of a
role in deciding its destiny. And only those with an independent base in the economy
were regarded as able to think and act independently, and so to deserve the right to vote.

78. The dense growth of civil society in the liberal core is associated with democracy in
yet another way. Only a democratic system can mediate among the powerful and
diverse interests that a modern economy produces. In the words of a Chinese economist: "The whole process of economic pluralism inevitably leads to pluralism in ideology and other spheres, because it leads to diversity of economic interest which in turn
produces distinctive needs and values . . . A specialized professional society like China
is becoming requires a more innovative, pluralistic ideology." Elisabeth Rosenthal,
"Riding Winds of Reforms, Yet Mired in Orthodoxy," *The New York Times*, November
17, 1999, p. A15. See also Francis Fukuyama, *The End of History*, p. 112.

79. Finer, op. cit., *Volume I: Ancient Monarchies and Empires* , p. 604; Richard Pipes, *Property and Freedom*, New York: Alfred A. Knopf, 2000, p. 105.

80. The traditional Islamic state might qualify. It was governed, in theory, by the religious
law but without either popular election of rulers or constitutional restraints on their
rule, which is not to say that that rule was unrestrained. Lewis, *Multiple Identities*, p. 98.

81. The relationship between property and liberty is the subject of Pipes, op. cit., Chapters 1–4.

82. The phrase is from *The Theory of Legislation*. It is cited, inter alia, by Holmes and Sunstein, op. cit., p. 59, and Finer, op. cit., *Volume I*, p. 604.

83. Property does not always lead to liberty. When very unequally distributed it can have
the opposite effect. The propertied class will block the extension of political rights for
fear that this will lead to the confiscation of what they own. This fear, prominent in
the nineteenth century, was a major reason for opposition to extending the franchise.
In the twentieth century, the redistribution of land in the Philippines and Taiwan

paved the way for political liberalism. Conversely, the lopsided distribution of wealth in Haiti and Pakistan obstructed the establishment of liberal government in these countries. The creation of the welfare state bestowed property, in the form of entitlements, upon every citizen, thereby diminishing opposition to the principle of private property by making it less unequally distributed.

84. Law without the state occurred in preliterate communities, but perhaps the one exception to this pattern in the mainstream of history is diasporic Judaism, in which communities dominated by law lacked a state to enforce it. Compliance was based on habit, a sense of community, hostile surroundings, and, of course, a strong belief in the law's divine origins and sanction.

85. "No modern market system can flourish outside a coercively enforced legal system. Private property is not an object but a social relation, a bundle of enforceable rules of access and exclusion that function properly only if public authorities use coercion to excluded nonowners and maintain owner control over resources, predictably penalizing force and fraud and other infractions of the basic rules of the game." Stephen Holmes, "Cultural Legacies or State Collapse? Probing the Post-Communist Dilemma," in Michael Mandelbaum, editor, *Post-Communism: Four Perspectives*, New York: The Council on Foreign Relations, 1996, p. 49. This is a major theme of Mancur Olson, *Power and Prosperity: Outgrowing Communist and Capitalist Dictatorships*, New York: Basic Books, 2000.

86. "A liberal government must refrain from violating rights. It must 'respect' rights. But this way of speaking is misleading because it reduces the government's role to that of a nonparticipant observer. A liberal legal system does not merely protect and defend property. It defines and thus creates property. Without legislation and adjudication there can be no property rights . . ." Holmes and Sunstein, op. cit., p. 60.

87. The role of the state is related to another point of similarity between the liberal approaches to economics and security. By enforcing contracts and so protecting property rights, the state provides a public good. It is, of course, the state's chief task and justification to provide such goods, and it is the absence of the equivalent of the state in relations between and among sovereign states that makes the provision of international public goods difficult.

88. Finer, op. cit., *Volume III*, p. 1450.

89. According to Kant, "Our age is the age of enlightenment, the century of Frederick." Quoted in ibid., p. 1448.

90. W. G. Beasley, *The Rise of Modern Japan: Political, Economic, and Social Change Since 1850*, New York: St. Martin's, second edition, 1995, pp. 91–95.

91. This is the major theme of Richard Pipes, *Russia Under the Old Regime*, New York: Scribner, 1974. It is reprised in Pipes, *Property and Freedom*, Chapter 4.

9. THE TRIUMPH OF THE MARKET

1. The creation of more money but not more goods on which to spend it is, of course, the recipe for inflation, which is presumably what the alchemists would have produced had they succeeded. One consequence of the sudden influx of precious metals in premodern Europe from sources in the New World was a rise in the price level. Peter Jay, *The Wealth of Man*, New York: PublicAffairs, 2000, p. 132.

2. On this point see Robert Skidelsky, *The Road from Serfdom: The Economic and Political Consequences of the End of Communism*, New York: Penguin Books, p.b., 1996, p. 88.

3. The divided nations offered the most striking contrasts in economic performance but

not the only instructive ones. "In 1950 Poland and Spain had roughly the same per-capita income. But whereas Poland's per-capita income increased from $775 a year in 1955 to $1860 a year in 1988, Spain's went up from $561 a year to $7740 in the same period." Skidelsky, op. cit., p. 145.

4. Their economic success offers one answer to an intriguing historical question: What became of the rampant nationalist sentiment that fueled their campaigns of conquest in the 1930s and 1940s? One obvious answer is that it was beaten out of them. Both were crushed in 1945 and occupied thereafter. But the pride and energy that they harnessed to destructive purposes before 1945 may also have been submerged into the creation of wealth. Occasionally it rose to the surface in political form, in the German reluctance to give up the Deutschmark in favor of the euro and the Japanese disinclination to buy foreign products.

5. The Cold War limited this familiar pattern for most of the second half of the century. For much of that conflict Communist Eastern Europe was off limits to Germany and Communist China to Japan.

6. The real incomes of East Asia's newly industrializing countries increased sevenfold in the last three decades of the twentieth century, and their share of world trade quadrupled. Chris Patten, *East and West*, London: Pan Books, 1999, p. 121.

7. "Already in World War I, all the most important belligerents had pushed through laws that effectively overrode their citizens' property rights and enabled governments to take those means into their own hands when necessary. These controls they used to decide who should produce what, how, where, at what prices, and with the aid of which workers possessing professional qualifications and working at which wages during how many hours a day or week." Martin van Creveld, *The Rise and Decline of the State*, Cambridge, England: Cambridge University Press, 1998, pp. 238. See also William McNeill, *The Rise of the West*, Chicago: The University of Chicago Press, 1991 (first published, 1963), p. 742.

8. Richard Pipes, *The Russian Revolution*, New York: Alfred A. Knopf, 1990, p. 673.

9. Occasionally, as in the case of agriculture in Communist Poland after 1945, a sector was spared nationalization.

10. John Kenneth Galbraith, *The New Industrial State*, Harmondsworth, England: Penguin Books, 1967, pp. 390–392.

11. The political parties from which Thatcher, Reagan, and Kohl came called themselves "conservative." But the economic approach they favored, giving preference to the market over the state in economic affairs, was what the nineteenth century had called liberal. The change in nomenclature coincided with a change of political opposition. In the nineteenth century proponents of the market were opposed by the forces of tradition, which were skeptical of all facets of modern life including the industrial revolution. In the twentieth century the opposition came from those who had no thought of returning to premodern politics or economics but who favored an expansive government role in the modern industrial economy, the proponents of socialism or social democracy. Not all core countries made the terminological shift. In France at the end of the twentieth century the champions of more scope for the market and less for the state were called—often scornfully and, in historical terms, accurately—"neoliberals."

12. The retrenchment of the state proceeded in all the countries of the core, not just the largest ones. "Socialist and labor parties in the industrialized democracies from Japan and Australia to Britain, Sweden and Israel have taken the road back to capitalism." Seymour Martin Lipset, "The Left Moves Right," *The Washington Post*, April 21, 1997, p. A17.

13. Skidelsky, op. cit., p. 139.

14. China and India, the two most populous countries in the world, in both of which new regimes took power after World War II with a commitment to rapid economic growth, naturally lend themselves to comparison. In the final two decades of the twentieth century China outperformed India. But this was not a victory for economic illiberalism. In political terms, to be sure, India, a democracy, was far more liberal than Communist-ruled China. But by 1991 a decade of economic reforms had made China more liberal in *economic* terms than the Indian license raj.

15. In both Latin America and India currency devaluation was part of the reform program. Currencies had been kept artificially high to make the import of capital equipment for local industry cheap, a policy that simultaneously discouraged exports.

16. The movement away from state control was also in evidence in a third region where state-led industrialization had been prominent, the Middle East. In Egypt, for example, an official program of privatization was launched in 1992, although progress in turning state-owned enterprises over to private hands over the next decade was sluggish. "A revolution to end the revolution," *The Economist*, October 25, 1997.

17. The results were spectacular. "Deng Xiaoping's decision to open China's economy in 1978 helped some eight hundred million peasants more than double their real incomes in just six years, arguably the single greatest leap out of acute poverty of all time." John Micklethwait and Adrian Wooldridge, *A Future Perfect: The Essentials of Globalization*, New York: Crown Publishers, 2000, p. 259.

18. Another familiar feature was stabilization, the reduction of inflation, which, in Russia, was the result of the money-creating policies of the last years of Communism. Anti-inflation measures were harsh, and so came to be called "shock therapy," which in turn became a term of opprobrium. The alternative, however, was unchecked inflation.

19. The *way* that traditional societies were destroyed—the timing, the methods, and the identity of the destroyer—was by no means uniform the world over, and the variations had important consequences for the kind of political system that succeeded the traditional one. This is the subject of Barrington Moore Jr., *The Social Origins of Democracy and Dictatorship: Lord and Peasant in the Making of the Modern World*, London: Penguin, 1967.

20. Communism "was the most rational and most intoxicating, all-embracing ideology for me and for those in my disunited and desperate land who so desired to skip over centuries of slavery and backwardness and to bypass reality itself." Milovan Djilas, a Yugoslav Communist turned dissident, quoted in John Lewis Gaddis, *We Now Know: Rethinking Cold War History*, New York: Oxford University Press, 1997 , p. 32.

21. None of the many answers to the question of why the industrial revolution began in England, or how it was possible for it to begin at all, invoke the features of the command economy.

22. They could increase savings, and thus investment, by keeping labor costs low, often by the expedient of branding people as criminals, putting them in camps, and forcing them to work for nothing.

23. This is the thesis of Alexander Gerschenkron, "Economic Backwardness in Historical Perspective," in Gerschenkron, *Economic Backwardness in Historical Perspective: A Book of Essays*, Cambridge, Mass.: Harvard University Press, 1962.

24. Martin Malia, *The Soviet Tragedy: A History of Socialism in Russia, 1917–1991*, New York: The Free Press, 1994, pp. 211–215.

25. "In the twenty-five years to 1985, India's per capita GDP barely rose at all (less than 0.25 percent a year)." op. cit., p. 275.

26. Karl Marx and Friedrich Engels, *The Communist Manifesto: A Modern Edition*, London: Verso, 1998, pp. 40–41.

27. This last was most emphatically true for advances in medicine. No one, no matter how wealthy, had access to penicillin before the twentieth century.

28. New York: Doubleday and Company.

29. "We can all look into each other's windows now. And as a result, people are less willing to accept a lower standard of living than their neighbors enjoy. By shrinking the world to a size small, globalization brings home to everyone just how ahead or behind they are." Thomas L. Friedman, *The Lexus and the Olive Tree: Understanding Globalization*, New York: Farrar, Straus and Giroux, 1999, p. 56.

30. Mass consumption and electoral politics came together in another way. Candidates presented themselves, and sought votes, using the techniques of advertising, notably paid messages—commercials—on television. Political parties and candidates had become consumer goods, striving to establish and retain brand loyalty. In 1960 his father said that John F. Kennedy would become president by the process of "selling him like soapflakes." Forty years later all of politics was an exercise in promoting consumer products.

31. A sign of how deeply the assumption of affluence pervaded the core came in the year 2000 in the United States, when political candidates lamented a "digital divide," which referred to the uneven distribution of access to personal computers and Internet across racial groups. Two decades previously no one had owned a personal computer; a decade before, the Internet had been the hobby of a tiny handful of academics. But in the year 2000 the fact that not everybody could use both was pronounced a national problem.

32. "The mainland Chinese are no longer satisfied to look back at the change in the past 20 years. They want to be like the Chinese in Hong Kong or the US, or they want to be like Japan . . . Politicians are not given much time these days." A Chinese official quoted in "Now comes the hard part: a survey of China," *The Economist*, April 8, 2000, p. 4.

33. Michael Dobbs, *Down with Big Brother: The Fall of the Soviet Empire*, New York: Knopf, 1997, pp. 317–318. In Communist Eastern Europe, the combination of the demand for consumer goods and the inability of the economic system to supply them caused the governments to borrow from Western banks. In 1971 the total hard-currency debt for the region was $6.1 billion. By 1988 it was $95.6 billion. Mark Mazower, *Dark Continent: Europe's Twentieth Century*, London: The Penguin Press, 1998, p. 373.

34. Paul Krugman, *The Return of Depression Economics*, New York: W. W. Norton, 2000, pp. 29–30.

35. Economic research in the twentieth century produced two different accounts of productivity. The exogenous approach took productivity to be what remained after all other elements of growth had been accounted for. The endogenous approach understood productivity as the result of changes in the composition of investment, often through the application of the fruits of scientific research and technological development. The endogenous approach had the advantage that, if fully articulated and definitively proved, it would provide the basis for increasing productivity and enhancing growth. If research and development could be shown, with some precision, to lead to higher productivity, a society could become more productive and therefore richer by spending more on the relevant kind of research and development. But as the new century began this approach was not proven.

36. Competition, the essence of liberal economics, is also one of the chief rationales for a pillar of liberal politics—free speech. In the marketplace of ideas, John Stuart Mill

argued in *On Liberty*, the truth will (usually) emerge triumphant. The clash of contrasting views is also central to science, a quintessentially liberal institution and one that depends on free speech and contributes to economic growth.

37. The historical importance of secure property rights for economic growth is a principal theme of Douglass C. North and Robert Paul Thomas, *The Rise of the Western World: A New Economic History*, New York: Cambridge University Press, 1973.

38. This perhaps represents, in part, the revenge of traditional society. The qualities of character and the patterns of conduct that it esteemed retained their prestige long after the conditions in which they had flourished—or were supposed to have flourished—had disappeared. The fierce aggressiveness of the successful warrior, the generosity expected of the noble, the indifference to worldly affairs and preoccupation with matters of the spirit of the priest were honored long after the court and the church had lost their power and war had become largely an impersonal contest of machines.

39. Adam Smith made this point. "It is not from the benevolence of the butcher, the brewer, or the baker, that we expect our dinner, but from their regard to their own interest. We address ourselves, not to their humanity but to their self-love, and never talk to them of our own necessities but of their advantages." Smith, *The Wealth of Nations*, New York: The Modern Library, 1994, p. 15.

40. John D. Rockefeller invented modern philanthropy for the purpose of changing the unfavorable reputation he had earned in making his money. This reputation, to be sure, stemmed not only from the fact of his fortune but from the way he accumulated it, which was subsequently made illegal.

41. Joseph Schumpeter, *Capitalism, Socialism, and Democracy*, New York: Harper and Brothers, 1950, third edition, p. 132.

42. The founder of *Time*, Henry Luce, also established a mass-circulation magazine devoted to the (largely favorable) coverage of business and businessmen. It was called, appropriately, *Fortune*.

43. It did have some effect. The low status of business contributed, according to one interpretation, to Britain's loss of its economic lead over all other countries in the twentieth century. Martin Wiener, *English Culture and the Decline of the Industrial Spirit, 1850–1980*, Cambridge, England: Cambridge University Press, 1982 paperback. And in France for most of the twentieth century the ablest young people, if ability is measured by performance on national academic examinations, aspired to become government officials rather than merchants or bankers or industrialists.

44. "Markets [are] a powerful organizing force, capable of inducing large numbers of people to form shared goals, dividing the work of achieving the goals among many specialists, and supplying the rewards and incentives needed to get the work done." Nathan Rosenberg and L.E. Birdzell, Jr., *How the West Grew Rich: The Economic Transformation of the Industrial World*, New York: Basic Books, 1986, p. ix.

45. Smith, op. cit., p. 745.

46. This was a central message of the influential 1944 book *The Road to Serfdom* (Chicago: The University of Chicago Press) by Friederich Hayek, an economist who, like Schumpeter, was born in Austria but emigrated to the West.

47. It did not matter how the government spent money. As Keynes put it: "If the Treasury were to fill up old bottles with bank notes, bury them at suitable depths in disused coal mines which are then filled up to the surface with the town rubbish, and leave it to private enterprise on well-tried principles of laissez-faire to dig the notes up again . . . there need be no more unemployment . . . " Quoted in Robert Heilbroner, *The*

Worldly Philosophers: The Lives, Times and Ideas of the Great Economic Thinkers, New York: Touchstone, revised seventh edition, 1999, p. 275. The evolution of Keynes's thought is described in Robert Skidelsky, *John Maynard Keynes: The Economist as Savior, 1920–1937*, New York: Viking, 1994. Government spending did help lift the economies of the Western core out of the Depression, and the most effective spending, because it took place on the largest scale, was the military expenditures made in preparation for, and then to wage, World War II. As with other influential figures, Keynes's message was misinterpreted (or distorted) and misused. He argued for deficit spending by governments to moderate economic slumps. Most governments after World War II adopted the practice on a continuing basis as a way to achieve other, political, goals, which contributed to the stagflation of the 1970s.

48. This was true of thirty-eight of the forty-six recipients of the Nobel Prize for Economics between 1969 and 2000.

49. "An appreciation of markets is common to nearly everyone, Right or Left, who has given the matter a decade or more of specialized study." Mancur Olson, *The Rise and Decline of Nations: Economic Growth, Stagflation, and Economic Rigidities*, New Haven: Yale University Press, 1982, p. 177.

50. The two disciplines also differed, not least in the fact that, while the constituent parts of economic life—individuals, firms, and governments—have minds of their own and can and do decide to alter their behavior in ways that affect the choices of others, the organs, limbs, and genes of the human body do not.

51. Paul Krugman, "The Myth of Asia's Miracle," in Krugman, *Pop Internationalism*, Cambridge, Mass.: The MIT Press, 1996. First published in *Foreign Affairs*, November/December, 1994. See also Martin Wolf, "The real lesson from Asia," *Financial Times*, October 2, 1997, p. 15.

52. "As I see it, in these days it takes an enormous amount of stupid policies or bad or unstable institutions to *prevent* economic development." Olson, op. cit., p. 175.

53. After a magisterial, 500-page survey of the subject, the economic historian David Landes writes, "If we learn anything from the history of economic development, it is that culture makes all the difference." Landes, *The Wealth and Poverty of Nations*, New York: W.W. Norton, 1998, p. 516.

54. Marx and Engels, op. cit., pp. 37–38. One hundred fifty years later the toll the market took continued to be high. See Edward Luttwak, *Turbocapitalism: Winners and Losers in the Global Economy*, New York: HarperCollins, 1999, pp. xi, 68.

55. Schumpeter, op. cit., Chapter VII.

56. The name was not used in the United States, where the impulse took a somewhat different political form from the one it assumed in Europe but where its goals, and achievement, were roughly the same.

57. In the United States, in fact, the earliest large-scale spending for social welfare took the form of pensions for Civil War veterans and their dependents. Theda Skocpol, *Protecting Soldiers and Mothers*, Cambridge, Mass.: Harvard University Press, 1992, Chapter 2.

58. To the question of how much of what society produced the government should spend, different Western countries arrived at different answers: The American government took 34 percent of the gross domestic product, the government of Sweden 61 percent. Skidelsky, op. cit., pp. 24–25; "Survey: The Twentieth Century," *The Economist*, September 11, 1999, p. 42.

59. The standard work on this subject is Peter G. Peterson, *Gray Dawn: How the Coming Age Wave Will Transform America and the World*. New York, Times Books, 1999.

60. Not only the wealthy countries faced this problem. It was even more acute in formerly Communist Eastern Europe, where the post-Communist governments inherited the extremely generous benefits the Communist regimes had granted in an effort to buy social peace, and was relevant as well in China. See Michael Mandelbaum and Ethan Kapstein, editors, *Sustaining the Transition: The Social Safety Net in Post-Communist Europe*, New York: The Council on Foreign Relations, 1998.

10. THE INVISIBLE CONSTRUCTION SITE

1. John H. Herz, *International Politics in the Atomic Age*, New York: Columbia University Press, 1962 paperback, p. 214n.
2. A concise summary of the differences may be found in Jeffrey Sachs and Wing Thye Woo, "China's Transition Experience, Reexamined," *Transition: The Newsletter about Reforming Economies*, The World Bank, Washington, D.C., Volume 7, Number 3–4, March-April 1996, pp. 1–5.
3. China was also able to attract money from abroad, much of it from ethnic Chinese residing in other countries. Russia did not have the benefit of a comparable diaspora.
4. This is well described in Barry Naughton, *Growing Out of the Plan: Chinese Economic Reform, 1978–1993*, New York: Cambridge University Press, 1995, on which much of what follows is based.
5. The spontaneous privatization from below practiced by Chinese peasants lends credence to Adam Smith's dictum that human beings have a natural "propensity to truck, barter, and exchange one thing for another." Adam Smith, *The Wealth of Nations*, New York: The Modern Library, 1994, p. 14. It suggests, as well, a natural propensity for ownership. See Richard Pipes, *Property and Freedom*, New York: Alfred A. Knopf, 2000, Chapter 2.
6. The "TVEs" operated within constrained budgets, as China's state-owned enterprises did not, and provided competition for these enterprises and for each other. The TVEs are discussed in Hehui Jin and Hingui Qian, "Ownership and Institutions: Evidence from Rural China," Development Discussion Paper No. 578, Cambridge, Mass., Harvard University Institute for International Development, April 1997.
7. The gradualist approach was not cost-free for China. It preserved the loss-making state sector. But China managed to postpone, through the first post-Cold War decade, paying the bulk of those costs.
8. The absence of a law-enforcing government was notorious in post-Communist Russia and organized crime filled the vacuum. "Practically all small and medium-sized companies, as well as several large ones, have what is known as *krysha* (roof, or in this context, protection). A krysha is a criminal organization that receives 10 percent to 20 percent of the profits from a business in exchange for protecting it from other gangs. In addition, a krysha offers the only real option to resolve disputes with clients who refuse to pay for delivered goods or with companies that do not pay off their debts." Vladimir Shlapentokh, "The Four Faces of Mother Russia," *Transitions*, October 1997, p. 62.

    Despite its impressive growth, China suffered from the same problem. "Probably in no other society today has economic good faith been compromised to the extent it has in China. Contacts are not kept; debts are ignored, whether between individual or between state enterprises; whole towns have gotten rich on deceitful schemes." Liu Binyan and Perry Link, "A Great Leap Backward?" (Review of He Qinglian, *China's Pitfall*), *The New York Review of Books*, October 8, 1998, p. 22.

9. "Cultures have had, as they still have, great intrinsic momenta, and they cannot be rapidly turned in new directions. The processes involved are often long ones . . . In his great chapter on the English Revolution of 1688, Macaulay writes of the French Revolution that 'had six generations of Englishmen passed away without a single session of Parliament,' then we too would have needed years of blood and confusion 'to learn the very rudiments of political science.'" Robert Conquest, *Reflections on a Ravaged Century*, New York: W. W. Norton, 1999, p. 29.

10. Indonesia under Suharto was a spectacular late-twentieth century example. "President Suharto's family dominates the economy, owning huge chunks of business, including power generation, an airline, construction, telecoms, toll roads, newspapers, property and cars. Family members and their cronies get first pick of government contracts and licenses, so it helps to have one of their names on the company letterhead. Paying off family members or well-connected officials can add up to 30% to the cost of a deal." "Survey: East Asian Economies," *The Economist*, March 7, 1998, p. 13. A common, if speculative, estimate of the wealth of the Suharto family at the end of his rule was thirty billion dollars. Benedict Anderson, "From Miracle to Crash," *London Review of Books*, April 16, 1998, p. 7.

11. An overview of government corruption is provided in Susan Rose-Ackerman, *Corruption and Government: Causes, Consequences and Reform*, New York: Cambridge University Press, 1999.

12. In a ranking of ninety countries by the degree of perceived corruption, of the twenty-five least corrupt only two—Hong Kong and Japan—were located in neither North America nor Western Europe. Transparency International, "The 2000 Corruption Perception Index," www.transparency.org/documents/cpi2000 html.

13. It is sometimes hopefully suggested that those who illegally acquire fortunes will then favor the construction of a sturdy legal order so as to protect what they have gained. In Russia in the first post-Cold War decade many fortunes were made illegally but those who made them did not seem inclined to follow this logic. See Joel Hellman, "Winners Take All: The Politics of Partial Reform in Postcommunist Transitions," *World Politics* 50, (January 1998), pp. 203–234.

14. This was the basis of post-Soviet fortunes in Russia. "In the spring of 1992 the state price of oil was 1 percent of the world market price; the domestic prices of other commodities were about 10 percent of world prices. Managers of state companies bought oil, metals, and other commodities from the state enterprises they controlled on their private accounts, acquired export licenses and quotas from corrupt officials, arranged political protection for themselves, and then sold the commodities abroad at world prices." Anders Aslund and Mikhail Dmitriev, "Economic Reform versus Rent Seeking," in Aslund and Martha Brill Olcott, editors, *Russia After Communism*, Washington, D.C.: Carnegie Endowment for International Peace, 1999, p. 96.

15. Konstantin Simis, *USSR: The Corrupt Society: The Secret World of Soviet Capitalism*, New York: Simon and Schuster, 1982.

16. In Russia, when Communism collapsed, "There was so much to steal that was so precious: oil, diamonds, nickel. It was the kind of opportunity that comes once in a millennium." John Lloyd, "Who Lost Russia?" *The New York Times Magazine*, August 15, 1999, p. 52, quoting Fritz Ermarth, a former American government official. "Soviet institutions did not simply atrophy or dissolve but were actively pulled apart by officials at all levels seeking to extract assets that were in any way fungible." Steven Solnick, *Stealing the State: Control and Collapse in Soviet Institutions*, Cambridge, Mass.: Harvard University Press, 1998, p. 7.

Similarly, in China, in the view of one jaundiced Chinese student of the subject, economic reform amounted to "a process in which power-holders and their hangers-on plundered public wealth. The primary target of their plunder was state property that had been accumulated from forty years of the people's sweat, and their primary means of plunder was political power." Chinese economist and author He Qinglian, quoted in Liu and Link, op. cit., p. 19. As in Russia, this was a matter of taking advantage of opportunities that the drift of events presented. "Decentralization of economic decision-making from the national to local levels in the late 1970s and early 1980s presented local officials with opportunities for graft. Weaknesses in the reform program also left openings for corruption, such as asset removal, which involves stripping state assets through 'spontaneous privatization' by managers and employees of state enterprises, often aided and abetted by local government officials." Neil C. Hughes, "Smashing the Iron Rice Bowl," *Foreign Affairs*, July/August, 1997, pp. 74–75.

17. "The Soviet system collapsed because a large portion of the *nomenklatura*, those with hands directly on state property, deserted the CPSU and the Soviet state to pursue business interests and nationalist political agendas. This had been going on *sub rosa* for years; the events of late 1991 only unveiled and accelerated the process." Fritz Ermarth, "Seeing Russia Plain: The Russian Crisis and American Intelligence," *The National Interest*, Spring 1999, p. 6. See also Solnick, op. cit.

    In the Chinese version the military, which had always had a more powerful role under Communism there than in the Soviet Union, itself entered the market. By the turn of the century it oversaw "perhaps 20,000 military businesses throughout China . . . " "No longer the army's business," *The Economist*, May 8, 1999, p. 34.

18. This is a major theme of Richard Katz, *Japan: The System that Soured*, Armonk, N.Y.: M. E. Sharpe, 1998. The greatest economic distortions were in agriculture, where, in the 1980s, more than seventy-five percent of farm income came from subsidies and price support programs. (Ibid., p. 83.)

19. By one estimate, at the outset of the twenty-first century government subsidies amounted to fully fifteen percent of the Indian gross domestic product. David Gardner, "India's Congress party may give up liberalization policy," *Financial Times*, July 20, 2000, p. 6.

20. In the Islamic Republic of Iran, for example, in the 1980s "the public sector was enlarged to the point where it now accounts for 80 percent of Iran's economic activity." Christopher de Bellaigue, "The Struggle for Iran," *The New York Review of Books*, December 16, 1999, p. 51.

21. Robert Skidelsky, *The Road From Serfdom: The Economic and Political Consequences of the End of Communism*, New York: Penguin Books, 1988 p.b., p. 137.

22. The protected sector of the economy was so large, and without competition prices were so high, that consumption faltered, producing a classic Keynesian slump. The Japanese government tried to end it by pumping money into the economy. The result, however, was a sharp rise in asset prices, leading to a financial bubble (Katz, op cit., p. 197). The protected sector also contributed to the "hollowing out" of the Japanese industrial base, as its artificially high prices drove Japanese industries to relocate their plants to Asian countries where prices, and therefore costs, were lower. Ibid., p. 215.

23. "Governments discovered that they could transfer resources to themselves without raising taxes by printing money. With the extra money the government could buy more goods; because of the rise in prices, the public could buy less." Skidelsky, op. cit., p. 46.

24. The stagflation of the 1970s in the core countries was due in part to governments

printing money to cover obligations—mainly for social welfare expenditures—that they could not or would not raise taxes to fund. Skidelsky, op. cit., p. 95.

25. Ibid., p. 177. The technical definition of hyperinflation is an inflation rate in excess of 500 percent annually. Inflation becomes hyperinflation when prices are rising so rapidly that the currency becomes useless for transactions because people refuse to hold it. Hyperinflation represents a failure of government comparable to the breakdown of law and order. It is the failure to protect not the lives of citizens but something almost as important: the product of their labors. Two of the major victories of illiberalism in the twentieth century, by the Nazis in Germany in the early 1930s and the Communists in China in the late 1940s, came about when popular support for the governments they were seeking to overthrow—the German Weimar Republic and Chiang Kai-shek's Kuomintang regime—evaporated because they presided over hyperinflation.

26. Economists distinguish between welfare and distortion, considering the direct payment of benefits to individual consumers to be less inefficient than subsidies, direct and indirect, to producers.

27. The design of the Japanese system of representation gave disproportionate influence to the most cosseted sector, agriculture.

28. Leyla Boulton and Martin Wolf, "Turkey's tightrope," *Financial Times*, December 20, 1999, p. 14.

29. "China's state enterprises as a group are efficient destroyers of wealth. It would be cheaper to close them all down, and still keep paying the workers." "Red alert," *The Economist*, October 24, 1998, p. 25.

30. On Russia, see Thane Gustafson, *Capitalism Russian-Style*, New York: Cambridge University Press, 2000, Chapter 9. In China, "Government tax revenues declined by two-thirds relative to output between 1978 and 1995. At the beginning of reform, taxes and other government revenues were equal to a third of the nation's output, a level well above the average of other transition economies. By 1995, revenues had fallen to about 10 percent, a level quite low in comparison with both other transition economies and emerging markets." Nicholas Lardy, "China's Unfinished Economic Transition," "Report of the Aspen Institute Conference on U.S.-Chinese Relations, March 30–April 4, 1999," p. 30.

31. In China, when a factory owned by an American firm was closed, "desperate Chinese workers expecting layoffs seized six foreign managers . . . and held them hostage in the factory for 40 hours." Elisabeth Rosenthal, "Factory Closings in China Arouse Workers to Fury," *The New York Times*, August 31, 2000, p. A1.

32. A good overview of the financial crisis of August 1998, is in Gustafson, op. cit., pp. 14–15.

33. The phrase was coined, and the phenomenon described, in Clifford G. Gaddy and Barry W. Ickes, "Russia's Virtual Economy," *Foreign Affairs*, September/October 1998, pp. 53–67.

34. By one estimate these costs might include the reduction of the workforce of the state-owned enterprises by two-thirds, entailing the loss of 70 million urban jobs. "China's political cage," *The Economist*, August 8, 1998, p. 16.

35. The direct and indirect subsidies to loss-making firms was estimated, at the end of the 1990s, to amount to ten percent of the gross domestic product. Nicholas Lardy, *China's Unfinished Economic Revolution*, Washington, D.C.: The Brookings Institution, 1998, p. 10. The book provides an overview and an explanation of the country's principal post-Cold War economic problems.

36. In that case the government might well choose to print money to bail them out, triggering an inflationary spiral.

37. The proposition that authoritarian regimes are capable of setting distorted economies on the proper course because only such regimes are impervious to the political backlash that the social consequences of economically sound policies are bound to trigger came to be known as the "Pinochet option," after the Chilean general who took power after the overthrow of the socialist Salvador Allende in 1973 and adopted—or was believed to have adopted—politically difficult policies that eventually brought prosperity to the country.

    Some explanations of the high growth of the countries of East Asia in the last three decades of the twentieth century imputed this in part to the ability of authoritarian regimes to pursue economically effective policies with a determination democratic governments could not have mustered. See, for example, Robert Wade, *Governing the Market: Economic Theory and the Role of Government in East Asian Industrialization*, Princeton, N.J.: Princeton University Press, 1990.

38. This is the thesis of Mancur Olson, *The Rise and Decline of Nations*, New Haven: Yale University Press, 1982. He called such groups "distributional coalitions" because they exert political pressure to affect distribution rather than to enhance production. He argued that they are ordinarily weakened or eliminated only through political upheavals and not by the normal routines of democratic politics.

39. "On balance, the hypothesis that there is no relation between freedom and prosperity in either direction is hard to reject." Amartya Sen, "Human Rights and Asian Values," *The New Republic*, July 14 and 21, 1997, p. 33. One of the best-known studies of the subject is Robert Barro, "Democracy and Growth," National Bureau of Economic Research, Working Paper no. 4909, Cambridge, Mass., October 1994. The study concludes that "With respect to the determination of growth, the cross-country analysis brings out favorable effects from maintenance of the rule of law, free markets, small government consumption, and high human capital. Once these kinds of variable and the initial level of GDP are held constant, the overall effect of democracy on growth is weakly negative. There is some indication of a nonlinear relation in which more democracy enhances growth at low levels of political freedom but depresses growth when a moderate level of political freedom has already been attained" (Ibid., p. 25).

40. "Democracy may be better than other forms of government at handling interest-group pressures that harm the economy . . . In a democracy all specially interested people and groups, not just those who happen to be favored by the ruler or the ruling group, are admitted into the fray and may freely seek to manipulate governmental policy to their benefit." John Mueller, *Capitalism, Democracy, and Ralph's Pretty Good Grocery*, Princeton: Princeton University Press, 1999, p. 237.

41. Ethan Kapstein and Michael Mandelbaum, editors, *Sustaining the Transition: The Social Safety Net in Post-Communist Europe*, New York: The Council on Foreign Relations, 1998.

42. Anders Aslund, *Building Capitalism: The Transformation of the Former Soviet Bloc*, New York: Cambridge University Press, 2001.

43. This is a major theme of Mancur Olson, *Power and Prosperity: Outgrowing Communist and Capitalist Dictatorships*, New York: Basic Books, 2000.

44. Robert Gilpin, *The Challenge of Global Capitalism*, Princeton: Princeton University Press, 2000, pp. 172–173. The old attitude had not disappeared everywhere. In India, K. S. Sudarshan, the leader of the Rashtriya Swayamsevak Sangh (RSS), a Hindu

organization closely associated with the ruling Bharatiya Janata Party (BJP), "told the BJP it must fence off the economy from rapacious multinationals that the RSS likens to the East India Company that preceded the Raj, because they want to pillage India's assets, flood it with imports and bleed it through debt." David Gardner, "A self-reliant seer," *Financial Times*, July 22/23, 2000, p. 9.

45. In nineteenth-century Europe it was sometimes said that private bankers were so powerful that they could decide matters of war and peace because no country could fight without a loan. In the twenty-first century bankers were less powerful—governments had found other ways to finance war—but the interruption of capital flows was still a threatening prospect because of its impact on economic growth. Niall Ferguson, *The House of Rothschild: Money's Prophets, 1798–1848*, New York: Penguin Books, 1999, p. 263, and Ferguson, *The House of Rothschild: The World's Banker, 1849–1999*, New York: Viking, 1999, p. 94.

46. "I pose a simple question to this Chinese economist: Can China afford to attack Taiwan? His unhesitating answer was: 'No—it would stop investment in China, stop growth, stop our last chance to catch up with the rest of the world.'" Thomas L. Friedman, *The Lexus and the Olive Tree*, New York: Farrar, Straus and Giroux, 1999, p. 202. The Chinese government was caught between two sources of legitimacy: protection of its own territory, which by its definition included Taiwan, and the promotion of prosperity.

47. Karl Marx and Friederich Engels, *The Communist Manifesto*, London: Verso, 2000, pp. 39–40. First published, 1848.

48. "All over the world, whenever economic reform has succeeded, trade opening was at the heart of the effort." op. cit., p. 240. See also pp. 244–245.

49. In the case of South Korea, "The scope of the IMF reforms is wide. The plan is to free the financial sector from intrusive state control while forcing the *chaebol* (industrial conglomerates) to make investments based on earnings potential rather than market share." John Burton, "Painful prospect," *Financial Times*, December 8, 1997, p. 18.

50. When the Kenyan government initially refused the demand the IMF stopped its support for the country. Three years later the Kenyans accepted terms that amounted to a "virtual surrender of sovereignty." *Financial Times*, August 5, 2000. On the initial refusal, see Robert Chote, "IMF warning to member over corruption, *Financial Times*, August 9, 1997, p. 4.

51. For an example see Friedman, op. cit., pp. 141–142. See also John Plender, "Russia hears the gospel of governance," *Financial Times*, November 24, 2000, p. 15.

52. Friedman, op. cit., pp. 86–88. In the role of foreign capital the twenty-first century resembled the nineteenth. In the earlier period, when European governments depended on loans from private bankers, the continental bond market functioned as "the opinion poll of the political class." Ferguson, *Money's Prophets*, p. 6. In the post-Cold War era, the credit rating assigned to countries seeking international capital had the same status. Friedman, op. cit., p. 32, 81–82.

53. "The German-based chemical giant BASF, which employs more than 2,000 people in China, has set up a management development center at Shanghai's elite Jiao Tong University . . . [Its] emphasis on leadership and communication is in marked contrast to the management style prevailing in Chinese state-owned enterprises, where, as the old Chinese proverb goes, the nail that sticks up will be hammered down." Michael A. Santoro, "Promoting Human Rights in China Is Good Business," *The Wall Street Journal*, June 29, 1998, p. 18.

54. James L. Watson, "China's Big Mac Attack," *Foreign Affairs* 99:3, May/June 2000. The

encounter between McDonald's and East Asia is described in Watson, editor, *Golden Arches East: McDonald's in East Asia*. Stanford: Stanford University Press, 1997.

II. THE GLOBAL UTILITY

1. New York: Penguin Books, 1988 (first published, 1920), p. 99.
2. See Robert Skidelsky, *John Maynard Keynes: Fighting for Freedom, 1937–1946*, New York: Viking, 2001, especially Chapter 10.
3. Adam Smith, *The Wealth of Nations*, New York: The Modern Library, 1994 (first published, 1776), p. 14.
4. "The certainty of being able to exchange all that surplus part of the produce of his own labor, which is over and above his own consumption, for such parts of the produce of other men's labour as he may have occasion for, encourages every man to apply himself to a particular occupation, and to cultivate and bring to perfection whatever talent or genius he may possess for that particular species of business." Ibid., p. 16.
5. "By means of [international trade] the narrowness of the home market does not hinder the division of labour in any particular branch of art or manufacture from being carried to the highest perfection. By opening a more extensive market for whatever part of the produce of their labour may exceed the home consumption, it encourages them to improve its productive powers, and to augment its annual produce to the utmost, and thereby to increase the real revenue and wealth of the society." Ibid., p. 475.
6. Ibid., pp. 20–22.
7. This has been well described for the first age of globalization, which ended in 1914: "There was hardly a village or town anywhere on the globe whose prices were not influenced by distant foreign markets, whose infrastructure was not financed by foreign capital, whose engineering, manufacturing, and even business skills were not imported from abroad, or whose labor markets were not influenced by the absence of those who had emigrated or by the presence of strangers who had immigrated. The economic connections were intimate . . ." Kevin H. O'Rourke and Jeffrey G. Williamson, *Globalization and History: The Evolution of a Nineteenth-Century Atlantic Economy*, Cambridge, Mass.: The MIT Press, 1999, p. 2.
8. On the uneven distribution of capital flows worldwide see Robert Gilpin, *The Challenge of Global Capitalism: The World Economy of the 21st Century*, Princeton: Princeton University Press, 2000, pp. 169–170, and Miles Kahler, "Introduction: Capital Flows and Financial Crises in the 1990s," in Kahler, editor, *Capital Flows and Financial Crises*, Ithaca: Cornell University Press for the Council on Foreign Relations, 1998, p. 11. On trade see David P. Calleo, *Rethinking Europe's Future*, Princeton: Princeton University Press, 2001, p. 218.
9. In their study of the first era of globalization, O'Rourke and Williamson, op. cit., often date it from 1870, although this may be in part because data are decreasingly reliable before then.
10. Ibid., p. 2. " The major fact about the nineteenth century is the creation of a single global economy, progressively reaching into the most remote corners of the world, an increasingly dense web of economic transactions, communications and movements of goods, money and people lining the developed countries with each other and with the undeveloped world." Eric Hobsbawm, *The Age of Empire: 1875–1914*, New York: Pantheon, 1987, p. 62.
11. O'Rourke and Williamson, op. cit., p. 4. Gilpin, op cit., p. 294.

12. Political developments were not irrelevant to the initial period of globalization. The European conquest and governance of much of the periphery helped, along with the steamship and modern medicine, to bring these regions into the world economy.

13. When, in July 2000, the Russian government promulgated an official foreign policy doctrine, prominent among the goals it spelled out was the "broad integration of Russia in the system of world economic ties" in order to foster "favorable conditions for Russia's economic growth." David Hoffman, "Russia Sets Guidelines Governing Diplomacy," *The Washington Post*, July 11, 2000, p. A17.

14. "Free trade," according to its leading nineteenth century proponent, Richard Cobden, "is God's diplomacy, and there is no other certain way of uniting people in the bonds of peace." Quoted in "All free traders now?" *The Economist*, December 7, 1996, p. 21. The idea was not a new one. Montesquieu wrote, in *The Spirit of the Laws*, that "Peace is the natural effect of trade. Two nations who traffic with each other become reciprocally dependent; for if one has an interest in buying, the other has an interest in selling; and thus their union is founded on their mutual necessities." Volume I, Translated by Thomas Nugent, London: G. Bell and Sons, 1914, p. 341.

15. On the postwar expansion of trade see Gilpin, op. cit., pp. 20–21.

16. "Every prudent man in every period of society, after the first establishment of the division of labour, must naturally have endeavoured ... to have at all times by him, besides the peculiar produce of his own industry, a certain quantity of some one commodity or other, such as he imagined few people would be likely to refuse in exchange for the produce of their industry." Smith, op. cit., p. 24–25.

17. Cited in Edwin Cannan, "Introduction," to Smith, op. cit., p. xxxi. See also pp. 485–486.

18. Douglas Irwin, *Against the Tide: An Intellectual History of Free Trade*, Princeton: Princeton University Press, 1998 paperback, pp. 3, 8, 217, 224–225. The book examines the various intellectual challenges to free trade in the nineteenth and twentieth centuries.

19. Adam Smith denied that the foreign wars of the eighteenth century were financed by the use of gold. Smith, op cit., pp. 468–470. But the transfer of gold to support British armies on the European continent in the Napoleonic Wars was one method by which the Rothschild family first accumulated the capital on which its great nineteenth-century banking empire was founded. Niall Ferguson, *The House of Rothschild: Money's Prophets, 1789–1848*, New York: Penguin Books, 1999 (paperback), pp. 85–90. Traditionally governments also imposed taxes on commerce for a different reason: It was often the most efficient way to raise revenue, the tax easiest to collect. And Smith himself conceded the legitimacy of restraints on trade for purposes of defending the country. On this basis he judged the protection of the British shipping industry to be justified. Smith, op. cit., p. 492.

20. The term acquired a variety of related meanings in the modern era, when gold and silver ceased to be necessary for the prosecution of war. It came to refer to economic policies favoring producers over consumers. Adam Smith anticipated this: "In the mercantile system, the interest of the consumer is almost constantly sacrificed to that of the producer; and it seems to consider production, and not consumption, as the ultimate end and object of all industry and commerce." Smith, op. cit., p. 715.

21. Communist regimes had another reason for closing their borders to trade. They sought to keep out anything that might subvert their rule, and almost anything from the outside world fit into that category.

22. An essay by Paul Krugman devoted to this point, entitled "Competitiveness: A Dangerous Obsession," first published in the journal *Foreign Affairs*, March/April 1994, and reprinted in Krugman, *Pop Internationalism*, Cambridge, Mass.: MIT Press, 1996,

evoked considerable controversy. (Krugman's reply to his critics is also reprinted in this volume.) Edward Luttwak interprets this enduring mercantilist sentiment, and the "geoeconomic" policies to which it gives rise, as a holdover from the long centuries when military rivalry was the chief business of states. "States tend to act geoeconomically simply because of what they are: territorially defined entities which exist precisely to outdo each other on the world scene in one way or another." Luttwak, *Turbocapitalism: Winners and Losers in the World Economy*, New York: HarperCollins, 1999, p. 137. The error of supposing sovereign states to be in fundamental economic competition with one another is different from the one Adam Smith identified as fundamental (and pernicious) in the eighteenth century: namely, that gold and silver, rather than farms, factories, and natural resources, were the source of wealth. Smith wrote his famous book in part to correct this error and its title—*The Wealth of Nations*—therefore had, when it was published, a revisionist implication.

23. Deficits are economically helpful if they bring in resources that are used to increase the country's productive capacity, just as individual firms incur debt by borrowing to increase their capacities. For this reason it is generally thought desirable for countries in the early stages of economic development to run current-account deficits. In the nineteenth century the United States, which was such a country, consistently did so. Peter B. Kenen, *The International Economy*, Fourth Edition, New York: Cambridge University Press, 2000, pp. 285–286.

24. Gilpin, op. cit., pp. 93, 259. A related misconception is that *bilateral* deficits have special importance. In economic terms this is not so. "Robert M. Solow, the Nobel economist, is fond of saying that he has been running deficits with his barber for 40 years straight, buying haircuts for cash and never selling him a single economics lesson." Peter Passell, "Economic Scene," *New York Times*, April 17, 1997, p. D2.

25. "The Achilles heel of the post–Cold War liberal world order is the poor public understanding of economic liberalism, of the functioning of the market system, and how capitalism creates wealth." Gilpin, op. cit., p. 18.

26. Jagdish Bhagwati, *A Stream of Windows: Unsettling Reflections on Trade, Immigration, and Democracy*, Cambridge, Mass.: MIT Press, 1998, p. xvi.

27. Kenen, op. cit., pp. 55, 189–190. If factories in a rich country and a poor one both make widgets, all other thing being equal, the wages in each will depend on how many widgets per unit of time each worker can make. If the better-equipped, better-trained rich country worker can make five times as many, his salary will be five times as great. The point is discussed and illustrated in "The World Economy," *The Economist*, September 28, 1996, pp. 31–32. This is not to say that wages are unaffected by foreign competition. To the contrary, one of the best-known and most widely accepted parts of modern economic thought, the Stolper-Samuelson theorem, holds that the factors of production in which a country is relatively well-endowed and that it uses intensively in the products it exports will be disproportionately rewarded by trade. While economists are virtually unanimous that countries increase their overall wealth through trade, the distribution of the benefits from commerce within political communities is an intellectually and politically more contentious issue. In the last decades of the twentieth century, in the core countries, especially the United States, where skilled labor was abundant, the wages of unskilled labor suffered a relative decline, suggesting that while trade benefited the United States as a whole it harmed one particular segment of the American workforce. Some studies of this trend, however, found that trade with peripheral countries was *not* the major cause of this development: Technological innovation had had a greater impact. The issue is discussed in

Paul Krugman and Robert Lawrence, "Trade, Jobs and Wages," reprinted in Krugman, *Pop Internationalism*. "The consensus today among the trade experts is that the evidence for linking trade with the South to the observed distress among the unskilled to date is hard to find." Bhagwati, op. cit., p. 44. The relationship between trade and wages remained, at the outset of the new century, unsettled.

28. For an overview of List's views and their enduring relevance to twenty-first century Europe, see op. cit., pp. 69–72.

29. Irwin, op. cit., pp. 38, 40, 44.

30. This is the theme of Irwin, Ibid., summarized on pp. 220–221.

31. Ibid., pp. 135–137. The validity of the infant-industry argument for protection thus came to depend upon the existence of industry-wide, or external, economies of scale—that is, benefits accruing to entire industries that could be provided only by government assistance to the industry as a whole and not by loans to individual firms. Such economies of scale proved elusive: As with the Loch Ness monster, sightings were occasionally reported but the creature was never firmly fixed, let alone measured. Irwin, op. cit., pp. 144–152. Kenen, op. cit., pp. 261–262.

32. Michael E. Porter, Hirotaka Takeuchi, and Mariko Sakakibara, *Can Japan Compete?*, New York: Perseus Books, 2000. In his book *Japan: The System that Soured*, Armonk, N.Y.: M. E. Sharpe, 1998, Richard Katz makes a valiant effort to reconcile the skepticism of professional economists about the worth of government support for selected industries with the apparent success of Japanese industrial policy. He argues that in the Japanese case government intervention made a modest but favorable difference because it was undertaken on behalf of industries that were likely to succeed anyway. By carrying out "market-conforming" industrial policies the Japanese government was pushing on an open door, accelerating the rise of export industries that would have grown, although not as rapidly, without it. But Katz also cites one estimate made in the 1990s that without the cartels and informal measures of protection, (not all of them, to be sure, put in place to nurture export industries), Japanese retail prices would fall by 41 percent. (p. 276).

33. Critical analysis of strategic trade policy is in Paul Krugman, *Peddling Prosperity: Economic Sense and Nonsense in the Age of Diminished Expectations*, New York: W. W. Norton and Company, 1994, Chapters 9 and 10, and Bhagwati, op. cit., Chapters 7 and 8.

34. In his essay "The Myth of Asia's Miracle," Paul Krugman argued that Asia's economic success was due to the old-fashioned tried and true practice of high investment. The Asian economies displayed no great advances in productivity. Thus there was no unique and uniquely successful Asian model of economic growth, as strategic trade theory implied. The essay, which originally appeared in *Foreign Affairs*, November/December, 1994, is reprinted in Krugman, *Pop Internationalism*.

35. Smith, op. cit., pp. 501, 527.

36. Irwin, op. cit., p. 181.

37. In countries such as France and India protection has been depicted not simply as a way to protect local jobs but as a means of safeguarding the local culture itself, which is portrayed as under assault from abroad. Foreign products, in this view of the world, become a form of aggression, or pollution, or both. Perhaps the most ingenious, or baroque, rationale along these lines for protection came from Japan. The Japanese kept out American wheat on the (entirely spurious) grounds that the Japanese people were anatomically different from North Americans and so could not digest it.

38. An early-twentieth-century appreciation of this point is cited in Jagdish Bhagwati, *Protectionism*, Cambridge, Mass.: MIT Press, 1988, p. 72.

39. Kenen, op. cit., p. 229, reprints a chart showing the total cost of protection in selected American industries, the number of American jobs saved, and (dividing the second into the first) the total cost per job preserved, which in every case far exceeds the likely average salary and benefits for the industry. On this point see also Bhagwati, *Protectionism*, p. 117. The structure of trade politics in the United States reflects the division between winners and losers from international commerce. The Congress is the home of protectionist sentiment. Each member of Congress represents a small part of the country and is thus susceptible to the influence of intense local interests. The executive branch, which is chosen by the entire country and on which the influence of any single industry will therefore be weaker, tends to be the champion of free trade.

40. Anthony Howe, *Free Trade and Liberal England, 1846–1946*, Oxford, England: The Clarendon Press, 1997, Chapter 1. Personal considerations—notably the change of mind on the part of the previously protectionist Tory prime minister, Sir Robert Peel—also contributed to repeal.

41. Continental countries did begin to liberalize their trade policies in the wake of the repeal of the Corn Laws, beginning in the 1860s. O'Rourke and Williamson, *op. cit.*, pp. 38–39.

42. "The nineteenth century French economist [Frederic] Bastiat once summed it up this way: Saying that our country should be protectionist because other countries do not practice free trade is like saying that we should block up our harbors because other countries have rocky coasts." Krugman, *Peddling Prosperity*, p. 240.

43. Howe, op. cit., pp. 93–105; O'Rourke and Williamson, op. cit., pp. 33–39; Kenen, op. cit., p. 210–211.

44. "[The GATT's] underlying essence is a concept of symmetric rights and obligations for member states, rather than unilateralism in free trade." Bhagwati, *Protectionism*, p. 35.

45. The circumstances in which unilateral tariffs can, in theory, increase welfare are discussed in Irwin, op. cit., pp. 108–116 and 167, and Kenen, op. cit., pp. 193–196.

46. The arguments, political and economic, for proceeding unilaterally were more common in the nineteenth century than in the twentieth, although after 1980 a number of countries in the world's periphery did undertake unilateral trade liberalization. Bhagwati, *Protectionism*, pp. 27–31.

47. There is, of course, an important difference between the two. If Freedonia reduces its arms while Sylvania does not, Sylvania is better off in that it has gained a usable military advantage. If Freedonia reduces a barrier to imports while Sylvania does not, *both* are better off economically, although in some circumstances Sylvania will gain more than Freedonia does.

48. Bhagwati, *Protection*, p. 80.

49. The conflict between the interests of import-competing sectors and industries and those that rely on exports has formed the basis for political cleavages in core countries. Two elaborations on this theme are provided by Peter Gourevitch, *Politics in Hard Times: Comparative Responses to International Economic Crises*, Ithaca: Cornell University Press, 1986, and Ronald Rogowski, *Commerce and Coalitions: How Trade Affects Domestic Political Arrangements*, Princeton: Princeton University Press, 1989.

50. If economic growth causes the market for shirts to double, the domestic shirt industry will be better off even if it loses a quarter of the home market to foreign competitors.

51. A good account of the gold standard is Barry Eichengreen, *Golden Fetters: The Gold Standard and the Great Depression*, New York: Oxford University Press, 1992. A shorter version may be found in Eichengreen, *Globalizing Capital: A History of the International*

Monetary System, Princeton: Princeton University Press, 1996, Chapter 2. The British commitment to gold was crucial. "Britain's dominant position in the world economy led one country after another to accommodate itself to the gold standard, in accordance with what economists infelicitously call 'the model of network externalities' (i.e., the advantages of doing whatever your economic neighbors are doing)." Peter Jay, *The Wealth of Man*, New York: PublicAffairs, 2000, p. 197.

52. To compound the difficulty of sustaining the nineteenth century monetary system in the twentieth, in part because of the same political developments prices and wages became more rigid, which meant that the burden of adjustment fell on employment, which in turn made it even less acceptable politically. Eichengreen, *Globalizing*, p. 31.

53. Ibid., pp. 35–36.

54. Ibid., pp. 73, 86. The Depression and the gold standard combined to form the basis for Keynes's heretical and temporary endorsement of protection. With the British balance of payments in deficit, with Britain committed to the gold standard, and with levels of unemployment already unacceptably high, Keynes reluctantly advocated the only remaining method of reducing the outflow of money: limiting the inflow of goods from abroad. Irwin, op. cit., Chapter 6.

55. "In an environment of formally or informally pegged rates and effective integration of financial markets, any attempt to pursue independent monetary objectives is almost certain, sooner or later, to result in a significant balance-of-payments disequilibrium, and hence to provoke potentially destabilizing flows of speculative capital. To preserve exchange-rate stability, governments will then be compelled to limit either the movement of capital (via restrictions or taxes) or their own policy autonomy (via some form of multilateral surveillance or joint decision-making). If they are unwilling or unable to sacrifice either one, then the objective of exchange-rate stability itself may eventually have to be compromised. Over time, except by chance, the three goals cannot be attained simultaneously." Benjamin J. Cohen, "The Triad and the Unholy Trinity: Lessons for the Pacific Region," in Richard Higgott, Richard Leaver, and John Ravenhill, editors, *Pacific Economic Relations in the 1990s: Cooperation or Conflict?* London: Allen and Unwin, 1993, p. 147. See also O'Rourke and Williamson, op. cit., p. 222.

56. In fact, with these two liberal features monetary policy was generally ineffective: If interest rates were lowered to promote economic activity, capital was likely to leave in search of higher returns. Kenen, op. cit., p. 499.

57. The trilemma is well described in Cohen, op. cit. See also O'Rourke and Williamson, op. cit., p. 22, and Paul Krugman, *The Return of Depression Economics*, New York: W. W. Norton, 2000, pp. 106–109.

58. The story of Bretton Woods is told in Richard Gardner, *Sterling-Dollar Diplomacy in Current Perspective: The Origins and Prospects of Our International Economic Order*, New York: Columbia University Press, 1980, and Robert Skidelsky, *John Maynard Keynes: Fighting for Freedom, 1937–1946*, New York: Viking, 2001.

59. A good general description of Bretton Woods in practice is in Eichengreen, *Globalizing*, Chapter 4.

60. Britain's effort to restore the current account (trade) convertibility of sterling failed when this triggered a demand for reserves—gold and dollars—on the part of holders of pounds that the British government could not meet. Ibid., pp. 102–103.

61. Ibid., p. 129; Kenen, op. cit., p. 457.

62. This was known as the "Triffin Dilemma," after the Belgian-American economist Robert Triffin who first noted it. The dilemma, concisely stated, was that "the quantity of reserves could be increased only at the risk of reducing their quality." Kenen, op. cit., p. 461.

63. Calleo, op. cit., pp. 156–157.

64. The technical term for this privilege is "seigniorage." Gilpin, op. cit., p. 120.

65. One of the main sources of dollar expenditure overseas was the American military presence in Europe and Japan. The dollars that the governments of America's allies had to accept could therefore be seen as the taxes they paid to the United States in return for it defending them. Calleo, op. cit., pp. 163–164.

66. This involves the "nth-country problem," discussed in Kenen, op. cit., pp. 277, 454, 501.

67. Calleo, op. cit., pp. 157–158.

68. Kenen, op. cit., p. 463.

69. Gilpin, op. cit., p. 124.

70. Calleo, op. cit., pp. 165, 204, 213.

12. THE FUTURE OF THE INTERNATIONAL ECONOMY

1. The various hypotheses about the underlying causes of these crises are summarized in Robert Gilpin, *The Challenge of Global Capitalism: The World Economy of the 21st Century*, Princeton: Princeton University Press, 2000, pp. 150–155.

2. Charles S. Maier, *Dissolution: The Crisis of Communism and the End of East Germany*, Princeton: Princeton University Press, 1997, pp. 227–244; Peter B. Kenen, *The International Economy*, Fourth Edition, New York: Cambridge University Press, 2000, p. 481.

3. The precipitating, as distinct from the underlying, cause of the attacks on the lira and the pound sterling was fear of a negative vote in the French referendum on the Maastricht Treaty, which established the common European currency to which the EMS was a stepping stone. This would have cast currency unification into doubt, leaving the British and Italian governments with no reason to defend the politically unpopular interest rates to which they had committed themselves to qualify for it. Peter B. Kenen, op. cit., p. 482. The story of the British exit from the EMS is told in Philip Stephens, *Politics and the Pound: The Conservatives' Struggle With Sterling*, London: Macmillan, 1996, Chapters 9 and 10.

4. Paul Krugman, *The Return of Depression Economics*, New York: W. W. Norton 2000, pp. 84–85; Miles Kahler, "Introduction: Capital Flows and Financial Crises in the 1990s," in Kahler, editor, *Capital Flows and Financial Crises*, Ithaca: Cornell Univeristy Press for the Council on Foreign Relations, 1998, p. 1.

5. Liberalization of capital movements was of particular interest to the United States, for which, as the world's greatest financial power, capital was an important export product and liberalization a form of export-promotion. The efforts of the American government to promote capital account liberalization are described in Nicholas D. Kristof and David E. Sanger, "How U.S. Wooed Asia to Let Cash Flow In," *The New York Times*, February 16, 1999.

6. Kenen, op. cit., p. 361; Barry Eichengreen, *Globalizing Capital: A History of the International Monetary System*, Princeton: Princeton University Press, 1996, p. 190; Krugman, op. cit., p. 53.

7. They often borrowed the local currency and converted it to dollars, counting on being able to reconvert the dollars and pay back the borrowed currency at a lower rate, thereby turning a profit.

8. Paul Krugman, *The Accidental Theorist and Other Dispatches from the Dismal Science*, New York: W. W. Norton, 1998, pp. 159–160; Kenen, op. cit., pp. 505–506.

9. At the time of the 1992 crisis of the pound sterling "[t]he Bank of England's total holdings of foreign exchange were equivalent to only 10 per cent of the *daily* turnover of the London market." Ferdinand Mount, "One-and-a-half cheers for the euro," *TLS*, June 28, 1996, p. 27.

10. The banks often borrowed on a short-term basis and loaned long-term, which aggravated their currency risk.

11. These and other, similar episodes are described in Charles P. Kindleberger, *Manias, Panics and Crashes*, New York: Basic Books, 1989, and Edward Chancellor, *Devil Take the Hindmost: A History of Financial Speculation*, New York: Penguin, 2000 (paperback).

12. "Institutions see their holdings in Latin American, Asian and east European security as part of a category, or class, of emerging market assets that moves together." Richard Lapper, "Slow-motion dominoes," *Financial Times*, August 17, 1998, p. 10.

13. Morris Goldstein termed the first of these causes of contagion the "'wake-up call' hypothesis and the second the "competitive dynamics of devaluation." Goldstein, *The Asian Financial Crisis: Causes, Cures, and Systematic Implications*, Washington, D.C.: Institute for International Economics, June, 1998, p. 18. See also Kenen, op. cit., pp. 486–488.

14. Krugman, *Return*, p. 123; David P. Calleo, *Rethinking Europe's Future*, Princeton: Princeton University Press, 2001, p. 191.

15. In the cases in which institutions or economies are basically sound and do not require major adjustments, transparency serves the same purpose as it does in common security: preventing a spiral of mistrust based on unwarranted fears.

16. "If there is one lesson from the experience of the last two decades, it is that banks are disastrous vehicles for large-scale capital flows across frontiers . . . It would be far better for international intermediation to be based, as a century ago, on long-term finance: direct investment, portfolio equity and long-term bonds." "The trouble with global finance," *Financial Times*, March 6, 1998, p. 17.

17. Useful discussions of the virtues and drawbacks of capital controls may be found in Barry Eichengreen, "Capital Mobility: Ties Need Not Bind," *The Milken Quarterly*, First Quarter, 1999, pp. 29–37, and Robert Wade, "The Coming Fight Over Capital Flows," *Foreign Policy*, Winter 1998–1999, pp. 41–53.

18. "They promote an unrealistic cost of capital and therefore the misallocation of investment; they undermine access to international capital markets; they encourage corruption and increase the risk of inflation." Samuel Brittan, "The control trap," *Financial Times*, October 1, 1998, p. 22, paraphrasing economist David Hale. Brittan adds that exchange control "is one of the most potent weapons of tyranny that can be used to imprison citizens in their own country," citing the experience of people trying to flee Nazi Germany before World War II.

19. "In a weekend speech, Malaysian Prime Minister Mahathir Mohamad, known for his anti-Western outbursts, singled out billionaire American trader George Soros as the demon behind the fluctuating money markets and compared currency speculators to international criminals and drug traffickers." Paul Blustein and Keith B. Richburg, "Thailand Seeks IMF Bailout To Shore Up Its Financial System," *The Washington Post*, July 29, 1997, p. A11.

20. Some therefore advocated expanding the IMF's powers and responsibilities. Gary C. Hufbauer and Edward A. Fogerty, "Bring on a bigger, meaner IMF," *Journal of Commerce*, April 13, 1998, p. 7A.

21. "The best definition I have seen comes from Charles Calomiris of Columbia: Moral hazard arises from bankers who know that future gains from taking on risks will be

private, but believe that losses will be borne by taxpayers." Samuel Brittan, "The three heresies," *Financial Times*, September 3, 1998, p. 10.

22. Precisely this argument was made by two former American secretaries of the treasury and the former chairman of a major American bank. George P. Shultz, William E. Simon, and Walter B. Wriston, "Who Needs the IMF?" *The Wall Street Journal*, February 3, 1998, p. A22. In response to this criticism, the deputy managing director of the IMF asserted that "most investors in Asian countries, and especially investors in Russia who bet on the 'moral-hazard play', have taken very heavy losses." Stanley Fischer, "Lessons from a crisis," *The Economist*, October 3, 1998, p. 27.

23. This was the economic medicine disastrously administered by Western governments in their initial response to the economic crisis the 1930s; hence the title of Paul Krugman's study of the Asian financial crises: *The Return of Depression Economics*. The IMF was subject to yet another criticism: that it had engaged in unwarranted meddling in the internal affairs of the countries to which it made loans. Martin Feldstein, "Refocusing the IMF," *Foreign Affairs*, March/April 1998.

24. The WTO included mechanisms and procedures for adjudicating trade disputes but no enforcement powers.

25. There was violence the following year, on a smaller scale, at a similar meeting held in Prague.

26. Edward Luttwak's term for the post-Cold War economic order, "Turbocapitalism," made the point vividly. Luttwak, *Turbocapitalism: Winners and Losers in the World Economy*, New York: HarperCollins, 1999, especially pp. 27, 37, and 46.

27. Kevin O'Rourke and Jeffrey G. Williamson, *Globalization and History: The Evolution of a Nineteenth-Century Atlantic Economy*, Cambridge, Mass.: The MIT Press, 1999, Chapters 6 and 10.

28. This suspicion was not entirely unfounded. See Jagdish Bhagwati, *A Stream of Windows: Unsettling Reflections on Trade, Immigration, and Democracy*, Cambridge, Mass.: The MIT Press, 1998, Chapter 24.

29. Jagdish Bhagwati, *Protectionism*, Cambridge, Mass.: The MIT Press, 1988, pp. 5–7. The exception to this pattern among the core countries was Japan, which engaged in far less "intra-industry trade" than did the countries of North America and Western Europe, which was one reason that political pressures for protection against Japan were stronger within those countries than pressure for protection against one another. Richard Katz, *Japan: The System that Soured*, Armonk, N.Y.: M.E. Sarpe, 1998, pp. 248–249. Another reason core-periphery trade was difficult to liberalize was that much of what peripheral countries produced for export was agricultural products, and throughout the Western core agricultural lobbies were particularly tenacious and successful.

30. Robert O. Keohane, *After Hegemony: Cooperation and Discord in the World Political Economy*. Princeton: Princeton University Press, 1984, p. 139.

31. The United States also used the grants it made to Western Europe in the early post-war period for liberal purposes: "Each recipient [of Marshall Plan aid] had to sign an agreement with America, promising to balance its budget, free prices (hitherto controlled), halt inflation, stabilise its exchange rate and devise a plan for removing most trade controls." "A gift from the Cold War," *The Economist*, July 9, 1994, p. 70.

32. Kenen, op. cit., p. 455.

33. Keohane, op. cit., pp. 145–146, 149; Eichengreen, *Globalizing*, p. 108. In this way the liberal international economic order was a kind of public good, with the United States paying the cost of sustaining it. The relationship between the post-World War II

openness of the western economic order and the dominant position of the United States is a prominent theme in the literature of international political economy, including Keohane, op. cit.

34. Eichengreen, op. cit., pp. 123, 130; Gilpin, op. cit., p. 61.

35. In 1995 the administration threatened a one hundred percent tariff on Japanese luxury automobiles unless Japan agreed to give a specific share of its auto parts market to American-made products.

36. Bhagwati, *Stream*, Chapters 12, 21.

37. Ibid., Chapters 10 and 11.

38. Bhagwati, Ibid., Chapter 4; O'Rourke and Williamson, op. cit., p. 108. A middle position is argued in Katz, op. cit. Japan did practice protection, and more extensively than other core countries, but the very policies that so annoyed Japan's American critics ultimately harmed Japan itself by contributing to the prolonged slump of the 1990s.

39. Eichengreen, op. cit., Chapter 6.

40. "Under a pure currency board the whole of a country's note issue and reserve deposits by banks have to be covered by holdings of dollars or other specified hard currencies." Samuel Brittan, "Yet more dollars," *Financial Times*, April 29, 1999, p. 10. Currency boards were operating, at the outset of the twenty-first century, in Argentina, Estonia, Lithuania, Bulgaria, Bosnia, and Hong Kong.

   "The best guess at the moment is that emerging economies will divide into two groups: those with flexible exchange rates and a relatively low level of integration into global capital markets; and those that bind their economies tightly through currency boards or currency unions, and as a result have heavily integrated financial systems with strong foreign ownership. Within a couple of decades, this division could result in two sizable currency blocks, the dollar and euro zones, together with a large number of countries with floating exchange rates." "Time for a redesign?" *The Economist*, January 30, 1999, p. 17.

41. "In 1990 there were 25 [regional trade agreements]; today [1998] there are more than 90." "Fifty years on," *The Economist*, May 16, 1998, p. 23. See also Gilpin, op. cit., p. 343.

42. Because it had a common external tariff, the EU qualified as a customs union. NAFTA, the members of which set their own external tariffs, was, by contrast, a free-trade area. Kenen, op. cit., p. 257.

43. The distinction between trade diversion and trade creation, an important one in the study of trade policy, is discussed in Kenen, op. cit., p. 250. The distinction was first noted in Jacob Viner, *The Customs Union Issue*, New York: Carnegie Endowment for International Peace, 1950.

44. Eric Hobsbawm, *The Age of Empire 1875–1914*, New York: Pantheon, 1987, pp. 66, 72–73.

45. The trend toward economic regionalism predated the outbreak of war. The post–World War I collapse of the gold standard led to the formation of loose regional monetary blocs, including one in the Western hemisphere centered on the dollar. Eichengreen, op. cit., pp. 86–87. The ancestor of all regional blocs, at least non-liberal ones in Europe, was perhaps the "continental system" that Napoleon tried to construct at the outset of the nineteenth century as part of his struggle with Great Britain. Paul W. Schroeder, *The Transformation of European Politics, 1763–1848*, New York: Oxford University Press, 1996 paperback, p. 310.

46. "'Unless we agree to act,' Mr. [Renato] Ruggiero [the head of the WTO] warned, 'the world will become divided in 20 years into two or three intercontinental blocs, each

CONCLUSION

1. "If we learn anything from the history of economic development it is that culture . . . in the sense of the inner values and attitudes that guide a population . . . makes all the difference." David S. Landes, *The Wealth and Poverty of Nations: Why Some Are So Rich and Some So Poor*, New York: W. W. Norton, 1999, p. 516. See also Lawrence E. Harrison and Samuel P. Huntington, editors, *Culture Matters: How Values Shape Human Experience*, New York: Basic Books, 2001, a collection of essays devoted to this theme.

    The use of culture as an explanation for economic performance has a distinguished history. One of the founders of modern social science, the German student of ancient history turned sociologist Max Weber, imputed the worldly success of northern European Protestants to their religious beliefs. Max Weber, *The Protestant Ethic and the Spirit of Capitalism*, New York: Charles Scribner's Sons, 1958.

2. Harrison, introduction to Harrison and Huntington, editors, op. cit., p. xxix.

3. "Culture" is the answer to one of the great questions of economic history: why China, despite having the prerequisites long before Great Britain, did not launch an industrial revolution of its own. Imperial Chinese society lacked the necessary values. Brief summaries of the large literature on this subject can be found in Landes, op. cit., Chapter 21, and Peter Jay, *The Wealth of Man*, New York: PublicAffairs, 2000, pp. 79–84.

4. "Even in the late twentieth century, when a far greater world consensus exists on the desirability of respect for civil rights, democratic processes and economic co-operation in international affairs, [than after the Wars of the French Revolution] the most an international order can be expected to do is to encourage these among member states, not produce or compel them." Paul W. Schroeder, *The Transformation of European Politics, 1763–1848*, New York: Oxford University Press, 1992, p. 577.

5. At the end of the Cold War the West had reached a high point of power and prestige but could not readily use them to bring about its most important foreign policy goals: the implantation of liberal institutions and practices in Russia and China. The situation recalled the instructive case of Nathan Rothschild, the richest man in the world in the early decades of the nineteenth century, who died in 1837 of an infection of which the poorest Englishmen could easily have been cured in the next century by readily available antibiotics. All of Rothschild's wealth could not purchase what had not yet been invented. Landes, op. cit., pp. xvii-xviii.

6. "During her Senate confirmation hearings, Secretary of State Madeleine Albright declared that Americans 'must be more than an audience, more even than actors; we must be the authors of the history of our age.'" Mark Danner, "Marooned in the Cold War," *World Policy Journal*, xiv:3, Fall 1997, p. 4. Just what this meant was not at all apparent but it was certainly intended to bespeak a great and commanding role in the affairs of the world and of other countries.

7. This political and etymological tendency appeared in most extreme form in the boasts of public officials that their policies had "grown" the economy. This was both a grammatical error and a dubious political claim: "to grow" is an intransitive verb that does not take a direct object and economic growth, while it is influenced by public policies (often negatively), cannot be produced by them.

8. "There was [before World War I] a fear of war in the abstract, but it was as vague as the perception of what form modern war itself might take. Stronger by far, particularly among the political classes in every major country, was the fear of the consequences of the failure to face the challenge of war itself." John Keegan, *The First World War*, New York: Alfred A. Knopf, 1999, p. 18.

with its own rules and internal free trade, but with external barriers
world.'" Paul Lewis, "Is the U.S. Souring on Free Trade?" *The New York*
25, 1996, p. D4. The concern is expressed in Gilpin, op. cit., especially p
and 349.

47. Gilpin, op. cit., pp. 240, 249, 288.
48. Calleo, op. cit., p. 196.
49. More than the loss of control over monetary policy was in prospect. Acco
president of the German Bundesbank, "a European monetary currency
member states transferring sovereignty over financial and wage policies
monetary affairs. It is an illusion to think that states can hold on to the
over taxation policies." Martin Wolf, "Crisis of identity," *Financial Ti*
1999, p. 12.
50. The task of economic integration in Europe had been made easier by
Europe had not had to conduct an independent security policy and so ha
decide, for example, how large a military role Germany should play.
51. The Maastricht Treaty committed the EU to constitutional changes to
problem. But just what the appropriate changes were, and how the EU
tion if they were implemented, remained unclear a decade after the Treaty
52. Gilpin, op. cit., p. 276
53. Henry Nau, *Trade and Security: U.S. Policies at Cross-Purposes*, Washingtoi
American Enterprise Institute Press, 1995, p. 40.
54. The Japanese economic slump of the 1990s weakened its claim to region;
In the wake of the Asian currency crises the afflicted countries needed to
reserves through exports. But Japan's economic weakness, combined with
disinclination to import on anything like the scale of the United States,
provided little help on this score. Katz, op. cit., pp. 254–255.
55. Calleo, op. cit., p. 185.
56. "All of the [regional trade] groupings to date have tended to increase the
rather than to restrict it, which suggests at first sight that they are econoi
ficial. None has yet adopted rules that are openly at odds with the W
years on," *The Economist*, May 16, 1998, p. 23. But the economic v
arrangements is controversial. A negative view is expressed in Jagdish Bł
track to nowhere," *The Economist*, October 18, 1997, and Bhagwati, *Str*
28. A generally benign appraisal of regional arrangements is in Milℓ
World of Blocs: Facts and Factoids," *World Policy Journal* Vol. XII, No 1,
57. In the negotiations leading up to Bretton Woods, Keynes proposed
function as just such an institution. Kenen, op. cit., p. 451; Robert S
Maynard Keynes: Fighting for Freedom, 1937–1946, New York: Viking, 2c
Later Robert Triffin made a similar proposal. Kenen, op. cit.., p. 46
Asian currency crises the financier George Soros offered a comparable
Soros, "To avert the next crisis," *Financial Times*, January 4, 1999, p. 18.
58. This was emphatically true of the European Union. Calleo, op. cit., pp. ;
59. Gilpin, op. cit., p. 231; Kenen, op. cit., p. 531. Common security was
innovation at the end of the first post-Cold War decade to have establ
tern or the other. To the extent that it endured in Europe and took ho
was likely to follow the first rather than the second.

9. John Maynard Keynes, "Economic Prospects for Our Grandchildren," in Keynes, *Essays in Persuasion*, New York: Harcourt Brace, 1951.

10. "Between 1960 and 1995, the ratio of income between the richest and poorest 20 percent of the world rose from 30:1 to more than 80:1. An estimated 1.3 billion people—about a quarter of humanity—were living on less than U.S. $1 per day in the 1990s, in a world whose average income was U.S. $14 a day and whose more affluent economies averaged over $50 per day." Jay, op. cit., pp. 246–247. The blessings of the twentieth-century revolutions in the technology of communications were just as unevenly distributed: "The city of Tokyo, whose population is 23 million, has three times as many working telephone lines as the whole of the African continent, whose population is 580 million. Only one person in ten in the world has even made a telephone call. A mere 1 per cent of the earth's population has access to the Internet." John Keane, "The humbling of the intellectuals," *TLS*, August 28, 1998, p. 14.

11. "The greatest test for human society as it confronts the twenty-first century is . . . how to find effective solutions in order to free the poorer three-quarters of humankind from the growing Malthusian trap of malnutrition, starvation, resource depletion, unrest, enforced migration and armed conflict—developments that will also endanger the richer nations, if less directly." Paul Kennedy, *Preparing for the Twenty-First Century*, New York: Random House, 1992, p. 12. See also Jay, op. cit., p. 307.

12. The Latin American version of the second doctrine was called dependency theory. An updated version of Marx's assertion that the wealthy few battened on the impoverished multitudes, it inspired proposals for reorganizing the global economy to produce a "new international economic order" more favorable to the south, which were tabled in international forums, to no effect, in the 1970s. The discrediting of the first doctrine by the sluggish economic performance it produced undermined the second. David S. Landes, "Culture Makes Almost All the Difference," in Harrison and Huntington, op. cit., pp. 4–6. On the proposals for a new international economic order see Stephen D. Krasner, *Structural Conflict: The Third World Against Global Liberalism*, Berkeley: University of California Press, 1985.

13. This critique of foreign aid appears in the many works of the Hungarian-born English economist P. T. (later Lord) Bauer.

14. "History tells us that the most successful cures for poverty come from within. Foreign aid can help, but like windfall wealth can also hurt. It can discourage effort and plant a crippling sense of incapacity." Landes, *Wealth*, p. 523.

15. The outlook for the world's poorest people was better than the aggregate statistics on the global distribution of wealth suggested because so many of them lived in the world's two most populous countries, China and India. Both countries achieved more than respectable rates of economic growth in the first post-Cold War decade and both had good although not unclouded prospects for sustaining these rates, which would benefit their poorest citizens.

16. In his 1974 book *An Inquiry Into the Human Prospect*, New York: W. W. Norton, 1974, Robert Heilbroner predicted that impoverished countries would come to be governed by stern, repressive "iron" regimes that would acquire nuclear weapons to extract money from the wealthy of the planet. (pp. 39, 43) A quarter century later the poorest countries were instead governed, insofar as they were governed at all, by what could more appropriately be called paper regimes, which were so weak that they could not even keep order within their own borders let alone build, buy, or steal weapons of mass destruction.

17. "If the developing world remains caught in its poverty trap, the more developed coun-

tries will come under siege from tens of millions of migrants and refugees eager to reside among the prosperous but aging populations of the democracies." Kennedy, op. cit., p. 46.

18. Such a scenario is depicted in the 1973 novel by Jean Raspail, *The Camp of the Saints*. Its relevance for the post-Cold War era is discussed in Paul Kennedy and Matthew Connelly, "Must It Be the Rest Against the West?" *The Atlantic Monthly*, 274:6, December 1994. In real life, however, neither the motive for a massive descent on the North by the people of the South nor the means of transport for such an invasion were likely to be available; nor was it likely that, as in the novel, in the face of an invasion of desperate but unarmed hordes the governments of the core countries would abandon their border controls and let them in.

19. At Bretton Woods in 1944, Keynes proposed the creation of global financial institutions with real powers. His proposals did not attract American support.

20. Industrially polluted air was not unknown in the nineteenth century, in the industrial cities of Great Britain.

21. The environmental movement took different political forms in different parts of the core. In Western Europe it gave rise to separate political parties, commonly called "Greens," which were independently represented in local and national parliaments but sometimes joined other parties to form governing coalitions. In the United States the independent Green party played a negligible political role (although Ralph Nader's 2000 presidential candidacy may have tipped a close election to the Republican candidate George W. Bush) but both major parties absorbed environmental principles and policies.

22. A good discussion of the economics of global warming, upon which the discussion that follows draws heavily, is Charles S. Pearson, *Economics and the Global Environment*, New York: Cambridge University Press, 2001, Chapter 14.

23. They depended more heavily on activities likely to be harmed, such as agriculture and fishing, and had bigger populations living in areas likely to be adversely affected.

24. In 2001 the American president, George W. Bush, pronounced the Kyoto Treaty dead.

25. Among the contributions to the ongoing debate on global warming was the argument that in the short term the wisest course was to do nothing, or at least nothing very costly. For this there were two reasons. First, although the evidence that the Earth's temperature was rising was increasingly persuasive, the precise effects of this trend were far from clear. It was therefore better to wait until they became clearer before taking action. Second, lowering the consumption of fossil fuels would inevitably reduce economic growth, and it was more sensible to obtain that growth and use its fruits to cope with whatever problems global warming turned out to cause. An ounce of prevention, by this logic, was worth *less* than a pound of cure.

26. There is an exception to this generalization. The Congress of Vienna, established after the Wars of the French Revolution to preserve equilibrium on the European continent, was the creation of powers none of which save Great Britain had anything resembling a liberal political system.

27. Her presentation described how, in response to Sputnik, the American Department of Defense placed increased emphasis on building secure networks of communication, an effort that led to the system that became the Internet.

28. Another sign of the change was the cover of the February 15, 1999, issue of *Time*. It depicted three American economic officials—Alan Greenspan, the chairman of the Federal Reserve Board (the American central bank), and Robert Rubin and Lawrence

Summers, secretary and deputy secretary of the treasury. The caption read "The Committee to Save the World" and the article to which the cover referred, entitled "The Three Marketeers," told of their efforts to keep the Asian currency and fiscal crises of 1998 from worsening and spreading. During the Cold War *Time* had reserved this kind of journalistic treatment for American officials dealing with national security affairs and for events involving an actual or potential war.

29. "[By 1998] the average GDP of the old eastern European economies (including the Baltic states) was still just below 1989 levels, and that of the former Soviet Union was down 45 percent, indubitably the worst peacetime economic setback experienced by any substantial economic area since—who knows? But maybe since the Black Death." Jay, op. cit., p. 268.

30. *The Collected Poems of W. B. Yeats*, New York: Macmillan, 1950, p. 309.

INDEX

PUBLICAFFAIRS is a publishing house founded in 1997. It is a tribute to the standards, values, and flair of three persons who have served as mentors to countless reporters, writers, editors, and book people of all kinds, including me.

I. F. STONE, proprietor of *I. F. Stone's Weekly*, combined a commitment to the First Amendment with entrepreneurial zeal and reporting skill and became one of the great independent journalists in American history. At the age of eighty, Izzy published *The Trial of Socrates*, which was a national bestseller. He wrote the book after he taught himself ancient Greek.

BENJAMIN C. BRADLEE was for nearly thirty years the charismatic editorial leader of *The Washington Post*. It was Ben who gave the *Post* the range and courage to pursue such historic issues as Watergate. He supported his reporters with a tenacity that made them fearless, and it is no accident that so many became authors of influential, best-selling books.

ROBERT L. BERNSTEIN, the chief executive of Random House for more than a quarter century, guided one of the nation's premier publishing houses. Bob was personally responsible for many books of political dissent and argument that challenged tyranny around the globe. He is also the founder and was the longtime chair of Human Rights Watch, one of the most respected human rights organizations in the world.

· · ·

For fifty years, the banner of Public Affairs Press was carried by its owner Morris B. Schnapper, who published Gandhi, Nasser, Toynbee, Truman, and about 1,500 other authors. In 1983 Schnapper was described by *The Washington Post* as "a redoubtable gadfly." His legacy will endure in the books to come.

Peter Osnos, *Publisher*